MODERN DEMOCRACIES

BY

JAMES BRYCE

(VISCOUNT BRYCE)

AUTHOR OF

"THE HOLY ROMAN EMPIRE," "THE AMERICAN COMMONWEALTH," ETC.

IN TWO VOLUMES

VOL. II

CONTENTS

PART II (*Continued*)

SOME DEMOCRACIES IN THEIR WORKING

UNITED STATES

CHAPTER		PAGE
	PREFATORY NOTE	1
XXXVIII	THE BEGINNINGS OF DEMOCRACY IN NORTH AMERICA	3
XXXIX	THE FRAME OF GOVERNMENT: STATE, LOCAL, AND FEDERAL CONSTITUTIONS	10
XL	THE PARTY SYSTEM	27
XLI	THE ACTUAL WORKING OF THE NATIONAL AND STATE GOVERNMENTS	47
XLII	THE STATE GOVERNMENTS IN THEIR WORKING	77
XLIII	THE JUDICIARY AND CIVIL ORDER	83
XLIV	PUBLIC OPINION	112
XLV	RECENT REFORMING MOVEMENTS	129

AUSTRALIA

XLVI	AUSTRALIAN HISTORY AND FRAME OF GOVERNMENT	166
XLVII	AUSTRALIAN LEGISLATURES AND EXECUTIVES	182
XLVIII	THE EXECUTIVE AND THE CIVIL SERVICE	193
XLIX	AUSTRALIAN PARTIES AND POLICIES	202
L	QUESTIONS NOW BEFORE THE AUSTRALIAN PEOPLE	214
LI	LABOUR POLICIES AND PROPOSALS	220
LII	CHARACTERISTICS OF AUSTRALIAN DEMOCRACY	243

NEW ZEALAND

LIII	THE COUNTRY AND ITS FIRST HALF CENTURY OF HISTORY	265
LIV	RICHARD SEDDON AND HIS POLICIES	273
LV	COMPULSORY ARBITRATION IN TRADE DISPUTES	299
LVI	THE WORKING OF THE GOVERNMENT	313
LVII	RESULTS OF DEMOCRATIC GOVERNMENT	322

v

PART III

CHAPTER PAGE

A. An examination and criticism of democratic institutions
in the light of the facts described in the survey contained in Part II. of the working of six democratic
governments.
(CHAPTERS LVIII.–LXVIII.)

B. Observations on certain phenomena which bear on the
working of Democracy everywhere.
(CHAPTERS LXIX.–LXXII.)

C. General reflections on the present and future of Democratic Government suggested by a study of the forms
it has taken, the changes it has undergone, and the
tendencies that are now affecting it.
(CHAPTERS LXXIII. to End.)

LVIII   THE DECLINE OF LEGISLATURES 335
LIX   THE PATHOLOGY OF LEGISLATURES 345
LX   THE EXECUTIVE IN A DEMOCRACY 358
LXI   DEMOCRACY AND FOREIGN POLICY 367
LXII   THE JUDICIARY 384
LXIII   CHECKS AND BALANCES 390
LXIV   SECOND CHAMBERS 398
LXV   DIRECT LEGISLATION BY THE PEOPLE 417
LXVI   THE RELATION OF CENTRAL TO LOCAL GOVERNMENT 435
LXVII   COMPARISON OF THE SIX DEMOCRATIC GOVERNMENTS
EXAMINED 446
LXVIII   TYPES OF DEMOCRATIC GOVERNMENT 461
LXIX   THE MONEY POWER IN POLITICS 477
LXX   RESPONSIBILITY 489
LXXI   DEMOCRACY AND THE BACKWARD RACES 498
LXXII   THE RELATION OF DEMOCRACY TO LETTERS AND
ARTS 519
LXXIII   THE RESULTS DEMOCRATIC GOVERNMENT HAS GIVEN 527
LXXIV   DEMOCRACY COMPARED WITH OTHER FORMS OF GOV-
ERNMENT 535
LXXV   OLIGARCHIES WITHIN DEMOCRACIES 542
LXXVI   LEADERSHIP IN A DEMOCRACY 552
LXXVII   THE LATER PHASES OF DEMOCRACY 564
LXXVIII   PRESENT TENDENCIES IN DEMOCRACIES 575
LXXIX   DEMOCRACY AND THE COMMUNIST STATE . . . 585
LXXX   THE FUTURE OF DEMOCRACY 597
INDEX 611

PART II (*continued*)

SOME DEMOCRACIES IN THEIR WORKING

UNITED STATES

PREFATORY NOTE

THE chapters that here follow are not an abridgment of the full description of the constitution and government of the United States presented in my book entitled *The American Commonwealth* which was first published more than thirty years ago, and has been since enlarged and frequently revised. They have been written as a new and independent study of American institutions, considered as founded on democratic theories and illustrating in their practice the working out of democratic principles and tendencies. Desiring to present a general view of what popular government has achieved and has failed to achieve, I have dealt with those details only which are characteristic of democratic systems, omitting as beyond the scope of this treatise all matters, such as the structure of the Federal Government and its administrative methods, which do not bear directly upon it or illustrate its peculiar features. Neither has it been my aim in these or any other chapters to bring contemporary history up to date. It is safer not to touch, and I have carefully abstained from touching the controversial questions of the moment, questions which indeed change their aspects from month to month. My wish has been throughout the book to give the reader materials for estimating the merits and defects of each form which popular government has taken, and for this purpose events that happened ten or twenty years ago are just as profitable as those of to-day, indeed more profitable, for we can judge them by their consequences.

Though the main conclusions to which I was led when writing on the United States in 1888 seem to me to be still true, new phenomena have since appeared which throw further light on the nature of popular government, and these I

1

have endeavoured to set forth and comment upon, studying the facts afresh and unbiassed by the judgments of thirty years ago. Since that year much has been done in America to vivify public interest in political theory and history by many books, excellent in plan and execution. To these, and to the American friends who have aided me by their criticisms and comments, I gratefully acknowledge my obligations.

CHAPTER XXXVIII

THE BEGINNINGS OF DEMOCRACY IN NORTH AMERICA

OF all modern countries the United States supplies the most abundant data for the study of popular government. It has been a democracy for a century and a quarter, and is now by far the largest of the nations that live under self-governing institutions. It shows the working of these institutions, on a great scale in its Federal Government and in the governments of the most populous States, on a smaller scale in the lesser States, as well as in counties, townships, and cities, some of which latter have a frame of government that makes them resemble autonomous republics. It has exerted an immense influence on other countries, for its example fired the French people at the outbreak of the Revolution of 1789, and its constitution has been taken as a model by the new republics of the Western hemisphere. Since Tocqueville published in 1832 his memorable book on American democracy, the United States has stood before the minds of European thinkers and statesmen not only as the land to which the races of the Old World are drawn by hopes of happiness and freedom, but also as the type of what the rule of the people means when the people are left to themselves, and as the pattern of what other peoples are likely to become as they in their turn move along the fateful path to democratic institutions. Whoever in Europe has wished to commend or to disparage those institutions has pointed to the United States, and has found plenty of facts to warrant either praise or blame.

No nation ever embarked on its career with happier auguries for the success of popular government. The friends of liberty in Europe indulged the highest hopes of what Liberty could accomplish in a new land, exempt from the evils which the folly or selfishness of monarchs and nobles had inflicted on the countries of Europe. The Americans themselves, although the Revolutionary War left

3

them impoverished as well as vexed by local jealousies, were full of pride and confidence. There was much to justify this confidence. Their own racial quality and the traditions they inherited, the favouring features of their physical environment and the security from external dangers which isolation promised, made up, taken in conjunction, a body of conditions for a peaceful and prosperous political life such as no other people had ever enjoyed. Those who settled Spanish America had an equally vast and rich territory open before them. Those who settled Australia and New Zealand had an equally noble inheritance of freedom behind them. But in neither of these cases were the gifts of Nature and those of a splendid Past bestowed together in such ample measure on the founders of a State.

Let us pass these gifts in brief review.

Temperate North America was a vast country fit to be the home of a North European race, and a practically unoccupied country, for the aboriginal tribes, though most of them fierce and brave, were too few to constitute an obstacle to settlement. There was land for everybody; and nearly all of it, as far as the Rocky Mountains, available for cultivation. It is only to-day, three centuries after the first English colonists settled in Virginia and on the shores of Massachusetts Bay, nearly a century and a half after the Declaration of Independence, that the unappropriated arable areas have become scarce. Besides the immense stretches of rich soil, there were superb forests and mineral deposits it will take many centuries to exhaust.

In such a country everybody could find means of sustenance. Among the earlier settlers and almost down to our own time there was no economic distress, no pauperism nor ground for apprehending it. Nobody was rich, nobody very poor. Neither were there any class antagonisms. Though the conditions of colonial life had created a kind of equality unknown to old countries, certain distinctions of rank existed, but they were not resented, and caused no friction, either social or political. The people were nearly all of English or (in the Middle States) of Dutch or Scoto-Irish stock, stocks that had already approved themselves industrious in peace, valiant in war, adventurous at sea. All were practically English in their ways of thinking, their beliefs, their social usages, yet with an added adaptability and resourcefulness such as the simple or rougher life in a new country is fitted to implant. In the northern colonies they were well educated, as education was understood in those days, and mentally alert. The habit of independent thinking and a general interest in public affairs had been fostered both by the share which the laity of the northern colonies took in the management of the Congregational churches and by the practice of civil self-government, brought from England, while the principles of the English Common Law, exact yet flexible, had formed the minds of their leading men. Respect for law and order, a recognition both of the rights of the individual and of the authority of the duly appointed magistrate, were to them the foundations of civic duty.

Though there were wide economic and social differences between the Northern colonies, where the farmers and seafaring men constituted the great bulk of the population [1] and the Southern, in which large plantations were worked by slave labour, these differences did not yet substantially affect the unity of the nation: for the racial distinctions were negligible, and no language but English was spoken, except by some Germans in Pennsylvania. Such divergences in religious doctrine and church government as existed were too slight to be a basis for parties or to create political acrimony. Finally, it was their good fortune to be safe from any external dangers. The power of France had, since 1759, ceased to threaten them on the side of Canada, and on the south neither from Florida nor from Louisiana, both then in the hands of Spain, was there anything to fear.

With conditions so favourable to peace only a small navy and still smaller army were needed, circumstances which promised security against the growth of a military caste or the ascendancy of a successful general.[2] These fortunate

[1] There were very few negroes in the North, though slavery existed in 1783 in all States except Rhode Island, Pennsylvania, and possibly (for the point seems doubtful) in Massachusetts and New Hampshire.

[2] The European Wars, which began in 1792 and ended in 1814, raised controversies with Britain which culminated in the war of 1812-14, but thereafter questions of foreign policy affected but slightly the politics and general constitutional development of America down till our own time.

conditions continued to exist for many years. Once, however, the unity of the nation was imperilled. The maintenance of negro slavery, which wise statesmen had hoped to see disappear naturally, and the attempt to extend its area so as to retain for the Slave States an equal power in the government, led to a long struggle between the Free and the Slave States which ended in the War of Secession, a war that retarded the progress of the South and has left behind it a still unsolved internal problem. Nevertheless, the cohesive forces proved strong enough to reassert themselves when the fight was over. The present generation knows no animosities, and honours alike those who, between 1860 and 1865, fought on one or other side. The old Slavery issues belong to a dead past, and need seldom be referred to in the pages that follow, for the tendencies that characterize popular government have developed themselves upon lines with which slavery had little to do, so the phenomena which we have to-day to study would (except as respects the suffrage in, and the political attitude of, the Southern States) have been much the same if no slave-ship had ever brought a negro from Africa.

What were the tendencies of thought and feeling wherewith the nation started on its course and which constituted the main lines of its political character? Some were inherited, some the outcome of colonial conditions.

There was a strong religious sense, present everywhere, but strongest in New England, and there fostering a somewhat stern and almost grim view of duty. This has continued to be a feature which sharply distinguishes native American thought and conduct from all revolutionary and socialistic movements on the European continent. There has never been any anti-Christian or anti-clerical sentiment, such as has embittered politics and disrupted parties in France, Italy, Spain, and Mexico.

There was a vehement passion for liberty, dating, in embryo, from the early Puritan settlements in New England and keen also among the Scoto-Irish of Virginia, the Carolinas and Pennsylvania, who had fled from the oppressions suffered by the Presbyterians of Ulster. Intensified by the long struggle against King George III., this passion ran to excess when it induced the belief that with Liberty in the van all other good things would follow. During the War of Independence the men of conservative opinions, branded as enemies of freedom, had been mostly silenced or expelled. The victory of the People over arbitrary power had glorified both Liberty and the People. It was natural to assume that the one would be always victorious and the other always wise.

With the love of Liberty there went a spirit of individualistic self-reliance and self-help, not indeed excluding associated action, for that they possessed in their town meetings and colonial assemblies, but averse to official control or supervision. In the great majority of the people these tendencies co-existed with a respect for law and a sense of the value of public order. But there were, especially in the wilder districts, restive elements which gave trouble to the Federal Government in its early days and obliged it to use military force to overcome resistance to the enforcement of revenue statutes. Lawlessness has never been extinguished in the mountainous regions of East Kentucky and East Tennessee.

Neither did the respect for constituted authority, general in the older and best-settled parts of the country, prevent a suspicious attitude towards officials, including even members of the legislatures. Here the individualism characteristic of the Puritan and of the settler asserted itself. Any assumption of power was watched with a jealousy which kept strictly within the range of their functions those whom the people had chosen for public service.

Lastly, there was a spirit of localism which showed itself in the desire to retain as much public business as possible under local control and entrust as little as possible to a central authority. The attachment to self-government in each small community was rooted, not in any theory, but rather in instinct and habit. Nobody thought of choosing any one but a neighbour to represent him in an elected body. This showed itself especially in the northern colonies which had grown up out of little rural Towns. The Town was not a mere electoral area but a community, which thought that no one but a member of the community could represent it or deal with its affairs.

These tendencies were fundamentally English, though

more fully developed in America, as an orchard tree grown
for centuries in one country may, when placed in a new
soil under a new sun, put forth more abundant foliage and
fruit of richer flavour. The Americans, however, began
soon after the Revolution to think of themselves, and the
less instructed sections among them have continued so to
think, as a new people. They fancied their history to have
begun from 1776, or at earliest from 1607 and 1620, forgetting, in the pride of their new nationalism, that both their
character and their institutions were due to causes that had
been at work centuries before, as far back as Magna Charta
and even as the Folk Mots of their primitive ancestors in
the days of Ecghbert and Alfred. Rather were they an old
people, the heirs of many ages, though under the stimulus
of a new nature and an independent life renewing their
youth even as the age of an eagle.

Such was the land and such the people in which the
greatest of modern democracies began to build up its frame
of government. On what foundations of doctrine was the
structure made to rest?

The Americans of the Revolution started from two
fundamental principles or dogmas. One was Popular Sovereignty. From the People all power came: at their pleasure and under their watchful supervision it was held: for
their benefit and theirs alone was it to be exercised. The
other principle was Equality. This had from the first covered the whole field of private civil rights with no distinctions of privilege. Equality of political rights was for a
time incomplete, voting power being in some States withheld from the poorest as not having a permanent stake in
the community, but in course of time all the States placed
all their citizens on the same footing.

Along with these two principles certain other doctrines
were so generally assumed as true that men did not stop to
examine, much less to prove them. Nearly all believed that
the possession of political rights, since it gives self-respect
and imposes responsibility, does of itself make men fit to
exercise those rights, so that citizens who enjoy liberty will be
sure to value it and guard it. Their faith in this power of
liberty, coupled with their love of equality, further disposed
them to regard the differences between one citizen and an-

other as so slight that almost any public functions may be assigned to any honest man, while fairness requires that such functions should go round and be enjoyed by each in turn. These doctrines, however, did not exclude the belief that in the interest of the people no one chosen to any office must enjoy it long or be allowed much discretion in its exercise, for they held that though the private citizen may be good while he remains the equal of others, power is a corrupting thing, so the temptation to exceed or misuse functions must be as far as possible removed.

CHAPTER XXXIX

HOLDING these dogmas and influenced by these assumptions, the people began after they had declared their independence to create frames of government for the colonies they had turned into States, and then in 1787–9, to substitute for the loose Confederation which had held them together, a scheme of Federal Government. To use the terms of our own day, they turned a Nationality into a Nation, and made the Nation a State by giving it a Constitution.

The instruments which we call Constitutions are among the greatest contributions ever made to politics as a practical art; and they are also the most complete and definite concrete expressions ever given to the fundamental principles of democracy. What we call the British Constitution is a general name including all the laws, both statutes and common law doctrines embodied in reported cases, which relate to the management of public affairs. But an American Written or Rigid Constitution is a single legal instrument prescribing the structure, scope, powers, and machinery of a government. It is, moreover, an instrument set in a category by itself, raised above ordinary laws by the fact that it has been enacted and is capable of being changed, not in the same way as statutes are changed by the ordinary modes of legislation, but in some specially prescribed way, so as to ensure for it a greater permanence and stability. This was virtually a new invention, a legitimate offspring of democracy, and an expedient of practical value, because it embodies both the principle of Liberty and the principle of Order. It issues from the doctrine that power comes only from the People, and from it not in respect of the

10

physical force of the numerical majority but because the People is recognized as of right the supreme lawgiving authority. Along with the principle of Liberty, a Constitution embodies also the principle of Self-restraint. The people have resolved to put certain rules out of the reach of temporary impulses springing from passion or caprice, and to make these rules the permanent expression of their calm thought and deliberate purpose. It is a recognition of the truth that majorities are not always right, and need to be protected against themselves by being obliged to recur, at moments of haste or excitement, to maxims they had adopted at times of cool reflection. Like all great achievements in the field of constructive politics, and like nearly all great inventions in the fields of science and the arts, this discovery was the product of many minds and long experience. Yet its appearance in a finished shape, destined to permanence, was sudden, just as a liquid composed of several fluids previously held in solution will under certain conditions crystallize rapidly into a solid form.

The Constitutions of the States

The student of these American instruments must note some features which distinguish the State Constitutions from that of the Federal or National Government, which we shall presently examine. The former came first, and express the mind of the people in the days of the Revolutionary War, when liberty seemed the greatest of all goods. These early constitutions have been from time to time amended, or redrafted and re-enacted, and thus they record the changes that have passed upon public opinion. Those dating from the years between 1820 and 1860 show a movement towards a completer development of popular power, while those from 1865 to our own time present certain new features, some of a highly radical quality, some enlarging the functions of government, some restricting the powers of legislatures.

To describe in detail the variations in these instruments and the changes each underwent might confuse the reader's mind. It will suffice to indicate in outline the principles from which the authors of the first Constitutions set out, and to which the nation has in the main adhered, though the mode of their application has varied according to the particular aims it has from time to time striven to attain and the evils it has sought to cure.[1]

These principles were:

To secure the absolute sovereignty of the People.

To recognize complete equality among the citizens.

To protect the people against usurpation or misuse of authority by their officials.

In particular, with a view to this protection, to keep distinct the three great departments of government — Legislative, Executive, and Judicial.

What a very high authority [2] says of the Federal Constitution applies to the State Constitutions also. " The peculiar and essential qualities of the Government established by the Constitution are:

" It is representative.

" It recognizes the liberty of the individual citizen as distinguished from the total mass of citizens, and it protects that liberty by specific limitations upon the power of government.

" It distributes the legislative, executive, and judicial powers into three separate departments and specifically limits the powers of the officers in each department.

" It makes observance of its limitations necessary to the validity of laws, to be judged by the Courts of Law in each concrete case as it arises."

These leading characteristics of the Constitutions as documents flow from the aforesaid three fundamental principles. Let us now see how these principles were worked out, and in what forms these characteristic features appear in the Constitutions, taking first those of the States, both as elder in date, and as most fully expressing the democratic ideas of the time which saw their birth.

Every State has to-day:

---

[1] This outline of the scheme of American government is given in order to enable those readers who have not time to study the Federal and State Constitutions to understand the institutional conditions under which democracy works and which have influenced countries so different as Switzerland, Australia, and Argentina.

[2] Mr. Elihu Root in an admirable little book entitled, *Experiments in Government and the Essentials of the Constitution* (1913).

(*a*) Its Constitution, enacted by the whole body of citizens voting at the polls.[1]

(*b*) A Legislature of two Houses, both elected by manhood (or universal) suffrage for terms varying from one to four years, but most frequently of two years. The smaller House, which is elected by larger constituencies, is called the Senate. In both the members receive salaries. The powers of both are substantially equal, though in a few States finance bills must originate in the larger House, and in a few the Senate is associated with the Governor in making appointments to office. In a few it sits as a Court to try impeachments.

(*c*) A Governor, elected usually for two or for four years by the citizens voting at the polls. He is the head of the Executive, and has (except in North Carolina) a veto on bills passed by the legislature, which, however, can be (though it seldom is) overruled by a two-thirds' vote in both Houses.[2]

(*d*) A number of administrative officials, some acting singly, some in Boards, elected by the citizens at the polls, or in a few cases by the legislature, and usually for short terms. These officials discharge functions prescribed by statute, and are independent of the legislature, though in some cases, directed or supervised by the Governor.

(*e*) Other minor officials, appointed, for short terms, either by the Governor or by the legislature or by the officials or Boards aforesaid.

(*f*) Judges, elected either for the whole State by its citizens voting at the polls, or for local areas by the citizens resident in those areas, and for terms of years usually short. In three States, however, the judges of the highest court are appointed for life by the Governor (subject to confirmation by the legislature, or by the Senate alone), and are removable only by impeachment, and in four others they are appointed by him (subject as aforesaid) for a term of years, while in four others they are elected by the legislature for terms, longer or shorter.

[1] There have been a few cases in which there was no direct popular enactment. See the author's *American Commonwealth*, vol. i. chap. xxxvii.

[2] There is also usually a Lieutenant-Governor, who succeeds to the Governor if the latter dies or resigns, and who, in some States, presides over the Senate.

The salaries of these officials vary according to the wealth of the State and the importance of the particular post, but are mostly small, averaging about $6000 (£1200).

LOCAL GOVERNMENT

Local Government has had such profound importance for democracy in America that the forms it has taken deserve to be described. Though every State has its own system, both for rural and for urban areas, all systems can be referred to one or other of a few predominant types. Those in force for rural areas, while varying from State to State, are the three following:

The New England type has its basis in the Town, a rural circumscription, dating from the first settlement of the country, which was originally small in population as well as in area. The Town, corresponding roughly to the English Parish, is governed by a general meeting of all the resident citizens, held at least once a year, in which the accounts of town expenses and receipts are presented, the general affairs of the community are discussed, the Selectmen (a small locally elected administrative council) are interrogated, and the officials for the ensuing year are elected. This Town meeting corresponds to the general meeting of the inhabitants of the Commune (Gemeinde) in Switzerland, and is the child of the old English Vestry, which was already decadent when the first settlers came to New England. No American institution has drawn more praise from foreign as well as American observers, and deservedly, for it has furnished a means of political training and an example of civic co-operation to every class of citizens, all deliberating together on the same level. It has been both the school and the pattern of democracy. It still flourishes in the agricultural parts of the six New England States, but works less well where a large industrial population has sprung up, especially if that population consists of recent immigrants. Above the Town stands the County which exists chiefly for the purposes of highways and as a judicial district, and which (in most States) elects its judges. It is governed by officials elected by the citizens for short terms, each official (or Board) having specific statutory functions. There is not, as in Great Britain, a County Council.

In the Southern States there are (broadly speaking) no Towns or Townships, and the County has always been the unit of local government. It has no council, but a number of officials elected by the citizens, each with his own prescribed functions. The most important of the smaller local authorities are the elected School Committees.

In the Middle and Western States both the Townships (for this is the name here given to the small local areas) and the Counties are important. In the latter single officials or small administrative Boards are elected for short terms. As their respective duties are prescribed by statute it has not been deemed necessary to have a council to supervise them. In those States which have been settled from New England, a Township has its Town meeting working on the old New England lines, but enlisting to a less extent the active interest of the people. The many different forms of local government that belong to this third type need not detain us. It is enough to say that in all the Northern, Middle, and Western States, though in varying degrees, the management of local affairs is entirely in the hands of the inhabitants, and thus receives more attention, and stimulates more sense of public duty, than it does in most of the free countries of Europe.

In Towns and Townships elections are generally conducted without reference to political parties, but County offices are frequently contested, this being due not so much to zeal for the public interest as to the influence of party spirit desiring to reward party services. The salient feature of rural local government is that everywhere local affairs are in the hands of persons locally elected, not, as in many parts of the European continent, of officials appointed by the Central Government. The citizens looking to no central authority for guidance, nor desiring (except for special purposes, such as education) the supervision which the central government gives in England, are content with such directions as general statutes give to the officials.

The principles of popular government are applied with unswerving consistency to the political arrangements of cities both large and small.[1] There are two forms of municipal

[1] " City " is the term used in the United States to describe any community organized as a municipality.

government. One, which till very recently was almost everywhere the same in its general lines, follows in most respects the model of a State Government.

There is a Mayor, but he is elected not by the City Council but by the whole body of citizens at the polls, and for a period nowhere exceeding four years.

There is a Legislature consisting in some cities of one Chamber, in others of two, elected in wards for a period which nowhere exceeds four years, and receiving salaries.

There are, in the larger cities, or many of them, officials, or Boards, also directly elected by the citizens for a period nowhere exceeding four years, as well as other inferior officials appointed either by the Mayor or by the Legislature.

There are judges and police magistrates elected by the citizens for terms of years, generally short.

All these elections are on the basis of manhood, or universal, suffrage. The Mayor, being directly chosen by the people, enjoys large powers, and has in many cities a veto on acts of the city legislature. He receives a salary which in the greater cities is large.

The other form of municipal government was introduced in 1901 in the city of Galveston in Texas, and having worked well there has spread widely, especially in the form of City Manager government into which it has recently developed. As it was adopted in order to cure evils conspicuous under the pre-existing system, and is an offspring of the new reforming movement, I reserve the account of it till these evils have been described (see Chapter XLV.).

THE FRAME OF NATIONAL GOVERNMENT

The Federal or National Constitution was drafted in 1787 when the country was depressed by economic troubles and the State legislatures had shown signs of feebleness and unwisdom, was enacted in 1788, and took effect in 1789. It resembles in its general lines the Constitutions of the thirteen original States (as they existed in 1787), subject to those variations which the nature of the case prescribed. The Convention which prepared it was not only under the influence of a reaction from the over-sanguine temper of war time, but contained many men of larger experience and more cautious minds than those who had led the States in the work of constitution making. Thus the National Constitution is not only a more scientifically elaborated but also a more "conservative" document, in the American sense of the word, than the State Constitutions. Moreover, some of the more "radical" or "democratic" provisions which were suitable to small communities, such as the States then were — only one had a population exceeding 500,000 — were ill suited to a country so large as the whole Union, and were therefore omitted. Ten amendments were made in 1791 in order to satisfy those who disliked some features of the instrument, two others in 1798 and 1804 respectively, and three others just after the War of Secession in the years 1865–70. Four others have been made between 1911 and 1920,[1] yet none of these materially affects the structure of the National Government. Under this Constitution there exist in the United States —

(a) A Legislature, called Congress, of two Houses. One, the House of Representatives, is elected, for a two years' term, by large districts approximately equal in population. The electoral franchise was that fixed by the law of the particular State from which the representative comes, viz. manhood suffrage in some States, universal suffrage in those which gave the vote to women, but now the right of voting in Federal elections has been extended to all women. Nearly all the Southern States have passed enactments which, without directly contravening the constitutional amendment of 1870 designed to enfranchise all the coloured population, have succeeded in practically excluding from the franchise the large majority of that population, although it is, in some States, nearly one half of the whole.[2] There are at present 435 members, and the number is periodically increased, according to population, after every decennial census. The other House, called the Senate, consists of two persons from each State, large or small, elected for six years. One-third of the number retire every two years. Formerly the Sen-

---

[1] One of these transfers the right of choosing senators from the Legislatures to the Peoples of the States, another forbids the production and sale of intoxicating liquors, and a third extends the suffrage to women over the whole Union.

[2] In S. Carolina and Mississippi it was in 1911 rather more than half.

ators were chosen in each State by its legislature, but now, by an amendment to the Federal Constitution adopted in 1913, they are elected by the citizens of each State on a " general ticket," *i.e.* a vote not by districts but over the whole State. The Senate has the right of considering and, if so advised, confirming nominations to office made by the President, and also of approving, by a two-thirds' majority, treaties negotiated by him. It also sits as a Court of Justice to try impeachments preferred by the House of Representatives against civil officials (including the President or his Ministers, or Federal judges), a two-thirds' majority being required for conviction. The salaries of members are large in proportion to those paid in Europe or in the British colonies, being at present fixed at $7500 (£1500), as also in proportion to the salaries of Federal officials.

(*b*) A President, head of the Executive, elected for four years by persons specially chosen by the people in each State for that purpose.[1] As these persons have been, in and since the election of 1796, always elected merely for the purpose of casting their votes for the particular candidate whom the voting citizen wishes to see chosen, this election by electors has become in practice a vote by the whole people. Each State chooses a number of Presidential Electors proportioned to its representatives in Congress, *i.e.* in effect proportioned to its population, but as all the votes belonging to a State are counted for the same candidate, irrespective of the number of votes cast by the citizens within that State for one or other set of the electors pledged to elect him, it may happen that the total vote given by the Presidential electors gives a different result from the total popular vote cast; *i.e.* a candidate may be elected (and has been more than once elected) who had not received a majority of the total number voting. The President frequently uses his right of vetoing a Bill passed by Congress, but his veto may be overriden if both Houses repass the Bill, each by a two-thirds' majority.

(*c*) Executive heads of departments, and a large number of other officials, the more important of whom (including

---

[1] They may be elected either by a " general ticket " vote over the whole State or in districts, according to the laws of each State. But the " general ticket " system is now universal.

those popularly called "the Cabinet"), are appointed by
the President with the consent of the Senate, as aforesaid.
Minor officials are appointed, some by the President, some
by higher officials or Boards, as the law may prescribe, but
none either by Congress or directly by the people.   The Cabinet Officers are responsible to the President, not to Congress, and, like all other Federal officials, are incapable of
sitting in either House.

(d) A Judiciary, consisting of a Supreme Court and such
inferior Courts as may be created by law.   The judges, appointed for life by the President with the consent of the
Senate, are removable only by impeachment.   Several have
been so removed.   Inferior Federal Courts have been created
all over the country, and from them an appeal lies to the
Supreme Court, which also enjoys original jurisdiction in
some kinds of cases.

This Frame of Government is less democratic than that
of the States in respect of the length of the Senatorial term,
of the life-tenure of the judges, and of the provision that
both administrative officials and judges are appointed, instead of being directly elected by the people, but is equally
democratic in respect of its placing the source of executive
as well as legislative power in direct popular election, and
of the shortness of the term of service allowed to Representatives.

Let us note how consistently the general principles have
been followed, both in the State Governments and in that
of the nation.

In the States the principle of Popular Sovereignty is
carried out (a) by entrusting as many offices as possible,
even (in most States) judgeships, to direct popular election,
so that the official may feel himself immediately responsible
to the people, holding office by no pleasure but theirs; (b)
by making terms of office short, in order that he may not
forget his dependence, but shall, if he desires a renewal of
his commission, be required to seek it afresh; and (c) by
limiting as far as possible the functions of each official to
one particular kind of work.   Similarly the doctrine of
Equality is respected in the wide extension of the electoral
franchise, in the absence of any kind of privilege, in the
prohibition of all public titles of honour, and practically also

in the usage which, taking little account of special fitness, deems everybody fit for any office he can persuade the people to bestow. Both in the States and in the National Government the apprehension felt regarding the possible abuse of power by holders of office, found expression (*a*) in the division of the Legislature into two Houses, (*b*) in the granting of a veto on legislation, in the State to the Governor and in the nation to the President, (*c*) in requiring the consent of the Federal Senate, and (in some States) of the State Senate, to appointments made by the Executive, (*d*) in the provisions for the removal of officials by impeachment, (*e*) by the Constitutional restrictions placed upon legislative and executive action. In these points we are reminded of the desire of the Athenian democracy to retain all power in the hands of the Assembly, and to watch with suspicious vigilance the conduct of all its officials, short as were the terms of office allowed to them.

Note also how the same principles run through the schemes of Local Government. Officials are all chosen by the direct election of the people, except those (a now increasing number) whose functions are of a technical character, such as surveyors or city engineers or public health officers. Many matters which would in Europe be assigned to elective county or city councils are left to the elected officials, who, uncontrolled by the supervision of a representative body, are simply required to act under statutes prescribing minutely to them their respective duties. This is supposed to guard the rights of the people, though in fact it makes the due discharge of those duties depend on whatever vigilance, often far too slight, some one in the people may display in instituting a prosecution for neglect or misfeasance.

The fact that the United States is a Federation in which there are everywhere two authorities, the National Government and the State Government, each supreme in its own sphere, concerns us here only in so far as it emphasizes and illustrates the American practice of limiting all elected authorities, whether persons or bodies. The powers of the National Government are defined and limited by the National Constitution, just as the powers of each State Government are defined and limited both by the National Con-

stitution, which has taken from them some of the attributes
of sovereignty, and by the Constitution of the particular
State.[1] Furthermore each branch of the Government, executive and legislative, both in Nation and in State, is limited. Congress has no such range of power as belongs to
the legislature of Great Britain or of a British self-governing Dominion, but is debarred by the Constitution from interfering with the functions allotted to the executive and to
the judiciary. So in each State the legislature, executive,
and judiciary are each confined by the State Constitution
to a particular field of action, which is further narrowed, as
respects the legislature, by the exclusion of a long list of subjects from legislative competence. This fundamental principle of American public law needs to be constantly remembered, because it has not only restrained popular impulses,
delayed changes, and protected vested rights, but also created a strongly marked legal spirit in the people and accustomed them to look at all questions in a legal way. It has,
moreover, by placing many matters outside the scope of
legislative action, compelled the direct intervention of the
people as the ultimate power capable of dealing with such
matters. Whatever powers cannot be exercised by an elected
authority have been reserved to the people, who exert them
by amending the Constitution. That stability in great
things coexistent with changefulness in small things, which
is characteristic of the United States, is largely due to this
doctrine and practice of limited powers, a feature foreign
to the French scheme of government, and less marked in
some other Federal Governments with Rigid constitutions,
such as those of Switzerland, Canada, and Australia.

Other points in which the observance of democratic principles appears are the following:

All members of legislatures receive salaries, so that no
one shall be debarred by want of independent means from
entering them.

Elections are frequent, so that no one shall ever forget
his constant dependence on the people.

No official of the Federal Government is eligible to sit in
Congress, no official of the Government of a State to sit in

---

[1] But whereas Congress possesses only such powers as have been expressly granted, a State legislature possesses all that have not been
expressly withheld.

its legislature. This provision, a tribute to the famous doctrine of the Separation of Powers, was meant to prevent the Executive from controlling the Legislature. Its effect has been to make the two powers legally independent of one another; but (as will be seen presently) it has not prevented the exercise of extra-legal influence, for just as Congress may hamper a President (or a State Legislature its Governor) by legislation narrowly restricting the sphere of his action, so a President may put pressure on Congress, or a Governor on his State Legislature, by appealing to the people against them; while a President may act upon the minds of individual legislators by granting, or refusing, requests made to him by them for the exercise of his patronage in the way they desire.

SUPERVENIENT CHANGES

We have now seen (1) what were the favouring physical and economic conditions under which the United States began its course as a nation; (2) what were the doctrines and beliefs, the hopes and apprehensions with which the schemes of government — State and Local and Federal — were framed; and (3) how these ideas and sentiments found expression in the institutions of which the frames consist. To test the soundness of the doctrines we must examine their results as seen in the actual working of the American government. But before considering these let us regard another factor, viz. the economic and social changes which have passed upon the United States during one hundred and thirty years of national life. The machinery has worked under conditions unforeseen when it was created. Never, perhaps, has any nation been so profoundly affected by new economic and racial phenomena, while retaining most of its institutions and nearly all its original political ideas.

The first of these changes was territorial extension. In 1789 the United States stretched westward only to the Mississippi, and did not reach the Gulf of Mexico, the coasts of which then belonged to France. The area of the thirteen States was then about 335,000 square miles, and the present area of the forty-eight States is now nearly 3,000,000 square miles. Its (free) population was then about 3,000,000, and is now (1920) over 110,000,000.

As the settlers moved into the interior, amazing natural resources were disclosed, an immense expanse of extremely fertile soil, vast deposits of coal, iron, silver, copper, and other minerals, forests such as had never been known to the Old World. The native free population grew swiftly, and had by 1840 risen to nearly 15,000,000. Soon afterwards a flood of immigrants began to come from Europe.[1] They and their descendants now form a majority of the American people. But as they came from many countries, and much the larger number from well-educated countries, such as the United Kingdom, Germany, and the Scandinavian kingdoms, and as those who settled on the land were quickly intermingled with and assimilated to the native population, the general standard of intelligence and conduct did not suffer in the rural districts. It was otherwise in the cities and mining regions. The growth of manufacturing industries, with the volume of trade that poured outward and inward from the great seaports, created enormous aggregations of labouring people fresh from the more backward parts of Europe, who being herded together were but slowly diffused into the pre-existing population. The gift of American citizenship, hastily conferred, found them unfit for its responsibilities. Another new factor was introduced by the Civil War, when slavery was first practically and then legally extinguished. The States were in 1870 forbidden to withhold the electoral suffrage from any citizen on the ground of "race, colour, or previous condition of servitude." This amendment to the Constitution placed under Federal sanction the right of voting conferred by Acts of Congress and State constitutions previously enacted upon a large mass of coloured citizens, the vast majority of whom were unfitted to exercise political rights with advantage either to the State or to themselves.

Meanwhile the material progress of the country had produced other not less significant changes. The development of agriculture, mining, and manufactures, the growth of commerce, foreign and domestic, which the use of steam for navigation and the construction of railroads had raised to gigantic proportions, created immense wealth, and concentrated a large share of it in the hands of comparatively few

[1] Many have recently come from Western Asia also.

men.[1] Three results followed. The old equality of fortunes disappeared, and though such distinction of ranks as had existed in colonial days melted away, the social relations of different classes lost their simplicity and familiarity when the rich lived in one quarter of great cities and the poorer were crowded together in others. That personal knowledge which made the feeling of a common interest a bond between the citizens was weakened. The power which money inevitably carries with it went on growing as the means of using it multiplied. Railroads and other business enterprises came to be worked on so vast a scale that it was worth while to obtain facilities for starting or conducting them by the illegitimate expenditure of large sums. The number of persons rich enough to corrupt legislators or officials increased, and as the tempters could raise their offers higher, those who succumbed to temptation were more numerous. Thus the power of money, negligible during the first two generations, became a formidable factor in politics.

As material interests grew more prominent and the passion for money-making more intense, policies and projects were more and more judged by the pecuniary prospects they opened up. That this did not exclude the influence of moral or humanitarian ideals is shown by the history of the Slavery controversy, for America, like England, is a country in which two currents of feeling have been wont to run side by side, sometimes apart, sometimes each checking or disturbing the course of the other. While the economic aspect of every question came more insistently into view, and tinged men's opinions on public issues, so also business enterprises had a greater attraction for men of ability and energy, diverting into other careers talents and ambitions which would in earlier days have been given to the service of the State. Men absorbed in business did not cease to vote, but were apt to leave their votes at the disposal of their political leaders. None of these changes could have been foreseen

[1] The improvement in the condition of the poorer class has, however, more than kept pace with the growth of millionaires, and it may be doubted whether these will be so numerous and play so large a part in the future as they have done during the last half-century. It is not true to say of America that the poor are poorer and the rich richer, for the number of persons moderately well off increases faster in proportion than does that of the wealthy, and the total wealth of the nation becomes more widely diffused.

by the framers of the early Constitutions, for although Jefferson and some of his contemporaries predicted for America a boundless growth of wealth, population and prosperity, they did not envisage the social and political consequences to follow.

The results of these geographical and economic changes may be summarized in a brief comparison:

The political institutions of the United States were created —
For a territory of which only about 100,000 square miles were inhabited.
For a free white population of little over 2,000,000.
For a population five-sixths of which dwelt in rural tracts or small towns.
For a people almost wholly of British stock.[1]
For a people in which there were practically no rich, and hardly any poor.
For a people mainly engaged in agriculture, in fishing, and in trading on a small scale.

These institutions are now being applied —
To a territory of 2,974,000 square miles, three-fourths of which is pretty thickly inhabited.
To a nation of over 110,000,000.
To a population fully one-third of which dwells in cities with more than 25,000 inhabitants.
To a people less than half of whose blood is of British origin and about one-tenth of whom are of African descent.
To a people which includes more men of enormous wealth than are to be found in all Europe.
To a people more than half of whom are engaged in manufacturing, mining, or commerce, including transportation.

It would not be strange if these institutions should bear signs of the unforeseen strain to which they have been subjected. The wonder is, not that the machinery creaks and

[1] There were about 150,000 Germans in Pennsylvania, but the other small non-British elements had been pretty thoroughly Americanized by 1789.

warps, but that it has stood the strain at all. But before examining the results of the changes referred to we must take note of a phenomenon of supreme importance which has affected in many ways the development of the institutions aforesaid. This is the growth of Party, and in particular of Party Organizations the most complete and most powerful that the world has seen. They constitute a sort of second non-legal government which has gained control of the legal government.

CHAPTER XL

THE three chief contributions which the United States has made to political science regarded as an Applied Science or Practical Art have been:

Rigid or so-called Written Constitutions, which, as being the expressions of the supreme will of the people, limit the powers of the different branches of government.

The use of Courts of Law to interpret Rigid Constitutions and secure their authority by placing their provisions out of the reach of legislative or executive action.

The organization of political parties.

Of these the first two are precautions against, or mitigations of, faults to which democracy is liable; while the third has proved to be an aggravation of those faults, undoing part of the good which the two former were doing, and impairing popular sovereignty itself. Yet party organization is a natural and probably an inevitable incident of democratic government. It has in itself nothing pernicious. Its evils have sprung from its abuses. We can now perceive that these evils are an outgrowth of the system likely to appear wherever it attains full development. But are they inevitable evils? Could they have been prevented if foreseen? Can they now be cut away without impairing such utility as the system possesses? This is a problem the American people have been trying to solve; and their efforts deserve to be studied.

Before describing the structure of the Organizations, let us enquire how Party came to cover the field and affect the working of politics more widely in America than elsewhere.

The political issues on which parties formed themselves after the establishment of the Federal Constitution were National issues. The first of these arose between those who sought to give full scope to Federal power and those who

27

sought to limit it in the interest of the rights of the States. This issue presently became entangled with that of the tariff; some groups desiring to use import duties for the protection of home industries, others preferring a tariff for revenue only. The question of the extension of slavery into the States which were from time to time formed out of the unorganized territories of the Union induced that bitter antagonism which ultimately led to the war of Secession. These issues overtopped and practically superseded all State and other local issues, and marked the lines of division between parties over the whole country. The fact that the Federal senators were chosen by the legislatures of the States made it the interest of each National party to fight every election of a State legislature on party lines, in order to obtain in that body a majority which would secure the choice of senators of its own persuasion, so State legislatures came to be divided on strict party lines, *i.e.* the lines of the National parties, though nearly all the questions which these legislatures dealt with had nothing to do with National issues. From the States the same habit spread into local elections, so that contests in cities and counties were also fought on party lines, though the work of these local bodies lay even more apart than did that of the States from the questions which divided the nation. It became a principle to maintain the power of the National parties in all elected bodies and by all means available, for the more the party was kept together in every place and on every occasion for voting, so much the stronger would it be for national purposes.[1]

Thus the partisan spirit extended itself to the choice of those administrative officials who were directly elected by the citizens, such as the State Governor and State Treasurer, the mayor of a city, the county commissioners. These elections also were fought on party lines, for a victory redounded to the credit and strength of the National party. Personal character and capacity were little regarded. The candidate was selected, in manner to be presently described, by the Primary or the Nominating Convention (as the case might be), as a party man, entitled to party recognition; and

---

[1] This was, however, never the case in the " Towns," the smallest areas of local self-government, and is not so generally the case in local bodies to-day as it was forty years ago.

the party machinery worked for him as zealously as it did for the candidate seeking election to Congress.

A further downward step was to require any official who had to appoint subordinate officers, or even to employ persons for some humble public service, to prefer members of his party for selection to the office or work. The official, himself chosen as a party man, was expected to serve the party by filling every place he could with men bound to vote for party candidates and otherwise serve the party. Even a labourer paid by weekly wages got employment on the condition of his voting and working for the party. Thus politics came to mean party politics and little else. People thought of party success as an end in itself, irrespective of the effect it would have upon the administration of many matters into which no party principle could enter. These evils were aggravated by the fact that the public service was not permanent. As the elected officials served for short terms, posts became frequently vacant. The tenure of those who were not directly elected but appointed lasted no longer than that of the authority who had appointed them, so when power passed from one party to another after an election, the employees appointed by the outgoing party had, however efficient they might be, no claim to be continued. They were dismissed, and their places given to successors appointed by the incoming party, which thus rewarded its friends and strengthened its influence. This practice, known as the Spoils System,[1] began in the State of New York early in the nineteenth century, and thence spread not only to other States but into the National Government also, so that the President, who by this time had an enormous number of posts at his disposal, was expected to use them as rewards for party services.

The Frame of Government, the outlines of which have been already described, was constructed in the belief that the people, desiring, and knowing how to secure, their own good, would easily effect their purposes by choosing honest

[1] The phrase, "the spoils to the victors," was first used by Marcy of New York, who described it as the practice in force in his State. It had been disapproved of in principle by the statesmen of the first generation, such as Jefferson and Madison, who saw its dangers, and desired to give the holders of Federal offices a permanent tenure. But President Jackson employed it freely, and the general treatment of offices as spoils dates from his time, 1829–1837.

legislators, and also by choosing officials who would be trustworthy agents, administering public affairs in accordance with the people's wishes. In a New England township, and even in the far larger county area of Virginia, the men of the eighteenth century knew personally the fellow-citizens whom they trusted, and could select those whose opinions they approved and whom they deemed capable; so, though the existence of parties was recognized, as were also the dangers of party spirit, the choice of legislators and officials seems to have been regarded as a simple matter, and it was not perceived that when population increased and offices became more important the old simple methods would not suffice, since elections must involve more and more work, and the selection of candidates be more difficult. Party organizations grew up unnoticed because unforeseen. There had been none in England, the only country where popular elections were known and party spirit had sometimes been furious. Thus it befell that in the United States, though parties appeared from the early days of the National Government, and their antagonisms were already fierce when the fourth presidential election was held in 1800, party organizations grew slowly, and attracted little attention. Tocqueville, writing in 1832, never mentions them, yet they were already strong in his day, and had covered the whole country before the Civil War broke out in 1861.

Some sort of associated action is incidental to every representative government, for wherever power is given to elected persons, those citizens who desire their particular views to prevail must band themselves together to secure the choice of the persons best fitted both to express their own views and to attract the votes of other citizens. Whether they devise a method for selecting a candidate or simply accept the man who presents himself, they must work in unison to recommend him to the voters generally, canvassing for him and bringing up their friends to the poll. Without concerted action there will be confusion, disorder, loss of voting power. An Election Committee formed to help a candidate pledged to its cause is the simplest form of party organization, legitimate and possibly inexpensive. Beyond this form party organization in England did not advance till our own time.

In the United States it was found necessary to go further. Under the constitutions of the several States elections were frequent, because many administrative as well as all legislative posts, both State and municipal, were filled by popular vote, and because these posts were held for short terms. As the population of cities and electoral areas generally grew larger, so that most citizens ceased to have personal knowledge of the candidates, it became more needful to inform them of the merits of those who sought their suffrages; more needful also to have lists of the voters and to provide for " getting out the vote." The selection of candidates also became important. In England, so long as the structure of rural society retained an old-fashioned semi-feudal character, some one belonging to an important land-owning family was usually accepted, while in the towns (after pocket boroughs had vanished) a wealthy merchant or manufacturer, especially if he had filled some municipal office, was likely to find favour. But in America, where Equality prevailed, neither wealth nor rank gave a claim to any post. The principle of Popular Sovereignty suggested that it was for the citizens not only to choose members or officials by their votes, but to say for what persons votes should be cast. Hence where any post was to be filled by local election, the local adherents of the party were deemed entitled to select the man on whom their voting force was to be concentrated. This was a logical development of the principle. Instead of letting a clique of influential men thrust a candidate upon them, or allowing a number of candidates to start in rivalry and so divide their votes, the party met before the election to choose the man they preferred to be their local standard-bearer, and it was understood that the votes of all would be given to whomsoever the majority chose. A meeting of this kind was called a Party Primary, and it became the duty of the party committee which managed elections to make the arrangements for summoning, and naturally also for advising, the Primary.

These being the two aims which called party organization into being, I pass to its main features, substantially, though not in minor details, the same over the whole country, and will describe it as it stood in 1888, before recent changes which cannot be understood till an account has been

given of the system as it existed before their adoption.
Though it has been almost everywhere altered, it may revert
to type, and in any case it has been a product of democracy
too remarkable to be ignored, for it showed how organizations essentially oligarchic in structure, though professing
to be democratic, can become tyrannical under democratic
forms.

The work of every Party Organization is twofold, corresponding to the two aims aforesaid. One branch of it
was to select party candidates by the process called Nomination, as practised before the recent changes. The other is
to promote the general interests of the party in every electoral area. Each party has, in most States, a party Committee in every city ward, in every city, in every township
and State Assembly district and Congressional district, in
every county, in every State, and at the head of all a National Committee for the whole United States, appointed to
fight the approaching Presidential Election.[1] Each of these
Committees is elected either by those who are enrolled as
members of the party in its meeting in a Primary (to be
presently described) or else by a Convention composed of
delegates from the Primaries. The Committees are appointed annually, the same persons, and especially the Chairman, being usually continued from year to year. They have
plenty to do, for the winning of elections is a toilsome and
costly business. Funds have to be raised, meetings organized, immigrants recruited for the party and enrolled as its
members, lists of voters and their residences prepared, literature produced and diffused, and other forms of party propaganda attended to, and when the day of election arrives party
tickets must be provided and distributed,[2] canvassers and
other election workers organized and paid, voters brought up
to the polls. Each Committee keeps touch with the Committee next above it in a larger electoral area, and with
that below it in a smaller, so that, taken together, these
bodies constitute a network, strong and flexible, stretching

[1] In some States it is only the larger areas that have Committees,
the county being the most important one after that for the State.
There is also a permanent Congressional Committee appointed by members of the two Houses from their own number.

[2] This part of the work has, however, now generally passed to the
officials who superintend elections. Party processions, once extensively
used, are obsolescent.

over the whole Union. They are an army kept on a war footing, always ready for action when each election comes round; and everything except the nomination of candidates and formulation of party programmes is within their competence.

Nominations belong to the other set of party authorities. These are either Primaries or Conventions. The Primary was — until recent legislation, of which more hereafter — the party meeting for the smaller election areas, in which a large proportion of the voters belonging to the party could be brought together in one room. It had two duties. One was to select a candidate or candidates for any elective office within its area, thereby putting its official stamp upon each person chosen as being the "regular candidate" entitled to the votes of all good and true members of the party. The other duty was to choose delegates to proceed to, and represent it in, a Nominating Convention for some larger election area or areas within which its own area lay. Thus a Ward Primary in a city would send delegates to a City Convention which nominates candidates for the mayoralty and other municipal offices, and also to a State Assembly District Convention, a State Senatorial District Convention, a Congressional District Convention, which nominates a candidate for Congress, and a State Convention which nominates a candidate for the Governorship and other elective State offices.[1]

The Nominating Convention consists (for Conventions are not extinct) of the delegates from the Primaries (or minor Conventions) within some large election area. Its function is to select candidates for elective offices within that area, such as members of the State Legislature, mem-

---

[1] The State Convention has now been in many States abolished by recent legislation, but while it existed it was an important part of the machinery. Sometimes, as in New York City, there may be a Primary for an Assembly District and in small cities a Primary may suffice for the whole city. It would be impossible to present, within reasonable limits, an account of the arrangements now in force in the several States, for these are nearly everywhere regulated by statutes, which vary from State to State. Federal legislation does not touch the subject.

Whoever desires to understand the whole machinery of the system as it stood in 1887 may refer to chapters lix.-lxx. of *American Commonwealth*, vol. ii., or to M. Ostrogorski's valuable book *La Démocratie et les partis politiques*, new edition of 1912. The local "Ward Leader" is an important factor in cities.

bers of the Federal House of Representatives, the Governor
and higher judges of the State. It selects and stamps as
"regular" the candidate it prefers, and in some cases it
also selects delegates to proceed from it to a Convention of
higher rank and wider compass, viz. a State Convention or
the National Convention which nominates the party candidate for the Presidency. A Convention also passes resolutions enouncing the views and aims of the party. These,
however, being usually cut and dried, seldom arouse discussion.

All these arrangements scrupulously respected the Sovereignty of the People. No member of a Committee, no
delegate to a Convention, was self-appointed. All were
chosen by the members of the party. Nobody was recognized as a candidate unless he had been chosen by a party
meeting. In theory, nothing could be more correct. Now
let us look at the practice.

Even before the system had matured and still more after
its full development, tendencies appeared disclosing inherent dangers. Those new phenomena, due to the growth of
population and wealth, which have been already described,
strengthened these tendencies, giving rise to grave perversions.

The Primary was in theory open to all members of the
party resident within its area, but in order to prevent persons who did not belong to the party from entering and
turning it into a public instead of a private party meeting,
it became necessary to have a roll of party members, so
that every one claiming to vote could prove his title. Now
the rolls were kept by the local party Committee already referred to, a body composed of the most active and thoroughly partisan local politicians. Wishing to make sure of
a subservient primary, this Committee took care to place on
the rolls only those whom it deemed to be trusty party men,
so any citizen suspected of independence was not likely to
be enrolled. If he were alleged to have failed to vote for
the "regular" party candidate at the last preceding election, that might be taken as a ground for omitting him, and
if, discovering that he was not on the roll, he demanded to
be entered, the demand might be evaded. *Prima facie,*
therefore, the Committee could make pretty sure that when

a Primary was held, it would choose the persons they desired to have nominated.

Now the Primaries were usually held in the evening,
especially in the cities, and it was chiefly in the cities that
the nomination methods here described were employed. The
attendance was seldom large, but it was sure to include all
the local party "workers," and others on whose votes the
managing Committee could count. Often it consisted entirely of persons belonging to the humbler strata of the
party. The richer sort, including the larger taxpayers,
though they had the strongest interest in entrusting administration to men who would conduct it economically, seldom
attended, preferring their social engagements, or a quiet
evening at home with their families. Few troubled themselves to see that their names were on the roll. Still fewer
desired the local posts, or cared to serve as delegates to a
Convention, so the choice of nominees for the offices, and for
the function of delegate, was usually left to the Committee,
who bringing their list cut and dried, proposed and carried
it without trouble. Now and then there was opposition, if
there happened to be a feud within the party, or if some
among the better sort of citizens, fearing the nomination of
exceptionally unfit men, thought it worth while to make a
fight. However, the Committee could usually command a
majority, and as the chairman was ready to rule every question in their favour, opposition rarely succeeded. Thus the
Committee, being master of the situation, almost always put
through its nominations both for the local posts and for the
choice of delegates. That having been done, the Committee
itself was reappointed, and the rule of the local managers
thereby duly prolonged from one year to another.

When the delegates proceeded to the Convention they met
other delegates from other Primaries within the Convention
area, persons similarly chosen, and similarly bound to carry
out the instructions which their respective Primaries had
given them. Sometimes these instructions directed them to
vote in the Convention for the nomination of the person
whom the party managers had already fixed on as the party
candidate for any particular office, but even if no direction
had been given, they followed the managers' lead. It need
hardly be said that the petty local politicians who managed

the Primaries were in close touch with the larger political figures in charge of the party business of the county, and with the still more exalted beings similarly charged with its interests in the State. If the Primary elections had been well handled, there was little trouble in getting the Convention to accept the list of nominations prepared by the managers, and this list, being official, then commanded the votes of all sound party men. The whole procedure was, in point of form, strictly democratic. The Voice of the People rang out in the Primaries. The delegates transmitted it to the Convention; so those whom the Convention nominated as party candidates were the people's choice. Hence the trouble taken to secure the Primaries was none too great. They were the key of the position.

Why did these methods succeed? Since about 1870, if not earlier, the more observant and thoughtful citizens had known the realities which previously, cloaked under democratic forms, had passed almost unnoticed. Yet for many a year they submitted tamely to the perversion of those forms, taking no pains to have good candidates selected, and voting for whatsoever candidates the Organization presented to them.

Several reasons may be assigned for this tolerance:

(a) The better sort of citizens, i.e. the educated and intelligent men, whatever their social status, who might have been expected to have an interest in good administration, were too indolent, or too busy with their own affairs, to attend the Primaries.

(b) The offices to which the Primary nominated were insignificant, and they did not care who filled them.

(c) The post of delegate had no attraction. It brought them into contact with persons whose company was distasteful; and if they went to a Convention they would have to choose between subservience to the managers and a troublesome and probably unsuccessful resistance.

(d) They did not, especially in the larger cities, know which candidates deserved support, for the offices to be filled were numerous, and how were they to select from a list of names that meant nothing to them? They wanted guidance, and as the party nominations gave it, they voted for the party nominees, asking no questions.

(*e*) Some of them had business interests which made it worth their while to stand well with party leaders in the city legislature, or State legislature, or Congress.

(*f*) Most of them were so possessed by the notion that democratic Equality means that every citizen is good enough for any place he can get, that they thought it mattered little who filled any but the highest posts.

(*g*) Nearly all were governed by the sentiment of party loyalty, exceptionally strong in America from 1830 to 1890, since which date it has been declining among the more thoughtful citizens.

All this implies that the citizens did not live up to the standard of civic duty which their democratic system contemplated. It does not mean that they were below the level of citizens elsewhere. On the contrary, they were probably above the point at which that level stands in Europe. What it does mean is that the legal duty imposed on them of voting frequently and the non-legal duty of sharing in party management were, taken together, too numerous and troublesome for average human nature. Overmuch was demanded from them. If less had been asked, more might have been given.

Nevertheless a time came when the combined influence of all these causes could no longer stifle discontent. The worm turned. From about 1890 onwards, dissatisfaction grew so strong that a demand for a reform of the Primaries, beginning in the great Eastern cities, spread over the country and secured in nearly every State the enactment of statutes intended to root out the abuses described and deliver the party voter from his tyrants. These changes will be described when we come to a general survey of the efforts recently made to improve the working of American institutions.

These vast party organizations, covering the country from ocean to ocean with a network of Committees, managing Primaries and Conventions, fighting the endless elections, raising and spending large sums of money, needed, and still need, a number of men to work them said to exceed that of all the elected officials of the country, if we omit those of ward and township. " The machinery of [party] control in American Government probably requires more people to tend and work it than all other political machinery in the rest of the civilized world." [1] These workers, except the secretaries and clerks, are almost all unpaid. Many chairmen of the more important Committees give their whole time to the work. Many of the humbler sort, who look after voters in the wards of crowded cities, throw zeal as well as labour into the duties assigned to them. What are the inducements? Whence comes the remuneration? One must distinguish three classes of persons.

From time to time, when some exciting issue rouses hope or alarm, men will work out of disinterested attachment to party doctrines. Many more, especially among the humble and less educated, are stirred by party spirit pure and simple, fighting for victory as in a football match. Keen is the pleasure of strife and competition, especially in America. The sympathy that springs from co-operation feeds this spirit. It is a joy to stand shoulder to shoulder, especially with a prospect of success. But the largest number of workers in all ranks work for their own interests, those at the top aiming at high political office, which may carry with it opportunities of gain exceeding its salary, those lower down desiring either a humbler public post or perhaps a profit to be made out of the Administration when their friends are installed in it, those at the bottom seeking employment in the police, or the fire service, or the gas service, or some other department of municipal work.

Thus the main inducement is Office, or the assured prospect of receiving an office when the party one serves is in power. "What are we here for except the offices?" was the oft-quoted deliverance of a politician at a National Convention. The Organization can confer the office and recognizes the obligation to do so, because it controls nominations and can require its nominees, when elected, to reward service rendered to it by bestowing any emolument, legitimate or illegitimate, that lies within the range of their official power or covert influence. It is largely self-supporting, like an army that lives off the country it is conquering, but while the party forces are paid by salaried posts, legislative, administrative, or judicial, the funds of the Organization are also replenished by contributions exacted from business

[1] Professor H. J. Ford, *Rise and Growth of American Politics*, p. 312.

firms or corporations which its power over legislation and
administration can benefit or injure. In this material aspect, the Organization is called by Americans the Machine,
because it is a well compacted and efficient set of contrivances which in its ordered working provides places for the
professional staff who serve its purposes by helping to win
elections.

Who were responsible for the rule of professional politicians? Where were the good citizens while all these things
were going on? Why did they vote at State and City elections for candidates of whom they knew nothing except that
they were the Machine nominees?

The system had grown up naturally as the business of
winning elections became more and more a matter needing
constant attention and labour. Those who had created the
original Committees came to be permanent party managers,
and had worked out of party spirit before they began to
work for their selfish interests. The " good citizens," occupied in making money and developing the resources of the
country, acquiesced and became unconscious accomplices.
Many of the urban constituencies had grown so large by the
increase of population that very few of the voters knew, or
could know, who were the fittest candidates. The bulk
were too much engrossed with their own business to be at the
trouble of enquiring for themselves, so when the party gave
them guidance by nominating candidates, they took thank-
fully what was given. In exciting times the vehemence
of their party spirit disposed them to overlook a candidate's
defects and accept any one who had received the party stamp
from nomination by the Primary or the Convention.
In duller times, they cared so little about the matter that
while many stayed away from the polls, others voted the
ticket like automata. Seldom was any protest raised in a
Primary or Convention.

From time to time questions arose which so deeply touched
either the emotions or the pocket of the good citizen as to
make him ready to swallow any candidate and turn a blind
eye to a want of honour in party leaders. The zealous
Anti-Slavery men of New England pardoned everything
for the sake of that cause; and in later days the Protectionists of Pennsylvania allowed their State to be domi-

nated by a succession of unscrupulous chiefs because the unity of the high tariff party must be at all costs maintained, and, even apart from any such motives, the loyalty to his old historic party was more deeply ingrained in the American nature than it had ever been in any other country where Party had no racial or religious basis. Thus it befell that party spirit supported the Organization through evil-doing and well-doing. Without such a spirit the Machine could not have won and kept power. But neither could the spirit have shown such tenacity of life without the Organization which gathered in and drilled recruits from the masses, turning into fervent Republicans or Democrats crowds of brand-new citizens who, neither knowing nor caring what the tenets of their party were, liked to be associated in a body which brought them into the life of their adopted country. They became partisans without principles, the solidest kind of voters. It must also be remembered that the party managers were not all professionals, at least in the lower sense of the term. Some were eminent statesmen who loved the party for the party's sake, and who, though not soiling their own hands, could not afford to scrutinize too closely the methods of the Bosses who controlled the votes which the party needed.

This brings us to another aspect of the subject. Who were those that led and ruled each Party, not as a professional machine with pecuniary aims, but as an association of citizens desiring to shape the policy of the nation? Who determined in what wise its traditional principles should be from time to time adapted to the circumstances and needs of the moment? Since a main object of every party is to foresee and follow the public opinion of the majority so as to catch votes at elections, it must, for this purpose, consider what views on current issues should be announced beforehand, what plans formulated and promises made.

The fundamental doctrine of democracy prescribes that the only authorized exponent of the views of the people is the People itself, and this means, for a party, all its members assembled by their representatives in a Convention. Accordingly every State Convention held before a State election adopted a Platform, which, though it might touch upon any important State issue, was chiefly concerned with na-

tional issues, and professed to express the national policy
of the party.   Still more authoritative of course is the platform adopted by the National Convention when it selects
the party candidate for the Presidency.   But in neither body
is there any real discussion of the planks in the platform.
There is not time enough, and a National Convention is a
body of more than a thousand delegates meeting in the presence of ten thousand spectators.   The State Committee or
National Committee (as the case may be) prepares the platform in advance, and the Convention usually adopts it after
two or three declamatory speeches, though alterations are
often made especially if needed to "placate" any critical
or possibly recalcitrant section of the party that may be
represented in the hall.   The part played by the Convention
is formal.[1]   Those who determine beforehand the contents
of the platform are, though the real leaders of the party,
persons whom it is hard to define and impossible to enumerate.   In England the Prime Minister and Cabinet declare
the policy of the party in power, and are usually accepted
as speaking on its behalf; while the leader of the parliamentary Opposition and the ex-Cabinet do the like for the
party in opposition.   But the existing Cabinet in America
counts for little in such a matter, and the last preceding
Cabinet for nothing at all.   So far as there is a leader of
the "party in power," it is the President, because he is the
choice of the people, assumed to retain their confidence till
some event shows that he has lost it.   Next to him in authority would come the Speaker of the House of Representatives, but only if personally influential, together with a few
of the leading senators of the party, and some other adroit
and experienced politicians, especially if they are in touch
with the President.   But with such men leadership depends
on personal qualities and reputation, not upon any official
position.   They will often be found in the permanent Congressional party Committee, which includes the shrewdest
of the party men in the House of Representatives; and
also in the National Committee, which though formed only
for the temporary purpose of each Presidential election, has

[1] Although large gatherings claiming to speak on behalf of each
party meet annually, little weight attaches (except in the case of the
Labour or Socialist parties, virtually without authoritative personal
leadership) to their deliverances.

become a sort of permanent party executive. But the public, knowing little of many among the members of these two Committees, is disposed to look chiefly to the President for leadership. Congress is not the centre of America's political life, as the House of Commons still is in England, and as are the Chambers in France, while the rank and file of those who fill the Conventions are not primarily concerned with policy but with the getting and keeping of places.

Two phenomena that have struck European observers deserve only a passing mention, because they are due to causes which have little or nothing to do with democracy. One is the fact that two great parties have since 1836 maintained themselves (except, of course, during the Civil War) in tolerably equal strength, neither able to disregard its opponent.[1] The other is that the minor parties which have been from time to time created have either died down or been pretty quickly reabsorbed, like the Know Nothings of 1852, the Populists of 1890–96, and the Progressives of 1912, or else have failed to attain truly national importance. This latter fact shows that democratic governments do not invariably, as some have inferred from the cases of France and Italy, cause the splitting up of parties into groups.

Note that this party organization forms another government, unknown to the law, side by side with the legal government established by the Constitution. It holds together an immense number of citizens in small party aggregates all over the country, each subordinated to and represented in larger State aggregates, and these in their turn represented in one huge party meeting, the National Convention which assembles once in four years to declare party policy and choose a presidential candidate. Thus the whole vast body is induced to follow a few leaders and to concentrate its voting power upon the aims and purposes which the majority prescribe. Though Bills are sometimes mentioned in a platform, legislation is not one of the chief aims of party, and many of the most important measures, such as the Prohibition amendment and the Woman Suffrage amendment, have had no party character.[2] Its chief purpose is

[1] The Republican party was founded in 1854 on the ruins of the crumbling Whig party, and maintained the two-party tradition.
[2] It is related that a noted politician, who was surveying the land-

to capture, and to hold when captured, the machinery, legislative and administrative, of the legal government established by the Constitution. That machinery, when captured, is used, mainly of course for discharging the normal routine work of legislation and administration, most of which has nothing to do with party doctrines and proposals, to some extent also for carrying out those doctrines by legislative action, but largely also for putting into public office " sound men," being those who profess the tenets of the party, and have rendered service to it. If the constitutional government of the country be compared to a vast machine set up in a factory to be worked by electric power, the party system may be likened to the dynamo engine that makes the electric current which, when turned on, sets all the machinery in motion. The two governments, the legal and the party, are in their structure very different things, but it is from the non-legal party machinery that the legal machinery of government derives its motive power.

Party organization has done much to unify the people of the United States and make them homogeneous, for it has brought city and country, rich and poor, native American and Old World immigrant into a common allegiance, which has helped them to know, and taught them to coöperate with, one another. Had the parties been based on differences of race or religion, those elements of antagonism which existed in the population would have been intensified. But they have been in fact reduced. Most of the Irish immigrants joined the Democratic party, most of the German the Republicans, but there were always plenty of German Protestants among the Democrats and of Irish Catholics among the Republicans. So, too, the Organizations have mitigated such inconveniences as arise from the provisions of the Constitution which disjoin the Executive from the Legislative power, for when the President belongs to the same party as the majority in Congress, he and the latter, having a common interest in the prestige of the party, are likely to work well together, though, conversely, when

scape from the back platform of a railroad car in motion, was warned by the coloured porter that he must not stand there, and when he remarked that he thought a platform was meant to stand on, the darky replied, " Oh no, sah, a platform ain't meant to stand on. It's meant to get in on."

they belong to different parties, the majority in Congress become the more disposed to " play politics " against him.

As compared with the legal Frame of National Government, the party system is more compactly built together and attains a completer concentration of power. It is an admirable contrivance for centralizing control and making effective the rule of a majority, and indeed the best instrument for the suppression of dissident minorities democracy has yet devised. Thus it has generally shown itself a conservative force, for in order to command a majority at elections, it is obliged — except when it can take advantage of some sudden impulse sweeping over the country — to conciliate various sections of opinion and try to keep them within its fold. It will even condescend to suffer cranks gladly, or to exploit temporary fads and follies, so long as it can do so without alienating its saner members. When a new question emerges, raising serious differences of opinion, the Organization usually tries to hedge. It fumbles and quibbles and faces both ways as long as it can. But when one section has gained the mastery of the party, the Organization may become almost ferociously intolerant, and enforce by the threat of excommunication [1] whatever it then declares to be its orthodoxy. It is conservative in another sense also, for it tends to restrain personal ambition and imposes a check upon the too obtrusive selfishness of prominent men. One who has risen by party support is rarely so indispensable, or so great a hero to the mass of voters, as to become dangerous by leading his party into violent courses or making it the accomplice in his schemes of personal ambition. He will have learnt that only by watching and following general opinion can power be retained.

Thus it may be said that Party Organization, which has done some great disservices to America, shows also a good side. It has, so far as concerns the lower strata, demoralized politics, and made them sordid. It has fallen under the control of an oligarchy. But it has also steadied the working of government over a vast country wherein are many diverse elements, by giving an authoritative solidity

---

[1] Thus in 1896 the " Free Silver " Democrats crushed opposition, and (for a time) drove the Gold Standard men out of the party, just as, after 1903, the Protectionists expelled the Free Trade men from the Conservative party in England.

to popular majorities. The tendency to abuse power, frequent in small communities, is reduced in this large country, because the party majority is held together by respecting the various elements of which it is composed, while as the party for the time being in the minority has also a strength and cohesion through its organization, it can criticize those who hold the reins of power and deter them from extreme courses. The greatest fault of the system, next to the selfishness and corruption its perversions have bred, has lain in the irresponsible secrecy of its influence over the official organs of government. An American party is, in one sense, so far made responsible that when its policy has been condemned by the results, it loses support, and may suffer defeat. But the leaders who direct its policy are usually so numerous, and some of them so little known, and the share of each in a misdeed committed so unascertainable, that it is hardly too much to say that in the State Governments only one person can be held responsible as a party leader, the Governor,[1] and in the National Government only one person, the President.

It may be thought that the description here given exaggerates the novelty of the American party system, seeing that Party rules both in Britain and her self-governing Dominions, and in France, and in some of the smaller free countries. But it must be remembered not only that the American Organization is incomparably more fully developed, but also that it stands forth more conspicuously as a system standing quite outside of the legal Government. In France, legislation and administration are carried on not by one party but by combinations of groups frequently formed, dissolved, and then re-formed. In England party conflicts fought all over the country, come only once in three, four, or five years, at a General Election; and when one party goes under and another comes to the top, only some thirty or forty persons change places, so the general machine of administration seems but slightly affected, and few are those who directly lose or gain. Party policy, moreover, rests with a half-dozen Parliamentary figures on each

[1] Nevertheless, a State Governor, though the choice of his party and presumably entitled to the support of his party friends in the legislature, may have less power than the State Boss who holds in his hands the threads of the Organization.

side, *i.e.* the leaders of the two Houses and their closest advisers and associates, whereas in the United States the National Convention is the supreme exponent of party doctrine and policy, universally recognized as the party oracle, though its deliverances may in practice be conveniently forgotten. Thus the American system, though it purports to regard measures rather than men, expends nearly all its efforts and its funds in getting men into places, and though it claims to give voice to the views and will of the whole party does in reality express those of an oligarchy which becomes, subject to the necessity of regarding public opinion, the effective ruler of the country, whenever the party holds both the Legislature and the Executive.

CHAPTER XLI

THE ACTUAL WORKING OF THE NATIONAL AND STATE GOVERNMENTS

WE may now return to the legal frame of Government, examining each of its branches, and noting how the working of each has been modified, and to some extent warped from its original purpose, by the influence of the parallel non-legal government constituted by the Party Organization.

First, as the foundation of all else, comes the part assigned by the Constitutions, State and Federal, to the direct action of the People at elections.

ELECTORAL SUFFRAGE

The electoral suffrage is left by the Federal Constitution to the States. In them, it was at first limited to citizens possessed of some property, often freehold land or a house, but in the period of the great democratic wave which passed over the country between 1820 and 1840, it was almost everywhere extended to all adult men; and since 1869, when Wyoming (then a Territory) gave it to women, many States have followed that example.[1] In 1919 Congress proposed an amendment to the Constitution granting equal suffrage everywhere to women, and this was ratified by the requisite number of State Legislatures in 1920. The change is the longest step towards pure democracy ever taken in America.

Whether the admission of women has made any, and if so what, practical difference remains still obscure, a matter for conjecture rather than proof, since under the ballot there is nothing to show how far women vote differently

[1] In 1919 eleven States had given the suffrage to women, viz. Wyoming, Colorado, Montana, N. Dakota, S. Dakota, Arizona, Oregon, Washington, California, New York, Massachusetts.

from men. It was, however, believed that, in 1916, the women electors (who voted in ten States) had turned the Presidential election, they being more eager than men to keep the United States out of the war then raging in Europe. Though it is often said that women generally vote for restricting or forbidding the sale of intoxicants, occasions are mentioned when this does not appear to have happened. Such evidence as is available indicates that women mostly vote much as men do, following the lead of their husbands or brothers and of the party organizations, that administrative government is in the woman suffrage States neither better nor worse than in others, and that the general character of legislation remains much the same. Nowhere does there seem to be any Women's Party, specially devoted to feminine aims. Only one woman has so far been elected to Congress, and few to State Legislatures.

In 1868 and 1870 Constitutional amendments were passed (Amendments XIV. and XV.) intended to secure the suffrage to the (then recently emancipated) negroes, but the apparently sweeping provisions of the latter enactment have been in nearly all of the former Slave States so far nullified by State Constitutions ingeniously contrived to exclude the coloured people, that less, perhaps much less, than one-fifth of these now enjoy voting rights. Members of Congress from the North and West at first resented, and sought means of defeating, these contrivances, but when a new generation arose, little influenced by memories of the Anti-Slavery struggle and the Civil War, interest in the question subsided. Common sense regained its power, and the doctrine that every adult human being has a natural right to a vote, though never formally abandoned, has been silently ignored.

The question whether any educational qualification should be prescribed, and how soon immigrants should be allowed to vote, is still discussed.[1] Some States prescribe such a qualification, some fix a term during which the immigrant must have resided in America. Others register him as a voter even before he has been naturalized as a citizen, argu-

---

[1] As a rule, a citizen can in the United States vote only in one place, that where he resides and pays local taxes.

Most States exclude from the suffrage criminals and persons receiving public relief. Minor differences between State and State as respects qualifications are not worth mentioning.

ing that this tends to accelerate the process of Americaniza-
tion. There is force in this view as respects rural areas
and small towns, where the newcomer quickly learns English and acquires the habits and ideas of his native neighbours. But in great cities and thickly-peopled mining districts, where he remains one of a mass of Italians, or Greeks,
or Serbs, or Finns, or Rumans, or Polish Jews, he learns
far less readily how to use his new citizenship, and falls
an easy victim to the party agents, often of his own race,
who sweep him into their net and use him as so much voting stock.

ELECTIONS

The number of direct elections by the people is far larger
in America than in any other country, (a) because there are
three sets of elections, Local (in which many offices may
have to be filled), State, and National; (b) because the
terms of office are short, so that the elections to each post
recur frequently; (c) because many offices (including judgeships), which in other countries are filled by Executive
appointment, are here filled by the direct act of the People.
This constant summoning of the citizens to vote has one of
two results. If National and State and Local elections are
held at different times, the elector, teased by these frequent
calls, is apt to refuse to go to the poll. If, on the other
hand, these elections are fixed for the same day, he is be-
wildered by the number of candidates for various posts between which he is expected to choose. The American practice has usually been for each party to put on one piece of
paper, called a Slip Ticket, and often adorned with a party
symbol, the names of all the candidates it nominated for the
various offices to be filled at the election. The voter could
mark with his cross all the names on the list, or could " vote
the ticket " simply by dropping it as it stood into the ballot
box. If, however, he approved of some of the candidates,
but disapproved of others, preferring some candidates appearing on another party ticket, he erased from his party
slip ticket those names (this is called " scratching ") and
substituted other names from the other ticket or tickets.
Where, however, as is now frequently done, the names of

all the candidates of all the parties are printed upon one
sheet, each name opposite the office for which each has been
nominated, that sheet becomes enormous, and the voter cannot, with the best will in the world, exercise an intelligent
choice by selecting the man he thinks best from the different
party columns in which their names appear; so he usually
abandons the task in despair and votes the names the party
recommends. With the rise of every new party, however
numerically weak, the confusion becomes greater by the
addition of a new set of candidates. The result is to make
all but impossible that judicious selection of the fittest men
for each particular post which the system of popular elections was meant to secure, a result which has of course
played into the hands of the party managers.

The gravity of the evil has provoked demands for curing
it by expedients to be presently mentioned. Meantime note
that a democratic principle may be so pushed to excess as
to defeat itself. The more numerous are the nominations
a party makes, the less likely are the bad to be detected.
Where the voter is expected with scarcely any personal
knowledge to select men fit for fifteen or twenty posts, he
ceases to try. Had there been only five he might have succeeded. To ask too much may be to get nothing. A beast
of burden that will carry half a ton's load to market will
get nowhere if the load is doubled.

Elections are now quietly conducted, neither side disturbing the meetings of its opponents (as often happens in
England), nor are voters at the polls molested, unless perhaps in a Ring-ruled city where the police are directed by
an unscrupulous party superintendent. Personation and repeating used to be frequent in some States. Ballot-box stuffing and false counting were habitually employed in the
South until less troublesome and more effective means were
invented for reducing the negro vote. All these malpractices have diminished, except, perhaps, in a few ill-governed
cities, in one of which an effective remedy was found by
providing glass ballot-boxes, so that the voters who came
as soon as the polls opened in the morning could assure
themselves that the officials in charge had not been beforehand with them. The proportion of electors who vote,
naturally much affected by the interest which the issues be-

fore the country excite, is highest in Presidential elections, and varies from 65 to 80 per cent, a figure which compares favourably with every other constitutional country except perhaps Switzerland. No State has adopted the plan of a Second Ballot, to be taken in case no candidate obtains an absolute majority of the votes cast, nor has proportional representation, though much discussed, already adopted in some cities, and regarded with growing favour, been tried long enough or on a large enough scale to enable its merits to be judged.

The cost of elections varies greatly, but is in general lower than in England. Official expenses connected with the polling do not fall on the candidate, and he is seldom, unless personally wealthy, left to bear the whole of the other expenses. Each party is required by Federal law to render at all Federal elections a full official account of its " campaign expenditure," with the names of the contributors and the sums they pay; while business corporations are now forbidden to subscribe to party funds. Similar legislation has been enacted in some States. The practice, now regrettably frequent in England, of gifts by members or candidates to various local purposes, such as charities and athletic clubs, gifts made at other times than elections, but with a purpose not purely altruistic, hardly exists in America.

Bribery is, or recently was, common in some districts,[1] such as parts of Ohio and South-Eastern New York, as well as in some cities, where a section of the less intelligent voters, especially the negroes in the Middle States, have been corruptible. Though prosecutions are sometimes instituted, the offence more often goes unpunished, the two parties agreeing not to rip up one another's misdeeds. The commonest method of corruption has been to give an agent a lump sum for all the votes he can deliver, and many of these he got without payment, perhaps by persuasion, perhaps, until Prohibition began to conquer State after State, by drinks and cigars.

Regarding elections as the means by which the will of the sovereign people is expressed, we may say that in the United States that will is —

---

[1] A remarkable instance occurred very recently at a senatorial election.

(*a*) Expressed freely, under no intimidation or undue influence.

(*b*) Not widely perverted either by bribery or by fraudulent handling of the votes.

(*c*) Expressed by as large a proportion of the registered voters as in any other country.

(*d*) Largely controlled by the party organizations.

(*e*) Likely to be better expressed if the elections were less numerous and the number of offices filled by election were not so large.

From the People, acting directly by their votes, we may now pass to those whom they choose as their representatives to act on their behalf, that is to say, to the Legislatures. Here there are four topics to be considered:

1. The quality of the men who fill the legislatures.

2. The methods by which legislation is conducted.

3. The value of the product, *i.e.* the statutes passed, and of the debates, in respect of their influence on the Executive and on public opinion.

4. The position of the Legislature in the system of government and the feelings of the people towards it.

1. *The Members of the Legislatures*

These are a great multitude, for besides the two Houses of Congress there are forty-eight State Legislatures, each of two Chambers.

They are citizens little above their fellows in knowledge and intellectual gifts. The average is higher in Congress than in any State, because a seat in Congress has a higher salary, carries more power, opens a better career, draws to itself a much larger proportion of well-educated men. About one half of them are lawyers. But even Congress, drawn from more than one hundred and ten millions of people, and wielding wide authority, contains few men who, uniting conspicuous talents to a well-stored mind and width of view, possess the higher gifts of statesmanship. It is not that such men are wanting in the nation, for they abound. It is that they either do not wish, or are not able, to find their way into the National Legislature. The three reasons for this cast so much light on the working of democracy that they need to be stated.

A seat in Congress fails to attract many men of high intellectual quality because much of the work it involves is dull and tiresome, for it consists in satisfying the demands of constituents for places, pensions, and help in their business undertakings, as well as in trying to secure grants of public money for local objects. One who has experience of the British House of Commons, where few such services are expected, is astonished to find how many of the calls upon a Congressman, or even a Senator, have nothing to do with the work of legislation. Moreover, the methods by which business is conducted in Congress, nearly all of it in Committees whose proceedings are not reported, allow few opportunities for distinction and give a member, at least during his earlier legislative years, few chances of proving his powers. Add to this the fact that a man of eminence who follows a profession, such as that of law or university teaching or journalism, cannot leave the city where he practises or teaches to live in Washington. Such a man living at home in London or Paris may continue his profession with a seat in Parliament.

The obstacles that block the path by which Congress is entered have still more to do with reducing the quality of its members. A custom old, universal, and as strong as law itself, forbids any aspirant to offer himself for election in any Congressional district except that in which he resides, and the same rule obtains in elections to State Legislatures. It is mere usage that imposes the restriction, for legally any citizen resident within the State is eligible for Congress or for the State Legislature, but the electors hardly ever dream of going outside the district. To do so would be to give away a good thing, and would seem to cast a slur on the district, as implying there was no one in it fit for the post. Eloquence, wisdom, character, the fame of services rendered to the nation or the party, make no difference. Europeans are surprised at the strength of this habit, and Englishmen especially, for they remember that nearly all the most brilliant members of the House of Commons during the last two centuries had no connection of residence, perhaps not even of family or previous personal acquaintanceship, with the constituencies they represented, and they know also that even where local interests are concerned — little as these

come up in British parliamentary life — a capable man re-
siding elsewhere is quite as fit to understand and advocate
such interests as a resident can be. In the United States,
as in other countries, the ablest and most energetic men have
been drawn to the cities, and especially to the great cities
where opportunities for success abound. New York, Boston,
Philadelphia, Chicago, Cleveland, St. Louis, could furnish
eminently gifted candidates for more than all the seats in
the States in which these cities are respectively situated,
but such men could be chosen only in those cities themselves.
Moreover, the city where such men are obliged by their professions to reside may be so entirely in the hands of one
party that no member of the other party can find in it a
district offering a chance of success, so that half or more
of the talent such a city contains is lost to political life.
This is the result of a habit deemed democratic.

The habit is perhaps more natural in a Federation than
in countries which have long had only one supreme legislative body, for in a Federal country each man is apt to feel
it his first duty to represent his own State or Canton or
Province, and this spirit of localism extends its influence
to smaller divisions also. Where a State or a district thinks
itself interested in a particular protective duty on imports,
its representative is expected to fight hard for that object
without regard to the general interest. There is said to be
more of this spirit now than before the Civil War, when
national issues filled men's minds. Local feeling disposes
the member to deem himself a Delegate rather than a Representative. Being chosen not solely or chiefly because he
is qualified by talent, but largely because his residence in
his district enables him to declare its views and wishes, he
comes to think that to " voice " them is his chief duty, and
is all the more disposed to subordinate his independent
judgment to what is called in America " the opinion of
the corner store." Yet with all this eagerness to catch
and obey the slightest indication of public opinion, Congress is a less perfect mirror of the opinion of the nation
than are some European Parliaments of countries, because
its members have been not the spontaneous choice of their
constituents but the nominees of party organizations with

of the constituency as a whole, and feel a more direct responsibility to the party managers than they may do to their electors. The Organization is interposed as a sort of imperfectly conductive medium between the member and the citizens by whom he is chosen.

This spirit of localism becomes explicable when one remembers the circumstances of the early colonies and States. In New England the Towns were autonomous communities out of which the State was built up. The settlers who went West carried their local feelings with them, and similar conditions strengthened the original habit. So too the County meant a great deal to the men of the South and they did not think of going outside it for a representative. Perhaps it is rather the English habit of going outside than the opposite American habit which is exceptional, and the habit did not, till recently, hold good in the English counties. It is right to add that although American localism excludes many of the best men from politics, it may be credited with also excluding such undesirable adventurers — city demagogues, for instance — as might by money or by plausible rhetoric win support from electors who knew little of their character, and thereby obtain access to legislatures they would be ill fitted to adorn. In the United States the constituency, however far away from Washington, expects the member to keep a residence within its bounds, and thus, having him among them for a part of the year, can form a personal judgment of his quality. If they wish him to be as like themselves as possible, thinking less of the interests of the United States than of what is desired in Oshkosh, Wis., they attain that end. There may be less knowledge and wisdom in the legislature, but they may deem it a more exact sample of the electors as a whole.

I do not suggest that a great deal of first-rate talent is needed to make a good legislature, for such a body might easily have too much of some kinds of talent. An assembly composed of orators all wishing to speak could ruin any country. But Congress has not enough either of that high statesmanship which only the few attain, or of those sensible men, mostly silent, who listen with open yet critical minds, and reach sound conclusions upon arguments presented.

2. *Methods of Legislation*

The methods by which legislation is conducted in Congress require a brief notice, not because they are specifically due to democratic principles, but because their defects have reduced the effectiveness of Congress, exposing it, and the whole Frame of Government, to strictures which ought to be directed rather against the methods than against these principles.

The mass of work which the National Legislature has to deal with, and the want in it of any leadership such as the President or his Ministers could give if present, has made it necessary to conduct all business by means of Committees. Many of these are small, consisting of from seven to fifteen members, and they are usually smaller in the Senate than in the House. They deliberate in private. The party which has a majority in the Chamber has always a majority in the Committee, and the Chairman belongs to that party, so that a sort of party colour is given to all Bills into which any controversial issue may enter, while even in dealing with non-partisan Bills there is a tendency for the members of each party to act together. Ministers are sometimes asked to appear before these Committees to explain their views on bills, and especially on the estimates for the public services, such as the army and navy, and on any administrative matters falling within the sphere of a Committee. But the Committee need not follow the advice tendered by the Minister nor grant his request for an appropriation, and it can recommend appropriations for which he has not asked. The Chairman, usually a man of some experience, enjoys a larger power than is yielded to the Chairman of a Parliamentary Committee in England or even to the *rapporteur* in a French Commission. He always belongs to the party holding a majority in the House (or Senate), and, in the case of some important Committees, practically occupies the position of a minister, independent of the President's ministers, and sometimes quite as powerful, because he can influence Congress more than it may be possible for a Minister to do, especially if the party opposed to the President has a majority in either House. Thus the Chairmen of the

Committees on Ways and Means and on Appropriations have at times more control of finance than the Secretary of the Treasury or the heads of the spending departments, a consequence of the disjunction of the Executive from the Legislature.

Another consequence is the want of that official leadership which in parliamentary countries such as England, France, Canada, and Australia is given by the Ministry. Since every legislative Chamber would without guidance be a helpless mob, means have been found in Congress for providing a sort of leadership. In the House of Representatives the Speaker, who is always not only chosen by the majority but allowed to act as a party man even in the Chair (though required by usage to give a fair share of debate to the minority), was formerly allowed to exercise great power over the course of business, especially in and since the days of Thomas B. Reed, an exceptionally able and resolute man. In 1910, however, the stringent rule of one of his successors provoked a revolt, which transferred the arrangement of business to the Committee on Rules (familiarly called the Steering Committee), while also transferring the selection of members of the Committees to the House itself. Another figure, now almost as prominent as the Speaker, is the Chairman of the Committee of Ways and Means, who is recognized by the Majority Party as their "floor leader," though they do not always follow him. Finally, when a question of importance arises on which the members of either party are not agreed, they meet in a separate room to debate it among themselves and decide on their course. This is called "going into caucus," and the decision arrived at is usually respected and given effect to by a vote in the Chamber. In these ways a general direction is given to the majority's action, and business goes on, though with a loss of time and waste of energy which the existence of a recognized and permanent leadership vested in a Cabinet might avoid. The rules for closing debate and for limiting the length of speeches are in constant use, being an indispensable instrument against obstruction, here called "filibustering."

3. *The Quality of Legislation*

Few Bills, except those relating to finance, are adequately debated, and the opportunities for members to distinguish themselves are scanty. All have a chance of doing useful work in Committees, but it is work unknown to the public.

The great majority of the Bills introduced [1] are what would be called in England "private," *i.e.* they have a local or personal object; and most of these used to be "Pension Bills" to confer war pensions upon persons who had, or were alleged to have, served in, or had perhaps deserted from, the Northern armies in the Civil War, and who for some reason or other did not come within the scope of the general Pension Acts, wide as that scope was. Members found in such a Bill an easy way of gratifying a constituent and his relatives. The practice was grossly abused, and indeed the Pension Acts as a whole, both general and special, have been a public scandal. In the fifty years that followed the Civil War (1865–1915) more than $4,000,-000,000 (£800,000,000 sterling) were expended in this way. Nothing like this could have happened had there been in Congress any Minister of Finance charged with the duty of protecting the public treasury. Private Bills in general have been a source of endless waste and jobbery, because regulations similar to those which exist in England have not been prescribed for examining into their provisions and for securing their impartial consideration by a small Committee which no lobbyist and not even a Parliamentary colleague should be permitted to approach.

As in most modern countries, many public bills are unsound in principle and meant to earn credit for their introducer from some section of the people.

The Senate

So far I have spoken of Congress as a whole, and in its character of a legislative body. The Senate, however, enjoys executive functions also, and is so peculiar and im-

---

[1] This number is enormous. In the sixty-second Congress (1913) it had reached 29,000 in the House of Representatives and 9000 in the Senate. Few pass.

portant a part of the general frame of government as to need
a more particular description, being indeed the most original
of American institutions, and one whose example has influenced other countries. It owes its origin to the Federal character of the United States, and was created primarily in
order to allay the fears of the States that they would be
absorbed or overridden by the National Government, partly
also from a wish to provide a check both upon the imagined
impetuosity of the popular House and upon the possible
ambitions of a President trying to make himself a dictator.
It was meant to be a cool, calm, cautious, conservative body
composed of elder statesmen, and chosen not by the people
but by the legislatures of the States who, being themselves
picked men, would be qualified to choose as Senators their
own best citizens. This mode of choice was supposed by
European observers, following Tocqueville, to have been the
cause of its superiority in personal quality to the House,
and thereby also of the preponderance over the House which
it acquired. This superiority was, however, really due not
to the mode of choice but to the fact that its longer term
of service, six years instead of two, its continuity, for it
is a permanent body, constantly renewed but never dissolved,
and its wider powers, made a seat in it specially desirable,
and therefore drew to it the best talent that entered political
life. In course of time the plan of choice by State legislatures disclosed unforeseen evils. It brought national politics into those bodies, dividing them on partisan lines which
had little or nothing to do with State issues. It produced
bitter and often long-protracted struggles in the legislatures
over a senatorial election, so that many months might pass
before a choice could be made. It led to the bribery of
venal legislators by wealthy candidates or by the great incorporated companies which desired to have in the Senate
supporters sure to defend their interests. Thus after long
agitation an amendment to the Constitution was carried (in
1913) which transferred the election to the citizens of each
State, voting at the polls.[1] This change has been deemed

[1] As is well observed by Prof. Gannaway (*Comparative Free Government*, pp. 129–130), this 17th Amendment finally disposed of the
old theory, which, however, had scarcely counted in later practice, that
a Senator represents his State as a distinct political entity. But it
does not affect the justice of Mr. Woodrow Wilson's remark that the

likely to reduce the partisan character of the State legislatures. But this may not happen: habits often outlive their original causes. Whether popular election will fill the Senate with better men remains to be seen. The labour and cost of an election campaign conducted over a large State is heavy, and gives an advantage to wealthy men and to those who command the support of powerful newspapers.[1]

The strength of the Senate consists not only in the higher average talent in its members, but also in their longer experience, for they have not only a six-years' term, but are more likely to be re-elected than are members of the House, while the small size of the body offers to able and pushful men better opportunities for displaying their gifts. There was no closure of debate until, in 1917, a rule was passed permitting it to be imposed by a two-thirds majority.[2] Real debate, which in the House is practically confined to financial Bills, exists upon all Bills in the smaller Chamber, and attracts some attention from the public. Even in finance the Senate has established itself as at least equally powerful with the House, although this does not seem to have been contemplated by the Constitution. Leadership belongs not to the presiding officer, who is the Vice-President of the United States, nor to any officially designated leader of either party, but falls to the man or the group deemed best able to lead, seniority being also regarded. Important issues are debated in a party caucus, while much influence is exercised by the chairmen of the principal Committees, who have now and then, when they added capacity to experience, become a sort of ruling oligarchy. The deference paid to seniority in the United States is a product of the respect professed for the principle of Equality. To prefer one man to another on the ground of superior ability would seem to offend against that principle, so length of service in

equal representation of States in the Senate has had the excellent result of securing full expression of the wishes of the less populous and especially the newer regions of the country. Under an election by large districts based on population these regions would have been virtually swamped.

[1] The "senatorial primaries" to be hereafter mentioned have increased the fatigue and expense of a candidacy.

[2] After closure has been imposed each speech is limited to one hour. This rule leaves an opening for filibustering when undertaken in the interests of a minority amounting to one-third.

a Committee gives, often with regrettable results, a title to its Chairmanship. That which makes a seat in the Senate the goal of a politician's hopes is the wider range of its powers, which are executive as well as legislative, since the more important administrative and judicial appointments made by the President require its concurrence. A Senator has thus a means of asserting his position in his State and in his party by threatening to " hold up " the President's nominations unless a certain number of these go to the persons whom he recommends. This control of patronage is the subject of a constant process either of bickerings or more frequently of what is called a " trade," *i.e.* a give and take between the President and the Senators of his own party. Every treaty negotiated by the Executive is laid before the Senate, and requires for its validity the approval of two-thirds of the Senators. Here is another engine of power, which can be effectively wielded to induce the President to oblige the Senators in various ways.

Though the Senate has filled a useful part in the constitutional scheme, it has never been, and is certainly not now, an assembly of sages. Jealous of its own power, it often allows that power to be misused by Senators who care more for the interests or demands of their own State than they do for the common good. It is as much moved by partisanship as is the House, and just as ready to " play politics," even in the sphere of foreign relations, when some party gain is expected. But the critics who have drawn from these defects conclusions adverse to the principle of a Second Chamber ought to consider what might have happened had there been no Senate. Neither the exercise of patronage nor the conduct of foreign affairs could safely have been left to a President irremovable (except by impeachment) for four years, and whose Ministers do not sit in the Legislature and are not answerable to it, nor could those matters have been assigned to a body so large and so short-lived as the House, which would have been even less responsible to the nation, and which is, under its stringent rules, unable to debate either Bills or current administrative issues with a thoroughness sufficient to enlighten the country. It is no more conservative in spirit than the House, contains fewer rich men than it did twenty years ago, and is no longer in marked sympathy with wealth. While with its smaller size, it gives men of talent more chance of showing their mettle and becoming known to the nation at large, it also does something to steady the working of the machinery of government, because a majority of its members, safe in their seats for four or six years, are less easily moved by the shifting gusts of public feeling. Whatever its faults, it is indispensable.

4. *Position and Influence of Congress, and the feeling of the People towards it*

How far has the Federal Legislature, considered as a whole, lived up to the ideal of a body which shall represent the best mind of a democratic nation? Does it give the kind of legislation that the people desire? Does it duly supervise administration, advising, co-operating, restraining, as the case may require? Does it truly mirror the opinion of the people, and enjoy their respect?

It is not that hasty and turbulent body which the Fathers of the Constitution feared they might be creating. Storms of passion rarely sweep over it. Scenes of disorder are now unknown. Party discipline is strict, an atmosphere of good-fellowship prevails, the rules of procedure are obeyed, power rests with comparatively few persons. It is eager, even unduly eager, to discover and obey the wishes of its constituents, or at least of the party organizations. Partisanship is no stronger than in Canada, and apparently weaker than in England. The tendency to split up into groups, marked in France, and now visible in England, hardly exists, for the two great parties have held the field. Though there is plenty of jobbery and log-rolling, the latter not necessarily corrupt, but mischievous and wasteful even when no bad motive is present, and though some members are under suspicion of being influenced by wealthy corporations, there is little direct corruption and the standard of purity has risen in recent years.

Nevertheless Congress does not receive the attention and enjoy the confidence which ought to belong to a central organ of national life. It is not, so to speak, the heart into which blood should flow from all sections of the people rep-

resented in it, and whence the blood needed to nourish all
the parts should be constantly propelled to every part of the
body.

Why is this?

One cause is to be found in its imperfect discharge of
the functions allotted to it. It seldom " faces right up "
to the great problems, not even always to the lesser problems
of legislation. It fumbles with them, does not get to the
root of the matter, seems to be moved rather by considerations of temporary expediency and the wish to catch every
passing breeze of popular demand than by a settled purpose
to meet the larger national needs. In the handling of national finance it is alternately narrow-minded in its parsimony and extravagant in its efforts to propitiate some class
or locality. The monstrous waste of money on war pensions, a waste for which both parties are almost equally to
blame, was prompted by mere vote-catching. Every year
sees the distribution from what is called " the Pork Barrel "
of grants of money to particular districts or cities for so-
called " local public works "— it may be for making a harbour which is sure to be silted up, or improving the navigation of a stream where there is just enough water to float
a canoe.[1] These things bring money to the neighbourhood,
and " make work," so a member earns merit with his constituency by procuring for them all he can. It is nobody's
business to stop him; and others who wish to earn merit in
a like way would resent the discourteous act. Another cause
may be found in the fact that Congress does not impress
the nation by its intellectual power any more than by its
moral dignity. Men who care for the welfare of the country as a whole — perhaps more numerous in the United
States than in any other free country — do not look to it
for guidance. The House scarcely ever enlightens them by
its debates, and the Senate less now than formerly. Its
proceedings, largely conducted in the dim recesses of committee rooms, do not greatly interest the educated classes,
and still less the multitude. The Legislatures of France

[1] Some instructive facts regarding the Pork Barrel and the amazing
expenditure of public money in appropriations for local purposes and
in the distribution of pensions by private or special Bills (as distinct
from the general Pensions Acts) may be found in the *National Municipal Review* for December 1919 in an article entitled *Pork.*

and England and Canada, whatever their defects, have a dramatic quality, and can be watched with ceaseless attention. They bring striking personalities to the front, turning on them a light which makes the people know them and take them for leaders. The House and Senate want that scenic attraction; and they have a rival in the President. The people read his speeches and do not read the *Congressional Record*. He is a Personality, a single figure on whom the fierce light beats.

We must also remember that Congress does not draw into itself enough of the best political talent of the nation. How often is the observer surprised to find that in the House there is a difficulty in finding any men marked out for the posts of Floor-leader or Speaker? How often do the parties realize, when the time for presidential nominations comes, that neither in the House nor perhaps even in the Senate do they discover more than two or three persons who can be thought of as candidates available for the great post, though Congress ought to be the arena in which the champions of parties or causes might have been expected to display their gifts? Why, then, does a Congressional career fail to attract?

One explanation has already been indicated. In no country are there so many other careers which open so many doors to men of ambition, energy, and practical capacity. The opportunities for power, as well as for winning wealth in the world of business, are proportionate to the size and resources of the United States, that is to say, they are unequalled in the world. To be president of a great railway system, covering many States, or of some vast manufacturing industrial company, gives a scope for financial and administrative talent which touches the imagination. The Bar is another career in which the pecuniary prizes, as well as the fame, are immense, and it can seldom be combined with political distinction, as it so frequently and successfully is in Europe. If a man who loves study feels that he has also the power of attracting and guiding young men, the large number of the American universities and the influence their leading figures can exert as presidents or professors, an influence greater than anywhere in Europe, offers another attractive prospect to one who desires to serve his country. In America political life can hardly be called a career, for it is liable to be interrupted by causes, irrespective of personal merits, which the lawyer, the university teacher, and the man of business have not to reckon with.

It is also a career the entrance to which is in most places neither easy nor agreeable. Services are exacted, pledges are demanded, which a man of high spirit does not like to render or to give. The aspirant to a seat in Congress, unable to make his way alone with a constituency, must get the party nomination, which is generally obtainable only by the favour of a Boss. The path is sentinelled by the party machine, which values party loyalty more than ability, and usually selects in each district the man who either possesses local influence or has earned his place by local party service.

It may seem paradoxical to suggest that in a country where every representative comes from the place of his residence, and he is eager to win favour by deference to every local wish, there is nevertheless a certain want of contact between the member and his constituents. Yet this impression does rise to the mind of whoever, having sat for many years in the British House of Commons, compares the relation a member holds towards his electors with that which seems to exist between the American Congressman and his district. The former is in direct touch with his constituents, holds his own meetings, manages his own canvas, and though of course on good terms with the local party organization, need not cringe to it. Many a Congressman seems to feel himself responsible primarily and directly to the Organization, and only secondarily to his constituents.

European critics used to attribute the defects of American legislatures in Nation, State, and City to the fact that the members, instead of working from motives of patriotism or ambition, receive salaries. Though it might be wished that no temptation of personal interest should draw a man to politics, or influence him there, it is doubtful whether, other things being what they are, the United States legislatures would be better if unpaid. Cynics used to say "Perhaps they would steal worse." Anyhow, the question is purely academic. In a country so large, and with a leisured class so relatively small, men could not be expected to quit their homes and avocations to reside in Washington without a remuneration to compensate for the loss of their means of livelihood as well as to defray the cost of residence in one of the most expensive places in the world. Even in the State legislatures the farmer or lawyer who leaves his work for weeks or months to do the business of the State must be paid for his time.

The President

That popular election has not succeeded in producing efficient legislative bodies is undeniable. But in America the people have other means of showing their capacity as judges of men. They elect the heads of the Executive, a President for the nation, a Governor in every State. To these let us pass, enquiring what it is that they look for in a high executive official, how they proceed to find what they desire, how they treat the man of their choice when they have found him, and what place he fills in the working of their system. The Presidency is one of the two or three greatest offices in the world; for only to the Pope do a greater number of human beings look, and it is the only office to which a man is chosen by popular vote. What are the gifts which commend a man to the people, and to those party managers who search for a candidate likely to please the people? These are matters in which we may study the tastes and discernment of the nation as a whole.

That which most attracts the people is the thing we call a Strong Personality. They want a Man, some one who is to be more than a name or a bundle of estimable qualities, a living reality whom they can get to know, to whom they can attach themselves, with whom they can sympathize, whom they can follow because they trust his ability to lead. Courage and energy are accordingly the gifts that most attract them. Some measure of intellectual power, some cleverness and command of language, are required, for without these qualities no man could have got high enough to come into the running. But neither statesmanlike wisdom, nor eloquence, though often deemed the road to power in popular governments, is essential. The average citizen has seldom either the materials or the insight that would enable him to judge the presence of the former.   He does not think of his statesmen as above his own level.   Eloquence he can feel, and by eloquence he is sometimes captivated.   Yet it is not indispensable.   No President, except Lincoln, has been a true orator: many, and good ones too, have not risen above the level of sensible and effective talk.

Honesty, or at least a reputation for honesty, there must be.   It is assumed, in the absence of evidence to the contrary, and rightly assumed.   A few Presidents have been surrounded by corrupt men, and have been too lenient to their faults.   But against none has any charge of personal turpitude or of making any gain out of his office been seriously pressed.   Such an offence would destroy him.   Not far behind these prime essentials of Honesty and Force comes what is called Geniality, the qualities whether of heart or only of manner which make a man popular — the cheery smile, the warm handshake, the sympathetic tone in the voice.   This gift seems to count for so much in England as well as in American electoral campaigns that people are apt to deem its absence fatal.   Nevertheless, there have been Presidents who wanted it, and some who failed even in the tact which, if it cannot always make friends, can at least avoid making enemies.

A forceful will, honesty, and practical sense being the chief qualities needed, what evidence of fitness do the Parties look for, since some is required, whatever the field of action whence it is drawn?   The candidate must be a man known as having " made good " in some branch of public life — it may be in Congress, it may be as State Governor, or Mayor of a great city, or a Cabinet Minister, or possibly even as an ambassador or a judge, or as an unusually prominent journalist.   The two first-named careers provide the best training for the Presidency, and the best test of fitness for it.   To be successful, a State Governor needs firmness, judgment, leadership, and the skill required for dealing with that troublesome body, his State legislature.   A man who has had experience and won authority in Congress has the advantage of knowing its ways.   Of the Presidents chosen since Lincoln only four (Hayes, Garfield, Harrison, and McKinley) sat there.   Hayes, Cleveland, Roosevelt, and Wilson had been State Governors.

These being the merits looked for, the party leaders proceed to make their selections of candidates by searching not so much for a good President as for a good candidate, *i.e.* a man likely to rope in votes in the largest measure from the largest number of quarters. To ascertain this vote-gathering quality other things have to be considered besides talent and experience, so the choice may fall on a person with neither force nor brilliance. There is the reputation already acquired or the hostility a man may have incurred, according to the French dictum, " It is an advantage to have done nothing, but one does not abuse it." There are the popular gifts summed up in the word " magnetism." There is also the hold which a man may possess over a particular State which has a special importance for the election, because its electoral vote is large, or because the parties in it are so equally divided that if one of its citizens is selected as candidate he will make sure of its vote.[1] These considerations may militate against the selection of the person fittest in respect of character and talents, and often draw the selection to States like Ohio and New York.

It goes without saying that the party must be united on its candidate, for division would mean defeat. Who then shall decide between the various aspirants? In the early days of the Republic this function was assumed by the members of Congress who belonged to each party, and their decision was acquiesced in. But presently this assumption was resented as an usurpation of the rights of the people. In 1828 extra-Congressional gatherings began to make nominations, and ever since 1840 party conventions of delegates from the whole country have met, discussed the claims of their respective party aspirants, and nominated the man whom they preferred. The plan is so plainly conformable to democratic doctrine that it is accepted as inevitable. The power of the people would not be complete if it failed to include not only the right of choosing its Chief but also the right for the members of any section to determine on whom the section should concentrate its voting force. Thus the

[1] The voting is by States, each having as many votes as it has representatives and senators, and the smallest majority in a State is sufficient to give all the votes of that State (New York has 45 and Pennsylvania 38) to the candidate who has carried it; New York and Ohio have long been doubtful States: Pennsylvania safely Republican ever since the Civil War.

Party Convention which nominates a candidate has become as real and effective a part of the constitutional machinery as if it had formed a part of the Constitution.

The framers of the Constitution contemplated nothing like this. They committed the election of the President to a College of Electors specially elected for this sole purpose, men who, possessed of wisdom and experience and animated by pure patriotism, would be likely to select the citizen whom their impartial judgment preferred. Boards of this type were twice elected, and on both occasions chose George Washington, who was the obvious and indeed the inevitable person. But the third College was elected (in 1796) largely, and the fourth (1800) wholly on party lines, and being expected to choose a party leader acted in a partisan spirit. Their example has been followed ever since, and what was to have been a council of impartial sages has consisted of nonentities, a mere cogwheel in the machinery of election, recording mechanically the wishes of the people.

Much depends on the questions before the nation at the time when the election approaches, and the amount of interest these questions evoke from those who think seriously about them, and influence their fellow-citizens. Such men desire to have in the Head of the Nation some one who will worthily represent their ideals, not merely a skilful party leader or administrator, but a man likely to guide the nation by his wisdom and courage along the lines which its needs prescribe. The mood of the nation influences its judgment on the candidates presented to it.[1]

During two years or more before each election of a Presi-

---

[1] " The Convention picks out a party leader from the body of the nation, not that it expects its nominee to direct the interior government of the party, but that it expects him to represent it before public opinion and to stand before the country as its represenative man, a true type of what the country may expect of the party itself in purpose and principle. . . . There is no national party choice except that of President. No one else represents the people as a whole, exercising a national choice, and inasmuch as his strictly executive duties are in fact subordinated so far as all detail is concerned, the President represents not so much the party's governing efficiency as its controlling ideas and principles. He is not so much part of its organization as its vital link of connection with the thinking nation. . . . His is the only national voice in affairs. . . . His position takes the imagination of the country."— *Constitutional Government in the United States* by Mr. Woodrow Wilson (then President of Princeton University), published in 1908.

dent, rumour and criticism are busy with the names of those persons in each party who are deemed " available," or to use the popular term, " Presidential Timber." [1] Sometimes there is one leader who so overtops the rest that his adoption is a foregone conclusion. But more frequently party opinion divides itself between several competitors, the adherents of each drawn to him either by sympathy with his views or by something captivating in his personality. Thus before the moment for choice arrives there are practically several factions within the party, each working for its own favourite.

The decision between these favourites is entrusted to a body called the National Convention, which meets about four months before the Presidential election in some great city, and consists of more than one thousand delegates from State Conventions. These State Conventions, it will be remembered, themselves consist of delegates from smaller local conventions or from those Primary meetings which have been already described, so the National Convention is a body representing the party over the whole United States, and representing it upon a population basis just as Congress does. It is in fact a sort of Congress, not of the nation but of a Party, charged with the double function of selecting a candidate and of discussing and enouncing that legislative and administrative programme upon which the party makes its appeal to the nation.[2] Most of the delegates come instructed by their respective State Conventions, or by so-called Direct Presidential Primaries, to vote for some particular person, since the merits of each aspirant have been already canvassed in those Conventions; but if they find themselves unable to carry their own favourite, they must ultimately turn over their support to some other aspirant, perhaps under instructions from their State Convention, or from the Direct Primaries,[3] perhaps at their own discretion, because

[1] This term conveys the same idea as the Italian word *papabili,* used of men who may be thought of for the Popedom.

[2] A full description of the National Convention may be found in *American Commonwealth,* vol. ii. chaps. lxix. and lxx.

[3] Recently the laws of some States have superseded the choice of delegates by a State Convention, and have provided for " Preferential Primary" elections, which are not private party meetings but public votings by ballot, at which the party voters in the State are given an opportunity of declaring their preference for a particular aspirant as

not all the contingencies that may arise can be foreseen.   All
the delegates from a State are expected to vote together, but
do not always follow this rule.   They meet from time to
time in secret to review the situation and discuss their course,
for the situation changes from hour to hour, according to the
rising or declining prospects of each aspirant.   In the hall
the proceedings are public — secrecy would be impossible
with such numbers — and are watched by some ten thousand
eager spectators.   The presence of the multitude, acclaim-
ing everything said in praise of the aspirant in whom each
section rejoices, adds to the excitement which prevails, an
excitement which, stimulated by bands of music and by displays of colours, badges, and emblems, grows hotter the
longer the contest lasts and the more doubtful its issue appears.   Sometimes this excitement, blazing into enthusiasm
for one name proposed, sweeps like a prairie fire over the
crowd and makes his nomination inevitable.   But more frequently each faction persists in fighting hard for its favourite, so ballotings may continue for days or even weeks.   As
many as forty-nine and even fifty-three have been taken in
the Convention of one or other party.   When the struggle
is thus prolonged, and it is seen that the knot cannot be cut
but must be untied, efforts are made to reconcile the opposing factions and effect an arrangement which may unite
them in the support either of one or other of the leading
aspirants or of some other person not objectionable to either.
Negotiations proceed in the vacant hours before and after the
forenoon and afternoon sittings of the Convention, sometimes even within the hall while speech-making goes on.
Compromises which might be impracticable if principles
were at stake become possible because the party managers who
support one or other aspirant have a personal interest in the

the person to be chosen by their delegates as the party candidate. This
effort to place the choice of a candidate in the people's hands has,
however, not so far worked perfectly, for, apart from other objections,
it does not meet the difficulty that circumstances may so change before, or in the course of, the sittings of the National Convention that
the chances of the aspirant indicated may have been reduced, perhaps to
a vanishing point. It has, moreover, developed the practice of starting
preliminary popular campaigns in behalf of particular aspirants, a
process which may involve heavy expenditure. In the National Convention of 1916 not much regard, and in that of 1920 (when these
Primaries were used in twenty States) still less regard was paid to
the preferences declared. Many think the plan a failure.

unity of the party stronger even than their attachment to their own man, since a disruption of the party would in destroying its chance of success shake their own influence and extinguish their hopes for all that victory could bring them. Each (or at least most) of the influential party chiefs commands a large number of delegates from one or more States, and can turn over a number of their votes to the aspirant who seems most likely to be either acceptable to the party as a whole, or to have a good chance of winning the election. Thus the few leading men — for here, as always and everywhere, real direction rests with a few — usually arrive, in secret conclave, at some sort of settlement, even if the candidate ultimately nominated be one for whom at the opening of the Convention no one prophesied victory. That such a method of choice, a strange mixture of Impulse and Intrigue, should not have borne worse fruit than it has in fact produced, may excite surprise. Now and then a Convention has seemed to be drifting straight on to the rocks. There have been cases when a majority of the delegates persisted in voting for an aspirant whom all men of discernment knew to be unfit to be President, and hardly fit to be even talked of as a candidate. But somehow or other the minority, just strong enough to hold out, prevailed at last and averted a disastrous choice. Sometimes the need for a compromise gives the prize to a mediocre, but never to a palpably incompetent man, nearly all having had a creditable if possibly commonplace record: and when the selections have been least happy, the candidate has been rejected by the people.

I have gone into these details because they show how the power of the party machine is limited by the need for pleasing the People, and show also how out of all the confused cross-currents of sentiment and interest, patriotism, selfishness, and partisanship, there may emerge a tolerably good result. A nominating Convention is the supreme effort a vast democracy makes to find its leader, and the difficulties of the process are instructive. The experience of eighty years has not lessened them.

It is a fear of the people that deters Conventions, bodies mainly composed of professionals, from nominating persons whom the more unscrupulous among the party managers would prefer. The delegates may be subservient or short-sighted, but the people have a sort of instinct which, asserting itself when a serious issue arises, saves the nation from windy demagogues and plausible impostors. The choice purporting to be democratic, because made by the citizens through their delegates, is at least as much oligarchic, arranged by a few skilful wire-pullers. In each delegation there are a very few only who count, and real control may rest with one man, perhaps belonging to another delegation or to none. Yet the influence of public opinion remains in the fact that no one can be chosen to be candidate who is not likely to attract the people. He must be a man to win with. Thus things have on the whole gone better than might have been predicted. Not many Presidents have been brilliant, some have not risen to the full moral height of the position. But none has been base or unfaithful to his trust, none has tarnished the honour of the nation.

The fear, once loudly expressed, that the President might become a despot has proved groundless, and this is due, not merely to the fact that he has no great standing army at his command but rather to the skill with which the framers of the Constitution defined his powers, and above all to the force of general opinion which guards the Constitution. The principles of the American Government are so deeply rooted in the national mind that an attempt to violate them would raise a storm of disapproval. It may seem unfortunate that the head of the nation, having been elected by a party, is obliged to be also that party's chief, and to look specially to it for support.[1] He is, however, expected not to let his duty to the party prejudice his higher duty to the nation; and a politic President will try to win from the public opinion of both parties the backing he may need to overcome sectional opposition within his own. When he gives bold leadership in an evidently patriotic spirit he will find that backing, sometimes even among those who voted against him. The nation values initiative, loves courage,

---

[1] " In the view of the makers of the Constitution the President was to be legal executive; perhaps the leader of the nations; certainly not the leader of the party, at any rate while in office. But by the operation of forces inherent in the very nature of Government he has become all three, and by inevitable consequence the most heavily burdened officer in the world " (*Constitutional Government in the U.S.*, already quoted).

likes to be led, as indeed does every assembly, every party, every multitude.

The power which the Executive can exert over legislation is conditioned by the party situation in Congress. If his own party controls both Houses he can accomplish much; if either House is hostile, and especially if there is a strong hostile group in the Senate, comparatively little, so far as regards controversial topics. But in any event he possesses five important powers.

He is Commander-in-Chief of the Army and Navy.

He suggests to Congress topics on which legislation is required, setting forth in his message or in speeches the substance of the measures needful, and getting some member to embody them in a Bill. This function, little used previously, has become frequent within the last twenty years, and helps to cure defects in the frame of government due to a too rigid deference to the doctrine of the Separation of Powers.

He has, and uses freely, the right of Veto, *i.e.* of refusing to sign Bills passed by Congress. His dissent can be overridden if the Bill is repassed by a two-thirds majority in each House, but as such a majority is seldom attainable, and the President is likely to have some good reason for his action, he is rarely overruled.

He has the function of nominating to the more important administrative diplomatic and judicial posts in the National Government.

Lastly, he has the conduct of foreign affairs. In these two last-mentioned functions, however, his power is limited by the right of the Senate to refuse its consent to appointments, and by the provision that the consent of two-thirds shall be needed for the approval of a treaty. The power of declaring war is reserved to Congress, but the Senate cannot prevent Executive action dangerous to peace from being taken, or negotiations from being brought to a point where war becomes almost inevitable.[1]

[1] As to the conduct of foreign affairs by the joint action of the President and the Senate, see *American Commonwealth*, vol. i. chaps. vi. and xi. The plan of the U.S. Constitution does not work smoothly, for the Senate has frequently rejected treaties negotiated by Presidents, but neither has any other plan given satisfaction in other constitutional countries, for though wherever, as in France, Italy and England, a

Into questions bearing on the personal relations of the President to Congress I need not enter, for they throw no direct light on those aspects of democracy which concern us. It may suffice to say that both the want of co-operation between the administrative departments and the Committees of Congress and the imperfect touch between the President himself and Congress as a whole have come to be recognized as defects to be cured. President Roosevelt was more active than his predecessors in pressing Congress to deal with matters he deemed urgent. President Wilson went further, for he frequently addressed Congress in person. In both cases the nation showed no disapproval. There is nothing in the Constitution to limit the interchange of views between the Executive and the Legislature. Congress has been jealous of its rights, but it might well gain rather than lose by more frequent personal intercourse with the President.

It used to be feared that a President, moved by personal ambition, or desiring to strengthen his position at home, might lead the nation into a policy of aggression abroad. That danger seems to have vanished. More recently alarm has been expressed that his influence might be used to bring about projects of sweeping constitutional or legislative change. This, however, he could not do without the sup-

Ministry leads a Parliamentary majority, that majority almost invariably accepts the engagements contracted by the Ministry, these engagements are sometimes distasteful to the people, and shake such confidence as it may have in the Ministry.

The adjustment of relations between Executive and Legislature in the conduct of foreign affairs has been in many free countries one of the most difficult and indeed insoluble problems of practical politics. At Rome it was divided between the Consuls and the Senate, the latter generally exerting a predominant influence. In the Greek democracies decisions were made by the popular Assembly. In Venice, and in oligarchical governments generally, a small Council took charge, and this is the plan adopted in the Swiss democracy, where, however, the Assembly has a right to be informed and to interfere if necessary. In such Parliamentary countries as England it belongs in theory to the Executive, but a Ministry must in exercising it make sure of being able to carry their majority with them. In the United States the Constitution, in dividing it between the President and the Senate and assuming that these two powers will maintain friendly relations and do their best to work together, does not provide for the case of a conflict à outrance between them. Things have gone most smoothly when a tactful Secretary of State has exerted himself to keep the Senate in good humour by informing them of the progress of negotiations and occasionally inviting their advice.

port of Congress and of public opinion. In all these matters public opinion must be the ultimate safeguard.

The powers of the Executive, considerable at all times, are of course most important in a crisis of domestic strife or foreign war, when prompt and decisive action, such as an assembly can rarely take, is demanded from the executive head of the nation, and is acquiesced in, even if it seems to go beyond the lines of the Constitution. At all times, however, much depends on the personal character of the President. It might almost be said that his powers are what his employment of them makes them. Looking at the succession of Presidents, and noticing how the nation is influenced by a chief magistrate whose energy impresses it or whose gifts take its fancy, we are reminded of the great emperors of the Middle Ages, such as Henry the Third and the two Fredericks of Hohenstaufen, whose personal character made all the difference to the support they could evoke, and still more reminded of those monarchs who ruled by the Word and not by the Sword, such as Pope Gregory the Seventh and Pope Innocent the Third. These latter ruled because they could command spiritual allegiance. A President prevails just so far as he can carry public opinion with him, according to the familiar dictum, " With the people everything succeeds: without the people, nothing." With opinion behind him, he may prove stronger than both Houses of Congress. Cases have arisen in which, when a Congress and the President were at variance, the sympathy of the people seemed to go more to the latter than to the former. Both he and they are the choice of the people, but if he is forceful and attractive, they take a personal interest in him which they do not feel for a large number of elected representatives, the vast majority of whom are to them mere names. If the elected king who governs as well as reigns during his allotted term shows himself worthy of the great position, he draws to himself, as personifying the Nation, something of that reverent regard which monarchs used to inspire in Europe.

CHAPTER XLII

FROM the National Government let us turn to the State Governments and observe how the democratic principles on which they were constructed have worked out in practice. Though the earliest State Constitutions existed before the Federal Constitution, they have been so often amended and so many new Constitutions have been enacted for both the older and the newer States, that the State Constitutions as a whole are now of a more democratic colour than is that National constitutional system whose workings have just been examined.

We have already seen that every State Legislature is elected either by manhood suffrage (except so far as coloured citizens are excluded [1]) or by universal suffrage, that each has two Houses, with practically equal legislative powers, and that neither the Governor nor any other official can sit in either. The men who compose the smaller House (Senate) and the larger one, both of them selected by the party Machines, are of the same quality, a quality nowhere high, but in which three grades of merit, or demerit, may be distinguished. [2] The legislatures of some of the older Eastern States where there is a large rural element are respectable, with a small proportion of half-educated men and a still smaller one of corrupt men. This grade shades off into a second, including the newer States in the Middle West and North-west. Their legislatures contain many farmers and

---

[1] A very recent decision of the Supreme Court has declared invalid one of the laws, adopted in some Southern States, which had the effect of excluding a number of coloured citizens from the Suffrage, but it remains to be seen what practical effect this decision will have in increasing the coloured vote.

[2] The new Direct Primaries (see Chap. XLV., pp. 141–145) have improved matters a little, but in most States there is a large "professional" element, and as the other members, especially the often inexperienced and credulous farmers, hold their seats for a short time only, the professionals have everywhere an influence disproportionate to their numbers.

many petty lawyers from the smaller towns, who are mostly honest, well-meaning persons, but of a limited outlook and a proneness to be captured by plausible phrases and to rush into doubtful experiments. Here, too, the quality of the legislatures is highest where the rural element is largest, and the party machines are least powerful. The third class, more distinct from the second than is the second from the first, includes States whose politics have been demoralized by large cities where Rings flourish and party Bosses distribute spoils to their adherents. Six or seven State Legislatures, among which those of Pennsylvania, New York, and Illinois are the worst, belong to this category. In these the level of honour and probity is low, for few men of public spirit, likely to disobey the party organization, would be permitted to enter them wherever the Bosses could close the door. Still their virtue has risen a little of late years, and in some of them a group of reformers may be found.

Legislation is conducted by a system of Committees resembling that of Congress, which in most States gives little opportunity for debate in public, though in many (as in Massachusetts) a Committee sits with open doors and receives evidence from all who come to offer it.[1] Debates excite little interest. Finance plays a smaller part here than in Congress, for the State revenue is not large, local requirements being provided for by county and municipal taxes. The tendency to borrow recklessly for public improvements, marked at one time, was checked by amendments to the State Constitutions. The stream of statutes flows freely, especially in the Western States, where new ideas " catch on " readily, the ardour of philanthropic progress being much in evidence. These social reform Acts are better than the men who pass them, because they are often dictated by groups of moral reformers whose zeal, though it outruns their discretion, is a wholesome factor in the community. If not defeated by the covert arts of persons interested in defending the abuses they are aimed at, they are passed with a glow of conscious virtue by those who find this kind of virtue easy; but such laws often fail to be enforced, sometimes because it is the

---

[1] This plan is most fully applied in Massachusetts, where it has worked usefully. See Mr. A. L. Lowell's book, *Public Opinion and Popular Government*, p. 250, for an instructive description and estimate.

business of nobody in particular, sometimes because they are practically unenforceable, so that, as an American philosopher has observed, " Western statute books are a record rather of aspiration than of achievement."

It is the special or " private Bill " legislation (to use the English term) which is the happy hunting-ground of the professional politicians who mostly compose the membership of these bodies, especially those of the six or seven States above mentioned.   This is what draws most of these professionals into the Legislature, for it is in this quarter that the opportunities for illicit gain are to be found.   The special or private Bills confer privileges or exemptions upon particular individuals or corporate bodies, authorizing them to do things the general law might not permit, as for instance to take private property for a public utility.   Such Bills are brought in and put through by any member, just as are public Bills of general operation, being subject to no such provisions for a quasi-judicial scrutiny of their preambles and enacting clauses as the system of Standing Orders and the rules of Private Bill Committees established long ago in England.   In these legislatures there is no duty thrown on any one to criticize faults or secure protection for any interest which the Bill may affect, so the door stands wide open to abuses of legislative power for the benefit of private persons or companies.   Through that door many filch their gains.[1]

The carnival of jobbery and corruption which such Bills have induced in State legislatures has done more than anything else to discredit those bodies.   Secret arrangements are made between the lobbyists who act for the promoters of the Bill, the members whom these lobbyists approach, and other members who usually have similar jobs of their own, and thus by the system called " log-rolling " support is obtained sufficient to put the Bills through.   Unscrupulous members use their powers in another way, introducing Bills designed to injure some railway company or other wealthy corporation, and then demanding to be bought off.   This form of blackmail is called a Strike, and has been frequent

---

[1] I describe these evils, as they were twenty years ago, because they indicate one of democracy's diseases, but they have now been reduced in many States.

in almost every State where there are large corporations to be squeezed. The threatened interests, obliged to defend themselves, justify their methods by the plea that their shareholders must be protected; and when legitimate means fail, because the composition and rules of the legislatures afford no protection, illegitimate means must be employed. When a Governor happens to be upright, courageous, and vigilant, he applies a remedy by vetoing the Bills he knows to be bad. But not all States have such Governors, nor can the most vigilant keep an eye upon every trick. In States where on the one side stand railway companies, street-car companies, and other great corporate undertakings commanding immense capital and anxious to obtain from the State what the Americans call " public franchises," rights of immense pecuniary value, and on the other side a crowd of men, mostly obscure, from whose votes these rights can be purchased with scant risk of detection and little social slur upon either the briber or the bribed if detection should follow, corruption must be looked for. The best evidence of the gravity of these evils is to be found in the attempts made by the better citizens to extirpate them, efforts which began many years ago and have taken more and more drastic forms. I reserve an account of these for the general survey of reform movements on a later page.

Every Governor is elected by the people of the whole State, having been nominated by a party convention. The qualities he ought to possess, while generally similar to such as are required in a President, are more distinctly those of a good man of business, viz. firmness, tact, common sense, alert watchfulness, and of course a pleasant manner, which helps to soften his refusals of the insidious requests that beset him. He need not have a creative mind, but must have a strong will. His chief tasks are those of vetoing bad private Bills, and inducing the legislature to pass good public Bills. His activity in this direction has recently increased in many States, and with good results, for legislatures need leading, and what he gives is likely to be better than that of party Bosses. The temptation to abuse his patronage is not great, since the chief State officials and Boards are directly elected by the citizens, and appoint their own subordinates, but that system is faulty, for it impairs administration, which might

be more efficient if the Governor were to appoint the heads
of the chief departments and use them as a sort of Cabinet.
As head of the Executive he is responsible for the maintenance of order, no easy function when industrial disputes
lead to rioting, and he has to choose between doing his duty
under the law and the anger which his enforcement of it will
rouse in a large section of the voters. Most Governors have
done their duty. So in the Southern States the merit of a
Governor is tested by his determination to protect the coloured population and enjoin a spirit of good feeling towards them.

As in these various ways a strong man may show his mettle,
the office attracts those who have begun to dream of the
Presidency of the United States, the possibility of reaching
that giddy eminence being always in the background of ambitious minds. It trains a man for the post, for it needs,
though in a narrower sphere, the same gifts of leadership,
firmness, and insight into men, coupled with the skill needed
in dealing with legislatures, singular bodies which are both
better and worse than are the individuals who compose them.
The judgment of the citizens on a Governor after his first
year of office is almost always fair and sound.

The tendency for the State Governor to overshadow his
legislature illustrates afresh the disposition of the masses
to look to and be interested in a Man rather than an Assembly. The Man becomes real to them, gets credit for what
he accomplishes, can be held accountable for failure or neglect. Much is gained by fixing on a conspicuous official
the responsibility which a hundred inconspicuous representatives elude. When he appeals to the people against the
politicians, the politicians may complain of his autocratic
ways, but the people are pleased and generally side with
him, as they did with Mr. Hughes when he defied the powerful party machine which controlled his own party in New
York State. As he was their own direct choice, they did not
care how much he threatened legislators who had been forced
upon them by the Organization rather than chosen by themselves.

Yet the Governor may not be the chief power. States
could be named in which there may stand above him, as there
has often stood in New York and has stood for many a

year in Pennsylvania, the mightier figure of the Boss, who as head of the Machine commands the Legislature, its members sitting by his favour. His extra-legal power is greater than any the laws of the State confer. So the State of California was ruled for a generation by a railway company, one of whose officials exercised the authority though he did not bear the name of a Boss; and that yoke lasted unbroken into the present century, till at last the Company grew tired of maintaining it.

CHAPTER XLIII

THE JUDICIARY AND CIVIL ORDER

Two features in the American judicial system have a special interest for the student of institutions. One is the part, more important here than in any other country, which the Judiciary holds in the constitutional frame of government, its functions under the Constitution making it, in fact as in name, an independent branch of the government side by side with Executive and Legislature. The other is the different effects on the quality of the persons chosen to the Bench which are traceable to the different methods of choice, and to the longer or shorter tenure of office. Let us note the results of the way in which certain principles held to be democratic have been applied.

(*a*) The place assigned to the Judiciary by the Constitution has turned out to be greater than the founders foresaw, because no country had, in 1787, tried the experiment of setting up a Rigid Constitution to limit the powers of a legislature.

In the United States, as also every State in the Union, a supreme Instrument of Government, the Constitution, stands above ordinary laws, so that if the Legislature should pass any statute or resolution contravening the Constitution, that piece of legislation is null and void, because inconsistent with the higher law contained in the Constitution. Whether such inconsistency exists in any given case is a pure matter of law, to be determined by examining their respective terms, setting the two documents side by side so as to ascertain whether and in what respects the law of less authority passed by the Legislature transgresses the law of greater authority enacted by the people in the Constitution. It is a question of legal interpretation. The interpreting Court does not review matters of policy, *i.e.* the intrinsic wisdom or propriety either of the statute or of the Constitution itself, but merely decides whether the former conflicts with the latter. But

as it is often hard to decide whether the general words used
in a Constitution are, or are not, consistent with the terms
of the statute which is alleged to transgress those general
terms, there is often room for difference of opinion as to
what the Constitution really means, *i.e.* what the people who
enacted it meant by the words they have employed.   This
may seem to leave a discretion to the judges.   It is hardly
to be called a discretion, for the honest and competent judge
tries only to ascertain the meaning and allows no personal
bias to affect his decision, but many persons are ready to
think that interpretation has been coloured by a Court's own
views, and may therefore complain when it decides against
what they desire.   Thus the charge is made that the judges
are legislating under the guise of enactment, and are, when
they declare a statute invalid, overruling the will of the
people as expressed by the legislature.   The answer is that
the will of the people is expressed in the Constitution also,
and there expressed directly, not through representatives,
so that the Constitution is a law of higher degree, the legislature having no more power than the Constitution allows
to it.   Only a Court can decide whether the two enactments
in question conflict, for if that decision were left to the legislature, a Constitution would be useless, because the legislature would always decide in its own favour.[1]

Any one can see what importance this duty of interpretation gives to the American Courts.   They become what
may be called the living voice of the people, because they
are in each State the guardians of that Constitution through
which the people have spoken and are still speaking till such
time as it pleases them to amend the fundamental instrument.   The judges need to be not only able and learned, but
also courageous, firm to resist any popular agitation, faithful to the constitution they are set to guard.   This is true
of State Judges, who have to interpret the constitutions of
the several States in which they hold office.   It is especially
needed in the Federal Judges, who have to interpret the
Federal constitution, declaring invalid any provision of a
State constitution or of a State law, or of a Federal act
passed by Congress, which transgresses that Constitution
which is the supreme law of the land.   Most of all is it

[1] See as to the Swiss view of this subject Vol. I. Chap. XXVIII.

needed in the Supreme Court of the United States, to which all questions affecting the Federal Constitution come ultimately either directly or by way of appeal from inferior Courts. Though that Court has been expounding and applying the Constitution for one hundred and thirty years, new questions raised by changing economic and social conditions are continually coming before it for determination. Its decisions as to what Congress may and may not do, and as to what the State legislatures may and may not do, have often an importance greater than any Act either of Congress or of a State legislature.

And now as to the judges and their tenure. The Federal judges, as already observed, are all appointed by the President with the consent of the Senate, and all hold office for life, though removable by impeachment. Those who constitute the Supreme Court, at present nine in number, always have been men of high character and distinguished ability. Those of inferior rank, Circuit and District judges, are sound lawyers, though seldom first-rate, for the salaries do not suffice to attract the most eminent men. Their integrity has been usually, though not always, above suspicion.

The State judges of every grade are elected by the citizens, except in seven States in which they are appointed by the Governor (with the approval of the Council or of the Legislature), and in four in which they are elected by the Legislature. Where the people elect, either by a State vote or in local areas by a local vote, the candidates are nominated by the political parties, like other elective officials, and usually stand on the same ticket with those officials as party candidates, though occasionally a non-party judiciary ticket is put forward by citizens dissatisfied with the party nominations. Such action, when taken, is apt to proceed from leading members of the local Bar. It seldom succeeds, and as a rule the best chance of securing good candidates is through the influence of the Bar upon those who control the party nominations.

The tenure of judicial office varies greatly. In two of the seven States where the Governor appoints, the judge sits for life, *i.e.* is removable only by impeachment or upon an address of both Houses of the legislature. In one of those where the legislature elects this is also the practice. In the remaining forty he is either elected or appointed for a term which varies from two years [1] to twenty-one, eight or ten years being the average. Re-elections are frequent if the judge has satisfied the Bar of his competence and honour.

The salaries vary in proportion to the population and wealth of the State, $6000 (about £1200) being the average. Only in one State (New York), and only to some of its judges, is a salary so large as $17,500 (£3500) paid,[2] even this sum being less than one-fifth of what some lawyers make by private practice.

No one will be surprised at what is, in most States, the combined effect on the quality of the Bench of these three factors — low salaries, short terms, and election by a popular vote controlled by party managers. The ablest lawyers seldom offer themselves: the men elected owe their election and look for their re-election to persons most of whom neither possess nor deserve the confidence of the better citizens.

We must, however, discriminate between different sets of States, for the differences are marked. Three classes may be roughly distinguished.

In some six or seven States, including those in which the Governor appoints, the judges of the highest Court, and as a rule the judges of the second rank also, are competent lawyers and upright men. Some would do credit to any court in any country.

In most of the other States (a majority of the total number) the justices of the highest Court are tolerably competent, even if inferior in learning and acumen to the ablest of the counsel who practise before them. Almost all are above suspicion of pecuniary corruption, though some are liable to be swayed by personal or political influences, for the judge cannot forget his re-election, and is tempted to be complaisant to those who can affect it. In these States the justices of the lower courts are of only mediocre capacity, but hardly ever venal.

Of the few remaining States it is hard to speak positively. A general description must needs be vague, because the only persons who have full opportunity for gauging the talents

[1] In Vermont.

[2] In England a judge of the High Court receives £5000, nearly $25,000.

and honesty of the judges are the old practitioners in their courts who see them frequently and get to " know their ins and outs." These practitioners are not always unbiassed, nor always willing to tell what they know. All that can safely be said is that in a certain small number of States the Bench as a whole is not trusted. In every court, be it of higher or lower rank, there are some good men, probably more good than bad. But no plaintiff or defendant knows what to expect. If he goes before one of the upright judges his case may be tried as fairly as it would be in Massachusetts or in Middlesex. On the other hand, fate may send him to a court where the rill of legal knowledge runs very thin, or to one where the stream of justice is polluted at its source. The use of the mandatory or prohibitory power of Court to issue injunctions, and of the power to commit for some alleged contempt of Court, is a fertile source of mischief. Injunctions obtained from a pliable judge are sometimes moves in a stock-gambling or in a political game, especially if the lawsuit has a party colour.

Taking the States as a whole, one may say that in most of them the Bench does not enjoy that respect which ought to be felt for the ministers of justice, and that in some few States enough is known to justify distrust. In these the judges of lower rank are not necessarily less scrupulous than are those of the highest Courts, but their scanty equipment of legal knowledge means that justice is not only uncertain, but also slow and costly, because the weaker the judge the greater the likelihood of delay and appeals, since American practitioners can always find some technical ground for a postponement or for trying to upset a decision.

All these things considered, it is surprising not that the defects described exist, but that they and the results they produce are not even worse. Worse they would be but for the sort of censorship which the Bar exercises, making all but the blackest sheep amenable to the public opinion of their State or neighbourhood.

How do these defects tell upon the daily administration of justice between man and man? As respects civil cases, seeing that the great majority of cases in contract or tort, or affecting property, come into State Courts, one hears fewer complaints than might have been expected. Evils of long

standing are taken for granted: people have in many parts
of the Union ceased to expect strong men except in the Federal Courts and those of a few States. Law is a costly luxury, but it is costly in all countries. In America its march
is slow, but in many States the rules of procedure are antiquated and absurdly technical, and most of the codes of procedure adopted in some States have been ill-drawn and cumbrous. The intelligence of juries, the learning and ability
of the Bar (legal education is probably nowhere so thorough as in the United States) help the weak judge over many
a stile; while favouritism and corruption, at all times hard
to prove, attract little notice unless the case affects some
public interest. Nevertheless, even if things are less bad
than the causes at work might have made them, clear it is
that the incompetence of judges does in many States involve immense waste to litigants through appeals and other
delays, and through the uncertainty into which the law is
brought by decisions in inferior courts likely to be reversed
on appeal.

Though the administration of civil justice leaves much to
be desired, that of criminal justice is far worse. There are
few States, perhaps only two or three outside New England
—New Jersey is one — where it is either prompt or efficient.
All through the rest of the country, South and West, trials
are of inordinate length, and when the verdict has been
given, months or years may elapse before the sentence can
be carried into effect. Many offenders escape whom everybody knows to be guilty, and the deterrent effect of punishment is correspondingly reduced. From among the high authorities who have described and deplored this state of things
it is sufficient to quote ex-President William H. Taft, who
with exceptional experience, and a judgment universally respected, has pointed to " the lax enforcement of the criminal
law " as one of the greatest evils from which the people of
the United States suffer.[1]

Many causes have combined to produce this inefficiency.
One is the extreme length of trials, especially trials for mur-
der. First of all, there is the difficulty of getting a jury.
In some States the jury lists are not fairly made up; but even

[1] *Popular Government, its Essence, its Permanence, and its Perils,*
1913.

where they are, the exercise of the right of challenging, on the ground that the person summoned is prejudiced or has already formed an opinion, is carried to extreme lengths. Sometimes hundreds of persons are rejected by one side or the other. There was a State prosecution in California a few years ago in which more than two months were spent in challenges before a jury was at last impanelled. Then there are the numerous intricacies of procedure and the highly technical rules of evidence. Every possible point is taken and argued on behalf of the prisoner if he has the means of retaining a skilful counsel. Objections taken to the judge's rulings on points of evidence, or to the terms of his charge, are reserved for subsequent argument before the full Court; and it is often a year or more before the Court deals with them. Distrust of authority and " faith in the people " have led nearly all States to limit strictly the functions of the judge. He may declare the law and sum up the evidence, but is not permitted to advise the jury as to the conclusions they ought to draw from the evidence, and he has generally less power than an English judge enjoys of allowing amendments where a purely technical mistake, not prejudicing the prisoner, has been committed.

Juries themselves are not always above suspicion. There are in many cities lawyers who have a reputation as " jury fixers "; and where unanimity is required by the law of the State, the process of fixing may be none too difficult.

If a verdict of guilty has been delivered, and if, months or possibly even years afterwards, all the legal points taken for the defence have been overruled by the Court, the prisoner has still good chances of escape. There is in the United States an almost morbid sympathy for some classes of criminals, a sentiment frequently affecting juries, which goes on increasing when a long period has elapsed since the crime was committed.[1] A conviction for murder, especially if there was any emotional motive present, is usually followed by a torrent of appeals for clemency in the press, while the Governor is besieged with letters and petitions demanding a

[1] Says Mr. Taft (p. 225 of book above referred to) : " The lax administration of the criminal law is due in a marked degree to the prevalence of maudlin sentiment among the people and the alluring limelight in which the criminal walks if only he can give a little sensational colouring to his mean or sordid offence."

reprieve or commutation of the sentence. Hardly a voice is raised on behalf of the enforcement of the law. Sometimes the matter gets into politics, and a Governor's sense of duty may be weakened by those who urge that his leniency will win popular favour.

The sentimental weakness which is indulgent to crime because it pities the individual offender while forgetting the general interests of society is common in democratic peoples, and perhaps even commoner in America than in Italy or France. It now and then appears in Australia. When to all these causes we add the intellectual mediocrity of so many among the State judges, the frequent failures of criminal justice become intelligible; and one wonders not at the practical impunity accorded in many States to violent crime, but at the indifference of the public to so grave an evil. Recently the Bar Association of New York has bestirred itself to secure reforms; but there are States where the conditions are far worse than in New York, and where the frequency of homicide and the feebleness of the law in coping with it rouse little comment. This is especially the case in the Southern States where the habits of violence formed in the days of slavery have not died out, and where racial feeling is so strong that it is just as difficult in many districts to secure the punishment of a white who has injured or even killed a negro as it has been to obtain justice in a Turkish court for a Christian against a Muslim. The practice of lynching is the natural concomitant of a tardy or imperfect enforcement of the law. Though not rare in some parts of the West, and sometimes applied to white offenders, it is specially frequent in the Southern States, but not confined to them. In 1910, at the little town of Coatesville in Pennsylvania, a negro criminal lying in the town hospital awaiting trial was seized by a mob, dragged out of the town, and roasted alive, no one interfering. Several persons were indicted, but all escaped punishment. This is one of the many cases in which there was no excuse for a violent interference with the regular process of law, for the victim would undoubtedly have been found guilty and executed for murder.

It is not solely from the incompetence of State judges and the defects of criminal procedure that public order and the respect for law have been suffering. In some States the ex-

ecutive officials fail to arrest or bring to trial breakers of
the peace.   In some few, bands of ruffians have been allowed
for months or years to perpetrate outrages on persons whose
conduct displeased them; and this, in the case of the White
Caps in Indiana and the Night Riders in Kentucky, with
practical impunity, the legislatures having provided no
rural police.   Train robberies by brigands resembling the
dacoits of India have not quite ceased in parts of the West,
though they no longer receive that indulgent admiration of their boldness which made Robin Hood a hero in
mediaeval England.   On the Pacific coast the Federal Government has found it hard to induce the State authorities to
secure to immigrants from Eastern Asia the rights which
they enjoy by treaty or by a sort of common law of nations.
It is urged by way of extenuation, both for the prevalence of
lynching and for other failures to enforce the law, that habits
of disorder — being a legacy from the days when a wild
country was being settled by bold and forceful frontiersmen,
and men had to protect themselves by a rude justice — disappear slowly, that the regard for human life is still imperfect, that the custom of carrying pistols is widespread, and
that the cost of policing thinly peopled regions is disproportionate to the frequency of the offences committed.   Whatever weight may be allowed to these palliations, it remains
true that in many parts of the United States facts do not
warrant the claim that democratic government creates a law-
abiding spirit among the citizens.

Why is there not a stronger sense of the harm done to the
community by failures of justice and the consequent disregard of human life?   Why does not a public opinion which
is in most respects so humane and enlightened as is that of
the American people, put forth its strength to stamp out the
practice?   As respects the defects of criminal procedure in
general, it must be remembered, that an evil which has become familiar ceases to be shocking.   The standard custom
has set comes to be accepted: it is only the stranger who is
amazed.   Those good citizens in the States referred to who
are shocked and desire a reform find it hard to know how or
where to begin.   The lower sort of lawyers, numerous in the
legislatures, dislike reforms which would reduce their facilities for protracting legal proceedings to their own profit, and

are apt to resist improvements in procedure. The ordinary
legislator has not the knowledge to enable him to prepare or
put through bills for the purpose. No body in a State is responsible for pushing reforms forward, for the Governor is
not represented in the Legislature and the members are often
jealous of his intervention. These explanations, the best
that are supplied to the enquirer, leave him still surprised
at the tolerance extended to the enemies of public peace and
order.[1]

Some one may ask, " Since the inferiority of the State
judges is a palpable and evident source of weakness, and one
which could be removed by improving their position, why is
that not done? Why not give better salaries with longer
terms and drop popular election? Cheap justice may be
dear in the long run."

The answer to this question casts still further light on
certain features of democratic government.

When the thirteen original States separated from England
all of them left the appointment of judges in the hands of
the State Governor, except two, where the legislature, and
one, Georgia, where the people chose them. The system of
appointments worked well: the judges were upright and
respected, and it might have been expected that when new
States made constitutions for themselves they would have
followed the lead given by their predecessors. But between
1830 and 1850 a wave of democratic sentiment swept over
the nation. The people, more than ever possessed or ob-
sessed by the doctrine of popular sovereignty, came to think
that they must be not only the ultimate source but the direct
wielders of power. The subjection of all authority to theirs
was to be expressed in the popular choice of every official
for a term of office so short that he must never forget his
masters, and with a salary too small to permit him to fancy
himself better than his neighbours. The view has persisted,
and still governs men's minds in most States. It is not

---

[1] The growing demand for judicial reforms in the States recently led
to the formation of a body called the American Judicature Society,
supported by many leading judges, lawyers, and professors of law. It
advocates a simplification of legal procedure, longer tenure and better
salaries for judges, and some method of selection more satisfactory than
popular election has proved to be. Progress has been made in improving the municipal court systems, and it is believed that public
opinion on the subject is being by degrees educated.

argued that the plan secures good judges. Obedience to a so-called principle disregards or ignores that aspect of the matter. Being in Kentucky in 1890, attending a State Convention called to draft a new Constitution, I enquired whether no one would propose to restore the old method of appointment by the Governor, and was told that no such proposal would be listened to. It would be undemocratic. In California in 1909 when, after hearing severe comments upon most of the judges, I asked whether the citizens could not be induced to secure better men by larger salaries and longer terms, the answer was that the only change the citizens would make would be to shorten terms and reduce salaries still further in order to prevent the judges from feeling class sympathy with the rich and the business corporations. Whether appointment by the Executive would work as well in Western and Southern States, or for the matter of that in New York and Pennsylvania as it works in Massachusetts and New Jersey it would be hard to say, for in the last-named States a tradition exists which the Governor is obliged to live up to; whereas in States where the elective system has set a lower standard a Governor might prostitute his patronage. But it is an indefensible system.

The Civil Service

Something must be said, before we pass away from the working of Government, about the Cabinet and the permanent Civil Service, for both differ widely from the institutions which bear those names in Europe.

The Cabinet is not a ruling group, as in France, Britain, Italy, Spain, Canada, Australia. It consists (1920) of ten heads of administrative departments, who act under the directions of the President in their several branches of work, and whom it is his habit, though not his legal duty, to consult. He appoints them, subject to the approval of the Senate, which is scarcely ever refused, and dismisses them at pleasure. They are responsible only to him, not to Congress. As they cannot sit in it, and are not obliged to address the people, they need not possess oratorical gifts, so it might be supposed that they would be selected as experts specially competent for the business of their respective departments.

This, however, is not so, any more than it is in England and France. Political, *i.e.* electioneering, considerations prevail, and men are appointed chiefly for the sake of pleasing particular sections of the country or of recognizing services rendered in the last preceding campaign.[1] Thus it may happen that the members of a newly formed Cabinet are most of them personally unknown, not only to the nation at large but to one another, some of them perhaps to the President himself. Though not necessarily men of outstanding ability, they have that American adaptiveness which enables them to get along almost as well as the average European Cabinet minister, and they are free from the parliamentary duties which distract him from his office work. As they may not have figured in politics before, so probably they drop out of politics when their four years' term ends, resuming their former profession or business.[2]

The Federal Civil Service comprises three classes of persons, (1) an enormous number of minor officials, such as custom-house officers and postmasters all over the country, (2) a considerable number of employees in the departments at Washington, including a large staff of scientific experts, and (3) diplomatic envoys and consuls. All these classes formerly held their posts at the pleasure of the President for the time being and vacated office when his term expired, unless he, having been re-elected, prolonged their service. The posts were party patronage, " Spoils of Office," which went to the victors in a presidential campaign. This system produced not only an inefficient civil service, but many other incidental results strange in a popular government. These may be summarized as follows :

The Party Machine filled the offices with men who were

---

[1] The Attorney-General is of course always, and the Secretary of State is frequently, a lawyer. Now and then a President may select a personal friend for the sake of having his constant counsel.

[2] The total volume of ability to be found in a Cabinet varies markedly according to the capacity a President shows for selecting able men. When a Cabinet is poor in talent, not only does administration suffer but fewer men of force and talent have the chance of becoming known to the nation, and the choice which a party has to make of a person to be put forward as its candidate for the Presidency is accordingly more restricted. In the early days this was less seen. Jefferson and John Adams had sat in Washington's Cabinets, Madison had been Jefferson's Secretary of State, and Monroe Madison's, and J. Q. Adams Monroe's, and Van Buren Jackson's.

often incompetent and always untrained. These men were changed whenever the Administration changed. Their allegiance was due primarily to the Organization, not to the nation. They were bound to contribute to its funds. Their first duty was to work for the party, and this duty they were compelled, on pain of dismissal, to discharge, so their efforts went to maintain the system by which the Machine paid its way and riveted its yoke upon the Government in Nation, State, and City. Public office was turned into a means of gain, not only to the Organization funds, but to its individual members through their opportunities of using their power for selfish ends. What went on in the National Government went on in the State Governments and in the city governments also, the same principles being applied everywhere by the same professional politicians, who indeed often reaped in the cities their largest harvests.

Through the operation of these causes, the Civil Service of the United States long remained not only inferior to that of the chief European countries, but far less efficient than the administration of great industrial. and commercial undertakings, such as railways or department stores, in America itself. Specially trained men were not looked for, because they were not desired: the salaries offered would not have secured them, and the places were wanted for partisans. Of experience there was little, because when a man had come to know his work he was likely to be dismissed to make room for some adherent of the opposite party. Neither was there a prospect of promotion as a reward for zealous service, since the service most required by the political heads of department was that rendered not to the public but to the Democrats or the Republicans, as the case might be. Yet the system was maintained, not so much because Congress was parsimonious, but rather because Congressmen, valuing patronage as a means of strengthening their hold on their constituencies, refused to part with it. At last, however, the pressure of a more enlightened public opinion, roused by a small but earnest group of reformers, compelled Congress to yield, the fact that the then dominant party feared to lose an approaching election contributing to make the majority in both Houses willing to save some at least of its partisan officials from the impending displacement. So in 1883

Congress, with a few growls, passed an Act empowering the President to place certain classes of offices under Civil Service rules which created examinations and gave permanence of tenure. This power, sparingly used at first, has been so far exerted that more than a half of the total number in classes I. and II. aforesaid are now "taken out of politics." This number includes most of the higher posts in the Washington departments, but the Assistant Secretaryships and some others of importance are still changed with the Administration as are also the foreign missions, and some of the consulates. The quality of the employees has improved as more and more have come in under the new system and been allowed to remain at the work they have learned. They are no longer compelled to toil for the party between elections as well as at elections; though some, especially among those who were appointed on the old system or still belong to the category of removables, may continue the practice. So, too, the custom by which the Organizations levied assessments, proportioned to the salaries, on the office-holders whose appointment party influence had secured, is now forbidden by law.

I have described what was one of the weakest points in the American government in order to show not merely how the interests of the people may be disregarded in a democracy, but also how in America the forces that make for righteousness can at last prevail. From the small beginnings of 1883 things have gone on improving, the professional politicians still snarling, but the reforms more and more carrying public opinion with them. The economic development of the nation, the swift diffusion and improvement of University instruction, the discoveries in physical science, the extension of State action into new fields, and a growing sense of the value of scientific methods in every kind of work, have combined to make the need for a competent Civil Service recognized.[1] While in the older departments the quality of the persons employed is rising as the old spoilsmen are superannuated or die out, fresh lines of work have been created in

[1] In 1914 there were more than 482,000 employees under the National Government, of whom 292,000 were in the Classified Civil Service, under the control of the Civil Service Commission. An interesting address to the National Service Reform Association, delivered in 1919 by Mr. Richard H. Dana, estimates the annual gain in efficiency as amounting to $30,000,000 per annum.

which men of special competence are sought for. Some of the new scientific departments in Washington, such as that of the Geological Survey, and that which has charge of the national collections, are now staffed by a large number of accomplished men equal in their respective lines of study to any whom the Old World possesses. As a home of science, Washington is no whit behind London and Paris.

A similar change has come over the public service of the more advanced States. The State Civil Service is comparatively small, and less organized than that of the National Government, partly because there has not been a Cabinet, the (few) chief State officials being elected along with the Governor, and not subject to his direction. As the functions of State Governments expand under the pressure for social reforms and for a development of the agricultural, pastoral, and mineral resources of each State by the provision of more elaborate technical instruction, new offices are created, and a new class of trained officials grows up. In 1920 ten States had good Civil Service laws, and there is an appreciation of the resulting benefits. In some States, as notably in Wisconsin, the State University has discharged with eminent success the functions of a State Bureau for education in many branches of applied science.[1] The leading State Universities of the West are a promising offspring of popular government, repaying its parental care by diffusing a wiser judgment and a more enlightened zeal for progress than is to be found elsewhere in the mass of citizens.

LOCAL GOVERNMENT RURAL AND MUNICIPAL

From the States I turn to the working of Local Government in cities and in rural areas. To what has been already said [2] regarding the latter only this remark need be added that the party system has been mischievous in some parts of the country, where local Rings put their adherents into local offices and perpetrate local jobs. In the rural areas one hears that officials, unwilling to offend persons of influence, are sometimes lax in enforcing the laws, and that

[1] See as to Wisconsin the book of Mr. Charles M'Carthy entitled, *The Wisconsin Idea.*
[2] See Chapter XXXV.

defalcations are frequent; but as the revenues of townships
and counties are mostly small, as their appropriation to public
objects is prescribed by law, as the public works to be locally
provided for are not costly, and the conduct of business tolerably well watched by the inhabitants who know the officials
and usually get to hear of malpractices, the Rings and Bosses
do no great mischief.[1]   The large sphere of independence allotted to local authorities has, at least in the Northern and
Western States, been so useful in maintaining a sense of
civic duty and a capacity for discharging it, that the advantages thus secured compensate for the harm which the
party system has done by bringing national issues into the
sphere of local administration.

The working of City government needs a fuller study, for
the United States is the country in which municipal affairs
have furnished the most striking illustrations of dangers incident to democracy.   Those who have in our time sought
to disparage it always base their charges on the record of
city scandals during the last eighty years.   Americans themselves, however proud of the successes of their system as a
whole, admit that here is to be found its one conspicuous
failure.   If Europeans knew what were and are the conditions under which the government of the cities has to be
conducted, they would throw less of the blame on democratic
principles, though they might well condemn the form in
which those principles have been heedlessly applied.   What
were these conditions?   They were unique in the world.   In
Europe the great cities have grown comparatively slowly —
Berlin is the only exception — and their civic organizations,
economic and social, have grown up with them, expanding as
they expanded.   In all but the largest there have been families in whom the mass of the people recognized a sort of leadership; neighbourhoods have had neighbourly feelings; local
divisions, such as parishes and wards, have meant something;
nearly all the inhabitants have belonged to the same race
and spoken the same language.

[1] County offices seem in many States to be too numerous and their
functions not well defined.   See as to the defects of County government especially in Middle Western States an interesting address by
Mr. Walker D. Hines to the Chamber of Commerce at Topeka, delivered March 30, 1917.

American cities have grown with unprecedented rapidity.[1] Men of the last generation who remembered New York as less than a mile in length and a half a mile in width, lived to see it fill the whole of an island fourteen miles long and spread out still further over an adjacent island and on the mainland. Chicago began as a tiny frontier port on Lake Michigan, and had after eighty years a population of two millions. This growth was due not only to industrial development and the building of railroads, but also to the flood of immigrants which began to pour in from about 1840 till 1910, most of whom could not speak English, very few of whom knew anything of the country or its institutions, and practically all of whom had no experience of the exercise of civic rights and no conception of civic duties. They formed a heterogeneous mass, at first chiefly of Irishmen and Germans, to whom were presently added Italians, Poles, Czechs, Slovaks, Croats, Serbs, Slovenes, Magyars, Russians, Greeks, Finns, Armenians, Syrians, and vast swarms of Russian and Polish Jews.[2] This crowd knew as little of the men into the midst of whom they came as they did of the city government. But they found themselves, within a few weeks or months, turned into citizens and entitled to vote at elections — City, State, and Federal. Each political party wanted voters, and bestirred itself to rope in the newcomers and enrol them as adherents. With no social ties in their new home, living in quarters removed from the better-housed native inhabitants, having no notions about voting or for whom they ought to vote, they were an easy and indeed a willing prey, pleased to find themselves of some consequence in their humble surroundings, glad to make acquaintance with the lower sort of professional politicians in the liquor saloons, and knowing no other public opinion than that which pervaded those resorts.[3]

[1] The nearest parallels to this growth may be found in Buenos Aires and in some of the cities of Siberia, such as Novo Nikolaievsk.

[2] The vast majority of Swedes and Norwegians did not remain in the cities, but went to take up farms, chiefly in the north-west.

[3] This describes conditions as they were before the Prohibition Amendment to the Constitution had been passed.

See as to the problems caused by the swift growth of cities, chap. lii. of *American Commonwealth*, by the late Mr. Seth Low, at one time Mayor of New York.

While the volume of ignorant voters was thus swelling, the cities grew faster than ever in wealth, and new work was being thrust upon their governments as docks had to be improved, public buildings erected, street railways constructed, drainage, paving, and other city needs cared for on a large scale. Taxation rose almost as fast as did wealth, lucrative contracts were being placed, immense sums disbursed. All this had to be done under the pressure which the quick growth of population and expansion of trade involved. The richer people could not spare time from money-making to attend to these things. Rarely did one of them think of standing for any city office, or entering a City Council, so the management of affairs was left to a set of persons with whom educated men had no social relations and whose action they were too busy to watch. Such men, moreover, or at least the public spirited among them, were in the years from 1835 to 1865 so keenly interested in the great national issues that city politics were neglected, or regarded only in so far as the victory of one or other political party affected its prospects in congressional or presidential elections. Good citizens, themselves upright and disinterested, turned a blind eye to the offences of those who professed to be working for the party whose success seemed supremely important. Not only were city elections fought on national lines, but party spirit gripped city politics in another way also. The Organization which controlled a city because it could deliver a heavy vote in State elections influenced the State Legislature, and probably the State Governor also, and this meant that the heads of the organization could procure from the State legislature the kind of municipal legislation which they desired in order to fasten their yoke more tightly on the city and carry through whatever schemes promised benefit to themselves. This habit of interference with the structure and working of city governments, instead of leaving them to take their regular course under the general statutes, entangled the city in a web of secret and sordid intrigues.

These then were the conditions:

A swiftly growing population of ignorant citizens, paying no city taxes, having no interest in good administration, tools in the hands of party leaders.

A rapid increase in the wealth of individuals, as also in

the revenues of the city and in its expenditure on a multiplicity of public services.

A neglect of city affairs by the well-to-do and educated
citizens, except in so far as the success of their party in the
city promised to strengthen it in the nation.

An inveterate habit of voting the national party ticket,
irrespective of the particular State or City issues involved,
and practically irrespective of the personal merits of candidates.

The party managers whose methods have been described
in a preceding chapter were not slow to profit by such a
situation. Every city had a government framed not with
a view to efficiency and economy but on political lines similar
to those of the State Governments. The differences between
one " City Charter " (as the frame of government is called)
and another were numerous, but the general character of
these instruments was the same, and so were the economic
and social phenomena which the cities presented. There
was a Legislature, sometimes of one, sometimes of two Councils, composed of persons most of whom belonged to the half-
educated class and were unknown to the respectable citizens.
There was a mayor and a number of other officials, each directly elected by the people for short terms; and there were
judges elected also for short terms with a wide civil as well
as criminal jurisdiction.[1]

The process by which a little group of selfish professional politicians gained in each city, first the control of the
party organization and then through it the control of the

---

[1] A high authority, Dr. F. J. Goodnow, President of Johns Hopkins
University, says: " By not providing for either property or educational qualification, and by requiring merely a short term of residence,
the United States city election laws thus generally bring it about that
the number of voters at city elections is from eight to fifty per cent
greater than elsewhere. Finally, the fact that these laws do not accord the vote to non-resident tax-payers prevents the exercise of a possible conservative influence on city elections.

" Although the conditions of population in American cities are such
that the voters are much more heterogeneous than they are elsewhere,
or even than they once were, the election laws of the United States
give no consideration to that fact, but confer the city suffrage on vast
numbers of people who cannot be said to have a permanent stake in the
city, who, indeed, in many cases may not be *bona-fide* residents of the
city, and may not have sufficient political capacity, because of lack of
power to read, or because of previous associations, to cast a vote intelligently " (*Municipal Government*, p. 146).

city, can seldom be traced, for the Ringsters conspired in secret, and the public records give only the outer aspect of their actions. Usually a few of the wiliest and most plausible who became prominent in the primaries were elected to the managing committees. There, getting to know one another, and having a common aim, they found it profitable to work together, filled the committees with dependants on whose obedience they could rely, and so grew to be a small irresponsible junta, who kept power because they proved themselves fit to use it. Sometimes they formed a sort of ruling Ring, always small. But in this Ring there was generally some one conspicuous either by his craft or by the popular talents which disposed the rank and file to follow him. If he had the gifts of leadership, boldness, self-confidence and the capacity for quick decision, he became the Boss. Democracies talk of Equality, but Efficiency is after all the first requisite in all governments, be they governments of a nation or of a faction; so in the midst of equality oligarchies and autocracies rise by a law of nature. Where the control of one strong, swift will makes for success, that will brings its possessor to the top. Thus the party organization, based on democratic principles, and respecting those principles in its rules, fell under what may be called an autocratic oligarchy with the Boss for its head, while the rest of the Ring formed his Cabinet council. So highly do American business men value efficiency, that they are more disposed to vest wide powers in a single hand than are the English, witness the concentration of the management of railroads in a President instead of a Board of Directors, and the far larger authority given to the President of a University than that allowed to the head either of any British university or of a college at Oxford or Cambridge. Thus, despite the sacred principle of equality, Bossdom prevailed in the party organizations; and in New York, for instance, the dynasty of Bosses who during eighty years have reigned purely by the gifts of political leadership may be compared with that line of monarchs, neither hereditary nor elective, but most of them rising by their military talents, which ruled the Roman Empire from Nero down to Constantine.

The party organizations laid hold of the city governments. They managed the Primaries and Conventions, nominated the party candidates, looked after the elections, resorting, when necessary, to personation, repeating, and other frauds, and adding to these, if their party controlled the officials in charge of the elections, intimidation at the polls, ballot stuffing and false counting. Most of their candidates were so obscure as to be unknown to the majority of the voters, who were thus obliged to vote the party ticket. Thus a Ring might by the use of those ignorant masses who constituted its voting stock, fill the offices with its creatures, the chief among whom found many ways of making illicit gains out of contracts or the sale of franchises (such as the laying of street railways) or by levying blackmail on firms who desired permission to transgress the law. Sometimes these practices went long unchecked, for the system grew up silently, unnoticed by good citizens who were thinking of the Slavery question or the Tariff. It was hard to fix responsibility upon offenders. Who could say which of the members of the Councils were the most guilty parties, who could examine records and documents in the custody of dishonest officials, who could hope much from legal proceedings likely to come before a judge who owed his election to the party dominating the city? While ward politicians made their petty gains in the lower strata of city life, and the ward leader directed his voting regiment like a colonel, members of the Ring installed themselves in offices where money could be scooped in by large operations; and the chiefs of the party in the State, seldom soiling their own fingers, winked at the methods of the professionals and profited by the voting power placed at their disposal.

These things, which need description because they have been used to discredit democracy, went on in practically all the great and most of the smaller cities, being generally worse in proportion to the population and the wealth of each. I take New York as a sample, because the largest, and because the facts of its case, though they have drawn the attention of the world, are little understood outside America.

In New York there was founded in 1789 a social and charitable club which after 1805 described itself as the Tammany Society, the name being taken from an Indian Sachem called Tammanend. It soon acquired a political character, and in

1822, having then thrown out tentacles all over the city, put its government on a representative basis, the General Committee being composed of delegates elected at meetings of the enrolled (Democratic) party voters. Its members were at first native Americans, many of them men of good social standing; but after 1850 the rank and file came more and more to consist of immigrants from Europe, while leadership passed to adventurers of a low type, native and foreign. Since then Tammany Hall has included a great mass of the new citizens — Irishmen, Germans, Jews, Italians, and Slavs. It came to be practically supreme in the Democratic party in the city, as well as the mainstay of that party in New York State, being therewith also a power in the National Democratic Convention, since the vote of New York State often turns the scale in presidential elections. In 1863 a man named William Marcy Tweed, who had failed in business as a chairmaker, a jovial, boisterous, swaggering fellow of vulgar tastes and scanty education, became Chairman of the General Committee, and therewith virtual ruler of the city, for (manhood suffrage having been introduced in 1842) the Tammany vote was omnipotent. He and his three leading associates who formed a ruling group called the Ring " had at their disposal," wrote Mr. S. J. Tilden a few years later, " the whole local Government machinery, with its expenditure and patronage and its employment of at least 12,000 persons, besides its possession of the police, its influence on the Judiciary, its control of inspectors and canvassers of the elections." This last-mentioned power was used to manipulate the taking and counting of votes on a gigantic scale, while three unscrupulous lawyers, creatures or confederates of the Ring, were placed on the City Bench to facilitate its operations. The press was largely muzzled by lavish payments made to it for advertisements, and some of the minor journals were subsidized. Confident in their strength, the " Boss of the Hall " and his three associates began to rob right and left. In thirty-two months they raised the city debt by $81,000,000 (£16,200,000), more than twice the figure at which the debt had stood before. This was done chiefly by means of payments for public works which were divided among the confederated Ringsters, with practically nothing to show for the expenditure.

A trifling quarrel between some of the accomplices led to the discovery of these frauds, and an uprising of the " better element" among the citizens of both parties (1871) drove the thieves out of power and sent to prison two of them, as well as two of the three corrupt judges. But what happened thereafter? Within six years Tammany Hall was again in power under another Boss. Its voters did not care how much the city was robbed, for few of them paid taxes, and many regretted Tweed as a good fellow. The " better element," having once asserted itself, relapsed into apathy, and was again immersed in business excitements and social enjoyments. Tammany, however, was thereafter less audacious, and has had to fight hard for its power.

The history of New York since 1876 has been a chequered one. When the good citizens have exerted themselves and effected a fusion of the reformers with the Machine of the Republican party they have been able to defeat Tammany.[1] When the Republicans ran a party candidate of their own, Tammany triumphed. Now and then, however, it put forward respectable candidates for the mayoralty. The new Frame of Government introduced in 1902 cut at the roots of some mischiefs. Election frauds are now almost gone, nor can the treasury be robbed with impunity, but some branches of administration, including the police department, remain unsatisfactory.

What has been said of New York may, as respects the essential features of municipal misrule, be said of every great city, though of course with endless local variations. San Francisco, with its mixed and changeful population, has been conspicuous for violent oscillations. At the end of last century it was ruled by a formidable Boss, a blind man, but of remarkable gifts for organization, who had at his command the votes and the partisan work of the employees of

[1] Why, it may well be asked, did not the Republican party organization always work with the Reformers against Tammany? Because the Republican Bosses wished to keep their own Machine in good working order by running only their own candidates, because many of their wealthier supporters were too indifferent to turn out to vote, perhaps also because some of their party managers had a secret professional sympathy with the Democratic Ringster opponents. Pure government is distasteful to Machine men in both parties alike, and party antagonisms do not prevent private co-operation, according to the dictum, " There's no politics in politics."

the Fire Department. After his fall — he fled when indicted for peculation — the city fell for a time under the dominion of a Ring chiefly composed of labour leaders. Some of these leaders were convicted of corruption, and a period of better government followed. Space fails me to speak of Pittsburg and Chicago, St. Louis and New Orleans and Cincinnati. The phenomena are everywhere substantially the same, as are their causes: the Rings are similar: the reformers fight and win and flag and fail and prepare to fight again. The combatants come and go, but the combat is always the same. As used to be said of revolutions in France, " *plus cela change, plus c'est la même chose.*" The case of Philadelphia was peculiarly instructive, for comparatively few of its inhabitants are foreign, and the poorer classes are better off than in most cities, the number who own their houses being so large that it is called " The City of Homes." In it maladministration and corruption have been flagrant: and though the " good citizens " have frequently risen against and overthrown their oppressors, every success has been followed by a collapse, and a new Ring has climbed into power. A great victory was won in 1912, yet in a few years its results seemed likely to be lost. Misgovernment has, however, been not quite so bad since 1881 as it was before the defeat then inflicted on the Gas Ring, and in 1920 the sky had once more brightened under a new charter and a capable Mayor.[1]

Be it noted that in the cities generally there has been nothing to choose between the political parties, neither of whom has been better or worse than the other. The Tammany Ring is Democratic. The Philadelphia Ring has always been Republican, and has held its power mainly because the wealthy manufacturers have so valued the maintenance of the protective tariff as to be ready to support in their city the party which contributed to make Pennsylvania a

[1] The charter of 1919 is described as a considerable improvement on any preceding scheme of city government, and likely to deliver Philadelphia from the control of contractors. In a short sketch of its provisions Mr. Penrose, U.S. Senator from Pennsylvania, and long a prominent leader in his party, remarks, " Municipal government increases in efficiency in the exact ratio in which it is divorced from partisan politics; party efficiency and capacity for public services increases in the ratio in which it disentangles itself from municipal politics."

safe Republican State. The moral which the student of
democracy may ponder is well conveyed in words which the
most eminent Philadelphian of our time (Mr. Henry C. Lea,
the distinguished historian) wrote to me in 1888. They are
still applicable:

" In existing social conditions it would be difficult to conceive of a large community of which it would appear more
safe to predicate judicious self-government than ours. Nowhere is there to be found a more general diffusion of property or a higher average standard of comfort and intelligence,
nowhere so large a proportion of landowners bearing the
burden of direct taxation and personally interested in the
wise and honest expenditure of the public revenue. In these
respects it is almost an ideal community in which to work
out practical results from democratic theories. The failure
is not attributable to manhood suffrage, for in my reform
labours I have found that the most dangerous enemies of
reform have not been the ignorant and poor, but men of
wealth, of high social position and character, who had nothing personally to gain from political corruption, but showed
themselves as unfitted to exercise the suffrage as the lowest
proletariat, by allowing their partisanship to enlist them in
the support of candidates notoriously bad who happened by
control of party machinery to obtain the ' regular ' nominations.

" The spirit of party blinds many, while still more are
governed by the mental inertia which renders independent
thought the most laborious of tasks, and the selfish indolence
which shrinks from interrupting the daily routine of avocations. In a constituency so enormous the most prolonged
and strenuous effort is required to oppose the ponderous and
complicated machinery of party organization, which is always in the hands of professional politicians who obtain control over it by a process of natural selection, and are thus
perfectly fitted for the work. Recalcitrants are raw militia
who take the field with overwhelming odds against them
both in numbers and discipline. Even though they may gain
an occasional victory their enthusiasm exhausts itself, while
the ' regular ' is always on duty and knows, with Philip
the Second, that time and he can overcome any other two."

Among the consequences of municipal misgovernment two

stand out conspicuous. The progressive and philanthropic spirit, now active in America, has been demanding an extension of the functions of city authorities. Better provision is needed for the health of the masses, for their comfort, for their delectation by music and by art exhibitions, for a still further extension of public parks and all sorts of city amenities. The so-called "public utilities," such as street railroads, gas, and electric lighting, might be taken out of the hands of grasping private companies, who are in league with the Rings, and be run more cheaply or made to yield a revenue for city purposes. But there is an obvious objection. Can the Machine politicans who control the cities be trusted with functions they are sure to abuse? Must not municipal reform precede attempts at municipal socialism?

The other palpable consequence of the recurring palpable scandals in city government has been to lower the standard of political morality. Sins frequent and patent which go unpunished cease to excite reprobation. The "boodling alderman," and the aspiring young lawyer who, coming from a pious home, succumbs to temptation and becomes a "grafter," are familiar figures on the American stage and arouse more amusement than blame. Since nobody expects virtue in a city politician, nobody is disappointed when he fails to show it, and many live down to the level expected from them.

The warning which the phenomena of American cities teach is essentially the same everywhere. The so-called "good citizens" are scarcely less responsible than the bad citizens for the maladministration and corruption of which they complain. A democratic frame of government assumes, and must assume, that at least a majority of the ruling people will know and discharge their duty. The richer and larger a community the more will birds of prey flock to it. But though vigilance is all the more needed, experience shows that the larger the community, the more apt is the citizen to neglect his duties, because there are so many others equally bound to discharge them. The habit of letting base politicians make their gains out of the cities was formed before people realized how great those gains might become. With indolence there went a good-natured tolerance, commoner in America than in Europe, which perpetuates the evils it endures.   Thus was city democracy turned into a sordid city oligarchy.

Another reflection is suggested by the history of these cities. Without asking what Democracy meant to those who founded it in Athens, to Pericles who guided or to Aristotle who described it there, or to Rousseau whose theories gave it a new birth in the modern world, let us consider what a City meant to the inhabitants of an Italian or German town in the Middle Ages, or to those of an English borough in the seventeenth, or those of an American borough in the first half-century of the United States.   It meant a community organized for common aims by men who had a long experience of rights they claimed and duties they were expected to discharge, a community held together not only by traditions but also by a sort of social cement, one in which, even after the trade guilds had become obsolete, men had a personal knowledge of one another, where the humbler classes respected the prominent figures to whom leadership belonged, sometimes by wealth, sometimes by intelligence and superior talents and education, or by the eminence which office, worthily discharged, secures.   In such a community men had grounds for trusting one another.   Workmen knew their employers, and employers felt some responsibility for their workmen.   The churches put the rich and the poor in some sort of touch with one another, and helped to create a sense of human fellowship.   Those were real Communities, because men had something tangible in common.   When citizens had to choose a man for an office, they had grounds for preferring A to B or C.   Merit (or the semblance of it) told: there was a record behind the candidate from which the likelihood of performance could be conjectured.

But what is a modern American city?   A huge space of ground covered with houses, two or three square miles appropriated by the richer sort, fifteen or twenty, stretching out into suburbs, filled with the dwellings of the poorer. More than half of these lower strata had lately come from their far-off Old World homes, leaving their former social ties behind them, and having not yet formed new ties in the strange land whose language many among them could not speak, and of whose institutions they knew nothing.   They were not members of a Community, but an aggregation of

human atoms, like grains of desert sand which the wind
sweeps hither and thither. They got work, but they knew
nothing of the man they worked for: probably he was the
manager of a great corporate company. They began to read
the newspapers, but the only part of the news that they could
follow was the record of crimes and accidents with which the
meaner newspapers are filled. Naturalization made American citizens of them, and they were pleased, for it seemed to
improve their position. But when election day came, and
their fellow-workmen who had lived longer in the city told
them they could vote, they did not know for what to vote, or
indeed what voting means, any more than they had done in
Lithuania.

Not long, however, are they left thus unguided. The ward
politician appears, tells the newly fledged citizen to join his
party, enrols him, takes him to the poll, gives him a ticket,
shows him how to mark his ballot-paper. He casts his vote
accordingly, and it counts for as much as does that of the
best instructed among his fellow-voters. Having no other
advice, no interest in good government, or in anything except
protection from the consequences of any breach of law he
might, perhaps unwittingly, commit, knowing nothing of the
candidates whose names are on the ticket, he takes such advice as is proffered, that of the Party. He is now part of
the "voting stock" by means of which Tammany or some
other such organization fills the city offices, counting this
stock by many thousands. The facts being what they are,
and human nature being what it is in the wily party manager and in the passive voter, could any other result have
been expected than that which the American cities present?
Democracy cannot be fairly judged under such conditions.
Yet the voters were the People. Statesmen continued to
flatter them, and to repeat that the People can do no wrong.
Carlyle would have observed that Nature takes her revenge
on those who live by shams.

What lessons are to be drawn from these scandals — the
thefts from the city treasury, the jobbing of contracts, the
sale of public franchises, the malign influence of those whom
President Roosevelt used to call "malefactors of great
wealth," the granting of immunity, for payment, to law-
breakers, the complicity of the police with one of the most

odious classes of criminals, and all the evils of fraud or violence that were needed to perpetuate the rule of Rings and Bosses?

They teach nothing that was not known before, though never before on so grand a scale.

A mass of ignorant voters, untrained in self-government, becomes the natural prey of unscrupulous leaders.

A government controlled by those who have no interest in economy will not be economical. It was said by them of old time, "No taxation without representation." Here was representation without taxation.

Where men practically irresponsible dominate those nominally responsible, responsibility disappears.

The members of a self-governing community need to have some social bonds of union, and if the men whom talent and character mark out for leadership stand aloof, their places will be filled by the less worthy.

CHAPTER XLIV

PUBLIC OPINION

THERE is no better test of the excellence of a Popular Government than the strength of public opinion as a ruling power. I have sought to explain (see Chapter XV. *ante*) wherein its rule differs, and differs for the better, from that of a numerical majority acting by votes only. In the United States, though votings are more frequent than in any other country, yet Public Opinion is, more fully than elsewhere, the ruling power. The founders of the Republic expected from the average citizen a keener sense of his duty to vote wisely than he has shown, but in the function of giving, by his opinion, a general direction to public policy he has done well. The doctrine of Popular Sovereignty and the structure of the Government made it specially necessary that he should respond to the call made upon him of giving such direction, because the functions of government are divided and parcelled out between its several organs. There are many checks and balances. Where each organ is watched and restrained by others, where terms of office are short, and changes in the persons who administer are consequently frequent, the watchfulness and directive control of the citizens are essential in order to keep the complicated machinery working and to guide each of its parts to a common aim. The citizen must feel his constant responsibility, both to form an opinion and to make it known between the periods at which he delivers it by an electoral vote. Though this duty is not perfectly discharged, public opinion is on the whole more alert, more vigilant, and more generally active through every class and section of the nation than in any other great State. The Frame of Government has by its very complication served to stimulate the body of the people to observe, to think, and to express themselves on public questions.

To explain why this is so, and what are the wholesome

results it has produced, let us note some features of public opinion as determined by the character of the national mind.

Not even in the United States are politics the first thing in the citizen's thoughts. His own business, his domestic life, his individual tastes, come first, yet more here than elsewhere does one discover a people seriously interested in public affairs. Nobody says, as men so often say in France, Germany, and Italy, " I never trouble myself about politics." Current events are constantly discussed among the ordinary rural folk, and though the country newspaper is chiefly filled by farming topics and " local happenings," still the affairs of the nation figure somewhere in the landscape of nearly every native American. It is, moreover, the good fortune of the country to possess a real national opinion as well as an ardent national patriotism; that is to say, there exists on most political topics a certain agreement which rises above and softens down the differences between the various sections or types of view. In some countries — France for instance — those differences are so marked that no such general concurrence of opinion can, as regards domestic issues, be discerned. It is usually antagonisms that are conspicuous. But in the United States, vast as the country is, there are many matters on which the great majority seem to be of one mind all the way from one ocean to the other. During the first two years of the late war there were diversities of attitude and feeling between the North Atlantic States and the South and the Middle West and the Far West, easily explicable by the fact that the first-named were in much closer touch with Europe and felt themselves more affected by what was passing there. But America's entrance into the conflict effaced these diversities. The same wave of feeling, sweeping over the whole continent, brought its sections into full accord. Considering how dissimilar are the conditions of economic and social life in the East, in the South, and in the West, this similarity of opinion is remarkable. It is qualified only by the feeling, still strong in the South, that, whatever happens, the coloured men must not be allowed to regain any considerable voting power. Racial diversities may be found everywhere, for one-third of the inhabitants were born abroad or of foreign parents, but such diversities affect but slightly the opinion of the nation, because the most recent immigrants have neither the education nor the experience needed to enable them to influence others; while those who have been born and bred in the country have already become substantially American in their interests and ways of thought. Though in some cities masses of Slavs or Italians remain unabsorbed, the only large minorities which retain an attachment to the country of their origin sufficient to have political importance are a section of the Germans and a section of the Irish. It is, however, only in so far as questions of foreign relations are affected that these two elements stand out of the general stream of opinion. The solvent and assimilative forces of education, of companionship, of all the things that make up social environment, are stronger in America than in any other country. Religious differences also count for very little. In some few matters Roman Catholics may be influenced by respect for the head of their Church, and they usually support the demand of their clergy for grants to denominational schools. But there is nothing resembling that strength of ecclesiastical sentiment which used to affect the political attitude of many Nonconformists and many members of the Established Church in England, much less any manifestations of the bitterness which in France arrays in hostile camps the Roman Catholics and the anti-clerical or the non-Christian part of the population.

Class distinctions have during the last hundred years become in Continental Europe the forces which chiefly split and rend a people into antagonistic sections of opinion. This tendency has increased with the spread of the revolutionary school which preaches the so-called " class war " of the " proletariate " against the " bourgeois." It is only within the last three decades that this doctrine, brought from Europe by German and Russo-Jewish immigrants, has been making way, and what support it receives comes almost wholly from the still unassimilated part of the immigrant population. America had been theretofore exempt from class antagonisms, because opinion had been divided, not horizontally along the strata of less or greater wealth, but vertically, so that each view, each political tenet, was common to men in every social class. The employer and his workmen, the merchant and his clerks, were not led by their different social positions to think differently on politics any more than they would think differently on religion. They have been Republicans or Democrats for reasons unconnected with pecuniary means or station in life, neither of these two parties having any permanent affinity either with the richer or with the poorer, though from time to time one or other might, in some parts of the country, enlist the support of the moneyed class on a particular party issue, like that of Free Silver in 1896.[1]

This fact suggests another reflection. In many of the largest and gravest questions, public opinion does not move on party lines. This is partly because the tenets, or at least the professions, of the opposite parties sometimes come very near to one another. A famous journalist observed to me in 1908 : " Our two parties are like two bottles, both empty, but bearing different labels." He spoke truly, for though there were strong currents of opinion discernible, none was flowing in a party channel. One observes in America that men accustomed to support their party by their votes, frequently disapprove both its acts and its promises. Thus the power and cohesiveness of party does not prevent the existence of a common sentiment in the bulk of the nation, often more united than the vehemence of party language leads foreigners to suppose. There are, in fact, only two fairly well-defined types of class opinion. One is that of the small financial class, including the heads of great industrial concerns, the other that of the advanced Socialist party,[2] largely under the influence of European syndicalistic or even anarchistic ideas. Among the rest there are no sharp and permanent oppositions of political tenets or of social sympathies.

Political opinion is better instructed than in Continental Europe, because a knowledge of the institutions of the country and their working is more generally diffused here than there through the rank and file of the native population. This is mainly due to the practice of local self-government

---

[1] This statement is not inconsistent with the fact that in the Eastern cities most of the rich belong to one party, and that in the former Slave States nearly all of that class belong to the other, but in the latter case this predominance is due not to economic reasons but to recollections of the Reconstruction period after the Civil War.

[2] Socialism has made less progress among the Labour Unions than it has among the working men of European countries. Some of the chiefs of the American Unions are definitely opposed to it, and occasionally denounce doctrines of a revolutionary tendency.

and to the publicity given by the newspapers to all that passes
in the political field.   Something may be attributed to the
active part in public affairs that has always been played by
members of the legal profession, and even more, in recent
times, to the influence of college teaching.   The number of
men who have graduated in some place of higher instruction
is probably ten times as large (in proportion to population)
as in any part of Continental Europe, and much more than
twice as large as in Great Britain.   These men have done
much to leaven the voting mass.   Most of them have not received what Europeans would call a complete university
education, and the so-called literary or humanistic studies
have been often neglected.   But they have been led into the
realms of thought, and their horizons have been widened.
They are often the leaders in reform movements, with higher
ideas of good citizenship than the average business man
used to possess, and they are less inclined to a blind support
of their party.   One of the most significant and most hopeful features of American life has been the increase during the
last forty years of the number and the influence of the universities, and of the extent to which their alumni, business
men as well as lawyers, teachers, and clergymen, make themselves felt in the higher forms of political activity.[1]

What, then, of the Press, which is in all modern countries
the chief factor in forming as well as in diffusing opinion?
This is not the place to describe its general features, nor to
enquire how far it deserves the censures which many Europeans, repelled by the faults of the worst newspapers, have
unfairly bestowed upon it as a whole.   These faults are due
not to democracy, but to the social and economic conditions of
the lower strata in city populations, conditions that produce
in all countries results generally similar, but more marked
here, because nowhere are there so many newspapers which
find their circulation in that vast reading mass which is
chiefly interested in records of crime and of events in the
field of sport.

[1] Complaints are sometimes heard that the Universities are too much
controlled by the boards of trustees drawn from the business world
and occasionally intolerant of opinions they dislike; but whatever
foundation there may be for these complaints so far as regards the
academical staff, the services rendered to the political life of the
nation are evident.

The press, including many weekly and some monthly magazines which handle political questions, is a chief agent in
forming opinion by letting everybody know what everybody
else is saying or is supposed to be thinking. This tells
on the minds of undecided or unreflective people. Having neither the time nor the knowledge to think for
themselves they feel safe in thinking with the majority.
In this sense the press makes opinion more effectively
here than in any other country, because the habit of
reading is more general, and prominent men, though
less given than are the English to writing letters to the newspapers, are more wont to confide their views to an interviewer. The papers have their defects. The reporting of
even the best speeches is full and exact only in a very few
of the best journals, the rest confining themselves to abridg-
ments which often miss the really important points. As
everything is done in haste, the truth of facts fares ill; but
in the general result the whole opinion of the country is
mirrored more completely than anywhere in Europe. It is
the statements of events and of the opinions of public men
that tell. They would tell even more but for the inaccur-
acies frequent in papers of the second rank and rarely corrected, yet here, as elsewhere, these do not prevent the average man from assuming that what he sees in print is likely to
be true. Editorial articles count for less than in England
or France: few people swear by their favourite paper, as
many still do in England, and the names of editors and of
writers of leading articles are scarcely known to the public.
Hardly more than six or seven men have, during the last
thirty years, become familiar and personally influential figures in the world of political journalism, great as is the literary talent which many have displayed. Thus the profession does not offer that opening to a public career which
it has often done in France and sometimes in England,
though the proprietor of a widely circulated paper or group
of papers may become a political figure, and even seek high
office by bringing himself before the public. Scarcely ever
has a leading statesman controlled, as in France, a newspaper which habitually pushed his views or urged his personal claims, so it may be assumed that this form of advocacy
or advertisement would prove unprofitable. Press hostility

directed against a statesman, not by mere abuse, which seldom tells, but by persistently recalling errors he has committed, or (more rarely) by inventing and repeating gross calumnies, can injure his prospects more than praise, however lavish, can improve them.   Men have been " boomed " into popularity and power more frequently in England than in America.   Does this argue the presence of more discernment in the public?

Partisanship also, *i.e.* the indiscriminating support of a political party, is rather less marked in American than in European journals, the former holding a more independent attitude, and bestowing their censures on one or other party with reference less to their professed political principles than to their action at any particular time or their attitude on any particular issue.   This increases their weight with thoughtful readers, and has a wholesome influence on party chiefs, who know they must expect criticism even from the organs to which they usually look for support.   To be wounded in the house of your friends, though a painful, is sometimes a profitable experience.

Though the Press as a whole is at least as important a factor in the working of government as it is anywhere else in the world, no single paper is as powerful as some have been in England, in France, in Italy, in Australia, and in Argentina.   This is due to the size of the country.   The range of a journal which can be read in the forenoon of its issue is confined to some few hundreds of miles, and though the utterances of the very best papers are widely read and largely quoted much further off, or may have their views telegraphed all over the Union, they have no great hold on a distant public.   The ascendancy of any wealthy proprietor or group of proprietors influencing a large proportion of the voters by impressing on them, day after day and week after week, one set of views and the same one-sided statement of facts or alleged facts, is a danger only in the sphere of foreign relations.   In that sphere plausible falsehoods and persistently malignant misrepresentation of the character and purposes of another people may do infinite mischief.   One form of such misrepresentation is to pick out and reprint any unfriendly utterances that appear in the newspapers, perhaps contemptible and without influence, of the country which it is desired to injure.

The exposure and denunciation of municipal misgovernment and corruption is among the greatest services which the American Press — including some religious and other non-political weeklies — performs.   We have seen how largely these evils sprang from the ignorance or apathy of the " respectable classes," who constantly need to be awakened from their torpor, and driven to support the too scanty band of civic reformers.   European observers, offended by the excesses to which the passion for publicity can run in the United States, sometimes fail to realize how many evils the incessant vigilance of the press prevents or helps to cure.   Whether its faults, which were thought to have been aggravated with the upspringing of some papers of a low type in the end of last century, have tended to decrease in later years is a question which some judicious observers answer by saying that the best papers have grown better and the worst papers worse. On several great occasions, and notably during the course of the recent War, the Press rendered conspicuous services to the nation as an exponent of instructed and thoughtful opinion.

Since it was on the Average Man and his civic virtue that the founders of the Republic relied for the working of its institutions, it is well to consider that generalized being, taking a sort of composite photograph from many individuals, and enquiring how far his power of forming a sound opinion has justified the confidence reposed in him.   As the characteristic type of the Average Man, take the native American landowning farmer in the Northern and especially in the Middle Western and North-Western States, where he is seen at his best, for in New England he has been largely replaced by the new immigrant not yet thoroughly Americanized.   With the farmer one may couple the storekeeper or artisan of those smaller towns which have a sort of rural colour.   These two classes, and particularly the former, are specifically American products, the like of whom one finds nowhere else, independent and fairly well educated.   Though sometimes querulous, as are agriculturists generally, accustomed to complain of the weather, they would, but for their resentment at the exploitation they suffer at the hands of financial interests, be as nearly satisfied with their lot as man is ever likely to be.

The normal member of these classes has a great pride in his country and a sense of his own duty to it. He follows the course of national and State politics, not assiduously, but with fair intelligence and attention, usually voting at elections, though apt to leave political work to be done by the party organization. He is overprone to vote the party ticket, whatever names are put on it, and needs to be made to feel his own interest affected before he will join in a reforming movement. Shrewd, and critical of the motives and character of politicians, he is rather less suspicious than is the English or French peasant, because he has confidence in his own shrewdness, is socially the equal of the politicians, and quite as well instructed as most of them. But his horizon is limited. His thought, like his daily work, moves in a small circle; his imagination fails to grasp conditions unlike those of his own life. Thus he is not well qualified to form a judgment on the larger questions of policy. Working hard to secure decent comfort for his family, he does not understand the value of special knowledge, thinks one man as good as another for official work, refuses to pay salaries to a judge or an administrator twice or thrice as large as his own net income. Not versed in economic principles, and seldom fitted by education to comprehend them when stated, he may fall a prey to plausible fallacies and be captured by vague promises to redress grievances of which he feels the pinch.

But if he be no good judge of measures, he is no bad judge of men. Here his shrewdness helps him: here his respect for honesty and courage comes in. When he recognizes in any public man uprightness, firmness, and a sincere desire to serve the public, he is ready to trust and to follow, rarely withdrawing a confidence once given. A strong State Governor or Mayor who fights the politicians of the Legislature in the public interest, speaking clearly to the plain people, and above the suspicion of selfish motives, can count upon his vote, even against the party organization. It was by the confidence of average men of this type that Abraham Lincoln was carried to the Presidency, and that Governor

Hughes of New York was enabled to bend to his will the party machine that had been ruling that great State. These men who till the land they own are solid and intelligent, one of the great assets of the republic.

Of some qualities which the American people as a whole show in their political life little need be said, because it is hard to determine how far these are due to democratic habits, how far to national character, *i.e.* to the original English character as modified by physical and economic conditions in a new country, as well as (in a lesser degree) by admixture with other races. Still, as we are considering how American democracy works, it may be observed that they are an impressionable people, among whom excitement rises suddenly and spreads fast, quickened by the contagion of numbers. Communication is so easy and swift over the Continent that the same impulse seems to possess every one at the same moment, as if all were assembled, like the Athenians, in one huge public meeting. It is then that the cunningly devised divisions of power and other constitutional checks are found serviceable, for at such moments opinion is apt to be intolerant of opposition, and may even resort to extra-legal methods of suppressing it. But this seldom happens. In ordinary times that tyranny of the majority [1] which Tocqueville described and feared as an evil inherent in democracies no longer exists. Independence of mind is respected. Even cranks are borne with, nor does any country produce a richer crop. Americans are, moreover, a kindly and in normal times an indulgent people.[2] This was seen half a century ago when after the Civil War an unprecedented clemency was extended towards those who were then talked of as rebels. Still less are they, as most Europeans suppose, a materialistic people. The race for wealth, not really greater than in Western Europe, is a passion rather for success in making

---

[1] As to this, and as to that tendency to acquiesce in the overmastering power of a large majority which I have ventured to call the Fatalism of the Multitude, see *American Commonwealth*, vol. ii. chaps. lxxxiv. and lxxxv.

[2] The intolerance of opposition occasionally shown during and just after the Great War was perhaps no greater than might have been expected in any country in like circumstances; and these were so exceptional that it would be hardly fair to judge the people generally by such an incident as the expulsion from a State Legislature of certain members whose views had roused hostility.

than for pleasure in enjoying a fortune. Nowhere is money so freely given to any charitable or other public purpose. Nowhere, except perhaps in Italy and France, are intellectual attainments so widely honoured. These two last-named characteristics may be credited to Democracy, which has here instilled a sense of a rich man's duty to return to the community a large part of what individual energy has won, and which respects achievements that reflect credit upon the nation and give it a pride in itself. Both sentiments flourish wherever, as here, class antagonisms are overborne by the sense of a higher common national life.

In saying that Public Opinion is the real ruler of America, I mean that there exists a judgment and sentiment of the whole nation which is imperfectly expressed through its representative legislatures, is not to be measured by an analysis of votes cast at elections, is not easily gathered from the most diligent study of the press, but is nevertheless a real force, impalpable as the wind, yet a force which all are trying to discover and nearly all to obey. As Andrew Marvell wrote:

> There is on earth a yet diviner thing,
> Veiled though it be, than Parliament or King.

In and through it, not necessarily at any single given moment, but in the long run, irrespective of temporary gusts of passion, the conscience and judgment of the people assert themselves, overruling the selfishness of sections and the vehemence of party. Illustrations of its controlling power are supplied by the progress of the various reform movements I must now describe, beginning by a short account of the most noteworthy changes which have passed upon American public sentiment during the last fifty years that have elapsed since I had first the opportunity of studying the country.

The Civil War (1861–1865) was a turning-point in the history of opinion, because for the twenty years that preceded it the growing gravity of the Slavery conflict had distracted men's minds from those constitutional and administrative questions which were not directly related to that issue. After 1865, and still more after 1877, when Federal troops were finally withdrawn from the South, the people were set free to think of many domestic topics that had been neg-

lected. It is a testimony to the vitality of the nation that
opinion is always changing not merely because new questions
emerge, but because the national mind has been constantly,
and is now increasingly active. Few of these changes have
been due to the recognized leaders of the parties. They began, like most American movements, from a small group, or
several small groups, of thinkers who saw the evils and
sought a cure. Wheresoever they started, they usually found
support in both parties, because the evils were felt to be real.
The professional party politicians, high and low, at first
discountenanced them, fearing for party solidarity. Various
was their fate. Sometimes, like the seed that fell in dry
places, they withered away, because the public feeling they
tried to appeal to was hard ground, and failed to respond.
Sometimes, slowly pervading one party, they captured it,
and their doctrines passed into its orthodoxy. Sometimes
they caused a schism and created a new party, which did its
work in affecting the views of both the older parties, and
then subsided, its adherents returning to their former allegiance without abjuring their tenets. These phenomena,
which may be traced far back in the annals of America, illustrate the tendency of its party organizations to become
ossified when left to themselves. They need to be shaken
up and have new life breathed into them by the independent
thought of individuals or groups. They exist for Offices
rather than for Principles. If the party system had exerted
the same power over minds as it did over offices, it would long
ago have ruined the country.

Among the changes and tendencies characteristic of the
democratic spirit in America, none has been better worth
studying than the dying down of the old tendency to aggression abroad. The sentiment which favours peace and
respects the rights of neighbouring States has grown
slowly but steadily. It is true that there have been
two wars within the last twenty-two years. That against
Spain might probably have been avoided, for with a
little more patience Spain could have been forced
to retire from Cuba, the long-continued misgovernment
of which had roused American sympathy, but the
war, though it brought about the annexation of the Philippines, had not been prompted by the lust for conquest. A

significant evidence of disinterestedness was given when the United States abstained from annexing Cuba, and again when having been subsequently obliged to despatch troops thither to restore order, those troops were soon withdrawn. From 1911 onwards the disturbed condition of Mexico, where American citizens were frequently injured, suggested armed occupation, to be probably followed by the acquisition either of the northern provinces or of the whole country. But the temptation was resisted. A financial protectorate has been established over the so-called " republics " of Haiti and San Domingo, whose disorders seemed to call for a benevolent intervention, but there are no signs of any wish to take over the general government of communities, one of which is no better than a piece of savage Africa placed in the Caribbean Sea.[1] The old talk about forcing or tempting Canada into the Union has ceased to be heard, and the relations between the two peoples, dwelling peaceably along an undefended frontier of three thousand miles, are more cordial than ever before. Of the unselfish motives which brought America into the Great War to defend what she held to be a righteous cause, there is no need to speak. The immense army which she raised and the prowess which her soldiers and sailors showed have fostered among the people no militaristic spirit, no desire for the conquest of new dominions.[2]

When he turns to the domestic sphere, the observer discerns two tendencies that may seem, but are not really, divergent. One is the disposition to leave the Southern States alone to deal with the difficulties which the presence of a large negro population creates. The Fifteenth Amendment to the Constitution, intended to secure equal electoral rights to the negro, has been successfully evaded by the whites of the South, yet the proposals made thirty years ago to restore those rights by Federal action have been quietly dropped. But while in this matter Federal intervention was disapproved, the powers of the National Government were simul-

[1] Some measure of financial control has also been assumed over Nicaragua and Honduras.

[2] Upon the changed attitude of the U.S. to world questions the recent book of Professor Max Farrand, *The Development of the United States*, and upon the relations of the U.S. to Great Britain and Canada the book of Professor Dunning entitled *A Century of Peace*, may be usefully consulted.

taneously growing in other directions, and the rights reserved to the States by the Constitution have been correspondingly narrowed. Decisions of the Supreme Court have
extended, and Federal legislation by Congress has made more
effective, the powers exercisable over railways and commerce.
Public sentiment went still further and induced Congress to
pass Acts for the regulation of child labour, which the Supreme Court held invalid because invading a province clearly
reserved to the States. An Amendment to the Constitution
(the Sixteenth) has authorized Congress to levy an income-
tax, another (the Seventeenth) has changed the mode of
electing the Senate, and more recently (1919) the world has
been startled by an Amendment (the Eighteenth) prohibiting
the production and sale of intoxicating liquors over the whole
Union, this having been hitherto a matter which seemed,
on the old constitutional lines, to be altogether within the
sphere of the States.[1] So, too, an Amendment extending
the electoral suffrage to women over the whole Union was
carried in 1920, a change which, whatever its merits or
demerits, deprives the States of what the framers of the
Constitution held to be an essential principle of the Federal
system.

This apparently light-hearted readiness to alter a Fundamental Instrument which had, save for the three Civil War
Amendments, stood unchanged from 1804 till 1912, and the
proposal of other amendments now treated as matters for
serious discussion, indicate a decline in that veneration for
the time-honoured Constitution which had ruled the minds
of preceding generations. The three first-named amendments were carried by large majorities, neither party organization opposing.

The United States has felt, quite as fully as any European
country, the influence of that philanthropic impulse which
has stirred the more advanced peoples of the world within

---

[1] Experienced observers declare that this amendment which was enacted by Congress and the requisite number of State Legislatures would
unquestionably have been carried if submitted to a popular vote. Its
success is ascribed partly to the dislike for the "saloons," as owned
and run by powerful incorporated companies, but is also deemed to be
largely due to the belief that it would not only diminish crime and
poverty but would increase the productive power of the nation. Both
these results are said to have shown themselves within the last few
months.

the nineteenth century, growing stronger with the years as they pass.

The legislation which that impulse has prompted seems to be the result of three converging forces — the sentiment of human equality which creates and accompanies democratic government, a keener sympathy with human suffering, and a fear among the educated classes that if they do not promote laws securing better conditions of life to the masses, the latter will attain those conditions for themselves by an over-hasty use of their votes, or, failing legal methods, by violence. For more than half a century American public opinion, warmly philanthropic in the more advanced and best educated parts of the country, has caused the enactment of many measures for bettering the health, comfort, and education of the poorer classes, and improving in every way the conditions of labour. As these things have to be effected by laws, and laws have to be administered by public authorities, reformers invoke the State; while the Labour organizations, desiring to throw more and more into its hands, advocate the nationalization of some great industries. The old doctrines of individual self-help and *laissez faire* have been thrown overboard, and the spirit of paternalism waxes strong. So far as respects regulation of conduct and the protection of the worker, the State has already become a significant factor, though it does not police the citizen as in Germany, nor undertake the direct management of industries after the manner of Australia and New Zealand.[1] All this has been the doing not of the parties, but of a public opinion at work in both parties, which aims at amending institutions, because it is hoped to obtain from them when amended certain social and economic benefits which the people desire. The machinery is to be repaired in order to secure a larger output.

Though often described as socialistic, this movement has had its source in a sense of human brotherhood seeking to mitigate the inequalities of fortune, rather than in any Collectivistic theories imported from Germany by the disciples of Marx. The professedly Socialist parties of America count some native Americans among their leaders, but find most of their support in the recent immigrants from Europe, and

[1] As to the movement in N. Dakota, see p. 136 *post*. There is no great tendency towards " nationalization " of industries except in the advanced sections of the Socialist party.

they grow slowly.   One of them runs candidates in national
elections, but its vote has hitherto been small.[1]

More important, and more directly operative in politics,
are three streams of opinion so intimately connected each
with the others that they must be considered together.   These
are: (1) hatred of the Money Power, and especially of those
large incorporated companies and monopolistic combinations
through which wealth chiefly acts; (2) disgust at the workings of the party Machine, and the methods of nomination by
which it distributes offices to its adherents; (3) anger at the
corruption and maladministration which have prevailed in
the great cities.   These three sources of evil are linked in
the minds of public-spirited and energetic citizens as three
heads of the hydra which must be shorn off together if the
monster is to be destroyed.   The great corporations have
used the party Machine to get what they want.   The party
Machine is seen at its worst in the cities, and draws from
their bad conditions most of its illicit gains, so to kill the
Machine would be both to reclaim the cities and to crip-
ple the power of money in politics.[2]   Three voices of discontent or aspiration were heard: Free the people from the
yoke of the Money Power and the monopolies; Free the voters
from the tyranny of the Machine; Free the masses from the
depressing conditions of their life.   How were these objects
to be attained?   By the People itself, that is, by its direct
action in law-making.   Legislatures have been tried, and
failed, for they have been corrupted by the money power and
controlled by the Machine.   Let us invoke the People to set

[1] Anarchism and Syndicalism are of course also at work here and
there, and labour disputes have led to some murders and to much
violence, especially in the mining districts, where there are large masses
of new immigrants.   But both the volume of industrial unrest and
the strength of extremist sections are less than in France, Italy, or
England.

[2] Speaking of the action of the money power, ex-President W. H.
Taft said: "Not all was brought about by direct corruption, but much
was effected through more insidious influence, and by furnishing the
funds that political exigencies in important electoral contests called
for.   The time was, and we all know it, when in many of the director-
ates of the great corporations of the country, orders for the delivery
of delegates in a convention and of members of the legislature for purposes of corporate control were issued with the same feeling of confidence in their fulfilment as an order for the purchase of machinery or
the enlargement of the pay-roll" (*The Signs of the Times*, address
before Electrical Manufacturer's Club, November 6, 1913, pp. 11–12).

things right. Thus there arose a wave of democratic sentiment which swept over the country, prompted by the sense of
practical grievances, but drawing strength also from that
doctrine of Popular Sovereignty to which the multitude respond now as they did in the days of Jefferson, and again
in those of Andrew Jackson.

CHAPTER XLV

Efforts to reform the Primaries

THE changes which this reforming spirit seeks to effect in the structure and working of the government (National, State, and Municipal) may be classed under four heads:

Reforms in the working of party organizations.
Reforms in the modes of appointing officials.
Reforms in the structure of city governments.
Transfer of legislative power from representative assemblies to the citizens voting at the polls.

The second and third of these are closely connected with and largely dependent on the first, which may be briefly described as the reform of the system of party organization by breaking the power of the Machine and restoring to the people at large that right of choosing candidates which the Machine had wrested from them. Its history is instructive.

It will be remembered that the scheme of party organization was based on the Primary meeting of all members of a political party within a given electoral area for the purpose of (a) selecting party candidates, (b) naming delegates to sit in a party convention, and (c) appointing a Committee to take charge of local party work. This scheme, sound in principle, for it was a recognition of the right of the members of a party not only to formulate their own policy, rejecting the dictation of leaders, but also to settle beforehand who should be their candidate, rested on three postulates:

All good citizens will attend their Primary.
When met in their Primary they will honestly try to find the best candidates, *i.e.* those trustworthy men who are most likely to win the election.
Capable and trustworthy men will be willing to become candidates if chosen by the other members of the party.
The second and third postulates seem to follow naturally

129

from the first. If the members of the party as a whole attend
the Primary, the sense of public duty which brings them
there will make them take pains to select trustworthy men,
and will dispose such men to accept the candidacy tendered.
There may be mixed motives, as everywhere, but since the
aim of the majority will be to secure a good choice, the meeting will go right.

None of the conditions which theory postulated had been
in fact fulfilled. Comparatively few members attended,
while some who would have attended were excluded because
too independent. Thus the Primaries did not truly represent the party. When the Primary met, opposition, if any,
to the names put forward by the Committee was over-borne
by its henchmen, and often outwitted by a partisan Chairman
who ruled questions of order against them. Accordingly in
the cities and wherever there was a pretty dense population
dominated by a Ring, the choice of candidates, delegates, and
Committee men was dictated by the Ring. The reform
needed, therefore, was to eliminate fraud in making up the
party roll, and force as well as fraud in the conduct of
business at the Primary. This was sought by the novel and
drastic method of turning what had been a (private) party
Meeting into a (public) Election (by polling) at which the
citizens should be entitled to vote (a) for the selection of
party candidates, (b) for the selection of delegates to a party
Convention, (c) for the members of the local party Committee. All this has now been done in practically every
State, though with an endless variety of details in the provisions of the various State laws. Rules are laid down for
the making up of the roll of members of a party, for the
conduct and modes of voting at the Direct Primary election
(as it is now called), for the prevention of bribery, fraud,
and violence, in fact for all the matters that have to be prescribed as respects the regular public elections to a legislature
or any public office. This legal recognition of Party as a
public political institution, this application of statutory
regulation to what had theretofore been purely voluntary
and extra-legal associations of citizens, strikes Europeans as
a surprising new departure in politics. American reformers, however, had been so long accustomed to regard their
parties as great political forces, national institutions which

for good or for ill ruled the course of politics, that they jumped at any method of overthrowing a corrupt system, and were not in the mood to be arrested by anything savouring of constitutional pedantry. Nothing weaker than the arm of the law seemed to them capable of democratizing that nominating machinery which had been worked by a selfish oligarchy.

The movement, which began in the last decade of the nineteenth century, ran like wildfire from State to State over the Union, for much as the professional politicians disliked it, they found it hard to resist what upon the face of it was meant to enlarge the freedom of the ordinary citizen. Some States, however, went further than others, applying a Primary Election to candidacies for all State offices, including those of Governor and Senator, and allowing the voter, in a Presidential year, to indicate his preference for a particular party man who aspires to be selected, in the nominating National Convention of his party, as its candidate for the Presidency. Some States recognize what they call " unofficial Primaries," and some allow Conventions to retain nominating functions which others transfer to Direct Primaries.[1] The most important difference between these State laws is that between the Open and the Closed Primary. In the former kind of election citizens belonging to any political party are admitted to vote together for any of the persons put forward to be chosen as candidates, so that a Democrat may vote for a Republican, or a Republican for a Democrat, though it is sometimes provided that all votes cast for any person shall be counted for him only as a candidate of the party upon whose ticket his name is written. The power to vote irrespective of party may seem in so far good that it

---

[1] The general use of Direct Primaries has not destroyed Conventions. These continue to be held for the purpose of adopting a platform and selecting members of the State Committee, and in some States they choose delegates to the National (Presidential) Convention. Sometimes, moreover, they are used for securing party agreement upon the persons to be voted for at the legally provided Direct Primaries for the selection of candidates, since the party voters need guidance as to how they shall vote thereat. Thus a third or preliminary voting is added.

In some places candidates for Congress, for State offices and for local offices are nominated in Direct Primaries, subject to the requirement that to succeed a candidate must secure 35 per cent of the votes cast. If no one receives that percentage the choice goes over to a Convention. Nominations for State and District judges are made at Conventions.

enables members of one party to "give a lift" to able men
or moderate men who belong to the other, but it might doubtless be turned to less worthy uses. The Closed Primary permits the enrolled members of a party to vote only for persons who belong to their own party, and this is sometimes
secured by requiring each party ticket to be of a distinctive
colour, so that no Republican can use a Democratic ticket,
his vote being rejected if he does. Some State laws require
every voter to declare himself to belong to a particular party
before he can vote; some go so far as to make him pledge
himself to support that party at the election next following
with a view to which the Primary is held. The persons
whose names are on the ballot-paper have of course been
nominated as the law directs, either by their respective party
organizations or by a prescribed number of citizens through
a petition, this latter giving a chance to independent candidates. The whole process is hedged round by an elaborate
code of rules often so complicated as to invite quibblings
and evasions, opening doors to controversy and litigation.

The Direct Primary is, constitutionally regarded, a large
addition to the electoral machinery of the country, throwing
upon it a new function the practice of which had become too
formidable to be left as a custom unregulated by law. It
prefixes to the election for office a preliminary secret election
by which the electors determine who are to be the party candidates for or against whom they are subsequently going to
vote, *i.e.* they vote to decide for whom they are going to vote
subsequently. An elector enabled to vote for any person, no matter by whom proposed, whose name appears
on the list of candidates for nomination, is set free
from one of his former difficulties, that of finding himself
obliged to choose between two sets of men whom he probably
equally distrusts, the candidates of his own party, whom its
Organization has forced upon him, and the candidates of the
other party, presumably no better. But the other old difficulty remains. How is he to know when he comes to vote
at the Direct Primary which of the men on the tickets are,
and which are not, capable and trustworthy? Unless the
office to be filled is an important one, like that of Senator
or Governor, he may know nothing of the names on a ticket.[1]

[1] On the official ballot for the Primary Election of one of the parties

He needs to be informed and advised.   Who so fit, or at any
rate so ready, to advise him as the Organization of his party ?
It knows everything about everybody.   It has put on the
ticket the names of those upon whom it wishes the candidacy
to fall.   Accordingly, while the educated " good citizen "
who gives constant attention to public affairs has more independence than under the old system of packed Primaries, the
average members of the party — and they are the vast majority — will still be inclined to follow the lead the Organization gives.   Thus the new Direct Primaries have not killed —
perhaps not even crippled — the Machine, though they have
given it a great deal of trouble, compelling it to add the worry
of a preliminary campaign and preliminary polling for
nominations for office to the pre-existing campaign and polling at the election to office, and obliging it to devise new
contrivances for hoodwinking and roping in the voters.
Some one has remarked, " A new set of reforms will always
be needed so soon as the professional politicians have learnt
how to get round the last set."   It is not, however, the Machine only that is worried.   Although the official expenses of
a Direct Primary are a charge (like those of the elections to
offices) on the public treasury, the other expenses which a
man desiring to be selected as candidate must incur, and the
labour of the campaign he must oratorically conduct if he
aspires to such an office as a Senatorship, are practically
doubled.[1]   He must create a special campaign organization
for the Primary elections and must travel over the State
recommending himself to the electors of his own party as the
fittest man to be their standard-bearer in the fight.   If he
wins, a second campaign against the candidates of the other
parties awaits him.[2]

in New York County in March 1912, in the 15th Assembly District,
there were 157 names of persons proposed to be voted for as the persons to be nominated as party candidates for delegates and alternates
to the State Convention, for members of the State and County Committees, of the Congressional District Committee, of the Fifth Municipal
Court District Committee, and for delegates and alternates to the National Convention.

[1] The cost of a Primary Campaign in Wisconsin some years ago cost
the candidates more than $800,000 (about £160,000).

[2] Though the Primary Campaign is a contest not between parties but
between rival aspirants for office within the same party, it often happens that the views of the candidates are not the same, so there may
be a certain amount of political as well as of personal controversy

Which is the best form of the Direct Primary and how much good its introduction has effected are questions, much debated in the United States, on which it may be still too soon to pronounce a final judgment. The power of the Machines in the cities has not been overthrown, and it may be feared that the professional politicians are discovering how to circumvent the new laws and regain all the power which these have tried to wrest from them.[1] For European readers the details just given have little interest, but they point two morals for Europeans as well as for Americans. The enactment of such laws witnesses to the influence which the zeal of a few earnest reformers, well served by the press, can exert upon a public which has begun to feel that something is wrong. Yet on the other hand the remedy adopted seems almost a counsel of despair, for it is an admission that the bright illusions of those early days, when it was believed that good citizens would bestir themselves to find good candidates and elect fit men, have been so belied by events that when the faults of a bad system have been long tolerated it becomes scarcely possible for the action of individual citizens, honest, but busy with other things, to effect a cure. That must be expected not from them but only at the hands of the law.

Why is this so? Wherein lies this extraordinary strength of the party Machine which enables it, like one of the giant climbing plants of a Brazilian forest, to grasp so tightly the tree which it encoils that it has grown to be strong as that tree itself?

involved, which creates feuds within the party, and reveals a dissidence which is made the most of by opponents when the parties contend at the official election.

[1] Professor Merriam says: "Some Bosses are wondering why they feared the Direct Primary law, some reformers are wondering why they favoured it." (Quoted by President Goodnow, *Municipal Government,* p. 147.)

On the other hand, the late Professor Jesse Macy (of Grinnell, Iowa), author of some admirably thoughtful and impartial treatises on politics, wrote to me in 1919 that "the (new) primary elections have been accompanied by a lessening of party spirit. Except where the parties are substantially equal they call forth more effort and arouse more interest than do the contests between the parties which follow. Voters become accustomed to criticisms of their own party by members of the party." Another judicious observer writes to me that the Direct Primary has lessened the influence upon nominations of the railroads and "Big Business" generally, but has not given the States any better officials than they had before.

The American party Organization has four roots, each of which has struck deep, and from these it draws its sustenance.

One is the Spoils system, which supplies what may be called the fuel for stoking the furnace.

The second is the existence of opportunities for illicit gain which attach to the position of a legislator in a State or a city, and to many city official posts.

The third is the multiplicity of elections, so confusing to the ordinary man that he needs to be told for whom, among a large number of names on the ticket, he is to cast his vote, and involving such a mass of organizing work that a large body of active workers, directed by superior officers, is needed to keep the party going and give it a chance of winning elections and rewarding its adherents with offices.

The fourth, itself partly due to the immense number of elections, has been the habit of voting at all elections the ticket of one or other of the National parties, whatever the local issues, a habit the more remarkable because few of the really significant issues coincide with the lines which divide the parties.   To the rank and file party allegiance became a sort of religion, but one consisting in external observances rather than in feeling.

REFORMS IN THE METHOD OF CHOOSING STATE OFFICIALS

A capital fault of the electoral system has been the practice of requiring the citizens to vote at the same time for an enormous number of elective posts, Federal, State, and Municipal, the names of the candidates for all of these being on the same ballot-paper, with the inevitable result that the voters, unable to judge between the fit and the unfit, were obliged to vote as the party Organizations bade them.   The remedy of placing these two latter elections at a different time from the Federal [1] is open to the objection that the calling the citizens too often to the polls leads to abstentions. For State elections another expedient is available.   It is to reduce the number of elective posts, transferring all but the

---

[1] These, however, are only (*a*) of the Presidential electors, (*b*) of representatives in Congress, and (*c*) of a Senator.

most important of these to the nomination of the State Governor. To give to the voters the election of a State Secretary of State, who may in some States be little more than a head clerk, or of a Surveyor-General or State Printer, or State Superintendent of public instruction, is merely to hand over these posts as spoils to the party Machine, which puts on its ticket the men it selects for them. Better leave these offices to the appointment of the Governor, who will be responsible to the opinion of the people for the exercise of the function.[1] The nominal power of the citizens when they have to mark a ballot-paper containing many names, only two or three of whom they know, acquires some reality when officials, whom the Governor can use as a sort of Cabinet, are appointed by him, for he is the one prominent figure whose action the public can watch, and who can be judged by the quality of the men he chooses as well as by the sort of work he does. This so-called " Short Ballot " movement, applicable also to municipal elections, has made great progress of late years. It deserves support, for the more the voting paper is reduced by taking out of it offices whose occupants can be as well or better chosen in some other way, the more efficiently can the voter discharge his functions.

The discontent which seeks to remedy economic hardships by using the State to oust the action of companies held to be oppressing the people has recently been found in a remarkable new departure made by North Dakota. There recently arose among the farmers, who constitute the majority of the inhabitants of this vast but thinly peopled State, a movement embodied in an organization called the People's Non-Partisan League, which captured the legislature and the governorship, ousting the old parties, and entrusted to State authorities the management of those branches of work in which the farmers are most interested, such as the running of grain elevators

[1] One of the most prominent Governors of recent years, Governor (now Senator) Johnson of California, has observed: " The minor offices on a State ticket are not really chosen by the people, because in the nature of things the people cannot know the candidates or their qualities. With the attention of the Electorate focussed on one or more of the conspicuous offices, the power with respect to these minor offices is much more certainly in the hands of the people." (I quote from a book entitled *Story of the California Legislature of 1911*, by Mr. Franklin Hichborn, worth reading for its interesting details regarding the workings of a State Legislature.)

and the handling of freight consigned to Eastern markets. This experiment, prompted by a sense of grievances suffered — that, for instance, regarding the use of elevators was a very real one — is the boldest which any State has yet tried in the field of economic action.   Europeans would call this State Socialism, but it is meant to be merely a practical attack on existing evils, and there is no sympathy, beyond that which one kind of discontent may have with another, between the Socialistic Communism of a theoretic European type and these landowning farmers who are thinking of their own direct interests.   The movement has seemed to be spreading in the North-Western States; but it may not last.

Want of space forbids me to describe with the fulness its significance might demand another notable improvement in State Government which consists in a reorganization of the administrative departments, placing these under heads appointed by the Governor, making these heads into a sort of Cabinet (resembling the President's Cabinet in the National Government), which while discharging executive functions under his supervision can also act as his advisers on general policy.   They are appointed by him, so that he is responsible to the people for their conduct; and they serve for the length of his term, but may be reappointed by his successor, as they will probably often be if they have " made good."   Each of them is also morally answerable to public opinion, because the scope of his work is clearly marked out.   This reform is, or will be, in many States, accompanied by the presentation of an annual Budget setting forth in a clear and orderly form the items of revenue and expenditure.[1]   Five or six States have already adopted schemes of this nature, and others are following in their wake.   The plan, while it reduces the undue number of popular elections, and conduces to economy and efficiency, has the further merit of strengthening the foundations of the Federal system by checking the tendency towards centralization, and by giving the State Governments a further hold on the people, stimulating their interest in honest non-partisan administration.[2]

[1] This improvement, interesting as a further illustration of the reforming spirit in the States, had up till 1919 been adopted in 39 States, the preparation of the Budget being entrusted (in most of them) either to the Governor or to a Board of which he is a member.

[2] Of this reform in the great State of Illinois, Governor Lowden writes

For the Judiciary, though it is the branch of State government which most needs attention, the reform movement has not yet accomplished much. In some States terms of judicial service have been lengthened, larger salaries allotted to the judges of the higher courts, and efforts made to simplify procedure.[1] So in some States there have been attempts to " take the Judiciary out of politics " by announcing that candidates for the Bench are not being run by the parties or included in the party ticket. But the plan of choosing State judges for life, or long terms, and giving the choice to a responsible Governor instead of to popular election, makes little way against the inveterate suspicion which assumes the Bench so likely to be influenced by the " interests " that the people must needs retain and frequently exercise the power of direct choice. In retaining it, the people defeat their own wishes wherever a Ring rules, because since it is to the Ring that the judge looks for re-election, he is more its servant than if he sat for life either by election or by appointment.

REFORMS IN CITY GOVERNMENT

It was in the cities, and especially the larger cities, that the reforming spirit found the grossest evils and the hardest tasks. Those evils sprang from two sources, the defective forms of city government, and the power of the party system. The division of power and responsibility between an elected Mayor, elected municipal councils, and officials directly elected on the model of the State governments, offered abundant opportunities for peculation, corruption, and job-

in his Message of 1919. " The Civil Administrative Code amounted to a revolution in Government. Under it a reorganization of more than 125 Boards, Commissions, and independent agencies was effected. Nine departments with extensive real power vested in each head have taken the place of those bodies which were abolished. . . . The scheme has more than justified the expectations formed of efficiency and economy under it. The Governor is in daily contact with his administration in all its activities. Unity and harmony of administration have been attained, and vigour and energy of administration enhanced." I quote from a Supplement by Mr. A. E. Buck to *National Municipal Review* for Nov. 1919. Mr. Buck's article presents an interesting view of the various forms this reform is taking in different States.

[1] In some States such as New York, the civil procedure in cases involving small sums has been simplified and cheapened so as to bring justice more within the reach of the poor.

bery, offences it was hard to discover, and the blame for which it was even harder to fix. After many experiments, the view prevailed that simplicity was the best security: the functions of councils were narrowed and their power reduced, while that of the Mayor was increased by entrusting appointments to him and giving him a general responsibility for the control of affairs. Along with this the pernicious practice of interfering by State statutes with municipal governments was checked and the principle of " Home Rule for Cities " largely enforced. This concentration of power in a Mayor, tried in various forms, gave good results whenever the " better element " among the voters could be worked up to rise out of their apathy and vote for a strong and honest man irrespective of party affiliations.[1]

Before this improvement had spread widely another plan was invented, which the reformers seized upon and used to good purpose. First tried at Galveston in Texas, where a tidal wave had destroyed half the city and driven the citizens to extemporize some plan for rapid reconstruction, it worked so well as to excite general attention, and was adopted by a large number of cities both great and small. Under this plan the whole body of citizens elect a small body of persons, varying, in different cities, from three to nine, the most frequent number being five, as Commissioners to take charge of the chief branches of municipal administration, one branch being specially allotted to each. The terms of office vary from city to city, two or four years being the most frequent. Usually one of the Commissioners (or Council) bears the title of Mayor, but his powers are much less wide than have been those of nearly every Mayor under the older scheme. The election works best when made by a general vote over the whole city and not by wards. Now and then there is a " freak election," but on the whole the men chosen are capable and honest. The principle of accountability yields its appropriate fruit, for the officials are made more fully responsible to the people than when they are subordinated to a city legislature, perhaps so numerous that it is difficult to fix blame on any members in particular. The ordinary administrative work is better done, especially when

[1] Chicago voted in November 1919 to make its ballot non-partisan in municipal elections.

the Commissioner at the head of a department works it by
experts whom he chooses, and the blame for jobs is more readily fixed on the person in whose department they occur. A
new development of this form has been to appoint five directors of city affairs, taken from the prominent commercial
men of the city, at small salaries, empowering them to engage and pay salaries larger than their own to business managers as heads of the city departments, or even to commit the
whole administrative work to a single highly paid " City
Manager " under the control, in matters of policy, of the
Commission, or other supreme elective authority, whatever
name it may bear. This plan, being believed to save money
and promote efficiency as well as to take the city offices out
of politics, has found much favour and been widely adopted.[1]
It is the latest word in municipal reform.

I have dwelt upon these details, some of which may have
little interest for the European reader, because they indicate
the active spirit of reform which has arisen in America,
where for many years people had " let things slide," and also
for the sake of showing how public opinion can effect reforms outside the parties and with no help from them, relying solely on the appeal to reason and a sense of civic duty.
These victories for good government were won in principle
before legislatures began to carry them out by law.

DIRECT LEGISLATION BY THE PEOPLE

From the attempt to mend the party system I pass to
a change of wider import for the world at large, a reform
which cuts deep into the framework of representative government. The faults of nearly all State Legislatures, such as
corruption, log-rolling, the passing of laws at the instance
of powerful corporations, and the " side tracking " by the
intrigues of the liquor trade or other selfish interests of bills
for effecting social and moral reforms, have long excited
popular displeasure. The first remedy applied was the imposition of constitutional restrictions on the powers of the
Legislature. Sessions were shortened and made less fre-

---

[1] This new " City Manager " plan had in December 1919 been adopted
by charter in 106 cities, and by ordinance or in a modified form in
59 others (*National Municipal Review* for December 1919).

quent, while public opinion more and more encouraged Governors to veto bad bills and to coerce the legislatures into passing those which the reformers demanded. These modes of action proved insufficient, because constitutional restrictions could be evaded. However few or short the sessions might be, the legislatures found time to play their old tricks, for the members were no better, and the temptations offered to them increased with the wealth of the tempters and the value of the benefits they intrigued to secure. The more drastic method sought for was ultimately found by the bolder Western States in the supersession of legislatures by the direct action of the whole body of citizens when invited either to enact laws at the initiative of some among their own number, or vote on the acceptance or rejection of laws which the legislature has passed. These methods are called the Initiative and the Referendum. With them a third scheme has also been brought forward and adopted in some States. This is the Recall of legislators, officials, and judges by a popular vote before the expiry of the term of office for which they were elected. As this last affects not merely the Legislative but also the Executive and Judicial departments of government, I reserve an account of it till the Initiative and Referendum have been dealt with.

The origin of the demand for Direct popular legislation is traceable to three sources.

First: A deep-rooted distrust of the State Legislatures as not truly representing and obeying the popular will, because they fail to pass bills which the people desire, and do pass bills which the people do not desire.

Secondly: Anger at and suspicion of the power of wealth, and especially of great incorporated companies which, by their influence over legislators, officials, and party organizations, are believed to oppress the people and to enrich themselves at its expense.

Thirdly: A desire on the part of certain sections of opinion to carry certain particular measures which — so these sections believe — could be carried by popular vote more easily than by pressing them on the Legislatures. Instances have been the Single Tax Law and, in some States, anti-liquor laws.

Fourthly: A faith in the wisdom and righteousness of

the People which expects from their direct action better work
for the community than can be had from persons chosen to
represent them. It is thought that a sort of mystical sanctity
not susceptible of delegation dwells in the Whole People. Its
sacramental quality is deemed to be weakened in an attempt
to transmit it, as if it were a wire so imperfectly conductive
that the electric current was lost in transmission.

The idea of direct popular legislation is of course not new.
From the early days of the Republic, Constitutions were enacted by popular vote, and the practice of amending them by
submitting amendments, proposed by a Convention or by the
Legislature to a vote of the whole State, has never been in-
termitted. Such a submission was in effect a Referendum
similar to that of Switzerland; and it existed before the
Swiss Confederation had begun to refer to the people bills
passed by the Assembly.[1] The two things that are new in
American State practice are the provisions which allow
private citizens to prepare and propose to the people, without the intervention of the legislature, a bill or an amendment to the State Constitution, and those which enable a
prescribed number of private citizens to demand that an act
passed by the legislature shall be submitted to the people for
its approval or rejection. The former of these methods, the
Initiative, was in the year 1919 in force in 19 States for laws
and in 14 States for Constitutional Amendments, while the
latter, the Referendum, was in use in 21 States. Most of
the States exempt from the application of the Referendum
any acts which the legislature may declare to be urgent, and
this power was so often resorted to in Oregon that the Governor felt bound to check its abuse by vetoing some bills
which contained an urgency clause not justified by the nature
of the measure. The number of citizens who may submit an
Initiative proposal varies in different States, ranging from
5 per cent to 15 per cent; and the number who may demand
a Referendum varies from 5 per cent to 10 per cent. (There
are States in which a fixed number is prescribed.) Many
complaints have been made in some States regarding the
methods employed to obtain signatures.[2] Associations, some

[1] As to the Referendum in Switzerland, see Chap. XXIX. in Vol. I.
Its use there deserves to be compared with the American practice.

[2] See Burnett, *Operation of the Initiative, Referendum nad Recall in
Oregon*, pp. 64–74.

political, some consisting of interests that conceive themselves to be threatened, spend much effort and large sums in hiring persons who go round pressing citizens to sign, often paying them at the rate of five cents (twopence halfpenny) and upwards, for their names. The average cost of an Initiative petition in California is given as $7500 (£1500). It is admitted that many sign on the mere request, some who sign adding that they mean to vote against the proposal when the time comes. A more serious evil has been here and there discovered in the insertion of large numbers of forged or unreal signatures; and as an illegible signature is not held invalid, the temptation to resort to this form of fraud is obvious. " Log-rolling " between the promoters of different proposals intended to be submitted at the same time is common.[1]

Little or no distinction is made in practice between the use of the Initiative in the form of an Amendment to the Constitution and in the form of the proposal of an ordinary law, so matters which properly belong to the category of Laws are constantly put into the form of Amendments, because this places them, if carried, out of the reach of repeal or alteration by the legislature. The natural result is to fill the Constitution with all sorts of minor or even trivial provisions unsuited to what was originally meant to be a Fundamental Instrument.[2] This process had, however, already gone so far as to have practically effaced the distinction between the two kinds of enactment. A graver abuse is that of trying to mislead the people by hiding away some important change, likely to excite opposition, among other proposals calculated to win support, while describing the amendment by the name of one of these latter. This trick has been attempted in Oregon. Many proposals made, and some adopted, are what Americans call " Freak Legislation," originating in the " fads " of small sections of the citizens, lightly accepted under the pressure of zealous advocates, and likely to be before long repealed. Moreover, the amendments and bills submitted are often so unskilfully drawn as to be obscure or even

---

[1] Another unfortunate result of the exercise of the Referendum power has been the uncertainty produced as to the continuance from one year to another of an appropriation to a public purpose, such as a State university.

[2] This has happened in Switzerland also. See Vol. I. Chap. XXIX.

self-contradictory. But in both these respects popular action is hardly worse than has been that of the legislatures, for the latter frequently pass freak bills, at the instance of some persistent group, merely to escape further worry, and many statutes have been so loosely expressed as to keep the Courts busy in trying to give them a rational interpretation.

For the guidance of the citizens summoned to vote on amendments or bills a pamphlet is in some States circulated by the State authorities containing the arguments adduced by promoters and opponents respectively. These documents have in Oregon, where they are published fifty-five days before the voting, run to a length so great as to deter all but the most conscientious citizens from studying them. They are generally well composed, though with occasional lapses from truth in the statement of facts. The more important propositions to be voted on are copiously discussed in the press and sometimes at public meetings, yet one is told that only a small percentage attend the meetings or follow the discussions. The average citizen who goes unprepared to the poll often takes up his voting paper in doubt and great perplexity, so large is the number of issues presented. At the election of 1912 Oregon set no less than thirty before him,[1] in addition to the names, often numerous, of the candidates for offices or seats in the Legislature. Colorado and California have sometimes laid nearly as heavy a burden on their citizens. How can any man, however able and earnest, think out and give an intelligent vote on half of issues so numerous, some of the Bills being intricate and technical, some relating to matters outside the range of his knowledge. The voter, if he does not modestly abstain, or in a fit of temper write " No " against every proposition, must be guided by what he has heard from some one else, perhaps no better informed. The ballot he marks conveys no judgment that can be called his own. But it was to elicit the judgment of each individual citizen that the plan of Direct Popular Legislation was devised.

As to the practical results of the system, the evidence is conflicting. The only incontestable data are those furnished

[1] Including six Constitutional Amendments which had been proposed by the Legislature to be voted on by the people. In 1909 the voters in the city of Portland voted on 35 measures at an election in which they chose a mayor and other municipal officers.

by the figures showing the number of proposals submitted to the people, the total number of persons who vote, and the majorities for or against each proposition. Space fails me for these; but the general result may be briefly stated.[1] The votes cast are usually much smaller than those cast at the same time for the State Governor or other chief officials to be elected at the same polls, and bear a still smaller proportion to the number of registered voters. In Colorado the percentage of voters on an Initiative has sunk as low as less than half of the largest number voting at the same time. In Oregon and California it is higher, but everywhere it indicates that the people take more interest in, or have a clearer view regarding, the choice of men than the enactment of laws.[2] The same holds good as to the Referendum, which in these States is less used than the Initiative, whereas in Switzerland the reverse is the case. Many proposals have been carried by a majority consisting of less than half the registered voters. Some complain of this as being anything but "majority rule," but others retort that those who fail to vote have only themselves to blame. Roughly speaking, the number of Initiative proposals rejected is slightly larger than that of those accepted, and the same holds true of the Referendum.[3]

The other arguments most frequently used against Direct Legislation, especially in Oregon, which has experimented more boldly than any other State, may be summed up as follows:[4]

(a) Though advocated as a Reserve Power whereby the

[1] It seems needless to discuss what is called the Local Referendum, i.e. the taking of a vote of the people of a city or rural local area on a question affecting them only, such as the expenditure of local taxation on some local purpose. This is an old institution, and usually works well, especially in rural areas.

[2] A case, however, recently occurred in which an amendment to the constitution of Michigan relating to the sale of intoxicants elicited a vote larger by 200,000 than that cast for the election of a Governor. The size of the vote is, of course, usually proportioned to the interest the question evokes.

[3] Oklahoma requires an Initiative proposal to be first sent to the Legislature which, if it does not pass the measure so proposed, may prepare an argument against it which will then go to the advocates of the measure and be circulated along with the counter arguments they adduce in favour of their proposal.

[4] Oregon would appear to have voted on as many Initiative proposals between 1904 and 1913 as had been submitted in all the other States put together.

people can keep the Legislature up to the mark, it has not in fact raised that body's tone or improved its work, which is done as crudely and hastily as before.

(b) Neither by Referendum nor Initiative has the malign power of the moneyed " Interests," and of the Bosses whom the Interests use, been expunged. They have still many devices left for influencing the fate of Bills submitted and of Initiative proposals.

(c) The Initiative produces many faulty laws, devoid of continuous policy or purpose and sometimes, by unintentionally reversing previous Acts, they render the statute-book more obscure and confused than before.

(d) The Initiative gives no opportunity for amending a measure or arriving at a compromise upon it; it is " the Bill, the whole Bill, and nothing but the Bill."

(e) An Initiative Constitutional Amendment, since it expresses the direct will of the people, overrides all such restrictions, imposed on legislative power for the protection of the individual, as every Constitution contains, and thus enables the people to disregard in its haste principles it had deliberately adopted for the guidance of legislation.

(f) There is no longer any responsibility for legislation fixed upon any person. Those who sign the petition merely ask that the people shall express its will. Formerly, though it was sometimes hard to know whom in the Legislature to blame for a bad law, men looked to the Governor, whose duty it was to kill such a law by his veto. But he has no veto on an Initiative proposal, nor on a Bill approved by the people in pursuance of a Referendum petition.[1]

One argument only, an argument formerly used by Swiss opponents of the Initiative, is never heard in Western America. No one alleges that the people in judging of proposals laid before them by the Initiative lose the enlightenment that might have been derived from debates on it in the legislatures, for nobody, except as Mark Twain said, a person suffering from senile decay, reads those debates.

The friends of the Initiative reply to these strictures by insisting that it brings government nearer to the people; that it prevents the legislature from refusing to submit to the

[1] Sometimes, it would seem, the friends of a Bill petition for a Referendum, in order, when they expect a favourable vote, to prevent the Governor from vetoing it.

people reforms which a large section desire; that it takes legislation out of those committee rooms and purlieus of the legislature where private interests intrigue with pliable members; that it gives measures a chance of being considered on their merits apart from the influence of political parties and their Bosses; that it is necessary in order to carry out schemes of social welfare; and that the opposition to popular legislation is led by selfish plutocrats who fear that business would suffer from those reforming schemes which the people would enact if they could give prompt and direct effect to their will. They point to the fact that no State which has once adopted the Initiative and Referendum has repealed either, or seems likely to do so. Such defects as have been revealed in working are, they affirm, due to inexperience, and will disappear as political education advances.

True it is that the people relish their power and are unlikely to relinquish it; nor can it be doubted that the habit of frequently voting on many kinds of questions does stimulate thought and strengthen a sense of civic responsibility, for though many vote heedlessly, and many more are unfit from want of knowledge to vote on most of the propositions submitted, there are enough left whose sharpened intelligence tends to permeate the mass and raise the level of political capacity. It is a noteworthy illustration of the trend of public feeling that in 1918 the Constitutional Convention of Massachusetts, after a very long and exhaustive discussion of the subject,[1] recommended to the people the enactment of both Initiative and Referendum, though in a form less wide than that which the Western States have employed. Nobody can think of Massachusetts as what Americans call a " Wild Cat State." Her Western sisters would rather describe her as a sedate old tabby; so her adhesion to this new idea is good evidence of the hold it has laid on the national mind.

As in a later chapter the general merits of Direct Legislation by the People will be discussed on the basis both of Swiss and of American experience, a few brief observations may be enough to sum up the results as visible in the United States.

In those States which have used the Initiative most freely,

[1] Reported at full length (1062 closely printed pages) in vol. ii. of *Proceedings of Massachusetts Constitutional Convention.*

many amendments and laws passed have been clumsy and confused, raising difficulties of interpretation, and some enactments carried have been, so far as a stranger can judge, unnecessary or unwise.

The character of the State legislatures has become neither worse nor better by the lessening of their powers. It is alleged, though with what truth I do not venture to pronounce, that the fear of the Referendum prevents many bad Bills from being passed. Yet one also hears that members still job when they can.

Some measures which well deserved consideration and which the legislatures had failed to pass have been submitted by Initiative, and some jobs which the legislatures were likely to perpetrate have been prevented. The people have, considering the number and the intricacy of many of the questions submitted, shown more care and discrimination than was predicted by the opponents of the Initiative. They have rejected not a few extreme and ill-considered proposals, and, although less conservative than the Swiss, who use the Initiative less, they do not make it an instrument of revolution. Mistakes have been made, some of which, as shown by subsequent reversals, are recognized as mistakes, yet no State appears to have suffered permanent injury.

The application of the Initiative might be safeguarded by provisions excluding it from topics outside the knowledge or experience of the citizens at large, such as details of judicial procedure; and by forbidding more than a small number to be submitted at the same voting.[1] Moreover, the form in which proposals are put to the vote could be improved by previously submitting these to draftsmen qualified to bring them into an intelligible shape, free from the vagueness, confusion of thought, and obscurity of expression charged against them.

It need hardly be said that the experience of American States even so large as Ohio and Michigan, throws little light on the suitability to the great countries of Europe of either Initiative or Referendum.

Not less significant of the spirit which seeks to cure by

[1] The advocates of Direct Legislation, however, deprecate any such restriction, alleging that it would enable the opponents of measures proposed to be submitted to prevent them from being voted on by bringing forward a large number of trivial propositions which would jostle out those which they sought to defeat.

the direct action of the people the misuse of delegated authority is the institution, new to modern politics,[1] which is called the Recall. It extends that action from the legislative into the executive and judicial spheres, empowering the citizens to remove by popular vote, before the expiry of his term, a person who has been chosen to fill the post of a representative, of an administrative official, or of a judge, and thereupon to proceed to the election of another to fill the place from which the deposed occupant has by transgression fallen. The Oregon law — for there are differences between the laws of different States, though the general effect is similar — provides that where a prescribed percentage of citizens in any local elective area have signed a petition demanding a vote on the dismissal of an official, such a vote shall, unless the official promptly resigns, be forthwith taken. If the vote is taken and goes against him, a fresh vote is thereupon held for the election of his successor for the unexpired residue of his term. This procedure has during the last few years been applied in a good many cases, chiefly in cities for the displacement of a Mayor or some other administrative officer, very rarely to displace a member of a legislature. It has in a few cases been abused, from motives of personal enmity. But there have more frequently been grounds for a belief that the official impugned was perverting his functions for selfish ends, and the vote has in most of such cases ejected him. The arguments used against the Recall are obvious. It will — so the opponents declare — create in officials a timorous and servile spirit. Executive authority will be weakened, for every official will be at the mercy of any agitation started against him, possibly supported by groundless allegations in the press. A Governor or Mayor will hesitate to deal firmly with a strike riot, lest labour leaders should threaten a proposal to depose him; or he may be attacked in respect of some administrative decision which, though taken for the general good, displeases any section of the citizens. A courageous official striving to protect a city against the Interests is no less exposed to such charges than is the corrupt official whom the Interests have captured, for

---

[1] Some of the Greek republics occasionally deposed their elected officials, and it was proposed during the course of the first French Revolution to provide for terminating the mandate of a delegate by those who had elected him.

the interests themselves may start a campaign against him. Few will be strong enough to stand up against such tactics: public-spirited men will refuse to accept office, and reformers be less than ever disposed to enter political life. The experiment has not been tried long enough to enable these predictions to be tested. There have been instances in which the Recall has worked well, especially as against a corrupt Mayor, but the older and more cautious States have hitherto looked askance at it. Massachusetts rejected it when she accepted the Initiative.[1]

So far of the Recall as applied to administrative officials and representatives. A wider question is raised by its application to judges, for this is advocated not only for the sake of ridding the community of a bad magistrate, but also for another reason peculiar to the United States. Statutes passed by a State Legislature being inferior in authority both to the Constitution of the United States and to the State Constitution, may, if and so far as they transgress either of those instruments, be pronounced invalid by a Court of Law. This is the duty of the Court as the authorized interpreter of the laws which are alleged to be in conflict, and the views of the judges as to the intrinsic merits of the statute have nothing to do with the matter. Now it sometimes happens that when a Court, in a case raising the point, decides a State statute to be invalid because it transgresses the State Constitution, there is an angry outcry from those who procured its enactment, as, for instance, from farmers or handworkers. Complaints arise that the judges are over-technical or old-fashioned, or that they are moved by class prejudice, or perhaps even that they have been " got at " by incorporated companies whose interests as employers would suffer from the statute.

It is partly a deficient respect for the judiciary in general, partly this resentment at decisions which cut down statutes popular with some section of the citizens, that have produced a demand for the power of dismissing a judge before the expiry of his term. Why, it is asked, should not the

[1] When the people of Arizona applied to be admitted to the Union as a State, Congress insisted that a provision for the recall of judges should be struck out of the Constitution. To obtain admission, the people submitted and struck out the provision, but, after the State had been duly admitted, it was restored by an amendment to the Constitution.

people who have chosen the judge be able to unmake him so
soon as he has lost their confidence? The legal method of
removing is by impeachment, but, apart from the uncertainty
of a trial, you cannot impeach a man for having interpreted
a law in a particular sense.[1] Popular feeling calls for something prompter and more flexible, in order to secure that the
judge shall be in harmony with that feeling. This demand,
which in a few States derives strength from the belief that
there are judges in office fit for nothing but to be turned out
of office, has secured the embodiment in the constitutions of
some Western States of amendments providing that a judge
may, like any other official, be " recalled " by a popular vote
taken upon a requisition signed by a prescribed number of
voters in the area for which he has been elected.[2] The plan
has evoked strong disapproval from the bulk of the legal
profession, especially in the more conservative States. All
the arguments against Recall in general apply with special
force to a method which would subject the Bench to popular
caprice and prevent the best men from consenting to sit on it.
Such opposition led to a proposal put forward as an alternative compromise. Instead of getting rid of the judge whose
decision is disapproved, why not get rid of the decision by
enabling the public through a vote to reverse the decision
and declare that the law does not transgress the Constitution
and shall accordingly be deemed valid?[3] As the people —
so it is argued — have enacted the Constitution, why should
not they be the best judges of what they meant by its terms?
Such a Recall of Decisions would be a shorter and simpler
process than that of amending the State Constitution, and
would give effect to the purpose with which a statute was
passed without dismissing the judges who delivered the decision, delivering it in good faith, but with minds warped
by their professional love of technicality.[4]

[1] In a few States a Judge may, without impeachment, be removed
by a vote of both houses of the Legislature, but only for improper conduct.

[2] The recall of all elective officers (including judges), is in force in
6 States, that of such officers except judges in 10.

[3] The Recall of decisions has been adopted in Colorado only.

[4] The Courts may sometimes be unduly conservative in temper, but
whatever may be said of a particular Judge here and there, I know of no
case in which a majority of the highest Court in any State have been
improperly influenced in any decision on the constitutionality of a
statute.

So far of the State Courts. Bold apostles of change desire to apply this device even to the Federal Courts, whose decisions have from time to time limited the operation of acts of Congress, passed to gratify what was thought to be, a popular demand, even when the constitutional power to pass them was more than doubtful. At the election of 1896 certain radical politicians argued that the interpreting power of the Supreme Court should be reduced, and more recently it was proposed to amend the Federal Constitution by inserting a provision permitting the people to reverse interpretative decisions of that Court.

These proposed changes, both as respects the States, in some of which they have been effected, and as regards the National Government, in which they have been generally disapproved, are of far-reaching significance, for they affect the foundations of the Frame of Government. A Constitution is the expression of the settled and permanent will of the people, reached after full deliberation, and expressed in a carefully considered form. The true meaning of such an instrument is a matter of legal construction fit only for minds trained by learning and practice. To allow a majority of persons voting at the polls, by a vote taken hastily and possibly in an excited mood, to over-rule the interpretation which these trained minds had given, would not only introduce confusion into the law, but also destroy the utility of constitutions.[1] The legitimate authority and regular application of the Constitution, as a supreme law, would be gone, and questions involving both personal rights and rights of property, as guaranteed by the

[1] " How could uniformity of fundamental or any other kind of law be possible under such a system? Instead of a Constitution consistent in its construction and uniform in its application, it would be a Government by special instances, a Government that in the end leads to despotism " (Ex-President Taft, *Popular Government*, p. 179).

Mr. Root observes: " The power exercised by the people under such an arrangement would be not judicial but legislative. Their action would be not a decision that the Court was wrong in finding a law unconstitutional, but the making of a law valid which was invalid before because it was unconstitutional. . . . The exercise of such a power would strike at the very foundation of our system of Government. It would be a reversion to the system of the ancient republics where the State was everything and the individual nothing except as a part of the State. When a judge's term has expired he is judged upon his general course of conduct while in office, and stands or falls upon that as a whole. But under the Recal he may be brought to the bar of public judgment upon the rendering of a particular decision which excites public interest, and he will be subject to punishment if that de-

Nation and the States, would be placed at the mercy of chance majorities, who would think only of the particular case, not of the general principles involved. Such a majority might, moreover, be a minority of the whole body of citizens, voters brought to the polls by the exertions of an eager section, while the bulk stayed away indifferent. Thus regarded, the Recall of Judicial Decisions might, if less dangerous to the Bench, be more dangerous to the general scheme of government than the Recall of Judges, and would virtually destroy what has been one of America's chief contributions to the art of orderly government.

This outline of the forms which efforts for the bettering of political conditions have been taking indicate not only the present tendencies of democracy but also the difficulties incident to movements of reform in an enormous country where organized and responsible leadership may at any given moment be wanting. Plans put forward are not always the fruit of mature reflection. The remedies suggested are often crude, and may be as bad as the disease they are meant to cure. Popular Initiative in legislation may seem needed where a legislature is corrupt, but it strikes a blow at representative government. The Recall of administrative officials and judges are a confession that the direct election of officials works little better than the election of legislators has worked; so the critic asks why, if the people are heedless in exercising their power of choosing men for administrative and judicial work, should they be less heedless in exercising a power of dismissal. The Direct Primary, from which much was hoped, has annoyed the professional politicians and driven them to new devices, but it has not, so far, sterilized the bacilli of the party Machine nor secured appreciably better nominations. These schemes of reform deal rather with the symptoms of the malady than with its root in the indifference, or subservience to party, of a large part of the voters. To raise the standard of civic duty is a harder and longer task than to alter institutions.

cision is unpopular. Judges will naturally be afraid to render unpopular decisions. They will hear and decide cases with a stronger incentive to avoid condemnation themselves than to do justice to the litigant or the accused " (*Experiments in Government and the Essentials of the Constitution*, p. 68).

Cf. also Supplement (by Mr. W. D. Guthrie) to the Report of a Committee of the New York State Bar Association (1913).

Nevertheless, every effort, even if imperfectly successful, to improve machinery which has worked ill, is an evidence of healthy discontent. The present generation will not tolerate evils which the last generation bore submissively. Fifty years ago administration was worse and politics more corrupt than they are to-day, but reformers were fewer and found far fewer listeners. To-day they are heard gladly, because the public conscience and the public sense of what America means for the world is more sensitive. Every fresh effort stimulates these feelings and keeps the need for improvement before the minds of those who lead. When I compare the volume of discussion of political, social, and economic subjects which issues from the American press to-day, descriptions of present evils, analyses of their sources, suggestions for their extinction, with the scanty consideration these matters formerly received, and with the spirit of lugubrious despondency that chilled the reformers of those days, I am astonished at the change, and welcome it as auguring well for future progress.

GENERAL REVIEW OF AMERICAN DEMOCRACY

We may now review and sum up the points in which defects have revealed themselves in the working of popular government in America, indicating the causes to which each of these defects is attributable and dwelling on some of the lessons which American experience provides for the instruction of other countries, lessons that may be profitable for a time which sees many old institutions thrown into the melting-pot, and sees many peoples trying to replace them by something better.

(1) State Legislatures do not enjoy the confidence of the people, as is shown by the restrictions imposed upon them, and by the transfer, in many States, of some of their powers to the citizens acting directly. Congress maintains a higher level, yet one below that to be expected in a nation proud of its institutions as a whole.

(2) The Civil Service (with the exception of the scientific branches of the National Government) is not yet equal to the tasks which the extension of the functions of government is imposing upon it.

(3) The State Judiciary is, in the large majority of the

States, inferior in quality to the better part of the Bar that practises before it, and has in some few States ceased to be respected.

(4) The administration of criminal justice is slow, uncertain, and in many States so ineffective that offenders constantly escape punishment.

(5) The laws are in some States so imperfectly enforced that the security for personal rights, and to a less extent for property rights also, is inadequate.

(6) The government of cities, and especially of the largest cities, has been incompetent, wasteful, and corrupt.

(7) Party Organizations, democratic in theory and in their outward form, have become selfish oligarchies worked by professional politicians.

(8) The tone of public life and the sense that public service is an honourable public trust, though now rising, are not yet what they should be in so great a nation.

(9) The power of wealth, and particularly of great incorporated companies, to influence both legislatures, and the choice of persons to sit in legislatures and on the judicial Bench, has been formidable.

(10) Though there are and always have been in public life some men of brilliant gifts, the number of such persons is less than might be expected in a country where talent abounds and the national issues before the nation are profoundly important.

To what cause shall we attribute each of these failures of democratic practice to attain the standard required by democratic theory? Has it lain in some misconception or misuse of democratic principles, or is it to be found in the emergence of unforeseen economic phenomena which have injured the working of institutions sound enough in principle, but not built to bear the new strain? After indicating in each case the proximate cause of the defects noted, we can enquire what relation such cause bears to the fundamental doctrines of Popular Government.

(1) The want of respect for legislatures is due to the quality of the men who fill them, few of whom are superior in knowledge and intelligence to the average of their fellow-citizens, and many of whom are (in some States) below that average in point of character.

(2) The Civil Service was recruited without regard to competence, and the Spoils System not only disregarded fitness, but taught the official that his party Organization had the first claim on his loyalty.

(3) The mediocrity of most State Judges, and the delinquencies of a few, are the natural result of popular elections, short terms of office, and low salaries.

(4) The delays and uncertainties of criminal justice are due partly to the weakness of the judges, partly to an antiquated and cumbrous procedure which provides endless opportunities for delay and technical quibblings. Why is not the procedure amended? Because, while nobody in particular has the duty of amending it, the selfish interest of petty legislative groups discourages reforms.

(5) State laws are ill-administered, partly because some of them, having been passed at the instance of a small but insistent section, are found hard to enforce; partly because elected officials (in cities and counties) are slow to prosecute offenders who can influence their re-election; partly also because in many States there is no rural police force.

(6) The scandals of city government may be ascribed (a) to the voting power of masses of immigrants ignorant of the institutions of the country; (b) to the faulty frames of municipal government which so divided responsibility that it could not be definitely fixed on a few persons; (c) to the failure of the " respectable " taxpayers to select and support by their votes trustworthy candidates; (d) to the power of party Machines.

(7) Party Organizations, long neglected by the great bulk of the members of each party, fell into the hands of persons who made personal gain out of them, and whose sins were ignored because the multiplicity of elections created a heavy mass of work, and they performed it.

(8) The men of fine quality who entered politics were, after the first thirty years, too few to maintain a high tone, while the ordinary politicians were liable to be demoralized by machine methods and by the impunity which the negligence of a busy public accorded to delinquents.

(9) The power of wealth has been immense, because the benefits which rich men and corporations sought to buy from legislatures were worth a high price, because secret bargains

could be easily made either with Bosses or with obscure legislators, and because these recipients of money or whatever else was offered were below the fear of social censure since they had no social position to lose. The bribe-givers sometimes thought and usually professed that they were "developing the resources of the country," an argument constantly on the lips of those who were impounding the resources for themselves.[1]

(10) The comparative rarity of well-stocked and thoroughly trained minds among politicians of the second rank — they are of course to be found in the front rank — is largely due to the attractions, greater here than in most parts of Europe, which other occupations offer. In the professions, in the Universities, and in business there are careers, open and continuous, which claim the best capacities, whereas in politics party Organizations hold the door of entry and a promising career is liable to be interrupted.

Some of the causes I have indicated are the outcome of phenomena with which democracy has nothing to do. A new land with immense sources of undeveloped wealth, in creating opportunities for swiftly acquiring wealth, creates temptations larger than the virtue of European legislators has had to resist. The vast areas and scanty population of many Western States make the maintenance of law and order by an efficient police more difficult than it is in Europe. The flooding of cities by hosts of immigrants imposes unusually heavy tasks upon municipal governments. Thus the defects that have been numbered (5), (6), (8), (9) and (10) are partly explicable by causes not political. So the portentous power of the party Organization owed its development to what may be called a historical and almost accidental cause, the absorption of men's minds in business during the years from 1830 to 1870 to an extent which made them neglect to notice weeds striking root so deeply that it became hard to rid the field of them. But the other defects are referable either to an undue confidence in the power of democratic principles to overcome the permanent weaknesses of human nature, or to the particular forms given to the institutions in which it was sought to apply those principles.

---

[1] It is a proverb in the Far West that the man who is "developing the country" thinks that he may appropriate whatever is not screwed on, and that whatever is screwed on may be unscrewed.

Take the doctrine of Equality in civil rights and political rights. It had to be asserted in 1776, and still more in France in 1789, as against the systems of privilege which then covered the world. But it was misconceived and misapplied when it induced the notion that any citizen was good enough for any public function, and when it refused deference and stinted honour to the occupants of high public posts. Thus the conception of public office as a public trust, worthy of respect because the people had committed to it a part of their power, was suffered to decline.

So the principle of the Sovereignty of the People was taken to require that the people should restrict as much as possible the functions of their legislatures, and should directly elect as many as possible of their officials. The application of this doctrine, along with the Equalitarian tendency already described, led directly to the popular election of judges and to the provisions (short terms and small salaries) which were intended to keep them in constant subservience to popular sentiment. The doctrine was further misapplied when taken to mean, not indeed by the founders of the Constitution, but by a later generation, that every human being has a natural and indefeasible right to share by his vote in the government of the country where he resides, irrespective of his fitness to use that right to the advantage of the community. Hence the fond illusion that to confer a right is to confer therewith the capacity to exercise it. In politics it is not false principles that have done most harm. It is the misconception of principles in themselves sound, prompting their hasty application without regard to the facts of each particular case.

Against the defects noted in the working of the American Government let us set some of the points in which democracy has shown its strength and attained a success the more remarkable because the Republic has been at times exposed to perils no one foresaw. Though its material progress must be mainly ascribed to the immense natural resources of the country and the stimulus their development has applied to an energetic and inventive race, much of its present greatness remains to be credited to the ideas with which the people started and to which they have sought to remain faithful.

Americans have been true to the principle of Liberty in

its social as well as its political sense. The right of the individual man to lead his own life in his own way is better recognized now than ninety years ago, when Tocqueville noted what he called the Tyranny of the Majority. Many regard the prohibition of intoxicating liquors as an infringement of these rights, but since the principle of protecting a man against his own propensities, when these are injurious to the community also, is deemed legitimate if sufficient grounds for legal interference have been shown, the question comes in each case to be what grounds are sufficient, and how to balance the admitted discomfort to some individuals who need no protection against the admitted benefit to others who do need it. The Prohibition movement has not proceeded from any one class or section of the community. Neither party took it up, because both feared to alienate a part of their supporters. It grew partly because employers thought it made for efficiency, partly perhaps because Southern men desired to stamp out the risks of intoxication which make the negro dangerous, but mainly because it appealed to the moral and religious sentiment of the plain people.

The love of peace and a respect for the rights of other nations have gone hand in hand with the love of liberty. Such aggressive tendencies as belonged to United States policy two generations ago have disappeared. The temptations to encroach upon Mexico have been resisted. No State possessed of gigantic power has shown in recent years so little disposition to abuse it.

If a faith in the doctrines of political equality has been pushed too far in some directions, it has in others worked for good, preventing the growth of class distinctions and enmities, and enjoining a respect for the lawful claims of every section in the community which gives to the nation a unity and solidarity of incomparable value. This was most conspicuously seen in the quickness with which the Northern and Southern States became reconciled when the first ten years of resettlement after the War of Secession had passed. To this solidarity has been due the stability of American institutions. No great State has suffered less, perhaps none so little, from the shocks of change. Almost the only revolutionaries are those who bring from Europe a bitter fanaticism born of resentment at injuries suffered there.

The risks arising from the presence of masses of immigrants, many of whom cannot speak or read English, and the majority of whom, possessing no experience of constitutional government, have not had time to acquire a knowledge of the institutions they are admitted to bear a share in working, cannot be discussed here, and it may not yet be possible to form positive conclusions on the subject. The argument used to defend the policy of extending the suffrage to them has been that since they are in the country, the sooner they are made to feel themselves at home in it the better, for they might be more dangerous if left unenfranchised. It is, however, to be remembered that, enfranchised or not, they are specially liable to be led astray by misrepresentations and demagogic incitements, and that the influence of native American opinion has not yet been able to play fully upon them. The danger, whatever it may be, to be apprehended from their voting power, will probably be slighter in the next generation, which will have been to some extent Americanized by the public schools and other assimilative influences.

To the peaceable fruits of democracy above described let us add the education in political thought and practice which democratic institutions have been giving. Though the citizens have not rendered all the civic service which those institutions demand, the deficiency seems great only in proportion to the greatness of that demand. If we test their fairness and good sense not by an ideal standard, but by what is seen in other free countries, we shall find that nowhere (except in Switzerland) is a sane, shrewd, tolerant type of political opinion so widely diffused through the whole native population. There have been more learned men in the great European countries. There have been in those countries as many men who have thought and written wisely on political subjects. What is peculiar to America, and what makes its political strength, is the practical good sense and discriminative insight of the native citizens taken in bulk, qualities which appear not so much in their judgment of ideas or proposals — for they are, like other nations, liable to be fascinated by phrases or captured by fallacies — as in their judgment of men. Nowhere does there exist so large a percentage who have an opinion, and can say why they have an opinion, regarding the merits of a question or of politicians. In listening to their talk one is struck by their shrewdness in "sizing up" (as they say) a statesman, and estimating his courage, honesty, and power of "getting there." To judge well of men is, in a democracy, more essential than to judge well of measures, for the latter requires more knowledge than can be expected from the average man, who must be mainly guided by his leaders. In no form of government therefore is the faculty to choose leaders wisely so much needed.

Some other conclusions, drawn from American experience, may be suggested as fit to be considered in other countries, especially in those States of the Old World which are now (1920) making their first essays in popular government.

It is not wise to overburden the people with functions to be frequently exercised. If too much is expected from them the results obtained are scantier than they would have been had less been demanded. Citizens required to vote incessantly between candidates of whom they know little or nothing, will end either by neglecting to vote or by blindly following the party lead. Few of those who are frequently summoned to the polls to deliver an opinion on a crowd of candidates as well as on matters submitted by Initiative or Referendum possess the knowledge to cast a well-considered vote or the leisure to acquire that knowledge. Votes so delivered do not truly express the opinion of a community.

The effective control of administration by the people is not necessarily secured by the direct election of officials, not even when elected for short terms. If seven officials have to be chosen for various administrative posts, the voters, unable from want of knowledge to select, will vote for those whom their party recommends. But if one head official is to be elected, and the selection of the other six who are to be his subordinates is left to him, with the power of dismissal if they fail to make good, responsibility will attach to him. It will be his duty to find good men, and his own conduct in office will be judged by his selections and by their discharge of their functions. The people will, through their right to call him to account, exercise a more real power than if they chose all their officials by direct vote. The fixing of responsibility upon the agents of the people, whether for administration or for legislation, is specially needed in a democracy. In a monarchy or an oligarchy there is little difficulty, for power is concentrated in few hands. Such governments as those of France or Canada, framed on the British model and having grown up out of monarchies, throw responsibility on the Cabinet, a small body, which leads in legislation as well as administration. But in the United States power is so much divided between public authorities each independent of the others, that it is hard to find any to whom praise or blame can be definitely allotted except the President as respects the Union, and the State Governor as respects his State. Each of these, moreover, is so restricted by Congress (or the State legislature) that it might be unfair to charge on either what was perhaps the fault of the legislators. Very often real authority dwells not with any official or body but with the party Organization which secretly controls officials and legislatures. Being a government outside the law, legally responsible to no one, and scarcely even morally responsible for those who control it, it may work in darkness and remain unknown except to a few behind the scenes. But within the Organization, responsibility exists, for in that well-compacted oligarchy there are always some few fit to comand the many who obey.

The founders of the American Constitution feared to entrust huge powers to one hand, and in creating a President they imposed a check upon him, finding that check in the Senate. They did well, for they could not foresee that a check and guide wiser and stronger than the Senate would ultimately grow up in the power of public opinion. In France there is still some dread of one strong magistrate, for the republic has seemed not yet absolutely secure, and public opinion is too deeply divided on some great issues to play the part it plays in America, where the Frame of Government stands " firm as Ailsa Craig." Opinion is in the United States so sure of its strength that it does not hesitate to let the President exceed his constitutional rights in critical times. It was the same with the dictatorship in the earlier days of the Roman Republic and for a like reason.

Free peoples, like those of Switzerland, Canada, and Australasia, do not need to be reminded of the value of traditions and of training in self-government, but those new States which are only now beginning their free constitutional life have still their traditions to make, and may profit by American experience, finding in it many things to imitate and some things to beware of.   They can learn the importance of cultivating from the first those habits of strictly observing constitutional forms, and that respect for every legal right of every citizen and class of citizens which have built up for America, as for Switzerland, the principles that guard freedom and secure internal peace.   These habits were formed in the field of local government before any national government was created, and in that field also the new States may profit by American and Swiss examples.   Politics should not be allowed to become a source of private gain. The salaries paid to administrative officials must be sufficient to secure the abilities which each particular kind of work requires; and all officials, except the few at the top who must from time to time be chosen as chiefs to direct general policy, ought to stand apart from party politics and be neither chosen nor dismissed for their opinions, but required to serve the country and their departmental heads with equal loyalty whatever party may be in power.   The neglect of this principle was a fertile source of mischief in America, and the recent disposition to respect it is becoming one of the best auguries for purity and good administration in the future.

All the democratic peoples may learn from America that no class in the community can with impunity withdraw from active participation in its political life.   In the United States the business and professional classes did not indeed withdraw, for they voted with their party and subscribed to its funds.   But they did not take the share that naturally belonged to them in the work either of political thinking or of legislation or of administration.   Not many entered the Legislatures; few were candidates for any but the highest posts; few gave their minds to the solution of the social and economic as well as political problems that were thickening on the country.   This aloofness contributed to bring about that degradation of politics, and especially of city politics, from which the country has now begun to recover.   A new spirit is happily now visible; such non-partisan bodies as the Good Citizens' Clubs and Civic Federations, and on some occasions the Bar Associations, the Chambers of Commerce, and the University Clubs have become potent agencies for reform, and for the promotion of social betterment in the interest of all classes alike.

There are clouds in the American sky to-day, threatening labour troubles such as exist in other great industrial countries; and if I have not discussed them here, it is not from any failure to note them, but because they are in substance the same as those which vex the internal peace of European States. These troubles are in the United States rather imported than of native growth. Comparatively few of the extremist advocates of the General Strike and the Class War are of American birth; most of the votes which support them come from recent immigrants crowded into the great cities. America is better fitted than are European countries to face any industrial strife that may arise, for no other people, except the Swiss, values so highly its institutions and the principles of ordered liberty embodied therein. In America Democracy has been the best guarantee against Revolution.

The history of the Republic furnishes an instructive example of the perpetual conflict between the forces of Idealism and the forces of Selfishness. The first generation set out with an idealistic faith in Liberty, in Equality, and in the Wisdom of the People. The second and third generations, absorbed by the passion for the development of their country's resources and distracted by the struggle over negro slavery, allowed abuses and corruptions to grow up, left practical politics to be dominated by a self-constituted oligarchy of professionals, and without losing their theoretical devotion to Liberty forgot that monarchs are not its only enemies, and that it may be threatened by money as well as by arms. Then in the fourth and fifth generations there came an awakening. The recuperative forces in the nation reasserted themselves. Both the old parties (so far as their Organizations went) failed to give the guidance needed, and there was much groping and stumbling in the search for remedies to cure the evils which all had begun to perceive. But the forces that were making for good have continued to gain strength. The old ideals of a government which shall be pure as well as popular, and shall unite the whole people in a disinterested patriotism that values national righteousness as well as national greatness, have again become beacon lights of inspiration.

No Englishman who remembers American politics as they were half a century ago, and who, having lived in the United States, has formed an affection as well as an admiration for its people,— what Englishman who lives there can do otherwise ? — will fail to rejoice at the many signs that the sense of public duty has grown stronger, that the standards of public life are steadily rising, that democracy is more and more showing itself a force making for ordered progress, true to the principles of Liberty and Equality from which it sprang.

AUSTRALIA

CHAPTER XLVI

THERE is no such thing as a Typical Democracy, for in every country physical conditions and inherited institutions so affect the political development of a nation as to give its government a distinctive character. But if any country and its government were to be selected as showing the course which a self-governing people pursues free from all external influences and little trammelled by intellectual influences descending from the past, Australia would be that country. It is the newest of all the democracies. It is that which has travelled farthest and fastest along the road which leads to the unlimited rule of the multitude. In it, better than anywhere else, may be studied the tendencies that rule displays as it works itself out in practice.

A few preliminary words about the land and the people may make it easier to comprehend the political phenomena we have to consider.

The Australian continent, with 2,974,581 square miles (rather smaller than Europe), is a vast plain, enclosed on the east by a long range of mountains, nowhere reaching 7500 feet in height, with a few groups of hills in the south-west corner and others scattered here and there in the interior. This plain is so arid that parts of it seem likely to remain for ever a wilderness. It is waterless, except in the south-east, where a few rivers descending from the inland side of the eastern range pursue languid courses towards the southern sea, with currents that are in summer too shallow for navigation. The only well-settled districts are those which lie in the hilly region along the east and south-east coasts. These districts were colonized from a few towns planted on the edge of the sea, the settlers spreading slowly inland and spreading also along the shore, until at last there came to be a practically continuous population along a line of some six hundred miles. This population is, however, still sparse in many regions, and the thickly peopled part of one state, West Australia, lies far away from all the others, its chief town communicating with the nearest city in them (Adelaide in South Australia) by a railway journey of forty-six hours, or a sea voyage of nearly three days, while another, Tasmania, occupies a separate island. Thus during its earlier years, when the character of each colony was being formed, each lived an isolated life, busied with its own local concerns, knowing little about the others, and knowing still less, until telegraphs were laid along the ocean bed, of the great world of Europe and America. Not only each colony, but the Australian people as a whole, grew up in isolation, having no civilized neighbour states except New Zealand, cut off by twelve hundred miles of stormy sea.

Fortunate has it been for a land lying so far apart that Nature has furnished her with nearly everything needed to make a community self-sufficing.

Want of moisture is the weak point of the country, for more than one-third of its whole area has less than ten inches of rain in the year, and another third less than twenty. It is a common saying that in Australia a purchaser buys not the land but the water. Nevertheless, there is not only along the east and parts of the south coasts a vast area of cultivable soil, with sufficient rain, but in the drier parts of the interior immense tracts fit for sheep, which have thus become the greatest source of the country's wealth. The recent discovery of subterranean reservoirs of water which can be made available by artesian wells offers a prospect of extending the region fit for settlement. The climate is temperate, except in the tropical north, and so healthy that the average death-rate is only ten per thousand. Its variety enables all sorts of products to be raised, sugar, cotton, and the fruits of the tropics in the hotter regions, wheat and other cereals in the more temperate. Coal, found in all the States but two, abounds in several wide areas, and there are rich mines of silver, lead, and copper, besides those gold workings which drew a sudden rush of immigrants to Victoria in 1849. These resources, taken together, suffice to promise prosperity and comfort to its inhabitants. They now number about five millions.

Those who have colonized this favoured land were well fitted to develop it. Nearly all came from the British Isles — 98 per cent is the figure usually given — and the proportion of the English, Scottish, Irish, and Welsh stocks is almost the same as that which these four elements bear to one another in the British Isles, the Scots and the Irish being slightly in excess of the other two, as both these are races of emigrative tendencies. Similarly the proportion of Anglicans, Nonconformists, and Roman Catholics differs little from that in the United Kingdom. Nearly all belonged to the middle and upper sections of the working class, for the cost of a long voyage debarred the very poor, so that class was represented almost solely by the convicts, who in days now long past were transported to New South Wales, Tasmania, and Western Australia.[1] The criminal strain thus introduced is deemed to have been now washed out, for there is, it would seem, a tendency for the average type to reestablish itself in the third generation, not to add that in the old days offences now thought comparatively slight were punished by transportation. In this sunny climate the British stock has wonderfully thriven. The rural Australian is tall, lithe, and active. Now that the great majority of the population is native born, one can begin to speak of an Australian bodily and mental type, for though there are differences between the several colonies, the population is practically homogeneous, more homogeneous than that of France or Great Britain or the United States. Each settlement grew up separately, but under similar influences, and with a flow of population hither and thither, unchecked (save as regards West Australia) by natural barriers.

The influences that have moulded this type are due partly to climate, partly to the conditions of life and industry in the new country. The Australian is fundamentally an Englishman, differing less from the average Englishman in aspect, speech, and ideas than does the man of British stock either in Canada or in the United States. But the sunnier climate enables him to live more in the open air than does the Briton. He has preserved something of the adventurous

---

[1] The transportation of convicts ceased in New South Wales in 1840, in Tasmania in 1853, in Western Australia in 1868.

spirit and easy-going ways of the bush settler. Poverty has
not weighed him down, for in Australia a healthy man need
never remain poor, so high are wages and so ample the opportunities for rising in the world. He is hopeful, confident, extremely proud of his country, which he thinks " the
latest birth of Time." It is natural to compare him, as he
compares himself, with the American. He has the same
energy and resourcefulness, but takes life less hardly, does
not exhaust himself by a continual strain, loves his amusements, thinks more of the present than of the future.

Of the five great races of Western and Central Europe the
British has so far shown the greatest capacity for developing
" sub-types " under new conditions. Until he is absorbed
into the surrounding population, the German, the Frenchman, the Italian, the Russian remains in other lands substantially the same as he was at home. But the Englishman
in the United States, in Upper Canada, and in Australasia,
though retaining what may be called the bony framework of
his English character, has in each country undergone a sea-
change when he has crossed the ocean into new climes whose
conditions have evoked latent qualities in his nature.

The economic conditions of Australia have determined the
occupations and distribution of the people, and these have
in turn exerted an influence upon its political life which we
shall presently have to note.

When settlement extended to the interior, the most obvious
source of wealth was to be found in sheep-raising, and immense tracts of land were taken up for this purpose. Sheep
have not generally been profitable except on large runs, partly
because in the dry areas a wide run is needed for even a
moderate flock, partly also because the loss of stock in the
occasional droughts is so heavy that only large owners possessing some capital can escape ruin, though latterly smaller
runs have begun to be combined with the tillage of wheat
fields. The great size of sheep runs checked the growth of
small agricultural holdings and kept population low in these
rural areas, because a pastoral estate needs few hands, except
at shearing time, of which more anon. Moreover, as the
land suitable for tillage was usually wooded, some capital
was needed to get rid of the forest before cultivation could

begin. This retarded the growth of such comparatively small farms as prevail in the north-western prairies of the United States and Canada.

For the same reason the country towns, centres of distribution for their neighbourhoods, also remained small. The vast quantities of wool and such other produce as was raised for export by the slow extension of timber-cutting and of agricultural production gave plenty of employment to those who handled it at the ports, which were few, for nearly all the export trade of New South Wales centred at Sydney, almost the only good harbour on the coast of that State (then a colony); while similarly most of the trade of Victoria centred at Melbourne. Thus these two cities grew to dimensions altogether disproportionate to the whole population of their respective colonies. The growth of Melbourne was further accelerated, first by the discovery of gold not far from it, which drew a vast swarm of adventurers, and subsequently, after the gold fever had died down, by the adoption of a policy of protection for local manufactures by the Victorian legislature in order to secure employment at high wages for the workers of that colony. The only other considerable industry in Australia, at the time when gold production diminished, was coal-mining. It has collected a large population in a few districts, but has not led to the growth of manufactures on a great scale over the country, and the towns of the second order are still small. There is, except in Tasmania with its considerable rainfall, practically no water power. Thus Australia shows a contrast between two very large and two somewhat smaller cities (Adelaide and Brisbane), which together include more than one-third (about 40 per cent) of the whole population of the continent, and vast thinly-grassed and sparsely-peopled rural areas, shading off into an arid wilderness. Population grows slowly, for immigration has received lukewarm encouragement, and the rate of natural increase is extremely low. Those small land-owning farmers, who are so valuable an element in Canada and the northern United States, are in Australia a slender though no doubt an increasing body. The middle class is the weaker through the want of this particular element; yet there are no great extremes of wealth and poverty. Poverty indeed there is none, for the wage-earning classes live so much more comfortably than do the like classes in France, Germany, or England, as to be up to what is there called a middle-class standard. Neither are there huge fortunes on the European or North American scale. A few of the ranch-owners or "squatters," called "pastoralists," and still fewer of the leading business men, have amassed considerable wealth, but rarely does any one leave property exceeding £1,000,000. The fortunes of the rich are not sufficient either to sharpen the contrast between social extremes or to make possible those vast accumulations of capital which are in the United States denounced as a political danger. Neither does wealth flaunt itself: no stately mansions in the country: no sumptuous palaces in the cities, and as the wealth is all new, it has not had time enough to turn itself into rank. Nowhere can one find a stronger sentiment of equality, that antagonism between the wage-earning and the employing class which the traveller feels in the atmosphere as soon as he lands in Australia, being economic rather than social, for the rich do not presume on their position and have never oppressed — they never had the chance of oppressing — their poorer neighbours.

The Australians brought from England, along with its other traditions, a respect for law, so order was firmly enforced from the first days of each colony. There was not, as in North America and South Africa, serious frontier warfare against natives, accustoming men to the use of firearms. The occasional brigandage of early days, known as bush-ranging, has long been extinct, nor did lynch law ever come into use. Political party organizations were not so fully developed in the old country, when the settlers left it, as they are now, but the settlers, though they belonged to a class which in the Britain of those days furnished few candidates for Parliament, possessed the average Englishman's interest in public affairs, with the habit of holding public meetings and forming associations for every sort of purpose. They were bold in speech, independent in thought and action, showing no such tendency to look to and make use of the government as has become conspicuous in their descendants of this generation, scantily equipped with knowledge, but full of the spirit of adventure and the love of freedom. All expected that self-government would in due course be granted to each

colony when its population became sufficiently large; and
when self-government came they relished it and worked it as
to the manner born.

Responsible self-government, *i.e.* a Legislature with a
Cabinet on the British model, was bestowed upon New South
Wales (the oldest colony), Victoria, South Australia, and
Tasmania in 1855–56. The Constitutions, prepared in each
colony by its Council, were, with a few changes, enacted by
the British Parliament. Queensland received a self-governing constitution in 1859–60 (when it was separated from
New South Wales), Western Australia in 1890. In South
Australia universal male suffrage existed from the first for
the popular House of Parliament; in the others it was introduced before long and with little opposition. Much later, the
suffrage was extended to women. The questions that occupied the Governments of these colonies were chiefly economic, some relating to the allotment and enjoyment and
taxation of land, others to fiscal policy, including tariffs.
However after 1883 the general scramble among the great
European Powers for unoccupied territories all over the
world began, when it extended to the Western Pacific, to
bring external affairs to the minds of Australians, who felt
that their interest in the islands, especially New Guinea and
the New Hebrides, which lie north and north-east of them,
could be more effectively pressed if the whole people spoke
through one authority. This helped to revive the project,
often previously discussed, of creating a federation of all the
Australian colonies, a scheme naturally indicated by commercial and fiscal considerations, but retarded by the jealous
care with which each community sought to guard its local
independence. After long debates in two Conventions
(1891 and 1897–99), a draft Federal constitution was at
last adopted by a vote of the people in every colony, and submitted to the British Parliament, which passed it into law
(with one slight change) in A.D. 1900. Thus was created a
new National Government for the whole continent under the
title of the Commonwealth of Australia, while the old colonies
were turned into States, each retaining its local government,
and exercising such of the former powers as it had not surrendered to the Federal authority.

The constitutional system of Australia and its practical

working are interesting both in respect of their slight differences from England and of their wider differences from the United States, but for the purposes of this treatise attention must be concentrated on what is most distinctive in the politics of the country, that is to say, upon those points in which it has given to the world something new, methods, schemes, or practices containing a promise or a warning for the future.

Four points stand out as specially noteworthy.

Australia is the land in which the labouring masses first gained control of the legal government and displayed their quality as rulers.

It is the country in which first a closely knit party organization, compelling all members of the Legislature who belong to it to act as a compact body, became absolute master of a representative Assembly.

It has extended further than any other country (except New Zealand) has done the action of the State in undertaking industrial enterprises and in determining by law the wages and hours of labour.

It is the country in which material interests have most completely occupied the attention of the people and dominated their politics, so that it affords exceptional opportunities for estimating the influence which the predominance of such interests exerts on the intellectual and moral side of national life. These four points, however, though the special objects of our study, cannot be understood without some account of the machinery of government and the way in which it works. I begin with the Commonwealth.

THE GOVERNMENT OF THE COMMONWEALTH

The Federal Government has received narrower powers than those enjoyed by the Dominion Government in Canada and by the Government of the Union of South Africa, but in some respects wider than those of the National Government in the United States. Powers not expressly allotted to it are, as in the United States, deemed to be reserved to the States, whereas in Canada the Provinces retain only such powers as have been expressly delegated to them, the residue not specifically enumerated being vested in the Dominion.

Trade — interstate and external — tariffs, currency, banking, patents, weights and measures, marriage and divorce, are in Australia Federal matters, as are also old-age pensions and arbitration in labour disputes which extend beyond the limits of one State, while the States retain legislation on property and most civil rights, industries, land administration, mining, railways, education. Reasons to be hereafter explained have led to proposals which would considerably extend the range of Federal authority, and many decisions have been rendered by the High Court of Australia, which is the ultimate Court of Appeal in the Commonwealth, upon the questions that have arisen as to the interpretation of the general terms employed in the Constitution.

The Commonwealth Parliament consists of two Houses. The Senate has thirty-six members, six from each State, all the States, great and small alike, being (as in the United States) equally represented. The senators are elected for six years by universal suffrage, not in districts, but by a general popular vote over the whole State. One-half retire every three years, so the Senate is a continuous body except when specially dissolved in consequence of a deadlock between the two Houses. The House of Representatives has seventy-five members, chosen in one-membered constituencies by universal suffrage. Its term is three years, subject to the power of earlier dissolution which the Governor-General can exert on the advice of his Ministers. Members of both Houses now receive a salary of £1000 a year.[1] The British Crown legally retains a power of veto, but this is in practice not exercised unless where some grave imperial interest might be deemed to be involved.

Executive power resides nominally in the Governor-General, as representing the British Crown, but virtually in the Cabinet of high officials who form his Ministry, and who must be members of the Legislature and must (in practice) have the support of a majority in the House of Commons. Subordinate officials are, as in Britain, appointed nominally by the Crown but practically by the Ministry, and form, as in Britain, a permanent Civil Service.

[1] Originally £400, it was in 1907 raised to £600, and the action of the Parliament which voted to itself the addition was severely commented on. In 1920 it was suddenly further raised to £1000. The same thing had happened in the United States and in France.

In order to make the Commonwealth Government independent of any State influences, its seat has been placed at a spot (called Canberra, formerly Yass Canberra) almost equally distant from Sydney and from Melbourne, lying in a thinly-peopled region far off the main lines of railway communication, and at present equally difficult of access from both cities. A space of about 900 square miles has been ceded by New South Wales for this purpose to the Commonwealth, and buildings are being erected there to provide accommodation for the Parliament and the administrative offices. Meantime the seat of government is at Melbourne.

The Federal Constitution can be amended by Parliament, *i.e.* by an absolute majority in both Houses, or by an absolute majority in one House, given twice, with an interval of three months intervening, and *plus* submission to the other House; but amendments must be thereafter approved by a majority of the States and also by a majority of the whole people voting simultaneously over the whole Commonwealth. In this case only does the Australian people exercise as of right that power of direct legislative action which is so frequent both in many of the United States and in Switzerland, where it is called by the names of Referendum and Initiative. It was, however, held to be within the power of Parliament, in such exceptional circumstances as were those of the Great War, to refer a matter to the vote of the people for their advice, a course taken in 1915 and 1917, when their opinion on the subject of compulsory military service was desired. This procedure for amendment is prompt and easy compared to that prescribed for the amendment of the United States Constitution, a natural result of the familiarity with swift parliamentary action which the framers of the Australian Constitution possessed.[1] When a question is submitted to the people to be voted on by them, every voter receives a docu-

[1] The Constitution of the Canadian Dominion can be changed only by the Imperial Parliament which enacted it in 1867; but this arrangement, which seems to leave less power to the Dominion Parliament than the Australian Parliament possesses, does in reality give the former more power, for the Imperial Parliament is accustomed to comply as a matter of course with requests for amendments proceeding from the Canadian Parliament, when satisfied that they represent the general will of the people, whereas in Australia a bare majority only of the States and also of the people is required.

ment setting forth the arguments for and against the proposals, as well as the full text of the proposals themselves.

The Commonwealth administers two Territories not included in any State, besides the Federal district of Canberra. One is the large region (532,620 square miles), lying along the north coast of the Continent, between Queensland and West Australia, and extending a long way inland. It was transferred by South Australia to the Federal Government in 1911. The other is the South-Eastern or British part of the great Asiatic island called Papua or New Guinea (90,540 square miles), which was annexed by Great Britain in 1888, and by an Act of 1906 entrusted, along with some groups of islands lying near it, to the administrative care of the Federal Government. To this part there has recently (1920) been added another part, about 70,000 square miles, formerly owned by Germany, but now allotted to Australia as mandatory of the League of Nations.

The State Governments

The Constitutions of the six States, all of course older than that of the Commonwealth, are reproductions of the British frame of government, having been originally created by statutes of the British Parliament, though subsequently modified by acts of the State Legislatures. In each there are two Houses. The smaller, which is called the Legislative Council, consists, in New South Wales and Queensland, of persons who have been nominated by the Crown, *i.e.* by the Ministry of the day, for life. In Victoria, South Australia, Western Australia, and Tasmania its members are elected for six years by voters possessing a certain small property qualification. The voters so qualified are between 30 and 40 per cent of those who elect the Assembly by universal suffrage. These Councils are continuous bodies, a part of the members retiring every second or third year. Members are usually re-elected. The larger House, called the Assembly, is in every State elected by universal suffrage for three years. Members receive salaries which vary from £150 (in Tasmania) up to £500 (New South Wales), and have also free passes over the Government railways. Each State has a Governor appointed by the Crown (usually for five years), and a Cabinet selected

from members of the Legislature by the person whom the
Governor summons to form an administration, such person
being usually the leader of the party which at the moment
constitutes the majority of the Assembly.   The Governor,
acting on the advice of his Ministers, can dissolve the Legislature, and can also, acting on behalf of the Crown, refuse
consent to a Bill or refer it to England for the consideration
of the Crown, but this right is now so very rarely exercised
that it constitutes no check on self-government.   Judges are
appointed for life by the Governor on the recommendation of
his Ministers, being removable only (as in Britain) upon
a resolution passed by both Houses.   The State Constitutions
(as already observed) can, like that of the United Kingdom,
be changed by the ordinary process of legislation.

The Judiciary in the Commonwealth and the States

Both in the Commonwealth and in the States, the judicial
arrangements follow those of England.   All the superior
judges are appointed for life by the Governor, acting on the
advice of his Ministers, and are removable only upon an address passed by the Legislature.   They receive salaries sufficient to attract the best men from the bar.   In the Commonwealth there has so far been created only one court, viz. the
High Court, which is the final Court of Appeal for all Australia in all matters, whether arising under Federal or under
State law.   Its decisions are enforced by State machinery,
while, conversely, the Commonwealth Parliament may invest
State courts with Federal jurisdiction.   There is also in the
Commonwealth a Court of Conciliation and Arbitration
(whereof more anon), and also a semi-judicial, semi-administrative body called the Interstate Commission with members
irremovable during their seven years' term, among whose
functions is that of investigating commercial matters and
watching the operation of the tariff.

General Character of the Australian Governments

In its practical working from year to year, the Commonwealth is, and each State also continues to be as a State

what it was as a colony, a Crowned Republic, *i.e.* a community monarchical in its form, but republican in its spirit and operation, and indeed more democratic than many republics are. Each community is attached, not only legally, but by what are now the stronger ties of sentiment and reciprocal interest, both to the mother country and to the other British self-governing Dominions. The growth of a strong Australian national patriotism has not diminished the feeling of the Unity of the British peoples all over the world.

These Australian frames of government, Federal and State, the legal outlines of which will be presently supplemented by a description of their working, are highly democratic. In the Commonwealth we find:

Universal suffrage at elections for both Houses of Legislature.

One-membered districts equal, broadly speaking, in population.

Triennial elections.

No plural voting.

Payment of members.

No veto by the Executive.

Complete dependence of the Executive upon the larger House of the Legislature.

Scarcely any restrictions on legislative power (other than those which safeguard State rights).

Prompt and easy means of altering the Constitution.

These democratic features exist in the States also, save that in them Second Chambers, not based on universal suffrage, impose a certain check on the popular House. On the other hand the State Legislatures, having full power to alter their Constitutions by ordinary legislation, are not required to invoke a popular vote for that purpose.

One can hardly imagine a representative system of government in and through which the masses can more swiftly and completely exert their sovereignty. Of them may be said what Macaulay said, not quite correctly, of the United States Government. It is " all sail and no ballast." The voters may indulge their uncontrolled will for any and every purpose that may for the moment commend itself to them.

The Federal Constitution is more democratic than are the State Constitutions in respect of the fact that its Senate is not a conservative force, being elected by the same suffrage as is the Assembly, and by a method which gives greater power to an organized popular majority. It will be seen presently that this has contributed to make the Labour party desire an extension of the powers of the Commonwealth to the detriment of the States.

Comparing the Commonwealth Constitution with that of the United States, the former is the more " radical," for it contains neither a veto power, like that of the American President, nor those numerous restrictions on legislative power which fetter Congress, while its method of altering the Constitution itself is more promptly applicable. On the other hand, most of the American State Constitutions depart further from English precedents than do those of the Australian States, for the former vest the elections both of judges and of administrative officials in the people, and many of them contain provisions for direct popular legislation by Initiative and Referendum. Yet as the American States give a veto to the State Governor, and limit in many directions the power of the Legislatures, the Australian schemes of government seem, on the whole, more democratic than the American, though some of the reasons for this view cannot be given till we have examined the practical working of Australian institutions. Whoever has read the chapters on Canada will not need to be told how much less democratic is the form of its government than is that of Australia.

Some one may ask, What of Britain herself? Has not her Constitution become in recent years almost as democratic as is the Australian? The electoral suffrage is practically universal, and the working-class commands a majority in almost every constituency? And is not the House of Commons supreme, though one delay is still interposed before its will can be carried into law, supreme even over those fundamental laws which are vaguely called the Constitution? Did not Parliament, early in the recent war, suspend, with scarce any debate, nearly every constitutional guarantee, and place the executive in uncontrolled power?

All this is true. The United Kingdom, which is now, so far as respects its frame of government, more of a democracy than the United States, is almost as much a democracy as the Australian Commonwealth. In practice, however, this is not yet the case. The difference lies in the different social and economic phenomena of the countries, and in a few traditions of public life, which, though now fast disappearing, have still more influence in old nations like England and France than tradition can have in any new community. Some of these phenomena I may here indicate, in order to explain the conditions under which Australian institutions have to work, reserving for a later stage remarks on those features of Australian character which determine the public opinion of the nation.

1. Australia presents a striking contrast between four great cities and a vast, sparsely-peopled rural area. The capitals of the greater States contain more than a third of the whole population.

2. The bulk of the wage-earning class is concentrated in these four cities, and most of the rest dwell in several mining areas.

3. In every State much of the land is owned by a small number of proprietors holding large estates.

4. These large estates being almost wholly pastoral, provide employment for comparatively few workers.

5. The small farmers, whether freeholders or lease-holders, and whether of arable land or of dairy farms, are a less important element in the population than in Canada or the United States, and constitute but little of what can be called a "middle class." Their voting power, such as it is, is lessened by the difficulties which those who dwell in thinly-peopled areas find in reaching polling places.

6. There is no sort of so-called "aristocracy" either of birth or of rank, and hardly even a "plutocracy." No family has possessed wealth for more than forty or fifty years.

7. There is, consequently, no class which has a hereditary interest in, or influence on, political affairs.

8. There is less social intercourse between employer and employed than in Britain. That sort of semi-feudal or semi-family relation that used to exist in some parts of England between the landowner and his tenants, and which sometimes included labourers as well as farmers, could not of course be expected in a new country. But in cities and at the mines also there has been and is nothing but a hard "cash nexus" (as Carlyle calls it) between the manufacturer or mine-owner

and the workman, seldom redeemed by the kindly interest
which, before the days of incorporated companies, the best
sort of Lancashire or Yorkshire millowners often took in the
mill hands and their families.[1]   The largest class of Australian rural workers, the sheep shearers, are migratory,
moving from station to station to do this most important part
of the year's work, while a numerous section of the city
labourers, those who load and discharge ships, are not in any
permanent employment.

9. The sentiment of social equality is extremely strong,
for there were hardly any distinctions of rank to begin with,
and such habits of deference as had belonged to Europe did
not attach themselves to those whose only claim was a more
rapid rise towards wealth.   Gold-digging, moreover, which
powerfully affected society (especially in Victoria) for some
years after 1850, is of all occupations the most levelling.

10. The passion for equality has induced social jealousy.
There is no such deep gulf fixed between classes as that which
divides " bourgeoisie " and " proletariat " in France, but
there is a feeling of latent antagonism or suspicion, an apparent belief among the workers that the interests of the
richer and those of the poorer are and must be mutually opposed.   No similar feeling has existed in Great Britain or
in the native population of Canada or of the United States.

[1] Two exceptions were, however, mentioned to me, and there are
doubtless others.

CHAPTER XLVII

AUSTRALIAN LEGISLATURES AND EXECUTIVES

In Australia, as in Britain, Parliament is the centre of political activity, the mainspring of the mechanism of Government. It is complete master of the Executive. No veto checks it. Every Minister must sit in it. There is no other avenue to public life, for there are no offices in the direct election of the people, and in Parliament the popular House is the predominant power, for it makes and unmakes the executive government and has the chief voice in finance.

As already observed, every adult in the Commonwealth and in the States possesses the suffrage. The admission of women was carried both in the States and in the Commonwealth with little controversy. People merely said, "Why not?" No steps were taken to ascertain whether the bulk of the women desired the right of voting. The women who actually demanded it were a comparatively small section, but little or no opposition came from the rest. The ballot does not permit it to become known how the women vote, but it is generally believed that in the richer classes fewer women than men vote, while the Labour Unions bring the working women to the poll in as large numbers as the men. So far as can be ascertained, the introduction of female suffrage has had no perceptible effect on politics, except that of strengthening the Labour party.[1] Women of the richer sort seem to take little interest in public affairs, or at any rate to talk less about them than women of the same class do in England. They are said usually to vote with their male relatives, and no one suggested to me that their possession of the vote had induced domestic dissensions. Though plural voting exists nowhere, owners of property may in

[1] It was, however, believed at the time that in the two Referenda on the question of compulsory military service the women voters of all classes largely contributed to the defeat of that proposal. Western Australia, in which it was carried, has the smallest proportion of women.

Victoria and Queensland cast their vote either in their place of residence or in some other place where they are registered in respect of their property.

Electoral districts are, broadly speaking, equal in population, though sometimes the rural areas contain fewer voters, this being thought fair in order to secure due consideration for rural opinion. The Commonwealth Constitution provides for an automatic redistribution of seats in proportion to population. Except in Tasmania, where the introduction of Proportional Representation required the creation of districts, each of which was to return a number of members, constituencies have been generally single membered, but Victoria, Western Australia, and Queensland have tried various forms of "preferential" or "contingent" voting. New South Wales in 1910 substituted preferential voting for the second ballot, and has now nine city electorates, each returning five members, and fifteen rural, each returning three. Proportional Representation, once enacted for the Commonwealth, was repealed by the Labour party when they held a majority.

Voting by post is permitted in Victoria and West Australia. "Absent voting" (*i.e.* the right for an elector to record his vote at a polling place elsewhere than in his division) has been introduced for Commonwealth elections and in Queensland. Candidates are not required by law or custom to be resident in the districts they sit for, but residents are generally selected as being better known locally. There is a tendency, less strong than in England, but much stronger than in the United States, to re-elect a sitting member.

The counting of votes at elections appears to be everywhere honestly conducted, and one hears no complaints of bribery, common as that offence used to be in the United Kingdom, and is still in parts of the United States and of Canada. A member is, however, expected to use his influence to secure various benefits for his district, such as roads, bridges, and other public works, an evil familiar in many other countries. The expenses of elections, generally limited by law, are in the States mostly light, usually ranging from £50 to £200, while for Labour candidates they are borne by Unions or political labour leagues. As the Commonwealth constituencies are much larger, the cost is in these often heavy.[1] Where the legal limit (which is £100 for a House of Commons district and £250 for a Senatorial election) has to be exceeded, the candidate's party or friends supply the money needed.[2] Elections are said to be growing more expensive, and members of the richer sort are beginning to be called upon to subscribe to various public or quasi-public local objects, a habit which has latterly become frequent in England.[3]

We may now pass to the Houses of Legislature, beginning with those of the States as being the older.

THE TWO HOUSES IN THE STATES

The bicameral system established when responsible government was first granted to each colony, was suggested partly by the example of the mother country, partly to provide a check on the supposed danger of hasty and ill-considered action by the more popular House.

In all the States the popular House, called the Assembly, is the driving force and dominant factor. It controls finance, it makes and unmakes Ministries. To it, therefore, men of ability and ambition flow. Its importance, though reduced by the creation above it of a National Government, is still sufficient to secure among its members, especially in the largest States, men of shrewd practical capacity, accustomed to political fighting, and quickly responsive to any popular sentiment.

Very different are the Legislative Councils. They are comparatively quiet, steady-going bodies, whose members, mostly belonging to the professional or business classes, and enjoying a longer tenure of their seats, are of a more conservative temper. Their sessions are fewer and shorter, their debates quieter and scantily reported in the press. Sit-

[1] I was told that it may reach £2000, but as at the same election a Referendum on a proposed amendment to the Constitution may be voted on, it is not easy to distinguish how much of the total expenditure is attributable to each issue.

[2] A statute directs enquiries to be made regarding such help.

[3] An Act of 1909 imposes penalties on those who disturb an election meeting with intent to frustrate its purposes, and another (of 1911) subjects to a penalty offensive comments on a candidate at an election, if published without the writer's name.

ting for life or for six years at least, and usually re-elected at the expiry of their time, they acquire a valuable experience, and are less at the beck and call of a Ministry or of their own party than men are in the Assembly; indeed many of them claim to stand outside party, which has naturally less power in a body whose votes do not affect a Ministry's tenure of office. Though the scope of their action, as it does not include finance, is narrower than that of the Assembly, they sometimes amend or reject its Bills, and occasionally persist in their view, feeling it to be their function to arrest the more drastic or (as they would say) hasty and experimental measures of the popular body, on whose powers they constitute the only check. Thus many disputes have arisen between the two Houses, and many efforts made to get rid of the Councils, the Labour party having declared its purpose to extinguish them or to elect them by universal suffrage. As regards the nominee Councils it seems to be now settled that when deadlocks arise the Ministry in power may add a number of new nominees sufficient to carry its measures. Queensland deals with deadlocks by a popular vote or " Referendum." [1] For the case of the elective Councils, in which the consent of the Council itself would be required for a change, no complete solution has yet been reached. These bodies, being representative, usually offer a firmer resistance to Assembly Bills than do the nominated Councils, but both sets of Councils have in the long run accepted measures distasteful to themselves when convinced that these had behind them the permanent mind and will of the people and not the temporary wishes or electioneering artifices of a Ministry.

Except when the aforesaid disputes arise, these Councils play a subordinate and little-noticed part in State politics. They do not resemble the Second Chambers (Senates) of the States in the American Union nor are they comparable to the French Senate, for they contain few men of political prominence, and do not greatly affect public opinion. But their record, taken as a whole, supports the case for the existence of a revising Chamber, for though they have sometimes delayed good measures, they have often improved legislation by giving time for the people to look where they were going,

---

[1] In Queensland, when a popular vote (Referendum) was taken in 1917 on a proposal to abolish the Second Chamber, the proposal was rejected by 165,000 votes against 104,000.

and by thus compelling the advocates of hasty change to re-consider and remodel their proposals.

The Federal Senate

When the foremost statesmen of Australia drafted the Federal Constitution, they clung to the time-honoured precedent of a two-chambered Legislature. Not seeking to create a check on the democratic spirit, they rejected the notion of election by limited constituencies, and found reasons for the existence of a Senate not only in the benefits which the revision of measures by a Second Chamber may confer, but also in the need for some body to represent the equality of the States and guard the rights of the smaller States from the numerical preponderance of the larger in the House of Commons. The body contemplated was to be something stronger and better than the Councils in the States, a comparatively small body, in which cool and experienced men, who wished to escape frequent elections and the rough and tumble struggles of the House of Commons, might sit for six years at least, addressing themselves thoughtfully to the great problems of legislation. Thus it received legal powers equal to those of the House, save that it does not turn out Ministries and cannot amend (though it may reject) finance Bills. When in 1898 the question arose how the Senate should be chosen, the framers of the Constitution were informed that American opinion, having then come to disapprove that plan of electing United States senators by the State Legislatures which had formerly won the admiration of foreign observers, was turning towards the idea of an election by a popular vote all over each State.[1] Moved by this consideration, and probably thinking such a direct election more consonant to democratic principles, the Convention resolved to vest the choice of senators in the people of each State as one undivided constituency, while following the American precedent of giving to each State the same number of senators, though New South Wales had (in 1901) a population of 1,360,000 and Tasmania of 172,000 only.

[1] This sentiment went on growing in America till in 1913 it carried an amendment (the seventeenth) to the Federal Constitution, by which the election of senators was vested in the people.

All the expectations and aims wherewith the Senate was created have been falsified by the event. It has not protected State interests, for those interests have come very little into question, except when controversies have arisen between New South Wales and Victoria. Neither has it become the home of sages, for the best political talent of the nation flows to the House of Commons, where office is to be won in strenuous conflict. The Senate has done little to improve measures, though this is largely due to a cause unforeseen by its founders, which will be presently explained. Not having any special functions, such as that control of appointments and of foreign policy which gives authority to the American Senate, its Australian copy has proved a mere replica, and an inferior replica, of the House. Able and ambitious men prefer the latter, because office and power are in its gift, and its work is more important and exciting, for most of the Ministers, and the strongest among them, are needed there, while the Senate is usually put off with two of the less vigorous. Thus from the first it counted for little. When the same party holds a majority in both Houses, no conflict between the Houses arises, and the Senate does little more than pass hurriedly, at the end of the session, the measures sent up from the House. But whenever the Senate majority is opposed to the House majority, trouble may be looked for.

This comparative failure of the Senate, admitted on all hands, is partly due to an unforeseen result of the method of election by a popular State vote. Each elector having three votes for the three seats to be filled, a well-organized party issues a list of its three Senatorial candidates, and the issues submitted being the same, all the party electors vote that list without regard to the personal merits of the candidates, which, though they might count for much in a one-membered constituency, count for little in the area of a whole State. What chance in a vast constituency has a candidate of making himself personally known? He can succeed only through his party. The tendency is irresistible to cast a straight party vote for the three whom the party managers put forward, so it is the best organized party with the most docile supporters that wins. Thus in the election of 1910 the Labour party, being far better organized than its opponents, carried every seat in six States, being half of the whole Senate. In 1913, when another election of half the Senate arrived, the same party carried three seats in three States, while three seats in two States and one seat in another went to the less compact Liberal party. At a special dissolution of both Houses in 1914 the Labour party, while obtaining a majority of eight only in the Assembly, secured thirty-one out of thirty-six seats. The electoral majorities were narrow, but the majority in the Senate became overwhelming. Such a result turned men's thoughts towards some scheme of proportional representation which would enable the minority to secure more members, and might give a better chance to men of eminent personal qualities; and a scheme of that nature is now on its trial.[1]

The Commonwealth House conducts its business on the same general lines as those followed in Great Britain and Canada, Ministers sitting in it, leading the majority, and carrying their Bills through the regular stages. Questions are addressed to the heads of departments, and the Speaker is, as in Britain (but not in the United States), expected to be an impartial chairman, though he, as also the President of the Senate, is now always chosen afresh at the beginning of each Parliament from the dominant party.[2] The closure of debate, an inevitable safeguard against persistent obstruction, called in Australia "stone walling," is habitual, and a time limit is imposed on speeches. Bills levying taxation or appropriating money to the public service must originate in the House, but the Senate, which can reject, cannot amend them, for this would in practice amount to giving a power to initiate, though it may (and does) return them, suggesting amendments for the consideration of the House. The House is the vital centre of political life, but its vitality was impaired when the Labour Caucus (whereof more anon) was established, for the centre of gravity shifted to that caucus in

[1] In 1919 the application of a plan providing for preferential majority voting resulted in the election of 17 members of the largest of the four parties with 860,060 votes, one member of another party (Labour and Socialist), with 820,000 votes, and no member of the two smallest (the Farmers and the Independent) parties, which together aggregated 173,000 votes. This outcome has given scant pleasure to the advocates of Proportional Representation.

[2] In 1912 the Speaker was not wearing any robe of office, this having been disused, but in the Parliament of 1913 it was restored.

which the Labour senators sit along with their comrades of
the House.   When Labour holds the majority the caucus
controls everything; and debate, except so far as it relates
to details not settled by the caucus, or makes an appeal to
the public outside, is thrown away, since it does not influence
the decision, the majority having already determined in
secret how it will vote.

This being the machinery of parliamentary government,
the men who work it belong to what is practically the same
class in the Commonwealth and in the State Legislatures,
although the average of ability is somewhat higher in the
Commonwealth Legislature, because it opens a wider field
to ambition.   Successful State politicians sometimes transfer their activities to the Commonwealth.

Europeans must be cautioned not to apply to any of the
new countries the standards of education and intellectual
power by which they judge the statesmen of their own old
countries.   In Australia there is no class with leisure and
means sufficient to enable it to devote itself to public life.
Some few men there are rich enough to live in ease upon
the fortunes they have made in business or as sheep farmers,
but scarcely any of such persons choose a life of Australian
ease, for if they wish for idle enjoyment, they probably go to
England, if they stay at home, they continue to occupy themselves with their sheep runs or their business.   Not many
aspire to a political career, which lacks the attractions that
have hitherto surrounded it in European countries.   It is
(happily) not lucrative, and it carries no more social importance than the membership of a city or county council
carries in England.   Still less can the man who has his fortune to make turn aside to politics.   The pastoralist lives
on his station and must look after his flocks; the manufacturer or banker or shipping agent cannot sacrifice his morn-
ings to work in a State Legislature, and cannot, unless his
home is in Melbourne, think of entering the Commonwealth
Parliament, where constant attendance is required.[1]   This
applies largely to lawyers also, and in fact no modern legislatures are so scantily provided with lawyers as those of
Australia; they are fewer than in Britain or Canada, far

[1] Successful business men are more often than not managers of a
large company, and in so far not free to give their time to politics.

fewer than in the United States or France. In 1919 only one was sitting as a representative from Victoria. When the seat of Government has been transferred to Canberra, now a remote country nook among the hills, far from everywhere, even the possibility of a Melbourne barrister will be cut out. The level of attainments is not high among politicians, most of whom have had only an elementary, very few a university education. There is, moreover, a localism of spirit which thinks first of how a measure will affect a place or a trade, and there is a natural distrust of all reasonings that seem abstract. Of quick intelligence and shrewd mother-wit there is indeed no lack, but rare are the well-stored and highly-trained minds capable of taking a broad view of political and economic questions.

One may regret that a larger number of men, trained to affairs by business or professional life, do not give to their country the benefit of their intellectual resources. But it is to be remembered that such men live chiefly in the large cities, and would be almost unknown in country constituencies, distances being greater than in England, and many electoral districts in the " back blocks " so large that to canvass them requires a great deal of time and expense. Putting all things together, only a quite exceptional public spirit will induce a man in good business to seek election to a seat in a State Parliament, for he must neglect his work, he has a good deal of rudeness and possibly even abuse to face, and he is expected, far more than formerly, to fetch and carry for his constituents and toil for the party. Local fame and £600 a year were not, nor, probably, will £1000 a year be sufficient to outweigh these drawbacks, not to add that such a man, unless possessed of an attractive personality which can meet the ordinary elector on his own ground, is exposed to prejudice or suspicion on the ground of his belonging to the richer class. This kind of suspicion or aversion, scarcely known in Britain or in Canada, is dwelt on in Australia as an obstacle in the path of the educated man seeking to enter politics.

Both before and since Federation politics have been unstable in the States and the Commonwealth, with frequent shiftings of the majority, and, by consequence, frequent ministerial changes. Victoria once enjoyed eight ministries in seven years, South Australia had forty-one in forty years, and the Commonwealth had, between its birth in 1900 and 1910, seen seven administrations. The consolidation in 1909 of three parties into two, with a stricter party cohesion, made for a time these shiftings of power less frequent. But elections recur every three years, and in the legislatures of the States, comparatively small communities, personal feelings count for much. Want of tact in a Minister, some offence taken by, or selfish motive acting on, a little group of members, has sometimes led to the turning over of a few votes and the consequent fall of a Ministry. Party discipline was lax until the rise of the Labour party drove its opponents to greater stringency.

There was plenty of vigorous debating in the State Assemblies of last century, which saw the conflicts of strong and striking personalities, such as Robert Lowe, Sir Henry Parkes, Sir Graham Berry, William Bede Dalley, C. C. Kingston, G. H. Reid, Alfred Deakin, and others, not to speak of some who happily survive, though now no longer in Australian political life. One is often told that the present generation of parliamentarians does not equal the men of 1860 to 1890, that the debates are on a lower level, that there is less courtesy and dignity, that the term " politician " begins to be used in a disparaging sense. Such *laudatio temporis acti* is so common everywhere that one would discount these regrets for a better past were they not so widely expressed by thoughtful observers. There are to-day, as there have always been, a few men of eminent ability in public life. It would seem that there has been a decline in manners.[1] Australian politicians fight " with the gloves off." Offensive remarks are exchanged, as usually happens in small bodies where each knows the weaknesses of his fellow-members, imputations freely made, speeches constantly interrupted by interjected remarks. But scenes of violence, such as occasionally disgrace the Parliaments of Europe and America, seem to be almost unknown, and personal feuds are rare; personal attacks seeming to be no more resented than is roughness in a football match.

Neither the growth of the States nor the creation of the

[1] But Sir G. H. Reid remarks in his autobiography on the rudeness common in the legislature of New South Wales in his day.

Commonwealth has caused a seat in Parliament to carry any more social prestige now than formerly, and it has added immensely to the work expected from a member. His constituents weary and worry him more than ever with requests, since the increase of State-controlled industries has so enlarged the number of State employees that the grievances which the member has to bring before the notice of a Minister or of Parliament grow in like proportion. The richer Australians dilate on the harm done by the payment of members, saying it has brought in many uneducated persons who come for the sake of the salary, and whose loyalty to their party is enforced by the fact that their income depends on their loyalty. But no one could tell me how it was possible to avoid the payment of members if it was desired to have the wage-earning class duly represented, nor were the old days adorned by quite so much dignity and disinterestedness as it is now pleasant to imagine.

CHAPTER XLVIII

THE EXECUTIVE AND THE CIVIL SERVICE

Both in the Commonwealth and in the several States the Executive Government consists of a group of Ministers, seldom exceeding seven, who are normally heads of one or more of the administrative departments, though there may often be found a "Minister without portfolio." These form the Cabinet. All have seats in one or other house of the Legislature, and are supposed to represent the best political capacity of the party for the time being in the majority. The place of Prime Minister [1] is, according to British usage, taken by the statesman who has been commissioned by the Governor to form the administration.

The personal characters and careers of most ministers are pretty familiar to the whole community but, partly for this very reason, their dignity and social influence are not equal to those of ministers in Europe. It is only when a Prime Minister is a man of exceptional popular gifts or indispensable by his talents and the force of his will that he can dominate the Legislature through the confidence reposed in him by the people. Under the organization of the Labour party, ministers who belong to it are selected by and must obey, often (it is said) reluctantly, the directions of the party caucus, so that it is rather their personal influence in that body than their official position that counts. If this caucus system lasts, it may reduce the importance of oratorical talent, and make shrewdness in council and the capacity for handling men as individuals the qualities most helpful in the struggle for leadership. [2]

[1] In the States usually called "Premier."

[2] A very careful and experienced observer wrote to me in 1920 as follows: "There has been a good standard of personal integrity in public men and this has generally been maintained, but in recent years there have been some grave scandals leading to the retirement of Min-

Cabinet Ministers are, as in Britain, practically the only members of the executive who are changed with a change of government. The rest of the regular civil service is permanent, *i.e.* removable only for misbehaviour or incompetence. In South Australia the person removed by the minister in charge of the department may appeal to an independent non-political Board, usually composed of high officials. For the lower posts there is everywhere a qualifying examination, the fairness of which is not questioned. In South Australia it is conducted by professors of the university. The minister usually appoints those who stand highest in the examination. Where the age of admission is low (in Victoria and Tasmania it is sixteen) tolerably good clerks are secured, but there is no certainty of getting talent of a higher kind. The more important appointments, and those which are more or less temporary, outside the regular service, are filled by the minister, who often selects with more regard to political services than to merit; but apart from these, and taking the State Governments generally, appointments seem to be fairly made, neither nepotism nor political motives seriously affecting them.

In all the States promotion goes practically by seniority, a method deemed necessary to prevent favouritism, but ill calculated to bring ability to the top. In filling the highest posts, especially where technical knowledge comes in, the Minister has a wider discretion. Tasmania, and (I think) other States also, permit a Minister when he can find no one in his department fit for some particular work, to get leave from the Civil Service Commission to bring in an outsider.

The salaries of employees, including those earning wages in constructional work or in Government industrial enterprises, are said to be in excess of those paid by private persons for services of the same kind, and there are persistent efforts to increase their numbers, efforts kept more or less

isters or members from public life, and in some cases these suspicions have been so strong that the whole matter has not been thrashed out and that others were implicated. In some States the establishment of a practice whereby Members of Parliament are regularly employed by persons having dealings with Government exercises a pernicious influence on the tone and standards of public life." This is said to happen especially where land transactions are concerned. I gather that the level of purity has declined somewhat during the last decade or two.

at bay by the Public Service Acts. Government employees
are in so far a privileged class, that they can make sure of a
hearing and of easy treatment, but the rest of the wage-
earners would resent their being generally paid on a higher
scale. The pressure exercised, especially at elections, by the
railwaymen in Victoria on members of the Legislature had
in 1903 become so serious that the then Prime Minister, a
man of exceptional force of character, induced the Legislature
to pass an Act taking out of the territorial electoral divisions
all persons in government employment, and placing them
apart in two constituencies, each returning one member.
This Act was of course unpopular with the working men,
and was, after three years, repealed at the instance of another Ministry.[1] The creation of Railway Commissioners
has reduced but not altogether removed the evil, for Ministers still retain a power, exercisable in the last resort, which
exposes them to parliamentary pressure. Government servants have formed themselves into several powerful Unions,
and therethrough bear a part in determining the policy of
the Labour party.

There exists in every State a Public Service Commission,
which acts under the elaborate provisions of statutes defining
the conditions of admission, promotion, salary, and discipline
of the State services, matters which in Great Britain have in
the main been left to departmental regulation. These Commissions have done good in keeping the civil service pure and
outside politics. A similar Commission exists in the Commonwealth also, the laws of which permit greater freedom
in promotion for efficiency. This freedom, however, opens
a door to political patronage, and means are found for ex-
empting particular appointments from the Civil Service
rules. The statutory provision which had, as in the States,
prohibited public servants from joining in active political
work, was in the Commonwealth repealed, and they were
merely forbidden to comment publicly on the conduct of any
department or to disclose official information. In the Commonwealth, and also in New South Wales, government employees may appeal to the statutory Arbitration Courts for

---

[1] It was observed that, although the employees themselves might be
confined to the two constituencies, their sisters and cousins and aunts,
as well as their wives and daughters, could continue to vote in all the
others.

an increase in their salaries, a concession justified as less harmful than a permission to exert political pressure through Parliament.

Public opinion, alive to the dangers incident to the abuse of civil service patronage for political purposes, has, so far, succeeded in maintaining a fairly good standard. In the higher posts men of marked ability and efficiency are not wanting, but in some, at least, of the States, the supply of such men is insufficient. The Premier of a small State deplored to me the absence of any official corresponding to the permanent Under-Secretary of the chief departments of Government in London, declaring that for the lack of such men more work was thrown on ministers than they could adequately perform. It may be hoped that with the growth of the country and the increasing burdens laid by recent legislation on the administrative departments, posts in them will more frequently attract thoroughly educated men of exceptional capacity such as those who now in Britain win their places by a competitive examination at the age of twenty-two. But it will be necessary either to have more searching entrance examinations or to allow wider discretion to the selecting authority. At present less efficiency in the upper posts is the price paid for more impartiality in patronage.

Some few branches of administration have been committed to semi-judicial, semi-administrative Boards. In the Commonwealth the most important of these is the Inter-State Commission, already referred to, and suggested by the United States Inter-State Commerce Commission. Such non-political authorities have the advantage of being free to employ methods unhampered by routine regulations, and of exercising a better discrimination in selecting specially qualified subordinates.

In the Judicial system the example of England has been followed, and with the like salutary results, both in the States and in the Commonwealth. Judges are appointed by the Crown (*i.e.* by the responsible ministry) and for life, being removable only on an address by both Houses of the Legislature. The High Court of Australia, consisting of seven judges, has the right of determining constitutional questions, subject to an appeal to the British Privy Council when leave has been given by the Court. The judicial Bench, every-

where filled by men of ability and learning, selected, as in
Britain, from the Bar, enjoys the confidence of the people,
and no serious proposal has ever been made to fill it (as in
most of the American States) by popular election, though it
has been attempted in Parliament to obtain from ministers
an announcement of the persons whom they meant to appoint.
Partisans sometimes complain of decisions given when these
lay down principles they dislike, or narrow the operation of
measures they specially value. But no foreign critic or domestic grumbler has, so far as I know, impeached either the
personal integrity of the judiciary or their conscientious desire to expound the law according to its true meaning and
intent. This is the more satisfactory because many of the
judges have, as in England, played a leading part in politics.
That such men should put off their politics when they put
on their robes is one of those features of the British system
which have, at home and abroad, worked better than could
have been predicted. No friend of Australia could wish
anything better for her than that the power of appointing to
the Bench, and particularly to the High Court which inter-
prets the Constitution, shall continue to be exercised in that
honest and patriotic spirit which searches for men of the
highest character and most unbiassed mind, unregardful of
their personal opinions upon any current questions that have
a political aspect.

There is, however, one cloud in the sky. Questions affecting labour and wages which approach the confines of
politics have been coming to the front in recent years. Acts
have been passed by the Commonwealth Parliament, by or at
the instance of a political party, the validity of which, contested on the ground that the Constitution had not given
Parliament the power to deal with the subject, has become a
party issue, just as questions of Constitutional interpretation
regarding slavery became political issues in the United
States before the War of Secession. Moreover, an important
Commonwealth statute (to be referred to later), establishing
compulsory arbitration in labour disputes, entrusted to a
judge of the High Court the determination of disputes regarding wages and other conditions of labour, a function that
is really rather administrative than judicial. Though no
charges of unfairness have been made upon members of the

High Court for their action in any of these issues, whether practical or purely legal, it may be difficult for Ministers who have to weigh the merits of persons considered for appointment to the Bench, to keep out of their thoughts the attitude such persons would be likely to take, as judges, upon the aforesaid delicate and highly controversial matters.[1] It would be a misfortune for Australia, as well as a blow to the authority of the Constitution, if it came to be supposed that judges were appointed with a view to their action in judicial controversies. The strength of long tradition has, except at a few moments, kept English judges, though appointed by party Ministers, within the strait and narrow path, and a similar tradition now fortifies the Supreme Court of the United States. But Australia has hardly yet had time to form traditions, so her position is less assured.

Of Local Governments in Australia one may say what Pericles said of the Athenian women, that the highest praise is given by saying nothing about them, because silence means that local authorities have been discharging their daily duties quietly and well. The system is in all the States generally similar to that of England, save that some functions there left to the local authority are here undertaken by the State. In one respect it is in practice better, because both the municipal councils and those which administer the shires are elected without the intrusion of political partisanship. Election is on a rate-paying franchise.[2] The Mayor, chosen by the Council,[3] is only its chairman, not, as in most American cities, the holder of wide executive powers. Australian municipalities show few of the evils from which the larger cities of the United States and two or three of the larger cities of Canada have suffered. In one city only has administration been marked by scandals. There is doubtless in others a little occasional jobbery, but on the whole things are as honestly managed as in the towns of England and Scotland. The provision of gas, electricity, and water is usually made

[1] A high authority told me that this consideration was believed to have influenced some judicial appointments during the last decade, and that judges of the inferior courts are sometimes selected with too little regard to their attainments.

[2] Sometimes (*e.g.* in Hobart) the ratepayer has a number of votes proportioned to his valuation.

[3] The proposal that the Mayor should be elected by the citizens has not so far received much support.

by the cities, which in some cases derive revenue also from markets and cattle saleyards. Their financial condition is described as satisfactory, for though some have incurred large debts, the expenditure is represented by valuable property, and there are sinking funds for reducing city indebtedness. All municipal work is unpaid, but in large cities a sum is granted to the Mayor for defraying the expense of public hospitality; and this extends (in Victoria) to the presidents of Shire Councils. The maintenance of public order, together with asylums, prisons, and the expenses of justice, are left to the State, which, there being no poor law, votes money for charities and subsidizes some benevolent institutions. Old-age pensions are now a Commonwealth matter. Roads are made sometimes by the State, but generally by the shires and municipalities, with the aid, however, of a State subsidy. Much money has been expended upon tramways, which, except a few in private hands, belong to the States, as do nearly all the railroads.

Rural local government has, owing to the sparseness of population in the interior, never attained the importance it has long held in Switzerland and in the northern United States, nor has it done much to cultivate the political aptitudes of the people and vivify their interest in good administration.

Throughout Australia the police is efficient, a fact the more creditable because there exist large mountainous and thinly peopled areas not far from the great cities which would afford a convenient refuge to malefactors, as they did in the old days of the bush-rangers. Lynch law is unknown. The people, as in England and in Canada, take their stand on the side of the law, and the administration of the law justifies their confidence.

Education,[1] which in early days it had been left to the denominations to provide, is now entirely taken over by the States, though there remain a good many private Roman Catholic elementary schools and a number of private secondary schools, unsectarian and sectarian. The conditions of a country where the population was widely scattered, and

[1] A lucid and interesting account of education in Australia, from which I have derived help, may be found in chaper xii. of the *Federal Handbook*, prepared in 1913 for the British Association which then visited Australia

in the rural areas very sparse, compelled State action, and the want of local interest and local resources ended by completely centralizing it. The localities resisted every attempt to make them bear part of the charge of erecting and maintaining schools, while ministries and politicians found in the allocation of grants from the State treasury means for strengthening their position in doubtful constituencies. The State, as bearing the cost, exerts all the control; the teachers are deemed to be a part of the civil service. In recent years State Governments have shown an increasing zeal for the extension and improvement of education, Labour ministries certainly no less than others, and the sums expended on public instruction have continued to grow, till in 1912–13 they had reached the sum of £4,101,860 (or 17s. 8d. per head) for all the States as against £3,000,000 (13s. 10d.) per head in 1908–9. School buildings are still often defective, but the salaries of teachers and the quality of teaching have been rising steadily. In elementary schools no fees are charged; attendance (though imperfectly enforced) is legally compulsory; and in districts where schools are few and far between, public provision is often made for the conveyance of the pupils. No religious instruction beyond the reading of the Bible is provided, but the clergy of the denominations are permitted to give it in the schools, at stated times, to the children of their respective flocks, if the parents desire it for them. The Roman Catholic Church complains that its members are required to contribute as tax-payers to the support of schools it disapproves, and demands support for those it maintains at its own cost, which are, however, in New South Wales where the Catholics are most numerous, attended by only 40 per cent of the Roman Catholic children.

The provision of secondary education, if still imperfect, is improving in quantity and quality. Schools of all grades are being brought into closer relations with the universities, and in some States the number of teachers who hold degrees is increasing. There are excellent agricultural colleges, but technical instruction in other branches is still deficient.

Whether education is suffering, or is likely to suffer, from being not only centralized but standardized and reduced to an undesirable uniformity, is a question on which Australian opinion is divided, though no one alleges that it has, as in many American cities, and in France also, "got into politics." The teachers seem to be left free, and they come nearer than in England to being a united profession, in which merit can rise from humbler to higher posts.

Each State aids its university by a considerable public grant, but exercises no more authority than is implied by its being represented on every governing body.

Though State subventions are a proper recognition of the importance, especially in a new country where men's minds are chiefly occupied with business and amusement, of institutions dedicated not only to instruction but also to learning and science and research in all the fields of human activity, and though among the professors there are many men of conspicuous ability and distinction in their several spheres of work, the Universities have hitherto counted for less in the progress and the development of Australian life than the Universities have in that of America; and they have not, owing to their limited resources, had the chance of doing so much as the latter to raise the standard of knowledge and thought in the country. This, assuredly not the fault of their teaching staffs, seems due to a deficient appreciation among the people at large of the services seats of learning may render. It is to be hoped that men of wealth will, as has been done on a grand scale in the United States, add freely to the endowments, still small in proportion to their requirements, which the Universities have already received from donors who saw their value as factors in national progress. Nowhere in the world is there more need for the work which Universities can do for an advancing people.

CHAPTER XLIX

THAT political parties would grow up in each colony so soon as responsible government had been granted was a matter of course, for where the powers and emoluments of office are prizes offered to the leaders of a majority in a legislature, its members are sure to unite and organize themselves to win these prizes. But upon what lines would parties be formed? The Whigs and Tories of the Mother Country lay far behind, and most of the questions which had been party issues in England did not exist here. There were, however, those opposite tendencies which always divide the men who reach forward to something new from the men who hold fast to the old, and there was also sure to come the inevitable opposition between the interests of the few who have a larger and the many who have a smaller share of the world's goods.

Some of the questions which have been the foundations of parties in Europe were absent. There were no race antagonisms, for the settlers were all of British stock, and hardly any religious antagonisms. Apart from local questions, important wherever a new community is making roads or railways or laying out towns, the matters that first occupied the assemblies were constitutional and economic. The former were easily disposed of by the enactment in every colony first of manhood suffrage and then of adult suffrage for elections to the popular House, but in Victoria, and somewhat later in South Australia, there were long struggles over the structure of the Upper Chamber.

Economic issues cut deeper and have been more permanent. They turned first upon the tenure of land, and took the form of a conflict between those called the squatters, who had early obtained large leaseholds, and others, the "free selectors," who, coming later, were granted rights of acquiring freeholds out of such large leaseholds in order to increase the number of cultivating owners. Simultaneously, or a little later, fiscal controversies emerged, and in some colonies the two parties were for a long time distinguished as respectively the advocates either of a tariff for revenue only, or of a tariff for the protection of domestic industries. Other questions, such as the provision of religious education and the restriction of the sale of intoxicants, from time to time arose, but the most vital differences till near the end of last century concerned land and financial policy. The Free Trade party was generally dominant in New South Wales, the Protectionist in Victoria, which had a relatively larger manufacturing population.

Every party organization is compact and efficient in proportion to the forces it has behind it, be they those of racial or religious passion, or of political doctrine, or of attachment to a leader, or of material interest.

In the United States, besides those motives of traditional loyalty to a doctrine or a phrase or a name which prompt men to unite for political action, the pecuniary interest felt by the enormous number of persons holding or desiring to hold public office built up the party Machine. In England there was a driving force during most of the eighteenth and the first three-quarters of the nineteenth century in the influence exerted by the landowners and supporters of the Established Church on the one hand, and by the commercial classes and Nonconformists on the other. In Australia none of the aforesaid forces, except, to a slight extent, that of interest, was operative till recently, nor did any leader arise who exerted a strong personal fascination. Accordingly, the party organizations were loose and feeble. There were only two parties in the legislatures, the Ministerialists and the Opposition, the Ins and the Outs, but, except at moments of high tension, members passed easily from the one to the other. The leaders frequently made new combinations, and sometimes took up and carried measures they had previously opposed, while the mass of the voters were not permanently ranged under one or other party banner. Nothing was seen like that elaborate system of local committees which has existed in the United States for nearly a century, nor even like those local Liberal and Conservative Associations which grew up in Britain from about 1865 onwards. Australian conditions did not furnish, except in respect of the land question, such a social basis for parties as England had, nor was there, outside the legislatures, any class which had aught to gain from office, so party activity was less eager and assiduous than it has been in America. The fluidity of parties and want of organization were, however, to some extent compensated by the power of the newspapers, which led the voters at least as much as did the party chiefs, while the fact that nearly half of the electors lived in or near great cities made public meetings a constant and important means of influencing opinion and determining votes.

Towards the end of last century a change came, and other forces appeared which were destined to give a new character to Australian politics.

While in the legislatures the ceaseless strife of the Ins and Outs went on in the old British fashion, though with more frequent swings of the pendulum, the leaders of the working men were beginning to exert themselves outside the regular party lines. They pressed forward Labour questions, such as that of the Eight Hours' Day. Chinese immigration had been stopped under their pressure, because it threatened to affect the rate of wages. The English Dockers' Strike of 1889 had quickened the activities and roused the hopes of Australian trade unions, already well organized. In every colony Trade and Labour Councils, embracing and combining the efforts of a number of the existing Unions, began to be formed, and their leaders began to busy themselves with politics in a way distasteful to Unionists of the older type. Already in 1881 the Labour Unions of a New South Wales constituency had returned a member to the Legislature to advocate their aims. The example was followed in South Australia in 1887, in Victoria in 1891, in Queensland in 1892, in Western Australia in 1897, and in Tasmania in 1903, so Labour parties grew up in every Legislature. The movement received a stimulus from the great strike which, arising in Melbourne in 1890 out of a dispute between the Marine Officers' Association and their employers, spread far and wide over the country, and involved many industries. This, and another great strike (in 1894) of the wool-shearers, was attended with many disorders, in dealing with which the

State Governments incurred the wrath of the Union leaders. The Unions continued to grow in membership and influence till their large membership, led by energetic men, came to constitute a vote with which candidates and ministers had to reckon. For a time they were content to press upon successive ministries the measures they desired, but when they came to form a considerable element in the legislatures, they adopted the plan, familiar from its use in the British House of Commons by the Irish Nationalists, of voting solidly as one body, and transferring their support to whichever of the old parties bid highest for it by a promise to comply with their demands. This was the easier because the two pre-existing parties, divided chiefly on Protection or Free Trade, could practise a facile opportunism on labour issues.

When the first Parliament of the Australian Commonwealth was elected in 1900, there appeared in it a Labour party already numbering, in House and Senate, twenty-four out of a total of one hundred and eleven members. The two older parties, which had existed in the former colonies (now States), reappeared in the Federal Parliament. One was practically Protectionist, the other largely composed of Free Traders. The existence of these three parties promised ill for stability. The first ministry fell (after three years), defeated by a combination of Free Traders and Labourites. A Labour ministry came in, but although the General Election of 1903 had raised the numbers of the Labour party to twenty-six in a House of seventy-five, their strength was obviously insufficient, and after three months they fell, to be succeeded by another ministry, whose head was a Liberal, but which included both Protectionists and Free Traders. This administration was in its turn overthrown, after ten months of life, by the other two parties voting together against it. A ministry of a Protectionist colour followed, and held office for three years by judiciously " keeping in touch " with the Labour party. When the latter, having obtained many of the measures they desired, suddenly withdrew their support, these ministers fell, to be succeeded by a second Labour Cabinet. Its life also was short, for after six months the leaders of the other two parties, alarmed at some utterances of the Labour men, which seemed to be taking on more and more of a socialistic tinge, resolved to effect

a fusion.   Thereupon, by the joint efforts of two sets of
politicians theretofore mutually hostile, the Labour men were
turned out, and a Coalition Government installed at the end
of 1909.   Next year came the regular triennial dissolution
of Parliament.   The Labour party had been continuing to
gain strength in the country, and on this occasion it was favoured by the occurrence, while the canvass was proceeding, of
a strike among the coal-miners of New South Wales, which
led to grave disorders and irritated the working class.   The
coalition of two theretofore antagonistic parties had, moreover, displeased many electors who had previously given
their support to one or other; and many of these seem to
have now abstained from voting.   The result was a victory
for the Labour party, who secured a working majority in the
Assembly and an overwhelming majority in the Senate.
Thus ended that triangular conflict which had caused six
changes of Government within the first ten years of the
Commonwealth, rendering ministries unstable and breeding
constant intrigues and cabals.   Those who had formerly been
Protectionists and Free Traders were now united as one Opposition, following one group of leaders, and offering what
resistance they could in a conservative or anti-socialist sense
to the dominant Labour caucus.   In 1915 the Labour party
split up on the question of compulsory military service, its
smaller section retaining office by a coalition with the Liberals, some of whose leaders entered the Cabinet.   The new
party thus formed took the name of National.   In 1920 it
held a majority in the Commonwealth Parliament.[1]

While this was happening in the Commonwealth, politics
were taking a similar course in the six States.   The Labour
parties which grew up found it at first expedient to play off
the two pre-existing parties against one another, and so to
get legislation from whichever was in power as the price of
support. Ultimately the Labourites succeeded, first in
Western Australia in 1904, in securing majorities which
placed them in control of most States till the split of 1915,

---

[1] The Roman Catholic Church has latterly, especially in New South
Wales, where there is a large Irish element, and in Queensland given its
support to the Labour Party, which largely consists of men of Irish
stock, and it has become an ardent advocate of Irish claims to self-
government.   Thus religion has come, practically for the first time, to
be a factor in Australian politics.

after which they lost the other States, except Queensland, to the Nationalist party. The coalescence in the States of the two old Liberal and Protectionist parties came the more easily because the tariff, having been transferred to the Commonwealth Parliament by the Federal Constitution of 1900, no longer furnishes a State issue. Thus everywhere in Australia the two-party system came again to hold the field, though at the general election of 1919 many votes were in three States given for a party called the Farmers' Union and in two other States, a smaller number of votes for those who called themselves Independents.

Against the contingency of schism within its ranks the Labour party has, by its organization, long taken every precaution to provide. The system deserves a short description. It is novel: it is effective: its example may probably be followed elsewhere.

The organization has two objects — to select the party candidates and to formulate the party doctrines. The former is primarily a local task, the latter is for the whole of the party in the State, or in the Commonwealth, as the case may be.

In every constituency there is a Trade Union Council and a Political Labour League. Every member signs its constitution on entrance, and is bound thereby. These two bodies work together, the Labour League selecting the party candidate for that constituency, while often conferring with and influenced by the central Labour Council of the State. Every candidate is required to take the party pledge, *i.e.* to declare that he accepts the authorized programme for the time being in force, and will, if elected, vote as the majority of the party in the legislature decide.

In each State there is held, shortly before the approaching triennial general election, a Conference of delegates from all Trade Union Councils and Political Labour Leagues, at which a legislative programme of the State party is discussed and adopted. Once adopted, it is binding on all members of the party, and especially on candidates and members of the legislatures. The State party becomes, for the purposes included in the platform, both as respects the general election and for the duration of the incoming legislature, an army under discipline, moving at the word of command. The members of this Conference are elected in each State according to rules prescribed by the State party authority. Similarly in the Commonwealth there is held once in three years, shortly before the impending Federal elections, a Conference consisting of six delegates from the central authority of the organized Labour party in each State. This Conference discusses and determines the party platform for political action in the Federal Parliament, and by this document, when adopted, every member of the party in Parliament is bound, as respects both the points set forth in the platform and also his own votes on any " questions of confidence " that may arise in Parliament, *i.e.* when the question is that of supporting or opposing a ministry on issues involving its tenure of office.

The terms of the pledge, as first settled, were as follows:

I hereby pledge myself not to oppose the candidate selected by the recognized political Labor organization, and, if elected, to do my utmost to carry out the principles embodied in the Australian Labor party's platform, and on all questions affecting the platform to vote as a majority of the Parliamentary party may decide at a duly constituted caucus meeting.[1]

When a Legislature (either Commonwealth or State) is sitting, the members who belong to the Labour party meet regularly in caucus once a week, or oftener if some emergency arises, to deliberate, with closed doors, on the course they are to pursue in debate and in voting. Each member is bound by every decision arrived at by the majority upon questions within the scope of the party platform, including all amendments to Bills falling within that programme. As the total number of Labour members in the two Houses is considerable, secrecy is not easily secured. The debates in caucus are said to be thorough, so every member can master the questions on which he is to vote. When the party commands a majority, its unanimity enables it to run its Bills through quickly, because there may be little or no debate on its side, while the resistance of the minority can be overcome by the use of closure, which is in fact constantly applied.

---

[1] I quote them from the book of Mr. W. M. Hughes, *The Case for Labor* (first published in 1910), p. 66, where the pledge system is explained and advocated. So far as I know, these terms have remained in force, but whether that is so or not the principle they embody continues to rule.

Sometimes the whole party, except one or two left to keep the debate going in the House, withdraw into caucus to consider their action, and return to vote when they have reached a decision.

This parliamentary caucus has also the right, when it constitutes a majority in the legislature, of selecting the members of the Administration. The leader of the party in the Assembly whom the Governor has summoned to form a government, is not free to choose his colleagues, but must take those whom the caucus names. Much canvassing goes on in the caucus on the part of aspirants to office, and when a minister has been chosen, he holds his post at the pleasure of the caucus, which is entitled to require his retirement if he fails to give satisfaction. To them, and not to Parliament, each minister is responsible. This is in effect a supersession of Cabinet government, and largely of Parliamentary government itself, because a majority in an Assembly, debating secretly, is not the same thing as the Assembly debating openly, and also because the caucus itself is largely ruled by a power outside its own body.[1]

Until this organization of the Labour party, both in the constituencies and in Parliament, had been built up, the two old parties, and, after their fusion, the united party, which was generally called Liberal, but now (1920) constitutes the large majority of the Nationalists, had possessed very little organization. In each electoral area the local heads of the party arranged who should be their candidate, and in Parliament the members followed their party leader upon the main issues, retaining their independence in minor matters. The bonds of party allegiance were not drawn tight in Australia any more than they had been in Great Britain before 1890–1905. When, however, the Labour party became a formidable fighting organization, the other party, obliged to follow suit, created a political machinery approximating to that of its opponents, though less complete and much less stringent. As respects the Commonwealth, its supreme party authority, called the Aastralian Liberal Union, was made to consist of all organizations recognized by the Executive, and its direc-

[1] This caucus system has been retained by the present Labour party, which is now the regular Opposition in the Commonwealth, both in the Commonwealth Parliament and in any States in which it happens to be in a minority.

tion vested in an Annual Conference of six representatives from each State. This Conference appoints a Council of three members from each State, and the Council, which must meet at least once a year, appoints an Executive of six, one from each State. The platform is adopted by the Conference, but business connected with Federal elections is left to the State party authorities, while the formation of a ministry belongs to the party leader summoned by the Governor-General to undertake that duty.

Under this system accordingly no pledge is exacted from a candidate except that of adhesion to the general party platform, and the formulation of the party programme is left to the parliamentary chief. In practice, the member of a legislature who belongs to what is now the " National " party seems to enjoy a much greater latitude in his action than is allowed to the Labour member. More freedom, of course, means less discipline and therefore less fighting efficiency, than belongs to the Labour party. Both the party organizations, although they purport to leave the selection of parliamentary candidates primarily to the localities, exert a greater influence upon the choice than British practice has usually recognized, and both organizations bind the member to the support of the party platform more strictly than did either of the two old British parties forty years ago, or than the practice of American parties does to-day.

Any one can see what advantages the Labour party has derived from the system above described. It had in every local trade union and Council of trade unions, as well as in the Political Labour Leagues, a firm foundation on which to build, for the Unions had their officials, were already accustomed to work together, and had a claim on the allegiance of their members. The adoption of a programme, in settling which every member had, either directly or through his delegates, an equal voice, made the system in form democratic. The platform, setting forth definite aims, gave every member of a Union an interest in their attainment. Canvassing was hardly needed, because the members of the organizations were personally known, and could, with their female relatives, be readily brought up to the poll. While the other parties exerted themselves chiefly when elections were approaching, the Labour organization was always at work,

costing little, because special political agents were not required. Thus the party was able to cast its full and undivided vote; and when women were admitted to the suffrage,
their vote was cast along with that of the men to a greater
extent than was possible in the other parties, in which many
of the women, especially those of the richer class, did not
trouble themselves to go to the polls.[1] The Labour party
was moulded into a sort of Spartan or Prussian army, to
which perfect union gave strength. It was in practice, if
not in theory, an undemocratic system, but, in view of aims
that were dear to all, individual freedom was willingly sacrificed to collective victory. Other causes also helped the swift
growth of the Labour party. A positive and definite programme is always attractive. This one made a direct appeal to the hand-workers. Shorter hours and better wages
need little advocacy, especially when they promise the attainment by legal and pacific means of objects for which
men have been fighting by repeated strikes, a warfare in
which there had been many defeats with consequent suffering. Clear and coherent in its aims, solidly united in its
action, the Labour party stood at first over against two parties
which it had forced reluctantly to concede measures they
were both known to dislike. Afterwards it was arrayed
against a coalition of politicians who had been differing on
an issue deemed fundamental, and who were now united only
in their anti-Socialism. The two most prominent leaders
of this coalition, Mr. Reid and Mr. Deakin, were men of
high character, long experience, and eminent capacity, men
whom to know personally was to like and to value. But
there was slackness among their supporters. A purely defensive attitude is even less inspiriting in politics than in
war. The economic arguments on which the Liberal leaders
relied went over the heads of the average voter, and had been
discredited in principle by the frequent divergence of Australian legislation from sound economic doctrine. Those
leaders could, of course, appeal to something stronger than

---

[1] Nearly all of my informants regarded woman suffrage as having
materially added to the strength of the Labour party. Women seem
to vote less than men. In a recent New South Wales election for the
State Assembly the percentage of men voting, where seats were contested, to the total number on the roll was 76, that of the women voting
65.

principles — the self-interest of the richer class, who saw themselves threatened by a constantly growing taxation. But most business men thought it less trouble to go on making money than to descend into the political arena. They voted, but they did not throw themselves into the fight as did the Labour men.

In point of education and knowledge the Liberals had an advantage; yet not so great an advantage as Europeans may suppose. Among the Labour chiefs there were a few men who, gifted with natural talents, had educated themselves by reading, and in some cases had entered the legal profession and made a reputation there. There were others who, with little book learning, had forced their way upwards from day labour through the offices of the trade unions, and been trained by assiduous practice to be alert observers, skilled organizers, capable debaters.[1] The career of a Unionist organizer and secretary gives a fine schooling to an active and tactful man, turning him out all the better fitted for his work because not encumbered with tastes or attainments which might impair his sympathy with his own class and their sympathy with him. Setting aside a few eccentric persons who owe their rise to boisterous good-humour or to a somewhat wayward energy, the average ability of the Labour Ministries that have held power in the Commonwealth is said to be little, if at all, inferior to that to be found among the Liberals, and possibly not below that of men prominent in the House of Representatives at Washington or in the Parliament of Canada. These Australian leaders understand the questions they have chiefly to deal with as thoroughly, on the practical side, as do their antagonists. They know human nature — which is after all the thing a politician most needs to know — quite as well, and the particular type of human nature to which most Australian voters belong, very much better. The Liberal politicians suffer from that suspicion which the average worker feels towards a member of the richer class. In Great Britain a candidate for Parliament gains with the electors, though less to-day than formerly, by being a man of means and education. In

[1] The present generation of Labour members is, however, described as rather inferior to those whom the early struggles of the Labour party brought to the front, and there would seem to be to-day fewer leaders of the calibre I noted when visiting Australia.

Australia he loses.   His social advantages are political draw-backs.   He may overcome them by popular manners and a frank honesty of purpose, but drawbacks they remain.   This is more noticeable in Australia than in the United States or Canada, because though equality reigns in all three countries alike, there is more of British aloofness among the richer Australians.

The weak point of Australian politicians, with some ex-ceptions among the leaders, is their deficient education, and that narrowness of view which the concentration of attention on a particular set of questions and interests produces.   This is natural in people who live far apart from the rest of the civilized world, and in a country which has had only a short history.   They miss something which Europeans, possessing no more school education, obtain by a sort of infiltration. Those who visit Europe generally return with their horizons notably widened.   Such deficiencies may be expected to dis-appear with the growth of the country and its more frequent intercourse with Europe and North America.

CHAPTER L

WE may now turn from the machinery of Government, the methods of administration, and the party organizations, to enquire what are the concrete questions which actually occupy the statesmen and people of Australia. What ideas guide them? What objects do they seek to attain? and by what means?

As these questions are, allowing for minor local differences, the same in all the States and in the Commonwealth Parliament, it is convenient to treat them together, as common to the whole country, though the forms they have taken vary slightly in the several States.

They may be classified under three heads: (1) Those on which the people of Australia, as a whole, are substantially agreed; (2) those on which there is a preponderance of opinion sufficient to remove them from the forefront of controversy, and (3) those which acute differences of opinion have made the battle-ground of politics.

The first class includes, happily for Australia and for the other Dominions as well as for the mother country, the maintenance of a political connection between Australia and the rest of the British people dispersed over the world. Most of those whose opinion carries weight regard this connection as equally beneficial to all the territories of the British Crown. There is among the more thoughtful a general though vague desire for some constitutional changes which may draw those relations even closer than they are now, so that the means of common defence may be more perfectly organized, and that the Dominions may receive a share in the direction of foreign policy corresponding to that share in the responsibility for common defence which they have themselves been undertaking, as Australia did when her naval force co-operated with that of Britain. How this object may best be attained is not yet clear. But the growing feeling that union is strength has been emphasized by the Great War, which, while developing in Australia a strong national self-consciousness, made it also evident that the safety of each part of the British dominions depended on the safety of every other part. The recognition given to Australia as a nation by her admission as a Signatory of the Peace Treaties of 1919 and 1920 and as a member of the League of Nations marked an epoch in her position in world politics. Sentiment and interest alike prescribe some system under which, while the fullest independence in local affairs is maintained for each of the self-governing divisions of the Empire, its collective energy for common affairs shall be regularized and increased; but those who desire to propound any scheme for creating a closer constitutional relation must not forget that the expression of a wish for it must, if success is to follow, come from Australia herself as well as from Britain.[1]

There is in Australia an even more general agreement that the continent must be strictly reserved for the white European races, excluding persons of East Asiatic or South Asiatic or African origin. The watchword, " A White Australia," is proclaimed by all parties alike. The philanthropic and cosmopolitan philosophers of the nineteenth century would have been shocked by the notion of keeping these races perpetually apart, and warning black or yellow peoples off from large parts of the earth's surface. Even now most large-hearted Europeans dislike what seems an attitude of unfriendliness to men of a different colour, and a selfishness in debarring the more backward races from opportunities of learning from the more advanced, and in refusing to all non-European races, advanced and backward, the chance of expansion in lands whose torrid climate they can support better than white men can. Nevertheless, there is another side to the matter. Whoever studies the phenomena that attend the contact of whites with civilized East Asiatics in Pacific North America, not to speak of those more serious difficulties that arise between whites and coloured people in large re-

---

[1] Even the use of the words " Empire " and " Imperialism " excites in some quarters a suspicion lest self-government should be encroached upon by the establishment of any sort of central authority however restricted its functions.

gions of America and in South Africa, perceives that there are other grounds, besides the desire of working men to prevent the competition of cheap Asiatic labour, which may justify exclusion. The admixture of blood, which is sure ultimately to come wherever races, however different, dwell close together, raises grave questions, not only for white men, but for the world at large. Scientific enquiries have not so far warranted the assumption that a mixed race is necessarily superior to the less advanced of the two races whence it springs. It may be inferior to either, or the gain to the less advanced may be slighter than the loss to the more advanced. One must not dogmatize on this subject, and many of those who know the yellow races at home deem their intellectual quality not inferior to that of the white races. Be that as it may, facts as they now stand prove that social and political friction, harmful to both races, would follow from their contact on the same ground.[1]

On the subject of a compulsory universal military training (*i.e.* preparation fitting the citizen for possible war service) there had been before 1914 a pretty general concurrence of opinion. Until 1915 the question of compulsory service had not (except as regards home defence) been raised. Compulsion was twice rejected by popular votes taken during the War.

In the second class of questions two only need mention. One is Immigration. As the population of Australia grows very slowly by natural increase, there is urgent need for settlers to fill up and develop the tracts which are fit for tillage, not to speak of the still larger areas which supply pasture for sheep but in which population must needs be relatively scanty. But the working class does not wish to see any afflux of incomers which could bring down the wages paid in handicrafts, while those who want land for themselves think they ought to be provided for before any competitors from without are introduced. Thus the proposals for attracting settlers from Europe have been half-hearted and feeble. Few votes are to be gained by advocating them; many votes might

[1] What is said in the text is of course said with reference to the world as at present existing. To think of a future centuries ahead is to think of conditions under which race fusion may be advancing much faster than it advances to-day, and should our planet, or human life upon it, last till another Ice Age returns, the process of fusion may by then have blent all the races into one.

be lost. Latterly a little more has been done, but even the Liberal party, more disposed to favour immigration than is the Labour party, did not venture to advocate any large and bold scheme. The European visitor thinks that there is a lack of wisdom as well as of altruism in discouraging an immigration which would increase prosperity by raising the number of consumers, and thus making needless the incessant enhancement of prices which is caused by building the tariff wall higher and higher. But though no one opposes immigration in principle, the matter drags on, and nothing happens.

The other question is that of Protection *versus* Free Trade. This issue — protective import duties or tariff for revenue only — was the chief dividing line between parties before Confederation. It still divides opinion within the parties; that is to say, there are some Free Traders in the Liberal or Nationalist party and some few in the Labour party. But the Protectionist majority in both parties is large enough to have forced the minorities to acquiesce, and the question is no longer one on which elections are fought.[1] The rich manufacturers and sugar planters see direct profit in a tariff which raises prices by excluding European competition. The working men believe that they gain more by getting higher wages from the protected manufacturers than they would gain by the lower prices of commodities which the competition of imported manufactures would secure. Owing to the high wages paid for labour, Australia exports no large amount of manufactured articles, except agricultural implements to Argentina. If the domestic market for her manufacturers were swamped by foreign competition, the manufacturing industries would — so it is argued — disappear. Now there exists in all classes a sort of feeling that Australia, a vast ocean island far from other civilized countries, ought to be self-sufficing, and possess within her own limits the means of producing everything she can need. This is not a view grounded, as was a similar doctrine in Russia, on the need for self-defence in war, because Australians knew that if they were at war with a great naval power, they would either have with them the naval strength of the

[1] The adjustment of details in the protective tariff has, however, sometimes led to lobbying in the Commonwealth Parliament.

British Empire as a whole, or else, if that navy were unable to command the seas, be left in a position where their domestic resources would avail little. It is rather due to the patriotic wish to be a complete and fully equipped Continental microcosm, rejoicing in a variety of industries and capable of maintaining and developing them without fearing foreign competition.

Last of all, we come to those "live" and highly controversial issues which now divide the existing parties, or, in other words, to the plans and proposals of the Labour party, these being practically the aggressively positive policies chiefly before the people, since the Liberals are in effect a party of resistance or caution, the proposals they put forward being designed to attain in a gradual or tentative way some of the aims which the Labour men seek by more drastic methods.

Now the Labour policies may be summed up in the general statement that they seek to gain by constitutional means those objects which trade unions had previously sought by strikes, *i.e.* higher wages, shorter hours, easier conditions of labour, preference in employment for the members of trade unions, the recognition of Unions as alone entitled to bargain with employers, and the extension of Unions to include the whole wage-earning population. Strikes were a defective method, inflicting hardships on the strikers, often attended by violence, always involving economic loss to the country. Moreover, they often failed. Where the workers command the popular majority, why not use their voting power to obtain what they desire?

To these old aims there have been added others which strikes could not have attained, such as heavier taxation of the rich, a progressive land-tax, a fiscal system designed to secure for the workers a share in whatever the producer gains by a tariff, more stringently protective navigation laws, the "nationalization" of all monopolies, perhaps of all "great scale industries," a Commonwealth bank, a public system of insurance, an extension of the powers of the Federal Government by Constitutional amendments, and the introduction of the Initiative and Referendum.

It would be impossible to examine in detail the plans proposed for these various purposes and the arguments used to support them. All I can attempt is to select some of the more important topics which present novel features or helpfully illustrate Australian tendencies. I begin with the question which has longest occupied the nation.

CHAPTER LI

LABOUR POLICIES AND PROPOSALS

The Land Question

OMITTING the earlier stages of the tangled history of Land legislation in Australia, let us regard the later developments it has taken in the hands of the Labour party.

Under the short-sighted policy that prevailed when Australia was being first settled, and for many years thereafter, much of the best land was suffered to pass into the hands of comparatively few owners. So far as regards land fit only for sheep, the existence of large estates may be justified by the fact that the small sheep-masters are less fitted to stand the risks of occasional dry seasons than are the large proprietors. On a small estate nearly all of a flock may perish by drought, with ruin to the owner, whereas the large pastoralist may pull through, not only because he has more capital accumulated from good years to fall back upon, but also because there is almost sure to be water available, even in droughts, at some point on his sheep-run.[1] This reason, however, does not apply to lands fit for dairy-farming or for tillage, and the holders of such small farms are few in proportion to the land available. To extend their number and facilitate the acquisition of land by men of moderate means is therefore an object desirable on non-controversial economic and social grounds.

In seeking this object, recent legislation has proceeded chiefly by two methods. One is the imposition of a Land Tax, progressive in proportion to the quantity, or rather to the value, of land held.[2] This taxation, though in some

---

[1] The extension of railway communications has been tending to reduce this source of loss, because when water cannot be found for the sheep it has become easier to take the sheep to the nearest water.

[2] Estates below £5000 in value are exempt, and the rate, beginning at one penny in the £ (*i.e.* $\frac{1}{480}$) for estates between that and £18,000, rises thereafter by one half-penny in the £ up to sixpence in the £ on

States either proposed or not resisted by the Liberal leaders, has in the main been due to the Labour party. The large landowners have usually opposed it, but so far they have proved able to bear it. The aim of bringing more land into the market has, however, been only to a slight extent attained.

The other method is that of compulsory acquisition by the State of land suitable for sheep or for tillage, to be resold to small purchasers. This process, applied for some time past, but only on a small scale, has proved expensive, for purchase by the State tends to raise prices, and the price the State obtains on a resale may be less than that which it has paid. It has happened that the State, while purchasing land with a view to re-sale, is at the same time selling some of the remaining Crown lands for prices lower than those at which it has been purchasing land of like quality.

Other expedients have also been adopted. Sometimes the land is leased on a system whereby the tenant becomes owner after he has paid the price by instalments spread over a number of years. Sometimes long leases, perhaps virtually perpetual, are granted either at a fixed rent or with provisions for periodical revaluations, thus giving an opportunity for raising the rent (if the value has risen), so as to secure for the State the so-called " unearned increment." The experiment has also been tried of perpetual leases, resembling what is called in Scotland a " feu," whereby the tenant holds for ever, at a fixed rent, but cannot assign his interest without the consent of the State, which therefore can count upon having a solvent working tenant.[1] Failure to pay the rent of course forfeits the lease.

The general result of all these plans has fallen short of the needs of the case and the expectations formed. Australia ought to have a much larger element of persons owning and living off the land, such an element as gives social stability to the United States and Canada. It may be added that while the Socialist party disapprove of permanent individual property in land, the Single Taxers, not so numerous

estates of £80,000 or more. An additional one penny in the £ ($\frac{1}{240}$) is charged on all owners who do not reside in Australia.

There are also progressive income taxes in force, but these are now too common in other countries to require description here. In some States there exist both Federal and State income taxes.

[1] This may be compared to the tenure called in the Roman law *Emphyteusis*.

here as in Western America, consistently condemn the exemption from taxation of any piece of land, however small.

The law relating to the distribution and tenure of the public land has been since the dawn of history one of the most difficult problems which economists and politicians have had to deal with. It was so all through the life of the Roman Republic. Every nation has committed so many errors that none is entitled to reproach others for their failures. But there is something peculiarly regrettable in seeing the vast vacant lands of a new continent so dealt with as to cause widespread discontent and involve, if not the waste, yet the unduly slow development of the wealth Nature has bestowed upon a new nation.

Financial Policy

The long struggle between Free Trade and Protection was for the time closed by the adoption of the Federal Constitution and the predominance of the Protectionist party in the Commonwealth Parliament. This result was partly due to the need for raising money for Commonwealth purposes by indirect taxation; and the policy has received further help from the steady raising of wages by the Wages Boards and Industrial Arbitration Courts, to be presently described. As wages went on rising, the manufacturers complained they could no longer make a fair profit unless import duties were also raised to enable them to exclude foreign competition. The workmen, already disposed to believe that constant employment and good wages depended on protective tariffs, accepted this view, so a plan was devised under which tariffs, prices, and wages were all to rise together as parts of a comprehensive scheme. This plan has received the name of the New Protection.

"The term 'New Protection' expresses the idea that the protection which the manufacturer receives should be made conditional on his paying what is considered a fair wage to his employees and providing labour conditions otherwise satisfactory. In the view of those who supported this policy, it was considered that the protective tariff might become a shield for trusts and combines, which might reap the benefit of monopoly prices while keeping the 'real' wages of workmen at a low level. The next step was therefore to make legislative provision for the repression of monopolies, and the prevention of 'dumping,' and then to ensure that a protected manufacturer should charge a reasonable price for the products of his factory, and also that the benefits of a protective duty should not be monopolized by the employer, but be shared with his workmen." [1]

Among the Acts passed to give effect to this idea, one, the Excise Tariff Act of 1906, imposed upon agricultural machinery manufactured in Australia one half of the duty chargeable upon similar machinery imported, but provided for the exemption from this duty of such home-made machinery as had been manufactured under conditions either declared to be reasonable by a resolution of both Houses of the legislature, or approved by the President of the Commonwealth Arbitration Court. [2] This Act was, however, pronounced invalid by a decision of the High Court holding that the matter belonged to the States and not to the Commonwealth. But the principles of the New Protection are being to some extent carried out in practice. When wages are raised by a Board or the Court, the manufacturer insists that in order to enable him to pay the higher wage he must be helped by a higher scale of duties. His demand finds favour and the import duty is screwed up accordingly. This adjustment of tariffs to wages in the joint interest of manufacturer and employee has been represented as an attempt to fix the prices at which goods are to be sold, but some of its defenders declare it to be no more than a proper effort to ascertain to just what point duties must be raised in order to enable the manufacturer to obtain a reasonable profit while he pays a reasonable wage. It seems to be no illegitimate development of Protectionist principles.

Europeans may ask why consumers do not complain when they find that in the effort to benefit the working class the price of articles is being constantly raised upon the workers themselves, who are the largest class of consumers and the class on which indirect taxation chiefly presses. The answer seems to be that the consumer, who is also, as a worker,

---

[1] *Handbook for Australia*, p. 468, where a valuable discussion of the whole subject, too long for quotation here, may be found. No proceedings against dumping have in fact been taken. The matter, however simple it may look in principle, proves puzzling in practice.

[2] To leave to Parliament the determination of what were "reasonable conditions" was to impose on it a duty difficult to discharge in an independent and impartial spirit.

a producer, feels, in Australia as in the United States, less interest in what he pays as a consumer than in what he receives as a producer, not because he gains more, for he probably loses more than he gains, but because wages are something direct and palpable, paid into his hand, whereas the higher cost of commodities, being diffused over many small transactions, is not directly felt, and seldom traced to its tariff source. It is nevertheless argued with some force that the New Protection ought to protect the consumer also, and that the fixing of the prices at which protected products should be sold would be a logical extension of the doctrine, if this proved practically workable, and could be done under the Federal Constitution.[1]

State aid to the producer is in Australia given also in the form of bounties upon the products of some industries. "The Bounties Act 1907, the Manufacturers Encouragement Act 1908, and the Shale Oil Bounties Act 1910, in providing for the encouragement of certain industries, provide also for the refusal or reduction of a bounty if the production of a commodity is not accompanied by the payment to the workers employed in that production of a fair and reasonable rate of wage."[2]

The most conspicuous instance of bounties was the large subvention paid to the sugar planters of Queensland for the maintenance of that industry, now that in pursuance of the "White Australia policy" they are forbidden to use the cheap labour of aborigines from the Pacific Islands. In response to this demand not only was the duty on imported sugar raised, but a large bounty also was granted.[3] Given the will to maintain a "hothouse industry" and the resolve to have neither Kanaka labour nor that of immigrants invited from Southern Europe (who would, indeed, if they came, soon insist on an Australian rate of wages), this was the obvious course that remained. Bounties on the iron and kerosene oil industries are given on the ground that other-

[1] What is said in the text about legal enactments regulating trade and labour is to be taken as referring generally to the facts as they stood in 1913, when things were fairly normal. I have not found it possible to keep abreast of the changes, legal and economic, that have come to pass since that year, and conditions were, of course, abnormal during the Great War and for some time afterwards.

[2] *Federal Handbook*, p. 471.

[3] This has now ceased.

wise they would go to the ground. Kerosene was an article
so generally consumed that it would have been unpopular to
raise the price, so the solitary producing company was encouraged to go on producing by the gift of 2d. a gallon up
to £50,000, as otherwise foreign competition would have
stopped local production.[1]

LEGISLATION ON LABOUR CONDITIONS

The policy of safeguarding by law the health and comfort of persons employed in factories and workshops, and of
limiting the hours of labour for women, with limits of hours
and age for young persons, was adopted from Great Britain
before the advent of the Labour party, and needs no special
notice here. The eight hours' day for adult males was established by custom, though in some States laws also deal
with these matters, prescribing holidays and fixing the hours
at which shops must be closed. The extension of legal compulsion to working hours in such occupations as those of sea-
men and household or farm servants, and to places of public
entertainment, has raised difficulties. A guest arriving in
the later part of the evening in any hotel, except a large
one where several shifts of servants are kept, finds it hard to
get served. The restriction of employees to the special kind
of work covered by their trade union makes it illegal for a
farm servant to groom a horse.

In some States a minimum wage has been fixed by statute.[2]
No great opposition was made, even by those who objected to
the principle, because the argument that everybody ought to
be paid enough to support a family in tolerable comfort was
deemed irresistible.

TRADE DISPUTES AND THE FIXING OF WAGES

The significant feature of the Australian methods of dealing with these questions, now of the greatest gravity in all

[1] See Turner, *First Decade of the Australian Commonwealth*, p. 303.

[2] It was originally fixed in New South Wales at four shillings a day,
but this was not meant to be necessarily a living wage, that being left
to be settled by the Arbitration Courts from time to time. A prominent
politician once said that a minimum wage of seven shillings a day was
" fixed like the law of gravitation."

industrial countries, is that they apply compulsion to disputes which everywhere else except in New Zealand and since 1917 in Norway (possibly now in other countries also) are left to be settled by a trial of strength between the parties.

The Treatment of Industrial Disputes.— Few countries had suffered more from strikes during the later years of the nineteenth century than had Australia. The frequent defeats of the striking Unions, the losses resulting to both parties, the accompanying disorders, and the ill-feeling which strikes and lock-outs left behind, together with the failure of methods of conciliation, and finally the example of New Zealand, disposed the wage-earners to advocate the principle of compulsory arbitration as a means of raising wages preferable to the strike. After much discussion, two methods were devised, Wages Boards for fixing the rate of wages and hours of work in particular industries, and Courts of Conciliation and Arbitration for investigating and determining particular disputes between employers and employed.

A Wages Board is, in the five States wherein it exists, a body consisting of an equal number of persons chosen by the employers in any particular industry, and of persons chosen by the workers in the same industry, the Chairman, who must not be connected with the industry, being either elected by the other members or appointed by the State Government A Board may be appointed either by the Ministry or (in the case of a new industry) by the Governor in Council. There need not be any dispute either pending or in immediate prospect. Once established, the Board goes on indefinitely, deals with disputes, in the particular industry, as they arise, and has power to review its own decisions. Its function is to fix, for the particular trade it has been appointed to deal with, both wages and hours of labour, but it has no power to determine other questions that may be in dispute. Its decisions apply to the whole of the industry throughout the State, binding the employers to pay and the workmen to work as the Board prescribes. In most States the enforcement of the awards is entrusted to the Factories Department in the State Government.

Courts of Conciliation and Arbitration, also created by statute, exist in New South Wales and West Australia. More important, however, is the Commonwealth Court, established by an Act of 1904, which has been subsequently amended. The chief differences between these Courts and the Wages Boards is that the former are set in motion only by an existing dispute, and deal with that dispute only, whether it covers a single industry or more than one, not (as do the Wages Boards) with the whole body of employers and employed in any given industry. The Commonwealth Court has jurisdiction in those disputes only which extend beyond the limits of a single State. It is presided over by a judge of the High Court, who may be assisted by assessors. Its action is usually invoked by a complaint proceeding either from a trade union on the one side, or an employer or group of employers on the other, but it may also be set in motion by a reference from a State industrial authority, or wherever the Registrar certifies the existence of a dispute. The proceedings, being in the nature of litigation, are judicially handled, but professional lawyers are not admitted to argue unless by consent of both parties, a consent not often given by the Unions.[1] The powers of the Court extend not only to wages and hours, but to all conditions of labour and all questions in dispute, including the employment of Union labour only, or a preference for such labour, or the dismissal of employees. Though the award may not legally cover the whole of an industry in which the dispute has arisen, for some employers may not have in their service members of the Union which has intituted the proceedings, still the number of respondent employers may be so large (in one case it was 200) as to affect the vast majority, and so become virtually a rule for the trade. Very often the action of the Court is able to bring about a compromise, which can then be made, by consent, an award binding the parties.

One of the questions most frequently brought before the Court is that of a minimum wage, and the chief difficulty that had to be faced at the outset was that of finding what that minimum should be. The principle upon which the Commonwealth Court has proceeded is that of " securing to the employee a wage sufficient for the essentials of human existence."

" After ascertaining the proper wages, basic and secondary, it

---

[1] A high authority, head of an Industrial Court, testifies to the great saving of time when lawyers conduct the cases of the parties.

considers any evidence adduced to show that the employer ought
not to be asked to pay such wages. It will consider grounds of
finance, of competition with imports, of unfairness to other workers, of undue increase in prices of the product, of injury to the
public, etc., etc." [1]

The tendency both of the Wages Boards and of the Courts
has been to raise wages, but as prices have risen from other
causes, it is doubtful whether legal regulation has done more
than regularize and somewhat accelerate the process, and
though an increase in wages need not necessarily result in
increased prices, still in many industries the employers have
been able (through trade associations and by other means)
to pass on to consumers a considerable proportion of the increased amount of their wages bills. The suspicion that in
this way part of the benefit of increased wages is lost naturally suggests to the wage-earners that what they are gaining
is a nominal rather than a real increase. [2]

There is much difference of opinion in Australia as to the
comparative merits of Wages Boards and Courts of Arbitration. Some prefer the former, because they cover the whole
of a trade and are composed of experts; and it is alleged
that as they come into being before a dispute has arisen, they
can anticipate disputes and settle points with less friction
than when those points are already in sharp issue. On the
other hand, the Courts have the advantage of a wider range,
covering every kind of controversy; they can proceed upon
general principles, and the judge soon acquires experience in
the questions that recur. Moreover, where a dispute ex-

---

[1] I quote from an instructive article in the *Harvard Law Review* for
November 1915 by the President of the Court (Mr. Justice Higgins),
in which the principles on which the Court acts, the mode of applying
those principles, and the results so far attained, are set forth with
singular clearness and fairness. Those who are interested in the subject are recommended to consult this article, and a later one by him
in the same *Review* (volume for 1919).

[2] " While the percentage of wages paid on the total value of the output
of manufacturing industries increased between 1908 and 1912 from 19.08
to 21 per cent, the percentage available for interest, depreciation, other
charges, and profit also increased uniformly from 16.5 in 1908 to 17.9
in 1911, though it decreased slightly (to 17.2) in the following year,
showing that, in spite of the increased wages, the percentage available for interest, etc., had increased. Available evidence, therefore, indicates that the effect of the legislative control of wages and conditions
of labour has been of benefit both to wage-earners and employers."—
Federal Handbook (*ut supra*), p. 478.

tends beyond one State, some authority higher than that of a State is needed.

Few allegations of prejudice or unfairness have been charged against either the Courts or the Boards. Their wish to bring about peace is admitted. The Commonwealth Judge, whose decisions have been most closely watched and frequently canvassed, has generally, though not quite invariably, ordered a rise in wages, but this action seems to have had, no doubt with exceptions, the support of public opinion, and it must be remembered that the cost of living had even before the Great War been rising. Though it was at first the Unions that invoked the Court, the employers having become less suspicious than they were, sometimes set the Court in motion. The most humane and liberal among them often welcome a decision which, when it applies practically to the whole trade, screws up the men of harder hearts or more niggling minds to the level which these better men hold to be wholesome for themselves and the community. The employing class taken generally would rather have been left without the Court, but do not ask its abolition; and the growth of prosperity up to 1914 showed that the system of compulsory wage-fixing had not caused an industrial set-back.[1]

As in Europe and in America the bulk both of employers and of employees have hitherto agreed in deprecating recourse to compulsion for the settlement of labour disputes, a word may be said as to the reasons which enabled Australian workmen to enlist public opinion in its favour. Europeans deem it open to three chief objections. One is the interference with freedom of contract. Australians care nothing for that. They would call it a theoretical objection. The workers thought that compulsion would help them, and it did help them, for though wages would doubtless have risen anyhow, much strife might have been needed to secure the rise.[2] A second is that the matter is not strictly judicial, but rather

[1] A well-informed Australian friend, not belonging to the Labour party, wrote to me in 1912: "Whatever may be said in detraction of the system of legal regulation of wages, it is undeniable that at no time in the history of Australia has the general level of return on capital been higher than it is at present or has been during the last few years."

[2] A Labour organ wrote in 1914: "Compulsory arbitration, in Labour's conception of it, is an instrument of progress, a means for bringing about, without violent dislocations of the social fabric, a more equal distribution of wealth."

for the discretion of the Court (an argument like that used
against the jurisdiction of the English Chancellor in the sixteenth century), and that as there is no general rule to guide
the Court, different judges may apply different principles.
And, thirdly, it is urged — this point being strongly pressed
by Australian employers — that the method operates unequally upon the two parties to a dispute.[1] The employer
can be compelled to pay certain wages so long as he keeps
his factory open, and he can escape liability only by closing
it, whereas the individual workman cannot be compelled to
work. The power given to the Court to meet this difficulty
by fining the Union has not proved effective. In the earlier
days, the awards were usually obeyed, but it is to be remembered that they have almost always prescribed a rise in
wages. The gravest test will come when, in less prosperous
times, workmen are denied some increase they ask for, or employers begin to ask for a reduction. In 1912 the system
was working more smoothly than had been predicted. Recent accounts are less satisfactory. The Court still does excellent work in many of the main disputes; but it is alleged
that when a strike has been compromised by an award con-
ceding part of what was asked, another strike soon follows to
obtain the rest of the demand, and that this process often
repeated produces constant unrest. The frequent delays in
the proceedings of the Wages Boards, the inevitable technicality of some of the rulings in the Courts, give rise to irritation. Strikes have not ceased, and some have attained
alarming dimensions. In 1916 there were in various places
506 separate strikes, in one of which the (then Labour)
Government surrendered, through the agency of a Commission, to the Unions in a strike entered on in defiance of the
Act providing for adjudication by the Court. This gave a
shock to the authority of the law. The Unions have sought
to widen the range of the Commonwealth Court by so amending the Constitution as to give it jurisdiction over all disputes arising anywhere in the country. On the other hand,
that extreme section of the wage-earners, sometimes described
as Syndicalists, who call themselves the Industrial Workers
of the World (I.W.W.), denounce all peaceful methods for
settling trade disputes, since they desire to overset by gen-

[1] See as to this *Harvard Law Review* (*ut supra*), pp. 33 and 37.

eral strikes the whole industrial, or so-called " capitalistic,"
system as it now exists.[1]

A review of the compulsory system as worked during the
last fifteen years points to the conclusion that its failure to
prevent strikes has been due to two causes, first, that as there
could not be finality in the awards, the temptation to the
Union leaders to make fresh demands soon after a rise in
wages had been secured kept up irritation and uncertainty,
and secondly that there was no means of compelling the
wage-earners to comply with the awards. An eminent Australian of long experience has written: " The introduction
of penalties in the form either of imprisonment or of fine,
is an illusory protection. If the organizations concerned are
reasonable and imbued with a spirit of obedience to the
spirit and letter of the Law, neither imprisonment nor any
other sanction is necessary. If the organization is strong,
aggressive, and unreasonable, the threat of fine or imprisonment will not be a deterrent." [2]

One result of the legal regulation of wages, and of the attempts at a legal regulation of prices also, has been to bring
the employers in every industry into closer relations with
one another. They are made respondents together in proceedings taken by Unions to obtain higher wages or better
conditions. They are forced into frequent conferences and
combinations, and thus a sense of class interest is strengthened, and occasion given for those " friendly agreements "
and " honourable understandings " in respect of prices and
distribution which excite much displeasure in Labour circles.
Those of the Labour leaders, however, who look forward to
the nationalization of all property and all industries, probably regard with satisfaction whatever makes against the old
individualism, even if in the meantime it induces those
" combines " which in Australia, as in America, are objects
of public aversion. The completeness of the organizations
on both sides makes for strife, just as the possession of great
armaments disposes nations to war. As employers leagued

---

[1] In 1895, when in charge of a measure brought into Parliament to
deal with the matter, I found British working men just as generally opposed to a compulsory settlement of trade disputes as were employers,
and this seems to be still the attitude of both parties.

[2] *Australia, Problems and Prospects* (published in 1919), p. 36, by
Sir Charles Wade (now a Judge of the Supreme Court of New South
Wales).

together harden themselves for defence, so trade union secretaries feel that they must justify their existence by making fresh demands: young men come into office in the Unions, and throw the militant Australian spirit into each fresh contest. Unceasing controversies create an atmosphere of disquiet and suspicion.

Want of space prevents me from pursuing this subject here, but a further discussion of the working of a similar system will be found in the chapter on New Zealand. Though in both countries the application of compulsion illustrates the tendency of the Labour party to extend the power of the State into new fields, a disposition common to all who think they can use that power for their own purposes, it must be understood that the public opinion of Australia as a whole, alarmed by the mischief which strikes were doing, and sympathizing with the desire of the wage-earners for a larger share of the products of labour, was generally favourable to the experiment. In 1919, though it had not satisfied the hopes it had at first raised, there were only two sets of extremists who would abolish it, the most rigid employers who dislike any interference with business, and the revolutionary Communists who wish to make an end of capitalism either by force of arms or by stopping the whole machinery of production and compelling capitalist governments to surrender.[1]

GOVERNMENTAL INDUSTRIES

The entrance of the State into the field of industry as an employer has been supported by various arguments, some of them but distantly related to the real motives. Can it not by appropriating to itself the profits on vast national undertakings which would otherwise be absorbed by the rich, and by taking to itself the control of the making or selling of the articles in which a monopoly is being created, relieve the people from the pressure of monopolies or " trusts " (to use the American term), benefit the workers by providing employment when work is scarce, and by paying good wages, set an example other employers will have to follow? To

[1] As these pages are passing through the press cablegrams from Australia state that a measure is pending in the Commonwealth Parliament for materially altering the constitution and functions of the Arbitration Court, and creating another body for settling disputes.

those who cherish Collectivist ideals, it seems to provide the easiest, because the least startling, approach to that absorption by the community of all the means of production and distribution which is the ultimate goal of their hopes.

It is not, however, to any Collectivist views that the State ownership of Australian railways is to be ascribed. That was the natural result of the economic conditions which existed when lines began to be built. Nothing could be expected from private enterprise, for there was little capital in the country, nor was it then easy for private persons to obtain large loans in England, so the duty devolved on a public authority of providing directly, or by way of subsidy, those means of communication which were indispensable to the development of the country. The States assumed the duty. 21,181 miles of government lines were open for general traffic in 1918, besides 1241 miles similarly open but under private control, four-fifths of which were in Queensland, West Australia, and Tasmania.[1] For a long time the railway administration remained in the hands of Ministries and the general managers they appointed, but political interference and favouritism were at last found so harmful that in each State control was transferred to Commissioners appointed by the Governor in Council (*i.e.* the Ministry). In New South Wales and Victoria there are three Commissioners, in the other States one only.

In every State the Minister for railways still directs legislation and answers questions in the legislature; otherwise the Commissioners have a free hand, though ministers can dictate the general policy to be followed, being in this respect subject to an embarrassing parliamentary criticism, for every member can bring forward any grievance a constituent, most frequently an employee, puts before him, and the unceasing pressure for higher wages is hard to resist. Railway construction is in some States assigned to the Commission, in others to the Public Works Department. Except in respect of the inconveniences arising from the existence of five different gauges, the railway system is worked with fair efficiency. Management is honest and the traffic grows. The

[1] Between 1912 and 1917 a trans-Australian railway 1051 miles long, connecting South Australia with Western Australia through a region largely uninhabited, was constructed.

general result shows a very small balance of profit after deducting from earnings the cost attributable to construction, equipment, loans, and working expenses.

Public management has its drawbacks when politics come in, as Australia has seen before and may see again. But there are also evils incident to the private ownership of those great lines of transportation which control the commerce of a country and hold in their hands the fortunes of large districts. From these evils the United States and Canada, and (in a less degree) France also, have suffered.

The undertaking by the State of industries usually left to private enterprise has been due to various causes. Besides the desire to secure good conditions of labour for the workers, there has been put forward the need for checking monopolies. This was made the ground for starting Government brick-works, when it was alleged that a ring of brickmakers was trying to secure exorbitant prices. So in West Australia the Government undertook the transport of beef to defeat the plans attributed to a " Beef Ring," and started a line of steamers to resist a Shipping Combine. The New South Wales Government recently opened a mine at Lithgow.[1] Some coal-mines have been acquired because the industry was deemed to be of national importance, and had frequently suffered from strikes, the miners being largely influenced by extremist propaganda. Australian opinion on the subject is still in a fluid state. While cautious men confine themselves to proposing to regulate by law industries in which sweating exists or monopolies threaten public welfare, the more advanced school seeks the extension of government action as a step towards Communism, and has carried in gatherings of the Labour party a demand for the " nationalization of basic industries." The same issues that perplex Europe are being pondered in Australia.

A very high and universally respected Australian authority wrote to me as follows : " With regard to those great services which stand out as fundamentals of the life of a civilized community, a time of comparative quiet should be chosen for proposing special legislation. Some means of direct control,

[1] In 1917 a Fire Insurance Office was set up by the Labour Government of Queensland, and employers were required to effect insurances for workmen's compensation either with the Government office or with private offices licensed by the Government. No licenses were issued.

by the Board of Trade or other body in which employers will
have a say, of freights, fares, wages, and working conditions
will be necessary. If some real and not illusory representation is given to the men, accompanied with powers of continual inspection and publication (if thought desirable) of
results, then but not otherwise will it be practicable to carry
and enforce provisions making strikes in these services an
offence against the law. . . . The fetish of trade secrecy
must not be permitted." [1]

It is no less difficult than important to ascertain the actual
results of the State assumption of industries. Some sections of State employees certainly gain in having better wages,
and all gain in greater security for employment. But what
of the community at large? Is the work efficiently done,
and done as cheaply as it would be on a system of private
employment? My stay in Australia was not long enough to
enable me to probe the matter to the bottom, and some of my
informants may have been biassed. But such evidence as
I obtained went to show that, in proportion to the wages paid,
less work was done than private employers obtained. The
workers were said to do as little as they well could. " The
Government stroke " has passed into a byword. " They
dropped the tools the moment the hour came for stopping,"
because " the slower the work goes, the more of it remains
to be done." One informant not hostile to the Labour party
remarked that the systematic practice of slack working to
make every job last long had a bad effect on character, because
it prevented men from doing their best. The foreman fears
to keep the men up to the mark, or to dismiss them, because
they may appeal to their Union, and the Union can influence
the member of the Legislature for the district, and he in turn
the Executive Government.[2] If a Labour Ministry is in

---

[1] In Australia, as in England, the possibility of granting to the workers some share in the management of industries, as well as in profits,
is beginning to be considered as its importance deserves.

[2] Sir C. Wade observes, *ut supra*, p. 45: " In Government undertakings laxity in discipline or efficiency was soon manifested by loss instead of profit. . . . As in construction [of works] so in the administration of Government Departments political interference should be
avoided. Experience shows that if a strike takes place in a Government
establishment, Ministerial intervention is enforced and a concession
made to the strikers. The Government position is always difficult. If
the Ministry resist the demands, votes may be imperilled; if they yield,
discipline may be threatened."

power, it cannot resist Labour pressure. Some of my informants declared that these things were notorious in the case of the great irrigation works undertaken by New South Wales and Victoria. Grievances real or fancied are constantly brought up in Parliament, wasting its time and lessening the authority of those who direct the work. When complaints accumulate, a Commission of Enquiry may be appointed, with further expenditure of time and money, and no relief of the disquietude. It is alleged that where Government owns the wharves, the workers, though paid twice as much per ton for loading and unloading as the ordinary market rate, loiter over their work to prolong it.

The Unions, practically controlling the Government whenever a Labour ministry is in power, are both employers and employed, and it is natural that where considerations of State business interest come into opposition with personal and political self-interest, State business interest should go to the wall. Some one has summed up the Labour policy as "more wages for shorter hours: less work, and more amusement."

The Australian idea seems to be that instead of setting out to get work done and paying wages for it, Government should set out to pay wages and find work as a reason for the payment.

State employment is an easy way towards this goal, and has been accompanied by the virtual acceptance, in some States, of the liability of the Government to find work for persons unemployed. The logical development of this policy will obviously be the absorption by Government of the means of production and distribution, a development contemplated by most of the Labour leaders, though by not very many of the followers, and by a still smaller proportion of those who, though not wage-earners, support the party by their votes, in the hope that it will better their condition. In all progressive or aggressive parties there are some who are hotter, some cooler, some who have clear, others muddled minds, some who fix their eyes on a distant goal and march steadily towards it, others for whom one step at a time is enough. The rank and file of the Labour party are not yet Socialists in the common acceptation of the term, but (to adapt a phrase of Aristotle's) " though they are not Socialists, they do the acts of Socialists." When a French observer had called them Socialists " *sans doctrine,*" another answered, " Say rather *sans declaration,*" but if that phrase suggests that they conceal their views it applies only to a minority. Socialist doctrine may grow, but at present they are divided not only as to aims but as to methods, for a section, stronger by youthful vehemence than by numbers, despises constitutional action, seeking, by frequent strikes and the use of violence in strikes, to overthrow the capitalistic system, while the more moderate elders complain that the recklessness of their young friends retards instead of hastening progress.[1]

Privileges for Trade Unionists.— Even before the creation of a Labour party it had been a prime aim of the leaders of the working men to strengthen the Trade Unions by drawing into them as many as possible of the workers. This was then desired for the sake of success in strikes, for the employers always fought a strike by bringing in non-Unionist labour (those who are in England called " black-legs " and in Australia " scabs ") to take the place of the strikers. After Labour parties in the legislatures arose, there was a further advantage to be expected from the growth of the voting power of the Unions, for they form the basis of the party organization, so efforts were made to prescribe membership of a Union as a condition for Government employment. Another plan was to provide in the awards of Wages Boards and Courts of Arbitration that a preference should be accorded to Union men in the competition for work. This issue, warmly debated when the first Compulsory Arbitration Act was before Parliament in 1904, and again when an amending Act was passed in 1910, was settled by a provision leaving to the Court a discretion to direct that prefer-

[1] When in 1919 the extreme Socialist (Marxian) party launched a scheme (similar to that of the I.W.W. of America) for the creation of one all-embracing union of Australian workers,— popularly called the O.B.U. (One Big Union),— in order to organize general strikes and reach its ends by revolutionary methods, strong opposition came not only from the moderate Labourists in general but from the powerful Union called the A.W.U. (Australian Workers' Union), which includes the bulk of the rural workers, and also from the politicians of the Labour party. See as to this *Round Table,* Nos. for June and for September 1919.

ence should be given to Unionists, " whenever it is necessary
for the prevention or settlement of the industrial dispute, or
for the maintenance of industrial peace, or for the welfare
of society." It would appear that such awards have been
sometimes revised, so as to add, as a condition, that admission to Unions shall be open, as some have been accused of
closing their doors against applicants, or of limiting the
number of apprentices. A third part of the Labour policy
is to restrict to the Unions the right to bring employers before the Arbitration Courts. When the Industrial Peace
Act was being discussed in the Queensland Legislature in
1912, it was opposed by the Labour members because it
omitted this restriction. The tramway strike of 1911 in
Brisbane had arisen from a demand that only Union men
should be employed. Though the number of members of the
Unions — estimated in 1910 at about one-tenth of the total
number of workers — has largely increased under the aforesaid provision for preference and through constant struggles
with employers, there are still trades in which they constitute a minority of persons employed.

In 1905 the Commonwealth Ministry of the day, then
receiving the support of the Labour party, passed, at its
instance, in a Trade Marks Act a section prescribing a so-
called " Union Label," to be affixed to goods wholly manufactured by members of Trade Unions. This section was
two years later declared invalid by the High Court, not only
because such a label was not a trade-mark in the ordinary
sense the term had when the Constitution was enacted, but
also because it attempted to extend Federal action beyond the
powers granted.

A request was seen in the Federal Labour platform of
1908 which included as a plank, " Arbitration Act amendment to provide for preference to Unionists," while the Australian " Liberal Union " platform of 1912 contained the
two following sections, which seem designed to pledge its
members to a different doctrine, viz.: " To maintain the
right of all men and women to work and enjoy the fruits of
their thrift and industry, and to secure equal opportunities
for all to do so," and " to oppose preference to, or the
penalizing of, any section of the community, whether as
employers or employees."

PROPOSED LABOUR AMENDMENTS TO
FEDERAL CONSTITUTION

There remains another important issue, raised by the Labour party, that of amending the Federal Constitution so as to enlarge the powers of the Commonwealth Government. Two currents of opinion have brought the party to this conclusion and proposal. The first is the desire to extend the jurisdiction of the Arbitration Court to deal with all industrial disputes wherever arising. The second is the wish to enact uniform legislation in the interests of Labour over the whole continent. A third aim is to get rid of the Legislative Councils which are the strongholds of conservatism in the States, and thereby to complete the sovereignty of universal suffrage. Every party, when it finds itself in a majority, desires to use its power drastically, doing all it can while it can, for the mere possession of overwhelming strength is an incitement to put it forth in action.

The Federal Constitution had left to the States legislation relating to commerce, industry, and labour disputes within their respective limits, while authorizing the Commonwealth to regulate foreign and interstate commerce, and to provide for the settlement of Labour disputes extending beyond the frontiers of any one State. When objects which it had been sought to effect by Commonwealth legislation proved unattainable because the laws had been pronounced by the High Court to be *ultra vires,* the only means of effecting those objects was by amending the Constitution. Thereupon the Labour Government of 1910 brought forward and passed through Parliament two amendments, extending the power of the High Court to deal with Labour disputes wherever arising, authorizing the Commonwealth Parliament to legislate on the conditions of labour and industry generally, including combinations and monopolies, and enabling the Commonwealth to carry on any industry which each House might declare to be the subject of a monopoly. These proposals, rejected by a popular vote in 1911 by a large majority were, when resubmitted in 1914, again rejected by a smaller majority on a larger vote, the difference being possibly in part due to the fact that this second voting coincided with a general election at which the Labour party gained a

victory.[1] To secure the fair consideration of any alteration of the Constitution, it ought to be put separately before
the people. The War having interrupted the further testing of public opinion, proposals for making particular
amendments to the Constitution have now passed into the
wider question of undertaking a general revision of that
instrument, especially for the purpose of readjusting the relations of the Commonwealth to the States. If this task is
to be undertaken,— and there seems to be a growing feeling
that it has become necessary,— it would be best committed
to a Convention specially chosen for the purpose, a plan
which American experience commends.

The conditions which ought to determine the allotment of
powers between a National Government and State Governments have changed in our time through the swifter means
of transportation, and consequent increase in internal trade,
and with the growth of huge incorporated companies operating all over a large country. Economically, therefore, there
is a case for enlarging Federal powers. But political considerations point the other way, for local needs and conditions require local treatment, and are better understood and
dealt with where local public opinion controls the legislature
than by a Parliament of the nation. Queensland is to some
extent, Western Australia and Tasmania to a greater extent,
cut off from the other States, and each has problems not always the same as theirs. Men can show in the local legislature those qualities which fit them for the wider parliamentary arena; experiments in legislation or administration can
be tried on a small scale, the other States watching the results
and profiting thereby. The same passion does not rage with
equal force over a whole country when it is checked by the existence of local divisions, even as in a large lake cut up into
smaller patches of water by numerous islands scattered over
its surface the waves run less high and subside more quickly
than happens where one whole unbroken sheet is swept by a
mighty blast. Local legislatures stimulate local political life,
and give a variety to political thought. The existence of the
States constitutes a certain check on the power of demagogues
and the vehemence of any popular impulse. To entrust the
destinies of the continent to one parliament and one set of

[1] Cf. *Federal Handbook*, p. 576.

ministers would throw on Australian statesmen a burden they may not yet be able to bear, and involve risks of a hasty action which might imperil the future.

If there is less respect in Australia for the Federal Constitution as a fundamental instrument than existed in the United States from the time of Washingon till the end of last century, this is due not merely to the fact that it is still young, but also to the dominance of issues which are the same all over the country. That which is called in America " States' Rights " sentiment is observable chiefly among the leaders in the State legislatures, who are attached to their local public life with which their own fortunes are bound up, and in men of the richer class, who are moved quite as much by their fear of the power of Labour as by any constitutional considerations. With the masses who have occasionally returned the Labour party to power theoretical and even practical arguments of a constitutional kind carry no weight. Labour policy covers the whole sky. Its leaders desire to take the shortest path to their goal, and " have no use," as the Americans say, for any checks or restrictions, or, indeed, for any scheme that cuts up political power into fragments.

These remarks are ventured with reference not so much to the aforesaid amendments, which have been dropping into the background, as to the general issue of virtually abolishing the States and giving Australia a Unitary Government like that of New Zealand or Great Britain, an issue raised in the South Australian Labour platform of 1909 under the heading, " Unification of Australian States," and which may again come to the front, though other objects are more immediately desired by the Labour party.

LABOUR POLICY IN OTHER CONSTITUTIONAL QUESTIONS

How far, it will be asked, has the most advanced political thought of Australia moved towards those expedients which radicalism favours in other countries, such as the election of judges, as in most of the American States and in the Swiss cantons, and those methods of direct legislation by the people which are practised in Switzerland and in many American States?

The answer is: Very slightly, because Australian radicalism has not found them necessary. A Queensland Labour Congress (in 1910) passed a resolution demanding "an amendment of the Constitution to deprive the High Court of power to declare unconstitutional bills passed by both Houses of the Federal Parliament," but it does not appear that Labour men generally are committed to such ideas. The introduction of the Initiative and Referendum found a place on the Federal platform of the Labour party in 1908, and is sometimes referred to by their leaders as desirable, but it was not pushed further after the party gained control of the Federal Parliament. In the United States direct popular voting has been widely adopted, first, because the State Legislatures were distrusted; secondly, because the power of the "party machine" had controlled the action of those bodies and delayed legislation which large sections of opinion desired; thirdly, because the faith in popular sovereignty had become a dogma of almost religious sanctity. None of these causes exists in Australia. The legislatures obey the voters and the ministers obey the legislatures so promptly that the people can obtain what they want without their own direct vote, and this is so conspicuously the case as regards the Labour party that it is hard to see what they could gain, so long as their organization does its work effectively, by exchanging for caucus rule the direct rule of the voters, who might act more independently when acting outside the Organization, refusing to obey its dictation upon issues directly submitted to their own personal judgment. Nevertheless, the march of democratic sentiment may ultimately lead Australia into the American path. There is no feeling of respect for the legislatures to deter her, and every people is liable to be attracted by the suggestion that their power will be best exerted directly by themselves.

CHAPTER LII

CHARACTERISTICS OF AUSTRALIAN DEMOCRACY

THE reader who has followed this outline of the trend of Australian legislation, and particularly of the policies of the Labour party, often the chief factor in legislation even when not holding a majority in Parliament, will probably ask, What is the attitude of public opinion towards the questions and schemes now in issue, and what are the characteristics of public opinion itself in Australia? Opinion is not necessarily the same thing as voting power, and may be imperfectly expressed in parliamentary elections or by parliamentary action. Large issues, going down to the foundations of economics as well as of politics in the narrower sense, issues fateful for the future, are being pressed forward in Australia more boldly than elsewhere, perhaps with less realization of their gravity. What is the nation's mind regarding them?

Public opinion is in all countries produced by the few and improved and solidified by the many. If we leave out of account the very few detached thinkers, and the very large number who do not care about public affairs at all, it consists in practice of the aggregate of the opinion of sections, local, or racial, or religious, or ocupational, or politically partisan. National opinion results from the intermixture of these sectional opinions, which on some few subjects coincide, in others modify and temper one another, in others sharpen one another by collision. Since the chief topics on which Australian opinion is practically unanimous, such as a White Australia, and the wish to make Australia a good place for the average man, have been already dealt with, we may go straight to the points on which opinion is sectional rather than general, first noting some facts which influence the formation of Australian opinion.

1. There is no such "leisured class" as exists in most European countries, and is now beginning to exist in North

America. Men rich enough to live at leisure usually either betake themselves to Europe, or continue to be occupied with their estates or their business.

2. There are no racial divisions, the people being almost entirely of British stock. The Irish element, larger than the Scottish, has not been till lately (when questions relating to Ireland began to be raised in New South Wales and Queensland), marked off, except in so far as it is Roman Catholic, from the rest of the population.

3. There are no religious dissensions, though the Roman Church, wherever there is a large Irish element, exerts political power, and has latterly co-operated with the Labour party.

4. There have been no questions of foreign policy, because these were left to the mother country, until in recent years the action of Germany in the Western Pacific Ocean began to cause anxiety.[1]

5. Questions regarding the distribution of political power have been long settled, for universal suffrage obtains everywhere, and the working class is master of the situation. Questions regarding the machinery of government and administration remain, but receive little attention from the people at large, and are discussed, less upon their merits, than as they affect party policies.

6. The matters which occupy the mind of the nation in all classes are accordingly its material or economic interests — business, wages, employment, the development of the country's resources. These dominate politics.

7. There is a love of out-door life, favoured by the climate, and a passion for all kinds of " sport " and competitions — cricket, football, and, above all, horse-racing — matters which overshadow political interests. A great cricket match is a more important event than a change of ministry.

8. Australia has been isolated from the movements of the Old World, and is only beginning to realize that not even so distant a continent can remain unaffected by them. She has thought her experiments could be tried, so to speak, in a closed vessel. Of actual conditions in Great Britain, economic and social, in spite of a real affection as well as a po-

[1] Papua has now become a sort of dependency on Australia, through the mandate given to Australia after she had been recognized as a member of the League of Nations.

litical connection, she knows little more than Great Britain knows of her. I was amazed to find in 1912 how many Australians believed Britain to be a declining and almost decadent country.

9. In point of natural mental vigour, as well as of physical activity and courage and enterprise, the Australians are abreast of any other modern nation. But intellectual interests play no great part in their lives. Theoretical arguments, constitutional or economic, are seldom heard.

10. Patriotism is intense, more self-confident than in older countries, and though compatible with strongly marked social antagonisms, capable of overriding these when a national interest is concerned.

In Australia, considering its vast size, there is singularly little localism in ideas and ways of thinking. Local pride there is, and local jealousies, but that is a different matter. The types of opinion are class types, social or occupational types, not State types, for though each State is chiefly occupied with its own interests and politics there is less difference of character between them than between the four component parts of the United Kingdom. Even in isolated agricultural Tasmania, even in far-off Western Australia, called the most " radical " of the States, the same classes hold everywhere much the same views.

These types are three: that of the wage-earners and the poorer part of the population generally, that of the land-owners and richer part of the commercial class,— merchants, manufacturers, large shopkeepers,— that of the professional men.

The hand-workers, clerks, shop-assistants, persons of limited means, are all educated. Illiteracy is practically unknown. Nearly all are what would be deemed in Europe comfortably off, i.e. they are well fed, well housed, except (to a slight, and rapidly diminishing extent) in some few city slums. " Sweating " practices have been eliminated, and there is no pauperism. Nobody need want, unless he is hopelessly unthrifty or addicted to drink; and drunkenness, once a grave evil, has been greatly reduced of late years. But though educated and blessed with more leisure than their brethren in most parts of Europe, the hand-workers of Australia are, as a rule, uninterested in what are called " the things of the mind," reading little but newspapers and light fiction, and more devoted to amusements, sports, and open-air life, particularly enjoyable in their climate, than the corresponding class in any other equally civilized country. Sunday is recognized as the day of pleasure to an extent unknown elsewhere in the English-speaking world. An Australian said " The sun is the enemy of religion." The average citizen cares less about public affairs than does the average Swiss or (native) American of the same class, and is less theoretically interested in democratic principles than are those two peoples. Civic responsibilities sit lightly upon him : nor does party feeling, except among Socialists, do much to stir his interest. Among the leaders of the Labour party one finds persons of natural shrewdness who understand politics from the practical side, having acquired experience in the management of trade-union affairs ; and there are also some few men of marked intellectual gifts, who have educated themselves by reading, have thought out political projects, and can defend them by argument. But the mass do little thinking for themselves, and take their cue chiefly from their leaders or their newspapers, not out of deference or self-distrust, for they carry independence to the verge of indiscipline, but because, taking no thought for the morrow, they are content to fall in with views that seem to make for the immediate benefit of their class. The same remark applies to the rest of the less wealthy sections, such as clerks and shop-assistants, perhaps even to elementary school teachers and the lower ranks of the civil service, and likewise to that politically unorganized stratum of the middle class, such as small farmers and shopkeepers, which has not gone over to Labourism.

The richer people, pastoralists, merchants, and manufacturers, form a class rather more sharply cut off from the wage-earners than is the like class in Switzerland or Canada or Norway, though it largely consists of those who have risen by business talent, for Australia is a land of opportunity, where talent quickly tells. Among them, too, intellectual interests are not keen ; business and pleasure leave little time for learning or thinking. The commercial man may keep an eye on politics, in order to resist what he considers the attacks made by Labour upon realized wealth ; he may even subscribe to electoral anti-Labour campaigns. But he conceives that he would lose more by neglecting business than he would gain by spending time in defending business from the onslaughts of Labour. From this class there have come some few political leaders of conspicuous capacity, but on the whole, it contributes little either to the practice or the theory of statesmanship, and does not seem to have realized, any more than the leaders of the Labour party, how much thinking is needed if the problems before Australia are to be solved.

The professional class, which includes lawyers, physicians, engineers, clergymen, men of letters, and the teachers in the higher schools, is very small outside the four great capital cities, and within those cities belongs socially to the mercantile class. Some leading politicians not of the Labour party, and several within that party, have been barristers or solicitors. As in all countries living under a Rigid Constitution where a legal instrument defines the respective powers of a superior and an inferior legislature, legal questions arise, which have to be argued in Parliament as well as in courts of law, and these ought to secure an important place for the possessors of judicial learning. But the legislatures contain few such persons. The men of high scientific and literary attainments, who are found among physicians, journalists, engineers, and in the Universities, enrich the mind of the community, but take less part in public affairs than does the corresponding class in the United States, France, or Britain; and they also are most scantily represented in the legislatures. Altogether, the men occupied in study, thinking, and teaching contribute less to the formation of a national opinion than was to be expected, considering that they hold a position less obviously affected by personal interests than do either the rich on the one hand, who are threatened by progressive taxation, or the middle and poorer classes on the other, who desire to pay little to the State and receive much from it. They might therefore, to a larger extent than heretofore, exert a mediating influence between capital and labour, recognizing what there is of reason and justice in the claims of the opposing sections.

There remains that great and pervasive factor in the formation of opinion, the newspaper press, through which each type of doctrine can speak to the others. In Australia it stands high as regards both ability and character. It is above suspicion of corruptibility or black-mailing, is well written, gives an efficient and a generally fair and honest news service, is not, so far as I could ascertain, worked by politicians behind the scenes for their own purposes. It has not (with a few exceptions) lapsed into that vulgar sensationalism and indifference to truth which belong to an increasing number of organs in some older countries. One does not hear of its publishing interviews which put into the mouth of public men words they never used, and refusing to publish contradictions of stories proved to have been false. Australian criticisms of politicians are often bitter, but not more unfair than those to be found in the French or English press. In the later decades of last century, the three or four greatest newspapers in Sydney and Melbourne exercised more power than any newspapers then did in any other country, being at times stronger than the heads of the political parties. Moments are remembered at which they made and unmade ministries. Till the fusion of parties in 1910, the controversies of Free Traders and Protectionists were fought out in their columns, and while they served to enable each party to argue with the other, they exerted a restraining influence on both. The Labour party has had no considerable daily organ in the press, and its victories, won without such an organ against most of the great journals, proved what skilful organization can accomplish. It makes slight use of the newspapers to expound or defend its policies, and their criticisms tell little on its members. Though the working classes in the cities read the papers for the sake of the news, chiefly to be sure for the racing intelligence and athletic sports reports, the rural folk of the "back blocks" usually see only small local papers containing local happenings, so journalism does less than could be wished to help the antagonistic sections to comprehend and appreciate one another's position; nor is this gap filled by the weekly or monthly magazines, which, however, cannot fairly be compared with those of Europe or America, so much smaller is the population which they address.

In Britain and France the legislatures do much to form, clarify, and formulate public opinion. In Australia, though there are seven of them, they do comparatively little.

Neither are there many associations, such as abound in the United States, devoted to the advocacy of particular doctrines or causes.

The types of Australian opinion I have sketched seem to run parallel along the lines of class rather than to blend in a unity within which they are mere variations. Except in matters appealing to patriotic sentiment, there is less of a general national opinion than in the United States and Canada, perhaps less than in Switzerland. In Australia certain elements needed to form breadth and to give variety, or to form a mediating influence between sharply opposing interests, have been wanting. The opinion of the richer sort as well as that of the masses runs in a groove with far too little of a sympathetic interchange of views. Class antagonism divides the people into sections almost as much as such antagonism, coupled with religious enmities, has divided France. Neither social equality nor the standard of comfort, much above that of England, which the workers enjoy, has softened the clash of economic interests. Each section, distrusting the other, sees its own case only, and it is hardly a paradox to say that the more the condition of the wage-earners rises, the more does their dissatisfaction also rise. The miners, for instance, receiving wages undreamt of in Europe, are always to the front in the struggle against employers, whether private companies or the State. Where other distinctions are absent, and a few years can lift a man from nothing to affluence, differences in wealth are emphasized and resented, deemed the more unjust because they often seem the result of chance, or at least of causes due to no special merit in their possessor. The people are gathered into a few large centres, where they lead a restless life, in which leisure means amusement, and there seems to be little time left for anything but business and amusement. Equal in inborn capacity to any other branch of the British stock, they have that want of intellectual curiosity and deficient love of knowledge for its own sake which foreign critics often note in that stock, as compared with the Italians, for instance, or the Celtic peoples, or the Norsemen, so the enjoyment of leisure tends less than was expected either to widen their intellectual interests or to stimulate their sense of civic duty. A distinguished Australian observed to me: "If our people had an intellectual vitality comparable to their physical vitality they might lead the world." All this is doubtless true of most European countries, but it strikes the observer most in Australia, because comfort and leisure have grown faster there than elsewhere. Moreover, leisure from work does not mean quiet and repose, for the life of Australians is preeminently a life in cities. "The world is too much with them." Men love to escape from the lonely inland plains where only the clumps of Eucalyptus break the uniformity of wide-spreading pastures, into the seaports, where ocean breezes cool the summer heat and the excitements of life are most attainable, a fact the more regrettable because along the eastern coast and in the mountains which border it, there are, especially as one approaches the tropics, many charming pieces of scenery.[1] There are, moreover, too few centres in which opinion is made, and these centres are far from one another, so that the leaders of thought in each are not in close touch. Sydney is New South Wales, Melbourne is Victoria, Adelaide is South Australia. Some one has compared these cities, with their "back blocks" of forests and far-stretching grasslands, to Athens dominating and almost effacing her Attica, as Rome did her Campagna, and Carthage her circumambient wheat fields and olive yards. Vast as New South Wales is, one thinks of its thinly peopled rural areas as a mere appendage to Sydney; for it is the urban population which impresses on the State its political character. No similar primacy is yielded to the capital in Britain, where Lancashire or Yorkshire or Scotland contribute as much to national opinion as does London; one must go to Buenos Aires for a parallel. Yet the four Australian cities are less efficient in stimulating thought, and in focussing and criticizing its results, than were city republics like Athens, or than are the greater cities of Continental Europe. Compared to Paris, Vienna, Berlin, Rome, they must needs have with their smaller populations fewer well-informed and powerful minds, but neither have they the intellectual vivacity and variety of those ancient cities which

---

[1] Many travellers in the British Antipodes, struck by the splendid snow mountains, valleys, lakes and fjords, of New Zealand, where the grandeurs of Switzerland are combined with those of Norway, have done less than justice to the quieter beauties of Australia; and few have spoken of its wealth of brilliantly coloured flowers.

like Rhodes, Croton, or Syracuse, did not approach them in point of population. In Australia it is material interests that hold the field of discussion, and they are discussed as if they affected only Australia, and Australia only in the present generation. Nobody looks back to the records of experience for guidance, nobody looks forward to conjecture the results of what is being attempted to-day. There is little sense of the immense complexity of the problems involved, little knowledge of what is now being tried elsewhere, little desire to acquire such knowledge. Yet economic problems are no simpler here than they are in Europe, the chief difference being that errors may not so swiftly bring disaster to a new and naturally rich and thinly peopled country. The average Australian, apt to think first of how a scheme will affect his own household, takes short views and desires quick results. With few data drawn from the past, the past means nothing to him; if he thinks of the future his pride in Australia makes him sure that all will go well.

It has been a political as well as an economic misfortune that an element conspicuous in the Northern United States and Canada is here scantily represented, viz. the occupying owners of small agricultural properties. This element has begun to grow, especially by an increase in the number of dairy-farms co-operating in the making of cheese and butter, but its growth needs to be quickened; it might have grown still faster in the interior had the railway system been better laid out. The rural areas fit for tillage are still insufficiently peopled, for immigrants come slowly, the growth of population is lamentably slender since the birth-rate is extremely low, the drain from the country into the towns, where life has more variety and amusements, seems irresistible. Moreover, the wool-shearers, a considerable section of the rural population, are migratory, not settled in villages but following their work from one sheep-run to another.

It may be thought that a country gains politically by having comparatively few subjects to think about and deal with, as Australia has only domestic and economic questions, with no foreign or ecclesiastical distractions. But is this really so? May it not be that the mind of a nation is stirred and widened when it has other problems to solve besides those that touch its business life? The Australian horizon is nar-

row and politics too much occupied with the consideration of
results directly measurable in money. This may be a reason
why, though all Australians are alike unfettered by theoretical dogmas, alike proud of their country, alike desirous that
it shall be a good place for everybody, classes seem unduly
suspicious of one another, and fix their minds upon those
matters in which interests seem to conflict rather than on
those which all have in common. It was hoped that the
fervour of feeling aroused by the Great War, and the pride
in the dashing valour of Australian regiments, would have
created a sense of national unity drawing classes together.
But this does not seem to have happened.[1] The rich give
scant sympathy to the reasonable aspirations of the workers;
the latter assume the opposition their plans encounter to be
due only to the selfishness of the rich, and themselves betray an exclusive spirit when it is a question of admitting
immigrant workers from England herself.

The Australians do not show in politics that fickleness of
which democracies have been often accused, for many of their
statesmen have through long and chequered careers retained
the loyalty of the masses. But though it is well that a
statesman whose honesty has once won their confidence should
retain it, their indulgent temper is apt to forget misdeeds
which ought to have permanently discredited an offender.
Memories are short, and it might sometimes be well if they
were longer. Tergiversation, and still more severely pecuniary corruption, are censured at the time, yet such sins
are soon covered by the charitable sentiment that " Bygones
are bygones."

Though parliamentary debates are acrimonious, and
though class antagonism prevents men from comprehending
and making allowances for the views of opponents, public
opinion is on the whole kindly, free from bitterness and
rancour against individuals. Here one sees a marked contrast between the English-speaking democracies and those of
the ancient world, where intestine seditions often led to fe-
rocious conflicts, or, as in the later days of the Roman republic, to wholesale proscriptions. The long-settled habit of

---

[1] It has been suggested that this failure to attain the expected unity
may have been partly due to the controversy which arose over the question of compulsory military service and to the way in which that
controversy was handled.

respect for law and the provision of constitutional methods for settling disputes have stood the children of England in good stead. However high the waves of party strife may ever rise, one cannot imagine a time at which such things could happen among them as happened in the Parisian Terror of 1793, or as we have seen happening recently in Eastern Europe. Nor must the traveller omit to note an undercurrent of prudence and self-restraint among the working masses, who are by no means so extreme as many who profess to speak for them. The notion of Direct Action by strikes and the scheme of one all-absorbing combative Union have not won the approval of these masses.

In forming their impressions of what Australia is and does, Europeans and Americans must never forget that the settled parts of this wide Continent have a population less than that of Belgium, with a number of thinkers and writers small indeed when compared with the old and large countries of Europe, and even with such countries as Switzerland and Holland. All these countries, moreover, are in close touch with one another, and profit by one another's writings and practical experiments in statesmanship. Australia lies so far away that, although the best books reach her and the great world events produce their impression, that impression is fainter. No such constantly flowing and bubbling stream of free criticism and debate upon all political and economic issues as one finds in Europe and North America can be expected here, so the stimulus to thinking is less keen and constant. Nor is it fanciful to add that the isolation of this continent has induced a half-conscious belief that it can try its experiments without fear of suffering from the disapproval or competition of the distant peoples of the northern hemisphere. Schemes are the more lightly tried because there is less sense of responsibility and a more confident faith in the power of a new country to make mistakes without suffering for them.

To wind up this survey of Australian conditions let me try to answer two questions — First, What has democratic Australia achieved both in the way of good administration, and by that kind of moral stimulation which, in ennobling national life as a whole, raises the thoughts and enlarges the horizon of individual citizens? Secondly, What conclusions

regarding the merits of popular government does its record
suggest?

The conditions which have affected politics have been already described. There is a homogeneous population, isolated, left free to shape its own institutions and steer its own
course, protected from foreign interference by the naval
power of Britain, to which it is now adding its own, with no
old animosities to forget, no old wrongs to redress, no bad
traditions to unlearn. Inequalities of wealth have grown
up, but there are few monopolists and no millionaires, and
nowhere does wealth exert less influence on legislation or
administration.[1] Social influences count for little or nothing in politics. Australia and New Zealand have provided,
better than any other civilized countries, an open field for
the upspringing of new ideas, new institutions, new political
habits.

Democracy has given the people the thing for which government primarily exists, public order and laws steadily
enforced. Except for the rioting frequent during strikes,
less serious latterly than similar troubles were in 1890, dis-
turbances are rare, and lynch law unknown. Convictions
for serious crime diminished between 1881 and 1912 from
a percentage of 69.3 per 10,000 of population to a percentage
of 26.2, though the police service was certainly no more efficient forty years ago than it is now.[2]

The administration of justice has been in upright and
competent hands, enjoying the confidence of the people.

The permanent Civil Service is honest, diligent, and tolerably capable.

Direct taxation presses pretty heavily upon the richer
people, who, however, seem able to bear it. Indirect taxes,
especially high import duties, affect all classes by raising the
price of commodities, but the consumers do not greatly complain, thinking they recoup themselves as producers. Financial administration is honest, though far from economical.
The public debt, both national and local, was too large for

[1] The only other democracies known to me in which money has counted
for so little in politics are the Orange Free State (as it was before
the war of 1899), Switzerland and Norway, all of them countries in
which there were hardly any considerable fortunes.

[2] Here as elsewhere it seems sufficient to give pre-war figures, because
the conditions from 1914 to 1919 were exceptional.

the population even before 1914, but much of it is represented by assets, such as railways, and it was not, when the Great War came, more than the resources of the country were then enabling it to support.

For education, elementary and agricultural, ample public provision is made, and the four greater States possess excellent universities. Tasmania and Western Australia, both comparatively small in population, are trying to follow. Secondary education has been hitherto less well cared for, and the buildings of the elementary schools need to be improved.

The railways are pretty well managed, and the roads good, considering the difficulties of maintaining them over immense stretches of thinly-peopled country. Public health is duly cared for, and the death-rate low in cities as well as in the country, in some States only ten per thousand. Intemperance has notably diminished, less through legislation than owing to a general improvement in the habits of the people.[1]

Great irrigation works have been undertaken in New South Wales and Victoria, whereby the cultivable area has been increased by many hundreds of square miles. Forestry, however, has been neglected, and little done in the way of replanting in districts where fires have wrought widespread devastation.

The machinery of government works smoothly. Elections are quietly conducted, ballots taken and counted with no suspicion of fraud. Bribery is practically unknown; public meetings less disturbed than in England.

The administration of some government departments is unsatisfactory and often wasteful, not merely from want of skill, but largely because political considerations have weakened disciplinary control and caused high wages to be paid to slack workers.

In the legislatures, as in all legislatures, there is selfishness, intrigue, and factious spirit, but little corruption, and no serious abuses connected with private Bills have arisen, such Bills being indeed few.

Local government has been imperfectly developed, for the difficulties it encounters in the thinly-peopled areas are

---

[1] So far as I could gather, it is not so fertile a source of crime and poverty as in Great Britain, where the failure of Parliament to deal effectively with it has been for many years a serious reproach to democratic government.

obvious, but it is reasonably efficient as well as honest. There is some little jobbery, but only in one or two great cities have scandals arisen.

State industrial enterprises (other than railways), if not conspicuous failures, have not been successes, and do not seem to have so far proved helpful to national progress. They are generally believed to be wastefully managed, with an output below that obtained under private management.

The number and extent of strikes were at first reduced by the system of compulsory arbitration, but they continue to break out from time to time, sometimes spreading widely, and involving heavy losses to all concerned.

Monopolistic and other combinations have scarcely yet become, but might become, a public danger requiring to be restricted by legislation or taken over by the State.

Except in bringing to the front some few Labour leaders of ability, democracy has done less than was expected to evoke talent or to awaken among the masses any keen interest in public matters other than wages and the conditions of labour, nor has it roused members of the richer class to take that active part in public life reasonably expected from educated citizens.

That the standard of comfort is nowhere higher over a whole people, if indeed anywhere so high, as in Australia, that nowhere is life more easy and leisure for amusements so abundant, cannot be set to the credit of democratic government, for it is largely due to the favours of Nature. It has, however, a significant influence on the national mind, encouraging a self-confident optimism which enters bodily on experiments.

Parliamentary debates do little to instruct or guide the people, nor do the legislative bodies inspire respect. There is singularly little idealism in politics.

What are the peculiar characteristics democracy here presents? To what sort of a future development do the existing phenomena point? What are Australia's contributions to the stock of the world's experience? What lessons does it teach fit to be learned, marked, and inwardly digested by those who are constructing popular governments elsewhere?

The Labour party, having in 1911 obtained a majority in both Houses, formed a Ministry and ruled the country

for some years. Thus for the first time in history (apart
from moments of revolution) executive power passed legally
from the hands of the so-called " upper strata " to those of
the hand-workers. Australia and the world saw a new kind
of government of the people by a class and for a class. Instead of the landowners or the richer people governing the
landless or the poorer, the position was reversed : the latter
imposed the taxes and the former paid them. Class government, which democrats had been wont to denounce, reappeared, with the material difference that the governing class
is here the majority, not the minority, of the nation. Yet
this new rule of the working masses showed fewer contrasts
than might have been expected with the old rule of the landed
and moneyed class in England before 1832, or the rule of
the middle class that followed. Hardly any political and
few large economic changes were effected. There was nothing revolutionary. The stream of change continued to flow
in the well-worn channels of parliamentary constitutionalism.
The bulk of the Labour men have not been Socialists, and
few of them extremists in their radicalism. Theoretic doctrines had little charm, and the common-sense moderation of
the majority restrained the impatience of doctrinaires or
fanatics. There was no passion, because there were no
hatreds, no wrongs to avenge, no abuses to destroy, like those
which have often roused ferocity among revolutionaries in
countries that had never known, or had lost, constitutional
government.

The power of a Class party has been built up on a local
and vocational foundation which covers the whole country
with a network of closely knit and energetic organizations,
working incessantly for common aims. These local organizations culminate in a parliamentary caucus in each of the legislatures, State and Federal, which concentrates the full
strength of the party upon its legislative and executive measures. Whenever a Labour party holds power, the parliamentary caucus, itself largely controlled by central Labour
organizations outside the legislatures, supersedes the free action both of representatives and of Executive Ministers, and
thus ministerial responsibility to the electors is for the time
reduced, since it is to the caucus that the Ministers are responsible. This caucus system has not been violent in its

action, but it works in secret, substituting a private conclave for public debate, depriving the people of that benefit
which open discussion coming from both sides was expected
to secure. All this has been made possible by the British
system of parliamentary government, a logical result of the
principle which concentrates power in the majority for the
time being, however small it may be, of the representative
assembly.

The action of State authority, both in limiting freedom of
contract between individuals and in taking over industries
previously left to private persons, has gone further than
in any other democratic country except New Zealand. Australia shows the high-water mark, so far, of collectivistic or
socialistic practice, though with very little of avowed socialistic doctrine. In particular, there has been a further advance than elsewhere towards the provision of employment
by public authority and increasing the payment made for it,
as well as towards the compulsory regulation by State authority of wages and other conditions of labour. This has
been effected not only by direct legislation, but also through
the judicial department of government, which has received
functions partly legislative, partly administrative, that seem
foreign to its normal sphere.

Let me note once more that these changes have been
effected:

Without violent party struggles or breaches of the peace.
" All things have been done decently and in order."

Without attacking the institution of private property as
an institution, or doing any conspicuous injustice to individuals.

Without, so far, seriously affecting the prosperity of the
country.

Without, so far, reducing the individual energy and self-
helpfulness of the Australian people.

It need hardly be said that the time during which these
novelties have been in operation has been too short, and the
scale of their operation too small, for any change in this last-
mentioned direction to become manifest. The present generation grew up under an individualistic system. They are
the children of the bold and enterprising pioneers who first

explored and settled the country. It may be forty or fifty years before the results of State control and State socialism can be estimated.

The evidence I gathered enables me to say no more than this, that the results so far obtained do not encourage the extension of the experiments tried, and that these results are due to tendencies permanently operative because inherent in human nature, known long ago and likely to appear wherever a democracy may embark on similar policies.

Happily exempt from many causes of strife that have distracted Europe, Australian legislatures have been busy with land questions and the respective claims of squatters and " free selectors," with tariffs, with taxation, with such industrial subjects as strikes, wages, and conditions of labour — all of them matters which touched not the imagination or the heart, but the pocket, and which were discussed not on grounds of economic principle, but as bringing gain or loss to some one class or group in the community. They were important but not inspiring themes. Chatham once enthralled a listening senate when he spoke of sugar; and silver once roused frantic enthusiasm at an American Presidential election. But the men and the occasions that can work these wonders come rarely. They have not come in Australia. Though its politics have not been dull, for they have been strenuous and changeful, they have been prosaic. What room for idealism among tariffs, trade marks, and land taxes? Patriotism no doubt there has been, a patriotism proud of the strength, the self-reliance, and the prosperity of Australia, and which glowed with bright hues when in 1914 the youth of Australia volunteered to fight in Europe not for Australia only, but also for a cause in which the fortunes of the world were involved. But this patriotism, this vision of a great Australia, Queen of the Southern seas, belonged to a different sphere from that of politics and did not tell upon the politicians. Thus there has been a sort of commonness in political life, a want of that elevation of spirit and that sense of dignity in conduct that should belong to men charged by their fellow-citizens with the affairs of a nation growing rapidly to greatness.

It might have been supposed that in such conditions of

political life the standard of honesty would have declined, and many Australians say this has happened. But though the air of Australian politics has neither an ennobling nor an intellectually bracing quality, it is not, broadly speaking, corrupt nor corrupting, While in playing the party game against adversaries every advantage that the rules permit is taken, it rarely happens that a statesman abuses his position for his own private profit. Constituencies are not bought, nor are newspapers; the permanent Civil Service is upright: one hears less said about the pernicious power of money than in any other democracy except Switzerland.

No one would desire that causes of strife such as those which made politics exciting in England and France during the nineteenth century should exist in any country merely for the sake of stimulating men's minds to higher flights than the conflict of material interests has produced. As well desire war because it gives opportunities for heroism and supplies themes for poetry. But there are human aspects in which material interests may be regarded that have failed to receive due consideration in Australia. There might have been more sympathy on the one side and on the other more comprehension of the difficulty of economic reconstruction, and on both sides an attempt to reconcile the claims of different classes in the spirit of a wide-minded philanthropy, together with a keener appreciation of the need for adjusting legislation to habits and motives that are a part of human nature.

What light do the facts here set forth throw upon the probable future of government in Australia?

The longer a man lives, the more is he surprised at the audacity of prophets, of the foretellers of evil no less than of the visionary enthusiasts of progress. I can well remember the gloomy forecasts in which not only European travellers but Americans themselves indulged in 1870 when they contemplated the political evils which then afflicted the United States, and which made municipal administration, and in some States the judicial bench itself, a byword and reproach among the nations. Most of those evils have now disappeared. Never despond: unexpected good arrives as well as expected evil. Less than twenty years ago a friendly and very intelligent French observer [1] predicted that if things continued in Australia to follow the course they were then taking, capital would disappear, the spirit of enterprise would be destroyed, employers would be terrorized, confidence would vanish, and at last there would come a revolution. Things have continued to follow the same course, at an accelerated pace, but none of these calamities seems appreciably nearer. Those who hold that certain economic laws operate as inevitably as the laws of nature are entitled to say that some of the causes already at work will produce certain effects, if conditions remain the same. But conditions never do remain quite the same, and who can tell which of them will change, and in what direction? Much may happen in Australia, a land which has seen many changes since 1890. Parties may break up; their tenets may be developed in one or another direction. In English-speaking countries parties are less fissiparous than in continental Europe, yet they are from time to time rent by differences of doctrine or by the rivalries of leaders. The caucus system, though it has given less offence to the general public than might have been expected, might by abusing its power induce a reaction, lose the confidence of sections among its supporters, and collapse. The secret of the effectiveness attainable by a pledge binding every member of a Parliamentary party, discovered by the Irish party in the House of Commons under the leadership of C. S. Parnell, was most successfully used, yet that party broke in two before his death, though national sentiment, the main factor in its cohesion, had remained unbroken. So a caucus system like that of Australian labour may be loosened if new issues arise, if mistakes discredit the leaders, if personal jealousies drive in a wedge of disunion and break up the party into sections.[2] Some observers expect a popular disappointment with paternalism, and a recoil from it should the defects continue which the management of governmental undertakings have shown.

The plan of raising wages by law, and then proceeding to raise duties on imports in proportion to the rise in wages, cannot go on indefinitely. It is possible, though hardly prob-

---

[1] M. Voisson in his book *La Nouvelle Australie;* M. Biard d'Aunet, in his *L'Aurore Australe,* is almost equally pessimistic.

[2] Signs of such schisms were visible in 1920.

able, that, before the limit has been reached, large further advances may have been made towards the supersession of private enterprise through the absorption by the State of a constantly increasing number of industries. The question of wages would then pass into a new phase; for when most of the workers are paid directly by the State, they can fix their own wages through their control of the legislative machinery, voting to themselves whatever wages they please. To make up what the State would lose by the difference between expenditure on wages and the value of the product of labour, further progressive taxation would be needed, if there were fortunes left to bear it.

Other possible economic changes lie in the lap of the future. A succession of dry seasons might bring bad times for all classes, with results unpredictable in their effect upon present labour policies.

Constitutional development, which, though perceptible only at intervals, is unceasing, being indeed as unavoidable in States as are growth and decay in a tree, may show new forms. Representative government, transplanted from the mother country, lost its old character when power passed from Parliament as a whole to the parliamentary caucus, and even from that caucus itself to a body standing outside and controlling the caucus, the Trades' Hall. A demand for the direct action of the voters by the Initiative and Referendum, devices which have won favour in the United States and Switzerland, might then arise. The Australian Labour leaders have hitherto been satisfied with a system which has brought them many triumphs, but the idea of direct popular legislation is more conformable to the democratic principle that the whole people should rule than is the domination of one class through a legislative caucus.[1]

New questions may emerge if the Commonwealth, already called to deal with high matters beyond its own limits, takes a more active part in world-politics than it has yet done.

Much may moreover depend on the unpredictable factor of the personal quality of the statesmen who will come to the front in the two parties within the next twenty years. Maladroit leadership on the one side, skilful and stimulating

[1] Queensland has already adopted a plan for referring to a popular vote the decision of conflicts which arise between the two Houses of its Legislature.

and inspiring leadership on the other, might make a great difference where class interests and the forces of opinion are so nearly balanced as they have been in Australia during the last twenty years.

Finally, there may be intellectual changes. The diffusion of higher education may raise the level of knowledge in all classes, may enable them to realize that neither statutes nor those who administer them can prevail against the facts of human nature, may cause the people, who have more leisure than any other people, to spend more of it in reflecting upon the conditions and principles which determine political progress and national well-being. The more highly educated class in particular may arouse themselves to take a livelier interest in public affairs, and to send more of their best men into a political career. Public opinion may become wiser and wider, riper, more truly national and less controlled by class feeling than it has latterly been.

Should any one of such changes occur, it would of course come slowly. In the United States the return of the more educated classes to activity in the field of state and municipal government began thirty years ago, and has not yet gone so far as reformers trust it will. Of the other changes indicated as possible, none seems likely to deflect the main stream of Australian ideas and wishes. The trend of sentiment and the political habits of the masses are already so clearly marked that the tendency to throw burdens upon the richer sort, and to use State power for objects that promise to benefit the citizen even at the risk of limiting his freedom, may hold its ground for some time, suggesting further experiments, the success or failure of which will accelerate or arrest the march towards communism. With its present prosperity the country can afford to lose money upon experiments tried at the expense of the few, even if failure may ultimately injure the many. Each of these will deserve to be studied by itself, and judged on its own special merits or demerits in working. Older countries will look on and be grateful for what Australia can teach.

Among the general lessons for democratic governments which Australian experience affords, that of widest import bears upon the character which Party government takes when Party coincides with Class, and upon the consequences to a representative assembly when it passes under the control of a pledge-bound majority of its own members, each forgoing his own liberty and owning the authority of an extra-parliamentary organization. It is hard to keep popular government truly popular, for power seems inevitably to slip back into the hands of the few, however strictly constitutional may be the forms. Australia has got no nearer than has any other country to solving the problem of government by the whole people with fairness to the whole people, but has given one more proof of what needed no proving, that a class dominant as a class will always govern in its own interest.

The Australians, like the Americans, may not have used to the best purpose all the gifts of nature, and especially the great gift of a new land in which they could make a fresh start, delivered from the evils that afflicted the old societies. They have committed some serious mistakes and tolerated some questionable methods. But they have a great recuperative power. The maxim that nations must not presume too far upon their hereditary virtues is one that no nation can venture to forget. Some have suffered from forgetting it. Yet in Australia it is hard not to be affected by the youthful vigour and optimistic spirit of the people. We may well wish that there were more of them, for they are an asset precious to the world, as well as to that Commonwealth of British nations whereof they form a part, a virile and high-spirited race, energetic and resourceful, a race which ought to increase and spread out till it fills the vast spaces, so far as habitable by man, of the continent that is its heritage.

NEW ZEALAND

CHAPTER LIII

OF all the British self-governing dominions New Zealand is that best suited by climate to be a home for men of British stock. Small as it is in comparison with Canada, Australia, or South Africa, it has a larger proportion of its total area available for the service of man, and it is unsurpassed, if indeed equalled, by any of these countries in salubrity and in natural beauty. Europeans and Americans are apt to associate it with Australia, because the two countries lie only twelve hundred miles apart. But they are very different countries, unlike in physical aspect, unlike in climate, unlike in their fauna and flora, unlike in the character of the aborigines whom the settlers found, and like only in the character of their white population and in the British traditions which it brought to a new land.

The country, consisting of two long islands and one much smaller isle to the south of the Southern island, measures 900 miles from north to south, and is so narrow that no point on it is more than seventy-five miles from the sea. The northernmost part has the climate of Lisbon or Gibraltar, the southernmost the climate of Edinburgh. Large parts are mountainous, the highest peak of the South Island reaching 12,349 feet, and those of the North Island — where the loftiest are extinct volcanoes,— exceeding 9000 feet. Of the total area 104,471 square miles, about two-thirds, are deemed fit for agriculture or pasture, and of the residue a large part is still covered by forests of considerable economic value as well as great beauty. There is a copious rainfall, plenty of water-power, and mines of gold, silver, and coal. A comparatively small part of the land has been brought under tillage, for the chief industry is the keeping of sheep (about

26,000,000, (1919) and cattle (over 3,000,000), but in large parts of the island the native herbage is so innutritious that it is necessary to sow European grasses, and in some regions the process is repeated every seventh year. Nature, while making ample provision for a very large population, has indicated pasture and agriculture as the chief occupations, for the coal deposits are not sufficient to provide fuel for great manufacturing industries, and New Zealand lies so far away from any large markets that manufacturers could not hope to do much more than supply the needs of the home consumer. Sheep-keeping is, moreover, pursued more profitably on a great than on a small scale, so that Nature might seem to indicate that economic causes, if left their full play, would make the country one of fairly large rather than of small holdings. An important development of pastoral industry, however, has recently appeared in the form of moderately sized dairy farms, worked on the co-operative system, and exporting butter and cheese to European markets. A study of the natural resources of New Zealand and of the economic phenomena springing from them suggests that the population will remain rather rural than urban, pretty dense in the arable, dairying, and fruit-raising districts, much more sparse in the pastoral and forest-covered lands. So, too, the towns will be important chiefly as ports for the shipping to foreign markets of agricultural and pastoral products, and as the two islands have a coast line about 4300 miles in total length, harbours are fairly numerous. No one of these ports, except perhaps Auckland in the north, the nearest point to the Panama Canal, and with a spacious haven, seems likely to outclass the others to the same extent as Sydney and Melbourne dwarf the other seaports of South-Eastern Australia.

These are the advantages Nature has bestowed on the country. What one may call the human conditions under which the white colony began were scarcely less favourable. The Maori aborigines belonged to one of the most intelligent branches of that brown Polynesian stock which is perhaps the most attractive primitive race that has ever been discovered. Though they were bold as well as chivalrous fighters, and had, unluckily, been allowed to obtain firearms, they were not numerous enough to be permanently formidable to a European population constantly recruited from without.

The first white settlers were of an exceptionally high quality, with no convicts among them. A good many belonged to old English county families, and not a few were persons of exceptional talent and character. No British colony ever started on its career under brighter auspices, with a larger promise of an equal distribution of wealth, ampler opportunities of prosperity for every industrious man, and greater freedom from the disturbing influences and bad habits of the European world.

The early history of the colony may be dismissed in a few words. In 1840 the islands were formally annexed by Great Britain and a treaty made with the leading Maori chiefs, by which they recognized British sovereignty, while the enjoyment of their lands was guaranteed to them. Disputes about landownership inevitably arose as the settlers spread out, and induced a series of wars, the last of which ended in 1870, since which time the natives have lived at peace with the whites, having a considerable region reserved to them, along with the right of returning four members to the House of Representatives. It has been customary to have one **Maori** in the Cabinet.[1]

In 1853 an Act of the Imperial Parliament created an elective Legislature, and 1856 a Ministry responsible to the Legislature, on the English model, was set up. This Parliament presently became a powerful centralizing force, for up to 1876 a large party of the functions of government had been discharged by Provincial Councils, one for each of the provinces (at first six, afterwards nine), into which the country was divided, and these councils had done good service by creating an interest in efficient government, and training not a few men for public life. In 1861 gold was discovered, first in Otago, a little later on the west coast of the South Island, still later on the east coast of the North Island, and this brought in a good many immigrants of a new type, for the most part rough and uneducated, but hard working and kindly. With the year 1870, however, there began a new era. Sir Julius Vogel, then Minister of Finance, seeing the need for land communication between the widely separated centres of settlement, carried through Parliament a plan for

---

[1] The Civil List Act of 1908 provides a salary for two Maoris as members of the Executive Council not holding ministerial posts.

borrowing £10,000,000, to be expended in public works, and especially on railways. As the country had then barely 250,000 white inhabitants, besides 45,000 Maoris, this was a bold venture, but Parliament went further, and within the next ten years the debt of the colony had risen from £7,841,-000 to £27,000,000. Long stretches of railway were built, many of which are said to have been laid out unsystematically and constructed wastefully. The expenditure of so many millions created a demand for labour, and drew into the country a swarm of immigrants so large as nearly to double the population between 1871 and 1881. Land values rose rapidly, the influx of miners continued, new industries were started and towns grew. A period of wild speculation in land and in business generally was naturally followed by a collapse and general depression, from which the colony did not recover for many years. Then first was it that distress and pauperism appeared, then first the unlucky immigrants whose hopes had been disappointed began to look to the Government for help. As the heavy debt compelled an increase in taxation, the duties on imports were raised, and a foundation laid for the protective tariff now in force.

The functions of the Parliament of the colony having grown more important after the Provincial Councils had vanished, party divisions in the Legislature became more marked, though for a good while there was hardly any electoral organization in the constituencies, while in the Assembly the tie of party allegiance was loose. For the next fifteen years the reins of government were usually in the hands of those who were then deemed Conservatives, and who defended the interests of the larger landowners and the wealthier business men. Among the opponents of this party, calling themselves Liberals, the most prominent figure was Sir George Grey (in earlier days twice Governor, and now a party leader), a remarkable man, radical in opinion, authoritarian by temper, brilliant by his intellectual gifts, but without the tact and forbearance which the conduct of business in an Assembly requires. His advocacy, while Prime Minister, of an enlargement of the franchise, compelled his successor to pass in 1879 an Act establishing manhood suffrage, and this, followed some years later by the abolition of plural voting, made New Zealand a democracy. At first, however, no great change in legislation was visible. The subjects that occupied Parliament were chiefly land questions and various financial difficulties which the growth of the debt and the depression in business had made acute. Some measures designed to benefit the working men were passed, and the disposition to play for their votes became more evident. Ministers and members, however, to whichever party they belonged, came almost exclusively from the richer and more educated classes. They were landed proprietors, merchants, lawyers, and other professional men, some more advanced in their views and sentiments than others, but not separated among themselves by any sharp lines either of social sympathy or of political opinion. Very few were radicals by theory, if indeed one can talk of theory at all among New Zealand politicians. They were occupied by the issues of the hour, and inevitably also by the getting and keeping of office, for the balance of party strength frequently shifted, and a disproportionate amount of time and effort was spent on the incessant game of replacing the Ins by the Outs.

In that game the working men had not yet begun to take a hand. They had, of course, voted since the suffrage had been extended to them, and most of them voted for the party called Liberal. But they were not keen politicians, their leaders being far more directly interested in the building up of the trade unions and the conduct of strikes and other labour disputes, these having grown more frequent with the increase of the wage-earning class.

This was the position when that election of 1890 which proved fateful for New Zealand was approaching. The Constitution had then already taken the completely popular character which now marks it, and as it has remained unchanged (except in two details to be presently noted) since 1890, this is a convenient point for a brief description of its main features as it stood when the days of effective democracy began.

The Parliament or " General Assembly " consisted of two Houses. The House of Representatives had, and still has, seventy-six members (besides four representing the Maori aborigines), elected by universal (then manhood) suffrage for three years, and for districts approximately equal in population. Each member has received a salary of £300 a year. No elector can vote in more than one district.

The Legislative Council contained in 1890 thirty-four members, appointed for life by the Governor, *i.e.* by the ministry in power at the time when vacancies occurred. It had practically no power in financial matters, and it did not make or unmake ministries, but otherwise its functions in legislation were legally the same as those of the popular House. The number of its members was not limited by law. As we presently shall see, this provision has been changed.

Executive authority was vested nominally in the Governor appointed by the British Crown (with a term of office usually of five years), but practically in the Ministry, *i.e.* the leaders of the majority in the House of Representatives. This is the regular form of government in all the self-governing Dominions of Britain, and it places the ultimate seat of power in the majority of citizens voting at an election, this power being exercised through the majority in the popular House and the Ministry which it supports. Its democratic quality was limited by only one check, viz. the right of the Legislative Council to amend or reject Bills other than financial.

The bulk of the voters, however, which here as elsewhere consisted of the poorer classes, had not realized how great their power was, just as the English working class did not realize theirs for many years after the Act of 1867. But now, in 1890, the awakening came. There was much discontent among the masses. The agricultural element among them had been disappointed at their failure to obtain those small holdings for which they had been calling during thirty years. They blamed the improvidence that had allowed most of the good land to get into the hands of large proprietors, and the ineptitude of successive Ministries whose plans for selling or leasing Crown lands in small blocks had failed to satisfy the legitimate desires of the people. The depression which followed the " boom " of the early 'seventies had never quite passed away, although the great sheep-masters were now prosperous through their wool exports, and beginning to profit by the newly discovered methods of sending frozen mutton to Europe, circumstances which raised the price of land against the small buyer. The considerable working-class population which had grown up in the towns since the days when loans had brought money and, for a

time, plenty of employment into the country, was restless and
unhappy. While many of those who had arrived in the
" boom days " were emigrating, there was distress among
those who remained, and what is called " sweating " was
complained of in some trades. The efforts of their chiefs
had hitherto been devoted to the raising of wages and the improvement of labour conditions generally by means of strikes.
But the greatest strike yet ventured on, due to an attempt to
prevent the use by the shipping companies of non-Union labour, had just failed, after having nearly drained the resources of the Unions. They were disheartened; and hard
times made them ready for some new and more promising
line of action. There was a sense in the air of coming
change, a feeling in all classes that a crisis in industrial problems was at hand. In this situation the leaders of the Liberal party, having already many adherents among the small
farmers, turned naturally for support to the leaders of the
wage-earners, and the latter gladly joined hands with them,
thinking, as were the Australians at the same time, that
what they could not get by strikes they must seek in some
other way. The election of 1890 gave a majority against the
Conservative Ministry, and brought in five working men as
supporters of the Liberal Government formed by Mr. Ballance as Prime Minister. When the bold programme of
legislation which he set himself to carry out was arrested by
the action of the Legislative Council, which rejected or materially altered some important Bills, he resolved to deal with
the Council itself, and passed through the House a measure
reducing the tenure of office of the councillors from life to a
period of seven years. The Council, in which there were
then only six Ministerialists out of a total of thirty-four, rejected the measure, whereupon the Ministry requested the
Governor to appoint twelve new members, there being, it will
be remembered, no limitation to the numbers of the Council.
The Governor, who thought this change too large, declined
to appoint more than nine. The matter was referred to the
British Government at home, which, adhering to its general
principle of letting the self-governing colonies settle their internal affairs for themselves, directed the Governor to comply. The twelve new councillors, four of whom were working men, were thereupon appointed, and the Bill reducing the

term of a councillor's office to seven years was passed.   Since
this change the Council, though for a time it showed fight,
and though it continues to meet and debate, has practically
counted for little, and constitutes no effective check on the
action of the popular House.   In 1893 another general election gave the Liberals a majority of 22 in that House.   The
Ministry now had the ball at their feet, and threw themselves with redoubled energy and confidence into that policy
of extending the action of the State in many new directions
which has made New Zealand's legislative experiments a
subject of curiosity and interest to the world.   This was done
under a new Prime Minister, Mr. Richard John Seddon, one
of the most remarkable leaders of the people modern democracy has produced.

CHAPTER LIV

RICHARD SEDDON, or King Dick as he was commonly and affectionately called, was born at St. Helens in Lancashire in 1845. Both of his parents were teachers in elementary schools, then on a far lower level than now. Despite these facilities, he carried away from school little education, being of a restlessly active temper which had no liking for books. After an apprenticeship of five years to an engineering firm, he went at nineteen to seek his fortune in the gold-diggings of Australia. Not finding it there, he crossed the sea from Melbourne to New Zealand, where, after some further experiences in gold-mining, he set up an inn and shop, which his friends called a store and his detractors a public-house, at Kumara, on the west coast of the South Island.[1] Here his hustling energy and "hail-fellow-well-met" spirit soon made him successful as a miner's advocate in the Warden's Mining Court, and also a leading figure in local politics. In 1879 he was returned to Parliament as a supporter of Sir George Grey, then Prime Minister, and sat thenceforth in the House of Representatives till he died in 1906, still in middle life, but broken down by a tireless activity which would allow itself no respite from work.

His character and career deserve more than a passing mention. He had little book-learning, no love of knowledge for its own sake, and in particular no acquaintance with even the rudiments of economics and legislation. In eloquence he was equally wanting. There was neither art nor grace in his speeches, which rambled on through a string of details tedious to the listener, with nothing even of that idealistic strain by which men of ardent soul but halting utterance sometimes rouse an audience. But he had Force and Drive. He could say what he meant when he wanted to say it, and said it in a way to command attention. " I believe "— so he once

---

[1] The house had a license, but taken out in the name of his uncle.

remarked to an interviewer —" in giving it to the great many-headed hot and hot, lots of pepper and seasoning, none of your milk-and water pap, no namby-pamby solemn beating about the bush, but straight-from-the-shoulder talk." It was well observed of him that he "never could estimate the precise value of comparatives and superlatives, and seemed to the last to imagine that strong language was the only language befitting a strong man." When he had to deal with a subject, he spared no pains to get up all the facts and to keep them accurately in mind. In Parliament his indomitable persistence and strenuous will bore down all opposition, and the air of determined resolution that sat well on his strong features was all the more impressive from his burly frame and a chest like Vulcan's.

But with this force there were coupled other qualities quite as serviceable. He had a genial manner, a cheery laugh, a crushing hand-grip. Though jealous, he was neither malicious nor vindictive. He was at home with the people. From them he had sprung, and they were proud of him. He got acquainted with everybody, remembered everybody's face, knew how to handle everybody, and thus did more to strengthen his power outside than inside Parliament. Even his opponents found it hard to hate him. With these gifts and a convenient absence of scruples, he was an adroit parliamentary leader, quick in apprehension, shrewd in his judgments, knowing even when to yield and how to yield without the appearance of weakness.[1]

He was accused of playing down to the crowd, and certainly did much to vulgarize New Zealand politics. Power was his passion, and, though his head was not turned by popularity, he had his full share of vanity. Yet he was something more than a mere self-seeker or vote-catcher. His heart was kindly, and he honestly wished to better the condition and brighten the lives of the class whence he came. He deserves to be remembered as one of the few leaders of the masses who began and remained throughout on the level of the masses. Seldom has any one of an origin so humble risen to the top, not even in France, in the midst of a revolu-

---

[1] A penetrating observer who had every opportunity of studying Seddon told me that he got on much better with the average elector than with men of intellect or education, their mental processes being unfamiliar to him.

tion, nor in the United States, nor in Switzerland. But the New Zealander, had he lived in the days of the first French Revolution, would have played a notable part there, as he would have done also in those cities of ancient Greece that were often torn by seditions. Revolutions give chances to everybody, but Seddon did not need troublous times to rise. There have been few more remarkable figures in our time than this popular dictator, who gained and kept power without education and without eloquence.[1]

The election of 1893 gave Mr. Seddon, who had become Prime Minister after the death of Mr. Ballance, a majority of 22, and three subsequent elections in succession confirmed his power. Though during the first few years the resistance of the Legislative Council occasionally delayed his measures, he carried through, during his thirteen years of office, a series of Acts, to which, having regard both to their number or their significance, few parallels can be found in recent history. Most of them were passed in the interests of the working class, and many of them extended the scope and power of State action. Seddon was not himself a Socialist, indeed he was not an -ist of any kind, being free from all theories, and looking solely to the needs of the moment and the exigencies of the political situation. Nor was his Ministry, as a whole, Socialist in the European sense of the term. Resting on the support of the Liberals and of the working-class vote, the latter already strong, though not yet organized, it met the more urgent desires of the latter without offending the former, and carried with it the poorer part of the agricultural class, and indeed the bulk of public opinion in the colony. But it was not by this support only nor by his personal ascendancy that his Ministry kept its grip on members and constituencies. Mr. Seddon was the most astute of party managers, and never hesitated to use Government patronage to win support or buy off opposition. He saw nothing wrong in this, and almost disarmed criticism by the frankness of his avowals. Appropriations for roads, bridges, railways, harbour improvements, every kind of work which could benefit a district or bring money into it, were freely

---

[1] M. Siegfried observes that the Frenchman from the country, who is said to have gone round Paris trying to find the being called *L'État*, and was at last shown a very large building full of public offices, might in New Zealand have simply been led to Mr. Seddon's room.

granted.   No one charged him or his Ministers with enriching themselves.   New Zealand is one of the purest of colonial
communities, and, indeed, of democratic communities anywhere, comparable in this respect with Switzerland.   But
though the grants were occasionally made to districts that
were not supporting his government, his abuse of public
funds for party purposes did much to lower the tone of
politics.

These methods and acts passed, with the support of the
Liquor interest, helped to secure his continuance in power,
though some thought that his prestige was beginning to wane
before he passed away.   The pace of legislation slackened
during his later years, when two or three of his ablest colleagues were no longer with him, and the trade union leaders,
always expecting some fresh concession, grew restive, and
were stimulated by the example of the rapid advance made
by the Labour party in Australia to think of detaching themselves from the Liberals.   After Seddon's death his two successors kept the Liberal majority together on the lines he had
followed, while slowing down the pace still further.   They
were beginning to be weakened by an increase in the class
of small farmers, which grew more conservative as it acquired
property; and when the wage-earners found that there were
limits to the raising of wages, the two sections began to draw
apart.   Moreover, the Ministry suffered, like every Ministry
long in office, by the sort of staleness it acquired in the view
of the voters.   " In the end the possession of great administrative power brings about destruction.   Security breeds
carelessness, perhaps corruption; length of office inspires mis-
trust, discontent, and envy." [1]   However, it held on, not
without the use of what are euphemistically called " administrative methods," though at the election of 1908 many of the
Labour men drew off, running candidates of their own.   Finally, at the election of 1911, the Opposition obtained a small
majority, and formed, under the name of the Reform party,
a Government, which devoted itself chiefly to financial and
land questions, and created a Civil Service Commission, but
did not attempt to repeal the measures of its predecessors.

In the election of 1915 the Labour party gained seats in

[1] Hight and Bamford, *Constitutional History and Law of New Zealand*, p. 303.

seven constituencies, and elsewhere gave its support to the Liberals, but the Reformers obtained a small majority over both these parties. Shortly afterwards (August 4, 1915) the European War brought about the coalition of Reformers and Liberals in what was called a " National Government," and it lasted till 1919, when the " Liberal " members withdrew.[1]

As it is the legislation passed by the Seddon Government that has chiefly fixed upon New Zealand the attention of economists and statesmen in other countries, their measures, and especially those which have a flavour of State Socialism, deserve to be examined in detail. Before, however, I proceed to such an examination, and thereafter to a description of the present political conditions and of the public opinion of the country, a few words must be said upon Local Government, Education, and the Civil Service, in order to complete the account of the machinery of government.

No British colony has developed a more complete system of local institutions. There are, in rural areas, County Councils, and under them Road Boards, both elected biennially on a system which allots one, two, or three votes to the citizen, according to his valuation.[2] Their functions cover every kind of rural work except Education, Poor Relief, and Police. The Borough Councils are chosen biennially, the Mayor being elected, not by the Councils, as in England, but directly by the voters, as in the United States. The qualifications are freehold or rating or residential, but the latter does not entitle its holder to vote on any proposal submitted to the electors regarding loans or rates. The functions of these Councils include the care of " streets, drainage, lighting, tramways, bridges, ferries, water-works and water-power, sanitation, fire prevention, workers' dwellings, markets, public libraries, museums, public gardens, and they may contribute funds for recreation, instruction, etc. More than one borough has a theatre." [3]

The total indebtedness of the various local authorities in

---

[1] The general election of Dec. 1919 gave to the Reform party 48 seats, to the Liberals 18, to the Labour party 10, and 4 others were described as Independents.

[2] A peculiar provision is that where a qualification, freehold, rating, or residential, is possessed by either husband or wife, it is deemed to be possessed by each.

[3] Sir R. Stout, *New Zealand*, p. 102.

New Zealand (excluding debts to the Government amounting to £3,851,000) was in 1918 £22,260,000. Considerable subsidies are paid annually by the Dominion to Borough Councils, and on a still higher scale to County Councils. No salaries are paid to the members of any of these local bodies. " When the large number of local bodies is considered, it will be seen," says Chief Justice Sir Robert Stout, " that some thousands of our people are concerned, without fee or reward, in managing our local concerns." And he adds, " Mistakes may have been innocently made, but up to the present time (1911) not a single charge of corruption or fraud has ever been made against any of our municipal bodies or any of their members." [1] Every one whom I questioned in New Zealand agreed in bearing like witness to the honesty with which local government is conducted.

In rural areas, party politics do not enter into elections, but in the cities it is otherwise. The Labour party ran candidates in the four chief cities in 1913. Municipalities are empowered to adopt in their elections proportional representation, but this right has been so far sparingly used. [2]

Police belongs entirely to the government of the Dominion, which has entrusted it to a Commissioner. In 1919 a police force of only 878 was deemed quite sufficient for a population of 1,160,000, being one policeman to every 1319 persons. Another cheering fact is that whereas persons born in New Zealand and over fifteen years of age constitute 60 per cent of the whole population, the percentage of New Zealand-born to the total number of prisoners in gaol was only 43. [3]

Education also is entirely supported by the Dominion Government, the administration being entrusted to thirteen district boards and to school committees elected locally. The question of religious teaching in schools has been much contested. In 1914 a Bill was introduced providing for the reading of the Bible and permitting ministers of religion to

[1] Sir R. Stout, *ut supra*, p. 108.

[2] Visitors from Europe have remarked on the neglect of civic amenities shown by some municipalities. Auckland, for instance — with an admirable situation and environs of great interest, possessing what is a sort of natural museum of geology and archaeology, for it is, I believe, the only city in the world with a number of small extinct craters in its suburbs, some of which the Maoris turned to account as forts, placing stockades around them — has not made proper use of these natural advantages any more than San Francisco has of hers.

[3] *New Zealand Year-Book* for 1919.

enter the schools at suitable times to instruct scholars belonging to their respective denominations, but it was warmly opposed and ultimately dropped, owing to the outbreak of war in Europe. Apart from this question, the schools did not "come into politics." In the elementary schools instruction is compulsory and gratuitous, while in secondary schools free places are provided for all children who reach a certain standard by a certain age. There is practically no illiteracy among native-born New Zealanders. But one part of the fabric remains unfinished. It is the top story. The University is merely an examining body, and no one of the four colleges affiliated to it, situated in each of the four chief cities, useful as they are and all of them well deserving to be maintained, possesses the equipment which a University needs.[1] No city will yield to any other, not even to Wellington, the capital, the honour of being selected as the seat of a true university of the European or American type, concentrating in itself the highest teaching power and the most varied learning of the country. The provision for engineering and other technical instruction is of good quality and sufficient for the population, but institutions created to give instruction in applied science, however valuable for practical purposes, do not fill the void. A first-class university staff is all the more necessary, because New Zealand lies far away from the intellectual influences of Europe. They do, indeed, reach her through books, but with the thin voice of a telephone.

THE PUBLIC SERVICE

In few countries, if in any, is the proportion of members of the public service to the whole nation so large as in New Zealand, and this because in few does the Government undertake so many tasks on behalf of the people. In 1909 a Minister stated that 130,000 persons out of a population then of 1,000,000 were directly dependent on the State, and this number is said to have now risen to 150,000. This estimate would, however, seem to have been reached by adding to the number of State employees, then 40,000, the old-age pensioners, then 14,000 (now over 19,000), and estimating the dependent families at two and a half persons to each of the

---

[1] In 1919 these four colleges had in all about 113 professors and lecturers.

above. The condition of the Civil Service is therefore a matter of special interest, for it affects the welfare of a large part of the people, as well as the efficiency of the many and diverse kinds of public work which they perform.

Four questions in particular need to be noticed here, the methods of admission into the Civil Service, the tenure of its members, the system of promotion, and the relation of the Service to party politics.

Admission to the public service is by a competitive examination, held at the age of fourteen, in elementary subjects and therefore affording no satisfactory evidence of the intellectual gifts of the candidates, though some evidence of their diligence. This arrangement does not apply to posts in the railway service, which are filled by the appointment of the Ministers for that department, while in the postal and telegraph services, appointments are entrusted to a non-political Commission. Members of the Legislature used to put political pressure on the Ministers to give places to their friends, and found this one of the least agreeable of the functions which their constituents expected from them. One member is reported to have said: "The applications I receive from candidates for the public service are the worry of my life; men, women, and children all seem to want to get Government billets." And another observed: "Members of Parliament are to a large extent Labour agents; there is none of us who is not supposed to possess some influence with the Government, and who is not expected to use that influence on behalf of persons seeking Government billets." [1]

Tenure.— The existing evils due to political patronage would be much graver had not New Zealand fortunately adopted the British principle of regarding the tenure of posts as practically permanent, *i.e.* making no dismissals except for serious faults or evident inefficiency. There is no "Spoils System," no wholesale turning out of officials on a change of Government, such as was once general, and still exists, to some extent, in the United States.

Promotion.— The efficiency of any service depends on the methods used for bringing superior ability to the top, but this implies the entrusting of a wide discretion to the head of the department, who cannot always be trusted to resist

[1] Quoted by Rossignol and Stewart (referred to later), p. 202.

political pressure exerted by members of parliament in the way already referred to. The alternative is promotion by seniority, which, even if coupled with examinations at different stages (an experiment tried in New Zealand), gives little security, beyond what mere experience furnishes, for administrative capacity. Thus New Zealand has suffered both from ministerial discretion and from the rule of seniority. As a new country, she had not the advantage of that long tradition and settled custom which in Great Britain has on the whole, if not invariably, controlled Ministers in the disposal of patronage, impressing on them the duty of selecting the best men for the higher posts. An effort to mend things was made in 1912 by an act creating a non-political Public Service Commissioner, with two Assistant Commissioners to exercise a general control over the public service, except the Railway, Defence, and Police departments. Appeals from a decision of the Commissioner may be brought to a Board of three members, one of them appointed from the ranks of, and another elected by the Civil Service itself. This Commission is independent of the Ministry, and its members are removable only by Parliament. An effort to bring its powers under direct parliamentary control has, however, been threatened.

The Participation of Public Servants in Politics.— Though it was long ago laid down that members of the Civil Service are forbidden to take an active part in political controversies otherwise than by recording their votes, this rule was not strictly observed. Members have been known to complain that in the days of the Seddon Government they found an array of public servants working against them at elections, and that it was felt in some places that a man could not get work under the Government unless he supported it by his vote,[1] but others have told me of many who, though they might not work against the Ministry, voted against them. In 1907, when a workman had been dismissed because he had moved a resolution hostile to the Government at a meeting of a Labour League, the matter was raised in Parliament and the action of the Government supported. It was generally felt, as some one said, that if the Government did not rule

[1] Quoted by Rossignol and Stewart, p. 212. It would appear that there is to-day little, if any, of such action by civil servants.

the Civil Service, the Civil Service would rule the Government. The public action, and even the votes, of a body so numerous and so constantly growing would, if steadily thrown for the party which promised them higher remuneration and more favourable conditions, be a dangerous factor in politics, as has happened before now, to some extent in Britain and to a larger extent in Australia, and would also be unfair to those workers who might, as taxpayers, be thus forced to pay more to others than they were themselves receiving for like work. I did not, however, hear that even the railwaymen, the largest single body of employees, have as yet gone far in this direction. Railway workers, though not long ago there was a strike among them, are to some extent kept quiet by the fear of forfeiting their pensions for long service.

The opinions expressed to me in New Zealand all went to show that the upper ranks of the Civil Service were reasonably efficient and entirely pure. One could not expect to find among them more than a few persons of the calibre of the permanent chiefs of the departments in the countries of Western Europe.

We may now turn to the experimental legislation which has won for New Zealand the reputation of a semi-socialistic State.

The boundless energy of Mr. Seddon, the enormous majority that supported him in the legislature, and the command he soon acquired over the minds of the people, made it possible for his Ministry to carry through in the years following 1893 a series of laws, conceived in the interests of the working class, to which few parallels can be found in any other modern country. Many of these require no special notice, because similar to measures enacted in European countries or in several States of the American Union, so I will advert only to those few which either throw strong light on the tendencies of democratic government or go farthest in enlarging the functions of the democratic State. Most of them did not spring from Mr. Seddon's brain, which was by no means creative, yet without his force and his ascendancy both in and out of Parliament they could not have been pressed through against the resistance of the richer section of the community. I begin with the land policy, in which it was not he, but his colleague John M'Kenzie, Minister of Lands, a masterful shepherd from the Scottish Highlands, who originated, carried, and set a-going the administration of the governmental measures.[1]

LAND LEGISLATION

When the Liberal-Labour Government of 1891 proceeded to tackle the Land question the problem was not new, but had already a history, long, changeful, and complicated. In the earlier years of the Colony, when all the land of the islands, except the parts reserved for the Maoris, lay at the disposal of the Government, sad mistakes were committed. There was abundance of good intentions, but very little foresight. Vast blocks were permitted to pass into the hands of speculators, so that in the early 'seventies, when immigrants desired to take up farms, much of the richest and best-situated arable soil was already gone, while the boom (consequent on Vogel's borrowings) which began in 1870 had run up the price against small buyers. Thenceforward many attempts were made by legislation to repair these original errors. Some experiments failed and were abandoned; none had in 1891 done much to meet the reasonable demands of the people. In that year 584 persons owned 7,000,000 acres out of rather less than 44,000,000 fit for agriculture or pasture,

[1] New Zealand has been fortunate in the authors who have devoted themselves to a description and criticism of her politics, and in particular to accounts of her recent experiments in the field of legislation. The first of these, and one of the fullest and best written, is *State Experiments in Australia and New Zealand* (published in 1902) by Mr. Pember Reeves, who was Minister of Labour in the administrations of Mr. Ballance and Mr. Seddon. It, however, brings the story down only to 1902. More recent are three works by French observers, the *Aurore Australe* of M. Biard d'Aunet, the *L'Australie Nouvelle* of M. Voisson, and the *Democratie en Nouvelle Zélande* of M. André Siegfried (published in 1904), one of the best studies in contemporary politics our time has produced. (An English translation was recently published.) Still more recent are Sir R. Stout's *New Zealand*, already referred to, the *New Zealand in Evolution* (published in 1909) of Mr. Guy Scholefield, very fair and sensible, the *Life of R. J. Seddon* (published in 1907) of Mr. Drummond, eulogistic but not partisan, and the *State Socialism in New Zealand* of Messrs. Le Rossignol and Downie Stewart (1910), very careful and impartial. Interesting, but perhaps unduly optimistic, is the still more recent book of Major Lusk, *Social Welfare in New Zealand*. From all these, and from the very well arranged and executed *New Zealand Official Year-Books* (published annually), I have derived much assistance. There is now room for another book, which shall bring the story down from 1890 to 1920, dealing fully with strikes and arbitration.

and in 1894, 470 persons held land of the unimproved value
of £15,000,000, while 38,465 persons held land of unimproved value to the amount of £23,000,000, *i.e.* one-eightieth
of the total number of holders owned two-fifths of the total
value of the land. To make farms easily procurable, and
to improve social and political conditions by reducing the
number of large and increasing that of small landholders, was
an object which all recognized as desirable, but about the
means there were great differences of opinion.

In 1892 the Liberal-Labour Government abolished the
then existing system of a perpetual lease of Crown lands at
5 per cent, with right to purchase, and substituted what was
called a " lease in perpetuity," at a rent of 4 per cent, without
the right of purchase, limiting, moreover, the area which
any one tenant could hold to 640 acres of first-class or 2000
acres of second-class land. Presently the tenants under the
tenure created by this law began to ask for permission to
purchase the freehold. This right they at last obtained in
1907, but with a provision that the price should be the capital
value which the land had, not at the time when the lease was
granted, but at the time of purchase. At the same time the
lease in perpetuity was abolished, and a lease for sixty-six
years substituted, with a provision for valuation and renewal
at the end of the term at a re-fixed rent. But many tenants
remain who hold under the older tenures, some under perpetual lease and some under the lease in perpetuity, and their
numbers make them a powerful body. A recent authority
remarks: [1]

The chief danger of a large State tenantry is the immense
political pressure they can exercise. There were, in 1909, 25,204
State tenants, holding 18,264,083 acres, and they will agitate for
the freehold so long as there is the slightest chance of getting it,
and will be supported in their demands by about 45,000 freeholders
of country lands, most of whom are strong upholders of the tenure
which they enjoy. Even if they do not succeed in obtaining the
freehold, they are quite likely to clamour for reduction in rents
in time of depression, as indeed they have already done. One
witness before the Land Commission of 1905, on being pressed
to give reasons for his belief in the freehold, said, " I believe in
the freeholder because the freeholder is the man to whom, in times
of trouble, the State will look, and the leaseholder the man who in
times of trouble will look to the State."

[1] Rossignol and Stewart, p. 33.

The questions connected with State ownership cannot be
yet deemed to have been settled, and the authority just
quoted expresses the opinion that

the advantages of State ownership have been much exaggerated,
and it is not easy to show that New Zealand has derived any
benefit that could not have been obtained from freehold tenure
combined with taxation of land values. Had the efforts of the
legislature in the past been concentrated upon the prevention of
land monopoly and closer settlement on freehold farms, more
progress would probably have been made than has been possible
on the lines attempted in the past.

While these different forms of State leasing were being
tried, the sale of Crown lands in freehold also went steadily
on, but with two important provisos, " that the purchaser
must reside and execute improvements, and that no one can
purchase who already owns a certain prescribed quantity of
land." The " Reform " Government, which took office
in 1912, has allotted the proceeds of land sales to the support of a fund, to be now referred to, for the purchase of
land.

Besides the measures dealing with the lands that had
belonged to the State from the first settlement of the Colony,
a further effort was made to meet the desire for small properties. In 1894 the Seddon Ministry passed an Act empowering the Government to acquire privately-owned land by
compulsory purchase for the purpose of furthering closer settlement. " The land so acquired is disposed of on perpetual
renewable leases of thirty-three years, at a rental of £4: 10s.
per cent on the amount paid for the land. At the end of
such lease the renewal rental is £4: 10s. per cent on the value
of the land." [1] The sum of £750,000 per annum may be expended in this way, and in fact sums very large in the aggregate have been so expended. Most sales have been effected by agreement, without compulsion. But the money
the State pays is obtained by borrowing in England, and
the rents which the State has been receiving have not quite
covered the interest upon the loans and the expenses incident
to the process of purchasing. Moreover, the recent prosperity of the country sent up the price of land, so that it had

[1] Stout, p. 174.

become before 1914 more difficult to purchase at a price permitting subdivision and letting at rentals which tenants can afford to pay.[1]   Thus, undeniable as is the benefit to the tenants of obtaining farms, that benefit was being secured at a loss to the community as a whole.   This was not sound finance.   Now that the rates at which loans can be raised in England have so greatly risen, can the process continue? So many countries have, since the days of the Roman Republic in the fourth century B.C., failed in their efforts to deal wisely with the problem of the management and disposal of the public land that it need cause no surprise that, even with the experience of the past to instruct them, successive Governments in the Australasian colonies have done little better.   New Zealand, specially favoured in one respect, because she started with no landed aristocracy already entrenched in their vested interests, has paid dearly for the errors of the first twenty years.   The Seddon Government, however, deserves the credit of having grappled boldly, if not always wisely, with the evils it found.   Without confiscation, though at a heavy cost in money, it improved the situation.   Under its successors, who are more definitely committed to the plan of freehold ownership, small properties have been increasing, and the large estates are being slowly reduced as the agricultural population grows.

It is only fair to add that the Governments of recent years have been embarrassed and distracted by the existence of three divergent currents of opinion.   One school desires to make the State the universal landowner, and to support its expenses by land revenues.   Others desire to extinguish private property in land as in all other means of production, in order to establish a Collectivist regime.   Opposed to these sections are those who, both on political grounds and for the sake of satisfying a popular demand, seek to create the largest possible number of small landowning cultivators, just such a class, in fact, as exists in North America and (with smaller properties) in many parts of France.   Sometimes trying to satisfy both these schools of opinion, sometimes yielding to one or other, New Zealand land policy has been wavering and changeful.[2]

[1] Rossignol and Stewart, pp. 43–45.
[2] The advocates of the leasing system say that the freehold system

FINANCIAL ADMINISTRATION

Revenue.— In New Zealand, as in all young countries where population is sparse and the rich are few, duties on imported goods constitute the most convenient form of taxation, so they continue to supply the chief source of revenue. They were at first imposed for revenue purposes only. Presently, however, when there seemed to be a lack of employment for the town workers, and when this was attributed to the competition to which home-made articles had to submit from the competition of British-made articles, the tariff began to be regarded as a means of raising prices for the home-producer, and thereby assumed a Protectionist character. This character it has since retained and developed. Import duties were further raised under Seddon, whose faith in Protection was so ardent that he insisted on preaching the doctrine in England, regarding it as of universal application, whatever might be the economic conditions of a country. The manufacturing employers, who had found their position strengthened against imports by a raising of duties originally adopted in order to add to the revenue in a time of depression, thenceforward pressed for a higher and higher tariff; while the workmen, thinking that this meant more employment for themselves, seconded that pressure, so that with the support of both classes Protection has become the established creed of the country. It gives revenue; it is popular with the townsfolk; and the agriculturists either have not perceived the burden it lays upon them or are willing to bear that burden in what they suppose to be the general interest. The fear of the competition of Australian-made goods was one of the grounds which deterred New Zealand from entering into Federal relations with Australia. Little objection was made when Seddon, who was a strenuous Imperialist, introduced a preferential scale favouring British imports, because the preference was given, not by reducing the tariff on goods brought from England, but by increasing it upon goods coming from foreign countries. Protection has doubtless helped to maintain in New Zealand some industries that might other-

gave opportunities for trickery and for wild speculation; but it is hard for a visitor to sift and decide between conflicting views in such matters.

wise have languished. But whether this has proved, or will in the long run prove, a benefit to the country is another question.[1]

Two other features of the financial policy instituted by Ballance in 1891 and continued by the Seddon Ministry, were both a Land-Tax and an Income-Tax graduated on all profits except those from land. The former was designed not only to raise money, but to break up the large estates, an object already sought by the other means above referred to. To make it effective for this purpose it was laid to fall more heavily upon estates in proportion to their value. The ordinary land-tax, which dated from 1891, applied to all properties exceeding £500 (unimproved value), estates below that sum being exempt. A graduated land-tax (first proposed in 1887 by the Stout-Vogel Ministry), applicable to all properties which exceeded £5000 (unimproved value), was added later, and in 1917 the distinction between the two was abolished, so there is now one graduated tax which, imposing one penny in the £ on land the unimproved value whereof does not exceed £1000, rises till it reaches a maximum of sevenpence in the £ at £193,000. The amount was increased for 1917–19 by a supertax of 50 per cent of the primary tax, making the maximum rate 10½d. in the £. For absentee owners there is a further increase of 50 per cent on the graduated tax. The object of reducing the size of estates has been only to some slight extent secured. The more it is secured the less, of course, is the return from the graduated tax. The graduated income-tax, not charged on the incomes of resident individuals below £300, rises by successive steps to a maximum rate of 7s. 6d. in the £, which rate is attained at an income of £6400. Both these taxes were of course resisted by the large landowners and by the rich generally, but were so welcome to the small farmers, as well as to the labouring class, that they were easily carried and have been maintained. Continued prosperity, with high prices for wool, mutton, cheese, and butter in British markets, has enabled them to be

[1] See note appended to this chapter. It need hardly be said that New Zealand manufacturers already enjoyed a "natural Protection" in the high cost of importing goods from Britain thousands of miles away, and that they would have gained more by the increase in their home market which larger immigration would have caused than they were gaining by duties which raised the cost of living to the whole community, including their own workmen.

borne. There are also progressive duties on property passing at death, a class of imposts now familiar. Great Britain
imposed graduated succession duties in 1894, and a graduated
income-tax in 1911. Congress imposed a graduated surtax
for the United States in 1916. New Zealand, however, led
the way so far as English-speaking communities are
concerned.

How is this taxation, large in proportion to the wealth of
New Zealand, expended? The net public debt amounted in
1914 to a sum of £91,689,000, in 1919 of £170,000,125,
with an annual charge of £8,000,000 for interest and sinking
fund, about £70,000,000 having been added to it during the
War of 1914–18. In 1891, when the Liberal-Labour Ministry came in, it was £39,000,000, in 1909 £70,000,000, in
1914 £91,000,000, while in 1919 War Loans had raised it
to £171,000,000, representing £151 per head of European
population. Why so rapid an increase up to 1914 in a country which had, theretofore, no naval and only a very small
military expenditure? Most of the money had gone into re-
productive public works, such as railways and roads, and
much in loans to local bodies, on which they pay interest.
Other parts had been expended in the purchase of lands for
closer settlement, the rents paid for which nearly equal the
interest on the sums so applied, and in advances to settlers
for farms and to working men to enable them to obtain dwellings of their own; and it would appear that on these various
items the State has lost little or nothing, while many a farmer
owes his success to this initial aid. Upon the agrarian policy,
taken as a whole, there has, however, been a certain loss,
for it has involved many incidental expenses, which have had
to be charged on general revenue. From such authorities as
are available in Europe I do not gather that the Seddon
Administration and its continuation down to 1912 can be
charged with recklessness — Seddon was personally averse
to waste — or with financial incompetence.[1] It showed
business capacity on more than one occasion. But it was
certainly lax in its methods of expenditure, and lax with
comparative impunity, because the direct taxes, which in
practice are the only taxes the citizen feels, are paid by a
comparatively small part of the community, and it was not

[1] The expenditure in railway construction will be referred to later.

this particular part that kept the Ministry in power. The
tendency of most branches of administration in New Zealand,
as in most democratic countries, has been to a steadily increasing expenditure. Old-age pensions, for instance, when
introduced in 1898, ten years before they were granted in
Britain, were surrounded by a number of restrictions and
qualifying conditions which were in subsequent years struck
off, one after another, so that the number of recipients has
increased much faster than it ought to have done in proportion to the increase in population. In 1919 it was 19,872.
The original amount of each pension was £18 a year. The
average was in 1919 a little over £37. The total amount
expended per annum, which in 1900 was £157,000, had risen
in 1917 to £480,000, and in 1919 it was £743,000.[1] The
large expenditure had not in 1910 reduced the amount spent
by the State on charitable aid to the poor, but it had diminished private contributions to charitable purposes.[2] The Poor
Law arrangements of New Zealand are alleged to encourage
extravagance by allowing local authorities to spend sums received from the central revenue; and the growth of pauperism in a community so new and so prosperous has been frequently commented on and was deplored even by the optimistic Seddon.[3]

The tendency to laxity, not to say extravagance, in expenditure was increased by that habit of constructing public
works with a view to the winning of political support which
has been already referred to; and it came all the more easily
because the Dominion was able to go on borrowing in England
at a rate of from 3 to 3½ per cent. Those were happy days,
not likely to return in our time. Though there has been for
many years past a Sinking Fund, it was a thing more for
ornament than use, and valuable, as a leading statesman
once observed, chiefly as indicating an intention some day or
other to pay off the debt.[4] The elasticity the revenue has
shown makes parsimony seem unnecessary, and every one
knows that the temptation to please the present generation

[1] In 1917 an increase of £13 a year was granted to continue till
twelve months after the end of the War with Germany.

[2] See as to this Rossignol and Stewart, pp. 183–94, where many interesting details are given.

[3] Rossignol and Stewart, p. 182.

[4] In 1919, however, the Sinking Fund was stated to amount to about
£5,951,000.

at the expense of posterity is particularly strong in popular governments.

UNDERTAKINGS CONDUCTED BY THE STATE

Among the enterprises and industries which Government has undertaken in New Zealand, the railroads are by far the most important. In a young colony, where there was hardly any private capital available for construction of costly works, and no chance of obtaining it from Europe save through State action, undertakings so essential for the development of the country inevitably fall to the Government. Some few small lines were built by the Provincial Councils, while they existed, but a far greater number by the Central Government, especially after the bold borrowings started by Vogel. At present, two lines which were privately owned having been bought up, practically all the railways are owned and worked by the State. Its action may be examined first as regards the constructing and then as regards the management of the railways.

Construction.— When the business of providing a country with proper facilities for railway communication is determined by economic considerations only, the problems of military or naval defence not needing to be considered, two principles ought to be observed. One is to lay out and construct the railroads on a systematic plan, both the trunk lines and the branch lines being in proper relation to one another. The other is to build lines where the commercial need for them is greatest, and prospects exist of a remunerative traffic, which will enable them to be worked at a profit, as well as maintained in perfect working order. Neither of these principles was followed by the New Zealand Government. Exposed to a strong and unceasing political pressure by those who wished to have the value of their properties improved by transportation facilities, it usually yielded. Trunk lines might be neglected, while some lines were built where they were little needed, and where, consequently, the receipts were, and have continued to be, small. The whole thing was done piecemeal, and consequently at a needless cost, though it ought in fairness to be said that the absence of any economic centre whence railroads might radiate increased the difficulty of planning a system. A Minister might try to resist, but when votes were to be gained or lost, he was apt to comply or be overruled by his colleagues. This went on from the first, and has been no worse under universal suffrage than it was when landowners ruled the country under a limited franchise, for the latter were just as insistent in desiring to improve their properties as a working-class constituency is in desiring to have employment provided at its doors. Less reprehensible, but almost equally unfortunate, was the clamour which arose from every part of the colony for " a fair share " in the distribution of the loans procured for railway construction. With his usual grasp of realities, Seddon said in the Assembly: " Until we have had a fair expenditure of public money out of loans upon each part of the colony, it is wrong of those parts that have had a fair share to say suddenly that there is to be no more borrowing." [1]   Districts where the need was small and the physical difficulties of construction great insisted that as much be spent within their limits as in places where the prospects of traffic were brighter. Much of the waste which from early days loaded the country with a heavy debt is due to this intrusion of political influences.

Management.— In early days the railways were both built and managed by the Minister of Public Works. The loss incurred in running them caused so much dissatisfaction, that in 1887 a permanent non-political Commission of three persons was established, who were thenceforth to control and manage the railways. This Board effected some improvements and many economies. But, as usually happens, the economies were unpopular, because the individuals whom they inconvenienced were more vocal than the general body of taxpayers whom they benefited. When the Commissioners tried to increase traffic by anything in the nature of a differential rate, they were charged with unfairness. Members of the Legislature could no longer obtain the favours for their constituents that had been squeezed out of a political Minister. Many New Zealanders declare that the merits of the Board — its independence, and its stiffness in recognizing nothing but its duty to the community as a

[1] Quoted by Messrs. Rossignol and Stewart from the New Zealand Hansard, vol. xcix, p. 291.

whole — proved its undoing. The matter is one still in controversy, but be that as it may, Seddon's Ministry abolished
the Board, creating a Minister for railways under whom
the politicians regained their influence while economy declined. Ministerial patronage, used, of course, for political
purposes, flourished once more, and was said to be flourish-
ing when I visited New Zealand in 1912. Patronage includes not only the bestowal of posts in the railway service
and the giving of employment to day-labourers, but also the
execution of improvements, such as a new station, in places
where a constituency can be gratified, and the creating of
work for the unemployed in a particular area. It is said that
political aims were at one time pursued in another ingenious
way by bringing into an electoral district, where the parties
may happen to be equally divided, a body of railway workers whose votes could be counted on for the Ministry employing them.

Two questions remain to be considered: the financial
position of the Government railways and the service they
render. The former is not easy to ascertain because the
form in which accounts are presented, with the habit of
sometimes charging to capital what ought to come out of
revenue, does not tell the whole story. It seems clear, however, that the lines have been, and are being, worked at a
loss, *i.e.* the receipts do not cover interest on the cost of construction as well as all working expenses, so there is a loss to
the general taxpayer. The explanation usually given, besides, of course, an admission of the errors which made the
original cost greater than it ought to have been, and which
also saddled the Department with unremunerative lines, is
that the rates are kept low with a view to the development
of the country and the benefit of the travelling public. As
regards " development," this is a term wide enough to cover
expenditure on unprofitable lines, and one of the results of
" political " and otherwise extravagant railway construction
and management has been to reduce those very railway receipts which might have been used for the building of new
lines where they were really wanted. It is alleged that the
higher branches of the railway service suffer because it is
hard to promote the most capable men without incurring the
reproach of favouritism, and it is further asserted that in

the lower departments less work is got out of railway employees of all kinds than private employers obtain.[1] The rates for passengers and even for freight traffic, admittedly low, considering the wages of labour, are justified on the ground that this policy helps the people to move about freely, and that producers would complain if rates were raised on the transport of agricultural products.

Station accommodation is poor, but the transportation service is fairly efficient, having regard to the physical conditions of the country, and the permanent way is kept in good order. Trains are few, for the rural population is sparse and the four great cities lie far apart. The total mileage was, in 1919, 3012 miles, of which 2983 belonged to the State. All lines have a gauge of 3 feet 6 inches, a fact which makes the heavy cost of construction all the more remarkable.

Nobody in New Zealand proposes to change the present system of administration. To sell the lines to private companies might, it is thought, lead to the creation of a formidable monopoly. To lease them to private companies would take them, more or less according to the method of leasing adopted, out of Government control. A more obvious remedy for the present defects would be to re-establish an independent non-political Commission, such as existed from 1887 till 1894, and such as exists in some Australian States. This course also would, however, be unwelcome to members of the legislature, whose political interference offends only a small number of thoughtful men. New Zealanders who admit the defects of their system remark that after all it is better than the control which great railway companies have sometimes in other countries exerted over Governments to the prejudice of public interests, as notably in the United States, and also in France.

Besides building railways, the Public Works Department constructs, or aids by money grants, the local authorities to construct, roads and bridges, forms of expenditure in which ample use is made of all opportunities for showing favour to localities. "I am not one of those (observed Seddon) who say that, other things being equal, I should not favour

[1] Some interesting remarks on the costliness of the working of American railways by the State during the War may (with figures) be found in Mr. Moorfield Storey's *Problems of To-day* (Boston, 1920).

the district that was represented by one who helped to maintain the Government in power." "It is unreasonable and unnatural to expect the Government to look with the same kindly eye on districts returning members opposed to the Government as on those which returned Government supporters." [1]

Minor Governmental Undertakings.— Some of these need only a passing mention. The State has taken over the oyster-beds at Auckland because they were suffering from reckless private treatment. It has established trout and salmon hatcheries to stock the rivers with fish, and thus created some of the best trout-fishing areas to be found anywhere in the world. It wisely took charge of the famous region of mineral springs and geysers at Rotorua, and has provided hotels for tourists there. It set up sawmills to get timber for its public works more cheaply. A more important enterprise was its undertaking to work coal-mines on the public lands. In 1901 coal had become scarce and dear, owing to a diminished importation from Australia, and it was alleged that a coal Ring was keeping up prices. An Act was therefore passed by the Seddon Ministry empowering the Government to work the coal-beds it possessed on the west coast.[2] This it has continued to do, supplying its own railways and also competing in open market with private mine-owners. The latter do not seem to have materially suffered, and the prices, though probably steadied down by the State mines, are still high. It is, however, possible that the entrance of Government into the business may have discouraged the opening of new pits. Mine-owners say that they can stand the competition, because the Government mines are worked at a higher cost, not from a difference in wages, because wages are regulated by law, but because the State workers take things easier and do less work for the same wages than private employers obtain. It may be added these miners have been found troublesome to deal with, for

[1] Quoted by Rossignol and Stewart, p. 109. Cf. as to the U.S.A. Pork Barrel, p. 68 *ante*, and as to Canada, Vol. I., p. 535, where a similar condition of things is described.

[2] The results of the working of coal-mines by the Government is discussed in *Round Table Studies*, pp. 332–337, and the conclusion from the facts there given seems to be that the mines are operated at a loss, owing to the higher working expenses. Strikes have occurred on these mines.

they are exacting in their demands, and their Unions much disposed to strike.[1]

Life and Fire Insurance.— The business of Life Assurance was undertaken by the State as far back as 1869, when no local New Zealand companies were engaged in it. It has been carried on with reasonable success, though in recent years private companies have distanced the State office and obtained most of the new business. These companies are said to put more energy into canvassing, and communication with the outer world is so much more frequent that State intervention may be less needed than in earlier days. State Fire Insurance was taken up by the Seddon Government in 1903, against strong opposition on the part of the private companies then already established, and which had become unpopular because supposed to have formed a combination which was charging exorbitant premiums. When the State office started with a system of lower premiums, they fought hard against it; and experience showed that the reduction it had made was too great for safe business, the percentage of fires being high in New Zealand, where houses are largely of wood, and earthquakes not unknown. The State office, which found itself obliged to raise its premiums, is maintained as offering a security against the formation of a monopolistic Ring, but should it be found to be continuing to do business at a loss, it will be accused of benefiting the insurers at the expense of the taxpayers.

This is the place to mention another enterprise which won much favour. In 1894, when prices had been falling, and there was a good deal of pressure from the farming class, Seddon carried legislation authorizing loans to be made to agriculturists by way of mortgage at 5 per cent, the interest usually charged on farm mortgages being then from 6 to 8 per cent, or even more. The Government could do this, because it could borrow in England at 3 to 4 per cent, and make a profit on lending at 5. Under the powers of this Advances to Settlers Act, it went into business as a money-lender, with the result of relieving the farmers and bringing down the rate of interest in the open market. Repayment

[1] I am informed that in the summer of 1919 the "go slow" policy adopted on these Government mines reduced the supply of coal by 30,000 tons per month, with the result of seriously disorganizing the railway service.

by small instalments was required, and the State has, in fact, profited by this enterprise.[1] The experiment was followed up in 1906 by another Act, authorizing advances to workers on first mortgage at 4½ to 5 per cent to enable them to acquire homes. The borrower's income must be under £200 a year, and the loan is not to exceed £350. This experiment also seems to have worked well financially, though critics observe that both schemes encourage the belief that whenever any class is suffering from economic causes, it may expect the Government to step in to relieve it. The same remark would apply to the practice of providing State work at times of unemployment.[2]

All the water-power of large streams has been taken over by the Government. It is still the owner of considerable natural forests, forests of great beauty which ought to be carefully preserved, and as these are disappearing, it has entered on a policy of afforestation with foreign trees, for the native trees, though many of them valuable, are of slow growth.[3]

NOTE ON PROTECTION

" The effect on the social structure can be traced if we ask ourselves what would have happened if New Zealand had adopted a different policy. Denmark, like New Zealand, has broken up the great estates by a Progressive Land Tax, and is relying on an elaborate system of co-operative credit to prevent the re-engrossment of the small holdings. But — and herein lies the difference between Denmark and New Zealand — the Socialist members returned by her one great city of Copenhagen have no influence on the policy of the Government. They are swamped by the representatives of the rural industry, who depend on foreign markets and insist on the maintenance of Free Trade. Supposing New Zealand had developed on the Danish policy, the factories of boots, clothing, agricultural machinery, and other manufactured articles would never have come into existence at all; for at present they

---

[1] See as to this Siegfried, chap. xv.; Rossignol and Stewart, p. 285; Scholefield, p. 253.

[2] The Factory Acts, and other laws for the protection of workers and limitation of working hours, are a subject too full of minutiae to be entered on here. Full information regarding them will be found in the works above referred to, and in the successive New Zealand Year Books.

The Social Democratic Party in its platform demands a recognition of the right to have work provided.

[3] In New Zealand, as was long the case in the United States, the people have not taken sufficient thought for the future of their charming woodland scenery. If protective measures are not soon taken, much will be irreparably lost.

only exist under one of the highest tariffs in the world. That large proportion of the population which they support would never have been collected in the great towns. On the other hand, the much lower cost of all manufactured articles would have made the profits of agriculture much greater than they now are, so great, in fact, as to attract the inrush of an agricultural population. And there would be ample room for an agricultural population many times larger than that which now occupies the land, for with lower costs of production, large areas would be worth clearing or ploughing, which at the existing cost of production it does not pay to clear or plough; just as in gold-mining lowered costs mean that a poorer grade of ore begins to be raised. It is evident that, given the existing measures to remedy or prevent the engrossment of land for sheep-walks, New Zealand, under Free Trade, would have accumulated a far larger rural population than it has done. It is equally clear that it would yield an infinitely larger output of its natural products — hides, wool, meat, butter, cheese, grain, and flax.

" The cities would, as we have said, be reduced by the absence of the manufacturing population, which exists under a high protective tariff. But, to an extent which can only be conjectured, this loss would be compensated in two directions. In the first place, the immense increase in exports and imports would of itself collect in the towns a larger population than is at present engaged there in the handling of trade. But, secondly, the natural products of New Zealand mean the establishment of subsidiary industries at the ports — meat works where cattle are slaughtered, and residuary products are canned or converted into tallow, manure, jelly, or glue, and freezing works for the meat, butter, and cheese. It is indeed conceivable that the whole volume of business done in New Zealand would be so great as to support towns as large as those now in existence, because the production from the land and the population living on it would be so much greater. The State would be a far larger one, and be growing much more rapidly; but its character would be wholly different. The rural population would have dominated the situation, and would continue to do so more and more." — " Notes on New Zealand " in *Round Table Studies*, p. 324.

CHAPTER LV

COMPULSORY ARBITRATION IN TRADE DISPUTES

NONE of the legislative experiments tried in New Zealand has excited so much attention in other countries as the application of compulsion to the settlement of disputes between employers and workmen, for no other economic question has caused and is causing so much friction all over the civilized world. I will here sketch first the provisions of the New Zealand law, then its working in practice, and lastly its general results, so far as yet estimable.

The wage-earners, having failed in the great strike of 1890, desired to find some better means of improving the conditions of labour, and the colony as a whole, alarmed by the strike, was in a mood to consider remedies. The first Act on the subject was introduced in 1891 in the Ballance Government and passed in 1894 by the Seddon Government. The drafting of the measure had been wisely left to the Minister of Labour (Mr. W. Pember Reeves), who was not only the most highly educated member of the Government, but did a great deal of its thinking down till 1896, when he left New Zealand. He stated its aims to be three: (*a*) To prevent strikes, (*b*) to strengthen Trade Unions, (*c*) to improve the conditions of labour generally.[1] Without describing the many subsequent amendments made in it, I give the principal provisions of the law, as it now stands, beginning with those which relate to Conciliation.

New Zealand is divided into eight industrial districts, for each of which there exists a Council of Conciliation. The

---

[1] W. Pember Reeves, *State Experiments in Australia and New Zealand* (published in 1902).

four Conciliation Commissioners who administer the Act set up a local Council on the application of a Union, or Association of Unions or Employers, or an individual employer, concerned. Assessors are nominated by the complainants and respondents. The Council hears the parties and endeavours to settle the dispute. If it succeeds, the settlement reached is filed as an industrial agreement, and becomes binding. If it fails, it refers the matter to the Court of Arbitration, since it does not itself possess compulsory powers.[1]

The Court of Arbitration, appointed for the whole country, consists of one of the Judges of the Supreme Court, detailed for that purpose, and of two assessors, one nominated by the association of employers throughout the country, and the other by the trade unions or associations of unions. These assessors hold office for three years. The Court hears the parties to each case referred to it by the Councils, and, if it has not effected an agreement by persua-sion, issues its award, which binds not only the parties, but individuals (whether or not members of Unions) who are working for the employer to whom the award applies. Every kind of question relating to labour falls within the jurisdiction of the Councils and the Court, and can be determined by awards, covering not only the minimum wage and the hours of labour, but also piecework, the distribution of work, permits to pay lower wages to less competent workmen, apprenticeship and the employment of boys, notices of dismissal, holidays, meal hours, modes of payment, provision of tools, the interpretation, scope, and duration of awards, and the power of extending them and imposing fines for their breach,— in fact every kind of condition affecting labour and in particular that most controversial of questions, the giving of preference in employment to members of trade unions. The Court exercises what is virtually a continuous power of legislation in everything that belongs to the relation of employer and employed. The right of applying to Council and Court is given to every union of workers with at least fifteen members, and to any union of employers with at least three. An award may cover the whole coun-

[1] See as to this subject Siegfried, pp. 109–43 (English translation, pp. 128–61); Drummond, *Life of Richard John Seddon*, pp. 238–68; Scholefield, pp. 212–43; and Rossignol and Stewart, pp. 216–68.

try, and employers on whom it is being imposed sometimes
ask for its extension in order to prevent unfair competition.
Every Union must be registered, in order to obtain the
right of application to the Court, and if it withdraws from
the register, or allows the registration to lapse, it is no longer
within the operation of the law.   An employer, however,
cannot similarly exempt himself.   A strike, when entered
on in breach of an award or industrial agreement, is punishable by a fine up to £200 for a trade union, and up to
£10 for an individual worker, and similarly a fine up to
£500 may be imposed on an employer who offends by declaring a lock-out.   Note also that a strike and a lock-out
in certain industries affecting the necessaries of life or a
public utility are made statutory offences, even when the
party in fault is not bound by any award, unless fourteen
days' notice of either has been given.

Working of the Law.— It has been often remarked that
whereas more was expected from the action of the Councils
(at first called Boards) of Conciliation than from the Court,
the reverse has turned out to be the fact.   The Boards
were found tedious and cumbrous, and fell into comparative
neglect, nearly all the cases brought before them being carried by appeal to the Court.   In their latest form, however, as altered by the Act of 1908, they have succeeded in
settling a number of minor disputes.   The Court, on the
other hand, had been incessantly resorted to in cases of every
description, and almost always by the workers.   Between
1894 and 1907 the binding agreements and awards imposed
reached the number of 535, and affected 78 industries.   In
1920 the number of existing awards and agreements was
530, and in all but two of these preference for employment
had been directed to be given to members of Labour Unions.
The decisions given have as a rule granted a rise in wages
or otherwise complied with the wishes of the workers, but
in one case the existing wage was reduced, and in a certain
number of cases no increase has been made or some other
demand of the Unions has been refused.   Preference to
Unions was usually given in the form of a direction that
Union men rather than others shall be employed, provided
that members of the Union, equally qualified with non-
members for the particular work, stand ready and willing

to undertake it. When granted, conditions were, where it seemed needful, imposed on the Unions, requiring them to admit to membership any applicant. To these the Unions have not generally objected, but they still demand an unconditional preference for their members in employment.[1] Trouble has also arisen over the employment of boys and the question of apprentices, whom the Unions seek as much as possible to exclude, in order thereby to increase the quantity of work available for adults enjoying the full minimum wage. In order to meet the case of the less efficient workers, such as elder men whom it would be wrong to throw out of employment, the law allows the granting of permits to such persons to work at less than the normal wage prescribed by the award. Such exceptions, however, are disliked, and as far as possible resisted by the Unions.[2] The awards are often extremely minute, going into numerous details. Their enforcement by proceedings against those who break an award is in the hands of the Labour Department, but either of the parties to an award can also sue a transgressor. It ought to be added that the Court has done useful work for improving the conditions of labour generally.

The principles on which the Court has proceeded in determining the fair wage are substantially those already set forth as followed by the Commonwealth Arbitration Court in Australia.[3] It has sought to find on the one side what is the minimum wage on which a worker — and presumably a married worker — can live in decent comfort, the New Zealand scale of comfort being higher than the average scale in Western Europe, and the price of most necessaries of life being higher. On the other hand, it has had to regard — and this consideration has sometimes received more weight than in Australia — what wages each given industry will bear, *i.e.* what an employer can afford to pay while continuing to make a profit on his business. The best proof of the fairness which the judges successively charged with this difficult duty have brought to it is to be found in the fact that while complaints against their decisions have come

[1] As to preference, see Rossignol and Stewart, pp. 235–6. See Scholefield, p. 220.

[2] Rossignol and Stewart, p. 232.

[3] See *ante,* p. 248.

equally from both sides, scarcely any one has questioned their uprightness and their desire to hold the scales of equity even, and to do the best that circumstances may from time to time admit. To satisfy everybody is an impossible task, so most of the judges have accepted those functions reluctantly, and been glad to return from them to their ordinary duties. The work is not truly judicial, except as regards the spirit of impartiality it requires, but rather administration, and administration of a singularly difficult kind; but since there exists in the country no other class of persons so generally trusted as the judges, it was perforce imposed upon them.

The result of a twenty years' working of the system has been to raise wages in practically every industry. The rise had been steady and large even before 1914, but within the same period the rise in the prices of articles had been nearly as great, so it may be argued that the worker is not substantially better off, and that in the natural course of things wages would have followed the upward course of prices. To have secured that rise might, however, have needed the rude expedient of strikes, with their attendant losses, so that by gaining the increase without these losses, both worker and employer have benefited materially and morally.

Sweating, which existed in some few trades so late as 1894, has been extinguished, but this would doubtless have happened in any case through factory legislation simultaneously passed, as well as by the sympathetic action of public opinion. The same may be said of workmen's housing and other improvements in the conditions of the working-class which statutes have dealt with. It is hard to assign these improvements to any one cause when several have been at work. Nevertheless, some credit is due to the Seddon policies.

The employer does not seem to have suffered seriously, if at all. Manufacturers say they have been worried by frequent appearances before the Boards and the Court, and that the conduct of their business has been interfered with, but they have continued to make reasonable profits, and have the advantage not only of a diminution in the number of strikes, but of feeling less anxious lest a sudden strike should prevent them from fulfilling a contract. Neither does it appear that there has been any unwillingness to start new industrial establishments and expand those that already existed. To all this some employers reply that the times have been good in New Zealand, so good as to enable them to support the Court's action, and to this, again, it may be answered that the Court felt it could safely raise wages with rising markets.

When the Bill of 1894 was introduced, the encouragement of Unions was announced as one of its objects. This has been largely attained, the awards of preference having strengthened their position and stamped with legal approval the plan of collective bargaining. Nevertheless, a large part, possibly a majority of the whole wage-earning class, still remains outside. The part which the protective tariff plays in this matter must not be forgotten. Were the manufacturers exposed to the competition of other countries, they could not afford to pay the minimum wage fixed by the Courts, so the compulsion imposed by the Court provides a ground for demanding that import duties be not only maintained but in some instances raised further. This gives the workmen also a motive for supporting a protective policy. Under free foreign competition the whole fabric would topple to the ground. Many New Zealanders who perceive this recognize that the experience of isles far off in the Pacific is too exceptional to set an example to European or American countries.

The third chief aim of the Act of 1894 was the prevention of industrial conflicts. During the first few years it seemed that this had been attained, for nearly all the Unions were on the register, and scarcely a strike or a lock-out occurred. Throughout those years the Court almost always granted an increase of wages, so the workers were pleased. But when, after the expiry of the first set of three-year awards, the Unions went again to the Courts to demand a second increase, they did not always succeed. Disappointment followed, signs of which appeared as early as 1901. In 1906 and the two subsequent years several strikes occurred, though none on a very large scale. Of those whose views I enquired, some blamed the Government, believing they showed weakness, while others thought that Seddon's death had made a difference, his strong personality having exerted a restraining influence on the working class. The passing of the Act of 1908 somewhat eased the situation, but there have been subsequently serious and prolonged strikes. One of these, at the Waihi gold mines, was in progress when I visited New Zealand in 1912, and could not be dealt with under the Arbitration Act because the Miners' Union had, by omitting to register, taken itself out of the Court's jurisdiction.[1] Not a few Unions have allowed their registration to lapse in order to obtain this result. Another serious strike took place in Auckland and Wellington in 1913, and failed, because the Government brought in a strong body of special constables from the rural districts, who repressed attempts at violence, while other farming volunteers loaded and unloaded the ships in the harbour. A recent Labour Disputes Investigation Act forbids a strike or lock-out, in cases where the trade is not subject to an industrial award, till the Labour Disputes Committee has publicly investigated the controversy and announced its opinion, and also requires that before any strike or lock-out takes place there must first be taken a secret ballot of the workmen and employers concerned, whether or no the Union is registered. Where an industrial award or (agreement) exists, strikes are absolutely illegal under the Act already mentioned.

What, it will be asked, is the present attitude of New Zealand opinion as to the practical value of the system? As already observed, the working-class is by no means so enamoured of it as in the first years, for wage-raising has not gone on latterly at the same pace. Since the Unions exist largely for the sake of securing better wages, the officials of these bodies, especially the younger among them, are tempted to justify their existence by constant activity, and contrive frequent appeals to the Court. When these have only a slender success, disappointment follows, and the impartiality, though not the honest purpose, of the Court may

[1] The case was a singular one. A section of the miners desired to form a new union of their own, register it so as to bring it within the Arbitration Acts, and then apply to the Court. The New Zealand Federation of Labour, a body largely Socialist, desired to prevent this, because any award obtained by the new union (if registered) would have bound all the miners, and therefore they organized the strike to arrest the attempt to have the proposed new union registered. The strike failed after six months.

be arraigned. Nevertheless, the workers as a whole desire to retain the Acts. It is only the more extreme and Communistic section, influenced by the body called Syndicalists, or "Industrial Workers of the World," that denounces the whole system as a part of "wage slavery," and seeks to obtain its ends by a succession of general strikes, which would "bring capital to its knees." Australian and European emissaries come to New Zealand on this mission, while the bulk of the native New Zealanders, led by the older and more experienced men, prefer to bear what evils they have and to keep the goods the Courts provide them. These uphold the Act, pointing to the sufferings which the strikes of former days entailed.

The views of the employers have undergone a sort of converse change. What depressed the spirits of the Unions cheered theirs. Though still grumbling at the interference of a Court with their private affairs, they found that their losses had been less than they feared, and the wiser among them, like the wiser among the working-class leaders, recognized that the prospect of peace, even for the three years an award runs, was no contemptible asset. Accordingly, though most of them still disapprove of the Acts in principle and often complain of them in practice, insisting, like Australian employers, that no effective compulsion is or can be applied to the workmen, they do not demand the abolition of the system.

Rising above these two classes, there is such a thing as the opinion of the country as a whole. This opinion seemed to me to be in favour of maintaining the Acts. It is not so proud of them as in the first few years of their working. It admits that they have not solved the industrial problem as a whole, that they are used by the Labour leaders to gain something by way of compromise, and soon after to reopen the dispute, and that a still longer experience than twenty-five years have supplied is needed to test them, but it conceives that, by invoking a trusted authority, they have enabled the public to hold the balance fairly between the parties, and have brought its judgment to bear on each dispute. Thus the Acts have made for peace, one of the highest interests both employers and employed can have. Things would be worse without them, because no means at all of settlement would be left; and the disposition to uphold them is all the stronger because they are denounced by the revolutionary Communist party. I saw no likelihood of their being repealed in the near future.

Into the general arguments for and against the plan of the State regulation of wages and other labour conditions and the elimination of freedom of contract [1] I do not enter. These considerations belong to the realm of legal and economic theory, little regarded in New Zealand.

The broad result of this remarkable experiment may be summed up in a few sentences.

It has had little success in the line of mere conciliation, and has perhaps done something to discredit that method of settling disputes, which, to be sure, was effecting but little in New Zealand when compulsion was introduced.

It began by strengthening the Labour Unions, but has latterly tended to create a division between them, some, under the influence of extremists, repudiating any pacific methods of settling industrial disputes.

It has raised wages, yet perhaps no more than they would have risen, ultimately, if not so quickly, by the action of economic causes.

It has not, to any appreciable extent, injured business or retarded the progress of the country.

If it has not extinguished strikes, it has reduced their frequency and their severity.

It has been a mitigation not a panacea. But, I must again repeat, the results have been attained during a period which has been, as a whole, a period of prosperity and expansion. The real test will come with hard times. Two dangers must not be ignored. One is the growth of a party among the workers which avows its wish to have done with peaceful methods. The other is the possibility that a government might some day, yielding to the pressure of the Labour vote, appoint judges virtually pledged to decide according to its wishes. In the present healthy condition of public opinion, such a danger seems remote.[2]

[1] The Chief Justice of New Zealand in 1900 (in delivering judgment in a case relating to the Arbitration Acts) observed: " All contracts regarding labour are controlled and may be modified or abrogated. The Court can make the agreement between the workman and the employer. It abrogates the right of workmen to make their own contracts."

[2] The only country (besides Australia) which has followed New

Two other pieces of legislation which belong to the Seddon period deserve a brief mention.

One is the extension of the electoral franchise to women, enacted in 1893. This measure, carried through the House of Representatives by Ballance, but rejected by the Council, had no great attraction for Seddon, whether he feared, as did some Australian statesmen, that it might help the conservative party, or whether it seemed to him likely to strengthen the Prohibitionist vote.[1] But, though he cared little for it, he chose, as was his wont, the line of least resistance, and let it pass the House, hoping (so I was told) that the Legislative Council would, as on previous occasions, reject it. The Council, however, not wishing to be always expected to do this kind of work, allowed it to become law. Such demand for it as there was in New Zealand had come chiefly from the Prohibitionists, but if there was little positive desire for it, neither was there any strong feeling against it, this easy-going democracy being always disposed to say Yes rather than No. Even among the women the demand for it was confined to comparatively few. Having got it, however, the women have come to the polls in almost as large numbers as the men. They usually vote with their fathers, brothers, or husbands, except to some exten'. upon liquor questions, when their tendency to cast a vote for the anti-liquor candidate, irrespective of his party affiliations, disturbs the calculations of politicians. Apart from these drink questions, and only slightly even as regards them, woman suffrage has — so I was everywhere told — made no practical difference to politics, and has not led to the introduction of legislation intended specially to benefit women.[2]

On the subject of immigration, Seddon held more decided views. In the years following the great borrowings of 1870, when money was being lavishly spent in building railways and otherwise developing the country, immigrants were invited from England and continental Europe, and aided by subsidies to come. Not a few Norwegians and Danes ar-

Zealand by establishing compulsory arbitration seems to be Norway, by a law passed in 1916.

[1] Mr. Seddon said, some years later, " By granting the franchise to women, Parliament plunged into an abyss of unknown depth."

[2] Women are now eligible to sit in the House of Representatives. Two were (unsuccessful) candidates at the general election of 1919.

rived, and made excellent colonists, but not all could obtain farms, and when an industrial depression succeeded the boom, many town workers could find no work. Suffering followed, and instead of emigration, men began, after 1880, to leave New Zealand for Australia or Europe. By 1890 the working class had become disposed to shut the door in the face of newcomers, who were now deemed intruders, because possible competitors for wages. Under the influence of the Unions the Ballance-Seddon Government dropped the subsidies theretofore given to attract immigrants. This might have seemed enough, for the cost of a passage from Europe to New Zealand was virtually prohibitive to the poorer class of labourers. But the Ministry went further, and brought in a Bill — the Undesirable Immigrants Bill of 1891 — which passed through the Legislature, but never became law, because the British Government at home objected to provisions it contained affecting the rights of British subjects. The Labour men have, however, maintained their hostility to immigration, although they have received the help of the Arbitration Court in keeping up wages. In 1898 it was found that some Austrian subjects, Slavs from Southeastern Europe, were working as gum-diggers in the kauri forests north of Auckland, and prospering so well that others of the same race were coming out. Nothing was alleged against them, for they were hard-working and frugal, except that they were lowering, or would lower, the rate of wages. The members for the district, however, complained to Government, urging that " the Colony could not be allowed to become a prey to the paupers of the Old World," so an Act was passed (1898, amended 1899) which stopped the immigration. The law now in force (Immigration Restriction Act of 1908) prohibits, *inter alia,* the landing of any person of other than British birth who fails to write out and sign in any European language a prescribed form of application. Trade Unions have, moreover, exerted themselves to dissuade emigration to New Zealand.[1] Nevertheless, there is a flow of immigrants, steady if not large, and Government, obliged to recognize the needs of agriculture and of domestic service, provides passages at reduced rates to *bona fide* farmers and agricultural labourers, under conditions

[1] Rossignol and Stewart, p. 282.

as to their possessing some pecuniary means, and also to domestic servants. A Report of the Minister for Labour called attention to the dearth of boys and girls, stating that there was in many trades too little labour to cope with the work offered, but this did not prevent the Unions from reiterating their protests. Their attitude, if not the result of, is in harmony with, the fiscal policy of the Dominion, for while the employer is protected by a high tariff against foreign competition, the workman has his wages raised by law, and could not have them raised but for the protection which the tariff gives to employers. As the products of his labour are protected, he thinks himself entitled to have his labour itself protected from any competition by newcomers, and defends his case by the argument that a State which does so much for the existing inhabitants cannot be expected to burden itself with any new citizens, and that it is better to have a small population raised to a high level of comfort than a larger one on a level not so high. But M. Siegfried seems to hit the nail on the head when he sums up the situation by remarking: " ' There is a cake to be divided,' think the workmen, ' let us be as few as possible when the division comes.' " [1]

Fifty or sixty years ago, democracy was supposed to be above all things humanitarian. The sentiment of the masses, themselves lately admitted (in the Old World) to full civic rights, went out to all their brethren of every race and country. All were equal, all equally entitled to the pursuit of happiness, all interested in one another's welfare. The growth of Socialism accentuated this feeling among the wage-earners, and it was even believed to constitute a powerful guarantee for international peace, illusory as that hope proved in 1914. To-day, however, neither in Australia nor in New Zealand do the workers generally or the Socialistic sections among them show any willingness to share with the workers of Europe the benefits they have secured for themselves. No more cosmopolitan humanitarianism, not even for white men seeking to better their lot. The same tendency is visible in the United States and in Canada, countries far more exposed to a large influx from the Old World. But there

---

[1] Siegfried, p. 121 (English translation).

the law excludes only immigrants really undesirable in respect of character or health, or likely to become a public charge, together with those who, being personally unexceptionable, are brought over under a contract of labour, and therefore presumably intended to replace striking workmen.

Few things in Australian and New Zealand policy seem to have so much surprised and grieved European observers as this apparently anti-social attitude of the working-class leaders, who, while striving for economic equality not only between the handworkers and other classes but also among all the handworkers themselves, yet seek to prevent European handworkers from coming to share in their own prosperity lest that should possibly affect questions of employment in Australia and New Zealand. The " class solidarity " for which they plead does not extend its sympathy to members of the same class in other countries. Whether immigration would in fact have the effect New Zealand wage-earners apprehend is a further question too intricate to be here discussed.

Asiatics also are excluded, as they are from Australia, and to some extent from Canada also. There is a strong dislike to them and a jealousy of their competition, which has gone so far as to forbid by law the owner of a laundry to work for longer hours than the statutes in force permit his employees to do, laundrying being a distinctively Chinese trade. A New Zealand law, passed in 1896, imposes a tax of £100 on every Chinese entering the country, and limits the number any vessel may bring to one Chinese for each 200 tons burthen. But as already observed [1] there are ethnological and social reasons, not necessarily disparaging to the races of Eastern and Southern Asia, which make it prudent to keep those races from flooding regions already peopled by whites. Though the working men of New Zealand are not interested in the ethnological aspect of the matter, their attitude is intelligible, and they have the whole opinion of the country with them. In 1911 there were 2630 Chinese in the islands, only 88 of whom were females; in 1916 they had fallen to 2147. The Japanese are extremely few, and so are the Polynesians, other than the native Maoris. Feel-

[1] See p. 236, *ante.*

ing being what it is, it may be safer to restrict the number of Chinese, for if they grew to be a considerable body collisions might arise similar to those of San Francisco forty years ago; and it is perhaps too much to expect of any nation that when it has a disagreeable thing to do it should take pains to do it in a courteous way.

CHAPTER LVI

THE WORKING OF THE GOVERNMENT

WHOEVER examines the phenomena of politics and public life as they exist to-day in New Zealand must never forget how many facts are there absent which control or colour political conditions in European States.

To begin with there are no racial questions. The white population is homogeneous, for though one region, Otago, in the South Island, is predominantly Scottish, that makes no difference for political purposes. The Maoris return their own four members and are on the best terms with the whites. Nothing does more credit to New Zealanders than this friendliness of the races.

There are no religious questions. Even the Roman Catholic Church, which exerts great political influence in Canada, and scarcely less in New South Wales, does not make itself felt politically here, for the Irish element is small, and weak in the legislature.

There are no questions of foreign policy, because that is left to the Motherland, nor of colonial policy, for the Cook Islands, the management of which was entrusted by Britain to New Zealand in 1901, are insignificant in size and population, and the only thing that needs to be done for them is to appoint competent and sympathetic administrators. The mandate given to New Zealand by the League of Nations for the administration of some of the Samoan islands increases the need for care in the choice of such administrators.

There are no constitutional questions, for democracy has got down as far as it can well go, unless indeed some should propose to shorten parliaments to one year from three, or to introduce the Initiative and Referendum in legislation, changes which would hardly make the system more effectively popular than it is at present.

There are no local disputes affecting general politics, *i.e.* none which set any considerable district of the country against another, or tend to make the views of districts on public affairs divergent. Questions affecting the distribution of money for public works are numerous enough, but they do not become party matters, though a local election may sometimes be won on them.

Think what a difference it makes to a people to be free from many causes of dissension and from many of those preoccupations with grave issues, often lying outside the knowledge of the ordinary man, which distract the minds of most free peoples! Undistracted by these, New Zealanders can better devote their thoughts to matters touching their domestic and especially their economic welfare.

There is in New Zealand no aristocracy of birth or rank or hereditary wealth, no great fortunes, no considerable class of indigent people, trembling on the verge of pauperism. Social distinctions and social ambitions have not quite disappeared, for there is a small class, colloquially known as "The Push," who consider themselves select, and desire invitations to parties at Government House, a privilege ungrudgingly accorded to those who have reached a certain position in the agricultural or business world. There is also a measure of suspicion or jealousy — it hardly amounts to the aversion evident in Australia — observable among the working-class towards the employers and the richer people generally. But class distinctions of this nature, in which, moreover, there are no sharp lines between poorer, middle, and upper, have no perceptible effect upon politics, except in so far as they make the wage-earners prefer one of themselves as a candidate for Parliament. Such slight antagonism as exists seems due to the bitterness aroused by labour conflicts, and to that sort of envy which is generally felt towards the richer in a community where differences of wealth exist, while the sense of equality has extinguished the old deference. The significant fact is that what Europeans would call the "upper class" exerts no more political in-

fluence than any other class.   It does not lead even so much
as the like class does in Switzerland or the United States,
not to speak of England or Italy, where social status and
wealth still count for something.   The one form of influence, operating as a slight check on the power of numbers,
which is still discernible in the older democracies, is here
conspicuous by its absence.

There are no constitutional checks such as exist in the
United States, and, to a less degree, in Switzerland.   Nothing inhibits the power of the popular House to carry any
measure it desires.   The Legislative Council of nominees
sitting for seven years has been a negligible factor.   So, too,
the veto of the British Government is practically no longer
used, though a case involving Imperial interests may be imagined in which it might be resorted to.   Whether a Referendum would prove a serviceable check may be doubted,
but it never has been tried except when submitted by the
legislature as respects the prohibition of the sale of liquor.
The House of Representatives is absolute master of the situation, being virtually able not only to pass laws but to alter
the constitution at its pleasure.

The conservative element in New Zealand — there is even
here, as there always must be everywhere, a certain conservative element — is to be found in the rural population.
In Australia each of the four great cities of the four chief
States contains one-third of the population of those States.
In New Zealand the four large cities (the other towns being
quite small) contain about one-fifth of the total, and the
proportion of the population occupied in manufacturing industries is even smaller.   The rural population, moreover,
consists to a larger extent than in Australia of small farmers,
who quickly acquire the so-called instinct of property.

Political Parties.— With these facts in mind, let us come
to the parties.   In 1915, when the European War caused
the formation of a Coalition or " National " Government,
there were two old parties, the Reformers and Liberals,
nearly equal in parliamentary strength, and the new Labour
party, a creation of the preceding eight years, with seven or
eight members in the House, but probably a larger proportionate strength in the country as a whole.   It was mainly
a party of urban wage-earners.   The Reform party includes

the bulk of the larger landowners, of manufacturers, and of merchants, the minority of these, as well as a good many of the poorer people, forming the Liberal party. Thus it is only the Labourites who are a class party, the two others, as in Australia before the Coalition of 1908, being drawn from both rich and poor.

Of the three, it is only the Labour men, now called the Social Democratic party, who have any regular organization, the Trade Unions having in many towns created political Trade and Labour Councils, whose delegates meet in an annual central Congress, the most powerful unofficial body in the Dominion, though it does not represent all the workers. The wage-earners are also organized in a body called the United Federation of Labour. The other parties have local political committees, but with no such complete and controlling organization as that which the " Liberal " (or anti-Labourite) party had created for itself in Australia in 1912. Candidates for the House of Representatives offer themselves to the electors, and if more than one of the same party come forward, the question who shall be the party standard-bearer is, if not settled locally, referred to the parliamentary chief. In New Zealand party ties are not and never have been strict, and party spirit, except sometimes in the Assembly during conflicts, has not been intense, much less bitter. Neither has the Labour party created any such powerful centre for its political action in the legislature as is the parliamentary Labour Caucus in Australia. Of its two sections, the larger and more moderate includes Socialists and Trade Unionists of the older type, while the smaller and more advanced is under Syndicalist and revolutionary influences, and goes by the name " Red Feds," as its leaders formed the kernel of the former Federation of Labour. The party programme for the election of 1915 demanded a Right to Work Bill, with minimum wage, a citizen army " democratically organized " on a volunteer basis, and never to be used in industrial disputes, and the Referendum, Initiative, and Recall. The extreme section has been much influenced by the most advanced Socialists of Australia, and seems to be growing. Being weaker than the Australian Labour party, and having had less immediate prospect of carrying

the legislation it desires, it is even more disposed to the
policy of strikes, yet hopes to secure some of its measures
by parliamentary pressure on the other parties.

The Liberals and Reformers were distinguished rather
by tendencies than by specific tenets. When the former lost
power in 1912, they had no bold legislative programme, for
the work done in the twenty years preceding had left them
comparatively little to accomplish. They have, however,
been more identified than their rivals with the extension of
State action and the promotion of the interests of the workers. The Reformers came into power on an unexciting platform, the chief features of which were the disposal of land to
small owners on freehold rather than leasehold tenure, with
retrenchment, *i.e.* small borrowings and careful administration, this being, as both parties admit, a chief need for the
country. Towards Labour questions their attitude has been
that of caution and criticism, for they conceive that the country has gone far enough for the present in the extension of
State action and in piling taxation upon the rich, but they
uphold compulsory arbitration and the system of advances
to settlers. Liquor legislation is the subject which rouses
most controversy, but upon it neither party has ventured to
announce a distinctive policy. When a sharp conflict arose
over a proposal that the Bible should be read in the public
schools the issue, though raised by a Ministerial Bill, was
fought not on party lines, but rather as between Episcopa-
lians and Presbyterians on one side and the secularist Social
Democratic party on the other, the latter supported by some
of the smaller religious communities.

The languor of party feeling and action in the country
had been, even before 1914, reflected in the Assembly, where
political life ought to be most vigorous. In point of composition, the House fairly represents all the elements of New
Zealand society. There are some few working men, and
about as many landowners, while all the other classes, manufacturers, merchants, shopkeepers, farmers, and professional
men contribute their quota. The lawyers are, as in Australia, a comparatively small element. Members of the
House receive a salary of £300 a year, those of the Legislative Council £200. There is a time-limit on speeches, a rule

needed to check obstruction, called here, as in Australia, " stone-walling." [1]

The House of Representatives is in one sense too representative, for its members are little above the average of their electors in knowledge or ability. That average is no doubt high, but nearly all my New Zealand informants declared that the quality of the legislature, instead of rising with the growth of the country, had declined during the last thirty years, and that the debates were now on a lower level than in the days of Sir George Grey or Sir Harry Atkinson. Some said the declension dated from the rise of Seddon, which led the more cultivated class to withdraw. Up till then every member was, according to M. Siegfried, *ex officio* admitted to the Wellington Club. The country has no lack of capable men, thoughtful and well educated,— none of the self-governing Dominions has a larger proportion,— but very few of those seem to find their way into the Legislature. When travelling through New Zealand I had the good fortune to meet in each of the four chief cities a group of men who used to come together to discuss the problem of the relations of each Dominion to the British Empire as a whole, and they impressed me, in every city, by their high intelligence and sound judgment. But hardly any of them belonged to, or seemed to think of standing for, the Assembly, which is left to persons five-sixths of whom do not rise above the level of the town councillors of an English town. English town councillors are good citizens capable of managing the daily business of their community in an efficient way, but their functions seldom require more than practical common sense, whereas the New Zealand Assembly holds in its hands the fortunes of a young nation which will some day be a great nation, and has to deal with most of those complex problems of law-making which tax to its utmost the capacity of every European legislature.

Why do not the electors choose men of marked ability? They abound, and are not excluded by the cost of elections, for there is no bribery in New Zealand, and legitimate election expenses are light. Except in the very few constituen-

[1] For some time there was a second ballot law, providing for a second election where no candidate obtained a majority of all the votes cast, but this was recently repealed by the Reform Ministry.

cies which the Labour Unions dominate, there is not, as frequently in the United States, a party machine which controls the choice of candidates, nor, as frequently in Australia, an aversion to candidates who belong to the wealthier class. Neither is the choice of a candidate confined to persons resident in the electoral district.

The reasons lie partly in the conditions of parliamentary life, partly in the competition of other careers. The position of a member carries very little social prestige, and has many disagreeable incidents. The member is expected to be the slave of his constituents, and to act, as one of them observed,[1] as a sort of labour agent. His chief business is to get something for the constituency, or for individuals who belong to it, by constantly preferring requests to Ministers, an ungrateful task, and one that distracts him from his proper duties. His merits are measured by whatever benefits he can manage to secure for the place or some of its inhabitants.

Other careers are more attractive. A lawyer or a college professor or a business man, unless he happens to live in Wellington (the capital), must neglect his duties or his private business if he has to attend the sittings of the House, for the other three chief cities lie far off, and two of them can be reached only by a voyage over a stormy sea. There is no leisured class in the country, although one finds some families retaining that tradition of familiarity with public life which used to be strong in England, and is not extinct in the older States of the American Union. The prizes of public life are few, not to add that here, as elsewhere, small is the number of persons who, while enabled by their private means to enter that career, feel themselves called to it by motives of pure patriotic duty.

It may be suggested that the Legislative Council, a Second Chamber in which work is lighter, and a seat is secure for seven years at least, might be used to gather in a number of persons who, when they had already secured a competence, or could leave their farms or business to the care of younger men, would be willing to place their experience and ability at the service of the country. The Council has,

[1] See *ante*, p. 308.

however, exercised little attraction, for its powers are limited, its life is sluggish, as it has nothing to do with installing or ejecting a Ministry, and its debates are little reported or read or regarded. With members selected for nomination chiefly because they had rendered steady support to their party it had become an almost superfluous part of the constitutional machinery. Now, however, it has by recent legislation been turned into an elective body, which is ultimately to consist of forty persons, to be chosen from districts, of which there are to be two in each island, so a prospect of usefulness is opening before it.[1]

These things being so, the standard not only of attainments, but of debates and of manners also, leaves something to be desired. Thinking bears a low ratio to talking. Legislation tends to be, as in most democracies, too copious and too hasty. There are — so far as I know — no scenes of disorder, but there is a good deal of rudeness, and personalities are freely bandied to and fro. A most acute and experienced observer (quoted by M. Siegfried) [2] noted in 1898

" an absence of refinement among politicians without distinction of parties, which is the result of the pioneer life they have led. What is more serious is the absence throughout the Colony of serious economic study, of scientific investigation of those industrial and social problems which the politicians themselves attempted to solve."

The first part of this judgment seems to me, as to M. Siegfried, rather too sweeping. But there is certainly what one may call a sort of commonness, a want of that elevation and dignity which ought to raise above their ordinary level those who administer the affairs of a self-governing community with a great future; and this lowers the moral influence of Parliament upon the community itself. Against these defects one must not forget to set the personal probity

1 The voting is to be on the preferential system. The Council's powers in finance Bills are limited to the right of suggesting amendments to the House of Representatives, but it may amend or reject other Bills, and if a disagreement between the Houses cannot be otherwise settled, the Houses are to sit and vote together as one body, and if the Bill whereon they differ is not affirmed by such a voting, a dissolution of both Houses may follow.

2 *Op. cit.* p. 75 (English translation).

in public affairs of nearly all the New Zealand politicians.
Innumerable jobs are done for constituencies and party interests, but rarely is any one charged with abusing office or
parliamentary position for the purposes of pecuniary gain.
In this respect New Zealand stands, and always has stood,
well above some older and larger democratic countries.

CHAPTER LVII

THE general good nature and absence of political passion noticeable in New Zealand are reflected in the Press, which is creditably fair and free from violence or bitterness. There were in 1917 63 daily newspapers, besides 34 tri-weekly, 32 bi-weekly, and 69 weekly, numbers large for a population of 1,100,000. No one among them has ever exercised so great a power as the chief dailies of Melbourne and Sydney enjoyed twenty years ago: none indeed could, for there is no city that holds a leading place in the nation. But the general tone is good, and several are written with marked ability. They seemed to me to be doing more for the formation of an enlightened public opinion than was being done by the debates in Parliament, which, to be sure, are scantily reported.

Opinion is rather less sharply divided on the lines of social class than is now the case in Australia; and this uniformity expresses the homogeneity of the nation. Still, one may distinguish between three sections, the wage-earners at the one end, the wealthier landowners and merchants at the other, and the large mass between these extremes. First of the wage-earners. Although less than half are said to belong to labour unions, it is these bodies and the United Labour Federation that dominate the whole, because they have an organization, and their programme makes a definite and positive appeal. Few of its members are revolutionary, though some have become imbued with communistic ideas. Whatever may appear in electoral platforms prepared by leaders more extreme than their followers, the aim of the great majority is not to create a collectivistic society but to secure further increases of wages and improvements in labour conditions. As already observed, there is an advanced party which, stimulated by Australian Syndicalists, and discontented with the Court of Arbitration, prefers the method of strikes, and has begun to advocate the nationalization of all the means of production and distribution, but the prospect of any such change is distant, for the moderate section is the more numerous, nor is the wage-earning element likely to grow large enough to dominate politics. Though the men of property are few, they carry weight, not by voting strength or by any power over the votes of their employees —for no attempt to exert such power would be tolerated — but by the sort of influence which persons of education and commercial importance cannot but possess in a community which feels that its prosperity depends on agricultural production and the export of its products. Such men are of course the stronghold of conservative opinion. Between these two extremes stands the bulk of the voters, including not only the middle but also a considerable part of the poorer class. Its opinion is the deciding force in the country. The principal articles of its faith may be summed up as follows:

It believes in equality, social as well as political, values constitutional freedom, knows that order must go with freedom, and condemns revolutionary methods. It is firmly — more enthusiastically perhaps than any of the other Dominions — attached to Britain and the unity of the British Empire. Proud of New Zealand, it likes to feel that New Zealand has by its experiments been giving a lead to older and larger countries. It has no fear of experiments, thinking it can try them safely, and drop them if they do not succeed, so, however far it may be from professing what are known as Collectivist doctrines, it would not disapprove of any measure merely because branded with that name. Its profound trust in the future makes it heedless of consequences. " This plan promises well: let us try whether it will benefit us now. The future will take care of itself."

Here is the answer to those Europeans who ask, after reading of New England's experiments in legislation, " Are the New Zealanders all Socialists, and if so, what has become of the Individualists? " They are in principle no more Socialists than Individualists. The great majority do not think in abstractions: they have no use for theories. If the most obvious way to avert some evil or obtain some good seems to lie in invoking the State's action, they invoke it. " What is the State but ourselves ? It is ours to use; why be jealous of it ? " There is in this none of the German deification of the State as Power. The State is not to them a mighty organism in which national life is to centre, and by which national life is to be moulded and controlled, but rather an instrument ready to hand to be employed for diffusing among themselves and their neighbours comfort and prosperity, the things they really care for, and which rather than the growth of power or population occupy the New Zealand mind, leading them to tolerate that working-class resistance to immigration which surprises Europeans and Americans.

Public opinion follows the doings of Parliament with intelligence, but with little deference and no keen interest. What one may call the " high voltage " of politics in France or England or the United States is absent. There are no great prizes and few small prizes offered to ambition.

Both here and in Australia one is struck by the absence of traditions. The institutions of course are not new, and the Speaker of the House wears a wig. But that flavour of the British House of Commons thinking and manners, which was brought by the most educated among the first Anglican settlers at Christchurch and the first Presbyterian settlers at Dunedin, has almost died out with them, and the present generation seems, patriotically British as it is, to have but slight sense of the long British past behind it. Traditions are needed, and great men are needed to create them in these new countries, striking figures that can touch the imagination and throw some rays of colour over the landscape of national life. Tame are those regions of the sky in which no stars of the first magnitude glitter. Leaders of some talent and force there will always be in every free country, but it is a misfortune when a nation's most forcible and most trusted leaders do not represent something more ideal than did Richard Seddon.

A description of the attitude of New Zealanders towards their Government and politics needs to be prefaced by a few words on their character and temperament.

They are all (except of course the fifty thousand aborigines) of British stock, and one often notes in them especially in Otago (the far South) a slightly Scottish tinge, whereas the Australians are more distinctively English, with now and then a touch of the Irish.   They are strong and healthy, frank, simple, courageous.   Before there was any talk of war they instituted a system of physical training and drill which public opinion, with some few exceptions, approved, and had created for defence a force, into the management of which politics scarcely entered.   What may be called the social atmosphere of the country is rural rather than urban,[1] for only one city counts more than one hundred thousand inhabitants, and outside the towns population is sparse, except where dairying or fruit-growing enables a small district to support many households.   Nowhere, not even in Western Canada, is the level of comfort higher.   The total private wealth has been calculated at £387,000,000, and the average wealth per head, for persons over twenty years of age, estimated at £604, and this although there are no millionaires and very few persons rich according to British or American standards.   A great number of the artisans own the houses they live in.   No class is sunk to anywhere near the margin of subsistence, and the traveller, from the moment of landing, feels that the economic pressure of life is light.[2]

Everybody is educated, and a large percentage well educated, for secondary schools are abundant.   The inhabitants, especially in the smaller towns and rural areas, have the same intelligent interest in literature and social questions and public affairs, civil and ecclesiastical, as has been traditional among the townsfolk and the peasantry of Scotland, and of Switzerland, and of New England until the

[1] Auckland had in 1916 133,000 inhabitants, Wellington 95,000, Christchurch 92,000, Dunedin 69,000. Only six other boroughs had populations exceeding 10,000.

[2] The birth-rate has continued to fall from 1886, when it was 35.40 to 1000 of population to 23.44 in 1918, but as the death-rate is extremely low, having been since 1896 below 10 in 1000 of the population, this, coupled with a steady though small immigration, gives a natural increase of population at the rate of 16.4 per 1000. Had the standard rate of increase recorded in the decade 1865–76 been maintained, the population, which in 1918 was 1,108,000, would have then been 1,621,000. The country could maintain three or four millions at least, but it may be argued that the people are right in preferring a high standard of comfort for few to a lower standard for many.

flood of new European immigrants began to swamp the off-spring of the old Puritan stock. The likeness to Scotland appears also in the religious habits of the people, for here (and especially in Otago) the habit of churchgoing seems to have maintained itself better than in any other purely British colony, except perhaps in Newfoundland and Ontario.[1] Visiting New Zealand soon after I had visited Argentina and Brazil, where men of the educated class have practically dropped Christianity, I was struck by this contrast between the descendants of the Spaniards and the Englishmen of the sixteenth century. In New Zealand life is taken more easily than in Europe, and far more easily than in strenuous North America. The people enjoy outdoor amusements, and are almost as addicted to horse-racing (with the use of the totalizator), cricket, and football as are the Australians. Their temper and view of life has a leisurely and indulgent cast, as of those who wish not only to be happy but also to make everybody else happy, to the extent even of dissolving for slighter causes than English law recognizes the marriages of those who think that they would be happier apart.[2] Though the level of knowledge and intelligence is fairly well maintained, men's interest in the greater world beyond the ocean lies in current events, especially those of the Motherland, rather than in following the movements of thought and literature and art. This may be attributed to the remoteness of the country from the European centres of intellectual life, the inevitable results of which it has not been attempted to meet by the establishment of a teaching university on the British or American scale. The country ought to possess, and all the more because Europe is so far off, a much larger number of persons occupied with the higher studies, both literary and scientific, for, over and above the direct influence of their teaching work, they help to keep up an intellectual atmosphere and to vindicate for learning and science a due place of honour. New countries are specially liable to be occupied with purely material interests, because those memorials and traditions of the past which touch imagination and inspire reverence are absent,

[1] I omit, of course, the Dutch-speaking parts of South Africa and the French-speaking parts of Canada.

[2] The number of divorces granted has risen in New Zealand much faster than the population. In the ten years 1898 to 1907 it rose from 31 to 147, in the ten from 1908 to 1917 it rose from 171 to 221.

and the first need of the settler is to subdue the land to his use and develop its resources for that export trade on which New Zealand depends. Material comfort and the volume of production may have for a time at least to take the first place, but they do not suffice for the full enjoyment of that leisure which New Zealand can command.

One may sum up the public opinion of the country by saying that it is temperate and reasonable rather than enlightened and foreseeing. In domestic affairs it thinks of comfort first, tolerates abuses, is glad to throw responsibilities upon Government, prefers to mitigate the consequences of political evils rather than exert itself to remove their causes, does not realize the need for a scientific study of the social and economic problems which its politicians try to solve.

The traveller in New Zealand is bewitched by the strange charm of its scenery, unlike any that is to be seen in the Old World or the New, lakes, and fjords like those of the Arctic Seas, running far into the recesses of snowy ranges like the Alps, volcanoes and geysers, trees and birds of families unknown elsewhere, and a race of aborigines in whose character, as seen by the first explorers, the extremes of savagery and chivalry seemed to have met. In such a land, remote and untouched by the influences of the old civilizations, he can hardly help expecting to find that simplicity and liberty which we associate with the conditions of primitive life. What is his surprise to find in New Zealand the most modern forms of modernity, a people who have given a lead to the nations of our time in extending most widely the functions of the State and superseding the action of the individual! Whatever he may think of this new departure, and however prosaic the machinery it has set working, he cannot quite escape the feeling, fantastic as it may appear, that the grandeur and beauty of the country and the element of romance that belongs to its scenery and to the misty twilight of its history will somehow or other mould or inspire the people. Those who inhabit such a land can hardly have a commonplace future. Will they not some day or other add something novel and striking, be it in letters or arts or institutions, to the stock of mankind's possessions?

It is now time to ask what Democracy has given to New

Zealand, what it has failed to give, what special tendencies it has here manifested, what lessons it suggests for other countries. Under it the people enjoy:

Honest government, without bribery or election frauds.

A tolerably efficient administration.

An upright and competent judiciary.

A pure and efficient unpaid local Government.

Good public order and a general respect for law.

An adequate provision of instruction in public schools.

These things, it may be said, existed before Democracy came, and are therefore not attributable to it. That is true. But universal suffrage and an unchecked legislature have not injuriously affected them.

The chief defects in the government of the country, not necessarily all of them due to its democratic character, are the following:

The average of knowledge and ability in Parliament is not high. It wants dignity: its debates neither instruct nor inspire the people.

Though there is no pecuniary corruption in public life, there is a great deal of jobbery, especially in efforts to gain the favour of constituencies.

Financial administration has been wasteful, both as respects the grants for local purposes and in the conduct of some of the many State undertakings. The debt is very heavy in proportion to the population, though part of it is represented by the asset of the railways. Here, as elsewhere, democracy is extravagant.

The growth of population is slow, partly owing to the desire of the wage-earning class to check immigration.

Too much land is in the hands of large proprietors, both through mistakes made in the first years of the Colony, and also because the Ministries that tried to deal with the problem lacked skill and foresight.

Of these faults the two last are not chargeable on democratic government, for they existed before it came, as did much of the public debt. Between 1850 and 1880 the landowning class were as keen in the advocacy of borrowings and in demands for local grants as the voters on a wider franchise have been since.

The distinctive boon Democracy is supposed to have conferred is the body of acts passed in the interest either of the poorer class or of the general public. Many of these have been already examined, but of them, taken all together, a few more words may be said.

That which has chiefly turned the eyes of older countries upon New Zealand is the extension of State action to new fields, partly by laws interfering with freedom of contract, partly also by the taking over of industries previously left to individual enterprise. This is, however, the subject on which it is most difficult to pass a judgment, and that for two reasons. One is that different schools of thought apply different standards to the evaluation of results. The Individualist condemns in advance a law which compels the employer to pay and the workman to accept a wage fixed by the State, and complains of regulations which make it difficult for him to obtain food in an inn after a certain hour. Another section of opinion is prepared in advance to approve both. The only test which these schools can agree in applying is that of tangible results. Does the State regulation of wages ensure industrial peace and give satisfaction alike to the employer and employed? Does the State, in working its coal-mines, obtain as large an output at no greater cost than private coal-owners obtain, and with no greater friction between employer and workman? To determine the results is, however, no easy matter, for in some cases, as that of coal-mining, they are disputed, while in others the experiment evidently needs to be tried for some time longer before its success or failure can be proved. Compulsory arbitration with the judicial fixing of wages has reduced the number and extent of strikes and prevented much loss of work and wages, but the hopes at first entertained that it had solved the labour problem have been dissipated. Just when the employers were beginning to acquiesce, the workmen became less and less satisfied, and a section among them prefers the strike to the Court. The system of loans to settlers and to workers for enabling them to acquire houses was working well so long as the Government could borrow in England at 3½ per cent, and lend in New Zealand at 5 per cent. But can it continue when the Government must pay interest at, or even above, the higher figure? Though the evidence I obtained regarding the management of Government enterprises seemed to show that the State pays more for the work it gets than private employers do, because its workers "go slow," and discipline is lax, it would be unsafe to treat this as an established fact, and hard to ascertain the amount of resulting loss. The future will have to settle these controversial issues, and throw some much-needed light on the question how far Paternalism can go without economic loss and galling restrictions on individual liberty.

Still more difficult is it to estimate the effects upon national character of the supersession by the State of individual initiative and enterprise, for such effects, always somewhat intangible, are slow in revealing themselves. They may not become evident until a generation has grown up under their influence, and in the meantime other causes may have modified that influence, making it hard to assign to them their share in affecting national character, for national character, though often talked of as if it were a permanent fact due to a racial strain, is always changing, and changes faster in our age, even in an isolated people, than it ever did before, because the influences that play on it are more numerous. Thus the field for speculation is still open. Neither those who hold nor those who deny that the increase of State interference weakens individual initiative are at present entitled to cite New Zealand in support of their doctrine.

It has already been observed how kind Nature has been in bestowing upon these isles all that could be needed for the growth of a vigorous race and a prosperous self-governing community. Philosophers like Plato in the ancient and Sir Thomas More in the modern world, have indulged their fancy in imagining an ideal State, in which wisely planned institutions and wholesome habits would ensure peace and happiness to a people placed on a fertile soil under genial skies, protected by their remoteness from external attack, unhampered by the resentments of a troubled past, and fitted by their intelligence and character to order life according to right reason. No people planted in a new country has seemed better fitted to realize that ideal than the men who settled in New Zealand. None had a better chance of creating institutions that might serve as a model to less favoured lands. These advantages they have possessed for eighty

years. The country has grown steadily and not over swiftly
in wealth, and has preserved the purity of its stock without
that inrush of ignorant immigrants which North Americans
have reason to regret. Its inhabitants have added education
to the inborn energy and intelligence of their race, nor have
any acute dissensions disturbed the public peace. Government, based on universal suffrage, and exercised (in practice) through one Chamber only, has been as entirely popular as any government can be. Yet a censorious critic can
remark that here, too, the defects characteristic of popular
governments in older countries have appeared. Want of
foresight allowed most of the land to fall into the hands of
large proprietors, while those who would have been better
occupied in tilling it have crowded into towns where they
live by artificially stimulated industries. The citizens are
not sufficiently interested in public affairs to observe them
with a constant vigilance. Public life attracts too little of
the nation's best intelligence, so the laws are often ill framed
and their administration imperfect. Expenditure is lavish
and sometimes wasteful. Local interests often prevail
against the common good. Industrial strife, which it had
been hoped to eliminate, constantly recurs. Political parties are more and more forming themselves upon the lines of
class distinctions, and the opposition of the poorer and the
richer, long familiar to the Old World, has reappeared.
There is rather more comfort and contentment than in the
great countries of Europe, but no approach to the ideals of
Plato or to those of Sir Thomas More can be discerned.

Nevertheless, true though it be that the dream of an ideal
democracy has been realized no more in New Zealand than
elsewhere, the critic would admit that she has escaped two
at least of the evils from which most democracies have suffered, the dominance of money and the control of party
organizations, and has made great economic changes with
no disturbance of order. Nowhere can we expect to find the
bulk of a people striving after ideals, not even when Nature and a secure isolation beckon them upwards. The New
Zealanders, after having gone a good way towards State Socialism, showed that they could pause to consider whether
they should go farther. They have never attempted a general levelling down, have never lost that reasonable temper

which the practice of self-government is fitted to foster. And so, far from being enervated by their seclusion in the midst of a vast ocean, they displayed, when a crisis arrived, their willingness to make every sacrifice needed to meet it. They raised a War Loan immense in proportion to their resources. They sent their youth freely to scale the heights that look across the Hellespont over the plains of windy Troy, and their youth gave proof on the battlefield of unsurpassable patriotism and valour.

PART III

This concluding Part contains —

A. An examination and criticism of democratic institutions in
   the light of the facts described in the survey contained in
   Part II. of the working of six democratic governments.

   (Chapters LVIII.–LXVIII.)

B. Observations on certain phenomena which bear on the
   working of Democracy everywhere.

   (Chapters LXIX.–LXXII.)

C. General reflections on the present and future of Democratic
   Government suggested by a study of the forms it has
   taken, the changes it has undergone, and the tendencies
   that are now affecting it.

   (Chapters LXXIII. to End.)

CHAPTER LVIII

THE DECLINE OF LEGISLATURES

EVERY traveller who, curious in political affairs, enquires in the countries which he visits how their legislative bodies are working, receives from the elder men the same discouraging answer. They tell him, in terms much the same everywhere, that there is less brilliant speaking than in the days of their own youth, that the tone of manners has declined, that the best citizens are less disposed to enter the Chamber, that its proceedings are less fully reported and excite less interest, that a seat in it confers less social status, and that, for one reason or another, the respect felt for it has waned. The wary traveller discounts these jeremiads, conscious of the tendency in himself, growing with his years, to dwell in memory chiefly upon the things he used to most enjoy in his boyhood,— the long fine summers when one could swim daily in the river and apples were plentiful, the fine hard winters when the ice sheets on Windermere or Loch Lomond gathered crowds of skaters. Nevertheless this disparagement of the legislatures of our own day is too general, and appears in too many forms, to be passed by. There is evidence to indicate in nearly every country some decline from that admiration of and confidence in the system of representative government which in England possessed the generation who took their constitutional history from Hallam and Macaulay, and their political philosophy from John Stuart Mill and Walter Bagehot; and in the United States that earlier generation which between 1820 and 1850 looked

on the Federal System and the legislatures working under
it in the nation and the States as the almost perfect model
of what constitutional government ought to be.   In the middle of last century most Liberal thinkers in France and
Spain, in Italy and Germany expected a sort of millennium
from the establishment in their midst of representative institutions like those of England, the greatest improvement,
it was often said, that had ever been introduced into government, and one which, had the ancient world discovered it,
might have saved the Greek republics from the Macedonian
conqueror and Rome from the despotism of the Caesars.   So
the leaders of the revolutions which liberated Spanish America took as their pattern the American Federal System
which had made it possible for a central Congress and legislative bodies in every State to give effect to the will of a
free people scattered over a vast continent, holding them together in one great body while also enabling each division
of the population to enact laws appropriate to their respective
needs.   By the representative system the executive would,
they believed, be duly guided and controlled, by it the best
wisdom of the country would be gathered into deliberative
bodies whose debates would enlighten the people, and in
which men fit for leadership could show their powers.   Whoever now looks back to read the speeches and writings of
statesmen and students between 1830 and 1870, comparing
them with the complaints and criticisms directed against the
legislatures of the twentieth century, will be struck by the
contrast, noting how many of the defects now visible in
representative government were then unforeseen.

These complaints and criticisms need to be stated and
examined, if only in view of the efforts which peoples delivered from the sway of decadent monarchies, are now making to establish constitutional governments in various parts
of Central and Eastern Europe.

As in Part II. the failings of the legislatures in the six
countries there dealt with have been already indicated, only
a brief reference to them is here required.   In the States
of the American Union a sense of these failings has led to
two significant changes.   Many restrictions have been everywhere imposed by constitutional amendments on the powers
of State legislatures; and more recently many States (nearly

one-third of the whole number) have introduced the Referendum and the Initiative, the former to review, the latter from time to time to supersede the action of those bodies. The virtue of members had so often succumbed to temptations proceeding from powerful incorporated companies, and the habit of effecting jobs for local interests was so common, that a general suspicion had attached itself to their action. Moreover, the so-called " Party Machines," which have been wont to nominate candidates, and on whose pleasure depends the political future of a large proportion of the members, prevented the will of the people from prevailing, making many members feel themselves responsible rather to it than to their constituencies. Like faults have been sometimes charged against Congress, though conditions are better there than in most of the States, but the Referendum and Initiative are of course inapplicable to the National government since the Federal Constitution makes no provision for them.

In France, while Paris is enlivened, the nation has been for many years wearied by the incessant warfare of the Chamber, divided into many unstable groups, with frequent changes from one Cabinet to another. The politicians have become discredited, partly by the accusations they bring against one another, partly by the brokerage of places to individuals and favours to localities in which deputies act as intermediaries between Ministers and local wire-pullers, while scandals occurring from time to time have, although few deputies have been tarnished, lowered the respect felt for the Chamber as a whole.

The same kind of brokerage is rife in Italy also. The deputy holds his place by getting grants or other advantages for his district, and is always busy in influencing patronage by intrigue.

In Great Britain these last-named evils have not appeared, partly because the Civil Service was taken entirely out of politics many years ago, partly because the passing of " private bills " for local or personal purposes is surrounded by elaborate safeguards. Yet the House of Commons seems to hold a slightly lower place in the esteem of the people than it did in the days of Melbourne and Peel. Its intellectual quality has not risen. Its proceedings are less fully reported. The frequency of obstruction and of the use of the

closure to overcome obstruction have reduced the value of
the debates and affected the quality of legislation, while also
lessening respect for a body which is thought — though this
is inevitable under the party system — to waste time in unprofitable wrangling. The " sterile hubbub of politics " was
noted by a non-political critic even thirty years ago.[1] The
independence of members has suffered by the more stringent
party discipline. The results of these causes are seen in the
diminished deference accorded to Parliament, perhaps also
in its slightly diminished attractiveness for able and public-
spirited men.

In the new overseas democracies — Canada, Australia, and
New Zealand — we cannot, except perhaps in New Zealand,
now talk of a falling off, for the level was never high. Corruption is rare, but the standard both of tone and manners
and of intellectual attainment is not worthy of communities
where everybody is well off and well educated, and where
grave problems of legislation call for constructive ability.

Setting aside the special conditions of each particular
country, because in each the presence or absence of certain
institutions may give rise to special defects, let us seek for
some general causes which in all the countries named, though
in some more than others, have been tending to reduce the
prestige and authority of legislative bodies.

The spirit of democratic equality has made the masses of
the people less deferential to the class whence legislators used
to be drawn, and the legislatures themselves are to-day filled
from all classes except the very poorest. This is in some
respects a gain, for it enables popular wishes to be better
expressed, but it makes a difference to Parliamentary habits. In England, for example, the old " country gentle-
men," who used to form more than half the House of Commons and from whom many brilliant figures came, are now
a small minority. Constituencies are everywhere larger than
formerly, owing to the growth of population and to universal
suffrage; while the personal qualities of a candidate do less
to commend him to electors who are apt to vote at the bidding of party or because the candidate is lavish in his promises. Not only do the members of legislatures stand more
than heretofore on the same intellectual level as their con-

[1] Matthew Arnold.

stituents, but their personal traits and habits and the way
in which they do business are better known through the
press. In some countries much of the space once allotted
to the reports of debates is now given to familiar sketches,
describing the appearance and personal traits of members,
in which any eccentricity is " stressed." " Scenes " are
made the most of, and the disorders which mark them have
left a painful impression. Legislators, no longer convention-
ally supposed to dwell in an Olympian dignity, set little
store by the standards of decorum that prevailed when, as
in France and England two generations ago, a large proportion of the Chamber belonged to the same cultivated
social circles, and recognized an etiquette which prescribed
the maintenance of external forms of politeness. The defect perpetuates itself, because men are apt to live up to no
higher standard than that which they find. The less the
country respects them, the less they respect themselves.
If politicians are assumed to move on a low plane, on it they
will continue to move till some great events recall the country and them to the ideals which inspired their predecessors.

The disappearance of this sense of social responsibility has
affected the conduct of business. Every rule of procedure,
every technicality is now insisted upon and " worked for all
it is worth." This stiffening or hardening of the modes
of doing business has made parliamentary deliberations seem
more and more of a game, and less and less a consultation by
the leaders of the nation on matters of public welfare.

A like tendency is seen in the stricter party discipline
enforced in the British self-governing Dominions. As party
organizations are stronger, the discretion of representatives
is narrowed: they must vote with their leaders. The member who speaks as he thinks is growing rare in English-
speaking countries. Whips called him a self-seeker, or a
crank, yet his criticisms had their value.

The payment of members has been supposed to lower the
status and fetter the freedom of a representative. First introduced in the United States, where it was inevitable because in so large a country members had to leave their business and their often distant homes, to live in the national
or in a State capital, it became inevitable in European countries also when the enfranchised wage-earners desired to send

members of their own class into Parliament. How far it
has affected the character of the representatives is not yet
clear, but it everywhere exposes the poorer members to the
imputation of an undue anxiety to retain their seats as a
means of livelihood.

Just as the increased volume of platform speaking by
leading politicians has lessened the importance of the part
which Parliamentary debate used to play in forming public
opinion, so has the growth of the newspaper press encroached
on the province of the Parliamentary orator. Only the very
strongest statesmen can command an audience over the whole
country, such as that which a widely read newspaper ad-
dresses every day. The average legislator fears the newspaper, but the newspaper does not fear the legislator, and
the citizen who perceives this draws his own conclusions.

Other organizations occupying themselves with public
questions and influencing large sections of opinion, have
arisen to compete with legislatures for the attention of the
nation. The Conventions or Conferences of the old and
" regular " parties, both in England and in America, have
no great importance; for, being practically directed by the
party leaders, they add little or nothing to the programmes
whereto the party has been already committed. But the
meetings of industrial sections and of the new class parties,
such as the Trades Union Congress in England and the Congress of the Peasant party in Switzerland, the Socialist Congresses in France, and the Labour Union Congresses or assemblies representing the farmers or miners in the United
States, the gatherings of farmers in Canada, and the still
more powerful meetings of Labour organizations in Australia — all these are important, for they represent a large
potential vote and their deliverances serve as a barometer
showing the rise or fall of opinion on industrial issues.
Those who lead them may win and wield a power equal to
that of all but the most outstanding Parliamentary chiefs.

Whether or no it be true, as is commonly stated, that in
European countries the intellectual level of legislative assemblies has been sinking, it is clear that nowhere does enough
of that which is best in the character and talent of the nation
find its way into those assemblies.[1] In this respect the an-

[1] This point has been examined in the chapters on France, the United
States, Canada, and Australia.

ticipations of eighty years ago have not been realized. The
entrance to political life is easier now than it was then, but
the daily round of work less agreeable, while the number of
alternative careers is larger.

These changes, taken all together, account for the disappointment felt by whoever compares the position held by
legislatures now with the hopes once entertained of the services they were to render. Yet may we not ask whether there
was ever solid ground for these hopes? Were they not
largely due to the contrast which the earliest free assemblies
offered to the arbitrary or obscurantist governments which
had been ruling everywhere but in America, Britain, and
Switzerland, and against which the noblest intellects in the
oppressed countries were contending? It was natural to
expect that when men of such a type came to fill the legislatures of France, Germany, Italy, and Spain, they would
rival the assemblies of the countries that were already thriv-
ing on freedom. That expectation was largely fulfilled as
regards the first free assemblies, for those who led them
were exceptional men, produced or stimulated by the calls
of their time. The next generation did not in days of peace
rise to the standard set in the days of conflict.

The issues of policy which now occupy legislatures are
more complex and difficult than those of half a century ago.
The strife of classes and formation of class parties were not
foreseen, nor the vast scale on which economic problems
would present themselves, nor the constant additions to the
functions of governments, nor that immense increase of
wealth which has in some countries exposed legislators to
temptations more severe than any that had assailed their
predecessors. The work to be done then was largely a work
of destruction. Old abuses had to be swept away, old
shackles struck off, and for effecting this a few general principles were thought to suffice. The next generation was con-
fronted by constructive work, a remodelling of old institutions in the effort to satisfy calls for social reorganization, a
difficult task which needed more hard thinking and creative
power than were forthcoming. Thus while the demands on
representative assemblies were heavier the average standard
of talent and character in their members did not rise. Never
was it clearer than it is to-day that Nature shows no dispo-

sition to produce men with a greatness proportioned to the scale of the problems they have to solve.

Taking all these causes into account, whatever decline is visible in the quality and the influence of legislatures becomes explicable without the assumption that the character of free peoples has degenerated under democracy. It remains to enquire what have been the results of the reduced authority of representative assemblies. The power which has departed from them must have gone elsewhere. Whither has it gone?

In the several States of the American Union it has gone to the Executive or to the People. The State Governor has become a leading figure whenever he happens to be a strong man with some initiative, some force of will, some gift for inspiring that confidence which legislatures fail to command. Not often perhaps does such a man appear, but when he appears he counts for more than he would have done forty years ago. In an increasing number of States, the introduction of the Initiative and Referendum has narrowed the power of the representatives and transferred legislation to the citizens voting at the polls, while the Recall has made members displaceable by a popular vote before their term comes to an end. All State legislatures have lost the function of choosing a United States Senator, which has been now assigned to the popular vote, this being the only considerable change made in the Federal system. Congress has fallen rather than risen, and the power of the President, when he knows how to use it, and happens to be a strong man who takes the fancy of the people, has been tending to grow.

The Constitutions of France and Great Britain have remained the same in form and on the whole in practice. But in France the recurring dissatisfaction with the frequent changes of Ministry which intrigues in the Chamber bring about continues to evoke cries for a more stable Executive. The discontent with " Parliamentarism " which nearly led to a *coup d'état* in 1888, may have serious consequences, especially if the steadying influence excited by the fear of external aggression should cease to operate. In Britain the House of Commons is still the centre of political life, and the driving-wheel of Government. But the power of the

Cabinet over the majority has grown as parties have stiffened their discipline, for majorities are strong in proportion to their docility. If that so-called " control of the caucus " which British pessimists bewail really exists, it is not so much the tyranny of a party organization acting under the committees that manage it in the constituencies as an instrument in the hands of the party chiefs.

In Italy a somewhat different process seems to have made the Chamber more subservient than formerly to the Ministry, for although the party system holds no great power, deputies are brought into line by the manipulation of patronage and benefits bestowed on powerful business interests or on localities. The Spanish Cortes, divided into a number of groups, each following its leader, are little regarded by the people, who have shown (except in Catalonia) scant interest in the exercise of their now widely extended suffrage.

In these European cases it is rather the moral ascendancy than the legal power of the legislature that has been affected. But when moral power droops legal power ceases to inspire affection or respect.

Can any useful conclusions, any lessons available for practice be drawn from these facts?

The mischiefs arising in the United States, and (to a less extent) in Canada from the abuse for electoral purposes of legislative power in local and personal matters might be removed by stringent regulations, such as those which the British Parliament has imposed on the examination and enactment of private Bills.

A scandal complained of in some countries might be reduced if a system of strict competitive examinations for posts in the Civil Service were to cut away the opportunities members have of misusing their position for the purposes of patronage, while the transfer to local self-governing bodies of the powers exercised in administrative areas by the central government, together with the discontinuance of grants from the national treasury for local purposes would, while saving public money, dry up a copious fountain of jobbery, for where the money to be spent comes from local taxes its expenditure is more likely to be carefully watched.[1] Any-

---

[1] Where, however, the undertaking extends over a wide area and has a national importance, national subventions may be unavoidable.

how the central legislature would be relieved from one form of temptation.

These are what may be called mechanical remedies for evils arising from defects in the mechanism of Parliamentary institutions. With those causes of decline which are either independent of the legislatures themselves, or arise from the intensity of party spirit, or the indisposition of men qualified to serve their country to offer themselves as candidates,— for these causes the remedies have to be sought elsewhere. Representative Assemblies must remain the vital centre of the frame of government in every country not small enough to permit of the constant action of direct popular legislation; and even in such countries they cannot be altogether dispensed with. The utility which Mill and Bagehot saw in them remains, if perhaps reduced. The people as a whole cannot attend to details, still less exercise over the Executive the watchful supervision needed to ensure honest and efficient administration.

CHAPTER LIX

THE PATHOLOGY OF LEGISLATURES

As new maladies assail the human body with advancing age or when the external conditions of life are changed, so with the progress of the years unforeseen weaknesses are disclosed in political institutions. The thinkers and statesmen of last century either did not discern or gave little thought to several such weaknesses incident to representative assemblies which have now begun to cause concern. Five of these chronic ailments, some of which have been briefly adverted to in the last chapter, deserve examination.

I. First comes the practice of what is called in England Obstruction, in America Filibustering, in Australia Stonewalling, in Germany *Dauerreden, i.e.* the systematic effort to delay the progress of business by speaking against time, or by a series of motions (usually amendments to a Bill) which are intended to keep the assembly as long as possible from reaching a decision on the main question before it. In a mild form this must have been an old device, pardonable or even justifiable when a party that found itself in a temporary majority tried to snatch a division. It could also be excused when employed as an honest protest by a minority which felt that it had not been allowed a fair chance of stating its case. In our times it has, however, been systematically used to paralyse the action of a legislature. In England, whose Parliament was formerly distinguished for a decorous propriety in the conduct of business, obstruction was raised to the level of a fine art,[1] with the result

---

[1] Some remarks of the Lord Chancellor in the House of Lords, in March 1919, during a debate on Devolution, contain an instructive account of the methods practised in the House of Commons.

not only of obliging the majority to spend excessive time over their measures, but of discrediting the House of Commons itself. The temptation to resort to it is strongest in countries living under the so-called " Cabinet " or " Parliamentary system," because in them the fortunes of the Administration are associated with the measures it proposes, so that when an important Bill fails for want of time to be passed, or when the disproportionate expenditure of time upon it compels the abandonment of other measures, the Cabinet suffers, having been unable to fulfil promises made to its supporters. In such countries, therefore, an Opposition is often tempted to waste time, for even if the particular measure obstructed is not disliked on its merits, the Ministry is prevented from proceeding to other measures which are actually so disliked, and is thus made to seem impotent in the eyes of the electors. This abuse of the right of free discussion has, in most countries, compelled the adoption of rules enabling the majority to close debate and proceed to an immediate vote. Such rules, however necessary as a remedy, are themselves an evil, for they are in turn abused to pass measures which, having been imperfectly discussed, will probably prove faulty when they come to be applied. No remedy, except closure, has yet been discovered against obstruction, nor any for the misuse of closure itself. In England the Administration, when it suffered from the former, used to believe that the electors would punish obstructionist members by refusing to re-elect them, and these members, when silenced by the closure, likewise believed that the electors would commiserate them and condemn the Administration. But neither of these things happened. The electors did not examine the merits of the quarrel, but blamed both parties, and regretted the good old days when neither majority nor minority pressed its rights to their utmost legal limit.

Obstruction is only one of the causes which have made it difficult for representative assemblies to meet the demands for legislation, more numerous now than ever before, that are made upon them. In France, in the United States, in England, arrears accumulate for overtaking which no means has yet been discovered.[1]

[1] In Britain proposals have been made for a scheme of federalization or devolution creating local assemblies to relieve Parliament.

II. A comparatively new feature in representative assemblies is the multiplication of parties. Most countries began with two — the party of Advance, called in England Whigs, and afterwards Liberals, and the party which defended existing conditions, called Tories or Conservatives. So in France there was the conservative party of the Right, and the party of the Left which pressed for changes, the former generally monarchical in its sympathies, the latter republican. But latterly, partly by the splitting up of these old parties, partly by the emergence of new issues, sometimes of race, sometimes of religion, sometimes of class, parties have grown more numerous. In the British House of Commons there were in 1914 three well-organized parties to which two or three much smaller groups have now been added. In the German Reichstag there were in 1914 five or six,[1] while in the French Chamber the eleven or twelve of 1914 have been but slightly reduced in number.

When a phenomenon appears simultaneously in several countries, one must search for a generally operative cause. Such a cause may be found in the fact that whereas the middle of last century was an era of destruction, when monarchical or oligarchic institutions were being rejected in favour of more popular forms of government, all the advocates of reform, while differing on some points, could agree in getting rid of what had become odious or obsolete. When, however, the work of construction had to be undertaken, divergences appeared between sections each of which had schemes of its own to propound. Thus Radicals drew apart from Liberals, and the classes which had special grievances tended to form class parties. Nevertheless there were also at work other causes, varying in different countries. Among these were Race and Religion. In Germany a Roman Catholic party arose many years ago, while the Poles formed a group by themselves. In the United Kingdom the sentiment of Irish nationality created a third party opposed to Liberals and Tories alike. In France the Catholic Church has kept alive a party which was at first Monarchist and still resists the anti-clerical Republican majority. This has happened in Holland and Belgium also. In Canada a Farm-

---

[1] It is not yet possible to define the position in the Reichstag of 1920.

ers' party, and even in Switzerland a Peasants' party, has
arisen. In these countries, as well as in Britain and Australia, Socialist or Labour parties have evolved themselves
on a basis partly of class interest, partly of theoretic doctrine. Only in the United States have the two old-established parties been strong enough to maintain their supremacy, doing this the more easily because it is not Congress but
a vote of the people every four years that gives executive
power to one or other party, so that the legislature is not, as
in "Parliamentary countries," the centre of political conflict.[1] That Republic has thus escaped two unfortunate results which the Group system has produced in countries lying
under the Parliamentary Frame of Government. One is
the instability of Cabinets, the other the difficulty of carrying through controversial legislation. Where there are more
than two parties, it is probable that no one party may hold
a majority of the whole Chamber. The Executive, being
dependent on the support of a majority, is in such cases
liable to be defeated by any combination of the minority
parties, and when power passes to the larger of those minorities, the new Executive, consisting of the chiefs of that party,
is exposed to a like peril. This affects not only the tenure
of office but the consistency and thoroughness of legislative
measures, which have to be so framed as to obtain from members of the Opposition parties a support sufficient to enable
them to pass. The only remedy lies in the making of bargains between the Executive and the leaders of one at least of
the Opposition parties, thus creating a combination capable
of keeping the Executive in power and helping it to pass
some of its Bills; but such combinations are unstable, and
legislation passed under such conditions becomes a matter of
compromise, showing the faults incident to measures founded
on no clear principle. Sometimes a minority party can, as
the price of its support, extort from the party in power
measures which the bulk of that party dislikes, and which
may not express the general will of the nation.[2] For these

[1] In the United States, moreover, the elements of religious animosity
are absent. See as to the causes which have prevented the new parties
that have been launched in America from maintaining themselves against
the old parties Chapters on the U.S.A. in Part II.

[2] See as to these phenomena in Australia Chapters on that country
in Part II.

evils, such as they are, members of the legislatures cannot be blamed. The sources lie in the nature of a representative system; and though racial and even religious antagonisms may in time by a process of assimilation disappear from the greater countries, the social or economic bases of parties are likely to last so long as no single type of economic doctrine becomes completely dominant. Within the party of Advance there will always be some desiring to move faster than others, and theorists, attracting bands of followers, will point out various paths into the Promised Land.

III. From groups in the legislatures one may pass to note the results of the existence in the electorate of small sections which exercise a power disproportionate to their numbers. Where electors having a personal interest, such as a particular trade (*e.g.* dealers in intoxicating liquors), or the votaries of a particular view, such as anti-vaccinationists, regard their special interest or tenet as of supreme importance, they are apt to make their support of a candidate depend on his promising to support it in the legislature, and where the contest is likely to be close, the candidate will probably give the promise. Thus the interest or view, possibly little better than a fad, secures an artificial support in the legislature, and the real wishes of the electors are misrepresented. In Britain, for instance, the postal and telegraph clerks were (in the larger towns) accustomed to tell a candidate that they would vote for or against him according as he promised or refused to promise to support in Parliament their demand for higher salaries; and by this method they secured in the House of Commons a majority of votes which represented not the views of the electors generally, nineteen-twentieths of whom took no interest in the matter, but only the pliability of complaisant candidates, so that the Ministry, which wished to resist the demand, found itself overborne. It is a weakness of the representative system that it gives undue importance to any section which, forgetting its duty to the whole community, puts its vote up to be bid for by a candidate to whichever party he may belong. In Australia such action by the railway employees once gave rise to serious trouble.

IV. To understand another malady which now threatens the utility of representative assemblies we must cast a glance back into the history of the representative system. It began in the Middle Ages with the sending to the national council, presided over by the King, of persons deputed to grant to him money for the State services, and was also used for the promulgation of the few laws which were then passed, the chief of which, in England, related to the tenure of land. I take England as the example to be described because in it the representative system has had an unbroken career, now continued in other English-speaking countries. The earliest representatives had a simple duty, that of granting money to the Crown for the national services. By degrees the House of Commons drew to themselves larger and larger powers in legislation and delivered their views on the great political issues of the time. Members were understood to be expressing the general mind and will of those who dwelt in the shires and boroughs whence they came, and they usually did so.[1] Little question was raised as to their obligation to precisely ascertain and obediently convey exactly what their electors desired. Practically they had a wide discretion, and felt themselves to be not merely representatives of particular localities, but also members of the Great Council of the Nation, successors of the (non-representative) Witan of Old England before the Norman Conquest, the Wise Men who were wont to consult with the Sovereign on all great matters touching the welfare of the realm, bringing to those matters not only the will of their constituents but their own wisdom, and therefore a freedom which could not be limited by positive instructions, because it was to be exercised after hearing what the Sovereign and his advisers, as well as their own colleagues, had to say to them. There were then, be it remembered, no newspapers, and public opinion expressed itself upon very few subjects. Broadly speaking, it was not till the eighteenth century that the question was seriously mooted how far a member's duty was to think, speak, and vote according to his personal views or according to the views of the majority of his constituents. The point was discussed by Edmund Burke in his famous

[1] Though in Tudor and early Stuart times the Crown, by giving the right of representation to many insignificant boroughs in which it could control the electors, tried to secure the presence of persons subservient to its will.

letter to the Sheriffs of Bristol. His argument that the member is not and ought not to be a mere delegate held the field till in our own time the stress laid upon the principle of popular sovereignty has led many to contend that in a true democracy the representative must be nothing more than a sort of conduit-pipe conveying the will of those who elected him. The growth of party organization makes possible the application of the principle, for the political committee which exists in each constituency can watch the votes of its member and is likely, especially if so requested by the Central Office of the party to which he belongs, to warn him that he must give unquestioning support to the party leaders.

The various views held regarding the grounds for choosing a representative, and the duties incumbent on him, may be reduced to three theories or types of theory.

(1) He may be chosen as the person whom the constituency selects to urge its special local demands, to state its special grievances, to obtain for it from the Government a full share of whatever is going in the way of money grants for local purposes, or any other favours.

(2) He may be chosen as a person eminently fitted by character and attainments to meet and consult with other representatives in the council of the nation on public affairs, while also in accord with the general views of the constituency regarding those affairs.

(3) He may be chosen as a spokesman of the party which holds a majority in the constituency, bound, whatever his personal opinions on any question, to speak and vote as the majority commands him, being thus a sort of telephone wire by which it transmits its wishes. This is the doctrine of the *mandat imperatif,* and has been strongly urged by those who carry furthest the belief that the people, *i.e.* the whole mass of voting citizens, hold a definite opinion and are prepared to declare their will regarding every question of some moment. Any other kind of representation seems to them undemocratic and delusive.

It is possible that the same man may combine the qualifications and fulfil the duties required and imposed by the first and third theories. He may serve the constituency for its local purposes and the party for its national as well as for local purposes. But he could not at the same time discharge also the duties prescribed by the second theory. No man can serve two masters. Cases arise in which the demands of a locality or the commands of a party are at variance with the interests of the nation, and the honest man who perceives this variance will have to sacrifice one or other. The third theory makes his duty to the party majority paramount.

Are there not here two duties each in itself clear, but at moments incompatible in practice? One duty of a member is that of securing full weight in Parliament for the opinion of his constituents, both as to the persons to be entrusted with executive power and as to the laws to be passed. The other duty, owed to the nation, is that of supporting whatever action, legislative or administrative, he believes to be best for the national interests. Does democratic theory require him to give a vote which his own judgment holds to be against those interests? Is he to be the mouthpiece of views he thinks mistaken? The matter is not so simple as it seems. The member may have been elected some while ago and conditions may have changed. Ministers may have so acted as to weaken the confidence his constituents then reposed in them. The question on which he has now to vote may be one on which he gave as a candidate no pledge, or maybe one which nobody foresaw at the time of the election. When his constituents chose him, can they have meant that he was not to profit by what he has learnt from debates in the legislature? If so, why have debates? It may be impossible for him to ascertain how the majority of his constituents would view the particular question now at issue. He may of course consult the local committee, but such a committee being usually more partisan than is the majority of his party, will probably tell him to support his party leaders, being naturally biassed in their favour whatever their conduct. Why should he become the slave of a small caucus? The electors must have meant to leave him some discretion, though it is hard to say how much.

It would seem, then, that the only way in which the system of the imperative mandate could be worked in practice would be to have in each constituency a committee constantly instructing the member how to vote, and for that purpose summoning a meeting of the party electors whenever an important issue arose. The objections to this need no stating.

The only way in which a member could defend himself from charges of breach of faith to his electors would be by his announcing while a candidate that he reserved his freedom upon all questions save those on which he gave a positive and definite pledge.

One thing is clear. If a representative so dislikes the whole policy of his own party as to wish to cross over to the other, his duty is to resign his seat forthwith. This is now the rule in Great Britain. So, too, if his opinions have so changed as regards one important measure that, having been elected to advocate it, he can do so no longer, he must resign. But where the Executive Ministers have announced a new policy on a new issue, is he bound to follow them into it because the bulk of their and his party supports them in it? This question arose in England when a large majority of the Conservative party adopted a Protectionist policy in 1904–5. It arose in 1899 when the Government of that day entered on the South African War. One of their supporters, a member of high personal character, who had been resident in South Africa and knew its condition, disapproved of their policy and spoke against it in Parliament. The issue was a new one, but his local committee, apparently with the support of the local majority, called on him to resign. Nevertheless he retained his seat till the next general election and seemed to be generally held justified in doing so.

The present tendency in England is to make the member more distinctly a delegate than he is in France or Italy, where people pass lightly from one to another of the various Liberal and Radical groups,[1] or than he is in America, where a straight party vote is exacted only on the main points of the party programme. In Switzerland the Constitution declares that he is not to consider himself a delegate, and the recent constitution of Esthonia enunciates the same view. To press hard the doctrine that a member is a mere delegate would result (a) in deterring men of independent character from entering Parliament; (b) in reducing the value of Parliamentary debate; (c) in increasing the control of local party committees; and (d) in making a Cabinet even more powerful over its followers in Parliament than it now is.

[1] In France, however, party discipline is rigid among the Socialists, who are the best organized party.

V. There remains to be mentioned a more serious menace to the healthy action of representative bodies.

Every party in a legislature is strong not only by its numbers but by its unity, *i.e.* by the freedom from internal dissensions which enables it to bring to bear its full strength and cast a unanimous vote on every important occasion. When a party has a definite programme and is earnest in pushing that programme, it may require those whom it approves as candidates to promise to hold together in the legislature and vote as one united body. They may be content to pledge themselves at their election to every item in the formally adopted party programme, and to give their votes accordingly. But as that document, like every other document, needs to be interpreted and applied to the circumstances of each case as it arises, this plan might not always secure unity, for members might interpret its terms differently, and circumstances might make the particular terms inapplicable. Hence some organizations have gone further by requiring candidates to undertake that they will, if elected, always obey any direction which the majority of the party in the legislature, assembled in a secret conclave — such as is called in America a " party caucus "— may pronounce. The member who has given such a promise foregoes his independence. He has his chance of influencing his colleagues in the conclave, but when a decision has proceeded from the majority of those present and voting, he, whether present or absent, will be bound, irrespective of his own convictions, to obey that decision.

This method enhances the power of a compact Group whether the group be a majority or minority of the whole Chamber. If it be a minority, the group are in a strong position to deal with the leaders of the majority party, for whenever the latter feel doubtful of success in a division, owing to differences in their own ranks, the group may offer to give its solid support upon certain terms favourable to themselves, and may thus extort from the other dominant party something the group desires. If, on the other hand, the group constitute a majority in the Chamber, it is omnipotent. The ball is at its feet; it can count on passing all its measures, and need not trouble to expound or defend proposals in debate except for the purpose of saving appearances and putting its case before the country. It has only to go on voting steadily what has been previously determined on in secret, uninstructed and unmoved by arguments from any other part of the Chamber, because there is no need for listening to words which cannot affect its predetermined action. The Chamber having ceased to be deliberative has become a mere voting machine, the passive organ of an unseen despotism. It may have even ceased to express the national will, for the majority of a majority party does not necessarily represent the view of the majority of the whole Chamber. Assume that whole Chamber to consist of 210 members, 110 of whom constitute the ruling Group. Suppose the majority of that group who decide upon a particular course to be 60 against 50 dissentients. Add to these fifty the hundred other members of the Chamber who are also opposed to the course proposed. That course will be carried by a compact majority of 110 against 100, although if the real opinion of the members were expressed by the vote, it would be rejected by 150 against 60. If we were to try to ascertain the probable will of the people on the matter by examining the popular majorities in each constituency by which the 60 members whose vote in caucus prevailed had been elected, as compared with the number of votes cast for the 150 members who disapproved, the contrast between the true popular will and the decision rendered by those who are supposed to represent it in the Assembly might become still more evident. Yet by this method of subjecting the whole Assembly to a bare majority of a majority the most far-reaching and possibly irrevocable decisions might be taken.

This may seem a sorry result for representative government to have reached, yet it is a logical and legitimate development of the principle of Majority Party Rule and there seems to be no remedy except by invoking the whole people to pass judgment upon Bills by a Referendum.

The Parliamentary caucus system here described was invented by the Irish party in the British House of Commons and worked there from 1880 to 1918. In its first ten years it proved effective, turning out two Ministries in succession after obtaining large concessions from each. It has also been practised with success in the legislatures of the Australian

States and in that of the Federal Commonwealth. It has been to some extent adopted as regards various subjects by Socialist parties in the French Chamber, and may spread wherever party spirit is strong enough to induce men to subordinate their views and wills to the attainment of a few aims they are united in desiring. The requisites for its existence are two — a definite programme and a fervent party zeal. The presence of a strong-willed leader, able by his hold on the party outside the Chamber to maintain discipline among his followers within it, facilitates its work. C. S. Parnell's possession of the advantages mentioned counted for much, but the Australian Labour parties have won their victories mainly by the loyal cohesion of their members and the pressure of the outside Labour organization to which all are responsible.

Every one of the defects in or perversions of representative government which I have enumerated arises naturally out of the conditions of political life, and none is peculiar to countries living under universal suffrage. In particular, Obstruction and the rule of a legislative caucus are natural weapons of war, ready to the hand of party spirit. No attempt to deal by law with any of these evils has a promise of success. They can be cured only by the action of public opinion, which can show its displeasure at practices that lower the character and utility of representative assemblies. But opinion is in most countries too much absorbed with the economic and social aims to which legislation should be directed to give due attention to legislative methods, and the leaders of a party are usually too eager for a temporary victory to forgo the means, however dangerous for the future, by which victory may be won. It is not that they are short-sighted: many foresee clearly enough the consequences of their acts: it is that in politics most men are prone to sacrifice the future interests of the nation to the temporary interests of the party, or, to give them the benefit of a common excuse, to attain by pernicious means a laudable end.

Though the dignity and moral influence of representative legislatures have been declining, they are still an indispensable part of the machinery of government in large democracies, since it is only in comparatively small populations that citizens can be frequently summoned to vote by Refer-

endum and Initiative.   Hence the quality of a legislature,
the integrity and capacity of its members, the efficiency of
the methods by which it passes laws and supervises the conduct of the Executive, must continue to be of high significance to a nation's welfare.   The dictum of a legal sage in
the seventeenth century, " England can never be ruined except by a Parliament," is true to-day of all countries in
which the Parliamentary system exists, and is still able to
hold its ground against revolutionary forces.

CHAPTER LX

THE EXECUTIVE IN A DEMOCRACY

As men are apt to estimate the merits of a religion by the influence it exerts on the conduct of those who profess it, so a form of government may be judged by what it does for the peace and welfare of the people who live under it. In applying this test to democracy, which purports to be a "government of the laws and not of men," we have to ask how far its legislative machinery succeeds in making good laws, its judicial machinery in providing for their just application, its executive machinery in carrying them out efficiently and in enforcing respect for them. The Legislature and the Judiciary have been already considered. It remains to examine the Executive or Administrative Department.

As freedom had been won by resistance to arbitrary monarchs, the Executive power was long deemed dangerous to freedom, watched with suspicion, and hemmed in by legal restraints, but when the power of the people had been established by long usage, these suspicions vanished, so that now it is only in countries where constitutional government is not well settled, as is still the case in most of the republics of Spanish America and in the small kingdoms of southeastern Europe, that the head of the Executive, be he President or King, can venture to aim at a dictatorship or can, as did the Kings of Greece and Bulgaria, betray the nation into a policy it disapproves. Only in France does enough of the old apprehension remain to make the people fear to extend the powers of their President. Thus it is unnecessary to treat here of the Executive as a danger to democracy. The world asks to-day, not how far that branch of government hankers after mastery but — how far is it an efficient servant, capable and honest?

The Executive Department has been often described as the weak point in popular governments. In them, as compared with oligarchies or autocracies, it is said to lack continuity in policy, promptitude in action, courage to enforce its decisions, judgment in the selection of officials, and the possession of that special knowledge and technical skill which administration requires in our day. To estimate the truth of these allegations let us examine such evidence to support or rebut them as is supplied by the six countries whose governments have been described in Part II. That examination may be taken under four heads — first, the quality of the Ministers, *i.e.* the political heads of Executive Departments, in the countries aforesaid; secondly, the subordinate officials, *i.e.* the civil service of the nation, which conducts all internal administration; thirdly, the departments concerned with national defence, army, navy, and air fleet.

A fourth head, the conduct of foreign affairs, presents different problems, and to it a separate chapter is devoted.

I. In all the countries described, except Switzerland, the ministerial chiefs of the departments of State are politicians, members of a party, entering or quitting office as their parties gain or lose power. There are always among them men of some prominence and generally of talent, who have risen either in the representative assembly by the gift of speech or by a service to their party which marks them out for promotion. Thus every ministry, especially in Parliamentary countries like France, Britain, Canada, Australia, and New Zealand, is sure to contain four or five, or possibly more, leading figures in the ruling party, and they may turn out capable administrators. But ministerial posts, even important posts, are often conferred upon mediocre men whom the Prime Minister, or (in the United States) the President, finds it well to include in his Cabinet for political reasons of various kinds, perhaps because they have influence in some particular part of the country or with some particular section of opinion. In none of these six countries is much regard paid either to special knowledge or to aptitude for administration, save that in the legal posts professional skill and eminence are essential. Otherwise political considerations come first, though in France it has been usual to choose as Minister of War a General, and as Minister of Marine an Admiral. Switzerland stands by itself as not changing its Ministers, for they are elected for five years and almost always re-elected. They are selected from politicians who have had legislative experience, and are chosen rather in respect of their general capacity and the confidence their character inspires than on the score of their special fitness for any particular kind of administrative work.

This method of choice (in the five first-named countries) is based on the idea that as the Government is a party government kept in office by a party whose policy is that of the majority in the legislature (or, in the United States, that of the party to which the President belongs), the departments must be administered on the lines of this policy, and be defended in the legislature (except in the United States) by men who are experts in politics if in nothing else. The two disadvantages of the system are that the Minister may have no special competence, and that, however competent, he will, when his party loses power, be ejected from the office he has successfully filled; but against these may be set the advantage that an able incoming Minister can bring in new ideas and help to keep his department in touch with the movements of public opinion. In France, England, Canada, and Australia there is the further merit of securing that there shall almost always be some competent critics in the ranks of the Opposition. On the whole, the system described gives good results, and would give better if more weight were allowed in constructing a Cabinet to the qualifications, general or special, of the politicians selected, and less to merely political reasons. This remark applies to England also, where, though family favouritism and social influence now count for very little, political considerations still take precedence of expert knowledge and skill.

II. In all the six countries described the working staff of the departments, *i.e.* the administrative Civil Service of the country, is outside politics, and posts in it are held (except to some extent in the United States) irrespective of the transfer of power from one party to another. Partisan influences have, however, their influence on promotions, especially in the higher grades. In all the six countries the civil servants are as a class competent and honest, equal to those to be found in any European monarchy, and of course incomparably superior to those of Tsarist Russia, where corruption flourished like a green bay tree from the top to the bottom of the official hierarchy. Nowhere, however, were they so admirably trained as was the German bureaucracy; nowhere was so large a proportion of the nation's ability to be found in the nation's service. Democracy has given a better if not a more economical administration in France than did the monarchies that preceded it, and in Britain a much better administration than was that of the oligarchy before 1832. The British service contains plenty of ability in its higher grades, and all grades work loyally for their chiefs to whatever party the latter belong.

III. National defence against attacks from without has been well cared for in France and Switzerland. If much less was done in the United States, that was because the risk of war with any powerful State had seemed negligible down till 1915. The administrative work of the naval and military departments has been everywhere efficiently, and for the most part honestly done, though malpractices have from time to time occurred in connection with naval contracts in France and in the United States. To examine the reproach sometimes levelled at democratic Governments of neglecting their armies is not here possible, for it would require an enquiry into the circumstances in each several case where neglect has been alleged. The wolf does sometimes come unexpected, but how often has the cry of " Wolf " been raised when he was nowhere in the neighbourhood! For a nation to be unprepared because it has itself no aggressive spirit is unwise, but to be so over-prepared as to grow aggressive and launch an unjustified attack may have a still worse ending.

Among modern democracies France and Switzerland alone impose compulsory military service. In the other countries and in Britain the need for it is matter of controversy. The United States imposed it when she entered the Great War in 1917, and so did Great Britain in 1915 after about three millions of men had volunteered, as did New Zealand and Canada also. The Australian people, twice consulted by way of Referendum, refused. Australia and New Zealand had before 1914, and with little opposition, prescribed a certain measure of military training in peace-time. On the whole, democracies seem at present disposed to peace, but the ancient and mediaeval republics were fond of fighting, and the United States, to-day the most pacifically minded among great States, was in 1846 and in 1898 drawn into wars which might easily have been avoided.

IV. Now comes a more difficult and controversial question, viz. the effect of democracy upon the enforcement of the laws and especially on the maintenance of public order. Some have argued that governments installed by the votes of the multitude will fear to resist and suppress manifestations of popular feeling even when they pass into violence and rioting. Others have replied that no government can so well afford to show firmness as one which stands solidly planted on the people's will. Where a monarch or an oligarchy may stumble or halt lest it provoke a revolution, men chosen freely by the nation may go boldly forward.

There are facts to support both these contentions. Much may depend upon the circumstances of the particular case, much upon the character either of the Government in power or of the particular official who is charged with the duty of maintaining public order. In the United States the National Government has almost always shown the requisite firmness. President Cleveland during the Chicago riots of 1894 quelled an outbreak by sending in Federal troops. So recently as 1919 the action of a Governor of Massachusetts, who had dealt energetically with a strike of the Boston police, was, when he stood for re-election, endorsed by an enormous vote coming from both political parties. On the other hand, there have been Australian cases in which State Governments — usually but not always Labour Governments — have shown timidity, leaving it to the action of private citizens to preserve order, and to bring a strike to an end by themselves undertaking the work of running tram-cars or discharging ships' cargoes which strikers were trying to impede.[1] In France a Ministry whose head was himself in sympathy with Socialist views showed great vigour and, aided by public sentiment, saved a dangerous strike situation.

[1] It is particularly difficult in Australia for a Labour Government which is ruled by a caucus of representatives pledged to act together, and is largely controlled by an outside labour organization, to do all it might otherwise feel bound to do to prevent strikers from resorting to violence.

Like energy was shown in a like case in Switzerland in 1918, the great bulk of the nation approving the energetic action of the Federal Council. The same may be said of Canada, which has faithfully preserved the British traditions which make the vindication of the law the first duty of the Executive. Strikes which pass into violence are in our own day the most frequent causes of trouble, and the most difficult to deal with, because, although workmen on strike admittedly possess the right of endeavouring to induce those whom employers are trying to hire in their place not to accept the work offered, "Peaceful Picketing" is apt to pass into threats or something more than threats, nor is it easy to draw the line.[1]

In some of the American State Governments there has been laxity on the part of officials and slackness in action by the citizens when summoned to aid in preserving order. Lynching prevails extensively in several of the Middle as well as in most Southern States, and, though the opinion of thoughtful men condemns the practice, some Governors or Mayors who have tried to repress it did not receive the support they deserved. It is also stated that locally elected officials are often remiss in enforcing the payment of taxes, and prone to acquiesce in minor breaches of the law lest they should incur enmities which would endanger their re-election.[2]

In trying to answer the broad question from which this chapter started, whether a democratic Executive can be a strong Executive, let us distinguish two different senses which the question may bear. An Executive is strong against the citizens when the law grants it a wide discretionary authority to command them and override their individual rights. There is nothing to prevent a democracy from vesting any powers over the private citizen it pleases in its elected magistrates. This kind of strength, strictly limited

---

[1] Leniency to law-breakers is by no means confined to labour unions or radical democrats. It was observed in England on two recent occasions that the law-respecting spirit is only skin deep, once when during the South African war attacks by mobs upon the houses of persons believed to be opposed to that war were palliated by persons of high official standing, and again when between 1907 and 1912 the destruction of churches (including the exploding of a bomb in Westminster Abbey) and the setting fire to houses by militant suffragettes were defended or excused by many members of the "most respectable" classes.

[2] See Vol. II., Chap. XLIII. *ante*.

in English-speaking countries, has been allowed to remain not only in Italy, Belgium, and Spain, but in France, where the Republican parties, though sometimes admitting that individual liberty is not duly safeguarded, do not like to part with a power they may need for crushing plots directed against the Republic.

But there is another sense in which the strength of an Executive is measured by its relation to the other powers in the State. The people may make it independent of the legislature, choosing it by their own vote, possibly for a long term of years. They may enable it to defend itself against the legislature by giving it a veto and a sole initiative in foreign affairs. The United States has gone furthest in this direction, and its President, independent of Congress for a four years' term, is the least fettered of all Executives in free countries, though his power declines in moral authority as that term draws to its end, and though the temptation to seek re-election may unduly affect his independence. Continuity in policy is hard to secure where the representative assembly and the Executive are liable to be changed by frequently recurring elections. Ministers who may be swept out of office by a hostile vote of the legislature, or may see the legislature itself pass under the control of the party opposed to their own, are often deterred from bold action by the fear that it may endanger their own position, or may be reversed by their successors. They are unwilling to propose measures, however salutary, that are likely to be unpopular, and tempted to bid for support by promising bills whose chief merit is their vote-catching quality. This sort of instability and discontinuity is the price which must be paid for that conformity to the popular will of the moment which democracy implies. It is of course more harmful where the people itself is inconstant or capricious. Such have been some democratic peoples, such may be some of those that are now starting on their career as independent States. But it so happens that none of the nations we have been studying presents this character. In all of them there often comes a "swing of the pendulum" from one party to another at a general election, and sometimes the change rises into what Americans call a "tidal wave." These oscillations are, however, mostly due not to changes of opinion on large principles, but to displeasure with errors committed by the Ministry. Even the French, supposed to be of an excitable temper, are at bottom a conservative nation, safely anchored some to one, some to another set of ideas and beliefs. Nowhere are changes of Ministry so frequent as in France; nowhere do they mean so little. Nevertheless, it remains true that the uncertain tenure of any particular Ministry both there and in Canada, Australia, and New Zealand — and this is true of England also — does operate to disturb the course of administration as well as legislation.

The results of this enquiry may be summed up as follows:

Ministries in democratic countries are no better in their composition, so far as ability is concerned, than they are elsewhere, for political reasons may do as much to prevent the selection of the fittest men, as secret intrigues do in monarchies or oligarchies. They are, however, more generally honest, being exposed to a more searching criticism than other forms of government provide.

The principle of equality has had the useful result of securing free access for all to the permanent Civil Service of the State and of restraining the tendency to favouritism in promotions. The United States, where patronage was most abused, has by degrees fallen into line with other democracies, and its Civil Service is correspondingly improving. Democratic governments, not being militaristic in spirit, are reluctant to vote money for war preparations, but when convinced that there is a danger of aggression, they rise to the emergency. The Executive in a parliamentary democracy suffers from its slippery foothold, which often prevents it from carrying through those legislative or administrative schemes of reform, the success of which depends on their maintenance for a course of years.[1] Uncertainty of tenure deters it from action, however otherwise desirable, that is likely to offend any body of voters strong enough to turn the balance against it at an election. So, too, Opposition

[1] No one can sit in a British Cabinet without being struck by the amount of time it spends in discussing parliamentary tactics, and especially how best to counter a hostile motion in the House of Commons. These things, small as they may seem, are urgent, for the life of the Cabinet may be involved, so the larger questions of legislation have to stand over, perhaps to be lost for the session.

leaders who hope to overthrow and replace the holders of power are apt to trim or "hedge" in order to win the favour of a section that may turn the scale in their favour.[1] On the other hand, a Ministry can usually count upon the support of the great majority of the people in a war, or at any other grave crisis, and will then be quickly invested with exceptional powers. Even on less serious occasions, a democratic community, be it the nation or such a unit as an American State or city, will usually rally to a courageous chief who gives it a strong lead. Politicians fail more often by timidity than by rashness.

As regards general domestic administration, democracies have nothing to be ashamed of. We have found the civil servants are fairly competent in all the six democracies examined — perhaps least so in the United States, where the results of the Spoils System are still felt — and the average of honesty is higher than it was in the less popular governments of the past. They are doubtless less efficient than was the bureaucracy of Germany before 1914, but efficiency was purchased at a price which free peoples cannot afford to pay.

[1] These phenomena may be studied in the history of British political parties in their dealings with Ireland, especially since the rise of the Irish Home Rule party in 1875-8.

CHAPTER LXI

DEMOCRACY AND FOREIGN POLICY [1]

STATESMEN, political philosophers, and historians have been wont to regard the conduct of foreign relations as the reproach of democratic government. The management of international relations needs — so they insist — knowledge, consistency, and secrecy, whereas democracies are ignorant and inconstant, being moreover obliged, by the law of their being, to discuss in public matters unfit to be disclosed. That this has been perceived by the people themselves appears from the fact that modern legislatures have left this department to officials, because it was felt that in this one department democracies cannot safely be democratic.

Per contra, popular leaders in some countries have, with an increasing volume of support, denounced Foreign Offices as having erred both in aims and in methods. They allege that the diplomacy of European States is condemned by the suspicion which it has constantly engendered and that the brand of failure is stamped upon it by the frequent recurrence of war, the evil which diplomacy was created to prevent.

These views, apparently opposite, are not incompatible. Oligarchies, and the small official class which in many democracies has had the handling of foreign affairs, may have managed them ill, and yet it may be that the whole people will manage them no better. The fault may lie in the

---

[1] This chapter, composed before the Armistice of November 1918, has been left unmodified (save by the addition of the last sentence), because the time has not come either to draw a moral as to what is called " secret diplomacy " from the negotiations of 1919–20, or to comment freely in a treatise such as this on the recent action of Governments and peoples in their attempts to restore peace and order in the world; not to add that the extraordinary events of the four preceding years had so disturbed the balance and normal working of men's minds as to make it unsafe to treat many things that have happened as supplying a basis for general conclusions.

conditions of the matter itself and in those tendencies of human nature which no form of government can overcome. What we want to know is not whether oligarchic and secret methods have failed — that may be admitted — but whether democratic and open-air methods will succeed any better. What light does history throw on the question?

Here at starting let a distinction be drawn between Ends and Means in the sphere of foreign policy, a distinction, which, though it exists in all branches of administration, is less significant in the domestic branches, because in them Ends, if not assumed as generally recognized, are and must be determined by the people through their representatives. Justice, the maintenance of public order, economy in expenditure are understood to be aims in every department, while the particular objects for which money is to be spent and the modes of raising it are prescribed by statute. But the relations of States to one another, varying from day to day as the circumstances which govern them vary, cannot be handled by large assemblies in a large country, but must be determined by administrators who are incessantly watching the foreign sky. Modern legislatures accordingly, though they sometimes pass resolutions indicating a course to be followed, or condemning a course which has been followed, by a Ministry, have recognized that in foreign affairs the choice of Means must belong to a small body of experts, and have accordingly left to these persons all details, and the methods which diplomacy must employ in particular cases, allowing them a wide, possibly a too wide, discretion.

But while Foreign Offices and diplomatic envoys may be the proper persons to choose and apply Means, the general principles which should guide and the spirit which should inspire a nation's foreign policy are a different matter, too wide in scope, too grave in consequences, to be determined by any authority lower than that of the people. There may be a divergence of opinion on these principles, *i.e.* on the Ends to be pursued, between the People of a country and those of their servants to whom the daily conduct of foreign affairs has been left, and it may be that the latter do not obey the real wishes of the people but seek Ends and apply principles which the people, if consulted, would disapprove. To this distinction as affecting conclusions regarding the range of popular action, I shall presently return.

About one aim there can be no divergence. The State must preserve its independence. It must be safe from attack, able to secure fair opportunities for its citizens to trade and to travel abroad unmolested; and these legitimate aims can be pursued in a spirit of justice and friendliness to other States. All States, however, whatever their form of government, have pursued other aims also, and pursued them in a way frequently at variance with justice and honour. They have attacked other States on trivial pretexts, have sought to acquire territory, to fill their own treasury, or enrich some of their own citizens, at the expense of their neighbours, have placed their State power at the service of men who pleaded that while enriching themselves they were benefiting the country by bringing money into it. Most States have, in pursuing these objects, been a law unto themselves. When strong, they have abused their strength, justifying all means by the plea of State advantage. They have disregarded good faith from the days when democratic Athens wantonly attacked the isle of Melos, killing and enslaving its inhabitants, down to the days of Louis XI. and Caesar Borgia, and from the days of Borgia's contemporary Machiavelli down to those of Frederick the Second of Prussia, who began his literary career with a book designed to refute the maxims of the Florentine statesman. Though in considering how popular governments have succeeded in the sphere of foreign policy, regard must be had to the moral quality of that policy both in Ends and in Means, the moral aspect may be in the first instance reserved, and the enquiry may go only to the question whether a democracy is in that sphere more or less efficient than other forms of government. Supposing " success " to mean the maximum of power a State can attain in the world arena, what kind of government will best attain it ? We can thereafter return to the moral side and enquire what sort of government will be most likely to observe justice and good faith, doing its duty by its neighbour States as a good citizen does his duty by his fellows.

Does Ignorance forbid success to a democracy? Let us hear the case which professional diplomatists make.

A monarch is free to select his ministers and ambassadors

from among the best informed and most skilful of his subjects, and in an oligarchy the mind of the ruling class busies itself with foreign relations, and knows which of its members understand and are fitted to handle them. The multitude has not the same advantage. It is ill qualified to judge this kind of capacity, usually choosing its ministers by their powers of speech. If, instead of leaving foreign affairs to skilled men it attempts to direct them either by its own votes, as did the Greek cities, or by instructing those who represent it in the legislature, how is it to acquire the requisite knowledge? Few of the voters know more than the most elementary facts regarding the conditions and the policy of foreign countries, and to appreciate the significance of these facts, there is needed some acquaintance with the history of the countries and the characters of the leading men. Not much of that acquaintance can be expected even from the legislature. One of the strongest arguments for democratic government is that the masses of the people, whatever else they may not know, do know where the shoe pinches, and are best entitled to specify the reforms they need. In foreign affairs this argument does not apply, for they lie out of the normal citizen's range. All he can do at an election is to convey by his vote his view of general principles, and, in the case of a conflict between two foreign nations, to indicate his sympathies.

If the masses of the people have been inconstant in their views of foreign relations, this is due to their ignorance, which disables them from following intelligently the course of events abroad, so that their interest in these is quickened only at intervals, and when that happens the want of knowledge of what has preceded makes a sound judgment unlikely. They are at the mercy of their party leaders or of the press, guides not trustworthy, because the politicians will be influenced by the wish to make political capital out of any successes scored or errors committed by a Ministry, while the newspapers may play up to and exaggerate the prevailing sentiment of the moment, claiming everything for their own country, misrepresenting and disparaging the foreign antagonist. Consistency cannot be expected from a popular government which acts under a succession of impulses, giving no

steady attention to that department in which continuity of
policy is most needed.

Secrecy in the conduct of diplomacy is vital in a world
where each great nation is suspicious of its neighbours and
obliged by its fears to try to discover their plans while concealing its own.   Suppose the ministry of a country to have
ascertained privately that a foreign Power meditates an attack
upon it or is forming a combination against it, or suppose it
to be itself negotiating a treaty of alliance for protection
against such a combination.   How can it proclaim either the
intentions of the suspected Power or its own counter-schemes
without precipitating a rupture or frustrating its own plans?
A minister too honourable to deceive the legislature may
feel himself debarred from telling it the facts, some of which
may have been communicated under the seal of confidence.
It is all very well to say that an open and straightforward
policy best befits a free and high-minded people.   But if
such a people should stand alone in a naughty world, it
will have to suffer for its virtues.   As a democracy cannot
do business secretly, it must therefore leave much, and perhaps much of grave import, to its ministers.   Herein the
superiority for foreign affairs of a monarchy or an oligarchy
is most evident.[1]

There is force in these considerations, yet a monarchy
in which the Sovereign may be either a fool, or the victim
of his passions, or the plaything of his favourites, may
succeeed no better than a democracy.   An oligarchy is better
qualified, for in it power rests with a few trained and highly
educated men who keep a watchful outlook on neighbouring
states.   The Roman Senate in which these matters were
controlled by leaders less numerous than a modern Cabinet,
showed singular tenacity and (in its best days) singular
judgment in directing the foreign relations of the Republic.
And the same may be said of the ruling Council at Venice,
who down to the eighteenth century were found able to keep
secrets, and who proceeded upon well-settled lines, exempt

---

[1] Though secrecy in diplomacy is occasionally unavoidable, it has its
perils.   There was a case in our time in which a secret agreement was
made which is now universally admitted to have been imprudent and
has been condemned by its results, and which would not have been
made had it been possible for public opinion to have been consulted
and obtained regarding it.   Publicity may cause some losses, but may
avert some misfortunes.

from the caprices which an absolute sovereign is prone to indulge.

To test the capacity of a popular government in this branch of its action, let us see how far such governments have shown wisdom in following sound aims and have succeeded in applying the means needed to attain them. Of the six countries examined, three — Canada, Australia, New Zealand — had no foreign policy of their own, but adopted, while more or less influencing, that of Great Britain, so we must consider the policy of Britain along with those of France, Switzerland, and the United States.

The case of France is peculiar in this respect, that the general lines of its policy have during the whole life of the Third Republic (1871–1920) been determined by its position towards Germany, the one enemy from whom hostility was always to be feared, and from whom it was hoped to recover territory lost in war. This fact coloured all France's foreign relations, forcing her to husband her strength and to seek for allies. As all parties felt alike on this supreme issue, all were agreed in keeping it out of party controversy. The incessant changes of Ministries scarcely affected the continuity of policy. Democracy was on its good behaviour; fickleness as well as partisanship was held in check. Some friction arose between Ministers and Committees of the legislature, yet secrets were generally kept and the people acquiesced in a silence felt to be necessary. It goes without saying that errors were now and then committed, but these taken all together were less grave than the two which marked the later part of Louis Napoleon's reign — the expedition to Mexico and the war with Prussia. And, as the result has shown, they were incomparably less than those which brought ruin on the three great monarchies which entrusted their foreign relations to militaristic bureaucracies — Germany, Austria, and Russia.

Switzerland's foreign policy has long been prescribed by the obligation to preserve a strict neutrality. Lying between four great military Powers, she, while maintaining her own dignity, strove neither to offend nor to seem partial to any of them. All this has been done successfully by the Federal Council (a Cabinet of seven) always in the closest touch with the small legislature. The suggestion made that treaties should be submitted to a Referendum has not received much support, though it would be consistent with the wide application given to the principle of the Popular Vote on all matters of importance.[1] Questions of foreign policy are seldom entangled with domestic issues, and rarely excite internal differences, just because the safety and independence of his country is the first care of every good Swiss. Particular steps might be blamed,[2] but one can scarcely imagine the Federal Council taking a course which, so far as principle went, public opinion would disapprove.

Of all the Great Powers, the United States is that which had, till recent years, the fewest foreign questions to deal with. Standing apart in its own hemisphere, and with no State of that hemisphere approaching it in resources for war, it had little to do except with Spain so long as Spain held Cuba, with Mexico and with Great Britain. The people have cared little and known less about foreign affairs, except when their national pride was touched, or when their one favourite principle of policy, the exclusion of European interference from the New World, might seem to be affected. In either of these contingencies public opinion, soon worked up by an alert press, speaks out quick and loud. In this sense, therefore, public opinion controlled the conduct of foreign affairs whenever it cared to do so. At other times it has left them, unnoticed or unheeded, to the Executive and to the Senate. The Constitution associated that branch of Congress with the President, because, since neither he nor his Ministers can be ejected from office during his four years' term, it was deemed unsafe to let him have sole control. The President has a Secretary of State to advise him, who is sometimes a man of first-rate gifts, but more frequently only a politician selected because of his party standing, and possessing little knowledge of world affairs. The staff of the office has been small, and too frequently changed. The Senate has been mainly guided by its Foreign Relations Committee, a fluctuating body, usually containing a few able men among others who know little of anything outside their

[1] See above, Vol. I. Chap. XXIX., and cf. the book of M. Edouard Georg, *Le Contrôle du Peuple sur la politique extérieure* (Geneva, 1916). The question of Switzerland's entrance into the League of Nations was submitted to and affirmed by a popular vote in 1920.

[2] As happened during the European War of 1914–1918.

own country, and may regard the interests of their own State rather than those of the Union. Jealous of its powers, and often impelled by party motives, the Senate has frequently checked the President's action, sometimes with unfortunate results.[1] It can debate with closed doors, but this does not ensure secrecy.

The President, however, who is always anxious to lead or to follow public opinion, and the Senate which is scarcely less so, concern us less than public opinion itself. As its rule is in the United States more complete than elsewhere, it furnishes the best index to the tendencies and capacities of a democracy.

The Republic has been engaged in three wars within the last hundred years. That against Mexico in 1846 was the work of the slave-holding party which then controlled the Executive and the Senate, and whose leaders brought it on for the sake of creating Slave States and strengthening the grip of slavery on the Union. It was widely disapproved by public opinion, especially in the northern States, but the acquisition, by the treaty which closed it, of vast and rich territories on the Pacific Coast did much to silence the voice of criticism.

The war against Spain in 1898 might probably have been avoided, for Spain had been driven to the verge of consenting to withdraw from Cuba when the breach came. But the nation, already wearied by the incessant troubles to which Spanish misgovernment had given rise during many years, had been inflamed by the highly coloured accounts which the newspapers published of the severities practised on the insurgents by Spanish generals, and the President, though inclined to continue negotiations, is believed to have been forced into war by the leaders of his own party who did not wish their opponents to have the credit of compelling a declaration. In obtaining, by the peace which followed a short campaign, the cession to the United States of Puerto Rico and the Philippine Islands, the President believed that he was carrying out the wishes of the people. This may have been so, for they were flushed with victory, and were moved not merely by the feeling that victory ought to bring

[1] See on this subject Mr. W. R. Thayer's *Life of John Hay.*

some tangible gain, but also by a sort of philanthropic sentiment which was unwilling to hand back the conquered territories to Spanish maladministration.   This war, therefore,
though it shows that a popular government may yield to
excitement and gratify its ambition for enlarged territory,
cannot be deemed a caste of mere aggression for the sake of
conquest.

The war of 1917 against Germany and Austria is too
fresh in our memories to need comment.   There was certainly nothing selfish or aggressive in the spirit that prompted
America's entrance into it.   The sinking of the *Lusitania* and other passenger vessels supplied a definite
casus belli; the mind of the nation had been stirred to
its depths by the sense that far-reaching moral issues were
involved.

Not wars only, but also the general diplomatic relations
of the United States with its neighbours to the North and
South deserve to be considered.   More than once, serious
differences arose as to the frontier line beween the Republic
and Canada.   One in which the State of Maine was concerned was amicably settled in 1842, after long negotiations.
Another relating to the far North West, where Oregon was
in dispute between Britain and America, was, after bringing
the nations to the edge of a conflict, adjusted by a compromise in 1845.   Another gust of feeling which swept over
the country in December 1895, roused by boundary questions between Great Britain and Venezuela, subsided as
quickly as it had arisen, when the British government made
a conciliatory answer to the American Note.   A fourth controversy, which had lasted ever since 1783, regarding the
rights of fishing in the North Atlantic, was referred to arbitration and disposed of in 1910 by a decision which both
sides accepted gladly.   By an exchange of notes in 1817
it had been agreed that only a very few armed vessels, just
sufficient for police purposes, should be maintained by each
country on the Great Lakes.   This agreement has been faithfully observed ever since, and along a boundary of three
thousand miles by land and water the reliance placed by
each on the good faith and good will of the other has made
military and naval preparations and defences needless.   The

example thus set to the world is creditable to the two peoples alike.

When in 1912 the long dictatorship of Porfirio Diaz vanished like melting snow, Mexico relapsed into anarchy. The property and lives of American citizens were frequently endangered. Some murders and many robberies were perpetrated by rebel bands which the nominal rulers at the capital could not suppress. Had the government of the United States wished to make these outrages a ground for occupying Mexican territory, it could have found justification for doing so. But the public opinion of the American people steadily resisted all temptations, perceiving that annexation would involve either rule over the Mexicans as a subject race, or their incorporation with the United States as full citizens. As both of these courses were equally fraught with danger, they determined to leave Mexico alone. A like disinterestedness had been shown in the case of Cuba, from which they had withdrawn their troops once (in 1903) after expelling Spain, and again a few years later when troubles in the island had compelled a second occupation. All these cases give evidence not only of the authority which popular opinion exerts over the main lines of foreign policy, but also of the growth in it of a spirit of good sense and self-restraint such as was not always seen in earlier years. The nation, when it came to full manhood, laid aside the spirit of self-assertion and the desire for conquest, and gave proof of a sincere desire to apply methods of arbitration and show its respect for the rights of other nations. An instance of this was furnished when in 1914 Congress, at the instance of the President and at the bidding of public opinion, repealed an Act by which it had in 1912 hastily asserted a particular power over the use of the Panama Canal, which the people, after the matter had been fully discussed, convinced themselves that they had disclaimed by the treaty with Great Britain of 1901. With this higher sense of justice there has also come a stronger aversion to war. No great people in the world is equally pervaded by the wish to see peace maintained everywhere over the world.

In Great Britain, the only other country which can be profitably referred to in this connection, the first long step towards democracy was taken in 1832, a second in 1868, a third in 1885. From 1848 onwards the opinion of the masses of the people, as distinct from that of the richer or more educated classes, became a factor to be reckoned with in foreign policy, though the conduct of diplomatic relations was left, and has indeed been left till now, in the hands of the Ministry of the day. During two years of revolution on the Continent (1848–1850), the sympathies of the masses were with the Italian, German, Hungarian and Polish revolutionary parties, but this was largely true of educated Englishmen generally, especially in respect of Italy, where tyranny had been most repulsive. Regarding the Crimean War no great difference showed itself between the governing class and the bulk of the people. Had the latter realized the detestable character of Turkish government and the hopelessness of reforming it, there would probably have been a stronger opposition to a resort to arms than Cobden and Bright succeeded in arousing. But the general hatred of Russian autocracy, personified in the Czar Nicholas I., made even the Radicals think that a war against him must be a righteous war. In 1857 the action in China of a British official led to hostilities, and roused a sudden and sharp controversy. The House of Commons condemned the Governor's conduct. The Ministry which defended him dissolved Parliament and secured a majority in the new House, the electors apparently considering that the high-handed behaviour of the Chinese justified the extreme steps taken by the Governor. The "insult to the flag" argument was largely used, and proved effective. Britain did not interfere in the two wars which secured the liberation of Italy (1859 and 1866), but popular sympathy was in both cases given to the Italian cause. When Garibaldi visited London in 1864 he received a welcome more enthusiastic than had ever before been given to any foreign hero.

The American Civil War of 1861–1865 was the first occasion on which a marked divergence between the sentiment of the masses and that of the so-called "classes" disclosed itself. "Society," i.e. the large majority of the rich and many among the professional classes, sided with the Southern States, while nearly the whole of the working class and at least half of the middle class, together with many men of intellectual distinction, especially in the Universities, stood for the Northern. Feeling was bitter, and the partisans of each side held numerous meetings, but it was remarked that whereas the meetings which were called by the friends of the North were open to the general public, admission to those summoned to advocate the cause of the Seceding States was confined to the holders of tickets, because it was feared that in an open meeting resolutions of sympathy with the South could not be carried. These and other evidences, showing that the great bulk of the nation favoured the cause of the North as being the cause of human freedom, as soon as President Lincoln's Proclamation had made it clear that slavery would disappear, confirmed the Cabinet in its refusal to accede to Louis Napoleon's suggestion that England and France should join in recognizing the Seceding States as independent.

In 1876 a question of foreign policy emerged which revealed an even more pronounced opposition between the opinion of the masses and that of the classes. The Turkish Government, fearing a Bulgarian insurrection, perpetrated a horrible massacre, attended with revolting cruelties. When this became known in Russia, the Czar Alexander II. summoned the Sultan to introduce certain reforms, and on his refusal proceeded to declare war. Lord Beaconsfield, who was then at the head of the British Government, did not conceal his sympathy with the Turks, and would probably have carried Britain into a war against Russia to defend them had not an agitation in the country, which had been shocked by the news of the massacre, deterred his Cabinet from that course. When in 1878 the Russian armies had approached Constantinople and compelled the Turks to sign a peace largely reducing their territories, Britain was again brought by the Prime Minister to the verge of a war on their behalf, and a fresh popular agitation arose which lasted until the signature of the Treaty of Berlin. Through the angry political strife of these years, the majority of the richer and more educated classes approved the Ministerial policy, while the anti-Turkish cause found its support among the masses. The line of political distinction did not coincide with that of class, for there were crowds which acclaimed the Prime Minister, and there were men of wealth and men of intellectual eminence who denounced both him and the Turks.

Still, the antagonism between the view of the multitude and that of what is called " Society " was well marked both in this momentous struggle and in that which followed over the Afghan War of 1878–1879, the moral issues arising in which were essentially the same as those which had been fought over from 1876 to 1878. This was not fully seen till the election of 1880, when the great majority recorded against Lord Beaconsfield showed how widely his policy had been disapproved by the voters. It was the first election since that of 1857 which had turned upon matters of foreign policy.

A like division of opinion reappeared in the years 1899 to 1901, during which a Ministry, which had become involved in a war against the two South African republics, met with opposition from a comparatively small section of the wealthier class, and a much larger section of the professional and middle and working classes. How far the sweeping defeat of that Ministry at the general election of 1905 was due to its South African policy cannot be determined, for other questions also were before the voters.

This is not the place to discuss the merits of these three great issues which in 1861 to 1865, in 1876 to 1880, and in 1899 to 1901 so sharply divided the British people. But if we may take the prevalent opinion of the nation to-day (1920) as a final judgment, *i.e.* as being likely to be the judgment of posterity, it is interesting to note that in all three cases the " classes " would appear to have been less wise than the " masses." Everybody now admits that it was a gain for the world that in the American Civil War the Northern States prevailed and slavery vanished. Nearly everybody now admits that Lord Beaconsfield's Eastern policy has been condemned by its failure, for while the Turks continued to go from bad to worse, the reduction of their power which he tried to arrest in 1878 has been subsequently found inevitable. There is a less complete agreement regarding the South African War, but the majority of Englishmen seem now to regard that war as a blunder, which would have led at the outbreak of the Great War in 1914 to the separation of South Africa from Great Britain had it not been for the election of 1905, one result of which was to bring about the restoration of self-government under the British flag to the

Orange Free State and the Transvaal as parts of the Union of South Africa.

It may seem strange that in all these cases the richer and more educated classes should have erred, while the poorer have been shown by the event to have judged more wisely. The causes are explicable, but to explain them and cite parallel phenomena from other countries would require a digression into history for which there is no room here. Summing up the results of this examination of the foreign policy followed by three great democratic countries during the last fifty years, we find that the case of France proves that it was possible for a democracy to follow a consistent policy, the conduct of the details whereof was left in the hands of successive administrations, and safely left because the nation was substantially agreed as to the general lines to be followed. The case of the United States proves that public opinion, which is there omnipotent, is generally right in its aims, and has tended to become wiser and more moderate with the march of the years. The case of Britain shows that the opinion of the bulk of the nation was more frequently approved by results than was the attitude of the comparatively small class in whose hands the conduct of affairs had been usually left. Declarations of the will of the masses delivered at general elections told for good.

There is another way also of reaching a conclusion as to the competence of democracies in this branch of government. Set the results in and for the three countries examined side by side with those attained in and for three other great countries in which no popular clamour disturbed the Olympian heights where sat the monarch and his group of military and civil advisers, controlling foreign policy as respects both ends and means. In Russia, in Austria-Hungary, and in Germany the Emperors and their respective advisers were able to pursue their ends with a steady pertinacity from month to month and year to year. No popular sentiment, no parliamentary opposition, made much difference to them, and in Germany they were usually able to guide popular sentiment. In choosing their means considerations of morality were in none of these countries allowed to prevent a resort to any means that seemed to promise success. Compare the situation in which Russia found herself in 1917, when the

autocracy crashed to its fall, and the situations in which
Austria and Germany found themselves in October 1918,
with those in which that momentous year found the three
free countries.   The temptations and snares which surround
and pervert diplomatic aims and methods in States ruled by
oligarchies or despots often differ from the temptations of
which popular governments have to beware.   But they proved
in these cases, and in many others, to have been more
dangerous.

In these last few pages Ends rather than Means have
been considered, though it is hard to draw a distinction,
for most Ends are Means to a larger End; and the facts
examined seem to show that in determining Ends the voice
of the people must have authority.   But what is to be said as
to the details of diplomacy in which, assuming the main ends
to be determined by the people, a wide choice of means
remains open?   It has been deemed impossible for the people
to know either which means are best suited to the purpose
aimed at or, if the people is kept informed of them, to apply
those means successfully, for in our days what is told to any
people is told to the whole world.   So long as each nation
strives to secure some gains for itself as against other nations
by anticipating its rivals in enterprises, or by forming profitable alliances, or otherwise driving bargains for its own
benefit, those who manage the nation's business cannot disclose their action without damaging their chances of success.
Hence even the countries that have gone furthest in recognizing popular control have left a wide discretion in the hands
of their Ministers or envoys and have set bounds to the
curiosity of parliamentary representatives.   Must this continue?   If it does continue, what security have the people
against unwise action or the adoption of dishonourable
methods?

One expedient used to overcome this difficulty has been
that of a committee of the legislature which can receive con-
fidential communications from a Minister and can bind its
members to keep them secret.   This is done in the United
States, where the Foreign Relations Committee of the Senate,
though it cannot dictate to the President (or his Secretary
of State), can through its power of inducing the Senate to
refuse assent to a treaty exercise a constant and potent influ-

ence. So also in France each Chamber has a Commission for foreign affairs. In both countries declarations of war must proceed from the legislature. The committee plan has its defects. No secret known to more than three men remains for long a secret; and a Minister can, if he likes, go a long way towards committing his country before he tells the committee what he is doing, taking of course the chance that he may be disavowed. Sometimes, moreover, action cannot await the approval of a committee, for to be effective it must be immediate.

The voices which in European countries demand the abolition of secret diplomacy and the control by the people of all foreign relations appeal to an incontestable principle, because a nation has every right to deliver its opinion on matters of such supreme importance as the issues of peace and war. The difficulty lies in applying a sound principle to the facts as they have hitherto stood in Europe. If publicity in the conduct of negotiations is to be required, and the mind of the people to be expressed before any commitment is made by its Ministers, there must be a renunciation of such advantages as have been heretofore obtained by international combinations or bargains secretly made with other nations. If, on the other hand, these advantages are to be sought, secrecy must be permitted and discretion granted to Ministers. The risk that secrecy and discretion will be abused will be gradually lessened the more public opinion becomes better instructed on foreign affairs, and the more that legislatures learn to give unremitting attention to foreign policy. In England as well as in America few are the representatives who possess the knowledge needed, or take the trouble to acquire it. It is this, as well as party spirit, which has led Parliamentary majorities to endeavour to support their party chiefs, even when it was beginning to be seen that public opinion was turning against them. If Ministries were to become more and more anxious to keep as close a touch with the feeling of the nation in foreign as they seek to do in domestic affairs, the risk that any nation will be irrevocably entangled in a pernicious course would diminish. So too if there should be hereafter less of a desire to get the better of other nations in acquiring territory or concessions abroad, if a less grasping and selfish spirit should rule foreign policy, fewer occasions will arise in which secret agreements will be needed. The thing now most needed by the people and its representatives is more knowledge of the facts of the outside world with a more sympathetic comprehension of the minds of other peoples. The first step to this is a fuller acquaintance with the history, the economic and social conditions, and the characters of other peoples.

The conclusions to which the considerations here set forth point to are the following:

In a democracy the People are entitled to determine the Ends or general aims of foreign policy.

History shows that they do this at least as wisely as monarchs or oligarchies, or the small groups to whom, in democratic countries, the conduct of foreign relations has been left, and that they have evinced more respect for moral principles.

The Means to be used for attaining the Ends sought cannot be adequately determined by legislatures so long as international relations continue to be what they have heretofore been, because secrecy is sometimes, and expert knowledge is always required.

Nevertheless some improvement on the present system is needed, and the experiment of a Committee deserves to be tried.

Whatever faults modern democracies may have committed in this field of administration, the faults chargeable on monarchs and oligarchies have been less pardonable and more harmful to the peace and progress of mankind.

If the recently created League of Nations is to succeed in averting wars by securing the amicable settlement of international disputes, it must have the constant sympathy and support of the peoples of the states which are its members. That this support should be effectively and wisely given, the peoples must give more attention to foreign affairs and come to know more of them. Ignorance is the great obstacle.

CHAPTER LXII

THE JUDICIARY

There is no better test of the excellence of a government than the efficiency of its judicial system, for nothing more nearly touches the welfare and security of the average citizen than his sense that he can rely on the certain and prompt administration of justice. Law holds the community together. Law is respected and supported when it is trusted as the shield of innocence and the impartial guardian of every private civil right. Law sets for all a moral standard which helps to maintain a like standard in the breast of each individual. But if the law be dishonestly administered, the salt has lost its savour; if it be weakly or fitfully enforced, the guarantees of order fail, for it is more by the certainty than by the severity of punishment that offences are repressed. If the lamp of justice goes out in darkness, how great is that darkness!

In all countries cases, sometimes civil, but more frequently criminal, arise which involve political issues and excite party feeling. It is then that the courage and uprightness of the judges become supremely valuable to the nation, commanding respect for the exposition of the law which they have to deliver. But in those countries that live under a Rigid Constitution which, while reserving ultimate control to the people, has established various authorities and defined the powers of each, the Courts have another relation to politics, and take their place side by side with the Executive and the Legislature as a co-ordinate department of government. When questions arise as to the limits of the powers of the Executive or of the Legislature, or — in a Federation — as to the limits of the respective powers of the Central or National and those of the State Government, it is by a Court of Law that the true meaning of the Constitution, as the fundamental and supreme law, ought to be determined, because it is the rightful and authorized interpreter of what the people intended to declare 'when they were enacting a fundamental instrument.[1] This function of Interpretation calls for high legal ability, because each decision given becomes a precedent determining for the future the respective powers of the several branches of government, their relations to one another and to the individual citizen.

Capacity and learning, honesty and independence, being the merits needed in a judge, how can these be secured? Three things have to be considered: the inducements offered to men possessing these merits to accept the post, the methods of selecting and appointing persons found to possess them, and the guarantees for the independence of the judges when appointed. The inducements are three: salary, permanence in office, and social status, this last being largely a consequence of the other two. The modes of choice tried have been three: Nomination by the head of the Executive, Election by the Legislature, Election by the Citizens generally at the polls. The differences in the practice of the free governments examined in Part II. yield instructive results.

In France the salaries of the higher judges are low compared to the style of living which a judge is expected to maintain, but as the position is permanent and carries social consideration, men of approved abilities and solid learning are glad to have it. The highest Court of Appeal enjoys great respect, and so do the chief judges in the great cities. All are selected by the Executive. Although party influences may sometimes affect the choice, the normally lifelong tenure of the office has practically secured judicial independence. Once, however (in 1879–83) what was called a " purification " of the Bench was effected by the removal of a good many judges whose loyalty to the Republic was suspected, a step which, though possibly justified by special circumstances, set an unfortunate precedent.[2]

[1] See as to this Vol. I. pp. 89–91. The new constitution of Germany appears to leave to the Supreme Court the decision of legal questions arising between the Reich (the Federation) and the States within it, but not the decision of the question whether a law infringes the Constitution. The Constitution of Czecho-Slovakia provides (§ 102) that " judges in passing upon a legal question may examine the validity of an Ordinance; as to a Law they may enquire only whether it was duly promulgated."

[2] See Vol. I. p. 305.

Switzerland pays small salaries both to Federal and to Cantonal judges. All hold office for terms of years, but as they are usually reappointed if they have given satisfaction, the tenure is virtually permanent. The members of the Supreme Federal Court are chosen by the Federal Legislature for six years;[1] those of the Cantonal Courts are elected by the people. No one proposes to alter the practice though some disapprove it. It is ancient, and is deemed the natural thing in a democracy. Most of the Cantons are so small that the electors are usually able to estimate the honesty and good sense of a candidate.

In the United States the Federal Judges are appointed by the President with the consent of the Senate, and are irremovable except by impeachment. They receive salaries small in proportion to the income which an eminent counsel can earn at the bar, but the dignity of the office makes the best lawyers willing to accept it. In five of the States the judges are appointed by the State Governor, in two they are chosen by the State legislature, in all the rest they are elected by the people for terms of various lengths, with salaries varying in amount, but almost always insufficient to attract the highest talent. The result has been to give an excellent Supreme Federal Court, a high average of talent in the other Federal Courts, a good set of judges in the States where appointment rests with Governor or Legislature, and in nearly all of the other States judges markedly inferior to the leading counsel who practise before them. In some States it is not only learning and ability but also honesty and impartiality that are lacking. The party organizations which nominate candidates for election for the Bench can use their influence to reward partisans or to place in power persons whom they intend to use for their own purposes. If the results are less bad than might have been expected, this is generally due to the action of the local Bar, which exerts itself to prevent the choice of men whom it knows to be incompetent.

The three British self-governing Dominions — Canada, Australia, and New Zealand — have followed the practice

[1] The (recently enacted) Constitution of the Esthonian Republic vests the election of the State (Supreme) Court in the Assembly, and the appointment of lower judges in the State Court.

of the Mother Country. In all of them the judges are appointed by the Executive, hold office during good behaviour, *i.e.* practically for life, and receive salaries sufficient to attract leading lawyers. In all alike the posts are filled by competent men who enjoy the confidence of the community, a fact the more remarkable because the persons appointed have often been party politicians. It is the independence which life tenure gives, and the custom, inherited from England, which prescribes perfect impartiality and abstention from all participation in politics, that have made the judiciary trusted.

Why does popular election which the Swiss do not condemn give bad results in the States of the American Union? Mainly because in the former the matters that come before the Courts are comparatively small, whereas in the latter it may be well worth the while of a great railway or other incorporated company to secure the election of persons who will favour its interests when they become the subjects of litigation, and such a corporation can influence the party organization to nominate the men it wants. In small communities, moreover, such as are nearly all of the Swiss Cantons, a large proportion of the voters have some direct personal knowledge of the candidates, so that no party guidance is needed or would be tolerated, and can watch their behaviour in office, while in communities which count their population by millions the bulk of the voters have no such knowledge, and follow the lead given by the party organizations, each of which has its own friends to reward or axe to grind, and cares more for the subservience than for the merits of a candidate.

It may, however, be asked, Why should popular election produce a worse Bench than appointment by an Executive, seeing that the Executive is in the countries named (except Switzerland) an officer, or a Cabinet, chosen by a political party and disposed to serve its interests. Why then should a Prime Minister be any more likely to make good appointments than is a party organiaztion? If the Boss of an American State party organization is a party man, so is a State Governor, so is the President of the United States himself. The explanation is that the President is responsible to the Nation, and the Governor to his State. Either official would damage himself and his party if he made bad appointments, whereas the party Machine has no official character, and cannot be made responsible for what is legally the act of the voters when they elect a person whom the Machine has put forward as a candidate. The choice is theirs, for they need not have obeyed the Machine. Except in small communities such as boroughs or counties, the average elector has no means of knowing which of several candidates, with names probably all unfamiliar, has the talent needed, or the character, or the special attainments. Law has become a science, and a modern judge needs to know his own science just as much as does a professor of chemistry, the voters being no more fitted to choose the one than the other.

So much for the modes of appointment. As respects salaries and tenure, the moral of the facts stated needs no pointing. Where the inducements offered are scanty, capable men will not offer themselves. Unfortunately the average citizen has not, in some democracies, realized that the qualities needed must be well paid for, nor that a judge who has not to think of his re-election or promotion finds it easier to be independent.

There are three of the countries described in Part III. in which apprehensions are at present entertained regarding the status of the judiciary. In France the power of the Executive to promote men from lower to higher posts is thought to influence the minds of some magistrates who wish to stand well with the ruling party. In the States of the North American Union the displeasure of those eager to see Labour legislation promptly carried out, a displeasure evinced by the proposals for the Recall of judges or of decisions,[1] may deter State judges from giving effect in their interpretation of State laws to those provisions of State Constitutions which inhibit the legislatures from interfering with rights of property and freedom of contract. In Australia the creation of a Court of Arbitration empowered to fix rates of wages and conditions of labour has made the selection of a person to discharge this delicate function a matter of keen interest to employers and employed alike, so that the Executive which appoints the judge is liable to be secretly pressed by persons

[1] See Vol. II. pp. 162–167, *ante.*

belonging to one or the other class to choose a man whose proclivities they think they know, yet whose moral authority will suffer if those proclivities are believed by the public to have affected the choice.

A review of the judicial branch of government in the countries already examined, suggests, except as regards some States of the American Union, nothing to discredit democratic government, for it has provided justice, civil and criminal, at least as good as did any of the European monarchies or oligarchies, and better than did most of them.   In Canada and Australasia public opinion has been vigilant.   Barristers promoted from politics to the Bench have, when once they take their seat there, breathed an atmosphere so saturated with the English traditions, now two centuries old, of judicial impartiality and independence that they have very seldom yielded to partisan sympathies or party pressure.   It has also been a benefit that in these countries they have been invariably selected from the Bar, with their former associates in which they maintain social relations, undisturbed by political differences, and to whose good opinion they are sensitive. Nor has the Bar been without its influence on the Government of the day in deterring it from appointing, in satisfaction of party claims, persons whose capacity or character fell below the accepted standard.

The new States that lately have been or are now being formed in Europe have not, nor had the republics of Spanish America, the advantage of like traditions and of an equally watchful opinion.   In none of the now liberated countries, and least of all in those that had suffered from Turkish tyranny, were the Courts entirely trusted.   It is much to be desired that they should regard the organization of the judiciary on a sound basis as one of the most important among the tasks that the creation of constitutional governments presents, seeing that nothing does more for the welfare of the private citizen, and nothing more conduces to the smooth working of free government than a general confidence in the pure and efficient administration of justice between the individual and the State as well as between man and man.

CHAPTER LXIII

CHECKS AND BALANCES

THAT a majority is always right, *i.e.* that every decision it arrives at by voting is wise, not even the most fervent democrat has ever maintained, seeing that popular government consists in the constant effort of a minority to turn itself by methods of persuasion into a majority which will then reverse the action or modify the decisions of the former majority. Least of all do revolutionaries respect majorities, for they always justify, even in governments based on universal suffrage, the use of force to overthrow what a representative assembly may have decided, declaring that once the admirable result of their action has been seen it will secure general approval. Every people that has tried to govern itself has accordingly recognized the need for precautions against the errors it may commit, be they injurious to the interests of the State as a whole or in the disregard of those natural or primordial rights which belong to individual citizens. Some sort of safeguard is required. A majority may be very small, or be uninstructed on the particular matter that comes before it, or deceived by those who speak to it, or be under the influence of temporary passion; and whether the action of the majority be directly given by popular vote, or proceed from a representative assembly, a majority vote may fail to express the best will of the people, who may regret to-morrow what was done to-day and blame the ignorance or the passion that misled them or their representatives. Nevertheless, the will of the majority must somehow prevail in the long run, for the acceptance of its decision is the only alternative to an appeal to force. Hence the problem arises: What can be done, while respecting the principle of majority rule, to safeguard the people against the consequences of their own ignorance or impetuosity? History records many a decision whose deplorable results might have been avoided had there been more knowledge, more time for reflection, more opportunity for reconsideration.

The annals of democratic governments largely consist in an account of the various expedients resorted to for this purpose. These have taken two general forms. One is the constitutional restriction of the powers either of a Primary or of a Representative Assembly by imposing on its action certain restrictions which it cannot infringe without transgressing the Constitution, such as directing certain delays to be interposed or certain formalities to be observed before a decision becomes final, or by prescribing a certain majority as necessary for specially important decisions, or, in the case of a representative assembly, by excluding certain subjects from the range of its functions. The other form is by a division of the whole power of the people, entrusting part of it to one, part to another authority. This may take place by making the Executive independent of the Legislature, or by setting up over against the Legislative Assembly (whether Primary or Representative) some other authority, a person or a body whose concurrence is to be required if the action of the Assembly is to have legal effect. The former of these modes may be called that of Checks, the latter that of Balances, each of the two authorities acting as a counterpoise to the other. Twenty-four centuries ago the ancient republics tried both plans, and their experiments have still an interest. The Greeks relied chiefly on Checks, the Romans chiefly on Balances.

In most of the Greek democracies the popular Assembly of the whole body of citizens, exerting a wider sway than belongs to any single body in modern republics, brooked no rival. Unwilling to restrict its powers, the Greeks devised other safeguards. One was the setting apart from the ordinary expressions of their will on current matters certain enactments passed in a specially provided way as being " Laws of the City," not to be changed except in the same special way, and so coming near to what moderns would call a Rigid Constitution. They could not give due legal protection to the peculiar character of permanence which they desired these Laws to bear, because there was no means of preventing the Assembly from doing what it pleased; and when it passed a " Decree " inconsistent with a " Law " no one could call it to account nor with impunity disregard the " Decree " on the ground that it had, or that he believed it had, transgressed the " Law." But as the sanction which protected the " Laws " was moral rather than legal, not invalidating the decree, though furnishing a ground for arguing that the decree should not be passed, the Athenians devised two methods for rendering more difficult a transgression of the enactments meant to be specially respected. One was to threaten with a penalty any citizen who should propose to repeal them. This had a certain awe-inspiring influence, but could of course be got round by first repealing the law which imposed the penalty and then proceeding to propose a repeal of the law that had been so entrenched against attack. The other and more ingenious plan was to permit a criminal process to be instituted by any citizen against the person who had induced the Assembly to violate the Law, much as in the seventeenth century in England a minister who had led the Crown into pernicious courses by giving it bad advice could be impeached and punished, or, to use a more familiar illustration, just as in some States of the American Union a saloon-keeper who had supplied to a customer the liquor that intoxicated him could be sued for damages by a person whose property the intoxicated customer had injured. This possibility of prosecution for wilfully misleading the people seems to have had a deterrent effect upon Athenian demagogues.[1]

The Romans, also unwilling to restrict the powers either of their supreme legislative body, the *Comitia,* or of their chief executive magistrates, or not knowing how to do so, resorted to the method of Balances, and worked their government by a number of authorities each set over against the other. Wide powers, deemed needed in a State that was always at war, were left to the magistrates, while other authorities were provided who might prevent the abuse of those powers in civil affairs. The Senate balanced the Consuls, the two Consuls balanced one another, the Tribunes by their veto power balanced all the higher magistrates. The Assembly itself could be arrested in its action not only by the Tribunes but by one Consul, for a quaint survival of ancient superstition permitted a Consul to send a message to the Assembly, when summoned at the call of his colleague

[1] See as to Athens, Vol. I. Chap. XVI., *ante.*

or of a Tribune, announcing that he was watching the sky [1] for birds that might give omens, favourable or the reverse, to the Assembly.   In this case the Assembly could not meet, and its meeting might be delayed from day to day while the piously obstructive Consul continued the search for cheering omens.

The United States has rivalled Rome in the pains taken to divide and subdivide power among various authorities and in the variety of the restrictions imposed upon most of them. The functions of government have been divided into the Legislative, Executive, and Judicial departments.   The two branches of the Legislature, the Senate and the House, are balanced against one another, and limited by the veto of the Executive.   The Executive is limited by the right of the Senate to disapprove his public service appointments and disallow treaties made by him, while the Judiciary as the interpreter of the Constitution has the function of declaring void any action of the other departments of Government which transgresses the will of the people as set forth in the Constitution.   The ultimate fountain of power, Popular Sovereignty, always flows full and strong, welling up from its deep source, but it is thereafter diverted into many channels, each of which is so confined by skilfully constructed embankments that it cannot overflow, the watchful hand of the Judiciary being ready to mend the bank at any point where the stream threatens to break through.

The only checks which France and England and New Zealand have provided are to be found in the existence of Second Chambers, and will be mentioned in the chapter next following.

Without setting forth in detail the methods adopted in other countries, I may proceed to classify the precautions against hasty action under four heads.   The first, that of rules regulating the procedure of legislative assemblies, is open to the objection that rules prescribed by the legislature itself, can be by it, if a sovereign body, repealed at its pleasure, destroying thereby the security they seemed to promise. If therefore they are to be effective, they must be placed out of its reach by being included in a Constitutional Instrument which the legislature cannot alter.

[1] *Servare de coelo* was the technical term.

A second form of restriction consists in withdrawing from the competence of a legislature certain classes of subjects, reserving these for the direct action of the people themselves, so that if the representative legislature attempts to deal with them, its acts are legally null and void. The outstanding instances of this plan are found in provisions of the Federal Constitution and State Constitutions of the American Union, which reserve many matters for direct action by the people in the form of Constitutional amendments. The defects of this method are that it may prevent the passing of a measure urgently required, for the process of amending the Constitution is inevitably slow, and that it raises questions as to the validity of a law which cannot be promptly settled, for when it is doubtful whether a legislature has exceeded its powers, the question of validity must remain unsettled till decided by the Courts. Thus the legislature is hampered by doubts as to its powers, while the citizen may be embarrassed by not knowing whether or not to obey the challenged law. Despite these inconveniences, the system continues to find favour in America, where it has prevented much unwise action by the legislatures. It is also used in Australia and Canada and in Switzerland, though to a less extent, since neither the Confederation nor the Cantons distrust their representatives as the citizens do in many American States.

Thirdly, some nations have entrusted to the Executive the right of rejecting bills passed by the legislature. This plan, adopted in the American Federation and also in all but one of the several States of the Union, is possible only in those democracies which choose their chief executive magistrate by a popular vote for a comparatively short term of office, so that he, equally with the legislature, holds a direct mandate from the people and is responsible to them. Democratic principles would forbid the vesting of a veto in a hereditary king, or even in a president elected for life. The British Crown virtually parted with its right of dissent from the Houses two centuries ago, though that right has never been extinguished by statute.[1] In the United States the

---

[1] " The term veto " is not constitutionally correct as applied either to the Crown or the House of Lords. Both are technically parts of the

veto of the President (in federal legislation) as also that of
the State Governor (in State legislation) is valued as curb-
ing the tendency of legislatures to pass faulty measures either
from a demagogic purpose to curry favour with some large
section of citizens, or at the bidding of powerful business interests which can get at the individual representatives or at
the local party leaders who command a majority in the legislature.   So largely and so beneficially is it used in the States
that the Executive often gains credit with the people by his
vetoes, and points, when he seeks re-election, to the list of bad
bills which he has killed.   The existence of this power has
formed in State legislatures the habit of passing, in reliance
on the Governor's " lethal chamber," measures they know to
be bad, thus contriving to earn merit with some person, or
some section of their constituents, without injury to the general public.

A fourth way of restraining the legislature is found in
submitting its acts to popular vote.   This is the so-called
Referendum, applied in Switzerland both in the Confederation and in the Cantons, and in many American States.   It
is separately examined in the chapter which deals with Direct Popular Legislation.   On the direct action of the people
by the Initiative no check is placed, but the instances in
which the Swiss have erred in the use of this unlimited
power seem to have been extremely few.   They are an extraordinary people.   The results in America are discussed
elsewhere.[1]

Lastly there is the method of subjecting measures passed
by the popular representative assembly to revision or rejection by another legislative body.   This is the so-called
Second Chamber scheme, preferable to a simple veto because
it provides opportunities for a second discussion and possible
improvement of a measure.   It is so extensively used in
democracies as to demand treatment in a separate chapter.

It is interesting to observe that in some of the countries
mentioned the checks and balances which exist, or have
existed, were not devised as safeguards, but were incident

same enacting authority, the " Great Council of the Nation under the
King in Parliament assembled."

[1] See Vol. II. Chapters XLV. and LXV.

to the process of transition from monarchy or oligarchy
to democracy, the old powers exercised by the Few being
allowed to subsist in a reduced form side by side with the new
powers conceded to the Many. This was the origin of the
English House of Lords, now acting as a Second Chamber,
which is a continuation of the ancient Great Council of
the Nation (*Magnum Concilium*) whence the representative House of Commons was evolved, as a section thereof,
in the thirteenth century.[1] So the Second Chamber of
Sweden survives as one of the old Four Chambers of the
Four Orders (nobles, clergy, burgesses, and peasants) which
had lasted down to our own time. Most of the Senates in
modern countries have been deliberately contrived as checks
on the popular House, in imitation of ancient Rome or of
England. The veto of the President and the State Governor
in the United States was suggested by the power, already disused long before 1787, which had formerly belonged to the
British Crown. The restrictions on legislative action contained in American Constitutions were new, but they arose
naturally as involved in the creation of Rigid Constitutions
and along with the arrangements of a Federal system which
allotted certain powers to the National Government while
leaving others to the several States.

The need for safeguards against imprudent action in a
democracy, and the practical utility of such safeguards in
any particular case, depends largely on the character of
each people. As there are individual men so impatient or
impulsive that they do well to make it their rule never to
post a letter written in anger till they have shown it to
a judicious adviser or re-read it after twelve hours, while
there are others whose coolness or caution renders such a rule
superfluous, so likewise there are peoples, such as the Swiss,
who can dispense with some of the safeguards others have
found needful.

How to find a means of restraining the hasty impulses
either of the whole people in a primary assembly or of a
representative legislature has always been a difficult problem, because a balance has to be struck between the need

---

[1] Scotland had only one House in its Parliament before the Union,
but a committee called the Lords of the Articles acted as a check on
the whole body. See the work of Professors Dicey and Rait, *Thoughts
on the Union between England and Scotland,* pp. 14 *sqq.*

for caution on the one hand and the need for promptitude on the other.   Checks may work ill by giving too much weight to minorities, or by retarding action when speed is essential. Delays and obstacles placed in the way of the majority's will may tend to exasperation, and exasperation may induce violence or even revolution.   The United States has gone farther than any other popular government in limiting and balancing the powers of each organ of government, and has doubtless escaped thereby some dangers while suffering some inconveniences.   Britain and the British self-governing Dominions have followed a different path, and provide, except to some small extent in the Constitutions of Australia and Canada, few effective checks.[1]   No one thought of imposing restrictions on the House of Commons.   Having won popular favour by extorting freedom from the Crown, it was allowed to reach a power with which it has never been willing to part, though the conditions of England have made its legal omnipotence a very different thing from what that was eighty years ago.

Though experience shows that no nation has ever been cool enough and wise enough to dispense with some restraint on its own impulses, the tide of fatalistic faith in the sovereignty of the people tends in nearly every country to sweep away such checks as exist, replacing them by no others; and the peoples who most need to be protected against themselves are the least disposed to provide such protection.

Here the spirit of Faith in the people and the spirit of Liberty part company.   The former is content to let a majority have its way forthwith.   The latter, not denying that in the end the majority must prevail, is concerned to secure for a minority the right of being fully heard, and for the people due opportunities for reflection.

[1] The Second Chambers in Canada, in Australia and its States, and in New Zealand have been described in the chapters relating to those countries.   The British Second Chamber can now do no more than delay the passing of a bill (other than financial) till it has been passed in three successive sessions, and until a period of two years from its first passing in the House of Commons has elapsed.   In financial bills it has no power at all.

CHAPTER LXIV

SECOND CHAMBERS

THOSE modern thinkers and statesmen, who have held that every well-framed constitution should contain some check upon the power of the popular assembly have usually found it in the creation of a second assembly capable of criticizing, amending, and, if need be, rejecting measures passed by the other Chamber. It was, however, to no such doctrine that the national assemblies of the European Middle Ages owe their division into several Estates: three in France, four in Sweden, two in Hungary and England. Neither had the idea of this restriction on democratic haste emerged in the ancient world, though the Councils of Greek republics and the Senate at Rome, however different their functions, may be cited as showing some benefits which the existence of two bodies exercising constitutional powers may provide. This duality may be found as far back as the early ages of Greece, in which the Homeric poems show us a primary assembly of the whole people, with a council of the wise elders [1] which holds its preliminary deliberations. With this one may compare what Tacitus tells of the primitive Germans, among whom the chiefs met in a small council to consider matters of minor importance, and held a preliminary debate on those graver questions which were to be brought before the Assembly.[2] When the first constitutions of the American States were drafted, a Second Chamber was deliberately introduced in imitation of the British Parliament with its two Houses. The example has been followed in most of the

---

[1] Βουλὴν δὲ πρῶτον μεγαθύμων ἷζε γερόντων (*Iliad* ii. 53).

[2] *De moribus Germanorum*, chap. xi. " De maioribus rebus principes consultant: de minoribus omnes, ita tamen ut ea quoque quorum penes plebem arbitrium est apud principes praetractentur." In the ancient world the functions of a " Second Chamber " seem to have generally been not to revise or further discuss the decisions of the popular Assembly, but to consider the topics that were to come before it, much as does a modern Cabinet. See as to the Athenian Council Vol. I. Chap. XVI.

countries that have given themselves frames of more or less popular government in modern times, including not only those which in the Old World have been influenced by the British model of Cabinet and Parliamentary government, but those also which in the Western hemisphere have taken the United States as their pattern. France, both in 1830 and 1875, created two, not regarding the dictum of Sièyés, who is said to have asked: " Of what use will a Second Chamber be? If it agrees with the Representative House, it will be superfluous, if it disagrees, mischievous," a dilemma which recalls that attributed to the Khalif Omar when he permitted the destruction of the library at Alexandria, " If the books agree with the Koran, they are not needed; if they differ, they ought to perish." [1]

In European States (as also in Iceland) except Greece, Bulgaria, Finland, Esthonia [2] and Jugo-Slavia the legislature consists of two Chambers.

The aim pursued in all these countries was substantially the same, viz. that of creating a legislative authority whose function it should be to review measures passed by the popular House in such a way as:

To prevent undue haste in the passing of important laws by securing a period during which the opinion of the people regarding a law may be duly formed and expressed.

To subject every project of law to a revision which might introduce improvements in form or substance.

While in some countries there were statesmen who desired for the Second Chamber powers practically equal to those of the " popular " House, it was, as a rule, intended that the latter should predominate.

METHODS OF CREATING A SECOND CHAMBER

Many are the ways in which nations have constructed

---

[1] As usually happens, these dilemmas owe their point to the omission of other possibilities. A Second Chamber may do work involving neither agreement nor disagreement with the Other House, and it may, where it agrees in aims, suggest other and better means of attaining them. The Khalif's remark would begin to have force only if the Koran were an encyclopaedia containing all a Muslim needs to know. Probably he thought it was.

[2] Esthonia has, however, provided a check on its legislature by the adoption of the Referendum. I have been unable to ascertain how matters stand in Poland and Lithuania, and in the Georgian and Armenian Republics and that of Azerbaijan.

their Second Chambers. To classify these let us begin by dividing Governments into the Federal and the Unitary or non-Federal.

In Federal States the need for providing a representation of the several communities which make up the federation suggested the creation of a Chamber to which each component entity should return members, and this naturally became a Second Chamber for the whole nation. The United States led the way in creating its Federal Senate, and its example has been followed by Switzerland, Australia, the Union of South Africa, Argentina, Brazil and some other American republics. This plan is simple, and has the great advantage of securing for the Second Chamber that weight which the representation of important communities such as the Swiss Cantons or the American and Australian States carries with it.[1]

Unitary countries have adopted one or other of the following methods: Some have assigned to the head of the Executive the right of nominating to sit in the Second Chamber any persons he thinks fit. Others, while giving nominations to the Executive, have restricted its choice to persons above a certain age or belonging to specified categories, *e.g.* men who have filled certain high offices, or who possess a certain amount of property, or who come from a titled aristocracy, or who occupy positions which qualify them to express the wishes of important professions. Thus the Italian Senators are nominated for life by the Crown, *i.e.* by the Ministry. Spain, and Hungary before the destruction of the Austro-Hungarian Monarchy, had Chambers with some hereditary peers and other persons chosen by electorates composed of persons holding property of a prescribed value. The Legislative Councils in four of the Australian States are elected by voters possessing a (low) property qualification.[2] Another method is to vest the election in the members of various local bodies, or persons se-

[1] The Dominion of Canada, a Federal State, has a Senate filled by the nominees of the Dominion Government, selected in certain proportions from the nine Provinces which make up the Federation and in so far representing those component communities, though not chosen by them Only two of the Provinces (Quebec and Nova Scotia) have a Second Chamber, and members of these are nominated for life by the Provincial Ministries.

[2] See Vol. II. p. 192, *ante.*

lected from them, such as are the "Electoral Colleges," created from the Councils of the Departments and of the Arrondissements, and from the Communes in France (see Vol. I. p. 259). This plan, adopted also in Sweden and Portugal, has been termed "indirect election," or "popular election in the second degree," because the electors have been themselves elected by bodies chosen by the citizens.

Finally, in many countries the members of the Second Chamber are directly elected by the people on the same suffrage as members of the other or "more popular" House, but in and by larger constituencies, so as to provide a Second Chamber less numerous than the First. This is the method used in all the States of the North American Union, in each of which the State Senate, a body much smaller than the State Assembly or House of Representatives, is elected on manhood (or universal) suffrage, but in larger electoral districts. Federal Senators also are now (since 1914) elected by the people on a general vote taken over each State, and so are the members of the Senate in the Australian Federation (see Vol. II. p. 190, *ante*). Direct popular election has also been adopted by the Czecho-Slovak Republic for its Senate, the electors being over twenty-six and the candidates required to be over forty-five years of age, and the term of office eight years.

In the functions and powers allotted to Second Chambers there is also a diversity so great that I must be content with indicating the three classes into which these assemblies fall, viz.:

1. Those which are equal in power, both legally and practically, to the First, or "Popular" House. These include the Second Chambers elected on universal (or manhood) suffrage, such as the Senates of American States, the Senate of the Australian Commonwealth, and the Federal Senate of the United States. The powers of the latter are indeed greater than those of the House of Representatives, for it is not only a branch of the legislature but also a sort of Council to the President, advising and to some extent controlling him.

2. Those whose functions are legally equivalent, or nearly so, to those of the First Chamber, but whose power is practically inferior, perhaps much inferior. To this class belong

the Chambers of France, Italy, Belgium, and most other European States, as well as those of New Zealand, the Dominion of Canada, and the Union of South Africa. Among these the French Senate is the strongest and that of Canada among the weakest.

3. Those whose powers are legally as well as practically slender, such as is the Senate in Holland and the Lagthing in Norway.[1]

The difference in functions between the two Houses turns chiefly on finance. An assembly not directly chosen by the tax-payers does not seem entitled to equal power with one directly elected as respects the raising of taxes and the appropriation of their proceeds to particular purposes, and since the control of revenue is the means of controlling the Executive, it follows that in countries where Ministers hold office at the pleasure of Parliament, such as France, Britain, and the British self-governing Dominions, it is the Popular House whose vote practically instals and displaces them.

Broadly speaking, the powers of the Second Chamber vary with the mode of its formation. They are widest where it is directly elected, narrowest where it is nominated or hereditary. The more it is Popular the more authority, the less it is Popular the less authority will it possess. Where not directly elected, it is always under the disadvantage of fearing to displease the popular House, lest the latter should seek to get rid of its resistance by rousing clamour among the people against it. The test of effective power is this: What happens when the two Houses disagree and each seeks to persist in its own view?

Now let us return to the methods of composing the Second House, and see which works best in practice.

None of the systems enumerated has altogether approved itself. Direct election by universal suffrage has doubtless the merit of securing for the Second Chamber a representative quality equal to that of the other Chamber. But in doing so it inevitably creates a competitive claim to equal authority. Springing directly from the people, and giving to each of its members this advantage over members of the larger House,

[1] It is really a sort of Committee of the Stor Thing or popular assembly.

that inasmuch as he is chosen by a larger electoral district he may claim to represent a greater volume of opinion, it is sure to become a rival of the First Chamber. The plan has, moreover, another fault. If the Second House has been elected at the same time as the larger House, it is likely to be controlled by the same political party, in which case its value as a moderating influence disappears. If, on the other hand, one of the two has been elected either earlier or later, whichever House has last come from the people will claim to be the true exponent of the people's mind. Moreover, the men who compose the two Houses will — an age limit makes no practical difference — have been drawn from the same class, so no new element of knowledge or wisdom is brought in to serve the nation. In the States of the American Union the Senates are no better than the Houses of Assembly; indeed, where corruption prevails the Senates may be worse, because as their members are fewer in number each member's vote is better worth buying and fetches a higher price. In Australia the Federal Senate, though smaller, is inferior to the House in the quality of its member-ship, because the abler and more ambitious men seek to enter the latter, from which Ministers are more frequently drawn. Nevertheless it asserts its equality. Little has been gained for that country except indeed that second consideration of Bills which their passage through another House implies, for the so-called " mental outfit " of the two Chambers is the same, or differs to the disadvantage of the Senate.

The plan of nomination by the Executive is even less to be commended, because members seem to be usually selected for party reasons; sometimes, as in Canada, not merely for the sake of securing for the Ministry a majority in the Second Chamber but also in order to reward its elderly supporters, who, weary of courting constituencies, gladly subside into a dignified armchair. There are countries in which secretly rendered political services or liberal contributions to party funds are believed to open the door of the Chamber to those whose merits the public had failed to discover. Election on a restricted franchise exposes the Chamber to the charge of being a class body, habitually opposed to the popular will. Election by Colleges drawn from local authorities has given to France a capable Senate, but it has brought party politics into the popular elections of those authorities themselves. Candidates seeking to enter a Departmental Council announce themselves as party candidates, and party organizations work for them, so each local body comes to be divided on partisan lines prescribed by national issues which have little or nothing to do with its proper functions. As in the United States the choice of Federal Senators by State legislatures helped to stamp upon those bodies almost from the first a partisan character, so the Departmental Councils in France are now more affected by national party influences than they might have been if a share in electing the Senate had not been assigned to them. Thus every method of choice has proved to have its defects, and nowhere have the results attained given complete satisfaction, a conclusion which does not in the least condemn the bicameral system in principle, for if no Second Chamber is perfect, neither is any First Chamber perfect. For each country the question is not whether it has got the perfection it desires, but whether it would not fare worse without some such addition to, or check upon, its popular House as a Second Chamber provides.

The reason which has made it more difficult to construct a Second Chamber than a " First " or " popular " Chamber is that the latter can be, and now is almost everywhere, created by direct election on a very wide suffrage. The application of this method has become a part of modern democratic theory, because it is supposed to be required by the fundamental dogma of Popular Sovereignty, and it has therefore led in America and Australia to the election of their Senates by universal suffrage. The objections to its application are (as already observed) that it creates two rival Chambers, and that they will be composed of the same kind of men. Why then have two? Cannot the will of the people be fully expressed through one? Accordingly, the most " advanced " theorists of our time seek to destroy Second Chambers altogether, while those who, because they have less absolute faith in the wisdom of the multitude, desire to check its impulses, are driven to look for some plan, other than direct popular election, by which a restraining authority can be created. But whichever way they turn they are stopped by the democratic dogma. Nomination by a Ministry, indirect election by local authorities, election in constituencies limited by property qualification, even election by the more popular House itself, all offend against that dogma. The ultimate issue comes to be whether the principle of direct and absolute Popular Sovereignty is incompatible with, or can be so far departed from as to admit, the imposition upon the legislature of such checks as will ensure that the deliberate will of the people itself shall be fully ascertained, after opportunity for deliberation has been afforded, before the final determination of any momentous question. If it is desired to make that departure from the dogma aforesaid by establishing a Second Chamber qualified to impose the check, such a Chamber must have some basis for its authority. What is this basis to be?

FUNCTIONS AND POWERS OF A SECOND CHAMBER

Let me now turn from this survey of the plans that have been tried and the results they have yielded to consider the Second Chamber problem in the light not only of experience but of the changed conditions under which popular government has to be carried on in the twentieth century. It is a double problem. What was said in the last preceding chapter makes it superfluous to restate the arguments used to prove that a Second Chamber is needed, so we may go straight to the two questions: If there is to be a Second Chamber how ought it to be constructed, *i.e.* how should its members be chosen? and, What powers ought to be assigned to it?

It may be said that the structure of the Chamber will depend upon the powers which it is meant to exercise. This is true. The powers will affect the structure. But so will the structure affect the powers. In discussing either branch of the problem we have to think of the other. If the powers are to be wide, the Chamber must be so constructed as to be fit, *i.e.* strong enough, to exercise them. If it is built upon a foundation not solid enough to bear a heavy weight the powers must be slender, otherwise it will totter under a shock. Bearing this in mind, let us begin with the Structure.

If we try to generalize some conclusions from the experiments heretofore made in divers countries, there will appear to be three sources from which a Second Chamber has in the past derived, or can now derive, the authority without which it would not be worth having. The first of these grounds is traditional respect felt for it by the people. If it has a long and dignified history, if its members belong to a powerful class which still enjoys social distinction, it may hold its place by the deference accorded to the persons who compose it. This deference maintained the House of Magnates in Hungary and the House of Lords in England, until the latter, in which both the ancient parties had been strong down till the middle of last century, passed so entirely under the control of one political party that it incurred the constant hostility of the other, its social status being at the same time rapidly lowered by the very large additions made to its number. Respect for antiquity has everywhere declined in our time, whose ways of thinking do not favour the maintenance either of time-honoured traditions or of any form of social deference.

The second ground of authority an assembly may enjoy comes from its representative character. If it is chosen by the people, it is deemed to speak the mind of the people and to have the weight of the people behind it. Upon this foundation the Senates of the several American States, whose members receive scant respect as individuals, and the Councils of the Swiss Cantons have been made to rest. Similarly, though to a slighter extent, the Second Chambers formed by Indirect or Secondary election, such as those of France, Denmark and (partially) Belgium, feel themselves, though weaker than the First Chambers because not the direct choice of the people, yet able, especially if adorned by men of talent, to exert considerable influence. Where, as is usually the case, the term of office is longer than that prescribed for the First Chamber, the Second Chamber draws some strength from the ampler experience of its members, but is in so far weaker as its representative authority has suffered by the lapse of time, since it seems to reflect the past rather than the present mind of the people.

The third ground is the personal merit and intellectual eminence of the members of the Second Chamber. If it were possible to discover in the nation, outside their popular First House, one hundred of the ablest men in the nation, men of experience and distinction in their several callings and also possessed of political knowledge and sound judgment, and to stock a Second Chamber with these men, it may be thought that the influence of their tested characters and personal eminence would compensate for the absence of popular election and would make their debates and decisions carry weight with the country. This does in fact happen, but to no great extent, with the Senates of Italy, Belgium, and Spain. For the best example of what authority intellectual power coupled with the glamour of tradition may give to an assembly, we must go back two thousand years to the long and splendid career of a body which was not elected, was not (in strictness) a Legislature, and cannot be classed as a Second House, because there was no First House but only the whole body of citizen voters set over against it.[1] The Roman Senate may well claim to have been the most successful of all the councils that have ruled in any state. It consisted, during the later Republic, of persons nominated, virtually for life,[2] by two magistrates of the highest rank and reputation called Censors, elected once in five years. Custom prescribed that every person who had held one of certain high elective offices, including of course the consulship and praetorship, should be nominated to a seat in it and left the choice of the rest to the discretion of the Censors. Thus the Senate had two sources of authority, the memory of centuries during which it had guided the fortunes of the State, and the high distinction and official service of a large proportion of its members. Sustained by this traditional reverence it survived the popular assembly and popular freedom itself to become a passive instrument of the Emperor's power, retaining a legal status which was sometimes usefully turned to account, and so lived on for more than fourteen centuries, till at the fall (in A. D. 1453) of the New Rome on the Bosphorus, all that remained of Roman greatness in the East was replaced by a brutal tyranny.

[1] The Senate could pass resolutions of an executive character, which the Consuls were, in practice, obliged to regard as authoritative, but was not entitled to enact laws until custom invested it with that right when free government was expiring. One may say that whereas during the Republic a *Senatus Consultum* had not the force of a *Lex*, the doctrine expressed in the words *Senatum ius facere posse non ambigitur* (Dig. I. 3. 9) soon became recognized under the Empire.

[2] Though liable, in very exceptional cases, to be removed from the roll.

Three theories have been and are held of the functions of a Second Chamber.

1. One is that it should have all the powers of the First or Popular House. We have, however, seen that such powers will not be granted to it unless it is directly elected, and the objections to two directly elected Houses confronting one another have been already stated. To make it the equal of the First Chamber is to invite it to contend for an equal right to popular support.

2. The second view is that it should be subordinated in financial legislation to the Popular House (and consequently should not be able to displace a Ministry), but should be for other kinds of legislation on the same footing. According to this theory it will be entitled not only to initiate bills, but also to amend and possibly reject bills sent up from the latter, though it will recognize that in a trial of strength it may prove the weaker.

3. The third is that its competence should be confined to the modest function of revising Bills passed by the " Popular " House, *i.e.* of suggesting amendments, and perhaps of recommending modifications of detail in financial proposals, but without power to reject or substantially alter a measure when returned to it by the Popular House in the form which the latter has approved. Let us take each of these three views in its probable working.

By common consent one of the functions of any Second Chamber would be that of revising the Bills brought to it from the more popular House. It is a great convenience to any Ministry passing a Bill to have an opportunity of setting right in another House mistakes or omissions overlooked in the House where the Bill originated, and the criticism of fresh minds, dealing with the measure in a calmer atmosphere, may correct various mistakes committed or overlooked. Though it is difficult to fix the extent to which revision should go, we may take it that those who hold this last view think that the Second Chamber must not enter on a conflict with the First, but submit after having made its protest. Note, however, a probable result. Were this view of a Second Chamber's functions to prevail, and revision be taken in the narrower sense of the term, such a body would become little more than a group of legal experts, a seat in which would not attract persons of ability and distinction. It would not constitute an effective check, even for the purposes of delaying hasty legislation, and the country might almost as well be without a Second Chamber.

If, however, the second view be adopted, and the Second Chamber be set up for the purpose of resisting ill-considered or unwise action on the part of the First House, the question arises: How far may such resistance go? How far may the material provisions of a Bill be altered? Alteration easily passes into practical rejection. Rejection is permitted to the Senate not only in the United States and in Australia, but also in France and Italy and Canada, though in these last the power is sparingly and cautiously exercised. Can it be refused to a Chamber which is to justify its existence by delaying action until the people have had full time for considering vital issues? Can financial questions be entirely excluded from its competence? Almost any change may be included in a measure professing to have objects primarily financial, and measures virtually revolutionary may thus be carried through in connection with the raising and the appropriation of public funds.

If the Second Chamber receives the right of offering some resistance, be it greater or smaller, to the First House, by what means are the differences between them to be adjusted? Five modes for reaching a decision have been suggested:

1. One mode is to fix a time after which the Second Chamber must accept any Bill passed a second (or third) time which the Second Chamber has rejected.

2. The two Houses may meet as one and the difference be determined by their joint vote after debate.

3. The votes taken in each House separately may be added together and the combined majority taken as decisive.

4. The Legislature may be dissolved and the Bill again voted on by both Houses after the general election, and ultimately by the Houses sitting together. This plan exists in the Australian Commonwealth.

5. A certain number of members of each House may be chosen to form a Joint Conference Committee, and the matter be settled by their vote after discussion.

6. The question may be referred to the whole people to

be voted on by them just as is a Constitutional Amendment in an American State or a matter submitted to popular Referendum in Switzerland.

Which of these methods of settlement should be adopted in any particular State would depend upon the population of the country, the respective numbers of the two Houses, and other local conditions. In France, Switzerland, the United States and some other countries no constitutional provision for terminating a dispute exists. One or other House gives way, in France usually the Senate, in the United States more frequently the House of Representatives.

REASONS WHICH IN OUR TIME INCREASE THE NEED FOR A SECOND CHAMBER

Before setting out the conclusions to which an examination of the two interdependent question of the Structure and the Powers of a Second Chamber seems to point, there is a further ground, besides those already mentioned, for creating a Second Chamber, a further value which such a body may possess.

A previous chapter has described the dissatisfaction with its representative Legislature which nearly every free people has come to feel; and I have sought to explain the causes which have produced the alleged decline in the quality and the consequent decline in the authority of legislatures. A decline in quality is not likely to be remedied so long as the conditions of membership in the Popular House remain so toilsome and exacting as they have become within the last thirty years, even in those European countries where the post of a representative is more attractive than it has been in the United States or Canada, in Australia or New Zealand. A French deputy is required to render to his constituents services that are incessant, laborious, often even humiliating. An English member is now expected to be constantly occupied in delivering speeches outside Parliament, on nonpolitical as well as political topics, and, if he be fairly rich, is also expected to subscribe considerable sums to many objects connected with his constituency: his independence has been reduced, for party discipline has grown stricter, while the fatigue of elections recurring at least once in five years, is far greater than formerly. Hence many men exceptionally qualified for public service but who are no longer young and strong, or who are deficient in fluency of speech or other popular arts, do not offer themselves as candidates. If their talents can be made useful to the nation, it must be by placing them in a different kind of assembly, such as a Second Chamber not popularly elected, or in which the pressure coming from constituents is less heavy.

We have already seen that the two defects most frequently charged upon legislative bodies in our time are the following:

1. Legislatures contain too little of the stores of knowledge, wisdom, and experience which each country possesses.

2. Legislatures are liable to fall under the control of one political party disposed to press through, in a hasty or tyrannical spirit, measures conceived in the interests of that party or of a particular class in the community, often without allowing sufficient time for full debate, sometimes even by means of an organization of the ruling majority which binds all its members to support whatever measures have been adopted by the larger part of that majority. Where this happens it is not the legislature as a whole that governs, but a majority of a majority which may frequently be a minority of the whole body.[1]

Taken together, these defects are a danger to democratic government. If a nation proceeds on the principle not only that the people are always right, but that their directly elected representatives are always competent to carry out in an efficient way the people's will, even when its action has been most hasty, then of course no check and little revising skill are needed. Or if, again, it be held that the harm caused by the errors of a representative body is less than the harm which would result from any attempt to delay its action, then again there need be no talk of a Second Chamber. But unless this view prevails, there must be some means for correcting the defects aforesaid, which tend to grow more dangerous because the functions thrust upon governments are becoming more numerous and complex, so that greater and greater special knowledge and skill are required to discharge them. More and more do they demand not only technical attainments, especially in the economic sphere, but also that

---

[1] See Vol. II. p. 389, *ante*.

power of steady and penetrating thinking not often present in the average legislator. The consequence is either that legislation and administration decline or that they fall into the hands of permanent officials constituting that sort of bureaucracy whose domination orthodox democracy denounces. Unless a nation is to lag behind its competitors it must rely upon a larger and stronger staff of officials to supply the defects of legislatures, or power will pass from it to those competing nations whose better-planned institutions are more practically efficient.

It has begun to be perceived that the existing legislative machinery of most countries does not sufficiently provide for the study of economic and social problems in a directly practical spirit by those on whom the duty falls of passing into law measures dealing with them, because legislatures incessantly occupied with party strife and with the supervision of the Executive in its daily work of administration have not the time, even if a sufficient number of their members have the capacity, for such investigation.

These considerations suggest that where such defects exist, with little prospect of curing them by improving the quality of directly elected legislatures,[1] a remedy may be found in the creation of a Second Chamber into which men might be gathered who are eminent by their ability and the services they have rendered to the nation or to the district in which they reside, men who have gained experience in various forms of public work, such as local government and the permanent civil service at home or abroad, or who possess special knowledge of important branches of national life, as for instance agriculture, commerce, manufacturing industry, finance, education, or who have by travel and study acquired a grasp of foreign affairs and the general movements of the world. Such a Chamber might be made a kind of reservoir of special knowledge and ripened wisdom to be added to whatever knowledge and wisdom have already been gathered into the more popular House. Place might be found in it for persons representing the great professions, such as scientific research, medicine, law, engineering, though, of

[1] See as to this, Vol. II. Chapter LVIII., *ante*, where reasons are stated which deter or prevent many men of political capacity from entering the Popular Chamber.

course, it ought not to be a mere aggregate of specialists, but predominantly composed of men familiar with public life and capable of dealing with political questions in a practical spirit, for the eminent man of science or man of letters is not always judicious, nor even cool and open-minded, when he approaches politics. No assembly can escape partisanship, but a calm and impartial spirit in a large proportion of its members would moderate that tendency in the whole body, and go far to secure popular confidence. The function of such a body in a country governed by Universal Suffrage would be not to aim at equal power with the Popular House but to approach all questions with as much as possible of a judicial mind and temper, recognizing its responsibility to the people, and resisting the Popular House only when there was good reason to believe that the matter in dispute had been hastily or rashly dealt with. It should not persist in opposition to whatever could be shown to be the people's will, but be content with trying to comprehend and give effect to that will when duly expressed, endeavouring to inform and influence the people through debates which would be conducted under freer conditions than is always possible in a large representative assembly. It would provide a forum in which foreign policy, seldom adequately handled in popular Chambers, might be dealt with at moments when the larger Assembly had no time to spare for them. Its Committees might study and report upon, either alone or in conjunction with Committees of the other House, questions of a non-partisan character upon which legislation seemed to be needed, and might prepare measures which would pass the more readily because proceeding from an authority not associated with one political party. In this way the labours of the Executive might be aided or relieved, and the longer term of service, say from six to nine years, assigned to its members would enable them to acquire an experience helpful in this branch of its work.[1]

If such a Second Chamber be desirable, how could it be

[1] The method of renewing the Second Chamber from time to time by the retirement, at intervals of two years, of a part of the body gives satisfaction in the United States. In the Australian Commonwealth half retire every three years. It need hardly be said that the observations here made are all general, and that every scheme would need to be adjusted to the conditions of the country for which it was being created.

created? Clearly not by direct popular election, which would tend to make it a mere replica of the First Chamber. Possibly by some one of the forms of Indirect Election previously referred to such as that used in France. If this method were disapproved on the ground that it might create a Chamber scarcely less partisan than the Popular House, and not much more certain to represent the special qualities and attainments which a Second Chamber ought to possess, other expedients might be tried. One would be that of election by the First House divided for that purpose into local groups,[1] and electing only a certain number of persons in each year, another that of Selection by a Commission appointed for that purpose, exercising by the appointment and in the name of the people a function resembling that of the Roman Censors.

The principle of making a Second Chamber strong and respected solely or mainly by the quality of its members and by the reputation their careers have gained for them, deserves to be considered by any nation which does not feel bound to press democratic principles to their full logical consequences. Let us imagine a small Selective Commission of men generally respected and trusted by the best opinion of their fellow-citizens to be specially appointed by the Legislature for the purpose of selecting persons fitted by ability, experience, knowledge of affairs — including of course high ex-officials — to sit in a Second Chamber for a term of not less than six or nine years. Such a Commission of Selection, created and renewed from time to time under the provisions of a permanent law, might choose, on principles and lines laid down in that law to guide their action, the persons who are to sit in the Chamber. The Commission ought to be a small (and as far as possible a non-partisan) body, both for the sake of fixing responsibility upon its members and in order to permit them to discuss freely and confidentially the qualifications of the persons to be chosen for the Chamber: and it might be desirable that most, though probably not all, of its members should be drawn from the existing Cham-

---

[1] It has been argued on behalf of this suggestion that it would tend to keep the two Houses in friendly touch with one another, while at the same time the members of the Second Chamber, sitting for a longer period, would not be a mere reflection of the First Chamber.

bers, as they would have exceptional opportunities for knowing where the ablest and fairest minds among men engaged
in public affairs were to be found. However conscientious
and impartial the Commissioners might be they would be
faced with one task of special difficulty. Capable and trusted
men may be found if only experience, capacity, and character have to be regarded. But as the Chamber must be
so composed as not to fall under the permanent control of
one political party, for that would impair the moral influence on public opinion desired for it, some regard must be
had not only to the eminence and wisdom of the persons to
be selected, but also to the political opinions they hold, for if
the Selectors should, however innocently, create a Chamber
in which one party was evidently predominant, other parties
would complain of unfair treatment, the prospects of success for the Chamber would be clouded and its influence be
discredited at the outset. Probably, therefore, the safest
method which a Selecting Commission could follow would be
to assign to each political party, in fair proportion to its
strength in the " more popular " House, a certain number of
the persons possessing the merits which marked them out
for selection, and then add to these a number of others who
were not avowed adherents of any section of opinion, but,
being also eminent in their several ways, were known as
men of impartial and independent minds, fitted to hold the
balance fairly between parties, and to exercise an unbiassed
judgment on each issue as it arose. In some such way as
this it might be possible to create a Chamber which, starting
without anything like a large predetermined majority for
any particular party, would be accepted by the people as entitled to speak with the authority which belongs to knowledge
and experience.[1] But so hard would it be to create a Selecting Commission not only capable of doing a work so delicate,

[1] The confidence accorded to the Committees of Selection in the two
Houses of the British Parliament, small bodies composed of members
of all parties appointed to choose other members to sit on Committees
with due regard to the representation thereon of all the chief parties
or groups, encourages the hope that such a Selecting Commission as
that mentioned in the text might be no less successful. The plan might
be varied by allowing the Second Chamber, when once constituted, to
fill up a certain number of the vacancies from time to time occurring
in its own body.

but also sure to be generally recognized as having done it in an honest and impartial spirit, that one cannot be surprised to find that the experiment is still untried.

Were any plan of this nature proposed, the old question would recur, whether in a democratic country a Chamber so chosen would be allowed the powers necessary to attract to it men of distinction, and necessary also to render it an effective part of the constitutional machinery. It might be decried as unresponsive, because not by direct election responsible, to popular sentiment. Only at rare moments, such as was that in which the American Constitutional Convention of 1787 met, are the people disposed to forgo any part of their power for the sake of their security. Thus it happens that the very conditions which make a moderating Second Chamber desirable are those which prevent its creation. Though the dangers which used to be feared from oligarchies of rank and wealth have been passing away in free countries, though nobody now ventures to defy public opinion, though it is against new perils that precautions are needed to-day, it still seems unlikely that any people could be induced to feel so much self-distrust or exercise so much self-restraint as the delegating of part of its authority would involve. Yet further experience of the defects of existing legislatures and of the undue control exercised over them by party or class organizations, may some day enforce the call for the safeguards a Second Chamber could best provide. Unfortunately the time when safeguards are most required is the time when they are least likely to be provided.

CHAPTER LXV

DIRECT LEGISLATION BY THE PEOPLE

No feature of modern democracy better deserves study than the methods recently introduced for enabling the whole body of citizens to enact laws by their own direct action; and this for three reasons.

These methods are a return to the earliest form free government took in the Primary Assemblies of ancient nations, such as the Greek and Italic and Phoenician republics. They witness to a distrust of the representative system of government, which had been for a long while the only form employed in large countries, and was deemed to be in them not merely inevitable, but to have marked a long step forward in free government. This latest novelty, having been approved by the experience of some communities, being warmly advocated in others, and seeming to indicate the line which changes in popular government are likely to follow, well deserves to be examined.

As the chapters on Switzerland and the United States have described the working in those countries of the Referendum and Initiative, this chapter need do no more than summarize the results which these two institutions as there worked have given, and state briefly the general arguments which commend and the objections which dissuade their introduction elsewhere.

The movement of opinion towards the direct action of the whole people in legislation springs from two sources, one theoretic, the other practical.

The theoretic source is to be found in the dogma of Popular Sovereignty, very ancient in its legal form, for it goes back to the law of Rome, but in its modern garb fascinating and familiar from the days of Rousseau. It is fervently preached both on the European Continent and in the United States by enthusiasts who hold not only that all power be-

longs by Nature and of right to the People, but that it is
truly and effectively their power only when exercised by
them directly, not through persons chosen to represent them,
for the so-called *mandat imperatif* by which the people instruct their representatives how to vote on their behalf has
been found insufficient and in practice unworkable. The
water must be drawn fresh from the spring among the rocks,
not from the brook in its lower and perhaps polluted course.

The other or practical source is that disappointment with
and distrust of legislative bodies which, more or less evident
in all free countries, has reached its maximum in the United
States. In many States the people, balked in repeated efforts to cure the faults of those bodies, have assumed the
power to review their action by subjecting acts passed by
the legislature to a popular vote of approval or rejection, and
have also authorized a prescribed number of citizens to prepare and submit to such a vote Bills to be enacted without
any intervention on the part of the legislature. It is this
sense of an actual evil that has helped forward the movement beyond the Atlantic, whereas in Europe its strength
has been chiefly drawn from abstract doctrine.

Decisions of the people may have their value for other purposes, also. Where a legislature consists of two Chambers,
and differences of opinion arise between them, each persist-
ing in its own view, then, unless the Constitution provides
that the voice of one of the Chambers shall prevail against
that of the other, a means of deciding between them may be
found in submitting the law, or those parts of it on which
the Chambers differ, to a vote of the whole people. This is
now done in the Australian Commonwealth, is talked of in
Norway and Belgium, finds a place in the new Constitution
of Germany, and has been suggested as an expedient fit to
be employed in Britain. There are also cases in which the
nature of a law proposed makes it specially desirable that the
wishes of the citizens should be so directly expressed upon
it as to ensure their cordial support of its enforcement if
enacted. A familiar instance is found in proposals to restrict the sale of intoxicating liquors. Legislatures have
sometimes, either for the reasons just mentioned or to relieve
themselves of responsibility, referred such questions to popular vote in a State or a city.

Direct Popular Legislation exists in Switzerland and in many States of the North-American Union, and that in two forms. One is the Referendum, *i.e.* submission to popular vote not only of amendments to the Constitution but also of ordinary laws passed by the Legislature. In some Swiss cantons all laws are required to be thus submitted — this is the Obligatory or Compulsory Referendum — in other cantons and in the Confederation, and also in the American States, the submission of a law takes place only at the demand of a prescribed number of citizens. This is the Optional Referendum.

The other form called Initiative is the proposal by a prescribed number of citizens of a Constitutional amendment, or a law, to be voted upon by the whole people. It exists in the Swiss Confederation as respects Constitutional amendments, as also in many of the Cantons and in many American States, as respects both Constitutional amendments and laws.

Let us now see (*a*) what use is made of each of these modes of legislation; (*b*) what matters can be submitted; (*c*) what is the proportion of citizens who vote; (*d*) what measures are taken to assist the citizens to vote aright; (*e*) what influence party spirit and party organizations exercise on the voting; (*f*) how far the people have shown themselves qualified for the function assigned to them; and (*g*) what has been the general result on the peace and welfare of the communities which have tried these new methods.

(*a*) *Use made of the Referendum.*— In the Swiss Confederation it has always been used sparingly, and in recent years less and less.[1] In those Cantons where it is optional it is little resorted to, but the output of laws in Switzerland is at all times and in all cantons very small as compared with that of English-speaking communities. Zürich, where legislation is exceptionally brisk, and all laws are submitted, passed only 254 in the fifty years from 1869 to 1919, and the large majority of those were accepted.

In the United States the Referendum is much more freely used, not only because the laws passed are more numerous than in Switzerland, but also because many are passed at the

---

[1] Between 1905 and 1919 a total number of 62 laws and decrees were passed by the National Assembly. In only three cases was a Referendum asked for, and in all three the law was accepted by the people.

instance of individuals or companies seeking benefits for themselves, and legislatures are distrusted. It is, however, now less frequently demanded than when it was first introduced, a change which may mean either that the legislatures are mending their ways or that the citizens have grown more indifferent, and less eager to deliver their judgment on enactments.

Use made of the Initiative.— This also is infrequent in the Swiss Confederation, where it is used only by way of Constitutional Amendment. Between 1905 and 1919 eight proposals were submitted under it, of which only two were carried. It is more freely used in the Cantons, but even in Zürich only on twenty-eight occasions for laws and thrice for Constitutional amendments between 1866 and 1908, both years inclusive.

In the American States many bills are proposed by Initiative, because there is a more active spirit of discontent or aspiration which desires to effect sweeping reforms by popular impulse, believing these to be retarded by sordid influences playing secretly on the legislatures. If the need for an institution is to be judged by the use made of it, that need was great in many States. The Initiative proposals accepted are, roughly speaking, about as numerous as those rejected, whereas in Switzerland the majority are rejected.

(*b*) *Nature of the Matters submitted.*— In the Swiss Confederation the Legislature has under the Constitution the right of withdrawing from the operation of the Referendum any Decrees or Resolutions (being of general application, and not including the annual Budget) which it may deem urgent, and this right is frequently used, sometimes even when the urgency of the measure was far from apparent.[1] A like power is allowed to the Legislature in American States, and has there also been occasionally employed under circumstances raising suspicion, so that Governors have vetoed Bills declared " Urgent " where the declaration seemed to have been made for the purpose of preventing the people from delivering their judgment.

In the American States Initative proposals made in the form of a Constitutional amendment are subject to no re-

[1] See Vol. I. Chap. XXIX. p. 420.

striction imposed by the State Constitution, because any such restriction would be overridden by a change in the Constitution itself; and in point of fact both there and in Switzerland matters which ought to be dealt with by Laws and find no place in a Fundamental Instrument of Government, are now constantly made the subject of a Constitutional amendment proposed either by a Legislature or by Popular Initiative.[1]

(c) *Proportion of the Citizens who vote.*— In Switzerland the proportion of persons voting to the whole number of qualified citizens is, both at Referendum and at Initiative votings, almost always lower than at elections of representatives to Legislatures. In the Confederation it has risen as high as 79 and sunk as low as 34 per cent. In rural Cantons it has occasionally sunk to 21 per cent. Abstentions are, of course, more frequent where there is no organization to bring up voters to the poll, and are in the United States often explicable by the fact that some Bills refer to purely local matters, out of the range of the average voter's knowledge or interest. One may say that the number voting, while varying with the interest felt in the particular question at issue, seldom exceeds half the total number of electors. This is true also of the American States, in which, however, the proportion voting is usually smaller.[2] Cases have occurred in which measures have been carried by a minority, even a small minority, of the registered voters. Where this happens, can it be said that the will of the people has been expressed? It is argued that those who do not oppose must be taken to assent, but abstention may be due to ignorance of the importance of the issue or to a modest consciousness of incapacity to express any opinion whatever.

(d) *Methods adopted to enable the Citizens to understand the Issues submitted.*— Both in Switzerland and in America copies of the Constitutional amendments, laws, and pro-

---

[1] This practice has almost effaced the distinction between Constitutional provisions and ordinary laws. See Vol. I. p. 427, and Vol. II. p. 156.

[2] President Lowell (*Public Opinion and Popular Government*, published in 1913) estimated the average percentage, in American States, of voters at Referenda and Initiatives to the whole number of qualified voters at about 60 per cent. It seems to be practically the same in Switzerland.

posals made by Initiative, sometimes accompanied by a statement of the arguments commending or attacking the law or proposal submitted are circulated officially, while supporters and opponents start their respective campaigns in the press and by public meetings.

(e) *Influence on the Votings of Parties and Party Spirit.* — In Switzerland, since party organizations are rarely active in discussing the issue submitted or in bringing up voters to the polls, the voting tends to convey the real judgment of the people unbiassed by party feeling. In the American States this is so far true that the party organizations, which exist rather for offices than for principles, seldom step openly into the arena, so the merits of the question submitted have a better chance of being fairly considered than an election would afford.

(f) *How far have the People shown themselves qualified for Direct Legislation?* — No nation has ever been better prepared for this task than the Swiss, for among them ignorance of and indifference to politics are least common. Every political issue to be voted on is abundantly discussed at public meetings and in the press; and the echoes of the discussion are heard far up in the secluded Alpine valleys. No one need want the means for forming some sort of opinion. The Swiss, shrewd, cautious, and inclined to conservatism, think before they vote. The minds of the peasants are slow working, somewhat narrow, as might be expected from rural folk living by tillage and dairying, thrifty and parsimonious, little influenced by abstract notions or plausible catchwords, but intelligent, willing to ponder any arguments within the range of their knowledge. The average citizen is withal independent and cool-headed, not surrendering himself to party leaders, and with a patriotism that qualifies the tendency to approve or condemn a proposal solely with a view to his personal interests. It was the right sort of people in which to try the experiment of the Referendum, and the success of the experiment has proved the people's competence. The fact that popular voting has been less and less used in the Confederation, though it has through the growth of population become easier than it was in 1874 to collect the signatures needed to bring a law before the people, is a further evidence of the good sense which confines the use of this power to cases in which there is a body of adverse opinion sufficiently large to make it worth while to put the country to the trouble and expense of a general voting.

Of the eighteen American States it is more difficult to speak in general terms, for though in most of them the population is agricultural, it is in others mixed with manufacturing or mining elements, and in some the recent immigrants from the backward parts of Europe are numerous. Hence both the proportion of educated and thoughtful men, capable of giving good leadership, and the average level of intelligence in the voters, differ greatly from State to State. The Western Americans take as intelligent an interest in public affairs as do Frenchmen or Englishmen, or Belgians, have had more political experience than Germans, are less impulsive and passionate than Spaniards or Italians or the Slav peoples.[1] They are more restless and rather more inconstant and decidedly less conservative than the Swiss, but taken all in all they seem quite as fit as any European people, and probably fitter than the races of Central and Southern Europe, to apply the methods of Direct Legislation. Thus their example, if the experiment succeeds, will not suffice to prove that peoples like those of Lithuania and Poland, Serbia and Rumania, destitute of the experience Western Americans have enjoyed, can expect results equally good.

(g) *What have these Methods of Legislation done for the Welfare of the Communities that use them?* — The test of the success of the system is to be found partly in the approval it has found and the satisfaction it has created in the peoples which employ it, partly in a scrutiny of the merits or demerits of the enactments which it has accepted or rejected.

For Switzerland the former question is readily answered. The people are so entirely content with the Referendum that while no one proposes to abandon or restrict it, some propose to extend it. Regarding the laws passed or rejected a

---

[1] The difference between the average citizen and the average member of a legislature is of course slighter in the United States than in European countries, so a law passed by a legislature carries a slighter presumption of being the product of superior intelligence and knowledge.

stranger must speak with diffidence, but the instances given
in a previous chapter [1] go to show that legislation has advanced on sound lines, and that under it the country and all
classes therein have attained an unusual measure of material
well-being and domestic concord. The spirit of conservatism and the spirit which seeks betterment by change have
tempered each the other. Some good enactments have been
delayed by the Referendum, but the loss has been slight, and
possibly compensated by the more general support which the
law obtained when ultimately passed. The results of the
Initiative are less easy to estimate, but it receives a more
general approval from the wise than it did thirty or even
fifteen years ago. No one suggests that it has done any
serious harm; many believe that it has accelerated several
needed reforms. That its immense power is not abused appears from the fact that it has been invoked, in the Confederation, only thrice within the last fifteen years.

In the United States there is no such general consensus of
opinion in the States which have experience of the Referendum: but it deserves notice that the number of States which
have adopted it since S. Dakota led the way goes on increasing, and that in none where it exists do the people seem
disposed to drop the power of direct law-making. Many observers, especially among lawyers, continue to dwell on the
defects of the plan, pointing to the occasional rejection of
Bills whose merits the people had not understood, to the
confusion brought into administration by haphazard decisions, and to inconsistencies in policy, as for instance in
the voting or rejecting of appropriations for educational purposes. Though the malign influence of the "money interests" has not been entirely eliminated nor the tone of the
legislatures raised, many of such jobbing Bills as these bodies
were wont to pass have been killed by Referendum or prevented from reaching that stage at which it would have killed
them. The working of the Initiative has proved more faulty,
because rejection of the bad is easier than construction of
the good, a task especially difficult when essayed by isolated
groups of citizens, each group anxious to push forward its
own projects. Many proposals submitted are not only ill-
drafted, but calculated to confuse the existing law; many

[2] See Vol. I. Chap. XXIX.

embody "fads," or contain schemes with a kernel of sound principle, but presented in an unworkable form. Although therefore no serious harm has resulted, for the common sense of the people rejects most of the "freak bills," the merits of the Initiative need to be tested by longer experience. Defects might be reduced by requiring all proposals to be put into a technically correct form by an official draftsman, and by limiting the number of issues to be placed before the citizens at the same voting.

In Oregon in 1912 there were submitted together at one fell swoop thirty-seven laws and Initiative proposals, while at the same time a number of officials had to be elected. The citizen on entering the voting compartment had to make up his mind on between forty and fifty distinct issues, merits of measures and merits of men. The best-informed and most experienced could hardly have an opinion on even one-fourth of the questions his vote was to decide.

This review of the working of Direct Popular Legislation in the countries where it has had a fair trial suggests some general reflections on its value for other democracies.

The arguments used to recommend it may be concisely stated as follows:

The Referendum corrects the faults of legislatures. Where those bodies act under the influence of corrupt motives or of class motives, or of purely party motives, an appeal from them to the whole people may prevent mischief. Legislative issues of permanent significance are disjoined from those transient party and personal issues which dominate legislatures. Where one party brings in a Bill from which it hopes to gain credit at an approaching election, its own fortunes, and especially those of its majority in the legislature, are bound up with the success of the measure, and the party in opposition has a motive for resisting it, because they will improve their chance of office by defeating the Bills of the party in power. Thus the merits of the case recede into the background. But if the Bill has to go to a popular vote, the decisive fight over it takes place before the people, for its enactment or rejection is their act. They may reject it without censuring the officials who prepared or the parliamentary majority which passed it. If the officials continue to be personally respected and trusted they may remain in office, though their Bill has failed, and the nation is spared the trouble of those general elections resorted to under the British Parliamentary system whenever a first-class Ministerial Bill has been defeated.

Take another case. In a legislature divided into groups one group specially anxious to carry a particular measure may by a "deal" with another group which dislikes that measure but is willing to accept it in order to carry some pet measure of its own, succeed in passing a Bill which the real mind of the majority of representatives, and still more the bulk of the electors, condemns. Or a section of the dominant ministerial majority may threaten to withdraw their support unless the Ministry consent to pass some Bill which it dislikes. The Ministry, in order to escape defeat, yields to the threat, so the Bill goes through, and in this case also against the real wishes of the majority. In both these cases a reference to the popular vote will checkmate the manœuvres of politicians.

An election is an Election, a choice between candidates as well as between policies, an occasion when so many issues of policy are simultaneously presented, that it is seldom possible to treat any one as having been really decided. After the election one party claims that the electors gave a "mandate" on one particular issue: another party or section makes a like claim, and there is no means of telling which is right. Only a consultation of the people can decide.

The Referendum helps the legislature to keep in touch with the people at other times than a general election, and in some respects in better touch, for it gives the voters an opportunity of declaring their views on serious issues apart from the distracting or distorting influence of party spirit. Thus representatives get to understand better the real mind of the electors as a whole, including those who are not their political supporters and therefore less known to them personally.

The Referendum gives security that no law is passed which is opposed to popular feeling. Legislatures may mistake the will of the people, or may, from party motives or class interests, take the risk of transgressing that will in the hope of doing so with impunity. An appeal to the people is the proper remedy.

Popular voting reduces Sectionalism in a nation, because men of different classes and parties find themselves working and voting together on issues which are outside the sphere either of class sentiments or of party programs.

A law receives strength from the approval which the people by their direct vote have stamped upon it. Because it is their own work they feel a fuller obligation to obey it and to make it obeyed.

The judgment of the whole people is a final judgment, from which there is no appeal. *Roma locuta est.* The ultimate authority having given its decision, controversy is stilled, at least until such time has passed and such new circumstances have arisen as may encourage a belief that the people will change its mind.

The three last-mentioned arguments recommend the Initiative also, but as it supersedes the legislature by enabling the people to pass a law without the participation of the latter, some further reasons must be advanced for introducing it. These reasons are in substance all one and the same, viz. that legislatures do not adequately express the people's will, so that the Referendum, which is confined to an expression of that will upon matters previously dealt with by the legislature, confers on the people only a part of their rights, giving no free scope for their action independent of the Legislature. Why should a body of persons chosen by the people close the door against the people themselves, allowing only such proposals of reform as take their fancy to pass through so that the people can deal with them? A party majority, perhaps corrupt, probably selfish, may for its own purposes hold back the people from getting what they desire, and the people must stand and wait, helpless till a general election arrives; and even then a new legislature may fail to carry out properly such wishes as the people have expressed. Thus while needed reforms are delayed, a sense of injustice is created which may break out in violence. Finally, if the people are fit to negative a Bill presented by the legislature, why are they not fit to frame one themselves?

In the American States — and wherever a Rigid Constitution limits the powers of legislatures — there is this further technical reason for employing the Initiative, that when employed by way of amending the Constitution, it overleaps all restrictions placed on the legislatures, because what the people put into the Constitution annuls those restrictions which their predecessors had imposed. This argument rejoices those who, desiring a free, swift unhampered course for the people's will, condemn the restrictions which Rigid Constitutions impose, while it repels those who value the restrictions just because they fear that swift unhampered course.

The objections urged against the Direct Intervention of the people can be even more briefly stated.

It reduces the authority and status of the legislature, lessens its responsibility to the people, and may induce it, yielding to a temporary and possibly factitious demand, to pass measures it does not approve in the hope that a voting by Referendum will reject them. It places matters that have been carefully considered and debated in a legislature — matters often beyond the comprehension of the average citizen — at the mercy of the voter's ignorance or prejudice. It is an appeal from responsibility to irresponsibility, from knowledge to ignorance. Not these objections only, but others of graver import apply to the Initiative. It brings before the people Bills that have never run the gauntlet of parliamentary criticism, which, if they have been carelessly or clumsily drafted, will, if enacted, confuse the law, creating uncertainty and inviting litigation. Citizens summoned by Referendum to vote on a Bill have at least the advantage of knowing that it has been scrutinized and amended by a competent legislative body, but an Initiative proposal has not had this advantage. It may contain many provisions, some which please, others which displease the voter, but he cannot amend it; and must either reject it as a whole or accept it as a whole, whatever its faults.

The Initiative offers a strong temptation to an excited faction or an unscrupulous leader to bring forward some scheme of sweeping change, promising to a section of the people benefits so alluring as to carry the law through on the top of the wave before its dangers can have been brought home to the nation. The fact that such attempts have failed when made in Switzerland because the good sense of the people repelled them, does not show that they might not succeed in some less intelligent and less cautious population.

Once a revolutionary step has been taken by Initiative, repentance comes too late. It is far harder to agitate for its repeal, even if there is time to do so before it takes effect, than to rouse the people to compel by Referendum the reversal of a decision given by a legislature.

The reader can weigh for himself the *pros* and *cons* of the case. Were I to express my own opinion it would be that the Referendum has worked well in Switzerland, and if less well in the American States, yet not fatally ill, for no conspicuous mischiefs have followed and some good may have been done. The Initiative was not really needed in Switzerland, but neither in the Confederation or in the Cantons has positive harm resulted. In the American States the reformers would have done better to improve the methods of their legislatures and raise the quality of their members rather than try to supersede them by the Initiative, but of this they seem to have despaired. In experimenting with it, they have given it not quite a fair chance, for it has been employed not only far more frequently than in Switzerland but with a neglect of obvious precautions which would have reduced the defects it has shown. American experience has, however, been too short to enable a final judgment to be pronounced.

Before proceeding to enquire what light the data supplied by Switzerland and America throw upon the general value and applicability to other countries of Direct Popular Legislation, let me enumerate certain provisions which might, if attached to the use of the Referendum and Initiative, tend to cure or mitigate the risks incident to the employment of either.

1. The number of signatures required to support the demand for a Referendum should be determined with regard not only to the total number of voting citizens, but also to the distribution of population, for signatures are more easily collected in densely populated areas. It would seem desirable that the percentage of persons signing required to the total number of qualified citizens should be not less than 8 to 10 per cent for a Referendum, and nearly twice that number, say 16 to 18 per cent, for an Initiative.[1]

---

[1] The number of 30,000 was fixed in 1874 as required by a Referendum in the Swiss Confederation and 50,000 (in 1891) for an Initiative,

2. The practical evil most complained of in the working of the Initiative is the obscurity and confusion, due to bad drafting, of the Bills proposed. This might be remedied in one of two ways. The proposers might be required to have their Bill prepared for them by a skilled official draftsman, or, seeing that the special object of the Initiative is to bring before the people some proposed enactment which the legislature refuses to embody in a law, this object might be attained by giving to the Initiative proposal the form not of an English or American statute drawn out in full, but of a concise statement of the object to be attained, with a command to the legislature to prepare a Bill dealing with the matter which would be in due course submitted to a popular voting.

3. When any Bill is to be submitted, every voter should be officially supplied not only with the text of the measure to be voted on, but also with an explanation of its purpose and a summary, concise and impartial, of its provisions.

4. In the case of an Initiative, the proposed law should be submitted to the Legislature for examination, and that body should be required to prepare a statement of its views upon the proposal, which statement should be officially circulated with the text of the Bill,[1] the legislature being also further entitled to draft and circulate an alternative Bill, calculated to effect such of the aims of the Initiative proposal as it approves. Another plan would be to entrust this function to a standing non-partisan Board.[2]

5. Some matters should be excluded from the operation of the Referendum, as for instance certain kinds of financial laws, and those which need immediate application. To these some would add all treaties with foreign countries.

but the population has so much increased since those dates (from 2,700,000 and 3,100,000 to over 4,000,000), that the collection of signatures has become much easier. Nevertheless Referenda have been fewer in recent years.

[1] This is provided by the Constitution of Oklahoma, which restricts every statement to two thousand words, divided between supporters and opponents.

[2] Another reason for having Bills proposed by Initiative carefully scrutinized is that in some of the American States attempts have been made to improve the prospects of the measure by putting in its forefront certain catching proposals, while hiding away, sometimes in words carefully chosen to conceal the effect, other proposals likely to rouse opposition, being of the kind called colloquially " jokers."

Whether Initiative proposals ought to be allowed to include Bills for imposing taxes and for granting money seems more than doubtful. The danger is obvious.

6. The number of propositions to be submitted at the same voting ought not to be larger than a citizen of average knowledge and intelligence can fit himself to vote upon.

7. To prevent the frequent repetition of an Initiative proposal, a time might be fixed within which a proposal substantially the same as one rejected should not be re-submitted.[1]

8. Inasmuch as the object of the Referendum is to elicit the opinion — if he has one — of the individual citizen, the influence of party organizations upon popular votings ought, so far as possible, to be reduced; and it would conduce to this if the votings were fixed for a time when no important election of a party character, such as the election of members of a Legislature, or of a President or other high official, is to take place.

9. To prevent important decisions from being determined by a minority of the whole people it might be provided that no Initiative should be carried at a voting in which less than a prescribed percentage, say three-fifths, of the qualified citizens took part.

10. Since in countries so large as France or Great Britain votings cannot be frequent, for the expenditure of time and money would be prohibitive, it would seem desirable to define the class of Bills on which a Referendum might be demanded. But can any definition be devised? In countries which, like Britain, have no constitution embodied in one instrument, there is no means of deciding what is a Fundamental Law; and in case it were thought proper to determine by a popular vote differences of opinion between two legislative Chambers, who shall say what differences are sufficiently important to warrant recourse to this solution? Some mechanical method, such as that of requiring a prescribed number of citizens, or of members of the Legislature, to demand a Referendum

---

[1] It has been objected to this suggestion that the opponents of a proposal intended to be submitted might, when they heard it was coming, hurry on ahead of it a number of other proposals which would take precedence and jostle it out of the way. There are, however, methods of preventing this artifice, for the discussion of which I cannot here find space.

might be adopted, but such a provision would be open to abuse, for it may be assumed that nine politicians out of ten will resort to any device for embarrassing an antagonist or delaying a defeat.

Two serious difficulties stand in the way of the use of the Referendum in large populations such as those of France, Italy, and Great Britain. One is that of determining the cases in which a Referendum may be demanded. In France, if the Swiss precedent were to be followed, the number of signatures required to support a demand for Referendum would exceed 300,000, so the verification of signatures would be an almost impossible task, yet a necessary one, if the plan were to be properly worked. The other is that as nothing but the activity of organizations could bring up the voters to the poll, the campaigns for and against a measure would fall into the hands of party or class organizations, and a large percentage of the votes given would come from persons who took little real interest in the matter; which means that the best-organized party would usually win, and the chief aim of a Referendum, that of eliciting the genuine judgment of the citizens themselves, rather than opinions imposed on them by their would-be guides and by the pressure of numbers, would not be attained.

A nation which, encouraged by Swiss and American experience in Popular Legislation, desires to follow in the same path, must begin by considering the conditions favourable or unfavourable to the experiment.[1]

The first of these is the size and population of the country. The larger these are, the more costly and less satisfactory will popular votings be, for the influence of party or class organizations will be greater since without them it is hard to " get out the vote." [2] Swiss success has been largely due to the comparatively small voting areas.

[1] The interesting and well-drawn Constitution of the Republic of Czecho-Slovakia (a Rigid Constitution, since it can be altered only by a majority of three-fifths in each Chamber) enables (section 46) the Government, if unanimous, to submit to a Referendum a Bill presented by the Government which the Parliament has rejected.

[2] It may be thought in a popular voting many citizens of moderate views will, since they can do so safely because secretly, break away from their class and party. This would happen in Switzerland and America, but be less probable in most European countries. In Australia the strong organization of the Labour Unions has given the Labour Party no small advantage for the purpose of a popular vote.

In a country where the citizens are divided by sharp antagonisms of race or religion, voting will tend to follow the lines of those divisions and the citizens be less likely to deliver an independent and well-considered opinion on the merits of a proposal.

Where classes stand opposed to one another by social antagonism or conflict of economic interests, and where each class reads only the newspapers that make it their business to state its case and support its claims, the tendency to class solidarity in voting may be strong enough to make a popular vote, especially where the voting masses are large, grow into a menacing crisis. In a legislative body each side has to listen to the arguments of the other, and bitterness is mitigated by friendly personal relations between opposing politicians; but a struggle in which the whole nation directly takes part knows no such mitigations.

The value of Direct Legislation in its working depends largely upon the amount of power party organization and party spirit exert. If they are weak, or do not interfere when the voting is on Laws, there is a good chance of getting the real and independent judgment of the citizens; otherwise not. In Switzerland and the American States aforesaid these favouring conditions are present. They are, of course, most likely to be present in times of comparative quiet, when no vital issues rouse excitement, and men are less disposed to blindly follow a party leader.

Thus it may be said that Direct Legislation is most likely to give good results in a small country, with a homogeneous population, intelligent and unemotional, not dominated by party organizations or inflamed by party bitterness. These are the conditions under which all democratic governments, great and small, have the best chance to flourish. As the function of direct law-making carries the citizens of a democracy a step further than that of choosing representatives who shall act on their behalf, the best proof of their civic competence is found in the successful discharge of this function. So far Switzerland alone has given that proof, her advantages having been such as few countries possess, and few can hope to acquire.

I have not dwelt, because it is obvious, on what is, if not the greatest, the most incontestable merit claimable for Direct

Legislation. It is unequalled as an instrument of practical instruction in politics. Every voting compels the citizen who has a sense of civic duty to try to understand the question submitted, and reach a conclusion thereon. Many, sometimes even a half, fail to come to the polls, yet even these may derive some benefit from the public discussion that goes on. Everybody can listlessly read articles in the press or listen to speeches in a meeting, but thinking is strengthened and clarified and concentrated when it leads up to a plain issue. It is a good thing for the citizen to be relieved from the pressure of those personal or party predilections which draw him to one candidate or another and to be taken out of the realm of abstract ideology to face concrete proposals. Here is a plan which throws on him the responsibility of declaring a definite opinion on a specific proposition, forcing him to ask himself, Is it sound in principle? Will it work? Shall I vote for it or against it?

CHAPTER LXVI

THE RELATION OF CENTRAL TO LOCAL GOVERNMENT

In an earlier chapter (Chapter XIII.) something has been
said of the origin of self-government in small communities,
and of the service it renders to democracy by implanting a
sense of civic duty in the citizens and training them to discharge it. We have here to consider in the light of the facts
described as existing in the several countries dealt with in
Part II., but without repeating details there given, (a) what
it is that a large democratic State may gain from the existence within it of a system of local self-government; (b) how
governmental functions should be distributed as between the
Central and the Local Authorities; (c) what is the best form
in which democratic principles can be applied to the creation
of the latter authorities, and (d) what defects in the working of local governments need to be guarded against.

In countries which, like France, Britain, and Australia,
are governed by representative assemblies it is desirable to
relieve, so far as possible, the strain upon the Central Government. A practically omnipotent legislature is liable to
sudden fluctuations of opinion, and the fewer are the branches
of administration which such fluctuations disturb, the more
regular and stable will be the general course of affairs.
Those of national importance must of course be dealt with by
the National legislature, but there are many matters in which
uniformity is not required, and the more these are left to
local control the less will representatives be drawn away from
national work. Where local discontents arise, it is better
for them to find vent in the local area rather than encumber
the central authority. Under a federal system of government, such as that of the United States, Canada, Switzerland,
where many matters are left to be settled by State, or Provincial, or Cantonal assemblies, controversial issues are
divided between those assemblies and the central national

legislature, and a political conflict in the latter need not coincide with other conflicts in the former. The same principle holds true with regard to local authorities in smaller areas, such as the county or municipality. Men opposed in national politics may work together harmoniously in the conduct of county or municipal business, as happens in Switzerland and England, and to a large extent in the United States also.

The wider the scope of a central government's action, so much the larger is the number of the persons employed in the administrative work it directs, and the larger therefore the patronage at its disposal. Patronage is a powerful political engine, certain to be used for party purposes wherever admission to the civil service and promotion therein are not controlled by rules which secure competence through examinations administered by a non-partisan authority. The fewer temptations to the abuse of patronage are left within the grasp of the central authority, necessarily partisan in all the countries we have been studying, the fewer abuses will there be. The United States suffered until recent years from the so-called Spoils system, applied in municipalities as well as in the Federal service, but the evils would have been even greater had the same party been steadily supreme at the same time in the National Government and in the local governmental areas.

Elementary education is a branch of administration assigned in some countries to a central, in others to a local authority. The argument for giving it to the latter is strong because the interest of parents in the instruction of their children ought to be stimulated by the function of choosing the local school authority as well as by the right of representing to it any local need or grievance. This function they have enjoyed in the United States, Canada, and New Zealand, as well as in Switzerland and Great Britain, but to a much smaller extent in France, Australia, and Ireland. Reformers, impatient with the slackness and parsimony common among local authorities, have, however, been everywhere advocating State intervention, insisting that the reluctance of the local citizen to spend freely makes it necessary to invoke the central government, both to supervise schools and to grant the money from the national treasury for the salaries of teachers and various educational appliances.   Here, as is often the case, the choice is between more rapid progress on the one hand and the greater solidity and hold upon the average citizen's mind which institutions draw from being entrusted to popular management.

In some countries possessing a highly trained civil service each department tends to lay undue stress upon uniformity, becomes attached to its settled habits, dislikes novelties, contracts bureaucratic methods, and may assume towards the private citizen a slightly supercilious air.   Progress is retarded because experiments are discouraged.   Popular interest flags because popular interference is resented, and officials fall out of touch with general sentiment.   The more the central bureaucracy controls local affairs, the wider will be the action of these tendencies.

Lastly we come to another benefit, of a more theoretical aspect, yet with real value, which local self-governing institutions may secure.   They contribute to the development of local centres of thought and action.   Many a country has had reason to dread the excessive power of its capital city.[1] There ought to be many cities, each cherishing its own traditions, each representing or embodying a certain type of opinion, and each, instead of taking its ideas submissively from the capital, supporting journals of the first excellence in point of news supply and intellectual force.   Such cities will be all the more useful in forming independent centres of opinion if they have also strong local governments which enlist the active service of their leading citizens of all classes.   France has in Lyons, Marseilles, and Bordeaux cities capable of fulfilling this function; and in the German Empire the influence of Berlin was qualified or counterbalanced by that of Munich, Frankfurt, Hamburg, Leipzig, Dresden, Cologne.

Upon the much-debated question whether the construction of public works not of evident national importance should be left to local authorities, their cost being defrayed out of local taxation, or whether this duty and burden should be under-

---

[1] Exceptions are the United States and Canada, in which the opinion of the capital cities is practically that only of the legislatures and officials, and Australia, where the future political capital (Canberra) is still a mere village.

taken by a central government, some light is thrown by the experience of France, Canada, New Zealand, and the United States. In all these countries a wide door has been opened to political intrigue and corruption by the practice of voting large sums for so-called " local improvements " from the national treasury in order to win support for the representative who presses for the grant of money and for the ministry which proposes or supports it. In the United States immense sums are wasted annually in this way, demoralizing both the legislature and the constituencies. Nobody is the better off in the end, but each locality, desiring to throw upon the State the cost of a work which it would otherwise have to pay in local taxation, forgets that in the long run it pays as much by the additional national taxation to which it contributes, indeed perhaps pays more, because it frequently happens that the " improvements " asked for are not needed, and are being undertaken for political reasons only. This is a habit to which democratic governments are specially prone, because the keepers of the public purse yield to the demands which representatives make. The principle that the cost of works undertaken solely for the benefit of a locality ought, in the interest of economy, to be defrayed out of local funds, would seem irresistible were it not for the fact that in many great cities a large majority of the voters, since they pay no local taxes, have no interest in thrifty management, and willingly support a council which spends lavishly on local purposes and wins popularity thereby. Where this happens the tax-paying class may think itself safer in the hands of the Central Government.

In the six countries examined in Part II. all the higher judges are appointed by the Central Government, as they are in Britain, but in some States of the American Union counties and cities are allowed to choose their judges, which they do by popular election, with results not always satisfactory. The detachment of the Bench not only from party politics but from all local influences is so evidently desirable that the choice of judges by local voting is a risky experiment.

Of such public institutions as prisons, reformatories, and lunatic asylums it is enough to say that their management by a central Government is likely to be more scientific and skil-

ful than that of most local authorities would be, while not less
economical. The questions that relate to pauperism are
more difficult. Where the indigent have a legal claim to relief, to throw the cost of that relief on national funds while
leaving the administration of it in local hands would be to
invite extravagance and waste. If the locality dispenses the
locality ought to pay, especially if outdoor relief is given.
This question, which was a grave one for England ninety
years ago, has fortunately little importance in other English-
speaking countries or in Switzerland.

Whether the maintenance of public order should be entrusted to a national force, such as the gendarmerie in France
and Italy and the Royal Constabulary in Ireland, or to local
county and municipal authorities as in most English-speaking countries, is a question which will be answered according
to the varying conditions of each nation. Experience seems
to show that the less the police acquire the character of an
army the better, and that character is more easily avoided
when they are (as in England) raised, controlled, and paid
by local authorities. There have, however, been in America
city governments in which politics had so much infected police management that the State felt itself obliged to create
within a city a police force under its own orders. Apart
from this case, and the exceptional case of Ireland, the practice of English-speaking countries seems justified by the
results.[1]

The composition or organization of local authorities in
rural areas needs only a few sentences, for in all English-
speaking countries, except the United States, and also in
France and Switzerland, the plan of elected councils has been
adopted; whereas in many States of the American Union
there is no elected council for a county, each executive official
being chosen by direct popular election for a particular
branch or branches of work, his duties wherein are prescribed
by the laws of the State. This plan has the disadvantage of
disjoining from each other the various administrative departments, and leads to laxity in administration, because the only

[1] The police of London are directed by the Central Government, but
this is due partly to the immense size of that city, whose suburbs
stretch far out into four counties, partly to its being the capital of the
country.

means of enforcing responsibility is by prosecuting an offending official.[1] The smaller unit called the Town (corresponding to the smaller communes of Continental Europe) is better provided for, because although each branch of local business is handled by elected officers, who may act independently, the area is so small that their conduct can be watched and reviewed in the annual Town meeting, a popular primary assembly.[2] In other English-speaking countries the counties, and any small areas such as the parish, are administered by elected councils, who appoint and supervise the officials. This is also the case in Switzerland and in France, where, however, the Central Government exercises a large measure of control.[3]

Municipal government presents more difficult problems, especially where the poorer sections of a large population inhabit one part or parts of the city, while the richer live in other parts or in the suburbs. In Canada, Australia, and New Zealand, as in Great Britain, boroughs and cities are governed by popularly elected councils, while the mayor is chosen by the council (except in some Canadian cities where he is elected by the people), and administration is carried on by committees of the council directing the officers whom it appoints. This system has, as a rule, been worked efficiently and honestly in Great Britain and New Zealand, while in Canada and (to a less extent) in Australia there have been occasional lapses into corruption or malversation. In Germany also there are elected councils, but their duty is not themselves to administer, but to supervise the trained permanent officials who handle the departments. The economy and practical success of this method are unquestioned, but some observers deem it too bureaucratic.

The Swiss system, which resembles that of Great Britain and her Dominions in assigning management to elected councils, differs therefrom by its free use of the direct popular vote or Referendum, by which measures of importance are submitted to the people for their approval or rejection. This plan works well, the cities being of moderate size, none with a population exceeding 200,000. Administration is efficient, economical, and honest. In France also every commune (a city as well as a rural area is a commune) has its popularly

[1] See Vol. II. p. 98.   [2] See Vol. II. p. 14.   [3] See Vol. I. p. 281.

elected council, the authority of which is, however, limited by
a right of interference allowed to the National Government.
The abuses which have occurred in a few of the largest cities
furnish justification for this check.[1]

It is in the United States cities that we find the most numerous and striking illustrations of the maladies to which
democratic government is liable, but he who seeks to draw
general conclusions from the scandals which have occurred
there must remember how exceptional their circumstances
have been.   The cities have grown with extraordinary swiftness by the influx of masses of ignorant immigrants from
Europe, and these immigrants, having no experience of politics and no social ties with the native American population,
become an easy prey to the wiles of the unscrupulous leaders
of party organizations.   Having started with a system which
left all power in the hands of elected councils upon whose
members it was hard to fix responsibility, the Americans
have been driven to withdraw power from these large bodies,
and transfer it either to a popularly elected mayor possessing
a wide discretionary authority or to small commissions acting (in many cases) through a business manager whom they
appoint.   These experiments are valuable contributions to
the science of practical politics.   Let it be added that American reformers prefer the plan of electing the commissioners
by a general vote over the city to the other method, generally
followed in the British Dominions, of elections in wards
(divisions of the city), holding that the " general ticket "
gives less scope for intrigue and secures better men.

Party organization and the microbe of party spirit, apparently endemic in National governments where large issues
of policy have to be decided at elections, would be transient
and practically negligible phenomena in local government
were it not for the habit, old and strong in the United States,
and often found in the municipalities of France and England, of fighting local elections on the issues of National
party politics, even when these have nothing to do with the
work of the councils to be chosen at those elections.   This
habit exists in the elections to the councils of departments
and arrondissements in France, but scarcely at all in those
of county councils in Great Britain, or of communal authori-

1 See as to French cities, Vol. I. p. 282.

ties in Switzerland. Three results which have proved harmful in America naturally follow. The minds of the electors are diverted from the personal merits of the candidates and from the local questions which the candidates, if elected, will have to deal with, to national partisan issues. The members of councils when elected are apt to act together as parties in those bodies, and such patronage as lies in the gift of a council is liable to be misused for partisan purposes, *i.e.* bestowed upon persons because they have served the party rather than because they are qualified to serve the city.

The plan has, however, been defended on the ground that it draws men of ability and ambition into local affairs, gives them a chance of showing their quality, opens a door to success in national politics. Without party guidance, moreover, the voter will not, at least in large populations, know whom to vote for, and the guidance which the party gives is worth something, since it must, for the sake of its own credit, put forward reputable candidates. Since a chief difficulty incident to municipal government is the reluctance of the leading men to devote their time and labour to work which interferes with the conduct of their own business and has little promise of any reward beyond the good of the city and the gratitude of fellow-citizens, the motive which party spirit and the prospect of an opening in national politics supply must be appealed to.[1] Nothing but the wish to serve his political party or to make his way in public life will suffice to induce a man, tired by a long day's work in his office, to take up a further burden and give his evenings to municipal committees in the centre of the town instead of seeking repose in his home far off in the suburbs. Many of the men who have risen highest in American politics, and a few who have attained like distinction in England, have begun in local politics a career which led them far.

There is weight in these arguments, yet on the balance of considerations it is better that bodies whose proper functions lie in local matters should be kept free from the dis-

---

[1] It may be suggested that some marks of honour might be bestowed on citizens who have rendered exceptionally good unpaid public service; but there are, unfortunately, few countries in which the National Government could be trusted to award such distinctions in a non-partisan spirit.

turbing influence of questions foreign to their sphere. One
of the values of local self-government lies in the habit it
forms among the inhabitants of a town or district of bringing their knowledge and capacities into common stock for
the benefit of the whole community, maintaining those
friendly personal relations which befit neighbours, and not
distracted by a desire for ulterior gains to their political
party. When such gains become a motive, men are less
scrupulous, suspicion thickens the air, a contentious spirit
is engendered.

There has emerged in recent years one question of national
moment which, since it belongs also to the sphere of local
government, furnishes grounds for party action there.
Where the State has assumed some functions previously
either uncared for or left to private action, such as the conduct of a business, the housing of the poor, the supply of
milk, the provision of music or theatrical entertainments,
the law may permit a local authority to carry out policies of
this nature at the expense of the local taxpayers. When a
Socialist or Labour Party runs its candidates for local office
as well as for the national legislature upon a platform including these policies, other political parties who resist such policies put forward their candidates also and use their party
organizations in the electoral campaign, so that the elections
inevitably take a party colour. If it is suggested that the national legislature should determine by general statutes the
principles involved, and leave to local authorities only the
mode of carrying them out, it may be answered that even in
the application of such laws many concrete cases must arise
on which Socialists and Individualists will differ, so that
each party will have a legitimate motive for trying to secure
the election of its own adherents.

The experience of the United States, conspicuous by the
number and variety of experiments tried in local government, suggests some conclusions fit to be considered in Europe, in Canada, and in Australasia.

It is possible to have too many elections. When there are
many posts to be filled, whether elective offices or seats in
administrative councils, the number of pollings and the number of persons to be chosen at the polls becomes so large that

the voter, unable to give an independent and intelligent vote, either stays away in weariness or votes blindly at his party's bidding.

Municipal administration has become more and more a business matter for experts in such sciences as sanitation and engineering. The chief duty of an elected council has therefore come to be that of appointing and supervising the permanent officials, and for this a comparatively small council can well suffice even in a large city.

The American and Swiss practice of submitting questions of moment to a popular Referendum has worked with results generally if not always satisfactory, and might if applied in Europe, at least in municipalities not exceeding a million of population, stimulate public interest and help towards a better definition of policy in municipal administration.

Human nature being what it is, favouritism and jobbery may always be expected, and the larger and richer communities grow, the greater will temptations be, so the one thing needful is to fix the constant attention of the people on the conduct of their affairs. Vigilance! unceasing Vigilance! What was said in an English city where the management of the police by a Committee of the Council had given occasion for criticism, " Watch the Watch Committee," may be said of all Councils and Committees.

In European cities the duty of watching and criticizing municipal councils and officials is usually left to the press, but in American cities there are frequently associations of men, belonging to all political sections, who being well known and respected for their judgment and probity, render to the community the service not only of keeping an eye on municipal authorities, but that of recommending candidates to the citizens as worthy of confidence. Such a service is needed in those large European cities where the bulk of the electors do not and cannot know for whom to cast their votes in local contests.

It was in small communities that Democracy first arose: it was from them that the theories of its first literary prophets and apostles were derived: it is in them that the way in which the real will of the people tells upon the working of government can best be studied, because most of the questions which come before the people are within their own knowledge.

The industrial and commercial forces which draw men together into large aggregations seem to forbid the hope that small self-governing units may reappear within any period to which we can look forward. Yet who can tell what may come to pass in the course of countless years? War and the fear of war were the chief causes which destroyed the little States. If the fear of war could be eliminated there might be some chance of their return.

CHAPTER LXVII

COMPARISON OF THE SIX DEMOCRATIC GOVERNMENTS
EXAMINED

The examination contained in Part II. of the institutions which Democracy has given itself in different countries and of the phenomena which their working in each has shown needs to be completed by a comparison of those phenomena, for the rule of the people, taking in each different forms, has shown resemblances as well as diversities, both in the spirit which the institutions evoked and in the tangible results that have followed. No democratic government is typical; each has its merits, each its faults; and a judgment on democratic institutions in general can be formed only by observing which faults are most frequent, and how far each of these is specially characteristic of Democratic government, or rather belongs to Human Nature as displayed in politics. This chapter is meant to present the comparison in three ways:

First by noting the salient features of popular government in each of the six countries examined, and what each has contributed to political science in the way of example or warning.

Next by showing in which of those countries and to what extent in each the faults commonly charged on democratic government exist.

Thirdly by noting the presence in each country of what may be called the mental and moral coefficients, viz. those qualities in a people that help democracy to work its institutions in the right way, so as to obtain in the largest measure the benefits which governments have been established to secure.

I begin with a brief statement of the features most characteristic of each country.

I. Summary View of Salient Features

In France administration is highly centralized, much business which is in English-speaking countries left to local authorities being managed by officials who are appointed by and take their orders from the central government, so local self-government, narrowly circumscribed in its functions, and exciting little interest, does comparatively little for the political education of the people.   France, having so far as methods of administration go, preserved the inheritance of the old monarchy, is the least democratic of democracies, for State authority is strong against the individual citizen.   Yet although Government is strong, Ministries are unstable, because dependent on majorities in the legislature which fluctuate under the influence, sometimes of party passion, sometimes of personal intrigues.   The legislature, or rather its directly elected branch, the Chamber of Deputies, is master of the political situation, and its individual members control individual Ministers, obtaining from them as the price of their support favours for their respective constituencies, and by means of these favours holding their own seats.   In matters of moment the Second Chamber, largely composed of able and experienced men with a longer tenure of their seats, exerts a useful guidance or restraint, and the high average quality of the Civil Service makes administration efficient.

Behind both deputies and Ministers stand the great financiers, powerful through their wealth and the influence it enables them to exert upon the newspapers.   Their influence, though sometimes steadying, can also be baneful, for it may induce the sacrifice of national interests to private interests, and it has sometimes enveloped public men in a mist of suspicions.   The sky is seldom free from signs of storm, for fifty years of republican government have not assuaged the bitterness which divides the various parties, yet the faults of politics which sometimes seem to be a game played in the legislature by a comparatively small class, have not seriously affected the strength and progress of the nation.[1]   Foreign-

[1] I speak of France as it was in 1914, for the time that has passed since the Great War ended has been too short to judge what effect it has had upon politics.

ers have judged France too much by its politics and its politicians, underrating its spirit and vitality and stability.

The emergence of strong organizations advocating communistic doctrines, and accentuating antagonism between classes, are phenomena now visible all over the world, and the revolutionary movements thence arising would be more threatening under a less popular constitution. French democracy, with difficulties to face greater than any that have tested the other countries we have surveyed, has nevertheless brought the nation safely through a time of unprecedented perils.

Switzerland presents a striking contrast. Nowhere is administration so decentralized, for functions and powers are parcelled out not only between the Federal and the Cantonal Governments, but also betwen the Cantons and the Communes. The people are called upon to take a more direct and constant part in public work than any other State requires from its citizens, being accustomed to review by their votings the measures passed by their legislatures; and the citizens can, by the Initiative, put forward, without consulting those bodies, legislative proposals which popular voting adopts or rejects. The practice of local self-government has trained the people to fulfil these functions efficiently, keeping their attention fixed upon those who represent them in their assemblies or are entrusted with official business. Party spirit is comparatively free from virulence; elections have aroused little passion; the same member is returned time after time to the legislatures; the same members are retained for many years in the Administrative Councils. The less agreeable side of what may be called " small scale politics " appears in the petty intrigues which affect elections to minor posts in some communes and Cantons. Though the absence of corruption, both in the Federal and in Cantonal Governments, and the high standard maintained in public life for many years, are partly due to the absence of those temptations which men of great wealth can apply to politicians, much must also be ascribed to the vigilance of public opinion in small communities. In no democracy has the power of money counted for so little, in none has political

life had so few prizes to offer.   But after all, the most interesting lesson it teaches is how traditions and institutions,
taken together, may develop in the average man, to an extent
never reached before, the qualities which make a good citizen — shrewdness, moderation, common sense and a sense of
duty to the community.   It is because this has come to pass
in Switzerland that democracy is there more truly democratic than in any other country.

As France shows at its maximum the power of the legislature,[1] and Switzerland the power of the body of citizens
voting directly, so the United States is the best example of
the strength which party organizations can attain and the
control they can wield.   Legal authority, divided between
the Federal Government and the Governments of the several
States, is in both divided also between the elected Executive
and the two elected houses of the legislature, the frequently
recurring differences between which complicate both administration and legislation.   Such co-operation as is needed to
make the machinery work is created by the party organizations, which nominate for election both the representatives
and (in the several States) the higher officials in each State
as well as its Executive head; and as persons elected in the
same area at the same time usually belong to the same party,
both officials and representatives are expected to carry out its
policy.   The work which the organizations have to discharge
has called into being a large class of professional politicians
who live off the offices which they are able to secure for themselves and the various gains which fall to those who can exert
private influence.   Next to the power of Party, the most
salient features of the United States system are the wide application of popular election to the choice of officials, including judges, and the recent introduction in many States of
direct popular legislation in the form of Initiative and Referendum, as also of direct popular action on administration in
the provisions for the Recall of executive and judicial officials

---

[1] In Britain also the legislature, or, rather, the House of Commons, is
legally supreme, but in practice it is much controlled by the Cabinet,
who can dissolve it, and can appeal to the party organizations over the
country to require members to render steady support.   Though, as
Bagehot observed, a committee of Parliament, they are a Ruling Committee.

by popular vote. Thus the inordinate number of elections throws on the voter more work than he can properly discharge.

Two of the faults charged on government in the United States are due to exceptional causes. That the Money Power has attained such huge proportions as to assail the virtue of officials and demoralize some State legislatures, must be largely ascribed to the prodigious fortunes which the swift development of a new country's resources created, the possessors of which found it worth while to buy favours from politicians who had them to sell. Similarly, the worst scandals of municipal misgovernment appeared where a sudden influx of old-world immigrants flooded cities that were already growing fast, phenomena unforeseen by those who granted universal suffrage to ignorant crowds who had no interest in honest and economical administration. These supervenient factors have told heavily against the working of democratic institutions. As against the evils they have caused must be set two points in which the institutions of the country have won the praise of foreign observers. One is the action of the Federal Courts in so interpreting and prudently developing the Constitution as to enable it to work well under new conditions that have imposed a heavy strain upon it. Another is the practice of local self-government which, diffusing an amount of political knowledge and creating a sense of civic responsibility, is surpassed only in Switzerland. It has helped to develop that public spirit which has from time to time, and notably in recent years, carried through movements of sweeping reform by which the political atmosphere has been purified.

Canada, Australia, and New Zealand have in common the English frame of parliamentary government, but their economic and social conditions are sufficiently dissimilar to have imprinted a different character on its working in each country.

In Canada two-thirds of the population live by work on the land, and nearly all the farmers own the soil they till. This has given stability to political parties and to the government as a whole. Ministries last on an average ten times as long as does a Ministry in France or in Australia. The legislatures, especially in the Provinces, have not fully maintained the best traditions received from England, for both they and some members of the administrations they install in power have been suspected of abusing their position. Responsibility is, however, pretty well secured by the power of questioning and dismissing Ministers, justice is honestly administered, order is effectively maintained over a vast and thinly peopled Western territory, and the difficulties which the presence of two races speaking different languages presents have been surmounted.

In Australia, where nearly half the population is gathered into a few great cities, the wage-earning class has been fully organized and obtained a political power which in other countries it is still only seeking. The rich, among whom there are no millionaires, take little part, at least openly, in politics. Frequent and hard-fought strikes have roused class antagonisms. The Labour Party created in the legislatures caucuses which, working along with the Trade Councils outside, obtained complete control of the Federal Parliament, and at one time or another of each of the State Parliaments; and their action has shown how the essence of parliamentary government may be destroyed with an apparent respect for its forms. Bold experiments in extending State action to industrial undertakings and in fixing wages by State authority have been tried by Labour Ministries and by others which depended on Labour support, but, except during strikes, law and order as well as a creditable standard of administrative efficiency and judicial purity have been maintained.

New Zealand has an agricultural landowning population larger in proportion to the whole than in Australia, but smaller than in Canada. The urban hand-workers, though they have never obtained a majority in Parliament, have been strong enough to secure legislation which in some points anticipated that of Australia in extending State functions, fixing wages, and taking over branches of business or industrial production. Parties, less organized than in Australia, have been less strictly disciplined. As the dominance of the parliamentary caucus has been Australia's most distinctive contribution to the art of politics, so has State Socialism been the contribution of New Zealand. Ministries have been stable, and public business not ill managed, though with scant regard to economy and a tendency to purchase parliamentary support by improvident grants to local purposes. Apart from this form of jobbery, government has been honest, and except among the wage-earners who show their discontent by frequent strikes, a spirit of general good-will bears witness to the country's prosperity.

In these three British Self-governing Dominions members of the legislatures receive salaries, but no class of professional politicians has arisen except in so far as the officials of Trade or Labour Unions, occupying themselves with politics as well as with purely industrial matters, can be so described.

II. Defects Observable in the Six Governments

(*a*) *Instability of the Executive Government owing to frequent changes.*

This, most conspicuous in France, has been conspicuous in Australia also, both in the Commonwealth and the State Governments. In the United States it is prevented by the constitutional arrangements which install an administration for a fixed period. It is not seen in Canada and New Zealand, and least of all in Switzerland.

(*b*) *Failure of the Executive to maintain law and order.*

In America this is evident in some only of the States, where lynching and other disorders have been tolerated. Against none of the other democracies is it chargeable. Strike riots have been frequent in Australia, France, and New Zealand, to a less extent in Canada; and though such breaches of the law occur in all countries, they are doubtless more frequent and more serious where the fear of losing votes by offending strikers deters an Executive from action.

(*c*) *Administrative extravagance.*

Economy, once expected to be among the strong points of democracy, has proved to be its weakest. Financial waste is worst in the United States National Government, owing to the desire to win votes by grants from the public treasury to localities, but the same evil is rampant in Canada and New Zealand, and to a less extent in France and Australia.

(*d*) *Want of honesty in Administrators, Legislators, and Voters.*

Though no democracy has sunk so low as either the ancient republics or many autocracies, such as those of Russia, Turkey, and China, the atmosphere has not been altogether wholesome in France, in Canada, and in many of the American States. In the United States Federal Government the tone is now satisfactory. Bribery occurs sporadically in the United States and Canada, but to a less extent than it did in England before that country had been democratized. Australia, New Zealand, and Switzerland have a good record.

(e) *Faulty Administration of Justice.*

In many of the American States where the Judicial Bench is filled by popular election, the Judges are far from competent; and in a few they are suspected of corruption. Everywhere the administration of criminal justice is so defective that a very high authority has called it " a disgrace to American civilization." [1] In France the inferior judges are not altogether trusted. In the other four countries the character of the Bench stands high.

(f) *The spirit and power of Party.*

Party spirit is no stronger in these democracies than it has often been under other governments, and it everywhere rises and falls according to the circumstances of the time. Party organization is a comparatively new phenomenon, first developed in the United States, where a strong and skilfully constructed system grew up between 1826 and 1860. It has rendered some services, but far greater disservices, in the land of its birth, and has been more or less imitated in Australia, New Zealand, Canada, and Great Britain, in all of which it is possibly the source of more evil than good. In France it counts for little, and in Switzerland for less.

(g) *Professionalism in Politics.*

The growth of a class which makes its living out of politics, due partly to the number of persons needed to work a party organization and partly to the existence of legislative

---

[1] President Taft speaking at Chicago in 1909, quoted in Mr. Moorfield Storey's book, *The Reform of Legal Procedure.*

A full and careful examination of this subject may be found in the work of Mr. Raymond B. Fosdick, *American Police Systems*, published while these sheets were passing through the press in Nov., 1920. He remarks with truth that the inefficiency of the police in the United States as compared with Europe is largely due to the immense mass of foreign-born population; but this fact does not excuse the faults of criminal procedure.

and administrative posts sought as a livelihood and obtainable by party patronage, tends to pervert and even debase politics by making it a business occupation, in which the motive of civic duty is superseded by the desire of private gain. The class, large in the United States, exists in the other democracies, again excepting Switzerland, but is nowhere numerous, though it may increase with that raising of legislative salaries, recently effected in France and Australia, and now demanded in Britain, which makes a seat in the legislature more desired.

(*h*) *The power of wealth.*

Democracy was expected to extinguish this ancient evil, for every citizen is interested in preventing men from using money to secure gains for themselves at the expense of the community. It has, however, proved as noxious in republics as it was in the days when the favourites of kings could be bribed, though the methods now in use are less direct. Of the six countries, the United States has been that in which money has been most generally powerful during the last sixty years, France that in which it is probably most powerful now, while Canada comes next, Australia, New Zealand, and Switzerland being practically exempt, though of course a party or a group of men with ample funds for elections and able to run newspapers in its interest enjoys everywhere an advantage.

III. Presence or Absence of Favouring Conditions

We have so far been considering the results which democratic institutions, differing more or less in their features, have produced in six countries. These results have, however, been due not merely to the greater or less excellence either of the institutions or of the external conditions of the countries described, but also to the intellectual capacity and public spirit of the peoples that work them. Let some paragraphs be therefore given to this branch of the comparison.

(*a*) The intelligence of the Average man, and the sense of civic duty which leads him to try to understand and vote honestly upon the questions submitted at elections, are most largely developed in Switzerland, next in the United States, in Canada, and in New Zealand, with Australia perhaps a little behind.   In France it is certainly not intelligence that is deficient, but a feeling among the peasantry and *petite bourgeoisie* that every citizen ought to make his opinion felt and his voice heard.   As nothing approaching an absolute quantitative test can be applied to determine the volume of the health-giving ozone of public spirit in the atmosphere, one can do no more than conjecture whether it is increasing. In all the countries, France included, it seemed to me to be growing, though slowly, while improvement is perhaps most evident in the United States, where a reforming spirit is abroad.

(b) The extent to which the best-educated class, including many besides those who would be called the intellectual *élite* of the nation, exert themselves in public affairs, is to be measured not merely by their taking a hand in legislative or administrative work, but also by the contributions they make to thought on public questions and by their influence in the formation of national opinion.

Here the results of observation are disappointing.   The extension of the functions of government and the increasing magnitude and complexity of the subjects falling within those functions have not elicited a corresponding will to serve the community on the part of those best fitted to serve it.   In some countries one is told of a decline: but this may be because the want is more felt, not because the supply has fallen off: there is not less water, but more thirst.   It is in France that public life seems to draw out most brilliance of talent, in Switzerland the most of sober wisdom.   In none of the other countries does the traveller feel that the class to which wealth or knowledge or capactiy gives social influence is doing its full duty to the State.   Administrative work attracts a fair number of competent men, but neither the legislatures nor more than a few of the Ministers seem equal to their tasks.   The causes of this, already explained in the accounts given of each country, are much the same everywhere, but have in some been increased by the disposition to require from candidates a pledge to speak and vote with the majority of their party, whatever their individual opinion, a pledge which men of spirit refuse to give.   It was thought, fifty years ago, that the extension of the suffrage and the growth of the sentiment of equality, coupled with the diffusion of education and the cheapening of elections, would draw new streams of talent, energy, and unselfish patriotism into the service of the State. But this has nowhere happened. Though the number of those who, belonging to classes formerly excluded, have now entered the legislatures, has increased, and though legislation is everywhere directed far more than formerly towards ameliorating the conditions of health and labour, there is no more talent, no more wisdom, no more of the disinterested zeal which subordinates all other interests to the common good. The more educated class, to whatever political party they belong, are in many countries heard to complain that public life is being vulgarized, that the laws which determine national prosperity are being misunderstood or ignored because abstract theories and vague sentimentalities fill the public mind, and that social classes are being alienated from one another for want of mutual understanding and the sense of a common interest. If and so far as there is any truth in these complaints, is not a principal cause to be found in the failure of the most educated and most thoughtful to take the part that belongs to them in public life?

(c) The existence of a sentiment of national unity and of an intelligently active public opinion. These two things go together, for if the former be weak, if the clashing of sectional interests and tenets diverts each section from its loyalty to the common good, sympathy is chilled and reciprocal comprehension lessened. I have dwelt in a previous chapter (Chapter XV.) on the advantages of government by Public Opinion as compared with the mechanical though indispensable methods of government by voting, and have sought to show that the value of Public Opinion depends on the extent to which it is created by that small number of thinking men who possess knowledge and the gift of initiative, and on the extent to which the larger body, who have no initiative but a shrewd judgment,[1] co-operate in diffusing sound and temperate views through the community, influencing that still larger mass who, deficient both in knowledge and in active interest, follow the lead given to them. Taking

[1] As to this distinction see Pericles as reported by Thucydides in Book II, chap. 40.

the rule of Opinion in this sense, it is most fully developed in Switzerland and the United States, rather less so in Canada and New Zealand. In France, great as is the devotion to national glory and the Sacred Soil, the assimilative and unifying influence of opinion is weakened by the sharp divisions on religious questions, as it is in Australia by a like division upon Labour and class issues, a source of acerbity which has begun to appear also in such countries as Belgium, Holland, and Italy. The diffusion from one country into another of new types of economic doctrine and new schemes for the regeneration of society preached by enthusiastic missionaries has increased those forces that disunite nations, as in the sixteenth century there were Protestants who renounced their loyalty to a Roman Catholic king, and Roman Catholics prepared to revolt against a Protestant. Such phenomena may be transient, but for the present they disintegrate national opinion and subject democracy to an unexpected strain.

Neither the presence nor the absence of the three conditions just enumerated can be ascribed to democratic institutions, for much depends on the racial qualities and the history of each people, but their presence or absence is nevertheless a credit or discredit to those institutions, because it indicates how far they tend to accompany and strengthen democracy, enabling the machinery to play freely and smoothly without shocks and jars. It is a sign that something is wrong with a government if it fails to attract to its service enough of such talent as the country possesses; it is an evidence of its excellence if the will of the people is amply and clearly brought to bear on the governing authorities through the means by which opinion expresses itself in the intervals between the moments when it is delivered at the polls.

The examination and comparison made above have shown that however marked the differences are between one modern democracy and another, all have some defects in common. Wherever rich men abound the power of money is formidable in elections and in the press, and corruption more or less present. I will not say that wherever there is money there will be corruption, but true it is that Poverty and Purity go together. The two best-administered democracies in the modern world have been the two poorest, the Orange Free State before 1899 and the Swiss Confederation. In every country but Switzerland financial administration is wasteful, and that form of political jobbery which consists in angling for political support by grants of money to constituencies is conspicuously rife. So, too, the rise of a class of professional politicians must be expected if large salaries are paid to representatives. Such a class grows in proportion to the work party organizations have to do, and patronage is misused for party purposes wherever lucrative posts or so-called honours are at the disposal of a party Executive. These phenomena are all natural, the inevitable result of tendencies sure to operate where circumstances invite their action; and only two, the habit of buying support by grants to localities and by bills intended to capture votes from some section of the voters, are directly due to the system of party government by the votes of the masses. The existence of a class who make their living by politics, though ascribed to democratic government, is no worse than was the bestowal of places and pensions on Court favourites, or on the relatives or friends of Ministers, in monarchies or oligarchies. Unscrupulous selfishness will have its way under one system as well as another.

These observations may be summed up by saying that the chief faults observable in the democracies described are the following:

(1) The power of money to pervert administration or legislation.

(2) The tendency to make politics a gainful profession.

(3) Extravagance in administration.

(4) The abuse of the doctrine of Equality and failure to appreciate the value of administrative skill.

(5) The undue power of party organizations.

(6) The tendency of legislators and political officials to play for votes in the passing of laws and in tolerating breaches of order.

Of these faults, the first three have been observed in all governments, and the first not worse under Universal suffrage than it is to-day, though the forms of all three are now different and their consequences more serious; for the number of useless or undeserving persons who lived off the public

revenue under the English oligarchy of the eighteenth century was smaller in proportion to the population than that of
persons of the same type who live off it in the United States
to-day, and the waste of public money in favours bestowed
on constituencies and individuals under that English oligarchy or under the Prussian oligarchy down to 1914 was less
in proportion to the total revenue than it is now in France or
the United States or Canada. As the third fault is in
Switzerland not visible, and the second only in a slight degree, these are plainly separable from democratic institutions. The evils attributable to the fourth, fifth, and sixth
sources may be more definitely connected with popular government. The new democracies in particular suffer from an
insufficient appreciation of the need in modern States of legislative and administrative knowledge and skill, an error
particularly unlucky in nations which have been piling upon
the State new functions for the discharge of which knowledge
and skill are required. The years of rapid constitutional
development in Australia and New Zealand coincided with
the spread of new ideas in populations less well equipped
for constructive work than were the older nations, and class
antagonisms sprang up before a thoughtful and enlightened
public opinion, able to profit by the lessons of experience,
had time to establish itself as a ruling force. These things,
however, may come: the defects of new countries are less dis-
heartening than the declensions of old countries.

Democracy has opened a few new channels in which the
familiar propensities to evil can flow, but it has stopped some
of the old channels, and has not increased the volume of the
stream. No institutions can do more than moderate or mitigate these propensities, but that which they can do is sufficient to make it worth the while of those who frame constitutions or lead reforming movements to study the institutions
which have in one country or another given good results.

Two dangers threaten all these six countries, and indeed
all modern democracies. One is the tendency to allow self-
interest to grasp the machinery of government and turn that
machinery to its ignoble ends. The other is the irresponsible
power wielded by those who supply the people with the materials they need for judging men and measures. That dissemination by the printed word of untruths and fallacies

and incitements to violence which we have learnt to call Propaganda has become a more potent influence among the masses in large countries than the demagogue ever was in the small peoples of former days.   To combat these dangers more insight and sympathy, as well as more energy and patriotism, are needed than the so-called upper and educated classes have hitherto displayed.

CHAPTER LXVIII

TYPES OF DEMOCRATIC GOVERNMENT

THE forms which popular government have taken are many, and the future may see the emergence of others, though mankind shows singularly little inventiveness in this field of action compared to the resourceful ingenuity it evinces in adapting the forces of nature to its service.

This chapter may be confined to representative Frames of Government, since the direct rule of popular assemblies, universal in the ancient world, but applicable only to very small communities, has disappeared except in the Swiss Forest Cantons, while the direct action of the people by voting in large areas has been dealt with already. Among representative Governments three specially deserve to be studied — the Parliamentary and Cabinet System of Britain, which, reproduced in the British self-governing Dominions and France, has been more or less imitated in other European countries, the Presidential system of the United States, adopted in many of the other American republics, and the Executive Council system of Switzerland. As each of these has been described in the chapters of Part II. dealing with France, America, and Switzerland, this chapter is intended only to compare each with the others in respect of characteristic merits and defects. All these Frames have in common certain features, viz. :

1. They can exist (in essentials) either under a Republic or a (Nominal) monarchy, for the form of Monarchy which exists in such countries as Britain and the British self-governing Dominions, in Italy, Holland, Belgium, Sweden, Norway, and Spain resembles the ornamental façade of a large public building behind which the work of the office is carried on in a number of rooms, the arrangement of which has nothing to do with the design of the façade.

461

2. They can exist either under a Rigid Constitution embodied in a single Fundamental Instrument (as in the United States, Switzerland, and Australia) or under a Flexible Constitution, where all laws can be made and repealed by the same authority at any moment (as in Britain and New Zealand), or where there are only two or three Fundamental Laws easily changed (as in France).

3. They are all based on the doctrine of Popular Sovereignty, recognizing the people as the ultimate and only source of Power, to whomsoever it may delegate that power.

4. As a consequence of this feature, the right of raising revenue and appropriating it to the several services of the State belongs in all these systems to the representatives of the people.

5. They are all worked by political parties, this being what the old logicians called an Inseparable Accident, a quality not essential, but in fact always present.

The distinctive features of each of these systems or Frames of Government may be concisely stated as follows:

I. The Cabinet or Parliamentary system has for its organs of government:

(*a*) A (titular) Executive Head of the State, either elected for a term of years (as in France, Germany, Finland, Czecho-Slovakia, Poland, Esthonia, Portugal) or hereditary (as in Italy, Britain, Holland, Belgium, Greece, Norway), who is not responsible to the Legislature nor removable by it.

(*b*) A group of Ministers, virtually, if not formally, selected and dismissible by the representative Legislature, and responsible to it. This group constituting the working Executive, is called the Cabinet, and its members must, everywhere by custom and in some countries by law, be members of the Legislature.

(*c*) A Legislature, of one or two Chambers, elected by the citizens for a prescribed term of years but (in some countries) liable to be dissolved by the Executive Head, which means in practice the Cabinet.

II. The Presidential System consists of:

(*a*) An Executive Head of the State, elected by the people for a term of years, removable (in many countries) by impeachment for grave offences, but otherwise irresponsible to the Legislature, not a member of the Legislature but entitled to address it, empowered to appoint and dismiss the chief officials and to conduct the external affairs of the country, though in these two functions the Legislature, or one branch of it, may be associated with him.

(*b*) A group of Ministers, called the Cabinet, appointed and dismissible by the President, acting under his orders and responsible to him but not to the Legislature, and incapable of sitting therein.[1]

(*c*) A Legislature, usually consisting of two Chambers, elected by the citizens for a term of years, and not dissoluble by the President. Their power of passing resolutions or statutes is subject (in the U.S. and some other countries) to a veto by the President, but (in the United States) any enactment so vetoed can be repassed and so become law by a majority of two-thirds in each Chamber.[2]

III. The Executive Council System, which for brevity's sake I shall call the Swiss, consists of:

(*a*) A small Administrative Council chosen by the Legislature for a short term of years to carry on the executive business of the State under its direction, its members not sitting in the Legislature though allowed to address it.

(*b*) A Legislature, consisting in Switzerland of two Chambers, elected for short terms, and not subject to dissolution.[3]

(*c*) The People, *i.e.* the whole body of citizens, who can, when any constitutional amendment or law or resolution is submitted to them in pursuance of a demand proceeding from a prescribed number of citizens, approve or reject by

---

[1] In Chile the Ministers are deemed to be responsible to the Legislature.

[2] A similar Frame of Government exists in all the States of the American Union with the difference that in nearly all the States there are, instead of a Cabinet appointed by the State Governor, various administrative officials elected by the people, and that in some States the people can legislate by Initiative and reject laws by Referendum.

[3] With this Swiss system may be compared a kind of government occasionally occurring in revolutionary times, that of a Legislature ruling through or along with an Executive Committee chosen from its own body. This was tried by the Long Parliament in England and by the French Convention in 1793 with the Committee of Public Safety, and later with the Directory overthrown by Bonaparte in 1799

their votes such enactment (Referendum), and who have also the power of enacting any proposal for a constitutional amendment, the submission of which has been demanded by a prescribed number of citizens (Initiative). The People are thus a second directly legislative authority, placed above the representative Legislature.

In all these equally democratic forms of government the sovereign power of the people is delegated, being in the Parliamentary form delegated entirely to the Legislature, in the Presidential form delegated partly to the Legislature, partly to the (elected) Executive and partly reserved to the People when they act by amending the Constitution, while in the Swiss form it is divided between the Legislature and the People acting on the occasions when they are summoned to vote by Initiative or Referendum.[1]

In comparing the aforesaid types three points have to be regarded:

(a) Which of them succeeds best in giving prompt and full effect to the Will of the People.

(b) Which is best calculated to guard against errors into which the people may be betrayed by ignorance, haste, or passion.

(c) Which secures the highest efficiency in administration.

The Parliamentary Type concentrates the plenitude of popular power in one body, the Legislature, giving to its majority that absolute control of the Executive which enables the latter, when supported by the Legislature, to carry out the wishes of the majority with the maximum of vigour and promptness. The only power which the Executive has against the Legislature is that of appealing to their common master the People at a general election; and in France the consent of the Senate is required for this purpose. The

---

[1] Other interesting types of free constitutional government existed in the Orange Free State and the South African Republic (Transvaal) before the South African War of 1899. In these the President, Head of the Executive, was elected by the citizens, could be removed by the Legislature, could and constantly did address it, but had no vote in it, and was assisted by a small Council elected by the Legislature. The scheme worked extremely well in the Free State, which had a small population of intelligent landowners scattered over a wide area. A description of these Constitutions may be found in the Author's *Studies in History and Jurisprudence*, published in 1901.

essence of the scheme is that the Executive and the majority in the Legislature work together, each influencing the other; the Cabinet being in fact an Executive Committee of the Legislature. The working of the scheme presupposes not only the existence of parties, but a sentiment of party unity strong enough to induce the majority in the Legislature to entrust a large discretion to the Cabinet, and to support it, except now and then in very grave matters, with a trustful loyalty which assumes its action to have been right till proved to have been wrong. The Cabinet on its side is bound to adhere to the principles which are dear to the party as a whole and to keep the majority in the Legislature in good humour, straining its loyalty no further than is absolutely necessary, and taking from time to time into its own body members of the majority who have won their way to the front.

The presence of Ministers in a Legislature has two other advantages. Being in constant contact with members of the Opposition Party as well as in still closer contact with those of their own, they have opportunities of feeling the pulse of the Assembly, and through it the pulse of public opinion, and can obtain useful criticism, given privately in a friendly way, of their measures, while the members can by their right of questioning Ministers call attention to any grievances felt by their constituents and can obtain information on current public questions. Like other things, the right to interrogate is frequently abused, but any one who has been a Minister in the British House of Commons values the means it gives him of correcting or contradicting erroneous statements, of refuting calumnies, of explaining the reasons for his administrative acts without being obliged to seek the aid of the newspapers.

This system is therefore calculated to secure swiftness in decision and vigour in action, and enables the Cabinet to press through such legislation as it thinks needed, and to conduct both domestic administration and foreign policy with the confidence that its majority will support it against the attacks of the Opposition. To these merits there is to be added the concentration of Responsibility. For any faults committed the Legislature can blame the Cabinet, and the people can blame both the Cabinet and the majority. In the long run the enforcement of Responsibility depends on the activity and sanity of public opinion in each party and the strength of its outside party. This Parliamentary system renders an incidental service in bringing able men to the front, giving them a position from which they can catch the ear of the nation and show themselves qualified for office. Power of speech is what first attracts notice, but if to that they add solid qualities of character — good sense, industry, loyalty, honesty — their colleagues in the Legislature come to respect them, and to trust them when they rise to be Ministers. Moreover, the alternation of power from one party to another provides in the leaders of the Opposition men who can criticize with knowledge the policy of their successors, and who if called upon to succeed those successors, bring in their turn some experience with them.

As the actual working Executive has necessarily a party character, it is a merit of this system that the Nominal Executive, be he King or President, should stand outside party, and represent that permanent machinery of administration which goes on steadily irrespective of party changes. An elected President cannot so easily fill this rôle as can a hereditary king, though some Presidents have filled it well in France. When a Cabinet falls, the transfer of power to another is a comparatively short and simple matter. The Executive Head (*i.e.* in England the Crown, in France the President, in Canada or Australia the Governor-General) commissions the leader of the Opposition to form a new Ministry; the occupants of the chief offices are promptly changed, and the ship, having put about, is soon under way on her new course, commanded by a new captain, and all this may happen without the worry and cost of an election.

These merits of the Parliamentary system are balanced by serious defects.

The system intensifies the spirit of party and keeps it always on the boil. Even if there are no important issues of policy before the nation there are always the Offices to be fought for. One party holds them, the other desires them, and the conflict is unending, for immediately after a defeat the beaten party begins its campaign to dislodge the victors. It is like the incessant battle described as going on in the blood-vessels between the red corpuscles and the invading

microbes.   In the Legislature it involves an immense waste
of time and force.   Though in theory the duty of the Opposition is to oppose only the bad measures and to expose only the
misdoings of the Administration, in practice it opposes most
of their measures and criticizes most of their acts.   Legislation is either, as in France, apt to be sacrificed to " interpellations " intended to damage the Cabinet, or, as in
England, to be delayed and clogged by the interposition of
party conflicts.

Debates over measures admittedly good are often vexa-
tiously protracted merely in order to prevent the Ministry
from carrying other measures which are disliked, or an angry
Opposition may seek to damage it by so obstructing all
business as to force them to present at the end of the session
a sorry harvest of statutes.

Crediting the close association of Executive and Legislature with the merit of avoiding friction, it is also true that
where either organ dominates the other, the consequences
may be unfortunate.   In the eighteenth century the Ministry
commanded a large section of the British House of Commons
by means of pocket boroughs which the Crown held, or could
obtain the use of from their owners.   In England, whenever
a Ministry has a strong party organization at its beck and
call, it can put pressure upon members through the local
party committees in their constituencies; and it has happened in Italy that a Minister may in one way or another
obtain control by unseen methods over a large section of the
representatives.   In France, on the other hand, it is Ministries that suffer, for members are able to extort all sorts of
favours for their constituencies from Administrations whose
instability compels them to angle for every possible vote; and
in Australia a Labour Ministry is a passive instrument in
the hands of a parliamentary caucus which is itself controlled by an organization outside Parliament.   A subservient Ministry loses the respect of the nation, as a dominant
one lowers the credit of the Legislature.

A system which makes the life of an Administration
depend upon the fate of the measures it introduces disposes
every Cabinet to think too much of what support it can win
by proposals framed to catch the fancy of the moment, and
to think too little of what the real needs of the nation are;

and it may compel the retirement, when a bill is defeated, of men who can ill be spared from their administrative posts.

The Cabinet system grew up in Britain when there were only two parties. When between 1876 and 1906, there appeared a third and, somewhat later, a fourth, it worked less well. The same thing happened in Australia after 1900, has since then happened in South Africa, and is now happening in Canada. In France for many years past no Ministry has been able to hold office except by getting several groups to unite so as to form a majority of the whole Chamber. Group alliances are what chemists call an unstable compound, and when they dissolve, down goes the Ministry.[1]

Lastly, the very concentration of power and swiftness with which decisions can be reached and carried into effect is a source of danger. There is no security for due reflection, no opportunity for second thoughts. Errors may be irretrievable.

The Presidential or American system on the other hand was built for safety, not for speed. Founded on the doctrine that the Executive and Legislative departments ought to be kept separate, because only thus could the liberty of the citizen be secured, it not only debars the Executive Head and his Ministers from sitting in the Legislature, but in the United States permits the latter both to narrow by law the President's field of action and to refuse him the money needed for carrying out any policy they disapprove. He is helpless against them, except in the narrow sphere which the Constitution reserves to him, and in that sphere the Senate can hamper him in the selection of his high officials.[2] These well-meant provisions, grounded on fears for liberty, have proved inconvenient by impeding the co-operation of representatives and administrators. The former cannot question the latter, except by means of Committees. The latter have not, unless through a Committee, the means of conveying the

[1] See as to France Vol. I. Chap. XX. In Australia Ministries have been singularly unstable, Vol. II. Chap. XLVII.

[2] The custom has been not to exert this power in the case of Cabinet Ministers, but it is applied to all other officers (including ambassadors and judges), and used to put pressure upon the President in matters of general policy. The reader need hardly be reminded that the President has against Congress the formidable power of veto.

needs of their departments to the representatives. Delay, confusion, much working at cross purposes are the result: and this is particularly felt in the sphere of finance where the legislature may refuse money when the Executive needs it, and may grant money for no better purpose than to purchase the political support of powerful sections or clamorous constituencies. The " Separation of Powers " has for some purposes turned out to be not the keeping apart of things really distinct but the forcible disjunction of things naturally connected. There is, moreover, no certainty that the Legislature will carry out the wishes of the Administration, however reasonable. They may even decline to pass the statutes needed to give effect to treaties duly ratified.[1]

The Presidential system leaves more to chance than does the Parliamentary. A Prime Minister is only one out of a Cabinet, and his colleagues may keep him straight and supply qualities wanting in him, but everything depends on the character of the individual chosen to be President. He may be strong or weak, wise or short-sighted. He may aim at standing above party and use his authority and employ his patronage with a single eye to the nation's welfare, or may think first of his own power and his party's gain, and play for his own re-election. The re-eligibility of the President has so often been supposed to unduly affect his action that many Americans think he should be legally disqualified for a second continuous term of office.[2] In some republics such a provision exists.

The United States has best shown the strength and weakness of the system, but just as it works differently in the hands of different men, so is it a different thing in different countries. In nearly all of the republics of Latin America racial and social conditions throw larger powers into the hands of the Executive chief than would be permitted to him in the United States. This has been seen in constitutional Argentina and Uruguay, as well as in those disorderly States

---

[1] This happened recently in the United States when Congress neglected to pass the legislation required to give effect to a treaty for regulating the fisheries in the Great Lakes which had been accepted by the Senate and which promised real benefits to the United States as well as to Canada.

[2] The American tradition which forbade a person to be chosen President more than twice seems to have recently lost nearly all its influence.

where a President is usually a military dictator. Legally the powers may seem the same: practically they are wider in the countries where constitutional traditions are still new and public opinion still weak or divided into sections by an economic or religious antagonism.

For administrative purposes it is a gain that the members of the Cabinet are not, like those of Britain, obliged to give constant attendance in the Legislature, and that when a Minister starts a promising policy he can count on carrying it on without being upset by a sudden change of government. The Legislature, too, since it cannot displace the President, nor even a Minister, is not distracted from the work of legislation by debates intended to discredit the existing and install a new administration.

Two other merits may certainly be credited to the Presidential scheme. Under it legislatures are less dominated by party spirit than those of Britain and France, of Belgium and Australia and Canada, for party discipline is not so strict at Washington as at Westminster, though the party organizations are stronger.[1] Under it there is also a greater sense of stability, partly because a shifting of the political balance can take place only at elections, points fixed by law, partly because the legislature can by withholding funds check the Executive in any project thought to be risky, while the Executive can by its veto arrest the legislature in a dangerous course. In either case, the appeal is to the judgment of the nation, to be given, if not forthwith by public opinion, then before long at the next general election. The moderate elements in the country need not fear a sudden new departure: the demagogue cannot carry his projects with a run.[2]

Is Responsibility to the People, a cardinal merit in every form of free government, better secured under the Parliamentary or under the Presidential system? Apparently under the former, because there is more unity, the Cabinet

[1] See as to this the figures as to voting collected by Mr. Lawrence Lowell from the records of divisions in the House of Commons and the House of Representatives respectively, in his *Government of England,* vol. ii. pp. 76–89.

[2] That the demagogic bacillus seems to be less rife or less harmful in the United States than in some European countries may be partly due to the fact that the American people (omitting recent immigrants) have by their experience of more than a century become more "immune" than are the European masses.

having over the whole policy and administration of the
country that full power which their majority in the Legislature has granted them.   If they err by omission or by commission, they cannot shift the blame to Parliament, for if
they do not receive from it the necessary support they can
either dissolve it or resign office, transferring responsibility
to it or to their successors.

Under the Presidential scheme the President is responsible,
except where the Legislature fails either to pass at his request
the laws, or to supply the money needed to carry out the
policy he recommends, in which case it is not he but the
Legislature that becomes answerable for any resulting evil.
The majority in a Legislature which prevents a President
from acting of course incurs a responsibility attaching to the
party which has elected it: and a party may so suffer, but it
is a responsibility far less definite than that attaching to a
Cabinet, or to the leaders of an Opposition, in a Parliamentary country.[1]   When President and Legislature belong
to the same party, it is to him that the nation looks, for he
can ask the Legislature for all that the conjuncture requires,
be it statutes or grants of money.   But when he and the
Legislature are at odds, and the country is not evidently with
the one or the other, there is nothing for it but to bear with
the deadlock and await the next ensuing election.

In the Presidential system the man chosen to be Head of
the Government becomes more definitely Head of the Nation
than does a Prime Minister in a Parliamentary country like
France, Canada, or England.   The eyes of the whole people
are fixed upon him even if he be a man of less than first-
rate quality, whereas in Parliamentary countries it is only
striking personalities such as Pitt or Cavour or Bismarck
that excite a similar interest and exert a similar authority.
An American President stands high above others, meaning
more to the people than leaders in Congress do, and always
sure to command attention when he speaks.   He need not
consult his Cabinet nor regard its advice as must a French
or British Prime Minister.   To his Cabinet he is a Master,

---

[1] Says Mr. Lawrence Lowell: " In countries where power is divided
among a number of bodies, or hidden away in Committees, responsibility
is intangible.   Every one can throw it off his shoulders and it may become the subject of a game of hide-and-seek " (*Government of England*,
vol. ii. p. 532).

to a French or British Cabinet only a Chief. A Prime Minister may fall at any moment if the Assembly tires of him: a President stands firm, and has to be taken by the nation for better or worse while his term lasts. Hence the method of choosing the Irremoveable Head becomes proportionately more important. No perfect method has been found, but this much may be said for popular election that whereas the method of natural selection from the Assembly in parliamentary countries gives a perhaps undue advantage to oratorical brilliance, the method of deliberate choice by a legal act of the whole people affords a wider field of choice for persons of other gifts, for men like George Washington, or of the type to which in their different ways such strong personalties as Grover Cleveland and Theodore Roosevelt belonged. It often fails to find the fittest men, but it has, at least in the United States, excluded the unworthy.[1] American experience cannot, however, be taken as a general guide. There are in Europe, as well as in those Spanish American republics in which a popular election without violence is now possible, countries where election by an Assembly is the safer method.[2] This was the view of those who framed the present Constitution of France.[3]

These two types of government so far resemble one another, having both sprung from the common root of a feudal monarchy, that it has been necessary to consider them together.[4]

[1] The method of Nomination by party caucuses in Congress was tried and abandoned, but the attempt to make nominations truly popular has not succeeded.

[2] One risk incident to an election by the nation instead of by an Assembly appeared in the United States in 1876 when a controversy arose over the results of the voting in several States which there was no authority capable of deciding. The American system of counting all the votes of a State for the candidate who obtains a majority, however small, in that State tends to concentrate the efforts of a party on those States in which parties are nearly equally divided, and makes a resort to illegal methods of influencing the electors or harvesting the results more likely.

[3] Election by a vote of the people had been discredited there by the two "plebiscites" taken under universal suffrage, which created in 1852 and renewed in 1870 the Empire of Louis Napoleon: yet it must be remembered that in both those cases no alternative was presented to the people; they had to choose between confirming the existing ruler and an entirely uncertain future which might have been one of civil war.

[4] The British Cabinet has inherited the old powers of the feudal king; the American President was created on the model of the English Executive, as it stood in the days of George III, modified by being made not

The third or Swiss type has a very different source, for Switzerland was never ruled by a single sovereign, and its legislature grew out of the diplomatic conferences in which the delegates of thirteen little States met to discuss their common foreign policy.[1] The mainspring of the Constitution is the National Assembly, which controls the Executive and in which the whole power of the People is embodied, except in so far as the Constitution limits legislative action and in so far as the people have a final voice in legislation by the Referendum and Initiative. The Swiss system has the advantage of simplicity and of a concentration of authority. The National Assembly chooses and supervises the small Federal Council which carries on administration. Both are watched by public opinion, and can be overruled if necessary by popular vote. Policy, both foreign and domestic, is continuous, moves with an even step, the ideas the same, the men the same. No time is wasted in party strife. Economy and efficiency are secured. The unchecked power which the people can exercise when by the Initiative their votes amend the constitution or enact a law, has not proved dangerous in a country with a population so shrewd, cool, and accustomed to the use of freedom. There are few prizes ambition can strive for beyond the respect and trust of fellow-citizens. A humdrum State, but it is prosperous and contented, and nowhere does patriotism glow with so steady a flame.

Can the advantages which this type of government has bestowed on Switzerland be secured elsewhere by like institutions? The conditions are peculiar: a small nation, its citizens not indeed poor, but very few of them rich, highly intelligent, long trained by local self-government, little distracted by party spirit. It is hard to suppose in any other country a coincidence of these conditions sufficient to give such an institution as the Swiss Federal Council a like chance of success. Nevertheless, we may imagine that even

hereditary but elective for a short term of years; the statesmen who framed the American Constitution not having realized how far effective power had been even by 1787 transferred from the Crown to the Cabinet. They did not see, says Bagehot, that the Sovereign had become "a cog in the mechanism of the British Constitution."

[1] The territories that now form the Swiss Confederation were all parts of the old Romano-Germanic Empire, but neither the Cantons nor the Confederation trace their origin to government of the Emperor or any other monarch.

in a country twice the size of Switzerland, a small Cabinet Council appointed by and in the closest touch with the Legislature, and itself appointing and supervising the heads of administrative departments might, in quieter times than the present, carry on public business with less friction and at less cost than has been found possible under either the Parliamentary or the Presidential system. An Administration not immersed in the whirlpool of party politics might devote itself to the task of bettering the condition of the masses of the people by measures none the less effective because they were not designed to win the momentary support of any section. Politics would be less spectacular: but after all politics were made for men, not men for politics. It would be hard to introduce such a system in any country where the passing of laws has been long associated with party strife, and where the distrust of opponents, intensified in our days by class sentiment, makes each side suspect whatever proceeds from the other; but since alike in France, in America, and in England the constitutional machinery that exists for investigating, preparing, and enacting legislation upon economic and industrial topics has failed to give satisfaction, light upon the problem of improving that machinery ought to be sought in every quarter.

Other schemes of government than the three here described might be invented, and one such, that of a series of local Assemblies, each sending one or more of its best men to a higher Assembly till they culminate in a Central Executive and a Central Council, has taken a sort of shape in the scheme of Russian Soviets. Many paths might be cut in the forest, but for the present it is enough to indicate those that are well trodden.

If we return to the questions whence we started, it would seem that of the three types examined the people's will receives a fuller and prompter effect under the Parliamentary system and the Swiss system than under the Presidential. The distinctive quality of this last which some would call a fault and others a merit, lies in the fact that by dividing power between several distinct authorities, it provides more carefully than does the Parliamentary against errors on the part either of Legislature or Executive, and retards the decision by the people of conflicts arising between them.

The Swiss, guarding themselves against mistakes committed by the Legislature but placing no check on the direct action of the people, seem to take the greatest risks; but they are really the most conservative in spirit of all the nations, and make the least use of the wide powers reserved to the citizens. Efficiency is most likely to be secured by the Parliamentary system, because whatever the Executive needs it is sure to obtain from its majority in the Assembly, subject, of course, to any check which the existence of a Second Chamber may provide.

As between these two systems the Parliamentary seems to be preferred by the new States which have arisen in Europe during the last hundred years, the newest adopting it in the French rather than in the British form. The Presidential system has found favour among the Latin American republics which drew their ideas of self-government from the United States, and has in most of them allowed the Executive a wider power, going so far as in the Argentine Federation to permit a President to supersede the elected officials of a State on the ground that this is necessary to secure a fair election, no party trusting its adversary to conduct elections fairly. So far as the experience hitherto acquired warrants any general conclusion, that conclusion would be that while the Parliamentary has many advantages for countries of moderate size, the Presidential, constructed for safety rather than promptitude in action, and not staking large issues on sudden decisions, is to be preferred for States of vast area and population, such as are the United States and Germany.

Those who hold the chief merit of a scheme of government to lie in the amplitude of its provisions for the expression of the popular will may observe that the Swiss system is the only one which brings out that will in an unmistakable and unpervertible form, viz. by an Initiative or Referendum vote, whereas under the other two systems a vote given at an election, being given primarly for a candidate, not for a law or executive act, does not convey the people's judgment on any specific issue.[1]

That is true, but the cumbrousness and cost of any frequent use of the Referendum in a large country are practically prohibitive, and the party which possessed a strong and

[1] See Chaps. LIX and LXV.

ubiquitous organization would have an unfair advantage at a voting. The opinion delivered would be for half or more of the citizens not their own, but an opinion imposed upon them by others. If the Will of the People means the personal mind and purpose of each individual citizen, to search for it is to search for the pot of gold at the foot of the rainbow.

CHAPTER LXIX

THE MONEY POWER IN POLITICS

PHILIP, King of Macedon, was wont to boast that he could take any city into which he could drive an ass laden with gold. Many statesmen from Philip's time down to our own have spoken to the like effect. So long as private property exists, there will be rich men ready to corrupt, and other men, rich as well as poor, ready to be corrupted, for " the love of money is the root of all evil." This has been so under all forms of government alike. The House of Commons in the days when Walpole, looking round its benches, observed, " All these men have their price," was no worse than were most of the Jacobin leaders among the French revolutionaries, and the fact that Robespierre's influence rested largely on his epithet " the Incorruptible " tells its own tale. Two absolute monarchies, Russia under the Tsars and China under the Manchu Emperors, were the countries in which corruption was seen in its most shameless luxuriance in our own time. The power money can exert upon Governments is to be specially feared in countries where two conditions, naturally connected, coincide, the existence both of large fortunes and of opportunities for making fortunes which the State, through its various organs, can grant or can withhold. Of many forms in which money can exert its power, corruption is only one, but as it is the most palpable and direct, it may come first in a summing up of the results which the survey of modern democratic governments contained in previous chapters has provided. " Corruption " may be taken to include those modes of employing money to attain private ends by political means which are criminal or at least illegal, because they induce persons charged with a public duty to transgress that duty and misuse the functions assigned to them.

Four classes of persons owing a duty to the public may be thus led astray, viz. (*a*) Electors, (*b*) Members of a Legislature, (*c*) Administrative Officials, (*d*) Judicial Officials.

(*a*) *Electors.*— The bribery of voters is a practice from which few countries have been exempt. To-day it is hardly discoverable in Switzerland, in Australia, and in New Zealand. Uncommon in France, not extinct in Belgium and Holland, and found also in Italy, it is pretty frequent in parts of Canada and of the Northern United States, where even well-to-do farmers are not ashamed to take a few dollars for their vote, sometimes excusing themselves on the ground that they ought to be paid for the time they spend in going to the poll; and it is also reported from the cities, chiefly among negro voters. The practice was a flagrant scandal in England till the enlargement of constituencies and a stringent law (passed in 1884) reduced it to a few towns in the southern counties. In Spanish America it was scarcely needed, because the Governments of most of the republics have been accustomed to take charge of the elections and secure such results as they desire, while in the cities of ancient Greece, it appeared chiefly in the bribing of orators to influence the general assembly of the citizens. But at Rome it became in the later days of the Republic so gross as to be one of the causes of the Republic's fall. Rich men bought consulships and praetorships from the lower class of citizens whose votes in the *Comitia* conferred these offices and more than reimbursed themselves for what they had spent in bribes by the spoils of the provinces which they were sent in due course to govern.

(*b*) *Members of a Legislature.*— Legislative power necessarily includes the power to pass measures, general or special, which involve some pecuniary gain or loss to individuals. A customs tariff, especially if designed to protect domestic industries, may enrich one man or impoverish another. The grant of what is called in America a franchise, *e.g.* the right to construct a railroad or tramway, may have vast possibilities of gain. A vote for the making of some public work may so raise the price of landed property in a particular spot as to make it well worth the while of the owner of such property to persuade the legislature to pass the vote. Where a member of a legislature has influence with administrative officials, as, for instance, with those who have contracts at their disposal, or who administer State possessions in a Colony, the member may be bribed to exert his influence. In these and other ways members of the legislature hold in their gift benefits sufficient to expose them to temptations from rich men willing to pay high. As on a rocky sea-shore one can tell how far the tide has fallen by observing how many limpets adhering to the rocks are to be seen above the level of the water, so the healthiness of public life may be judged by seeing how many rich men or their agents are found slipping into the halls of a legislature and approaching persons who can bring political influence to bear.

Bills affecting particular localities or persons have been, in American legislatures, and especially in those of the more populous States, a source of corruption surpassed only by the prostitution of their legislative functions by the members of municipal councils. In one such State the question " What sort of a legislature have you got ? " elicited the reply " As good a one as money can buy." In France such abuses have arisen chiefly over contracts or business operations in connection with public undertakings, sometimes in the colonies; and in Canada some of the Provincial assemblies are similarly suspected, but the adoption, in the self-governing Dominions, of British Parliamentary rules enacted seventy years ago regarding the treatment of private bills, have generally protected their legislatures from exposure to temptation.

(c) *Administrative Officials.*— An examination of the Civil Service in France, the United States, Switzerland, Australia, and New Zealand shows that in all these countries the highest ranks of this service maintain a good standard of honesty, though lower down, where salaries are small and the corporate tradition of purity is less strong, the seductions of wealth may sometimes prevail, especially where a secret commission is offered upon a naval or military contract.

Fifty years ago some Cabinet Ministers in the United States were compromised in scandals, as have been more recently some Canadian Ministers, especially in the Provinces. In neither country are the municipal officials of some large cities spotless. A frequent form of corruption is seen in those American municipalities where business firms bribe the police to wink at breaches of municipal regulations. Payments so made to escape prosecution have been in New York no inconsiderable source of emolument to officers in the police force and to the great political club of which most of those officers are honoured members.

(d) *Judicial Officials.*— Of all kinds of corruption that of the judiciary is the most odious, being one of the commonest ways in which the rich man gets the better of the poor. In the countries hereinbefore described one hears no charge of venality brought against the higher National judges. Frenchmen, however, do not seem to place implicit trust in their lower Courts; and in some States of the American Union the Bench is now and then discredited by the presence of men known to have been elected by the influence of great incorporated companies, or to be under the control of powerful politicians; and there are cities where some lawyers have made a reputation for " fixing a jury." [1] Neither are judges trusted in most countries of Portuguese or Spanish America, though there it is a family or personal friendship rather than money that is apt to pervert justice. In the British self-governing Dominions the traditions of purity brought from the mother country have been carefully preserved.

The means by which corruption is effected have, with the march of civilization, become in most countries more delicately elusive. Many are the devices available, many the cases that can be imagined in which there may be strong grounds for suspicion while the proof of a corrupt inducement is too weak to warrant prosecution. No coin, nor always even paper, need pass. Were Philip now seeking to capture a city council instead of a city, he would not load the

[1] That we hear little or nothing about the bribing of Athenian juries may be attributed to the great size of these bodies (see Vol. I. Chap. XVI). But the numbers of the juries who sat in the Roman *iudicia publica* to try criminal cases did not prevent bribery. It was, as we gather from Cicero, practised on a magnificent scale, and sometimes enabled notorious offenders to escape.

ass with gold, but would intimate that shares in a company being formed to work a copper mine were to be allotted below par to some good friends and would certainly go to a premium in a few weeks. In Russia under the Tsars a Minister, who was asked by some one from Western Europe for official sanction to a perfectly legitimate enterprise calculated to benefit the country, was accustomed, while inventing one objection after another, to rattle a drawer containing some loose roubles until the hint was taken; but in democratic countries, where a higher standard of purity is expected and the press as well as political opponents are prompt to detect and expose those who fall below it, more subtle methods are needed. Such methods often succeed.

From distinctly illegal modes of employing money in politics we may pass to others which are for any reason undesirable, as calculated to warp the spontaneous action of the citizens' minds and wills, or as giving to rich men an advantage which is undue, because derived from wealth and not from any superior fitness to serve the community. Some classes of such cases the law can reach; others it leaves untouched, perhaps because the motive that prompted the act may have been doubtful, perhaps because legal intervention would do more harm than good. A few illustrations may be given, beginning with cases wherewith the law has sought to deal.

Election Expenses.—In countries where power is conferred by the votes of the people the efforts of parties and candidates are chiefly directed to the winning of elections. Now Elections cost money. Money may legitimately be spent on them, but if it is spent lavishly, an advantage is given to the rich candidates and to the party which has the larger campaign fund. Hence, though there is nothing intrinsically wrong in flooding a constituency with canvassers, circulating an immense mass of printed matter intended to influence the electors, and spending money in conveying electors to the polls,[1] British legislation restricts the total expenditure which

[1] In Britain the conveyance of voters in vehicles hired for the purpose is prohibited, but as the conveyance in vehicles belonging to the candidate or his friends is still permitted, the possession by him of a large number of sympathisers who own and will lend motor cars is supposed to improve his chances.

a candidate may incur, the amount being determined by the
number of electors in a constituency. Similar statutes have
been passed in the United States also as respects Federal
elections, and in some States for State elections; and in the
United States the political parties have also been required to
furnish statements of their total National campaign funds.
These funds had often received large contributions from
great manufacturing or trading companies, usually because
such companies had an interest in the provisions of the protective tariff and expected the party to whose fund they
subscribed to repay the service by giving them the kind of
tariff they desired. Such practices come pretty near to
bribing, not indeed the voters, but a political organization
which might be able to " deliver the goods," so they have
now been forbidden by law.

These laws relate to elections. But golden seed intended
to bear fruit may be sown at other times also. In England,
and to a less extent in Scotland, a habit has grown up and
spread widely of expecting members of Parliament to subscribe to local purposes, and not only to charitable purposes,
such as hospitals, but also to all sorts of associations formed
for amusement, such as football and cricket and swimming
clubs. Rich men have been known to spend many hundreds
of pounds annually in such subscriptions, and prospective
candidates have also begun to do so, the practice being called
" nursing the constituency." It would be difficult to forbid
these things, for if the member or candidate resides within
the constituency, he would naturally subscribe to some of
these objects in his quality of a resident, while if non-residents
only were forbidden so to do, this might be held to give an
advantage to residents. The practice, however, tends to
demoralize the electorate and the candidate, and to deter
men of limited means from offering themselves.

Another regrettable habit visible at present only in the
United States, because it is only there that party organizations exercise a practically controlling influence on the selection of candidates for any post, is the use of pecuniary
inducements to influence a Boss, or any leading wire-pullers,
in the selection as candidate for office of an aspirant whom
the party that selected him is bound to support with its solid
vote. Here no offence is committed because a Boss, having

no legal position, has no statutory duty and responsibility, being merely a private citizen to whose counsels other private citizens are wont to defer. American legislation, though it provides penalties for bribery or other misfeasance in the conduct of nominating meetings, can hardly go so far as to recognize a Boss and surround his action, influential as it is, with safeguards, not to add that it would seldom be possible to pry into the dark corners where the spider spins his web.

The practice of " Lobbying," *i.e.* besetting and worrying members of legislatures with persuasions to vote for or against a bill which promises gain or threatens loss to some business enterprise, while occasionally discernible in France, and perhaps not unknown in some British countries, attains dangerous dimensions only in the precincts of American legislatures. When the lobbyist bribes he is of course punishable, but the employment of a crowd of professional agents, though it secures advantages for those who can afford to employ them, cannot well be forbidden. There is nothing wrong in persuasion *per se;* and who shall fix the limits of reasonable persuasion? [1] Lobbyists might, however, be recognized as a sort of profession and subjected, like parliamentary agents in England, to disciplinary rules.

The granting by railway companies of free passes over their lines, a practice formerly common in the United States, was in itself legitimate and often well employed. Ministers of religion, and sometimes others also whose journeys seemed useful for the community, such as University professors, received this privilege, which was, however, so much abused by the companies as a means of propitiating influential persons, especially members of legislatures, that it was forbidden by law.

These various forms in which the power of wealth has been felt and to some extent curbed, count for less than another which appears to defy all regulation. This is the manufacture of public opinion. A group of rich men who have a special business project or class interest, be it legitimate or deleterious, may combine to start a press propaganda on behalf of their interest or project, partly by

---

[1] A like difficulty has been found in distinguishing " peaceful picketing " in a strike of workmen from a picketing which becomes coercion.

pamphlets or books, partly by influencing or capturing journals, so as to deluge the public with facts and arguments advocating their schemes or helping a party whose chiefs are secretly committed to the support of those schemes.   Such a group may, by its control of a large part of the press, succeed in impressing its views on a public easily misled because one side only of the case has been constantly and ably presented to them while the opposing arguments are ignored or decried. The aim may be unobjectionable, but even if it be sordid, even if the facts be garbled and the arguments fallacious, how can such a propaganda be arrested ?   The only remedy, in a free country, is to disprove the facts and refute the fallacies. But it may not be worth anybody's while to incur the expense of a press opposition.

The great firms that manufacture munitions of war have been frequently accused of using their revenues to foster a warlike spirit and thereby dispose nations and their legis-latures to spend immense sums in military preparations.   I know of no evidence to show that this has happened in France or the United States or England, but it is generally believed to have happened in Germany, and might no doubt happen anywhere.   There have certainly been cases in which unscru-pulous men have, from selfish motives, used the press to push a nation into war.

The methods here enumerated are only some among the ways in which wealth can make itself felt in politics.   It commands social influences.   It can put politicians under personal obligations.   It can by subscriptions to party funds obtain, as has often happened in England, titles of rank, which carried, till they began to be lavishly distributed, some social influence.   Large sums may be expended for purposes sinister but not illegal, and where these tactics succeed, a bad precedent is set and the standard of honour is lowered. The most conspicuous example of a State demoralized and brought to ruin by the power of money is afforded by the history of the later Roman Republic.   The saying of the Numidian Jugurtha was prophetic: " The City is up for sale, and will perish if some day it finds a purchaser."

Among modern democracies the two which have been the purest, the best administered, and the most truly popular in spirit have been Switzerland and the Orange Free State as it

was in 1895 before the South African War.[1] They were
those in which there were no rich men.   On the other hand,
those free countries in which wealth has been most powerful
are the United States, France, and Canada.   In the United
States the swift growth of prodigious fortunes, and the opportunities for increasing them by obtaining favours from the
governments of States and cities, had coincided with the
building up of party organizations through whose help these
favours could be obtained.   The influence of what is called
" Big Business," wealth concentrated in a few hands and
finding its tools in politicians and party organizations, was
for many years a fruitful source of mischief, exploiting the
resources of the country for its selfish purposes.   These
abuses provoked a reaction.   " Big Business " began to be
bitted and bridled, and though it still shows fight, can hardly
recover the dominance it enjoyed thirty years ago, for public
opinion has grown more sensitive and vigilant.

To estimate the harm done in France by the power of
finance is more difficult, because the breezes of publicity do
not blow so freely as in America over the field of politics, and
where the facts are seldom ascertainable, rumour and suspicion are all the more active.   It is, however, beyond doubt
that Frenchmen believe the hidden influence of the heads of
some great undertakings, industrial and financial, to be a
potent force, manipulating the press, raising or depressing
the fortunes of statesmen, and by one device or another
turning the machinery of government to serve private ends.
I speak not as knowing but only as reporting what is believed.

In Canada there have been fewer charges and complaints,
but the close contact between finance, especially railway
finance, and the political parties has caused disquietude.   In
Australia the rich are supposed to support party funds, but
so far as I could learn, from political rather than directly
personal motives.

In England it has thrice happened that a group of men
who had made great fortunes abroad tried to use that wealth
for political ends.   The first instance was that of the so-
called Nabobs, men who had brought back wealth from the
East in the days of King George III.   They bought elector-

[1] It is now a part of the self-governing Dominion called the Union of
South Africa.

ates, and formed a group which, after rousing hostility by its prominence for some years, had vanished long before the Reform Act of 1832 abolished pocket-boroughs. The two other instances are too near our own times to be fit subjects for comment here. They did not permanently injure political life, but they disclosed some of the weak spots which wealth may assail. Apart from these passing, and in two instances pernicious, manifestations of the insidious influence money can bring to bear on the formation of opinion, England has not suffered from the malady since 1832, which never thereafter, not even while electoral corruption was frequent, seriously threatened its vital organ, the House of Commons. Were the centre of vital force to pass from the House of Commons to the press, there would be ground for anxiety. In every country unscrupulous wealth can, by artificially "making opinion," mislead and beguile the people more easily and with less chance of detection than in any other way.

Democracy has no more persistent or insidious foe than the money power, to which it may say, as Dante said when he reached in his journey through hell the dwelling of the God of Riches,[1] "Here we found Wealth, the great enemy." That enemy is formidable because he works secretly, by persuasion or by deceit, rather than by force, and so takes men unawares. He is a danger to good government everywhere, no more active, no more mischievous in popular than he is in other governments. Why then are we more shocked when we find him active and successful in a democracy? Is it because we are prepared to expect selfishness in monarchies and oligarchies, but not in States which live by public spirit and where the common good is the common aim? The hope that public spirit will guarantee purity is one which, however often disappointed, no one would like to lose. Yet why should it be supposed that the ordinary failings of mankind will be materially lessened by the form of government any

[1] "Quivi trovammo Pluto il gran nemico," *Inf. Canto* VI. l. 115. There can be little doubt that Pluto is to be here taken to mean Plutus the Roman God of Wealth, but perhaps his name was confused with that of Pluto, the king of the nether world, who represents in Roman mythology the Homeric ἄναξ ἐνέρων 'Αϊδωνεύς. H. F. Tozer's note in his eminently judicious Commentary on the *Divina Commedia* inclines to this view, which is also that of Mr. Paget Toynbee.

men live under? Can democracy do more than provide restraints and impose penalties less liable to be evaded than those tried elsewhere? Has not experience shown that safeguards may be more easily evaded where authority is vested in the multitude, for it is likely to be less vigilant, less prompt in detection and punishment, than is a well-organized bureaucracy?

The truth seems to be that democracy has only one marked advantage over other governments in defending itself against the submarine warfare which wealth can wage, viz. Publicity and the force of Public Opinion. So long as ministers can be interrogated in an assembly, so long as the press is free to call attention to alleged scandals and require explanations from persons suspected of an improper use of money or an improper submission to its influences, so long will the people be at least warned of the dangers that threaten them. If they refuse to take the warning, they are already untrue to the duties freedom prescribes.

The two safeguards on which democracy must rely are law and opinion. Laws, though they cannot cover all the cases in which the power of wealth is exerted against the public interest, and though strict proof may be wanting where the offence admits of little doubt, always render a service in providing a test and setting a standard by which men can recognize a temptation when it is presented to them. They help to keep the conscience of the people at a high level.

Public opinion is, however, even more important than law, since more flexible and able to reach cases not amenable to legal process. Opinion forms in public life that atmosphere which we call Tone and on whose purity the honour and worth of public life depend. Opinion is sometimes strangely lenient, with a standard purely conventional. The England of a century ago smiled at the candidate who gave a bribe, but despised the elector who took it. The habit was an old one, but so was the habit of duelling, so was the habit of intoxication, neither condemned by the code of custom. Those who conduct the affairs of a nation ought to be held to a standard of honour in some points higher and more delicate than any which law can set. Tone can decline as it declined at Rome, but it can also rise, as it rose among English politicians in the days of Chatham; and so has it

also risen in the United States since 1890, where modes of
gaining and using wealth once taken as part of the game are
now under the ban of opinion.   Money will always have
power, because the rich man has something to give which
others are glad to receive, so Power cannot be dissevered
from wealth so long as wealth exists.   All that democracy
can do is to watch its action with ceaseless attention, restraining its predatory habits, respecting its possessor only so far
as he devotes it to purposes beneficial to the community, and
regarding as " undesirable citizens " those who use it to gain
something from the public for their own benefit.

CHAPTER LXX

RESPONSIBILITY

Popular Government rests upon the principle that it is every citizen's business to see that the community is well governed. Each man, rich or poor, learned or ignorant, is alike bound to discharge his duty as a voter, or a representative, or an official, or a juryman, according to the measure of his powers. In this concentration of all the disinterested activity and wisdom the community possesses the strength of democracy was expected to lie.

Its weakness was long ago noted in the saying that What is everybody's business is nobody's business. In an oligarchy or a monarchy the few rulers have, because few, a comparatively strong and direct interest in seeing that State affairs are efficiently managed. The personal interest of an individual may sometimes override that of the privileged class, but the share of each member of that comparatively small class in whatever weal or woe befalls the community is larger than that of the citizen in a democracy. Where there are a hundred shareholders in a company each has more interest in the dividend than each has where there are a thousand. The citizen in a democracy of millions is prone to measure his own duty by his neighbour's, reducing his own obligations down to the level of the less conscientious, rather than raising them to the level of the most conscientious among his fellows. "Why," he thinks, "should I take more trouble about public affairs than I see my next-door neighbour do? He minds his own business and prospers; so will I. Let somebody else with more time to spare work for the public. The office-holders are paid to do it. I am not." He forgets that among those who profess to work for the public, office-holders and others, there will be many working for their personal interests only, perhaps to his detriment and that of the community.

The first and nearest duty of a citizen is to bear his part in selecting good men, honest and capable, to do the work needed by the community, and to make sure that they do it. In a small community like a little Swiss Canton or a New England Town this was a simple matter, because everybody knew everybody else and could see whether the work was being done or neglected, and if an officer neglected his work he was dismissed. A century ago the Town of Concord in Massachusetts met once a year, chose its Treasurer to gather and keep the scanty revenue, and its Road Superintendent, and its Hog Reeve — an office which local tradition says was discharged by Ralph Waldo Emerson. But when the work to be done for the State of Massachusetts or for the National Government of the United States had to be provided for, it became necessary to delegate the selection of officials and the supervision of their conduct to persons chosen for that purpose, *i.e.* representatives in an assembly, and these representatives again might have to delegate both selection and supervision to persons whom they appointed for those functions. Direct oversight by the citizens in Concord and the other Towns being impossible, there was constructed for the purpose machinery of securing wise choice and efficient oversight, a system of what is called a Frame of Government, representative and administrative, and one of its prime objects was to provide for all the citizens, as the ultimate rulers of the State, full means of knowing and judging how each part of the State's work was being done, carefully or negligently. Since they cannot personally oversee the work, they must know whether it is duly overseen by the persons appointed to this function, and whether these persons are in their turn watched and judged by those others placed above them, either official administrators or representatives, to whom has been entrusted the duty of overseeing the first set of overseers. There is thus created a chain of responsibility connecting every State employee of lower or higher rank with the People as the ultimate sovereign. If any link in this chain is weak, the right of the people to see that their work is duly carried out is infringed, and their power to secure efficient administration is reduced or destroyed. This is what we call the Principle of Responsibility, everywhere indispensable to good government. Each State servant, from a stoker at the furnace of a battleship up to the Secretary of the Navy, has his job, and is accountable to his immediate superior, who is in turn accountable to his superior, and so on. If his work, be it manual labour or direction and supervision, is done well, he is praised and continued or promoted. If it is ill done, he is warned or dismissed. Experience has shown that this principle, on which every private business is conducted, is the only guarantee of efficiency, for it relies on and uses motives common to all men. There are persons who work hard from a sense of duty. There are others who work hard because they like their job, and have an intellectual pleasure in seeing things well done. But far more numerous are those whose motives are chiefly self-regarding. They fear dismissal, they desire continuance or promotion. Fear, as well as whatever sense of duty they may have, helps them to resist temptation. Most people work better for the hope of some reward : everybody works better for knowing that he is watched and may suffer for default, for as an American philosopher has observed : True as it is that the wicked fleeth when no man pursueth, he makes better time when he knows that some one is after him. So let each State employee have his job. Let him be watched at his job. Let the watcher be himself watched to make sure that the watching is duly done, and let there be thus a line of responsibility all the way from the Minister at the one end to the weekly wage-earner at the other, so that when any fault is alleged to have been committed, there shall always be some one whose business it is to meet the charge, and the people shall always have some one to blame if the fault be proved.

In olden days the autocrat secured responsibility by Fear, which Montesquieu calls " the principle of Despotism," a sentiment echoed by a member of the French Convention when he said : " By Responsibility I mean Death." The people stand in the place of the monarch and must, in such a world as the present, rely upon Fear as well as Conscience to enforce Responsibility.[1]

---

[1] I quote this from a valuable little book by the late Mr. Arthur Sedgwick entitled *The Democratic Mistake.*

All this is common sense and common practice in commercial and industrial life, and so it is also inside any properly organized department of public administration. Every Frame of Government contemplates and purports to recognize it, but some Frames have failed to apply it thoroughly, and with unfortunate results. To understand these failures let us compare the arrangements already described (Chapter LXVII.), which exist in France and in the United States.

In France, as in England and in the British self-governing Dominions whose constitutions reproduce that of England, every member of the civil administration is responsible for the proper discharge of his duties to some superior in that department and ultimately to the Minister at the head of the department. The Minister is responsible to the legislative assembly, in which he sits and where he can be questioned in any matter relating to his department. If the explanation or defence he tenders for his own conduct or that of any of his subordinates is unsatisfactory, the assembly may express its disapproval, or demand an enquiry. If the matter is one of some consequence, and the Minister is censured, he resigns: if it is very serious and the Ministry as a whole support him, they will as a Cabinet resign.[1] This they will also do if their collective policy on any important subject is disapproved of by the Chamber of Deputies, since to it the Cabinet is responsible. The system works well inside each department, and pretty well as regards the relations between the Administration and the Legislature, though it sometimes happens that an error goes uncensured because nobody in the Chamber calls attention to it at the time, or because the majority in that body is unwilling to weaken the Ministry which it desires to keep in office,[2] and in that case the Chamber, by supporting the Administration, assumes a part of their responsibility. But the legislature is a large body, and the majority includes so many members that the share

[1] They may in Britain and the self-governing Dominions dissolve Parliament, but this course is infrequent and in France very rare.

[2] Upon one point there has been some difference of opinion and practice in the British House of Commons. Is it the duty of the Ministry to oppose bills brought in by private members of which they disapprove? In 1880 that duty was generally recognized. The House was deemed to be entitled to the advice of a Minister, and it was only he who could be

of each is small. Responsibility accordingly practically falls only to a small extent upon the members of the majority, and more fully on the Cabinet who are the leaders of the party. If the nation is displeased, it is primarily the Cabinet and secondarily its supporters in the Chamber that are the persons to be blamed.

To whom is the Chamber responsible? Only to the electors; and this responsibility can be enforced only at a general election. It is therefore possible for laws to be passed or executive action sanctioned by a vote of the representative assembly which the majority of the people would disapprove if they could be consulted. But as general elections cannot be ordered whenever a question as to the real wish of the people arises, this is an inevitable evil, the only remedy for which would be the taking of a Referendum as in Switzerland, or the Recall of members of the Legislature, as in some American States.[1]

Turn now to the United States. In its National or Federal Government the President is not responsible to the legislature, and his only responsibility to the people consists in the general approval or disapproval which his action evokes. Their favour is of course what every President strives to win for his party as well as for himself. But he cannot be practically deemed accountable for the incompetence or errors of his official subordinates, not even of that comparatively small number who belong to the higher grades, unless he has made so many unfortunate appointments as to discredit his capacity for selection. Nor are his Ministers responsible, for they are merely his servants, and do not sit in the Legislature. Committees of Congress may be appointed to investigate their conduct, but dismissal rests with the President only, and Congress cannot compel it. In

relied on to see that if it was a bad bill it should not go through because there was not enough resistance from non-official members to defeat it. Nowadays private members' bills have little chance of passing, so the question seldom arises, but it would seem that Ministries are less disposed to recognize and discharge their responsibility for stopping such bills if mischievous.

[1] As to Swiss administration and the position of the Federal Council, which, though responsible to the Chambers, differs otherwise from administrations in France and England, see Vol. I., chapters on Switzerland.

many branches of his duties he needs the help which Congress can render by legislation and by votes of money, but these he may be unable to obtain, for in one or other house of Congress the party opposed to him may hold a majority. Thus when things go wrong and the people complain, it is not clear who is at fault, for the President can throw the blame on Congress, and Congress on the President. Furthermore, the equality in legislative power of the two houses of Congress may make it difficult to fix upon either responsibility for the failure to legislate, since one party may hold a majority in the Senate while the other party holds it in the House. Add to this that the fate of most bills is decided in committees whose proceedings are not public, and it will be seen how hard it may be to apportion blame. Broadly speaking, and regarding only comparatively large issues, it is the political parties on whom responsibility can be most easily fixed. They can be punished by losing votes and seats at the next election, but individual culpability may escape any penalty except that which public displeasure inflicts on prominent figures.

Here the defect to be noted is the subdividing of responsibility till it almost disappears. In the several States of the Union another defect is visible. The chief officials of each State are, including the judges, not appointed by the Governor, as the Federal Ministers and judges are by the President. The wish to make these officials responsible dictated the assignment of their election to the people's vote, choosing them, as the Governor is chosen, for short terms, so that they may not forget their dependence on the people. They are not responsible either to the Governor or to the State Legislature, but to the people only, and in this sense only, that they may be rejected if they offer themselves for another term of office. This constitutional arrangement, adopted in order to recognize the sovereignty of the people and make the officials feel themselves directly accountable to the citizens, has had the exactly opposite effect. The people, having neither the knowledge required to select nor the time and knowledge needed to supervise these officials, have left the nomination of them to the party Organizations; each organization repays by a nomination those of its adherents

who have worked for it, and the candidates whom their party
carry at the elections owe their posts and their obedience to
it and not to the people.   So far as they safely can, they work
for the party, looking to it for renomination or some other
favour, and the party, so long as they are loyal, stands by
them if attacked.   Thus the plan which was meant to create
responsibility to the citizens has made such responsibility a
sham, while creating a real responsibility to the secret and
non-legal authority, the Organization or " Party Machine,"
which can reward or punish.   Inside that non-legal organization Responsibility is strictly enforced by a system of rewards
and punishments, so obedience and efficiency are secured.

The enforcement of Responsibility is a comparatively easy
thing in the sphere of administration where individual men
are concerned, and each has his specified work to do.   As in
a great manufacturing industry the foreman supervises the
workmen, and the head of each department supervises the
foremen, and the General Manager supervises the heads of
departments, and the Board of Directors, or proprietor,
supervises the General Manager, so in a government department the Minister, aided by the permanent secretary, can
keep everybody up to the mark by punishing default and
rewarding merit.   It is when bodies of men are concerned
that difficulties emerge.   A mob is dangerous because each
man in it feels that his own responsibility for a breach of the
law is lessened by the participation of many others.   A
representative assembly in which most men wait for some
one else to give a lead, each feeling that he will be blamed no
more than others for indolence or timidity, does not enforce
accountability on offenders so well as can an individual Minister, who knows that others are looking to him, and this is
especially true of the Minister in a monarchy or oligarchy
who has usually a freer hand as well as a more direct liability
to censure than any politician holding power by the favour
of an assembly can have.   Still more difficult is it to enforce
the responsibility of a representative assembly to the people.
The members are many; who can fix blame upon any in particular?   The people is a vast indeterminate body; who can
speak for it or get it to speak for itself?   This explains why
the trend of opinion in the United States has latterly been to

vest larger and larger powers in a State Governor and in the Mayor of a city or a very small Board. The citizens can watch him or them; they cannot so well watch a set of elected officials, or the aldermen in a municipal council. Like considerations have made thinking men tolerate party organizations, with all their defects. The Party is usually the only power that can be relied on to induce the people to inflict by their votes a penalty for misdoing, and upon the Parties some measure of responsibility can be fixed, for each has a motive for enforcing responsibility upon its opponents, and makes itself to some extent responsible if it fails in that enforcement. A " party in power " has a motive for avoiding gross scandals and maintaining a tolerable standard of competence in administration, because if offences are too flagrant, the people will rise and turn it out. A " party in opposition " has at least as strong a motive for detecting and exposing all the offences of the party in power whose fall will install it in office. Thus, whatever be the motives, the public interest is not wholly neglected, and abuses which might escape notice under a careless monarch or be hushed up by a selfish oligarchy have a chance of being corrected.

It remains true, nevertheless, that the enforcement of accountability on those appointed to serve the State is one of the abiding difficulties of democracy. Attempts have been made to control the member who represents a constituency in an assembly by exacting pledges and fettering him by instructions. Such a plan involves evils greater than those it could remove. Some American States have tried the experiment of giving to the citizens a power of ejecting from office, before the expiry of his term, an official or a representative, but reasons have already been given which dissuade this device of the so-called Recall. Experience has so far pointed out only one path worth following, that of making the way plain and simple by laying on the ordinary citizen only such tasks as he can be expected to perform. He cannot give much of his thought and attention to public affairs which for him come only in the third or fourth or fifth rank of his interests in life. To ask from him too much is to get from him too little. He can, however, concentrate his thoughts upon the election of a few men to do public work, and may try to watch these few, making each of them feel that he is being held responsible whether it be for what he does himself or for what he does in watching and directing others.   Keep the search-light steadily playing upon the few conspicuous figures, be it in a larger or a smaller area of government, in city or county, in State or nation, so that each person charged with public duties shall never forget that he has an account to render.

I have dwelt on this subject, familiar as it is, because the neglect to fix responsibility has been one of the most fertile sources of trouble in popular governments.   There is no better test of the value of institutions than the provisions they contain for fixing and enforcing it upon every one who serves the State.

CHAPTER LXXI

DEMOCRACY AND THE BACKWARD RACES

THREE causes have in our time set a new problem for Democracy by raising the question of its applicability to backward peoples. We see attempts made to create among races which, whether we call them civilized or semi-civilized, have had no practical experience of any but autocratic control, some form of popular government. Democracy which has been a natural growth in the civilized countries that now enjoy it, will in these despotically ruled countries be an artificial creation, built upon ideas brought in from outside, unfamiliar to all but the educated few, unintelligible to the masses.

The first of these causes is the contact, closer than ever before, which now exists between the more Advanced and the more Backward families of mankind.

The second is the immense influence and authority exercised by the Advanced Races over the minds of the Backward, an influence chiefly due to the development among the former of the sciences of nature in their application both to war and to the economic needs of life.

The third is the passion for Equality, civil and political, economic and social, which, having grown strong among the Advanced peoples, has not only spread among the more educated part — everywhere a tiny part — of the Backward peoples, but has disposed the Advanced to favour its sudden extension to the Backward through the creation of institutions similar to those which had slowly developed themselves among the Advanced. This love of equality is not found in Europeans who live among coloured races, who, so far from treating the latter as equals, generally contemn and exploit them. But human equality has become a dogma, almost a faith, with a majority of those who, dwelling in Europe, have no direct knowledge of the races to whom their theoretic sympathy goes out.

The subject has recently acquired a new and possibly disquieting significance. That military as well as intellectual predominance which the nations of Europe have held in the world since the battle of Salamis [1] may be threatened. The fierce rivalries of these nations, culminating in the war of 1914, and the internal strife by which each of them is now torn, have so reduced both the resources and the prestige of Europe as to disturb the balance between it and the Backward peoples of the Old World. Should the latter succeed in appropriating and learning to use the forces which scientific discovery places at the disposal of all peoples alike, Europe may one day have reason to rejoice that so many of her children have occupied the Western hemisphere. Thus it is now something more than speculative curiosity that leads us to consider what political developments may be in store for those Asiatics whom the Advanced races have been wont to regard with disdain. The problem has taken different forms in different countries. India has been governed by the British on lines necessarily despotic, though the despotism has long been more well meaning and disinterested than any one people had ever before exercised over others. Despotism would probably have continued but for the desire expressed by that extremely small section of the Indian population which has been instructed in British principles of government to see those principles applied in their own country, and to be permitted to share in its administration. This wish Britain has now set itself to meet. In the Southern States of the North American Union the extinction of negro slavery was followed by the over hasty grant of full political as well as private civil rights to the emancipated slaves. The suffrage has been gradually withdrawn from the large majority of the coloured people of the South, but a minority are still permitted to vote, and much controversy has arisen as to their moral claim and their fitness. In the Philippine Islands the United States Government, after conquering them from Spain in 1898–99, was faced with the difficulty of reconciling its rule with the doctrines of the Declaration of In-

[1] With a few brief interruptions, the latest nearly four centuries ago.

dependence.   In Egypt a demand is heard for the creation
of self-governing institutions under the sultanate set up by
European arms.   In Central and South America the colonial subjects of Spain, when they threw off her yoke a century
ago, formed republics in whose constitutions legal distinctions as respects political rights have not been generally made
between the Europeans and Mestizos (the mixed race) on the
one hand, and the aboriginal races on the other, although the
latter, who in most of these States constituted the large majority, were entirely devoid of the knowledge and the experience required for the exercise of the suffrage.   In these last-
mentioned cases supreme control has practically remained
with the educated class of European (or, to a less extent, of
mixed) stock, so the institutions set up have continued to
work, however imperfectly.   But to-day we see other cases
which raise the problem on a vaster scale and in a novel
way.   Not to speak of the farcical attempts to create parliamentary government in Turkey, or of the similar attempt
in Persia, which has fared little better, two vast countries
have proclaimed republican governments, intended to be
something more than shams, among populations which foreign observers had assumed to be absolutely unfitted for any
but an autocratic government.   In China the Manchu dynasty was overthrown by a few students, educated at American or Japanese universities, who, profiting by the incapacity of the Central imperial government and its failure to
quell local insurrections, set up a republic, there being no
person fit to mount the vacant throne.   A republic has continued to exist in name, not because the nation desired it,
but because the old dynasty had lost its hold, and no man
arose strong enough to obtain general obedience over an
enormous territory.[1]   In Russia the contempt aroused
among the educated classes by the folly and feebleness of the
Tsardom and the turpitude of its Ministers led to its sudden collapse; and control passed, after some months of inef-
fectual struggles by the moderate reformers, into the hands of

[1] Yuan Shi Kai's attempt to make himself Emperor seems to have
failed because as a new man he was unable to command the sort of religious awe which had consecrated the throne till its weakness forfeited
respect.

self-appointed revolutionary Committees, while the millions of ignorant peasants were left in a welter of anarchy, soon superseded by a ruthless tyranny.

All these cases, otherwise widely dissimilar, have one common feature. Each is an attempt to plant institutions, more or less democratic, in a soil not prepared for them either by education in political principles or by the habits of constitutional government. The races or nations summoned to work those institutions did not understand them in theory, and had never tried them in practice. Everywhere else the self-governing institutions that have grown up among the peoples now using them are suited to their ideas and habits, while in these backward countries they were thrust upon men, the vast majority of whom, ceasing to care for the old things, neither knew nor cared anything about the new.[1]

Here is the real difficulty. It is said, with truth, that knowledge and experience as well as intelligence are needed to fit a people for free self-government. But a still graver defect than the want of experience is the want of the desire for self-government in the mass of the nation. When a people allow an old-established government like that of the Tsars or the Manchus to be overthrown, it is because they resent its oppressions or despise its incompetence. But this does not mean that they wish to govern themselves. As a rule, that which the mass of any people desires is not to govern itself but to be well governed. So when free institutions are forced on a people who have not spontaneously called for them, they come as something not only unfamiliar but artificial. They do not naturally and promptly engage popular interest and sympathy but are regarded with an indifference which lets them fall into the hands of those who seek to use the machinery of government for their own purposes. It is as if one should set a child to

---

[1] The four new monarchies of South-Eastern Europe formed between 1829 and 1878 (for Montenegro was already independent) out of the ruins of the Turkish Empire in Europe are also instances in which constitutional self-government was bestowed upon peoples just delivered from a barbarous despotism. But in all of them the mass of the people, unprepared as each was to work a constitution, had at least actively desired freedom and had made efforts to gain it from rulers who were incapable and corrupt, as well as alien in race, faith, and speech.

drive a motor car. Wherever self-government has worked well, it is because men have fought for it and valued it as a thing they had won for themselves, feeling it to be the true remedy for misgovernment.

Some of the experiments that are now being tried might have been better left untried. But as they are being tried, let us consider what are the conditions and what the methods that will give them the best chance of success. Something depends on local facts, something on racial quality. It is easier to set up self-governing institutions in a country no larger than Switzerland or Bulgaria than in a huge country like Russia or China, where the people of one region know nothing about the leading men of another, and few know more than the names even of the most prominent national figures. Social structure is an important factor. Where men are divided by language, or by religion, or by caste distinctions grounded on race or on occupation, there are grounds for mutual distrust and animosity which make it hard for them to act together or for each section to recognize equal rights in the other. Homogeneity, though it may not avert class wars, helps each class of the community to understand the mind of the others, and can create a general opinion in a nation. A population of a bold and self-reliant character is more fitted to work free institutions than is one long accustomed to passive and unreasoning obedience. Men cool of temper, slow and solid in their way of thinking, are better than those who are hasty, impressionable, passionate; for the habit of resorting to violence is one of the prime difficulties in the orderly working of political institutions, as any one will admit who recalls the sanguine expectations entertained half a century ago, and compares them with the facts of to-day in nearly every free country. Swift wits and a lively imagination are not necessarily an advantage in this sphere. Education, that is to say the education given by schools and books, signifies less than we like to think. Native shrewdness and the willingness to make a compromise instead of yielding to impulses and pushing claims of right to extremes are more profitable.

The glib talk, common in our time, which suggests that education will solve the problems of China and Russia, of

Mexico and Persia misleads us by its overestimate of the value of reading and writing for the purposes of politics. Illiterate peoples have before now worked free institutions, or at any rate institutions which, being conformable to their wishes, were not oppressive, successfully enough to secure tolerable order and contentment, to enforce the rule of customary law and maintain both the solidarity of the community against external attack and a fair measure of domestic contentment.   The small self-governing groups of Norway and of Iceland in the tenth century had a kind of free government which perfectly suited them, with a strong or rich prominent man and a popular assembly for the central authority of each.   In the islands of the South Pacific Ocean, at the other end of the world, the chiefs were leaders in war and administered a rude justice, but their rule was controlled by public opinion almost as effectively as if there had been an assembly.   The people were satisfied.   All went well, because wants were few, the conditions of life simple, the areas so small that every one was virtually responsible to his neighbours, even the chief to his tribesmen.   The Basutos of South Africa are almost as much below the Tahitians as the Tahitians were below the Norsemen of Iceland, yet the Basutos have public assemblies which exercise some control over the chiefs and express the will of the nation.

So much for general considerations.   Let us, however, turn back to history, our only guide, and see what light on the prospects of self-government in Backward races can be derived from a study of the process by which popular governments have been developed in the past among the European peoples whose forefathers stood once where those races stand now.

The process has been a slow one, except in those few spots where small communities, protected from conquest or absorption by the inaccessibility of their dwelling-place, were able to retain a primitive equality and independence.[1]   Elsewhere there has been, usually with much fighting, a gradual

[1] The Valley of Andorra in the Pyrenees, where a little rural republic called officially the " Vallées et Suzeraintés," has existed since the days of Charlemagne, is a familiar example. Like San Marino and some of the oldest Swiss Cantons, it is a survival of the many small

wresting of freedom from the hands of local magnates, feudal lords, or bishops, or city oligarchies. It was the desire to escape from tangible grievances that prompted the struggle. Abstract doctrine and the love of independence for its own sake came later, when personal injuries and insults, or oppressive imposts, or the attempt to compel religious observances, had already roused the spirit of resistance. If the ruler, whether a monarch or an oligarchic group, had the prudence to abate the grievances, trouble would generally subside till some fresh abuses arose. Men who had been accustomed to be tolerably governed were willing to go on being governed in the same way, until new exactions enforced or new hardships suffered provoked them to claim for themselves a power whose abuse by others they were beginning to resent. The outburst which overthrew a tyranny did not necessarily create the love of self-government, which is by no means a natural growth in all soils, but was rather a child of circumstance, appearing spontaneously in small and isolated communities, and in others growing up because economic changes sapped the power of a ruling class. There must be also a sense that it is only self-government which can permanently cure the ills complained of. Revolts were usually led by persons prominent by their social position or their restless spirit, who, feeling insult or oppression more keenly, had something to gain by upsetting the powers that be, while the average man, too much occupied with making his daily livelihood to care about what did not directly concern him, desired to get back to his accustomed round of life as soon as the grievances were reduced. That which all insurgents had in common was to establish the primary right of the subject to security of life and property and be relieved from harsh exactions.

The first stage towards freedom was marked by the concession of these rights. The next was to provide means for their defence against any return of oppression. This meant self-government; and the effort to win it, unsuccessful in some countries, succeeded best in populations where the habit of joint action already existed; because groups linked to-

self-governing communities that once existed in Southern and Western Europe, itself a league of five tiny communes. Visiting it in 1873 I found the head of the State, a stalwart old peasant, in a red flannel shirt, thrashing out his corn.

gether, either by economic interests or religious feeling or tribal relationship, were better fitted for political freedom than others where the individual man, leading his own life in his own way, had little sense of obligation to his fellows. Self-government rests on the habit of co-operation, which implies the finding of capable and trustworthy leaders. Political leadership naturally grew out of social leadership, but the social importance of rank or wealth or any other kind of power (such as ecclesiastical office) was qualified or supplemented by the personal talent and energy of men without these advantages who sprang from the humbler class, and thus the ascendancy of rank was broken, another step towards freedom, and a means of bringing different strata of the people into closer touch with one another. Thus there came into being both a Frame, at first rudimentary, of constitutional government together with a set of persons fit to work it, and as the Frame developed, the extension of a share in government to the masses became only a question of time.

Let us see what help a consideration of these facts can afford to those who seek to create some kind of free self-government in peoples hitherto without it. Nature must be the guide, for it is by following or imitating the natural processes whereby the peoples now free obtained their freedom that the peoples hitherto unfree can hope to advance most steadily.

History, the record of these processes, suggests that one of the first things to be done is to secure for every man the primary right of protection against arbitrary power. His life, his personal safety, his property must be secured, the imposts laid on him must not be excessive nor arbitrary. When co-operation in the work of protecting and managing the affairs of the community is being organized, every actually existing kind of local self-government, however small its range, ought to be turned to account. Every social or economic grouping, every bond which gathers men into a community helps to form the habit of joint action and that sense of a duty to others which is the primal bond of civic life. If any existing local or social unit is fit to be turned into an organ of local self-government it ought to be so used. If there is none such, then such an organ must be created and entrusted with some control of those matters in which a neighbourhood has a common interest.

Small areas are better than large areas, because in the former men can know one another, learn to trust one another, reach a sound judgment on the affairs that directly concern them, fix responsibility and enforce it. Even family jealousies and religious enmities may subside when the questions touch the pecuniary interests of the neighbourhood. The older rural Cantons of Switzerland show what self-government in a small community can do for forming political aptitude, and the same lesson is taught by the tithings and hundreds of early England and by the Towns of early Massachusetts and Connecticut. The examples of these three countries suggest the value of primary meetings of the people in these small areas. The Folk Mot of Old England, the Town meeting of New England, the Thing of the Norsemen were the beginning of freedom.

Political institutions ought to be framed with careful regard to social conditions, for much depends on the relations of the more educated class with the masses, and the influence they can exert on the choice of representatives.[1] The people must have due means for choosing as leaders, be they officials or representatives, those they can trust; but if these posts go by free popular choice to the " natural leaders " in any community, small or large, so much the better, for they have more of a character to lose than has the average man. Leaders who have their own aims to serve may misrepresent mass sentiment, or may call for self-government only because they desire to make their own profit out of it. The more ignorant and inexperienced is the multitude, so much the more will power fall to a few, and the main aim must be to see that the latter are prevented from abusing it for personal or class purposes, and turning an attempted democracy into a selfish oligarchy.

The question of the suffrage by which persons are to be chosen for public functions, local or national, must depend on the conditions of each country. Those who hold the

---

[1] The " Intelligentsia " in Russia, the " Cientificos " in Mexico were too few to exert this influence. Even apart from their other deficiencies, there were not enough of them to form a public opinion, enabling them to hold their ground without an armed force.

right of suffrage to be a Natural Right, inherent in every human being, may feel bound to grant universal suffrage everywhere, but they can hardly expect that with the gift the power to use it wisely will descend by some supernatural grace upon the hill tribes of India, the Yakuts of Siberia, and the Zapotecs of Mexico. Nature does not teach the methods of constitutional government to an Egyptian fellah, any more than it teaches a Tuareg of the Sahara to swim when he first sees the Nile. Common sense does indeed suggest to him that he should vote for some one he knows and respects personally, but if the electoral area be large there will probably be none such among the candidates. As a wide suffrage gives advantages to the rich man and the demagogue, while a limited suffrage means the rule of a class, some have suggested the plan of allowing a local organ of self-government, whose members have been elected on a comparatively wide suffrage in a small area, to send its delegate to an assembly for a larger area, which will thus consist of persons of presumably superior competence.

Any frame of government must secure the responsibility of legislators and officials to the people, but responsibility presupposes publicity, and how is publicity as respects the conduct of officials and legislators to be secured in countries like China or Russia? Difficulties arise where there are differences of religion, especially if ecclesiastics have power at their command, but it so happens that this sort of power does not count for much in serious affairs among Hindus, Buddhists, or Muslims, though fanaticism is sometimes a source of danger. Political parties when they arise will doubtless make it their business to note and denounce every error of their opponents, but how can the multitude judge the truth of partisan charges as it could in times when the functions of government were few and the areas of self-government comparatively small? The populations of the countries we are considering are enormous, while to break them up into manageable political areas would run counter to those forces which have tended to unify and improve administration and to facilitate the intercourse of members of the same nation for commerce, for education, and for other kinds of intellectual and moral development. Liberty and self-government grew up in comparatively small and homogeneous populations. India, China, and Siberia are vast countries inhabited by diverse races in very different stages of civilization.

Among the dangers against which the institutions to be created among peoples devoid of constitutional experience must provide, three specially need to be guarded against.

One is the aggression of ambitious neighbour States. Could a Chinese republic, which has so far been able to assert only a precarious and intermittent authority in the Southern and Western provinces, defend itself against Japan, or a Russian republic defend itself against an intriguing neighbour? International guarantees would seem needed, but these have sometimes proved to be broken reeds. The new League of Nations may perhaps prove more effective.

Another is the maintenance of internal order. The old monarchies, though they had regular armies and the prestige of long-established authority, often failed to do this, and the difficulty will be greater in a people which, told to govern itself, has not yet learned that the constitutional scheme adopted must be supported. A government which has not stood long enough to inspire fear or acquire respect needs a strong army at its back, yet an army is a temptation to the Executive that commands it. Internal troubles subside when constitutional methods have become rooted in the minds of the people, but the process of subsidence may take centuries.

A third peril is the exploitation of the poorer classes by the stronger. If a restricted suffrage confines political power to the wealthier and more educated part of the people, because the ignorant are confessedly unfit to exercise it, the ruling section is likely to legislate and administer for their own benefit and oppress those beneath them. Were India governed by assemblies in the hands of the landowning and monied sections the ryots would be worse off than under the oversight of British officials, and similarly the native peons of Mexico would fare ill if left at the mercy of the landowners.

A fourth evil would be the corrupt abuse of their functions by officials and legislators, an evil frequent in many countries, but specially formidable where it has long permeated the ruling class.[1] In China that class was intellectually able, thanks largely to the peculiar institution of a mandarinate recruited from the ranks of those who had, under the old system, won their spurs at the examinations in verse-composition, but peculation and " the squeeze " had pervaded it under the successive dynasties which have reigned for uncounted ages. Not dissimilar are the phenomena of Russia and the risks that await her. Under the autocracy of the Tsars talent sometimes rose, but seldom had the masses the means of learning to recognize and honour either talent or virtue. When the Tsardom collapsed few men whom the nation could follow were ready to take its place, and the official class in which low standards of honour and public spirit had prevailed, shared the discredit into which the autocracy had fallen.

To give more concrete reality to these general observations, let us look more closely at the particular countries concerned, and see what foundations exist in each of them on which self-government could be built.

Europe has been wont to think of the Chinese as semi-civilized. It might be truer to say that they are highly civilized in some respects and barely civilized in others. They are orderly and intelligent. They have admirable artistic gifts. Many possess great literary talent, many observe a moral standard as high as that of the ancient Stoics. On the other hand, they set a low value on human life; their punishments are extremely cruel; corruption is general among officials, the most primitive superstitions govern the conduct of the immense majority. Diviners determine the exact spot in which a house ought to be built so as to enjoy the best influences proceeding from the unseen world, for a child born in a dwelling favourably located will be likely to become a mandarin, while another situation will give him a chance of winning fame as a poet. Walls or wooden screens are placed opposite a door or gate so as to prevent malign spirits from entering the house, because these beings can fly only in a straight line, making neither curve nor zigzag. Such a juxtaposition of highly cultivated minds with beliefs that elsewhere linger only in savage races is

[1] This malady is said to have already broken out in a virulent form in some of the new States recently established in Europe.

among the strangest of the phenomena that startle a traveller in China. But in some ways China furnishes no unpromising field for an experiment in popular government. Its people have five sterling qualities — Industry, independence of character, a respect for settled order, a sense of what moral duty means, a deference to intellectual eminence. They have the power of working together; they can restrain their feelings and impulses; they are highly intelligent and amenable to reason. Weak as they have seemed to be in international affairs, they have plenty of national pride and a sort of patriotism, though it does not flow into military channels. What one may call the raw material for popular government is not wanting, but unfortunately there have existed few institutions that can be turned to account for the purpose. The smallest unit is the village, ruled by the heads of the chief families, usually with one Headman, to whom any orders of government are addressed. So late as 1913 there was no larger rural area possessing any self-government, and the cities were ruled by officials appointed by the Governor of the province, who is himself appointed by Peking. More recently Provincial Assemblies consisting of popularly elected delegates from the districts have been created in some Provinces. These bodies advise the provincial Governor, who has hitherto been appointed by the central government, and been responsible to it only.[1] Thus a beginning, promising so far as it goes, has been made. It is for those who know China intimately to judge how far the system can be applied to cities and minor rural areas. One can imagine councils in cities, and a district council for a large subdivision of a province, which might be composed of delegates from the villages. The constitution-makers have assumed a Central Parliament for the whole country. But whoever considers the immense size of China, and the differences in language and custom between the provinces, and the strength of provincial feeling, may think that what is wanted is a sort of federal system, most of the functions of government being assigned to provincial assemblies and officials, with

[1] I learn from Sir John Jordan, late British Minister at Peking, and probably the highest living European authority on Chinese politics and character, that when he visited the Provisional Council in the province of Shan Si in 1918 he was favourably impressed by its working and by the useful relations between it and the Governor.

those only reserved to the Central Parliament which must be uniform in their action for the whole country, and provide for its common interests as respects commerce and national defence. It is an evidence of the practical sense and law-abiding quality [1] of the Chinese that though there has been a sort of intermittent civil war, more or less acute in different regions, ever since the fall of the Manchu dynasty in 1911, and though robber bands have sometimes ravaged the Western provinces, there was comparatively little disorder over the country as a whole. Internal trade continued, the steamers plied on the rivers, trains ran much as usual, the customs and salt-tax were collected under European supervision and the proceeds remitted to the capital.

A monarchy would probably suit China better than a republic, because the traditional habit of obeying the sacred autocrat has been hallowed by long tradition, and the veneration paid to him, which was paid to his Office, not to the dynasty, might have been passed over to a new hereditary constitutional sovereign. The only reason why there is a republic is because the tiny group of revolutionaries who, taking advantage of local risings, upset the Manchu throne, had learnt in American and Japanese Universities to deem the name Republic to be the badge of freedom, the latest word in political progress. At present obedience is enforceable only by the sword, because there is no power on which the mantle of reverence that clothed the old Empire has descended.

The prospects for popular government in Persia and in Mexico are dark.

Persia, with a long and brilliant record of literary achievement, and with the power of still producing remarkable religious leaders, is now, if not a decadent, yet a disordered and even disorganized nation, where there seems to be no firm soil on which to erect any constitutional government. The representative assembly created at the revolution of 1906 failed to work, and soon fell into contempt, while the Executive was hopelessly weak, tossed on the waves of turbulence

---

[1] It might be more correct to say " custom-abiding," for there is very little law, in the European sense of the word, in China, though well-established authority is usually obeyed, and well-settled usage almost always followed. Collections of Ordinances exist, but seem to be seldom used.

and intrigue. Left to itself, the country would probably fall
to pieces, or pass under the power of some leader of one of
the warlike tribes, fit to replace the enfeebled Kajar dynasty.
Had Russia been the only foreign power concerned, she
might well have virtually annexed the country before 1914.
At present it furnishes a striking instance of the impossi-
bility of establishing democratic institutions where there is
no Executive strong enough to guide, or carry out the will of
a popular Assembly. Were it possible to find any foreign
power willing to set up and direct such an Executive in a
disinterested spirit [1] such an expedient would offer the best
prospect of rescuing an ancient and famous people.

In Mexico, of which I have spoken in a previous chapter,[2]
an economic and social regeneration is called for as the necessary preparation for any kind of stable free government.
Porfirio Diaz, a statesman as well as a soldier, maintained
order and did much for economic development, but for educational and moral progress and for the welfare of the aborigines, nearly all of whom are either agricultural serfs or semi-
civilized tribes, little was attempted, while the very small
educated class, the so-called " Cientificos," were too few, too
much occupied with their own interests, and too little in
touch with the masses, to exert a reforming or enlightening
influence. The examples of Argentina and Uruguay show
that had a rule like his lasted for another half century the
country might have become rich enough to make settled government possible, because a large class, interested in the development of industry and commerce, would have arisen.
As things are now, a democratic constitution would probably
prove just as unworkable in practice as any of the constitutions that have been enacted during the century of independence. When elections were held under Diaz, ballot-boxes
were placed in the public squares, but so few voters appeared
to drop ballots into them that the local Colonel usually sent
a squad of soldiers towards evening with orders to cast into
the boxes the voting-papers which had been served out to
them. This indifference was due not merely to the sense
that the President was a dictator, but to the total want of
interest in the whole matter on the part of the population,

[1] As for instance under a mandate from the League of Nations.
[2] See Vol. I. Chap. XVII.

who desired nothing except tranquillity and amusements. For such a country the choice is at present — of the future one need not despair — a choice between oligarchy and a succession of short anarchies, each ending in a tyranny.

Of India I will not speak, because an experiment of the utmost interest is now being tried there under an Act of the British Parliament passed in 1920, the results of which may before long throw much light on the problem it is meant to solve. Under the guiding hand of the British Government, to which some departments of administration have been prudently reserved, good hopes for at least a partial solution may be formed. In Egypt there is a prospect that a somewhat similar effort will be made to create self-governing institutions, with the advantage that the population is fairly homogeneous and has learnt, since the deposition of the Khedive Ismail, to realize the value of an honest administration and impartial Courts of Justice. As to Russia, the events of the last few years have given evidence, if indeed evidence was needed, that a vast multitude of ignorant peasants is ill fitted to work the complicated machinery of a democratic government; but as the recollections of the system by which the Village Community managed its land have not yet vanished, there may be a chance of creating a scheme of local self-government in small rural areas and reconstructing the Zemstvos in larger areas to form a basis on which representative institutions may be erected, so soon as a strong Central Executive which the people can trust has replaced the present irresponsible tyranny.

The vital fact to be noted in all these cases is that in none of them has the demand for free institutions come from the masses of the people, though it is by them that those institutions would have to be worked, or even from any considerable section of those masses. The principles of democracy may be brought from the United States or Europe and scattered like seed, but it is only in soil already fertilized by European influences that they will take root; and even the few who understand them lack the skill to apply them. The group of Marxian Communists who seized control of the revolutionary movement in Russia, and the republican theorists who compose what is still called the Parliament of China have in neither country had more than a trifling following of convinced supporters.[1] The success which the former attained was due not to the good will of the peasants but to their war weariness and their desire to appropriate the land. The latter, once the Manchu dynasty was gone, lost control of events. That passed to those who could get money to pay the troops.

Let me now try to state the substance of views given to me by experienced observers in the countries above referred to, together with those of students of history whose opinions on the problem I have sought, men who, while they feel that change must come, and are not hopeful of its results, counsel wariness and patience in every effort to apply democratic principles among peoples hitherto ruled by arbitrary governments. I will summarize their views in a statement of the case for doubt and caution:

" Eighteenth-century philosophers who drew from the reports of travellers the material for their speculations upon the natural capacities of man did not greatly overestimate the possibilities of free government among unsophisticated men in small communities, where wants were few and conditions nearly equal. What is needed for the success of such government is the co-existence of a sense of personal independence with a spirit of intelligent co-operation in common affairs, the latter implying a willingness to obey the generally accepted authority, be it that of the chieftain or of the public gathering. Public opinion is strong in such a community, and gives a security for the rights of its members. There is not much for government to do except settle disputes (including blood fines), summon men to follow the leader in war, and manage the common land, pasture or forest. This is possible for administrative purposes where life is simple and social groups are small, possible also in a semi-nomad tribal system in which each community has little to do with any other except by way of tribal wars. Most of Arabia and Mesopotamia are in this condition, and civilized Powers might do well to leave the Sheiks alone, and let them raid one another, since that is the life they enjoy. When the

[1] I do not mean to disparage the intellectual quality of the Parliament of China, which seemed, when I saw it at work in 1913, to contain many alert and earnest young men, but it had no power at its command and no hold on the people.

question is of a population as large as was that of ancient
Egypt or Assyria, still more as that of modern China (or
even a province of China) or Russia, everything is different.
To break up vast populations into manageable political areas
would be to run counter to those forces which have been tending to unify peoples industrially and facilitate intercourse
not only for commercial purposes but for those also of education and various forms of intellectual development. Civilization has created countless needs and tasks of legislation and
administration. Large revenues are needed, much science,
many officials. Moreover, money is to be made out of government work as well as spent upon it. Many prizes bring
many temptations. Few of the people have any means of
knowing personally the officials or representatives who conduct their business. To watch them so as to gauge their ability and honesty, and to evaluate the technical side of their
work needs a capacity and experience beyond that of the average citizen. In India the difficulty may be reduced, for
there the guiding power of the British Government, as in the
Philippines that of the American Government, can retain
(at least for a time) those branches of administration which
require most technical skill or afford the largest opportunities
for malversation, and it can see that the work is properly
done. But how can the ability to watch and judge be expected from an untutored multitude in Russia or Egypt?
They must be guided by leaders belonging to the small educated class who have interests of their own to serve: how are
they to judge which of these leaders they should trust, that
being the judgment democracy expects from those to whom
it commits the power of ruling by their votes, though the only
judgment they are qualified to form is whether their own
grievances are being redressed and their own desires satisfied? In old days, as the body of the people slowly gained
control of government in a country like England, they grew
up to its tasks. Of them it could then be said, ' As thy day
is, so shall thy strength be.' Political institutions were the
machinery they made for themselves; and in making it they
learnt how to work it. It became more and more complex;
but increasing experience taught them how to handle it.
How different is the plight of inexperienced masses suddenly
called upon to work the vast and elaborate organization of a

great modern State, and that, too, without the help of the
officials who used to administer it, because these may, as in
Russia, be distrusted and rejected!   It is like delivering up
an ocean steamer to be navigated by cabin boys through the
fogs and icebergs of the Atlantic.   In such circumstances may
not the attempt to create democracy end in the creation of an
oligarchy unredeemed by the traditions and sense of social responsibility which imposed some check on the oppressions
often practised by European aristocracies in former centuries?

" What then is the use of giving democratic institutions to
those who neither desire the gift nor know how to use it?
Better let the people have what they understand, a national
monarchy or even an oligarchy under the name of a monarchy.   In China, Persia, Mexico, and Russia, apparently even
in Egypt, there exists a genuine national sentiment.   Respect it and let no foreign government dominate the country.
There are practical grievances, among them monstrous corruption in China, flagrant disorder as well as corruption in
Persia and Mexico.   Provide means whereby the people
can state and press for the removal of their grievances.
If the educated class desire opportunities for their careers,
let these be afforded.   This much can well be attempted without the complicated machinery of a representative democracy,
machinery which is sure to be perverted, because the people
have no means of restraining those who will seek to turn it
to their own ends.   You cannot build upon shifting sand,
nor effect by a single sudden stroke what in other countries
it has taken centuries of struggle and training to accomplish.   Neither individual men nor nations change their na-
tures at one swoop.   In the moral sphere there are doubtless
such things as Conversions, when some one, repenting of and
confessing his sins, renounces them under the influence of a
strong religious impulse.   Emotion can accomplish that.
So, too, emotion may string up a sluggish people to a forceful if only momentary activity.   But it can enable neither a
man nor a people to assimilate knowledge, to form new
habits of thinking, to work the complicated machinery of
institutions.   Precious for the battlefield and for religious
propaganda, it is unprofitable for the labours of administration or legislation.   By all means begin the work of fitting
the multitudes for self-government, but do it by slow degrees,

following as far as possible the process by which Nature worked during the centuries in which the free peoples of to-day made their gradual advance."

The case for doubt or caution which I have here stated is, however, not the whole case. Other considerations have to be regarded. Though lions stand in the path which leads the Backward peoples towards democracy, the movement has begun, and dread of the lions will hardly arrest it. The advocates of change point to facts which in our time qualify the application of arguments drawn from the past. They point to Japan. They cite the Philippine Isles where American administration has started a sort of legislative body which has been giving good results. Grounds for hope may be found in the earlier examples set long ago by the peoples that are now free and civilized which overcame difficulties as great as those which we see in China or Egypt. True it is that example has not the value of experience; it is their own direct experience that counts for nations as for individual men; yet it is also true that whereas the teaching of experience often comes too late for the individual to profit by it, each generation of a people can in the long span of national life go on learning from the successes or errors of its own ancestors. Errors and misfortunes there are sure to be, but so long as a nation is not enslaved or absorbed by a stronger neighbour, failures are rarely irretrievable; and one of the values of self-government lies in the fact that misfortunes bring knowledge and knowledge helps to wisdom, whereas under even a benevolent autocracy, the education of a people proceeds slowly if it proceeds at all. This is why the ancients held Tyranny to be the worst kind of government. No gains compensate for the sufferings it inflicts. The only thing it creates is the will to destroy it and start afresh. To-day the nations we are considering are faced by accomplished facts. The ancient despotisms have fallen and as the social structure of which they were a part has decayed, it will be better to replace them, not by tyrannies resting on military force, but by governments possessing some kind of constitutional character out of which truly popular institutions may in the long course of time be developed.

It would be folly to set up full-blown democracy, but it may be possible to provide (*a*) Guarantees, enforceable by law, for the civil rights of the individual.

(*b*) Full opportunities to the masses for stating their grievances.

(*c*) Means for declaring the wishes of the masses upon questions falling within their own knowledge.

(*d*) Protection by international agreement against aggression or exploitation by the civilized Powers.

Among modern conditions and under the stimulus of ideas proceeding from the more advanced peoples, intellectual development proceeds faster than ever before. The influences playing on the mind and habits even of a backward race are now unceasing and pervasive. There is more moving to and fro, more curiosity, more thinking and reading. Changes which it would have needed a century to effect may now come in three or four decades. Superstitions and all else that is rooted in religion hold out longest; but the habits of deference and obedience to earthly powers can crumble fast, and as they crumble self-reliance grows. Thus the capacity for self-government may be in our time more quickly acquired than experience in the past would give ground for expecting.

Moreover — and this is the practically decisive fact — there is a logic of events. In India or Egypt or the Philippines, for instance, when a government has, directly or implicitly, raised expectations and awakened impatience, misgivings as to the fitness to receive a gift may have to yield to the demand for it. There are countries in which, seeing that the break up of an old system of government and an old set of beliefs threatens the approach of chaos, an effort must be made to find some institutions, however crude, which will hold society together. There are moments when it is safer to go forward than to stand still, wiser to confer institutions even if they are liable to be misused than to foment discontent by withholding them.

CHAPTER LXXII

THE RELATION OF DEMOCRACY TO LETTERS AND ARTS

THE question whether democratic government either favours or discourages the power of intellectual creation and the growth of a taste for letters, science, and art, lies rather outside the scope of this treatise, yet deserves to be considered by whoever attempts to estimate the value of democracy for the progress of mankind.

Two opposite theories have been advanced. The Liberal thinkers of the generation which saw the American and French Revolutions expected the democratic form of government to make for progress in the intellectual as well as in the moral sphere. In delivering men's minds from bondage and arousing their civic activities it would stimulate the free development of thought and give fuller play to individuality in philosophy and art. Every man and every type of opinion would be sure of a hearing. A public enlightened by freedom and delivered from caste prejudice would have a finer appreciation of truth and beauty. With the greater simplicity of manners and the independence of view which equality would bring, the moral standard would rise, and the honour formerly paid to rank be transferred to virtue, to intellectual eminence, and to disinterested service.

The other theory holds that political equality tends to depress individuality and originality, disparaging genius. Equality, making the will of the numerical majority supreme, produces uniformity, and uniformity produces monotony, and monotony ushers in a reign of dulness by bringing every one down to the level of the average man, whose beliefs and tastes impose the rules which few are bold enough to defy. If here and there a solitary voice is raised to challenge them, no one gives heed, because the principle that the majority is right, and whether right or wrong must be obeyed, has become an axiom. No tyranny is so crushing as the peaceful tyranny of a stolid and self-satisfied multitude, because against it there can be no insurrection. Grey and cheerless will be the world in which excellence excites suspicion, and the weight of numbers passes like a steam-roller over the souls of men.

Both of these doctrines suggest points of view for which much may be said, but they are à priori doctrines, based not on facts but on conjectures as to what may happen under certain political conditions which are assumed for the purposes of the argument to be the only conditions worth regarding. The sphere of speculation is boundless and conjectures worthless, because political conditions cannot be isolated from other influences at work. There is only one test applicable to speculations, that of setting them side by side with such facts as we possess, so if any positive conclusion is to be reached it must be by noting what history has to tell us about the influence which forms of government have in fact exerted on intellectual life, and especially on creative intellectual power.

The view that democracy develops mental activity seems drawn from the fact that such a development has often occurred in times of transition, when the old maxims and practices of arbitrary governments were being broken down. The apostles of liberty who assailed such governments were men of force and courage, eager and sanguine, inspired by their ideas, and living a life of strenuous enthusiasm, so they naturally supposed that the lively play of mind round all the subjects on which discussion, once prohibited, was now being opened to all, would continue. Freedom had won those blessings, freedom would retain them. It did not occur to them that combat is more inspiring than undisputed possession, and that the high ideals which have inspired one generation may, just because they have triumphed, lose their vivifying power for the next. A striking instance is afforded by comparing the heroes of the Italian Risorgimento (1820 to 1870) with the men of the succeeding generation. A reaction almost always follows on times of exaltation, human nature dropping back to its normal level with the discouragement of disappointed hopes.

Just as there is nothing to show that democracy has intensified intellectual life, neither are there facts to support the
view expressed by Robert Lowe in a once famous speech that
it is a "dull and level plain, in which every bush is a
tree." Plato, with all his moral censure for the government
of his own democratic Athens, does not accuse it of inducing
uniformity but rather of encouraging an undue license and
irregularity in thought and manners. Travellers who visited the United States between 1820 and 1860 were struck by
the universal devotion to material progress, and complained
that only in a few Boston coteries could intellectual interests be discerned. This prosperous democracy, they remarked, even some years later, shows not only an overweening confidence in itself, but an overestimate of material success, with a corresponding indifference to the things of the
mind. If the facts were so, the swift development of the
country's natural resources, occupying nearly all its energy,
furnished a sufficient explanation. America has now been a
democracy for a second and longer period, yet she shows to-
day a more vigorous and various intellectual life than was
that of sixty years ago. The tyranny of the majority which
disheartened Tocqueville in 1830 is not now visible except at
times of unusual strain, when national safety is supposed to
be endangered. In France, where democracy is only half a
century old, social equality is older, and though both have
alienated many men of fastidious taste, there are no signs of
dreary monotony or an oppressive intolerance in the realm
of thought. No one has been able to point to any instance in
which equality in political rights and equality in social conditions, where they have come naturally and have not been
imposed by State authority, display a tendency to induce uniformity of thought, or to prevent genius from making its
way, irrespective of the accidents of birth. But if a popular
government were to attempt to enforce economic and social
equality by compulsory methods, and if this were carried out,
as some have suggested, by allotting to each man, without regard to his own wishes and personal bent, his work and
whatever remuneration for it the State authority might fix,
individual initiative might wither away and thought be compelled to revolve in the limited circle which the State approved. Certain devotees of democracy have indeed argued

that a democratic government must, when once installed in power, inculcate its principles not only through instruction in the schools but also by forbidding any other doctrines to seduce the minds of the citizens, an interesting return to the attitude of the Spanish Inquisition. Whoever is absolutely sure that he is right is only a step away from persecution. To make true doctrines prevail becomes for him a duty.

If we ask under what kinds of government letters and art and science have flourished, history answers, Under all kinds. Among the Greeks, the great philosophers and the lyric poets came from oligarchic as well as from democratic cities. Short was the age of Athenian glory in poetry, and it ended many years before free government was extinguished in the Hellenic world. The most illustrious Roman writers in verse and prose wrote within a period of seventy years covered by the lives of Julius Caesar and Augustus, during which republican institutions were disappearing;[1] and of these only one was born in Rome. In mediaeval Europe, and especially in Italy, the thirteenth century stands out as that illumined by the largest number of famous names, and in the fourteenth and fifteenth Florence produced, in proportion to her population, far more than her share of the finest genius in literature as well as in art. The explanations that may be given of these phenomena cannot be drawn from political conditions. The same may be said of the age of Shakespeare and Bacon in England, and of the age of Louis Quatorze in France. Both were periods of exciting events, of growing enlightenment, and of great mental activity, but popular government had not been born. The group of poets that was the glory of England and Scotland during the last quarter of the eighteenth and the first quarter of the nineteenth century arose under an oligarchy, and were the harbingers rather than the harvest of political freedom. This holds true also of the German poets and scholars and philosophers from Goethe and Schiller, Lessing and Kant down to Heine, Ranke, and Mommsen. The merit

[1] Lucretius, Catullus, Horace, Virgil, Ovid, Propertius, Tibullus, Cicero, Sallust, Livy. After an interval, a second period of fifty years covers Seneca, Lucan, Statius, Tacitus, Juvenal, Martial.

credited to democracy of occasionally producing brilliant orators is counterbalanced by the flood of commonplace or
turgid rhetoric which it lets loose.   If we turn from literature to art it is still more evident that painting and sculp-
ture have flourished alike under kings and in republics.
Music, the most inscrutable of all the arts, seems to be quite
out of relation to the other intellectual movements of the
world, except possibly to those which feel the touch of religious emotion.[1]

The causes that determine the appearance of genius in any
branch of intellectual or artistic creation have never been determined, and are perhaps beyond discovery, but though we
cannot tell why persons of exceptional gifts have been born
more frequently in particular times or at particular spots
than at other times and in other places, there are some data
for determining the conditions under which genius best rip-
ens and produces the finest fruit.   Into this fascinating enquiry I must not enter, for a long historical digression would
be needed to render probable the theory I should have to propound.   Enough to say that history does not prove the conditions aforesaid to have been sensibly affected by forms of
government, except perhaps where rulers have (as in Spain
after Charles V.) set themselves sternly and steadily during
a long period of years to repress the expression of any opinions except those which they approved.   The movements of
intellectual and moral forces are so infinitely subtle and
intricate that any explanation drawn from a few external
facts is sure to be defective and likely to be misleading.   It
is a common habit to seek the solution of large social or historical problems in a single obvious cause.   Any sciolist
thinks he can explain the characters of individuals by saying
that such and such a one has the Celtic, or the Slavonic, or it
may be the Jewish strain: and similarly it is easy to attribute to their form of government the political and moral tendencies of a people.   But just as the race factor, important as
it is, cannot be isolated from the whole environment of a race
or an individual, so it is with forms of government.   History finds much less than is commonly fancied to connect

---

[1] Palestrina, coming in the days of the Catholic revival, is usually
taken as the typical instance.

them either with the creative genius of individuals or with the innermost beliefs and mental habits of nations.

More than thirty years ago James Russell Lowell wrote: " Democracy must show a capacity for producing not an higher average man, but the highest possible types of manhood in all its manifold varieties or it is a failure. No matter what it does for the body, if it does not in some sort satisfy that inextinguishable passion of the soul for something that lifts life away from prose, it is a failure. Unless it knows how to make itself gracious and winning, it is a failure. Has it done this? Is it doing this? or trying to do it?"

Few will maintain that democracy has approached any nearer to Lowell's ideal since his words were written. But did he not ask more from democracy than any form of government can be expected to give? The causes that raise or depress the spirit of man lie deeper.

The citizens of a democracy do, however, show certain traits which, whether or no due to the form of government they live under, find full expression in it. One of these is the self-confidence of the man who, feeling himself, because he has an equal share in voting at elections, to be as good as any one else, is disposed to think that he and his neighbours of the same class are qualified for most public posts, and who, if himself imperfectly educated, underestimates the value of knowledge and technical skill. Equality tends not only to reduce the deference due to superior attainments, but also to the older forms of politeness and the respect which used to be paid to official rank. In the seventeenth century the Dutch and the Swiss were, as republicans, charged with rough manners by the French, but manners were no less rough among burghers and peasants in the monarchical states of Germany, the difference being that those classes did not in the latter come into official contact with French critics. Broadly speaking, one finds to-day no more rudeness in democracies than under other governments, though some races have by nature more tact and courtesy than others.

The manners which offended Dickens and other European travellers in Western America eighty years ago were the fruit of the conditions of a society in a country still raw, and no such criticisms could now be made.

The spirit of equality is alleged to have diminished the respect children owe to parents, and the young to the old. This was noted by Plato in Athens. But surely the family relations depend much more on the social structure and religious ideas of a race than on forms of government. In no countries do we see age so much respected and young children so kindly treated as in China and Japan: the passing traveller notes their gaiety and apparent happiness. May not this be connected with the conception of the Family implanted by the worship of ancestral spirits rather than with the nature of the government? Athenian women had a life less free than Roman women, but Athens was a democracy and Rome was not.

More truth may be found in the view that democratic peoples carry indulgence to wrongdoers further than a regard for the safety of the community permits, because the disposition to let everybody go his own way and please himself, perhaps also in some countries the weakness of a directly elected Executive, induces leniency. The peccadilloes of public men are too quickly forgotten. Whether a tendency to self-indulgence and licence is any commoner than under other kinds of government it is impossible to say, for many other causes come into play. Divorce has become easier and divorces more frequent in all free Protestant countries, but this is a phenomenon observable in nearly every modern country, scarcely commoner in America, and not commoner in Switzerland than it is in Germany. Its frequency is, moreover, no test of the sexual immorality of a country: there have been countries where divorce was unpermitted, while the laxity of morals was notorious. In this as in many other matters it is what may be called the spirit of " modernism," rather than the democratic influence of a form of government, that has been working a change in social usages and moral standards. The disappearance of the old theological conception of Sin, and the disposition to attribute a man's evil propensities to heredity or to surroundings for which he cannot be held accountable, have produced a tolerance more amiable than salutary, a reluctance to use severity where severity is the only means of repressing crime. This fault, though also a part of modernism, may not be specially frequent in democracies. It has not so far diminished their power of recognizing and admiring virtue. Shining examples of dignity, purity, and honour are to-day no less respected in the persons of men who have risen by their own merits than they were when exhibited by sovereigns or statesmen in the old days of inequality.

CHAPTER LXXIII

To test democracy by its results as visible in the six countries examined, it will be convenient to consider how far in each of them the chief ends for which government exists have been attained, taking these ends to include whatever the collective action of men associated for the common good can do for the moral and material welfare of a community and the individual citizens who compose it, helping them to obtain the maximum that life can afford of enjoyment and to suffer the minimum life may bring of sorrow.

These ends may be summed up as follows:

Safety against attack on the community from without.

Order within the community — prevention of violence and creation of the consequent sense of security.

Justice, the punishment of offences and the impartial adjustment of disputes on principles approved by the community.

Efficient administration of common affairs, so as to obtain the largest possible results at the smallest possible cost.

Assistance to the citizens in their several occupations, as, for example, by the promotion of trade or the regulation of industry, in so far as this can be done without checking individual initiative or unduly restricting individual freedom.

These may be called the primary and generally recognized functions of government in a civilized country. Other results, needing a fuller explanation, will be presently adverted to. I take first the five ends above named.

1. *Safety against External Attack.*— In all the Six Democracies this end has been attained as fully as in most non-democratic governments, and in one respect better attained, because the necessary preparations for defence have not given reasonable ground to other nations to fear

that armaments were being increased with a view to hostile aggression.

2. In most of the Six internal order has been well maintained, best perhaps in Switzerland, least perhaps in parts of the United States, where, although the Federal Government has done its duty faithfully, some State Governments have tolerated lynching and failed to check other breaches of the law. Rioting in connection with Labour disputes has occurred everywhere, but except in some Australian cases the constituted authorities have shown themselves able to deal with it.

3. Justice has been honestly and capably administered, quite as well as under other forms of government, in Switzerland, Canada, Australia, and New Zealand, and in France also, though perhaps with not so full a confidence of the people in the perfect honour of all the Courts. In the United States the Federal Courts are staffed (with few exceptions) by upright and capable men, and the same is true of certain States. In others, however, the Judiciary is below the level of its functions, and in a few it is not trusted, while criminal procedure is cumbrous and regrettably ineffective.

4. Civil administration has long been conducted with efficiency in France and Switzerland, and is now, since the partial abolition of the " Spoils System," beginning to be so conducted in the United States Federal Government and in many of the State Governments. A similar improvement is visible in Canada. Australia and New Zealand have permanent services which are honest but as yet not more than fairly competent. Still possessed by the notion that one man is as good as another, the new democracies have not yet duly recognized the increased call for thorough knowledge and trained skill in handling the widened functions now imposed on governments, both in determining the principles of economic and social policy to be adopted and in carrying them out in a scientific spirit. That the management of national finances has, in every country except Switzerland, been lavish and frequently wasteful is the fault not of the civil services but of Ministers and legislatures who have spent vast sums in that form of electioneering bribery which consists in making grants of money to particular classes (as

in the United States to those who professed to be Civil War
Veterans), or to constituencies under the pretence of execut-
ing public works.   This kind of bribery, like the indulgence
extended to law-breakers whose displeasure can be shown at
elections, is directly attributable to democracy.

5. What further services, beyond those already mentioned, Government may render to a community or to any
class of its citizens by acquiring property to be used for the
common benefit, or by embarking on industries or trading
enterprises, or by aiding individuals to do so, is a question on
which opinions differ so widely that no standard exists
whereby to estimate the merits or defaults of governments.
The only two countries that have gone far in this direction
are New Zealand and Australia, with results (described
already) which raise doubts whether democracy is a form of
government fitted for such enterprises.   Other matters,
however, which are now generally deemed to fall within the
sphere of legislation such as public health and the conditions
of labour and the regulation of the means of transportation,
have received in all the Six countries due attention, the newer
democracies being in no wise behind their elder sisters.

Of the conduct of foreign policy, once deemed a department in which popular governments were inconstant and
incompetent, nothing need be added to what has been said in
a preceding chapter except that the errors of the peoples have
been no greater than those committed by monarchs, or by
oligarchies, or in democracies themselves by the small
groups, or the individual Ministers, to whose charge foreign
relations had been entrusted.

Outside and apart from these definite duties, legally
assigned to and discharged by government, there is a sphere
in which its action can be felt and in which both its form
and its spirit tell upon the individual citizen.   When political institutions call upon him to bear a part in their working,
he is taken out of the narrow circle of his domestic or occupational activities, admitted to a larger life which opens
wider horizons, associated in new ways with his fellows,
forced to think of matters which are both his and theirs.
Self-government in local and still more in national affairs
becomes a stimulant and an education.   These influences
may be called a by-product of popular government, incidental,

but precious.   Whoever has grown up in a household where public affairs were followed with interest and constantly discussed by the elders and friends of the family knows how much the boy gains by listening, asking questions, trying to understand the answers given; and the gain to the budding mind is greatest when the differences of opinion he hears expressed are most frequent. In Britain and America every general Parliamentary or Presidential Election marked for many a boy an epoch in the development of his thought, leading him to reflect thenceforth on events as they followed one another.   In the Six Democracies described this kind of education is always going on, and the process is continued in an even more profitable form where the citizen, when he has reached the voting age, is required to vote not only at elections, but also, as in Switzerland and some of the American States, on laws submitted to the people by Referendum and Initiative.

Could this examination be extended to six other European countries, Italy, Holland, Belgium, Denmark, Sweden, Norway, the results to be described would not differ materially from those set forth as attained in the Six countries examined in Part II.   In none has justice or order or the efficiency of civil administration suffered in the process of democratization which all have undergone within the last ninety years, and in most these primary duties of government are better discharged.   We may accordingly treat the results our enquiry has given for the Six as substantially true for European democracies in general.

Here, however, a wider question arises.   Some one may say: " These attempts to estimate what government has done or failed to do for the citizen do not convey a definite impression of what is after all the thing of most worth, viz. the amount of satisfaction, be it greater or less, with life and in life which democracy has brought to the modern world.   What has it done for human happiness ?   Is it discredited, as some argue, by the fact that, after its long and steady advance, those civilized peoples which had hoped so much from popular government, have seen in these latest years the most awful calamities which history records ?   Has it, if we think of the individual man, made him more or less disposed to say, taking the common test, ' If I could, I would live my life over again,' or does it leave him still in the frame of mind expressed twenty-three centuries ago by the Greek poet, who wrote, ' the best thing for a man is never to have been born at all, and the next best to return swiftly to that darkness whence he came ' ? " [1]

Shall we say in the familiar lines of a later poet, that the question is idle, because governments have infinitesimally little to do with the matter ?

> How small of all that human hearts endure,
> That part which laws or kings can cause or cure.

What is Happiness ? Nations as well as men have shown by their acts how differently they conceive it. Some, like Albanians and Afghans, cannot be happy without fighting, and the exploits of the heroes recorded in the Icelandic sagas as well as the feats of warlike prowess which fill the *Iliad* seem to show that the first European peoples to produce great literatures cherished the same ideals. Yet the ideals of peace also were never absent. Eris and Atē, Strife, and Sin the parent of Strife, loom large in the Homeric poems as figures to be hated, because they are sources of misery. That impassioned little poem, the hundred and forty-fourth Psalm, begins with the stern joy of battle in the verses:

Blessed be Jehovah my Strength who teacheth my hands to war and my fingers to fight.
My goodness and my fortress, my high tower and my deliverer, my shield and he in whom I trust.

And ends with a prayer for the blessedness of peaceful prosperity which the Almighty bestows:

That our sons may grow up like young plants and our daughters be as the polished corners of the temple:
That our garners may be full affording all manner of stores:
That our oxen may be strong to labour, that there may be no breaking in nor going out, that there be no complaining in our streets.
Happy is the people that is in such a case; happy the people whose God is Jehovah.

So peace is for Dante the supreme good, which the government of an Emperor commissioned from on high is to confer upon an Italy distracted by internal strife, leading men to

[1] Sophocles, *Oed. Colon.* l. 1225.

the practice on earth of active virtue in this world, according to the precepts of philosophy, as the successor of Peter is to lead them to celestial felicity in the world to come. The Greek philosophers, however, and the Eastern mystics and the Christian theologians agree in regarding Happiness as a thing which governments can neither make nor mar, since it is unaffected by the possession or the lack of earthly goods. From this exalted view there is a long downward scale, for the pleasures of sense must not be forgotten: many Europeans would deem Happiness unattainable in a land where alcoholic stimulants were unprocurable; and among the various ideals of different modern countries there is that of the maximum of amusement with the minimum of toil, high wages and leisure for bull-fights or horse races and athletic sports, in which many, and that not in Spain or Australia only, place their *Summum bonum*.

Of Democracy and Happiness can more be said than this, that whatever governments can do to increase the joy of life is so slight in comparison with the other factors that tell on life for good and evil as to make the question not worth discussing on its positive side? With the Negative side it is otherwise. The establishment of popular freedom has removed or at least diminished sources of fear or suffering which existed under more arbitrary forms of government. France has never returned to the oppressions and injustices, even the religious persecutions which had lasted down to the days of Louis XV. In England, under the dawning light of popular power, the Slave Trade and the pillory and the cruel penal code and the oppressive restrictions on industry had begun to disappear even before the peaceful revolution of 1832; and slavery in every British dominion fell at once thereafter. In Germany, Switzerland,[1] and Spain torture-chambers had remained till the advent of the armies of republican France. Russia is the only country in which the overthrow of an old-established tyranny has not been followed by the extinction of administrative cruelty. Freedom of thought and speech, if not everywhere the gift of popular government, has found its best guarantee in democratic institutions.

It remains to see which among the things expected from

1 One is still shown to travellers in Appenzell.

it by its sanguine apostles of a century ago, Democracy has so far failed to bestow upon the peoples. To Mazzini and his disciples, as to Jefferson and many another fifty years before, Democracy was a Religion, or the natural companion of a religion, or a substitute for religion, from which effects on morals and life were hoped similar to those which the preachers of new creeds have so often seen with the eyes of faith.

What, then, has democracy failed to accomplish? It has brought no nearer friendly feeling and the sense of human brotherhood among the peoples of the world towards one another. Freedom has not been a reconciler.

Neither has it created goodwill and a sense of unity and civic fellowship within each of these peoples. Though in earlier days strife between classes had arisen, it is only in these later days that what is called Class War has become recognized as a serious menace to the peace of States, and in some countries the dominant factor in political and economic conflicts. Liberty and Equality have not been followed by Fraternity. Not even far off do we see her coming shine.

It has not enlisted in the service of the State nearly so much of the best practical capacity as each country possesses and every country needs for dealing with the domestic and international questions of the present age.

It has not purified or dignified politics, nor escaped the pernicious influence which the Money Power can exert. In some states corruption has been rife, and the tone of public life no better than it was under the monarchies or oligarchies of the eighteenth century.

Lastly, Democracy has not induced that satisfaction and contentment with itself as the best form of government which was expected, and has not exorcised the spirit that seeks to attain its aims by revolution. One of the strongest arguments used to recommend Universal Suffrage was that as it gave supreme power to the numerical majority, every section of the people would bow to that majority, realizing that their aims must be sought by constitutional methods, since a resort to violence would be treason against the People and their legal sovereignty. Nevertheless, in many a country revolutionary methods are now being either applied or threatened just as they were in the old days of tyrannical kings or oligarchies. If democracy is flouted, what remains? There was a Greek proverb, "If water chokes, what can one drink to stop choking?"[1] If the light of Democracy be turned to darkness, how great is that darkness!

Any one can see that these things which have not been attained ought not to have been expected. No form of government, nothing less than a change in tendencies of human nature long known and recognized as permanent, could have accomplished what philosophies and religions and the spread of knowledge and progress in all the arts of life had failed to accomplish. Christianity — a far more powerful force than any political ideas or political institutions, since it works on the inmost heart of man — has produced nearly all the moral progress that has been achieved since it first appeared, and can in individual men transmute lead into gold, yet Christianity has not done these things for peoples, because, checked or perverted by the worse propensities of human nature, it has never been applied in practice. It has not abolished oppression and corruption in governments, nor extinguished international hatreds and wars, has not even prevented the return of hideous cruelties in war which were believed to have been long extinct.

Yet the right way to judge democracy is to try it by a concrete standard, setting it side by side with other governments. If we look back from the world of to-day to the world of the sixteenth century, comfort can be found in seeing how many sources of misery have been reduced under the rule of the people and the recognition of the equal rights of all. If it has not brought all the blessings that were expected, it has in some countries destroyed, in others materially diminished, many of the cruelties and terrors, injustices and oppressions that had darkened the souls of men for many generations.

[1] Εἰ ὕδωρ πνίγει, τί δεῖ ἐπιπίνειν;

CHAPTER LXXIV

As everything in human affairs is relative, so also the merit of any set of institutions can be tested and judged only by comparison with other sets created for similar purposes. All institutions being imperfect, the practical question is which of those that are directed to like ends show the fewest imperfections and best secure the general aim of every political system — the welfare of the nation which lives under it. That form of government is to be preferred which gives the better tendencies of human nature the fullest scope and the most constant stimulus, permitting to the worse tendencies the fewest opportunities for mischief.

Accordingly, to judge democracy aright it must be compared with the two other forms of government to which it was in the ancient world and is still the alternative, Monarchy and Oligarchy. By Monarchy I understand the Thing, not the Name, *i.e.* not any State the head of which is called King or Emperor, but one in which the personal will of the monarch is a constantly effective, and in the last resort predominant, factor in government. Thus, while such a monarchy as that of Norway is really a Crowned Republic, and indeed a democratic republic, monarchy was in Russia before 1917, and in Turkey before 1905, and to a less degree in Germany and the Austro-Hungarian Monarchy till 1918, an appreciable force in the conduct of affairs.

The merits claimed for Monarchy as compared with Democracy are the following:

It is more stable, better able to pursue, especially in foreign relations, a continuous and consistent policy.

It gives a more efficient domestic administration because it has a free hand in the selection of skilled officials and can enforce a stricter responsibility.

It enables all the services of the State to be well fitted into one another and made to work concurrently and harmoniously together, because the monarch is the single directing head whom all obey.

It makes for justice between social classes, because the monarch, being himself raised above all his subjects, is impartial, and probably sympathetic with the masses of the people whose attachment he desires to secure.

Of these claims, the first is not supported by history so far as foreign relations are concerned, for monarchies have been as variable as democracies, and on the whole more disposed to war and aggression.

Some weight may, however, be allowed to the claims made under the second and third heads, whenever the sovereign happens to be an exceptionally capable and industrious man, or has that gift for selecting first-rate administrators which sovereigns occasionally possess, as did Henry IV., Louis XIV., and Napoleon in France, Frederick II. in Prussia, Peter the Great and Catherine II. in Russia. The seventeenth and eighteenth centuries saw many reforms in European countries which no force less than that of a strong monarchy could have carried through.

There have been a few kings whose action justified the fourth claim, but modern monarchs in general have chiefly relied on and favoured the aristocracy who formed their Courts, and have allowed the nobles to deal hardly with the humbler classes.

History, however, if it credits some kings with conspicuous services to progress, tells us that since the end of the fifteenth century, when the principle of hereditary succession had become well settled, the number of capable sovereigns who honestly laboured for the good of their subjects has been extremely small. Spain, for instance, during three centuries from the abdication of Charles V., had no reason to thank any of her kings, nor had Hungary, or Poland, or Naples. A ruler with the gifts of Augustus or Hadrian and the virtues of Trajan or Marcus Aurelius can be a godsend to a nation; and if there were any practicable way for finding such a ruler, he and public opinion working together might produce an excellent government. But how rarely do such monarchs appear! If a sovereign turns out to be dissolute or heedless or weak, power goes naturally to his ministers or his favourites, who become a secret and virtually irresponsible oligarchy. In most modern countries, moreover, the disposition to obedience and sense of personal loyalty which used to support a hereditary ruler who could win any sort of popularity, have waxed feeble, nor would it be easy to revive them. The fatal objection to autocracy is that it leaves the fortunes of a State to chance; and when one considers the conditions under which autocrats grow up, chance is likely to set on the throne a weakling or a fool rather than a hero or a sage.

Oligarchies deserve, both because they suffer less from the hereditary principle, and for another reason that will presently appear, more consideration than monarchies. There have been various types. The feudal magnates of mediaeval European countries ruled partly by armed force, partly by the respect felt for birth, partly because their tenant vassals had a like interest in keeping the peasants in subjection. In the virtually independent Italian and German cities of those ages the ruling few were sometimes, as in Bern and Venice, nobles drawing wealth from landed estates or from commerce, sometimes the heads of trading guilds which formed a strong civic organization.[1] The conditions of those days are not likely to return in this age or the next, so that in order to compare modern oligarchies with modern democracies it is better to take such cases as the British and French aristocracies of the eighteenth century, or the nobility and bureaucracy of Prussia since Frederick the Great, the last king whose rule was personal in that country, or the groups of men who governed France under Louis Napoleon, and Russia since the Tsar Nicholas I., and Austria since Joseph II. In these countries real power rested with a small number of civil and military officials, the sovereign being practically in their hands. To such cases there may be added in our own time countries like Chile and Brazil, both

---

[1] It is greatly to be wished that we should possess in English a history or histories of mediaeval city oligarchies based on a comparison of the civic institutions of Italy and those of Germany, not without references to those of France, Spain, and England in which there was less independence because royal power was more effective. Separate studies on a considerable scale of the history of such cities as Bern and Geneva, Siena and Genoa, Lübeck, Hamburg, Ghent, and Augsburg are also wanting in our language, though they might be made both instructive and interesting. Such books exist for Venice and Florence.

republics but hardly democracies, for the real substance of power is in few hands. The difference between these last countries and the monarchical oligarchies [1] of Prussia, Austria, and Russia is that in the latter not only did the personal authority of the sovereign occasionally count for something, but that to the power of the civil officials and of the leading soldiers there was added the influence of the strongest men in the fields of commerce and industry, great bankers, heads of railroad and steamship companies and manufacturing undertakings, for the power of wealth, considerable even in the days when Edward III. borrowed money from the Peruzzi in Florence and Charles V. borrowed it from the Fuggers of Augsburg, is now greater than ever.[2] Any oligarchy of the future will apparently have to be either a mixture of plutocracy and bureaucracy, or else composed of the leaders of labour or trade organizations; and the wider the extension of State functions, *e.g.* under a Communistic system, the greater will the power of the ruling few be likely to prove in practice. Being of all forms of government that best entitled to be called Natural, for it springs out of the natural inequality of human beings, it takes the particular form which the economic and social conditions of a community prescribe, military, commercial, or industrial, as the case may be; and however often it may be crushed, its roots remain in the soil and may sprout afresh.

Oligarchy has undeniable merits. It has often proved a very stable government, able to pursue a consistent policy and hold a persistent course in foreign affairs, paying little regard to moral principles. Rome could never have conquered the world without a Senate to direct her policy abroad. She escaped the inconstancies which belong to the rule of monarchs, one of whom may reverse the action of his predecessor, and of assemblies which are at one time passionate and aggressive, at another depressed by misfortune or undecided when promptitude is essential. Rome, and Venice in her best days were prudent as well as tenacious.

[1] German writers used to speak of Prussia as a Constitutional Monarchy — so Dr. Hasbach throughout his book, *Moderne Demokratie* — but in actual working it was, down till 1918, more oligarchic than monarchical; and only a superman could have made it a real monarchy.

[2] This element was least powerful in Russia because it contained fewer men of great wealth, and in particular very few who combined wealth with such intellectual capacity as distinguished the German plutocrats.

The two great errors of the English oligarchy, its high-handed action towards the North American colonies in and after 1775 and its failure to pass Roman Catholic Emancipation concurrently with the Parliamentary Union of Ireland with Great Britain in 1800 were not its faults so much as those of King George III., to whom it weakly yielded.

Domestic government has been often efficient under an oligarchy, because the value of knowledge and skill was understood better than has yet been the case in democracies. Unsympathetic to the masses as it has usually been, it has sometimes seen the need for keeping them contented by caring for their material well-being. The Prussian oligarchy, following no doubt in the footsteps of Frederick the Great, settled a tangled land question in the days of Stein, put through many beneficial measures and built up a singularly capable civil service along with a wonderful military machine. Even the government of Louis Napoleon, whose blunders in foreign policy were as much his own as those of his advisers, for he had unluckily taken international relations for his province, did much for the economic progress of France, and left the peasantry contented.

These and other minor merits which oligarchies may claim have, however, been outweighed by its faults.

Class rule is essentially selfish and arrogant, perhaps even insolent, and the smaller the class is, so much the more arrogant. It judges questions from the point of view of its own interest, and seldom does more for the classes beneath it than it feels to be demanded by its own safety. Legislation is stained by this class colour, and administration is likely to suffer from the personal influence which members of the dominant group exert on behalf of their friends.

Oligarchies are apt to be divided into factions by the rivalries and jealousies of the leading families. Where these do not lead to violence, as they often did in ruder ages, they take the form of intrigues which weaken and distract the State, retarding legislation, perverting administration, sacrificing public to private interests.

The pervasive spirit of selfishness and absence of a sense of responsibility to the general opinion of the nation, as well as the secrecy with which business is conducted, gives opportunities for pecuniary corruption. England under Walpole suffered from this cause, so did France under Louis Napoleon, so did Austria, so, and to a greater extent, did Spain also and the Italian Principalities, not to speak of Russia and China, where venal bureaucracies worked the ruin of both countries, creating habits which it may take generations to cure, and destroying the respect of the nation for the sovereigns who tolerated it.   England, in the years between 1770 and 1820, is almost the only case of a country in which this weed was quickly eradicated without a revolutionary change.

Lastly, where a people advancing in knowledge and prosperity finds itself ruled, even if efficiently ruled, by a class — and the example of Prussia shows that it may sometimes be so ruled — it is sure to grow restive, and troubles must be expected like those which England, and still more Scotland and Ireland, witnessed during the half century before the Reform Act of 1832.   That these troubles did not culminate in civil war, was due to the traditions and good sense of the Whig section of the aristocracy which espoused the popular cause.   When aristocracies are seriously divided the end of their dominion is near.   It was a scion of one of the oldest patrician families of Rome who destroyed the rule of the Optimates, though for this a civil war all over the Roman world was needed.   A people in which the springs of ancient reverence have run dry will trust no class with virtually irresponsible power.

There are points in which a democratic Government suffers by comparison with an oligarchic, for the latter is more likely to recognize the importance of skill in administration and of economy in the management of finance, since it is not tempted to spend money in satisfying the importunities of localities or of sections of the population.   It draws as much ability as democracy into the service of the State, for although the upward path is not so open, more trouble is usually taken to discover and employ conspicuous talent; and it is less disposed to legislate in a recklessly vote-catching spirit.   The executive vigour with which it is credited is, however, qualified by the fear of provoking resistance or disaffection by the use of force, just as in a democracy the Executive begins to shake and quiver when votes are in question.   The selfishness of those old days, when Venice kept her Slav subjects ignorant lest they should be restless, and when the English landowners enclosed commons with little regard for the interests of the humbler commoners, began in later years to be corrected — as in Prussia — by the need felt for keeping the masses in good humour. In the matter of purity, there is, if we look at concrete cases, not much to choose. The German Governments maintained a higher standard of honour among their ministers than some of the Canadian Provinces have done, and among their judges than some of the American States have done. The fear of social censure proceeding from the members of a highly placed profession may be as powerful a deterrent in an oligarchy as is the fear of public displeasure in a democracy.

Crediting Oligarchy with all these merits, it nevertheless remains true that few who have lived under a democracy would exchange its rule for that of an oligarchy; few students of history would honour the memory of a great oligarch like Bismarck as they honour the memory of men like Cavour or Cobden or Abraham Lincoln. Individual liberty has a better chance — even if not a complete security — with the People than with a class. There is less room for the insolence of power.[1] The sense of civic duty and the sense of human as well as civic sympathy are more likely to flourish. Government is more just and humane, not because it is wiser, for wisdom does not increase with numbers, but because the aim and purpose of popular government is the common good of all. An enlightened monarch, or even a generous and prudently observant aristocracy, may from time to time honestly strive to help and raise the masses, but wherever power rests with a man or a class, a scornful selfishness sooner or later creeps back and depraves the conduct of affairs. So long as democracy holds fast to the principle that it exists for the whole people and makes its officials truly responsible to the whole people it will deserve to prevail.

So far I have spoken of the Rule of the Few as being the rule of a Class. There is, however, another sense in which the Few may rule and do rule, which needs to be considered, for it is of wide import.

---

[1] The satiety that comes of great wealth breeds insolence (Τίκτει γὰρ κόρος ὕβριν ὅταν πολὺς ὄλβος ἕπηται), says a Greek poet who knew oligarchs.

CHAPTER LXXV

OLIGARCHIES WITHIN DEMOCRACIES

No one can have had some years' experience of the conduct of affairs in a legislature or an administration without observing how extremely small is the number of persons by whom the world is governed. Oxenstierna's famous dictum, *Quantula regitur mundus sapientia*, finds its exemplification every day, but it is a criticism not of the flocks who follow but of the shepherds who lead. In all assemblies and groups and organized bodies of men, from a nation down to the committee of a club, direction and decisions rest in the hands of a small percentage, less and less in proportion to the larger and larger size of the body, till in a great population it becomes an infinitesimally small proportion of the whole number. This is and always has been true of all forms of government, though in different degrees. The fact is most obvious in an autocracy. The nominal autocrat, except in so far as the fear of assassination or rebellion obliges him to regard popular feeling, can be a real autocrat, exercising direct personal government, only in two cases, viz. in a small community which he can, like the Sicilian tyrant Agathocles or Chaka the Zulu king, rule directly, or in a wider area when he is, like Julius Caesar or Napoleon, a superman in intellect and energy. In all other cases his personal will plays a small part, and the vast bulk of the business is done by his Ministers, so that the important part of his function lies in selecting those who are to govern in his name, and trying, if he be capable of the duty, to see that both they and their personal *entourage* continue to deserve his confidence. In a Court like that of Louis XV. the powers of the State were, subject to such directions as that voluptuary might occasionally give, divided between three or four high officials and the king's private favourites, with the reigning mistress or her favourites. The Ministers were themselves influenced by their secretaries and favourites, but the total number of persons who guided the destinies of France, exercising, say, nineteen-twentieths of the power over national as distinguished from local affairs, may have been less than twenty. Every Monarchy becomes in practice an Oligarchy.

British India furnishes an excellent example of an enlightened, hard-working, disinterested, very small official class ruling a vast country. Taking together the Central Government and the Governments of the Provinces, the traveller who has good opportunities for observation comes to the conclusion that the " persons who count "— that is, those from whom all the important decisions on policy proceed — do not exceed thirty or forty, including those private secretaries who may sometimes be quite as potent factors as their better-known chiefs. Within the large oligarchy of some hundreds of the higher British officials, this inner oligarchy rules, each member of it having an actual power which is often less or greater than that legally assigned to his office, his personal intelligence and industry making the difference. To take an example on a much smaller scale, that of a country which a democracy left to be governed practically by one man, though subject to the check imposed on him by the necessity of defending his acts in Parliament, and — when the matter was exceptionally important — of persuading his Cabinet colleagues that those acts were defensible, it may be said that the persons who aided and advised the Chief Secretary, and in that way bore a part in ruling Ireland, were, on an average, less than a dozen, viz. three or four of the most experienced officials, two or three of the popular leaders, and a very few private friends on whose advice the Chief Secretary set value,[1] the power of each, *i.e.* the share of each man in the decisions taken, being proportioned to the value which the Minister set upon that man's opinion.[2]   In Germany and

[1] Parliament governed Ireland in the sense that its wishes, or what were conjectured as likely to be its wishes, could not be defied, and that where legislation was needed, its consent to that legislation must be obtained, but the majority that gave general support to the Cabinet was usually so disposed to vote as the Cabinet wished that an extremely wide field was left open for the volition of the Irish Government and this volition was the work of the responsible Minister and the handful whom he thought it worth while to consult.

[2] The less the Chief Secretary happens to know of Ireland before he is sent there, the smaller will usually be the number of those whom he consults and the greater their influence on decisions.

The view stated in the text is based on the experience I acquired when, many years ago, responsible for the government of Ireland.

in Austria the determination of great issues, even the tremendous issues of war and peace which arose in July 1914. lay with seven or eight persons. In large democratic countries like England and France, and above all in the United States, the number of persons who count, swelled as it is by journalists and by the leaders of various organizations that can influence votes, is very much larger in proportion to the population, but that proportion is still infinitesimally small.

Conceive of Political Power as a Force supplied to a machine from a number of dynamos, some with a stronger, some with a weaker, current, and try to estimate the amount of that Force which proceeds from each dynamo. The force which comes from each dynamo that represents an individual man is capable of a rough evaluation, while that force which represented the mass of public opinion is not so evaluable, because it varies with the importance of the issue, which sometimes excites public opinion and sometimes fails to interest it. Whoever tries, in the case of any given decision on a political question, to estimate the amount of the force proceeding from the dynamos which represent the wills of individual men will be surprised to find how high a proportion that amount bears on the average to the whole volume, because in many cases public opinion, though recognized as the supreme arbiter, is faint or uncertain, so that in those cases decision falls to the few, and a decision little noted at the time may affect the course of the events that follow. This is plain enough in the case of the German decision of 1914. It is less evident in a democracy, for there public opinion is more active and outspoken, and when it speaks with a clear voice, omnipotent. But such cases are exceptional. Moreover, even in democracies opinion itself is in the last analysis made by a comparatively small percentage of the nation, the party chiefs being specially powerful among these. Public opinion is in ordinary times deferential to those who hold the reins of government, leaving to them all but the most important decisions.

The members of a representative legislature in a Parliamentary country are presumably men of exceptional ability, each being a sort of leader to his own constituents: yet within every legislature power is concentrated in a few, including the six or seven strongest men among the Ministers, five or six prominent leaders of the various Opposition groups and about ten per cent. of the rest, the others practically following the lead given to them, and not merely voting but also mostly thinking and feeling with their party.   In the United States House of Representatives business was for many years directed by a very few persons.   After the Speaker ceased to be a dictator, it passed to a small Committee, the exigencies of business as well as the interest of the dominant party prescribing this.   The selection of the persons to be nominated by the two great parties as candidates for the Presidency of the United States at their national Conventions falls in practice into the hands of a small group of politicians, so the nation may be shut up to choose between two men whom few citizens would have selected, the attempt made to ascertain the popular will by the plan of " Presidential Primaries " having virtually failed.   In a large popular Assembly, like that of a Greek republic, with hundreds of thousands listening to the speeches of orators, there was no party control, and every citizen voted as he pleased, but the contagion of numbers was powerful, and the dominant feeling swept men off their feet.   No ruling assembly ever contained so many men who had intelligence to guide their wills coupled with freedom to express their wills by a vote, as did that of Athens, but that will was the will rather of the crowd than each man's own, and was in the last resort due to the persuasive force of the few strenuous spirits who impressed their views upon the mass.   Even where the absolute equality of every voter was most complete, power inevitably drifted to the strong.

What has been said of governments and assemblies is equally true of non-legal organizations.   The two great parties in the United States, counting their members by millions, have long been ruled by small cliques: and in every huge city the Organization has its Great General Staff or Ring of half a dozen wire-pullers, usually with a Boss as chief.   The much less important party organizations in England are directed by two or three members of the Government and of the Opposition, with a few office-bearers of Conservative and Liberal Associations.   But the most striking illustration of the law that the larger the body the fewer those who rule it is furnished by the great Labour Unions that now exist in all industrial countries. The power which the members of the Unions entrust to their delegates to Trade Congresses and the docility with which in some countries they follow whatever lead is given them by a strong will, can, as an able writer who has given special study to the subject remarks, be in those countries paralleled only by the religious veneration given to saints.[1] Ferdinand Lassalle in Germany, Enrico Ferri in Italy, received a loyalty and adulation which hung upon every word. Millions of votes are controlled by perhaps a dozen leaders who have won confidence. This surrender of power by the Many to the Few is admitted by the leaders themselves, who, recognizing its abandonment of the principle of Equality, justify it by the needs of the case. A militant organization is an army which can conquer only as an army conquers, by Unity of Command. It may be said that after victory equality will return. Yes; but so will indifference. A party is most interested and excited when it is militant, and though the leaders may not be of the same type after the battle has been won, they will be still few and powerful.

We are thus driven to ask: Is a true Democracy possible? Has it ever existed?

If one finds everywhere the same phenomena they are evidently due to the same ubiquitous causes, causes that may be summed up as follows:

1. Organization is essential for the accomplishment of any purpose, and organization means that each must have his special function and duty, and that all who discharge their several functions must be so guided as to work together, and that this co-operation must be expressed in and secured by the direction of some few commanders whose function it is to overlook the whole field of action and issue their orders to the several sets of officers. To attempt to govern a country by the votes of masses left without control would be like

[1] The views stated in the text which I had reached by other paths are confirmed by an able writer who has given special study to the subject, R. Michiels, in his book entitled *Political Parties*, pp. 68–74. I may add that his description of the Socialist parties in Germany is well worth reading. He remarks that the Socialist leaders come mostly (as did Marx) from the bourgeoise, and are often idealists, led by their convictions, not by ambition,— though of course they, like all leaders, come to love power,— and maintaining an intellectual standard equal to that of German politicians generally. Some have been very striking figures.

attempting to manage a railroad by the votes of uninformed shareholders, or to lay the course of a sailing ship by the votes of the passengers. In a large country especially, the great and increasing complexity of government makes division, subordination, co-ordination, and the concentration of directing power more essential to efficiency than ever before.

2. The majority of citizens generally trouble themselves so little about public affairs that they willingly leave all but the most important to be dealt with by a few.[1] The several kinds of interest which the average man feels in the various branches or sides of his individual life come in something like the following order:

First, the occupation by which he makes his living, which, whether he likes it or not, is a prime necessity.

Secondly, his domestic concerns, his family and relatives and friends.

Thirdly, but now only in some countries, his religious beliefs or observances.

Fourthly, his amusements and personal tastes, be they for sensual or for intellectual enjoyments.

Fifthly, his civic duty to the community.

The order of these five interests of course varies in different citizens: some men put the fourth above the second, some so neglect the first as to be a burden to others. But the one common feature is the low place which belongs to the fifth, which for more than half the citizens in certain countries scarcely exists at all. For nearly all — and this will obviously be most true where women possess the suffrage, because domestic cares necessarily come first in the mind and time of most of them — the fifth fills a very small place in the average citizen's thoughts and is allowed to claim a correspondingly small fraction of his time.

3. Even those citizens who do take some interest in the welfare of their community are prevented, some by indolence, some by a sense of their want of knowledge, from studying political questions. Those who think, those who quickly turn thought into action, inevitably guide the rest. The " common will " to which Rousseau attributes rule, must

---

[1] As to the small minorities by which important questions are decided at votings on Socialist or Labour affairs, see Michiels, pp. 55–58, *op. cit.*

have begun as the will of two or three, and spread outwards from them.[1]

4. Inequality of Natural Capacity. Comparatively few men have the talent or possess the knowledge needed for thinking steadily on political questions; and of those so qualified, many are heedless or lazy, and leave politics alone, because they care so much more for other things that they confine themselves to delivering their vote at elections. Thus leadership naturally passes to the men of energy and boldness, especially if they possess also the power of persuasive speech. They become the Ruling Few. This sort of oligarchy is the natural and inevitable form of government. In a curious little collection of songs written to be sung by citizens during the First French Revolution there is a sort of hymn to Equality which begins, " O sweet and holy Equality, *enfant chéri de la Nature.*" But however sweet the child, Nature is not its parent. Monarchy was natural in some states of society: oligarchy in others, but the direct rule of all citizens equally and alike never has existed or can exist. The propensity to obey is at least as strong as the sense of independence, and much more generally diffused.[2]

As these things are of course familiar to any one who has either read a little history or seen a little of practical politics in any assembly down to a parish meeting, how then did the apostles of democracy come to talk as they did? Where is the Will of the People?[3] What becomes of the rule of the people by the people?

These enthusiasts were not the mere victims of illusions, but as they lived in times of revolt against the misgovernment of monarchies and oligarchies, governments of the Few who selfishly pursued their own class interests, they leapt to the

[1] Rousseau wrote in the *Contrat Social:* " A prendre le terme dans la rigueur de l'acception il n'a jamais existé de véritable démocratie, et il n'en existera jamais. Il est contre l'ordre naturel que le grand nombre gouverne et que le petit soit gouverné."

[2] Proudhon observed: " L'espèce humaine veut être gouvernée, elle le sera. J'ai honte de mon espèce." Quoted by Michiels, p. 421.

[3] The phrase " Will of the People " seems to involve two fallacies, or rather perhaps two implications which induce fallacies, and they spring from the habit of conceiving of the People as One. The first is that the Will of the Majority is apt to be thought of as if it were the Will of All. The second is that as it comes from many it is thought of as issuing alike and equally from many, whereas in fact it originates in few and is accepted by many.

conclusion that the one thing needful for good government was to place it in the hands of the Many, and that the Many, *i.e.* the whole mass of the citizens, would take the same interest in using it for the good of all as the oligarchs had taken in using it for their own class. They saw the people roused as they had not been roused since the religious conflicts of the sixteenth century, to take an eager interest in public affairs, and assumed that this interest would continue when the excitement had died down; and being themselves ardent politicians, they attributed to the mass a zeal like that which they felt themselves. The lapse of years has given us a fuller knowledge. It is time to face the facts and be done with fantasies. As Bishop Butler long ago observed: Things are what they are, and not some other things, and they assuredly are not what we like to believe them to be. The proportion of citizens who take a lively and constant interest in politics is so small, and likely to remain so small, that the direction of affairs inevitably passes to a few. The framers of institutions must recognize this fact, and see that their institutions correspond with the facts.

In one thing, however, the sanguine enthusiasts of whom I have spoken were entirely right. They saw that the chief fault of the bad governments they sought to overthrow lay in their being conducted for the benefit of a class. The aim and spirit were selfish: a government could be made to serve the people only by giving the people the right to prescribe the aims it should pursue. This was done by the overthrow of the oligarchs: and this is one great service democracy has rendered and is still trying, with more or less success, to render. It will have to go on trying, for Nature is always tending to throw Power into the hands of the Few, and the Few always tend by a like natural process to solidify into a Class, as the vapours rising from the earth gather into clouds. Fortunately the Class also, by a like process, is always tending to dissolve. The old Oligarchies of the Sword lasted longest, because in rude feudal times they had seized and anchored themselves to the land. The more recent Oligarchies of the Purse are less stable, because new men are always pressing in, and movable paper wealth may soon pass away from the descendants of those who acquired it. The Oligarchy of Intellect is still more fluid: talent easily enters it, and talent is not transmissible like the shares in a railroad. Philosophers who disliked the oligarchies of rank and feared the plutocracies that succeeded them have dreamed of an aristocracy of Intellect as the best kind of government, but though they knew that a State needs uprightness and public spirit as well as intellect in its rulers, they never succeeded in showing how the possessors of these qualities are to be found and chosen, and they forgot that to both sets of qualities there must be added another which only experience tests, that is, Strength, the power to move and control the minds and wills of men. " The Kingdom of Heaven is taken by violence, and the violent take it by force."

Thus Free Government cannot but be, and has in reality always been, an Oligarchy within a Democracy. But it is Oligarchy not in the historical sense of the Rule of a Class, but rather in the original sense of the word, the rule of Few instead of Many individuals, to wit, those few whom neither birth nor wealth nor race distinguishes from the rest, but only Nature in having given to them qualities or opportunities she has denied to others.

What, then, becomes of Democracy? What remains to the Many? Three rights and functions; and they are the vital strength of free government. Though the people cannot choose and guide the Means administration employs, they can prescribe the Ends: and so although government may not be By the People, it may be For the People. The people declare the End of government to be the welfare of the whole community and not of any specially favoured section. They commit the Means for attaining that end to the citizens whom they select for the purpose. They watch those selected citizens to make sure that they do not misuse the authority entrusted to them. Popular powers, however, though they determine the character and scope of government, are in practice more frequently Negative or Deterrent than Positive. The people can more readily reject a course proposed to them than themselves suggest a better course. They can say, " We dislike this: we will not have it " on many an occasion when they cannot say what else they wish to have, *i.e.* in what form such general benefits as they desire ought to be given.

Of these three functions the most important and most

difficult is that of choosing leaders, for though it seems simple to say that government must pursue the common good, the power to discern and decide in any given case what is that good, and what Means best conduce thereto, needs a wisdom and an unselfishness possessed by few. Since the people can seldom do this for themselves, their leaders must do it for them, and be held responsible for the consequences. A nation is tested and judged by the quality of those it chooses and supports as its leaders; and by their capacity it stands or falls.

To realize how much power does rest and must by a law of nature always rest with the few who guide the fortunes of any community, be it great or small, is to indicate the supreme importance of the choice which a free nation is called to make. The larger the nation the more difficult the choice, because opportunities for personal knowledge are slighter. And the choice is also more momentous, because the greater the body and the more numerous the various sections it contains, the more essential is it that strong leaders should be trusted with the powers needed to hold it together.

CHAPTER LXXVI

WE have seen that the quality of the leaders in a democracy is no less important than the quality of the people they lead, the conduct of affairs by the Few being a necessary condition in every government, no matter in whom State power is legally vested. The chief difference is that in an Oligarchy, where legal supremacy belongs to the Few, it is only they and those who are closest to them that guide the course of events, whereas where legal supremacy belongs to the multitude actual power is exerted not only by the persons to whom it delegates its legal authority, but by those also who can influence the multitude itself, inducing it to take one course or another, and to commit executive functions to particular persons. Whoever, accordingly, can sway the minds and wills of the sovereign people becomes a Leader, an effective factor in directing their action. Hence, while in a Monarchy or Oligarchy the ruling Few are to be looked for only in the small class in whom legislative and administrative functions are vested, one must in a democracy go further afield and regard not only ministers and legislators but also the men who are most listened to by the citizens, public speakers, journalists, writers of books and pamphlets, every one in fact who counts for something in the formation of public opinion.

In a Democracy every one has a chance — not of course an equal chance, for wealth and other adventitious advantages tell — of stepping out of the ranks to become a leader. The people are on the look out for men fit to be followed, and those who aspire to leadership are always trying to recommend themselves for the function. What, then, are the qualities which fix the attention and win the favour of the people?

Two are of especial value. One is Initiative. Leadership consists above all things in the faculty of going before others instead of following after others; that is to say it is promptitude in seeing the next step to be taken and courage in taking it. It is the courage which does not merely stand firm to resist an approaching foe but heads the charge against him. Nothing so much disposes men to follow as the swift resolution of one who is ready to take risks, the courage which makes one captain take his ship out from a lee-shore, under full steam, against a hurricane, while other captains are hesitating and trying to calculate the danger.

The other quality is the power to comprehend exactly the forces that affect the mind of the people and to discern what they desire and will support. These two gifts are precious because they are rare: they bring a man to the front under all kinds of popular governments, and by them, if he possesses the more ordinary gifts of a ready and telling speech, as well as industry and honesty — or the reputation of it — he can usually hold the place he has won.

Eloquence in some forms of government counts for more than in others. Where popular assemblies have to be frequently addressed it is indispensable, as in the Greek republics and at Rome. It is valuable in countries like France, Italy, and England where unending battles go on in representative assemblies, and is needed not only in the form of set speeches on the greater occasions, but in cut-and-thrust debates where a sudden onslaught or a telling repartee makes a member valued as a party fighter. Where, as in the United States, the Administration does not hold office at the pleasure of the legislature, neither the arts of debate nor those which enable a parliamentarian to wriggle out of a difficulty and to play upon the personal proclivities of individual supporters or opponents, are so much needed, and it is enough if a leader can deliver a good set oration, even if he reads it from notes. Nevertheless, in all countries that genuine eloquence which can touch the imagination or fire the hearts of a popular audience has often brought its possessor to the front, endearing him to the people, and perhaps concealing a lack of steadfastness or wisdom. France and Australia are the countries in which debating power most frequently brings men forward, while in Switzerland and New Zealand plain clearheaded good sense has been sufficient.

It is an old reproach against democracies that they are readily moved by a plausible tongue, and are beguiled by those who have, ever since the republican days of Greece, been called Demagogues (leaders of the people), furnishing a term of abuse freely applied in many a modern struggle. In current usage the Demagogue is one who tries to lure the people by captivating speech, playing upon their passions, or promising to secure for them some benefit. Such persons must obviously be expected in all countries where power lies with the people; and they may spread their nets by the press as well as by the voice, reaching larger numbers by the former method, and dangerous because often irresponsible, raising expectations which they are seldom called on to find the means of gratifying. Why they should have been, as is sometimes said, more frequent in Germany, Italy, and England than in France or the United States is an interesting question into which I must not digress.

Self-confidence, if it does not pass into the vanity which offers an easy target to ridicule, helps a bold man to make his way. To speak with an air of positive assurance, especially to a half-educated crowd already predisposed to assent, is better than to reason with them. A prominent statesman of our time, on being asked by a member of his party what arguments he had better use on behalf of the cause they were advocating replied, " I sometimes think that assertion is the best kind of argument."

There are other ways besides eloquence by which leadership is won. Journalism, a form of persuasive rhetoric which may be called oratory by the pen, has sometimes been an avenue to power in France and in the United States — even in Russia under the Tsars Katkoff was an effective force half a century ago. Benjamin Franklin exercised enormous influence by his writings, though he took little to do with the politics of his State. A book, coming at an opportune moment, may diffuse ideas which have their immediate reaction on popular opinion and so dispose sections of a nation to follow, perhaps for many years, the path it pointed out. Tolstoi, the latest of the prophets, told profoundly on the thoughts of his time, though how far he affected politics it is not yet easy to determine. Not to speak of Rousseau and Tom Paine, the writings of Karl Marx told upon a circle far wider than that of his associates in revolutionary agitation. Authorship gave to Henry George, the writer of *Progress and Poverty,* an influence which lasted through his life, though he never cared to enter either national or Californian politics.   Deeds as well as words, and deeds in war even more than service rendered in peace, have shed on some figures unversed in statecraft a lustre which led them to the highest posts.   Generals Andrew Jackson, Zachary Taylor, T. H. Harrison, and U. S. Grant all owed their Presidencies to their military fame.   There are among American Presidents many instances, like that of Jefferson, to prove that a man may be a popular favourite without eloquence.

When any one has risen high enough to be trusted with administrative work, his capacity is put to a new test, since some measure of honesty, industry, tact, and temper is required, and if it is a first-rate position, carrying leadership with it, he must show himself capable of inspiring confidence and attaching men to himself.[1]   What, then, of that higher kind of wisdom which looks all round and looks forward also?   It is not what the people chiefly seek for or often find: they and their representatives have generally to be contented with some one, be he forceful or seductive, who can meet the calls of the moment.   The busy life of a modern statesman leaves no time for reflection, and the partisans whom he has to please think of high statesmanship in the terms of a party platform.

Taking the gifts aforesaid to be those which attract the people, by what means do their possessors win the people's praise and confidence?   In Parliamentary countries the easiest way to prominence lies through the legislature, where influence is quickly won by effectiveness in debate, more slowly by a reputation for knowledge and diligence and judgment. The chiefs of parties come in these countries from the Chambers, and if there is a scarcity of first-rate talent among the party chiefs, it is because too little talent has found its way into the Chambers, as Talleyrand replied, when asked why the Generals of the time were not better: " Because they are chosen from the Colonels."

In the United States and in Switzerland men may become known by their work in local government or in some high

---

[1] Mazzini described democracy as " the progress of all through all under the leading of the best and wisest."   " Authority," he says elsewhere, " is sacred when consecrated by Genius and Virtue."

executive office, such as is, in America, the Mayoralty of a
city or the Governorship of a State. But the most potent
help to advancement in the earlier stages of a career is the
Party. In America, where it nominates the candidates for
every office as well as for seats in legislatures, it shows
little wish to find and push men of talent, reserving its favour
for those who have worked hard for the party and are sure
to be "solid" with it; and all the more pleased when they
are rich enough to contribute to election funds. This was
also, *mutatis mutandis,* the attitude of the Central Office of
the political parties in England from 1850 to 1900, for they
seldom cared to bring into Parliament men who could serve
the party by intellect, preferring the local wealthy man who,
not liable to the aberrations of youth and originality, could
be trusted to give a steady and, if possible, a silent vote.
Even the Parliamentary heads of the British parties did less
than might have been expected in this direction. The one
merit of the otherwise grotesquely indefensible system of
pocket boroughs lay in its bringing forward, now and then,
new men of conspicuous promise like Canning and Gladstone. In Switzerland, Canada, and New Zealand party
organizations have little to do with these matters, but in
Australia the Labour candidate has usually earned his selection by the work he has done in his Union or in his Political
Labour Leagues.

The newspaper press has become so effective an agency
in helping politicians to get on and to stay in, that some one
has well said that politics has in democracies become a
branch of the science and art of Advertisement. In certain
countries there have been persons, even among leading statesmen, who felt it so necessary to keep their names before the
public that they not only cultivated the goodwill of editors
and proprietors, but took pains to have their every daily act
of life recorded, thinking, perhaps correctly, that the way to
success is to fascinate everybody by making him believe that
everybody else has been fascinated. Keep yourself at all
hazards always before the public as if you were a patent medicine: on the principle of the painter who said to the newspaper critic, "If you cannot praise my picture, abuse it:
silence is the only thing I fear." These tactics succeed,

though of course, like well-advertised brands of tobacco, only if the article has some merit. Great is the power of iteration.

That publicity which the press alone can confer may everywhere do much to harm a politician, and still more to push him forward, but its power is not everywhere the same. In a small country like Switzerland the people have a personal knowledge of their prominent figures which relegates the newspapers to a secondary place. In a vast country like the United States the abundance of newspapers, and the restriction to certain areas of even the most important, prevents the people from falling under the sway of any, and forms in them the habit of judging men not by the praise or blame of contending journals, but by their acts, so though some may get more and others less credit than they deserve, still in the large majority of cases justice is done.

He who asks whether democracies have shown discernment in their choice of leaders must remember how different are the qualities of nations. Gifts that would commend a man in Italy might be less attractive in Switzerland or Holland. Some are more fastidious than others in their moral judgments, though generally disposed to pardon any means by which success has been secured. Some put reason above amusement, some reverse the order, but crowds seem everywhere to relish high-flown moral platitudes. In the small city republics of antiquity and of the Middle Ages the opportunities for personal knowledge were so abundant that we are not surprised to find that while the conspicuous figures were always men of some sort of brilliance, yet those whose power was merely rhetorical were seldom trusted with high office and did not hold their influence for long together. In large modern countries, where the citizens have to form their opinion from what they see in print, the task is hard, so much is there of misconception as well as of deliberate misrepresentation. How seldom are men correctly judged even by those who have good opportunities for judging and are not heated partisans! Even in a popular assembly it may be only the most intimate colleagues who are in a position to form a correct estimate of a man's real character; [1] who have learnt

[1] There are, of course, cases in which the sterling qualities do win due recognition and secure for their possessor an unhesitating confidence.

to appreciate and rely upon the honour and chivalry and goodness of heart and courage in emergencies of a man too modest or too proud to play for popularity; or who have to work with another colleague in whom they must tolerate selfishnesses and self-deceptions, pettinesses and lapses from truth, and posings before the public. It has been well said that you never really know any one till you have been his partner in business, or his companion on a long journey through a wild country. The peoples, however, need not know all these things — some of them are best left unrecorded — and may be well content if they can judge ability, courage, and honesty. Taking the six democracies already described, those which judge most shrewdly are Switzerland and the United States, and next after these, Canada.[1] The French are of course the keenest of critics, but the vehemence of partisanship is such as to make the estimate of a statesman's personal qualities unduly tinged by the attraction or repulsion of his opinions.

The charge of ingratitude so often brought against democracies finds little support in history.[2] Even among the

Mr. Gladstone was fond of telling how during the passing of the Reform Bill of 1832 a debate arose regarding the disfranchisement of a particular " rotten borough." Many speeches were delivered making so strong a case for sparing it that the House of Commons was on the point of omitting it from the schedule of disfranchisements, when Lord Althorp, who was then leading the Ministerial majority, rose and said that he had unluckily forgotten to bring with him the evidence supplied to him against the borough, but that this evidence was so conclusive that he felt sure it would have convinced the House. The House trusted him so implicitly that the borough was forthwith disfranchised. I may perhaps be permitted to add that the qualities which distinguished Lord Althorp reappeared in his nephew, the late Lord Spencer, one of the most admirable figures in the public life of his time.

[1] An interesting discussion of the causes which affect leadership in democratic countries may be found in an address by Mr. James A. Beck in vol. vi. pp. 1–23 of the American *Journal of the National Institute of Social Sciences*. He finds in the United States an excessive tendency to standardization.

[2] This was the view of Machiavelli, who had good opportunities for observing both. He remarks (*The Prince*, chap. vi.) that the charges brought against the multitude might be equally well brought against all men and especially against princes. Similar deliverances are quoted from the *Discorsi* by Mr. Burd in his edition of *The Prince*. Machiavelli observes, " Un popolo è più prudente, più stabile e di miglior giudizio che un principe."

R. Michiels, in his book published in English under the title of *Political Parties*, dwells upon the fidelity which the German Socialists have usually shown to their leaders through a long series of years.

volatile Greeks, where popular assemblies were often swept by gusts of passion, we are more often struck by their adherence to those they had once trusted than by their occasional anger at a general who had failed.   In the annals of the United States there is scarcely an instance of any statesman who lost his hold upon the people save by his own errors, and very few who did not even after those errors retain a fair measure of support.   In Canada, Australia, and New Zealand what surprises the observer is the undue indulgence extended to men whose faults ought to have brought their public career to a close.   Monarchs have been more ungrateful than free peoples.[1]   Compare the treatment of Benedek by the Hapsburg Court after the war of 1866 [2] with the fine loyalty of the Southern men in America after the fall of the Confederacy not only to the noble figure of Robert E. Lee, but even to others who might well have been censured for mistakes.

It is often said that every country has the leaders, like the newspapers, which it deserves.   This is not altogether true. Fortune takes a hand in the game, and takes it for evil as well as for good, sometimes sending, perhaps from an unexpected quarter, a man of gifts which quickly raise him to an eminence he may use or abuse with consequences fateful for the future.   The people who welcome and follow an Alcibiades or an Aaron Burr cannot be expected to know his capacities for evil.   The people who welcomed and trusted the rail-splitter from Illinois thanked Providence for the unlooked-for gift of one who was exactly fitted for the crisis and gave him their loyal trust thereafter.   That which we call Chance — it is the only available word where causes are undiscoverable — has had more to do with the course of events than the builders of scientific history have generally liked to recognize.

Notwithstanding such an instance as that of Abraham

---

[1] The critics of democracy have often drawn examples of its vices from the violence of city mobs which, like those of mediaeval Constantinople. turned furiously against dethroned sovereigns whom it had formerly treated like a god, but these cases furnish no evidence against democracy, because such mobs were composed of persons who had never shared the responsibilities of free self-government.

[2] As described in Mr. Wickam Steed's book *The Hapsburg Monarchy.* Queen Elizabeth, like her father, behaved very ill to some of the Ministers who had served her faithfully.

Lincoln, the first man who had ever risen from such small beginnings to the headship of a nation, it must be admitted that universal suffrage and the growth of equality in opportunity have done less than was expected to bring to the service of the State men of statesmanlike ability. Those who have compared the public life of France from 1815 to 1875 with its public life from 1870 to 1920, and that of the United States of the years 1850–1900 with that of later years, seem disappointed with the results. Similar complaints are heard from those who in England set the generation of Burke, Pitt, and Fox, and that of Peel, Disraeli, and Gladstone beside the England of later years. If the alleged inferiority exists, it can be explained without attributing the paucity of brilliant figures to any deficient capacity of democracies for recognizing talent and virtue when they appear. The cause may lie rather in changed economic conditions, and in the indisposition of the class from which statesmen used to be chiefly drawn to throw themselves into public work in the spirit of their grandfathers. Still the fact is there.

The predominance of Party in democracies has made us, when we talk of leadership, think primarily of the militant function of the general who directs a political campaign and bears, like the champions in ancient warfare, the brunt of battle in his own person. But the best kind of leader has a duty to the whole people as well as to his party. If he is in power, he must think first of the national welfare; if he is in opposition he has nevertheless the responsibility of directing the minds and wills of a large section of the people, and of aiding or resisting the policy of the Administration. In both cases his actions, as well as his views and arguments and exhortations, have weight with the whole nation for good or for evil; and this, most conspicuously true of the head of a party, is true more or less of all those to whom the nation is accustomed to listen. It used to be said of the British House of Commons that its tone and taste rose or fell with the Prime Minister who was guiding its deliberations. This applies to the body of the people also. A great man may not only form a school who assimilate and propagate his ideas, but may do much to create a pattern for the people of what statesmanship ought to be. If his honour is unblemished, his ideals high, his temper large, tolerant, and sympathetic,

his example is sure to tell.   Others try to live up to it.   He
may, without being a Washington or a Lincoln, a Pitt or a
Fox, not only deserve to be gratefully remembered as a light
of his time, but may, like Lord Althorp and Peel in one way,
Cobden and Bright in another, so influence his younger contemporaries as to strengthen the best traditions of public life
and maintain its standard.

So much is in our own time spoken and written on all the
great questions before civilized nations that leaders are not
expected to become, and indeed cannot for want of leisure
become, students or philosophers, creators of new ideas or
schemes.   It is enough if, availing themselves of what the
students produce, they can apply their experience to discern
which of the many doctrines and projects that are seething
up all around like bubbles in a boiling spring are most fit to
be made the basis of wise legislation.   Their function is to
commend the best of these to the people, not waiting for
demands, not seeming to be bent merely on pleasing the people, but appealing to reason and creating the sense that the
nation is not a mere aggregate of classes, each seeking its own
interests, but a great organized whole with a life rooted in the
past and stretching on into the illimitable future.   A democracy is tested by the leaders whom it chooses, and it prospers
by the power of discernment which directs its choice.

Leaders of this type stand in a wholesome and profitable
relation with the average citizen, who, despite all the flattery
he receives, is generally a sensible man, not conceited, willing
to listen and learn.   In Switzerland and America, though
of course much influenced by his neighbours, he wishes to be
independent and tries to form an opinion for himself.   But
independence is compatible with deference to the opinion of
those who know more and have had a longer experience.   Independence qualified by deference, an independence springing from the sense of personal responsibility, a deference rendered to moral as well as intellectual authority, creates the
best relation between the leader whom it steadies and the citizen whom it guides.

As this chapter closes the comments to be made on the
working of Governments in the Six Democratic countries described, I may here, before passing on to the present aspects

of democracy over the world, sum up in a few propositions certain broad conclusions that may be drawn from a review of modern popular Governments. They are stated subject to certain exceptions, already mentioned, in the case of particular countries.

Democracy has belied the prophecies both of its friends and of its enemies. It has failed to give some benefits which the former expected, it has escaped some of the evils which the latter feared. If the optimists overvalued its moral influence, the pessimists undervalued its practical aptitudes. It has reproduced most of the evils which have belonged to other forms of government, though in different forms, and the few it has added are less serious than those evils of the older governments which it has escaped.

I. It has maintained public order while securing the liberty of the individual citizen.

II. It has given a civil administration as efficient as other forms of government have provided.

III. Its legislation has been more generally directed to the welfare of the poorer classes than has been that of other Governments.

IV. It has not been inconstant or ungrateful.

V. It has not weakened patriotism or courage.

VI. It has been often wasteful and usually extravagant.

VII. It has not produced general contentment in each nation.

VIII. It has done little to improve international relations and ensure peace, has not diminished class selfishness (witness Australia and New Zealand), has not fostered a cosmopolitan humanitarianism nor mitigated the dislike of men of a different colour.

IX. It has not extinguished corruption and the malign influences wealth can exert upon government.

X. It has not removed the fear of revolutions.

XI. It has not enlisted in the service of the State a sufficient number of the most honest and capable citizens.

XII. Nevertheless it has, taken all in all, given better practical results than either the Rule of One Man or the Rule of a Class, for it has at least extinguished many of the evils by which they were defaced.

On what is the most important question of all, whether

democratic governments have been improving during the last
half century in their practical working and in their moral
and intellectual influence on the peoples who have established
them, it is hard to reach a conclusion, for the conditions of
the last few years have been abnormal.   In 1914 there were
signs of decline in some countries where decline was hardly
to have been expected, and of improvement in other countries, but nothing to indicate in any country either a wish to
abandon democracy or the slightest prospect that anything
would be gained thereby.   Disappointment is expressed,
complaints are made, but no permanent substitute has been
suggested.

CHAPTER LXXVII

THE LATER PHASES OF DEMOCRACY

THOSE whose recollections carry them back over the last seventy years will be disposed to think that no other period of equal length in the world's annals — not even the years between 1453 and 1521, nor those between 1776 and 1848 — has seen so many profoundly significant changes in human life and thought. We are here concerned only with those which have affected popular government. But political changes are — apart from the action of some extraordinary individual — always due either to changes in the external conditions of man's life, economic and social, or to changes in man's thoughts and feelings, or to both combined. It is therefore worth while to glance at the influences of both these kinds which have had their repercussions in political ideas and political practice.

The swift advance in every department of physical science, enlarging our command of natural forces, has immensely enlarged the production of all sorts of commodities, and has, by providing quicker and cheaper modes of transport, brought food from one part of the earth to another in vastly increased quantity. Population has increased. Wealth has increased. The average duration of life has been lengthened. Many things which were luxuries have become indispensable comforts. Nations have been drawn closer to one another, and commerce has become a far more important element in their relations to one another. In the more prosperous nations new avenues to wealth have been opened, so that a large number of men sprung from what were the middle and poorer classes have accumulated great fortunes, while the ownership of land, once the chief source of wealth and social influence, has sunk into a second place. The " economic factor " has attained a new importance not only in international intercourse, but within each country, changing the relation of so-

cial classes, effacing the old distinctions of birth and rank, and
not only placing the new rich almost on a level with the old
families, but destroying the old ties between the employer and
his workmen.   The isolated hand-worker has become rare, the
factories that have replaced him are filled by crowds of toil-
ers who have little or no personal touch with the incorporated
company that pays their wages.   As the number of such
workers grew, they learnt to organize themselves, so that presently their combinations as well as their numbers gave them a
power and an independence previously unknown.   Thus a
process of equalization set in which not only placed the new
rich on a level with the old rich, but raised and strengthened
the hand-workers as a whole, the processes of levelling down
and levelling up going on together.   Knowledge was no
longer confined to a small minority.   Nearly everybody
could read and write.   Books and newspapers were accessible
to all, so there was in the intellectual sphere also an equalization of opportunities and an emancipation of the masses from
that sense of inferiority which had formerly made them accept as natural the predominance of the better born, the
richer, and the more instructed.

These changes were directly or indirectly due to advances
in the sciences of nature and in their application to practical
ends, changes which, though they had been in process for
more than a century, were immensely accelerated and extended in their operation within the lifetime of men still
living.   But the advances had moral as well as material effects.   They changed what are called " the values."   Men
became more and more occupied with the ascertainment and
interpretation of facts, and especially of the phenomena of
nature.   Their thoughts turned to concrete facts.   They
questioned old ideas and long-established doctrines, demanding evidence of whatever they were asked to believe.   Principles which had gone undisputed for centuries were discredited.   Historical criticism of the Christian scriptures became more active and its results were disseminated widely.
The habit of respect for tradition, together with such obedience to ecclesiastical authority as had remained, began to disappear, except in a small circle which the growing scepticism
had affrighted, while the habit of looking to another world
as one which would provide compensation for the injustices

of this world declined.[1] There was a general unsettlement
of convictions, a disposition to get the most that was possible
out of this present life, along with a feeling that every one
ought to have a full chance for developing his own individuality and seeking happiness in his own way. This sense of
human equality and of the right to untrammelled " self realization " found its most striking expression in what is called
the feminist movement, an amazing departure from ancient
and deeply rooted custom, with hardly a parallel in the history of society in respect of its extent, of the passion which
inspired its advocates, and of the amount of sympathy it
evoked in unexpected quarters.

Either of these two streams of tendency, the economic
and the intellectual, was strong enough to effect great changes.
Coinciding in their operation, they have produced what is a
new world in the realm of what is called sociological thought
as well as in the material conditions of life and the economic
structure of society. Not a few views and proposals that
were derided seventy years ago are now accepted and welcomed. Economic doctrines, which all sensible men then
held are now treated as obsolete. What were fads or dreams
have become axioms. What were axioms are now despised
as fads or superstitions.

Such changes could not but affect the political movements
already in progress, expanding their aims and quickening
their march. Though the outburst of revolutionary fervour
in 1848 spent its force before permanent results had been
achieved, the forces that were making for democracy soon
recovered their momentum, since they had behind them the
assertion of human equality, the desire to break old shackles
and secure for everybody his chance in life. The loss of
respect for authority and for the persons who claimed it in
the State and in the Church cleared away much that had
barred the path of earlier reformers. The masses, now that
education had spread among them, could no longer be treated
as unfitted by ignorance for civic rights, and while the organizations they had built up gave them the means of show-

[1] Even so far back as 1884 I remember to have heard two distinguished
Americans, James Russell Lowell and Charles Eliot Norton, express to
another the surprise they felt at finding that, on returning to London
after many years, one could say whatever one liked about religious as
well as political matters without the risk of exciting horror.

ing their strength, the growing demand for legislation designed to benefit them by providing better conditions of health and labour made it seem absurd to prevent those for whom these benefits were intended from directly expressing their own needs and wishes.   So all over Europe, outside the despotisms of Russia and Turkey, power more and more passed to the people.   The United States had been for many years a democracy.   In England, which may be taken as fairly typical, because the changes it underwent were not revolutionary, but accomplished with a pretty general consensus of opinion, statutes of 1868 and 1885 made the wage-earners a majority in nearly every constituency; and an Act of 1918 extended the suffrage not only to all men but to all women over thirty years of age.   To-day the masses are, or could be if they asserted themselves, masters of the political situation everywhere in Europe; though in some countries, such as Spain and Rumania, they have scarcely yet seemed to realize their power.

Mention ought here to be made of two sentiments which, playing on conservatively minded men as well as on Liberals, brought about these changes quietly in England, and to some extent in other countries also.   One was the fear that if the constitutional demand for extensions of the suffrage were not granted, violent efforts to obtain it might follow.   The other was a belief that only by giving more power to the workers would their real grievances receive due attention and, above all, prompt attention.

The results of this change were not at once visible.   In Great Britain, for instance, little happened to show the difference.   The English Tories, after their victory in the Election of 1874, applauded the prescience of their leader (Mr. Disraeli) who had divined that his party need not suffer from the extension of the electoral franchise he had carried, an extension wider than that which his opponents had proposed.   I remember that when, in 1878, I remarked to a singularly acute observer, London correspondent of a German newspaper,[1] that it was strange to see the English working men make so little use for their own benefit of the power they

---

[1] Mr. Max Schlesinger, whom those who lived in London then will remember as one of the foreigners who best understood English thoughts and ways.

had come to possess, he replied that they did not yet know how great their power was. They must have time. Scarcely did they begin to know it till 1890, and not fully till 1905, by which year other changes had begun and a new spirit was at work.

The earlier victories of democracy in Europe, like its still earlier victory in America, had been won in the name of Liberty. Liberty meant the expulsion of tyrants, the admission of the bulk of a nation to a share in power, the full control of the people through their representative assembly, the abolition of privilege and hereditary rank, and the opening on equal terms of every public career to every citizen. These would have been the main articles of a radical democrat's creed any time between 1830 and 1870, and many, at least in England and France, would have added to it the suppression of the State Establishment of religion, the curtailment of public expenditure, the public provision of education, free trade, the reduction of armies and the cultivation of peaceful relations with all foreign countries. Once these things had been attained everybody could sit down and be happy in his own way, the free play of economic forces ensuring peaceful progress and a steady amelioration of the conditions of life. There were of course already those, especially among the revolutionaries of the European continent, who looked further ahead. But, speaking generally, political liberty and political equality, both taken in the widest sense, satisfied the aspirations of the democrats of those days. These were the ideals of orators and thinkers from Charles James Fox and Jefferson down to Mazzini. These hopes inspired Wordsworth in his youthful prime and Schiller and Shelley and Victor Hugo. These were the doctrines which offended Goethe,[1] and which repelled Carlyle in his later days.

When, however, political liberty and equality had been actually attained, or at least became certain of attainment, the leaders of the working classes began to ask what did it profit them to have gained political power if they did not turn it to practical account for their own benefit. Legislation for.

---

[1] Alle Freiheits Apostel, sie waren mir immer zuwider,
  Willkur suchte doch ein jeder am Ende für sich;
  Willst du viele befreien, so wag' es viele zu dienen;
  Wie gefährlich das sei, willst du es wissen, versuch's.

the improvement of labour conditions had, no doubt, been stimulated by the extension of the suffrage, both in England and in other countries, notably in Germany, where government sought to hold at bay demands for political change by propitiating the wage-earners. But more was wanted. The chief things which the working classes desired were higher wages and shorter hours. These had been heretofore sought by strikes. But political action in the legislature provided an easier and surer way, while the State might be required to better the condition of the wage-earners by providing at the public cost other benefits such as gratuitous education, pensions, or houses, or employment on public works when other employment was slack. Some went further, insisting on the so-called Right to Work, *i.e.* the duty of the State to provide employment for every one who sought it.

The growing power of the Labour Unions and the area over which strikes had begun to extend, led the employers also to combine for resistance, and their combinations further solidified the Unions, so that employers and employed were more and more gathered into hostile camps. Meanwhile, in many countries the consolidation of many industrial enterprises that had formerly been in many hands into a few great undertakings — such as those called in America Trusts — some of which created a virtual monopoly in certain branches of production, struck at that faith in the power of free and open competition on which the older economists had relied, and evoked demands that in order to protect the consumer such combinations should be broken up and their undertakings taken over and managed by the State. The simultaneous tendency to throw on public authorities an increasing number of services needed in the interest of the community made the supersession of individual action more familiar, while State action became less distrusted the more the State itself was seen to be passing under popular control.

Thus there came a new orientation in politics as the struggle for political equality died down, its goal having been reached. The movement towards Economic Equality, already visible in many countries, forged to the front and gained strength with those who thought that progress towards it might be made by extending the action of the State, perhaps in some new form. Though its chief support naturally came from the working class, which it would admit to a larger share in the world's goods, it had some backing among members of the richer class whose sympathy went out to the poor, or who held that theoretical justice prescribed equal enjoyment, or equal opportunities for enjoyment, for all alike, and that those whose labour was the chief factor in the production of wealth were entitled to a far larger share, perhaps to the whole, of that which was produced. If Economic Equality was to be taken as the aim in view, how was it to be attained? A mere redistribution of property as it existed, to be effected by taking from the richer to give to the poorer, was obviously no remedy, for differences of wealth would soon reappear.[1] It therefore became necessary to reconstruct society on a new basis so as to prevent inequalities from arising afresh. Thus various schemes were propounded by a host of thinkers in different countries, Frenchmen and Germans leading.[2] Some of these schemes proposed to transfer all the means of production, distribution, and exchange to the State (or to administrative authorities — local or departmental — within the State), gradually transferring one industry after another from individuals to public management, and bringing the products of the transferred industries into the public treasury, but not altogether superseding private effort or forbidding those who had produced some kinds of things to retain the product.

More extreme theorists advocated the entire extinction of private property, with an allotment of every form of labour to some specific form of production and the application of the commodities produced to satisfy the needs of all alike. This full-blown Communism considers Capital as the enemy to be destroyed, root and branch, and seeks to extinguish classes altogether, making all the members of a nation consist only of one body, the so-called " proletariate."

To describe even in outline the various types which the new doctrines have been taking, and the groups which in each

[1] As a Western American remarked, if a wooden city was burnt down to secure equality between poor and rich, some smart man would make his pile by buying up the ashes for potash.

[2] Modern Socialism was just heard of and no more in the first French Revolution, but in the second (1830) it came to the front, and in 1848 its votaries took up arms against the Republic, though it made no figure in the simultaneous revolutions in Hungary, Germany, and Italy.

country have embraced each type, would be beyond the scope of this book.   Three observations may, however, be in place.

The movement, which had been originally democratic, took in its new phase a different course in different countries. Anarchism, seeking to extend individual liberty so widely as to get rid of laws altogether, might have seemed to be a more natural extension of democratic principles than is Socialism, and there are those who so regard it.   But Socialists and Anarchists, despite their divergent theories, have in common their desire to overthrow existing institutions, the former in order to rebuild, the latter in order to leave the site bare for men to disport themselves thereon.   Agreeing as they do in the first step, there has been a certain amount of co-operation, if not of real sympathy, between them.   Communism throve best in France, Germany, Italy, and Spain, in some cities of which latter country Anarchism also was conspicuous.   Each set of theorists hoped to find a field for the full practical development of their respective doctrines in Russia.   In Australia and New Zealand, countries far less affected by abstract views, there were sustained efforts of the wage-earning class to secure higher wages, shorter hours, and various other benefits to be bestowed by the State, and these took shape in a well-compacted Labour party.   This happened also in Britain, which followed in the wake of Australia.   Many leaders of the Labour party held and hold socialistic principles, but these have not been generally inscribed on the Labour banner in any English-speaking land.   In the United States, where democracy had been longest established, a Labour party arose much later, now counting millions of adherents, but not yet strong in the legislatures, while Socialism and Communism have found almost all their support among recent immigrants from Europe, who give them a considerable and apparently increasing vote in Presidential elections.[1]

In France, Spain, Portugal, Italy, and Russia the Socialist movement has always had a strong anti-religious colour. The Church has been an object of attack, being represented as an enemy of the people and of progress.   This is much less true of Germany, and there is no definitely anti-Christian colour among English-speaking Socialists.   The demo-

[1] The causes which have retarded the spread of Socialism in America have been indicated in the chapters on that country.

cratic movements of last century were everywhere concerned
more with Destruction than with Construction. They sought
to sweep away privileges and restrictions, establishing political equality by knocking down the old barriers. This work
of abolition having been completed, there comes a call for
institutions which shall give to the masses the positive benefits they desire by organizing Society on new lines. This is
a Constructive work. Destruction is easy. Any fool can
with one blow of his hammer destroy a statue it took Michael
Angelo years to perfect. But to construct needs knowledge,
thought, skill, and at least so much experience as enables a
man to judge whether his plans can be put in practice. The
leaders of the Socialist and Communist parties have not had
the opportunities for acquiring such experience. There has
been plenty of intellectual force among German and French
Socialists, but they have been divided into many sects with
divergent doctrines, and chiefly occupied in denouncing the
existing state of society which no one defends, except indeed
by pointing out that every form of social structure known
to history has been indefensible.

Four methods of action have presented themselves to the
leaders of the new movements. One is constitutional action
through those representative legislatures in which a Labour
or Socialist party is able to secure a majority, or at least an
organized minority, strong enough to extort from an Administration in power the kind of legislation it desires. This
has been successfully done in Australia and New Zealand,
and to a less extent in Britain, in France, and in Germany.
A second method is the old one of organizing strikes to compel employers to raise wages, or shorten hours of labour, or
confine employment to the members of labour unions. This
expedient is everywhere resorted to, but as it is costly it
sometimes fails. A third plan is to organize a general or
" sympathetic " strike, so as to put pressure on the whole
community to yield to the demands of any particular body
of workers demanding something either from private employers or from the State, if they are in State employment.[1]

A fourth method, itself a development of the third, is to
apply either the general strike, or a strike of several asso-

---

[1] Some remarks on this method will be further found in the following
chapter.

ciated bodies of workers, for the purpose of compelling the legislature and executive to adopt, or to desist from, some particular policy, possibly a foreign as well as a domestic policy, which they have adopted or are deemed likely to adopt. This is called the method of Direct Action. It is expected to prove specially effective if the strikers are employed in a form of industry essential to the welfare of the community at large, such as work on railroads or in coal mines, or in electric lighting and power, seeing that the suspension of railroad traffic, for instance, paralyzes all industries and inflicts the gravest inconveniences on the whole population.

These facts, familiar to us all, are here noted for the sake of observing that whereas the two first-named methods are entirely constitutional and legal, not transgressing the principles of democracy, the two latter are revolutionary and anti-democratic. Democracy was meant to secure that the will of the whole people, as constitutionally expressed on the last occasion of voting, shall prevail, *i.e.* it was designed to avert revolution by enabling the people to obtain by their votes all the justice that revolution had been previously used to gain, whereas a general strike, whether directed against the whole community, or meant to compel a Government to take a particular course, is an attempt to override the legal methods of the people's rule, just as is an armed insurrection. Such action is therefore a declaration that democracy has failed, and must be replaced by that very violence it was designed to avert. It may seem strange that this method should be at this time of day so lightly resorted to, for violence is a game at which every party can play, and history warns us that a victory won by such means has no promise of finality, since, besides creating a sense of insecurity, it inevitably tends to provoke further violence.

Lastly, in the new phase described the idea of Liberty has been, though not renounced, yet forgotten or ignored. This is not merely because political Liberty, in the sense of the exercise of power by the people, has been won and needs no further thought, but also because the rights of the individual man to lead his life in his own way, work at what he will, take his pleasure as he will, save and spend for himself, are no longer, and that by many persons in all classes, deemed to be a part of Liberty. Every increase of State control, every supersession of individual action by State action more or less reduces them.   This may be — doubtless often is — for the general good; but it represents a profound change of attitude.[1]   Communism of course carries control furthest, for it prescribes to every citizen the work he shall do and the recompense he shall receive, and leaves him nothing he can call exclusively his own.[2]   Fraternity also, the old watchword of the revolutionist ever since 1789, has fallen out of sight. However little its spirit has ever ruled in France or elsewhere, it was respected as heralding a time when Liberty and Equality would bring friendliness and peace in their train. This kind of Idealism has disappeared; it is material benefits that hold that place in the minds of the most recent advocates of change which spiritual progress held in the earlier generation.   There is more hatred than love in the apostles of the Class War and proletarian rule.

[1] It may of course be argued — indeed it is argued — that a society in which men are dependent upon others for the means of subsistence is Servitude rather than Liberty, for what does it avail a workman to be uncontrolled if he will starve without work, and is thus driven to take work on the terms which the employer prescribes?   Thus any such laws as secure him both livelihood and a fair measure of leisure extend his freedom; and whatever restrictions may be imposed on the individual, there will be, after striking the balance, a credit to the Liberty side of the account.   Though it is necessary to call attention to this argument, it is impossible to attempt to discuss it in these pages.

[2] One of the leaders of the Soviet Government in Russia, L. Trotsky, has recently officially defended the system of compulsory labour enforced there, declaring that the Workers' State has the right to send the worker to any place where his labour is needed, and to lay hands on any one who refuses to carry out his labour orders, as also to punish any worker who " destroys the solidarity of labour," and justifies this by the argument that such compulsion is inevitable, and no worse than that which exists under the hiring system of the bourgeoisie.   He approves the payment of wages proportioned to work, in addition to the supply of the necessaries of life, as for the present required to increase production, but looks forward to a time when the motive of a voluntary wish to serve the community will be a sufficient stimulus.

CHAPTER LXXVIII

EVERY one who tries to follow the march of events in these chaotic days of ours asks himself the question: In what direction are things moving? Is Democracy spreading more widely? Is it improving or degenerating? Is it gaining or losing the confidence of the peoples?

To describe the conditions of the moment would be as if one should try to paint a landscape over which lights and shadows were coming and going every moment under clouds driven before a gale. What can be done, however, is to indicate the tendencies visible when the storm of war burst in 1914, since which time the minds of men have been everywhere so far from normal — shall we say shell-shocked? — that it is impossible to predict what they will be five or ten years hence. Some of these tendencies have, however, continued operative, assuming a more formidable significance.

I. Democracy is spreading. Seven new States have sprung up in Europe since 1918: Czecho-Slovakia, Austria, Poland, Lithuania, Latvia (Lettland), Esthania, Finland.

Three new States have arisen in Western Asia: the republics of Georgia, Armenia, and Azerbaijan, the latter specially interesting as the first attempt at republican government in a Mussulman country. The fate of Russia hangs and may continue for some time to hang in the balance. Hungary has not yet settled her form of government; nor has Poland nor has China.[1]

The ten new States aforesaid have given or are giving themselves democratic constitutions, as did Portugal in 1909, when she dethroned the Braganza dynasty. Thus the number of democracies in the world has been doubled within fifteen years.

II. In the form which it has almost everywhere taken,

[1] The present constitution of China is provisional.

that of government by a representative assembly, democracy shows signs of decay; for the reputation and moral authority of elected legislatures, although these, being indispensable, must remain, have been declining in almost every country. In some they are deemed to have shown themselves unequal to their tasks, in others to have yielded to temptations, in others to be too subservient to party, while in all they have lost some part of the respect and social deference formerly accorded to them.   Whither, then, has gone so much of the power as may have departed from them?   In some countries it would seem to be passing to the Cabinet — England is often cited as an example — in others to the directly elected Head of the State, as for instance to the Governors in the several States of the American Union.   In France, though there has been no definite change, calls are heard for a strong President, and in Argentina the President already overtops the Chambers. What is common to all these cases is the disposition to trust one man or a few led by one rather than an elected assembly.

III. Over against such cases stand those wherein power is taken for the citizen body to overrule the legislature by the Referendum or supersede it by the Initiative.   This Swiss method, which grew up naturally in the States of the American Union also, can hardly be made a regular organ of government in large countries where the process of voting is costly, and in some at least of such countries — indeed wherever party or class organizations are powerful — it is likely to work less well than it has in the lands of its birth, but its conformability to the doctrine of Popular Sovereignty recommends it.   The development of Local Government and transference to it of as many administrative functions as possible, though constantly preached by reformers, does not in fact advance.   Very little has been done in this direction by France or Australia, or in Spanish America, while in England the small parish units have failed to enlist popular interest.

IV. That extension in many directions of the sphere of government which began in the United States some forty years ago, and has been carried furthest in New Zealand and Australia, has by increasing the tasks laid upon administration affected the character of democratic government itself, for it compels the creation of a great staff of officials, and so a sort of bureaucracy grows up, handling many kinds of business. This swells the volume of patronage lying in the gift of Ministers, and adds to the temptations which the exercise of patronage presents. Such developments make effective popular control more difficult, because so many branches of work lie beyond the knowledge and judgment of the citizens, or their representatives, that the discretionary powers of government inevitably grow, and responsibility is less easily secured. Moreover, the larger the number of State undertakings and State employees, the larger is the influence which the latter can exert through their votes. They become a powerful class, with personal pecuniary interests opposed to those of the community as a whole, and Ministers have in many countries found it hard to resist their demands.

The tendencies here described may probably advance, for they are not revolutionary but the natural result of slowly developing economic and social conditions, and if the development of these continues, political institutions will change, if not in form, yet in substance. The larger the mass of citizens becomes, the more do they tend to look to the Executive, and especially to its head. They follow a man or a small group rather than legislators whom it is hard to make responsible, and this of itself tends to make legislative offices desired chiefly by those who seek in them an avenue to executive power. That the plan of entrusting law-making, or the ultimate decision of a contested issue, to the direct action of the community is attractive, is shown not only by its spread in America, but also by its adoption in some recent constitutions, as for instance in that of Germany. Bureaucracy is denounced, but it grows.

V. Another influence insensibly modifying popular government must not pass unnoticed, viz. the shifting of population from the country to the city, and especially to the great city, which grows the faster the larger it grows. Australia and Argentina are dominated by their capitals. New York, Chicago, and Philadelphia contained in 1920 10,145,000 persons, nearly one-tenth of the whole population of the United States, and there are now six other cities with populations exceeding one million. It is not merely the problem of maintaining order in such populations, and that of feeding them in case a railway strike cuts off supplies from the country, that raise disquiet, it is also the influence upon

character and the habits of life in centres of excitement and
amusement; and when we consider all that this means, democracy may be given some credit for having averted disorders
which the aggregation of such vast masses of human beings
might have been expected to involve, creating perils never
experienced in earlier ages. Can such immunity be
expected to continue?

So far of changes in or affecting the working of the constitutional machinery of democratic government. Two other
new facts are the appearance of forces which, coming from
without, threaten, one of them the disintegration of democracy, the other its destruction.

I have already observed that the immensely increased
scale of industrial undertakings, coupled with the desire of
those employed therein to secure higher wages and better
conditions of life as well as of labour, have led the workers
in the more important of these industries to organize themselves in Unions, sometimes including an immense number
of persons. Such Unions are in certain countries further
associated for joint action in a general League, such as are
the *Confédération Général du Travail* in France, the Labour
Leagues in Australia, the American Federation of Labour in
the United States, and the group formed in Great Britain by
three enormous Unions (miners, railwaymen, and transport
workers) called the Triple Alliance. These bodies, democracies within the national democracy, as in the Middle Ages
the hierarchy was within the Civil State an Ecclesiastical
State armed with tremendous spiritual authority, possess a
double power, that of their votes as citizens and that of
bringing industry and commerce to a standstill by ceasing
to work. Such an exercise of the right of each individual
to give or withhold his labour creates a difficult situation,
for if the Government happens to be the employer there is no
independent authority to arbitrate between it and the
strikers, and if the employers are private persons the cessa-
tion from work may affect so seriously the welfare of the
nation that the matter becomes a political one with which the
Administration must deal. But how? It is a passive insurrection, harder to meet than is a rising in the army, and an
insurrection directed against all the rest of the community
which cannot meet it by physical force. This is a disinte-

gration of democracy, for matters of the first importance to the whole community are discussed and decided by each of these bodies, or by their League, among themselves, while the rest of the population, which has no share in the decision, is faced by a threat operating in effect as a command.

The other new factor is the emergence of a doctrine primarily economic but in its consequences political, and embodying itself in the project of eliminating those sections of the community which either possess wealth or are earning it otherwise than by manual labour, so as to create and thenceforth maintain a uniformity of material conditions, perhaps along with the prohibition of private property.[1] This idea is the child, a child whose birth was to be expected, of the passion for Equality and of the feeling of injustice which resents the absorption by others than the hand-worker of a disproportionate part of what his labour produces. In order to secure both Equality and the whole of this product, it becomes necessary to get rid of those who are deemed to have unjustly captured it; and this can be done only by giving to the community all the means of production and distribution, and securing to all an equal share in the products. Since the possessors of wealth cannot be expected to dispossess themselves, force is necessary, *i.e.* a Revolution to be carried through by the hand-workers or so-called " proletariate."[2] The absolute power they must seize for this purpose is the " Dictatorship of the Proletariate," which, inasmuch as revolution cannot be carried to success except by a few commanding spirits, means a supreme control, exerted not by a multitude of hand-workers but by an educated oligarchy of their leaders, necessarily small and invested with a wide discretion; for the larger the enterprise the more essential is a concentration of executive power. What form this dictatorship will take when, ceasing to be militant, it has been permanently established is a further question, on which some light is thrown by the creation in

[1] Some of the advocates of this doctrine have been driven by necessity to recognize and use " brain-workers," but these seem to be regarded as exceptional cases, and it does not yet appear how they are to be dealt with.

[2] This vague term, drawn from the *proletarii* in the early Roman Constitution ascribed to Servius Tullius, is most conveniently rendered by the term " hand-workers," as they are the class usually in the minds of the writers who employ it.

Russia of what is called the Republic of the Soviets, elective councils of workers and peasants from which all but proletarians are excluded.[1] Democracy and the peaceful settlement of all issues by constitutional methods disappear, superseded by Revolution and Oligarchy. Writers of this school denounce the existing democracies, and especially their legislatures, as " bourgeois," and propose to destroy them.

These two developments of the class spirit, one of which expresses itself in the proclamation of a Class War, have startled the wealthier and middle sections of the most advanced, and especially of the English-speaking nations. They did not understand why class sentiment should become so suddenly bitter, nor why, where constitutional means for redressing grievances exist, that sentiment should take a form which threatens the welfare of the whole people. Yet a little reflection suffices to show that the phenomena are not unprecedented. The resentment of the wage-earners at the appropriation by employers of what seems an inordinately large part of the product of labour, and the vehemence of this resentment against the present generation of the wealthier class, which has shown far more sympathy with the aspirations of the worker than the two preceding generations had done, is an instance to verify the old saying, " The fathers have eaten sour grapes, and the children's teeth are set on edge." Injustice always brings punishment in its train, but the spirit of revenge often grows with time, and is stronger in the descendants of those who have suffered than it was in the sufferers themselves; while the penalties fall not on those who did the wrong, but on their more innocent successors who are trying to atone for the past. The wretchedness of the toiling masses in some industrial countries from 1780 till far down in the nineteenth century left a legacy of bitterness which became actively conscious in their grandchildren, even as the oppressions borne by the peasantry and workers of France before 1780 gave birth to the passions that found vent in the ferocities of 1792.

Men are shocked to-day at the selfishness that threatens to paralyze all the industries of a country, and bring famine into the homes of the poor by a strike on railroads or in coal mines. But is not this only an extreme instance of the

[1] See note at end of this chapter.

selfishness which springs up in every class accustomed to
think first and think always of its own special interests?
The feudal nobles of the Middle Ages oppressed the peasantry all over Europe.   The manufacturing employers in
some industrial countries recked little of the sufferings of
their work-people down to our own time.   The European
conquerors and settlers among uncivilized races have from
the time of the Spanish Conquistadores in America ruth-
lessly exploited the labour of those races and robbed them
of their lands, so that even to-day it is hard to secure protection for African natives from the intruding whites.   In
all these cases there were among the oppressors many men
kindly and reasonable in the other relations of life, but
constant association with their own class and the sense of
personal interest benumbed their natural human sympathy
and made them forget that property and power have their
duties as well as their rights.   Public opinion restrains the
selfishness of an individual, but the public opinion of a class
possessed by the sense of a common interest confirms the
individual in his selfishness and blinds him to his own
injustice.   Those who preach the Class War are in this
respect, except indeed as regards the ferocity of the means
they employ, in some countries, no worse than the leaders
of other selfish classes have been before, as they are also
certainly no better.   Nevertheless, the doctrine of the Class
War, which is to extinguish classes once for all, and the
weapon of the General Strike, sound a new note of menace
to the progress of mankind.   They are not the result of
Democracy.   It has, indeed, failed to prevent them, but it
has not induced them, for they have arisen not in any sense
from its principles, but out of historical and economic causes,
which would have been invoked more powerfully to produce
discontent and insurrection under an autocratic or oligarchic
Government, unless such a Government had possessed a
military force strong enough to hold down a vast population.
They are in reality an attack on Democracy, the heaviest
blow ever directed against it, for they destroy the sense that
a people is one moral and spiritual whole, bound together
by spiritual ties, and their instrument is Revolution.   The
sort of revolution contemplated will not be a matter of this
year or the next; it opens up a long vista of struggle by

armed force, which would subject democratic governments to a strain heavier than they have ever yet had to bear. Strange and unexpected evolution! Democracy overthrows the despotism of the one man or the few who ruled by force, in order to transfer power to the People who are to rule by reason and the sense of their common interest in one another's welfare: and after two or three generations there arises from the bosom of the democracy an effort to overthrow it in turn by violence because it has failed to confer the expected benefits. The wheel has gone its full round; and the physical Force which was needed to establish democracy is now employed to destroy it.

NOTE

The accounts that have reached England of the structure of the Soviet Government do not altogether agree, and that structure itself does not seem to be uniform over all Russia. The main lines, however, upon which it is constituted would appear to be as follows. The basis of the organization is a primary assembly or Soviet of all the workers in a particular factory and of the cultivators in a particular village, representatives going from these primary meetings to higher Soviets. The scheme is described in a statement purporting to come from Mr. Zinoviev, and prepared on behalf of the Third International, and embodied in a document issued in January 1920. I quote from it as printed in the book of Mr. R. W. Postgate, entitled *The Bolshevik Theory* (Appendix IV.): " The city workers' Soviet consists of one delegate from each factory and more in proportion to the number of workers therein, together with delegates from each local union.

" For the peasants each village has its local Soviet which sends delegates to the Township Soviet, which in turn elects to the County Soviet, and this to the Provincial Soviet.

" Every six months the city and provincial Soviets send delegates to the All Russia Congress of Soviets, which is the supreme governing body of the country, and decides upon the policies which are to govern the country for the next six months. This Congress elects a Central Executive Committee of two hundred which is to carry out these policies, and also elects a Cabinet (the Council of Peoples' Commissars) who are the heads of Government Departments. These Commissars can be recalled at any time by the Central Executive Committee, as the members of all Soviets can also be very easily recalled by their constituents at any time.

" These Soviets are not only Legislative bodies but also Executive organs. In the intervals between the meetings of the All Russia Congresses of Soviets the Central Executive Committee is the supreme power. It meets at least every two months, and in the meantime the Council of Peoples' Commissars directs the country. . . . The workers are organized in industrial Unions; each factory is a local Union, and the Shop Committee elected by the workers is its Executive Committee. The All Russia Central Executive Committee of the federated Unions is elected by the Annual Trade Union Convention; a Scale Committee elected by it fixes the wages of all categories of workers. . . . The Unions are a branch of the Government, and this Government is the most highly centralized government that exists. It is also the most democratic government in history, for all the organs of Government are in constant touch with the worker masses, and constantly sensitive to their will. Moreover, the Local Soviets all over Russia have complete autonomy to manage their own local affairs, provided they carry out the national policies laid down by the Soviet Congress. Also the Soviet Government represents only the workers and cannot help but act in the workers' interests."

It will be noted that whereas the City Soviets send their delegates directly to the All Russia Congress — there are few populous cities in Russia — the Peasants' or Village Soviets send their delegates to the Township Soviet, and it to the County Soviet, and it to the Provincial Soviet, which alone sends its delegates direct to the Congress. (The soldiers are also allowed to have delegates from their Soviets which seem to be military units resembling the old time regiments.) Moreover, the representation of the peasants is so arranged as to be much smaller in proportion to numbers than that of the city workers, the system having been framed upon the lines of manufacturing and not of agricultural industry, and the Provincial Congress containing delegates from the Town as well as the Village Soviets, so that the workers have a double representation. So far as appears, representation is not even in Workers' Soviets proportioned to the size of each Soviet, or in other words, it is not provided that constituencies should be approximately equal in numbers. It ought to be added that a well-informed authority, who obtained first-hand information from Communist leaders in Russia, states that the whole of this " constitutional machinery " is practically controlled by the separate organization of that comparatively small body, the Communist party (Dr. Haden Guest in the London *Times*, Sept. 1920).

This scheme of Government by a series of local bodies, primary assemblies both administrative and elective, sending delegates to bodies for larger areas, and these again to bodies for still larger areas up to the Supreme Congress for the whole country which appoints and supervises the small Supreme Administrative Council, is ingenious and interesting as a novel form of constitution. It is not necessarily connected with " Bolshevism " or any form of Communism, and deserves to be studied, apart from any doctrines, on its own merits. Nor need it necessarily be based on work in factories, for, so far as regards the agricultural population, it is apparently as much local as vocational. Professing to be, and being indeed on paper eminently democratic, it seems eminently likely to be worked as an oligarchy, for it gives every opportunity for intriguers to secure majorities in each of the bodies and

control the whole power of what is really — though the name is
repudiated — the old "State" in a slightly altered dress. If,
however, we imagine such a constitution honestly worked, in an
intelligent and educated people, by men desiring only the common
weal, it would have two merits, the one that of helping the best
talent of the nation to rise to the top, the other that of enabling
the opinion of the whole nation to be promptly ascertained without
the cost and delay of a General Referendum, for the same issue
could be simultaneously propounded to all the local Soviets, and
their answers forthwith transmitted to headquarters. It is a pity
that the experiment of working this constitution did not have a
fair trial, but it is admitted on all hands that the elections of
delegates were practically farcical, being so managed by those in
actual control as to secure the delegates they approved, and
thereby make the composition of the Congress and Central Executive Committee just what they desired. This was of course to be
expected, for revolutionaries rarely permit themselves to be stopped
by scruples. If they do, they perish like the Girondins in 1793.
Those to whom their aim is supremely sacred have in ecclesiastical
as well as civil strife usually justified the means, whatever they
may be, that promise to attain it.

CHAPTER LXXIX

DEMOCRACY AND THE COMMUNIST STATE

THE age in which we live has seen a phenomenon without precedent in world history. The old relation of the richer and the poorer classes has been reversed. Heretofore, with a few transient exceptions in some small republics, the richer class have ruled, usually legally, always practically. Now, however, with the establishment of universal suffrage over nearly the whole civilized world, legal power has completely passed to the poorer strata of society, for, being everywhere the majority, they have the whole machinery of government at their disposal. Of the old problems, " Who shall share in power ? " and " Under what constitutional forms shall power be exercised ? " the former has been settled by giving equal voting power to all, and the latter has fallen into the background because it is now everywhere assumed that the best forms are those which secure to the multitude the most complete and direct control of legislation and administration. The new and live question which fills men's thoughts is, In what ways will the masses use the power they have obtained to improve their material condition? Already the range of governmental action intended to benefit them and to bring economic equality nearer by laying constantly increasing burdens on the rich has been extended. Many schemes are in the air for extending that action still more widely. Such schemes agree in proposing to assign many kinds of functions to public administrators which have hitherto been left to private enterprise, and for some at least of which the existing machinery of free governments seems unfitted. Even the present structure of government, the present organization of departments, the present methods of legislation may prove inadequate.

The most extreme form of these efforts to secure what is called Social Justice by a more equal distribution of worldly goods takes the form of what is sometimes called Communism or Collectivism, a vague term, as the term Socialism is also vague, for both are taken in different senses by different writers and party groups advocating all sorts of theories or schemes. Communism I understand as that type of scheme (whatever its details) which proposes to extinguish (or greatly restrict) private property, and to supersede the free action of individuals in commerce and productive industry by the action of the State. Some plans go much farther than others, and contemplate more drastic methods; some would change existing conditions gradually and by peaceful methods, others suddenly and completely by revolution. These distinctions need not here and now concern us. To state and discuss them would be an endless task; it is sufficient for my present purpose to enquire what effect the application to a democratic government of Communistic principles will have upon the working of such a government.

It seems to have been generally assumed that existing constitutions and methods might continue, for few proposals for any great changes in them were propounded or discussed until the Soviets were set up in Russia in 1917. Still it is worth while to enquire how far such democracies as we see in France, Australia, Britain, and the United States, created for functions much more restricted than those which Communism would assign to them, will prove qualified to discharge these new functions. To put it shortly, What will Democracy be in a Communist State? Need such a Communist State, once established, be a Republic? Might it not have at its head a monarch, or an oligarchy of highly trained officials, who could be trusted to administer its affairs, the permanence of the Communist arrangements being guaranteed by the will of the mass of the people, since they would of course approve and maintain a system which was conferring on them the long-expected benefits? Theoretically such an oligarchy, steadier than a democracy, but controlled by a watchful public opinion, is possible, and might do its work efficiently. Practically, however, we may safely assume that a government created by the masses and maintained to secure their interests and protect them against a return of Capitalism or any other kind of exploitation would, whatever it became when it got to work, be proposed and created under forms purporting to place it under popular control, *i.e.* to base it on universal suffrage, whether acting in a large area through a representative assembly or in a small area or areas by direct popular voting. Universal satisfaction will, it is presumed, make force needless for its support.

What sort of a Government, then, will a Communist State have, and in what respects will it differ in scope and nature from such democracies as the world has hitherto known? For the sake of clearness and simplicity let us regard it in its full development as a State in which private property has disappeared, every man working for the community only, while the community, allotting to him the particular work which he is to do, gives him in return a due provision of food, lodging, and clothing for the daily needs of himself and his family (if the Family is allowed to remain).[1] To assume the extinction of private property is to go far. We need not argue whether the holding of property is a Natural Right, as the Frenchmen of 1789 said, or Theft, as Proudhon said. Enough to note that not a few thinkers have advocated its extinction, and that in the only country in which these thinkers have gained control they propose to extinguish it, though at present they are only preparing for that step, and have not got so far as to persuade the peasants to relinquish their land. Some carry it less far, allowing the worker to retain for himself a certain amount of property wherewith to gratify his own tastes. Yet another school, that which is called Guild Socialism, proposes to assign all the greater industries not to the State, but to organized bodies of workers, each of which is to control the management and dispose of the products of its industry. For the purpose of our present enquiry, however, I must not attempt to examine either these differences or other schemes for turning the State to Communistic ends, or reconstructing it on a Communistic basis. Let us assume that in one full-blown form of reconstruction or another private property has disappeared. All are to work for the State, and the State is to provide for all. It thus becomes a sort of business corporation for the purposes of production and distribution, every citizen being a shareholder in this vast industrial company and receiving his dividend in the form either of money (if money remains) or of food and other necessaries or comforts of life.[2]

[1] Some few Communistic theorists from the days of Plato have suggested its disappearance.

[2] I take this as the extreme form, and though the present rulers of

With the economic arguments advanced for and against the creation of such a State I have here nothing to do. Its advocates have the *prima facie* advantage of being able to denounce existing economic conditions to the top of their bent, for few defend those conditions, and the wish to better them receives much sympathy from all who feel that the good things of the world are and always have been unequally distributed, some getting more than they deserve (so far as any one can attempt to estimate deserts), others less, so that many readjustments are desirable, though, considering how much more the enjoyment of life is affected by such things as health, strength, and temper than it is by abundance of worldly goods, it will always be impossible to distribute happiness in any sort of equal measure. Assuming, however, that efforts must be made to reduce the inequalities due to Nature and Chance by creating the largest possible equality in material conditions, difficulties arise regarding the methods to be employed, and these lie as much in the spheres of ethics and psychology as in those of economic science. The critics of a Communistic system argue that it rests upon assumptions regarding the action of human motives and the possibility of raising the average moral level of human character which are discountenanced, or at least unverified, by experience. The Communist replies that under new conditions which will call out the best and reduce the worst impulses that level is sure to rise, and men will work as zealously for the Community as they have ever done for themselves.[1] The critic rejoins that history records no such moral progress, steadily advancing during the last three thousand years, as to entitle us to expect that man will become more unselfish and altogether more virtuous.

When the critic further remarks that under Communism men will soon begin to regret the loss of free self-determination, and will rebel against the control of their acts and opinions by the power of the community exercised through of-

Russia have shrunk from carrying it out, it seems to be the form they approve. But whether this be so or not, the principles and methods involved in any form which a complete governmental control of industry may take, need to be considered as respects their compatibility with existing democratic institutions.

[1] If men do not so work in Australia for the Government, the explanation given is that this happens because a capitalistic Government does not command their loyalty.

ficials presumably no better than themselves, the Communist answers that a new generation will quickly grow up which will not regret what it has never enjoyed, and will be so much more comfortable under the ordered paternalism into which it has been born than its ancestors were in their unchartered freedom, as to look back with pity and wonder on the Dark Ages of capitalist rule and selfish competition.

These questions belong to the study of Man as a social being, and the one test which can be profitably applied to all the schemes referred to is their conformity to the tendencies of Human Nature, for to political science, so far as it can be deemed a science, may be applied the maxim which Bacon applied to the physical sciences: *Natura non nisi parendo vincitur.* There is promise of good in any system which recognizes and turns to account the better tendencies in man and tries to repress the worse, and a prospect of failure for any system which ignores the latter. Some, we have reason to believe, are susceptible of improvement, but how far susceptible, no one can determine; and the maxim warns us that where any of them has the permanence and strength of that which we call a Law of Nature, it cannot be ignored. A Communist or an Anarchist who expects to reconstruct Society, each in his own way, must be an optimist, strung up to so high a tension as to believe that in the new world he seeks to create men will be renewed in the spirit of their minds and be themselves purer and nobler creatures. The fact that the conduct of such an one may lower instead of raising our hopes for human progress does not necessarily discredit his doctrines, nor do the violence and cruelty and perfidy which he or any other preacher of revolution may employ to reach his ends condemn those ends any more than the cruelties of the Inquisition condemn the religion in whose supposed interest they were perpetrated. Revolutionists intoxicated with their own aims recoil from no means needed to secure their ascendancy, because they have not learnt, in Cromwell's famous phrase, to believe it possible that they may be mistaken.

To see what kind of organization that huge Co-operative Company, the Communist State, will require, let us consider what functions its Government, once set a-going, will have to discharge. It will develop and manage all the natural sources of wealth, the land, the minerals, the water power.

It will establish and direct all industries, works, electric power stations, factories, iron and chemical works, and so forth. It will administer all the means of communication by land, water, and air, including those with foreign countries. It will provide State physicians and hospitals, and will found and manage all educational institutions, from the elementary school up to the university, appointing and remunerating the teachers and directing the curricula. It will plan, execute, and maintain all public works, including dwellings for the citizens; will provide public amusements and means of enjoyment, including theatres, concerts, picture galleries and libraries; will undertake the dissemination of news, conducting and supervising newspapers and magazines, and printing books. Presumably — and the practice of the Russian Communists suggests this course, which indeed had the approval of Rousseau and of Bebel — it will exercise a censorship, at least to the extent of forbidding the publication of any literature impugning the system of government or tending to create discontent, and may therefore have to forbid religions likely to distract men from their allegiance to the State; while as the obligation to work is universal, priests will not be excused from discharging it. The State authorities will of course feed and clothe the citizen, possibly allowing him, or at least her, so much choice in the kind of garments to be worn as is compatible with the principle of equal treatment for all. They must also maintain public order by providing a police, for though theft will have disappeared with property (except as an offence against the State),[1] offences against the person may continue, requiring the retention of penal laws and courts and prisons.

Whether an army and navy will be needed depends upon whether neighbouring or competing nations also have been converted to Communism. Such a conversion seems to be expected by Communistic thinkers generally, and is indeed almost essential to the success of the idea. If, however, there remain States which stand out, maintaining their old selfish and probably aggressive policies, this happy future cannot be expected, and defence will still have to be provided, with the incidental danger of creating military chiefs and an armed

[1] A man might of course steal articles belonging to the State, but as he could not, under the conditions which will then prevail, make much use of what he stole, there would be little temptation.

force dangerous to the system of government. Should Communism spread over the whole earth, not only will foreign policy be simplified, but internal economic arrangements also will gain. No country can within itself have the means of providing for all its needs. Few European countries can do so even as regards food. The abolition of customs duties on imports, peace being assured and private property gone, would make life easier for every country by cheapening many articles.

Against the many new functions devolving on this gigantic bureaucracy which will have taken over all that was formerly done by individual action, there must be set some functions hitherto exercised by governments which it may drop. Little legislation will be called for. Property having gone, there will be no contracts, and consequently no courts to try civil suits and no lawyers to argue them, a loss to which many persons will reconcile themselves.[1] No more family quarrels over wills, no calls by rate collectors to vex the householder! The house he inhabits will not be his own, but he will live rent and rate free, owing to the State nothing but his labour, which will, in the view of most Communists, be a light burden, cheerfully borne in an altruistic spirit.

In order to prepare the Communist State for these many tasks, its chiefs and guides must determine the principles on which work is to be allotted to each citizen, and what form his remuneration is to take. Equality and Justice are to rule. But how are Equality and Justice to be secured as between different classes of producers, hand-workers and brainworkers, the skilled and the unskilled, the strong and the weak, the industrious and the indolent? If the work assigned is more agreeable, shall it be remunerated on a lower scale? If it requires more skill, is the scale to be higher? or if the value of the work is to count, how is value to be estimated? A code of laws will be needed to settle these matters. Great will be the power of the officials who not only allot work but direct and superintend it, and select for the higher posts persons who have proved their superior fitness. Regulations must be enacted prescribing the modes of choosing officials, their terms of office, the method of superintending them, and the discipline to be applied to the workers of

[1] Whether actions for tort "sounding in damages" will remain when civil damages have been abolished with the extinction of private property is a question which, however interesting, can stand over.

all grades, since not even the sanguine optimist can rely on the absence of " slackers." But the most important matter of all will be to find means for securing the choice of the persons best fitted to manage the chief departments of the Company's work for the nation, and especially of the Board of Directors who provide for the proper correlation of these departments and select the departmental heads. Everything will depend upon the skill and judgment of this supreme Board of Control. Technical scientific knowledge would seem to be essential for its members as well as for heads of departments. Those who manage such vast branches of work as agriculture and mining, transportation and education, will be the real masters and mainstays of the nation, and it is for their capacity that they must be selected. Who is to judge capacity? If the Directing Board are to do so, they, as well as the managing heads, must possess not only the requisite mastery of applied science and administrative skill, but an unusual measure of discernment and honesty.

Similar questions arise with regard to the assignment of particular persons to particular kinds of work for which they seem to be, or represent themselves to be, specially qualified, intellectually or physically, for not every one who seeks the vocation of a cricketer or a metaphysician can expect his aspirations to be gratified; and such questions must arise also over promotions in the various branches of technical and administrative work. Efficiency can be secured only by promotion based upon merit. Excellence in the middle and lower grades of work can be judged only by those who in the higher grades know and can estimate the performances of their subordinates. As every one will be a worker, every citizen's career in life will depend upon the opinion formed of him by his superiors. In the civil services of Britain and Germany promotions have been generally made honestly, but in those countries the departments have been for many years kept apart from partisan, if not always from social influences. In a community where there is no property and all fare alike, no one will be able to obtain favour by giving good dinners, but can any barrier be erected capable of excluding feminine arts or the claims of relationship? How are officials to be prevented from putting their sons-in-law into " soft jobs," probably by way of secret log-rolling with friends in other offices? The most solemnly respectable of Directors, the most capable head of a department, will want watching in the exercise of powers which determine the fortunes and may arouse the suspicions of those beneath them. One cannot help using the word " beneath." It seems a relic of the old time when there were distinctions of rank. But although social rank will have vanished, there will still be, for there cannot but be, distinctions of official authority. There must always be some one to direct the work, others to perform it; and there must be, always and everywhere, some disciplinary enforcement of compliance, for if, in order to maintain equality, those elected to command are constantly changed, will not experience be lost and authority disappear? Nations which allow the soldiers to elect their officers find before long that the officers must be allowed to enforce stern discipline if the army is not to break down in face of the enemy. In a peaceful bureaucracy instant obedience is less supremely needed at a given moment, but obedience there must be, and unless human nature is quite transformed, it is unattainable without compulsion. Will not the Communist State have to choose between Efficiency and Equality?[1]

What, then, will be the relation of this kind of State to Democracy? In these new conditions, what will remain to those representative assemblies through which the people have declared their will? Although some extremist writers have denounced legislatures and democracy and the State itself as all " capitalistic," the People can hardly mean, in becoming a body of workers officered by bureaucrats, to relinquish the sovereignty they exercise by universal suffrage.

Much of the work hitherto performed by representative assemblies will doubtless have disappeared, and the basis of representation may be no longer territorial, but perhaps vocational. On many subjects there will be little legislation, no taxation, since every one's contribution will be rendered in his labour, hardly any debates on foreign affairs (if Communism spreads over the world), nor any on military or naval affairs. Some administrative subjects will remain, on which the citizens may express their wishes to the reigning bureaucracy, such as the kind of drinks, alcoholic or not, to be

[1] An interesting examination of the difficulties that may arise in the management of industries by the State may be found in a book published anonymously in England some years ago entitled *Vox Clamantis*.

supplied to the citizens, and the subjects to be taught in State schools. The questions now in controversy between the friends of the ancient classics and those of modern languages or physical science will probably have been ended by the extinction of the former subjects before Communism arrives, but conflicts between the advocates of cinemas, of the drama, and of concerts respectively, as pleasures to be provided for the people, may be more protracted; and if there is a surplus after providing for food, clothing, and housing, shall literature claim a share, the State, as being the only publisher, determining which poets shall be preferred? The main business will, however, be the supervision of the administrative departments, the examination of their accounts, reports on their work in production, a judgment of the wisdom of their policy in the appropriation of labour to competing demands for its application, and the way in which the powers of allotting work and bestowing promotions have been exercised. This last-mentioned topic will, if responsibility is to be enforced on the bureaucracy, be the most fertile field for criticism, for every member of the assembly as well as every one of his constituents will have a personal interest, all alike being servants of the country. Even if members of the legislature are exempted from any other work during their term of legislative service, it will be hard for them to criticize freely those who have been and may again be their official superiors. Will the same spirit of deference to authority come to pervade the soldiers of the Industrial Army as that which sapped the spirit of liberty in military Prussia?

What place will there be for political parties in the new Commonwealth, which will be not a State in the old sense, but a Co-operative Company for agricultural and manufacturing production and distribution, and on what issues will elections turn? If they be those of most consequence to every citizen, viz. the conditions of his own work and remuneration, are they to be settled by the people at elections or by their representatives in the legislature, or if the latter are to have the power of displacing officials whose exercise of their authority has displeased sections of the voters, who are, as workers, subject to that authority, how will discipline and the continuity of administrative policy be preserved?

Of the prizes offered in former days to ambition, only

Power will remain, for wealth will be unattainable, while eminence in art and letters will depend upon the favour of official patrons who have been chosen for their scientific knowledge and executive capacity. Without their favour neither poet nor painter will be able to reach the people, for the press will of course be in the hands of the ruling officials, who will provide for the people the proper views as well as the proper news. Of Power there will apparently be one kind only, that attached to a high place in the official hierarchy, to be won, if the system is to work, not by rhetorical gifts or lavish promises to the masses, but by the talent of the administrator. Eloquence and the demagogic arts that have flourished under popular governments will be as much out of place in the bureaucracy as in a meeting of railway directors. The qualities by which a man will rise will be those which bring men to the top of the Treasury or Admiralty or Post Office in the permanent civil service of countries like France, Germany, or England; but the men may probably be still more remarkable, for the civil service, being the only career, will draw to itself, like a magnet, all the talent of the country. The legislative assembly will doubtless still offer an arena to debaters, but if it interferes with administration and pitchforks men into high posts because they are fluent in speech, the principles on which the system is based will be violated and efficiency must suffer.

These observations suggest that schemes of a Communistic nature contemplate a condition of political and economic life, the latter overshadowing the former, to which the familiar institutions of Democracy seem ill adapted. Democracy as it exists to-day and Communism as it is preached, agreeing with Democracy (as against some other forms of Socialistic doctrine) in regarding the nation as one homogeneous whole, differ in this, that Communism regards it as primarily an Economic whole existing for the purposes of production and distribution, while the apostles of Democracy regarded it as primarily a Moral and Intellectual whole, created for the sake of what the ancient philosophers called the Good Life. It was to be expected that the political institutions established with a view to the latter theory and aim should be ill suited to the former purposes.

How the present forms and mechanism of Democracy

should be remodelled to do the work which Communist principles prescribe is a question to be answered by those who have formed for themselves a clear notion of what the Socialist or Communist State will be, a subject on which the different schools called Socialistic differ widely. I have here, for the sake of simplicity, taken for examination that particular form in which private property is not permitted, because it is well to see to what results a logical development of Equalitarian and Communistic principles will lead. Although some of the questions I have suggested as fit to be considered will not arise in States which allow property to survive, still in all communities where Government, or any authority created by the State, assumes the exclusive control of industry, problems of this kind cannot but emerge; and the nearer any form approaches to the extreme form here dealt with, the more need will there be for such a reshaping of existing institutions as will adapt them to the requirements of a State built on economic relations and making their adjustment on the principle of equality its primary aim.

CHAPTER LXXX

THE FUTURE OF DEMOCRACY

A STUDY of the various forms government has taken cannot but raise the question what ground there is for the assumption that democracy is its final form, an unwarranted assumption, for whatever else history teaches, it gives no ground for expecting finality in any human institution. All material things are in a perpetual flux. The most ancient heavens themselves, in which mankind has seen the changeless radiance of eternity, are subject to this law, moving towards some unknown destination, with new stars blazing forth from time to time only to vanish again into darkness; nor can we tell whether the substances which make up the Universe may not themselves be changing, so short has been the period during which we have observed them.

So, too, in human affairs the thing that hath been is not, and the thing that is can never return, because its having existed is a new fact added to the chain of causation; and therefore those Eastern cosmologies which tried to help men to conceive of infinity by imagining a succession of cycles endlessly repeating themselves, were obliged to make each cycle end with a destruction of all things in order that creation might start afresh, unaffected by what had gone before. That which the ancient poet said of the mind of man, that it changes with every returning sun,[1] is true of nations also, whose thoughts and temper vary from year to year, and true also of the institutions men create, which are no sooner called into being than they disclose unexpected defects, and begin to decay in one part while still growing in another.

Within the century and a half of its existence in the modern world free government has passed through many phases, and seems now to stand like the traveller who on the verge of

[1] Τοῖος γὰρ νόος ἐστὶν ἐπιχθονίων ἀνθρώπων
οἷον ἐπ᾽ ἦμαρ ἄγῃσι πατὴρ ἀνδρῶν τε θεῶν τε (*Odyss.* xviii. 136).

a great forest sees many paths diverging into its recesses and knows not whither one or other will lead him.

Whoever attempts to forecast the course systems of government will take must therefore begin from the two propositions that the only thing we know about the Future is that it will differ from the Past, and that the only data we have for conjecturing what the Future may possibly bring with it are drawn from observations of the Past, or, in other words, from that study of the tendencies of human nature which gives ground for expecting from men certain kinds of action in certain states of fact. We cannot refrain from conjecture. Yet to realize how vain conjectures are, let us imagine ourselves to be in the place of those who only three or four generations ago failed to forecast what the next following generation would see. Let us suppose Burke, Johnson, and Gibbon sitting together at a dinner of The Club in 1769, the year when Napoleon and Wellington were born, and the talk falling on the politics of the European Continent. Did they have any presage of the future? The causes whence the American Revolution and the French Revolution were to spring, and which would break the sleep of the peoples in Germany and Italy, might, one would think, have already been discerned by three such penetrating observers, but the only remarks most of us recall as made then and for some years afterwards to note symptoms of coming dangers were made by a French traveller, who said that the extinction of French power in Canada had weakened the tie between the American colonies and Great Britain, and by an English traveller who saw signs of rottenness in the French Monarchy. Men stood on the edge of stupendous changes, and had not a glimpse of even the outlines of those changes, not discerning the causes that were already in embryo beneath their feet, like seeds hidden under the snow of winter, which will shoot up under the April sunlight. How much more difficult has it now become to diagnose the symptoms of an age in which the interplay of economic forces, intellectual forces, moral and religious forces is more complex than ever heretofore, incomparably more complex than it had seemed to be before discovery had gone far in the spheres of chemistry, physics, and biology, before education had been diffused through all classes, before every part of the world had been drawn into relations with every other part so close that what affects one must affect the rest.

Nevertheless, since conjecture cannot be repressed, and the tendencies of human nature remain as a permanent factor, let us see whether men's behaviour in the past may not throw some glimmer of light upon the future. Frenchmen, Englishmen, and Americans find it so natural a thing that men should be interested in politics, that they assume men will always be so interested. But is it really true — so students of history will ask — that this interest can be counted on to last? For a thousand years, after the days of the last republicans of Rome, the most civilized peoples of Europe cared nothing for politics and left government in the hands of their kings or chiefs. Greek democracy had been destroyed by force more than a century earlier, and little regret was expressed at its extinction. The last blows struck for republican freedom in Rome were struck not by the people, but by a knot of oligarchs, most of whom had their personal reasons for slaying the great Dictator. No one thought of trying to revive free self-government in Italy or Greece or around the coasts of the Aegean, where hundreds of republics had bloomed and died. When the Italian cities shook off the yoke of local lords or bishops in the eleventh and twelfth centuries nearly all of these new republics passed before long under the sway of new despots, and few were the attempts made to recover freedom. The ancient doctrine that power issues from the people came to light when the study of the Roman Law was resumed, but nobody tried to apply it, not even under such teaching as came from Marsilius of Padua,[1] when he used the tenet as a weapon in the great conflict between the Emperor and the Pope. Cities and nations seemed to reck little of their rights: a tyrant might now and then be overthrown, but there was no reviviscence of the love of liberty. Since the days of Augustus the lives of the mass of mankind had been filled by labour in field or mine or workshop; the pleasures and the interests they had in common were given to War, and still more to Religion, which like a stream, sometimes full and strong, sometimes half lost in the swamps of superstitition, bore down the relics of the old civilization. Without the stimulus which the ecclesiastica struggles of the

[1] In his extraordinary book the *Defensor Pacis*, published in 1327.

sixteenth century gave to the sense of individual independence in the northern half of Europe, this stagnation of political life might have lasted longer than in fact it did.   If it be said that the conditions of the Roman Empire and the Dark Ages can never recur, now that the sense of civic right has spread widely, now when political equality is guaranteed by the passion for social and economic equality, the answer is that although those particular conditions will indeed not recur, we can well imagine other conditions which might have a like effect.   The thing did happen: and whatever has happened may happen again.   Peoples that had known and prized political freedom resigned it, did not much regret it, and forgot it.

Can we, looking back over the nineteenth century, think of any causes or conditions that might once again bring about this indifference?   We must not forget that the sense of civic right and passion for equality just referred to are nowhere felt by all the people, in many countries not even by a majority, in some only by a small minority.   Is it possible that a nation, tired of politics and politicians, may be glad to be saved the trouble of voting?   In France the peasantry and the educated bourgeoisie acquiesced in the despotism of Louis Napoleon, pleased to have the promise of a quiet life, as at Rome not only the multitude but the bulk of those who cultivated literature and philosophy had welcomed the rule of Augustus.   In Prussia, after the military triumphs of 1866 and 1870 had made monarchy popular, the middle and professional classes allowed themselves to be militarized and monarchized in spirit, preferring commercial prosperity, efficient administration, and the growth of the nation's power to a continuance of the efforts their fathers had made against Bismarck's rule when taxes were levied without the consent of the Landtag and constitutional reforms were refused.   So the forward movement passed into the hands of others who, desiring economic levelling rather than political liberty, sought the latter chiefly for the sake of the former, while the *Freisinnige Partei,* which represented the traditions of 1848–9, withered away, losing support in every class.

In Spain a republic, hastily set up in 1873, gained so little support that it was quickly followed by a restoration of the old monarchy; and when in 1890 universal suffrage was established the gift excited little interest and has made little practical difference to policies or to administration, though in a few of the Eastern seaports Socialist and Anarchist groups are occasionally enabled by it to return a few members of extreme opinions. Elsewhere constituencies are controlled and elections manipulated by local Bosses (commonly called Caciques [1]), whose rule, a source of profit to themselves, is acquiesced in by the bulk of the citizens. There could hardly be a more instructive refutation of the notion that a taste for the exercise of political rights is a natural characteristic of civilized man than this indifference to politics of an ancient nation which has produced wonderful explorers, conquerors, and statesmen, and made splendid contributions to literature, learning, and art.

In some countries we see to-day the richer class refusing to enter the legislatures, and voting only because they fear for their wealth, while in many the centre of gravity in political thought as well as in action has shifted from methods of government and legal reforms to economic issues. These last-named issues have, as already observed, come so to dominate the minds of large sections of certain peoples as to make them willing to sacrifice liberty itself, or at least the institutions which have hitherto safeguarded liberty, for the sake of that fundamental reconstruction of society which they desire. The revolution that is to effect this purpose is represented as a transient flood, needed to sweep away the barriers Capitalism has set up. But is the stream likely to return to its ancient channel? Will the forcible methods revolution uses be renounced?

Among the questions which men now ask about the Future none is more momentous than this: Will it be, as heretofore, a future of War, or — even if only in the middle distance — a future of Peace? If wars continue, the smaller free States may conceivably be vanquished and annexed or incorporated by their stronger neighbours. This was how the republics of ancient Greece and Italy perished; thus was freedom extinguished in Athens and Achaia; thus did the republic of Florence fall in the sixteenth century. In conquering Rome herself it was the vast extension of her dominions that made monarchy inevitable.

---

[1] A term from the name of a chief among American aborigines.

One road only has in the Past led into democracy, viz. the wish to be rid of tangible evils, but the roads that have led or may lead out of democracy are many. Some few of them may be mentioned.

If wars continue, the direction of Foreign Policy, a function which was of supreme importance in the city republics of the ancient and mediaeval world, may again become so, especially among those small new States of Europe and Western Asia which have territorial or commercial disputes with their neighbours. Till the relations of European peoples with one another become more stable than they are to-day, the spirit of nationality, accentuated as we see it by rivalry and hatred, a spirit which breeds discontent in some countries and in others prompts aggression against rival States, may keep alert and acute the desire of these peoples to share in the conduct of their governments. But it is also possible that the lust of conquest or the need for defence may lead to a concentration of power in the Executive dangerous to the people, inducing them to sacrifice some of their liberty to preserve national independence or to secure military ascendancy. Such things have happened.

He who has acquired ascendancy by brilliant success against the enemy and has thereby fascinated the people might, in some countries, establish his power. Even our own time saw a mediocre adventurer, pushed forward by a faction possessing wealth and social influence, who proved able, since believed to have the army behind him, to threaten the liberties of France; and this although he had no victories standing to his credit.

Dangers may also arise from civil strife, when it reaches a point at which one party becomes willing to resign most of the people's rights for the sake of holding down the other faction. This often happened in the ancient and mediaeval republics, and might happen in any country distracted by racial or religious hatreds, or perhaps even by the sort of class war which was carried on in 1919 in Hungary. There are European countries to-day in which it is, if not probable, yet certainly not impossible.

Thirdly, the less educated part of a nation might become indifferent to politics, the most educated class throwing their minds into other things, such as poetry or art, to them more

interesting than politics, and gradually leaving the conduct
of State affairs to an intelligent bureaucracy capable of
giving business men the sort of administration and legislation
they desire, and keeping the multitude in good humour by
providing comforts and amusements.[1]   The heads of such a
bureaucracy would, if wise, do little to alter the constitution,
content to exercise the reality of power under the old familiar
forms.   Such a change would scarcely happen so long as
there were questions rousing class bitterness or involving the
material wellbeing of the masses; we must suppose a time
in which controversies have ceased to be acute, and such a
time seems distant.   Free government is not likely to be
suppressed in any country by a national army wielded by an
ambitious chief.   If any people loses its free self-government
this will more probably happen with its own acquiescence.
But oligarchy springs up everywhere as by a law of nature:
and so many strange things have happened in our time that
nothing can be pronounced impossible.   Few are the free
countries in which freedom seems safe for a century or two
ahead.

Democracy has become, all over Europe and to some extent
even in North America also, desired merely as a Means, not
as an End, precious in itself because it was the embodiment
of Liberty.   It is now valued not for what it is, but for what
it may be used to win for the masses.   When the exercise of
their civic rights has brought them that which they desire,
and when they feel sure that what they have won will remain
with them, may they not cease to care for the further use of
those rights?   The politicians, who in some countries have
been more and more becoming a professional class, might
continue to work the party machinery; but that will avail
little if the nation turns its mind to other things.   If the
spiritual oxygen which has kept alive the attachment to
Liberty and self-government in the minds of the people
becomes exhausted, will not the flame burn low and perhaps
flicker out?   The older school of Liberals dwelt on the

[1] The passion for pleasure and amusement, as contrasted with the
taste for intellectual enjoyments, is often said to be growing with the
growth of civilization.   There certainly have been ages in which the
" things of the mind " were more and others in which they were less
cared for by the more leisured class, but men's judgment of the time
they live in is apt to be affected by personal bias, especially in those
who miss what they valued in their youth.

educative worth of self-government which Mazzini represented in its idealistic and Mill in its utilitarian aspects;
but who would keep up the paraphernalia of public meetings
and of elections and legislative debates merely for the sake
of this by-product? Much will depend on what the issues
of the near future are likely to be. If that which the masses
really desire should turn out to be the extinction of private
property or some sort of communistic system, and if in some
countries such a system should ever be established, the whole
character of government would be changed, and that which is
now called Democracy would (as indicated in a previous
chapter) become a different thing altogether, perhaps an
industrial bureaucratic oligarchy. Even if some less far-
reaching scheme of Economic Equality than that now presented to the wage-earners as the goal of their efforts be
attained, or enter a period of experiment which would end
in proving it to be unattainable, popular government cannot
fail to be profoundly modified.

A wider, indeed an illimitable field of speculation is
opened when we think of the possibilities of changes in the
interests, tastes, and beliefs of the different families of mankind. In Human Nature there are, to borrow a term from
mathematics, certain " Constants "— impulses always operative — ambition and indolence, jealousy and loyalty, selfishness and sympathy, love and hatred, gratitude and revenge.
But the ideas, fancies, and habits of men change like their
tastes in poetry and art. New forms of pleasure are
invented: the old lose their relish: the moral as well as the
intellectual values shift and vary. The balance between the
idealistic and the realistic or material view of life is always
oscillating. Humility, once revered in Christian and
Buddhist countries, has been described in our time as a Dead
Virtue. Even nations in which public life has been most
active may relegate a political career to a place as low as
soldiering has held in China and trading in Japan. The
masses may let the reins slip from their hands into those of
an oligarchy, so long as they do not fear for themselves either
oppression, or social disparagement, or the loss of any material benefits they have been wont to enjoy. They may trust
to the power of public opinion to deter a ruling group from
any course which would displease the bulk of the nation, for

the power of public opinion will survive political mutations
so long as an intolerant majority does not impose its orthodoxy to fetter the play of thought.   Such phases in the
never-ceasing process of evolutionary change might well be
transient, for oligarchies are naturally drawn to selfish ways,
and selfishness usually passes into injustice, and injustice
breeds discontent, and discontent ends in the overthrow of
those who have abused their power, and so the World-spirit
that plies at the roaring loom of Time discards one pattern
and weaves another to be in turn discarded.

That physiological factor which we call Heredity must
not be overlooked.   In the most civilized peoples there is an
evident tendency for those family stocks which are wealthy
or of exceptional intellectual quality to die out, so that the
perpetuation of the human species is left to be maintained
by sections of the population in which self-restraint and the
mental faculties are less fully developed.   This phenomenon
becomes more significant when we remember that sooner or
later, though of course in a still distant future, the races of
mankind will in some regions be inevitably so commingled
as to efface many of the distinctions which now separate
them.   About the effect of such a fusion upon human character and the institutions which are the outgrowth of
character *plus* experience, we cannot guess.   Since some
among the Backward races are both more numerous and more
prolific than the Whites, the prospect thus opened may seem
discouraging.   Yet not all of these races are intellectually
inferior to the European races, and may even have a fresh-
ness and vitality capable of renewing the energies of more
advanced races whom luxury has enervated.   In regions
where fusion has come to pass, the " composite man " of the
remote future may prove to be as well fitted for self-government as the more advanced races are to-day.   But fusion,
with the assimilation of language, ideas, and habits, though
it may extinguish race-enmities, need not make for peace
either in nations or between nations.

Whatever happens, such an institution as Popular Government will evidently take its colour from and will flourish
or decline according to the moral and intellectual progress
of mankind as a whole.   Democracy is based on the expectation of certain virtues in the people, and on its tendency to

foster and further develop those virtues. It assumes not merely intelligence, but an intelligence elevated by honour, purified by sympathy, stimulated by a sense of duty to the community. It relies on the people to discern these qualities and choose its leaders by them. Given the kind of communal spirit which Rousseau expected, given the kind of fraternally religious spirit which Mazzini and the enthusiasts of his time expected, self-government, having the moral forces behind it, would be a comparatively simple matter, living on by its unquestioned merits. With intelligence, sympathy, and the sense of duty everything would go smoothly; and a system which trained the citizen in these virtues would endure, because each successive generation would grow up in the practice of them. Thus the question of the permanence of democracy resolves itself into the question of whether mankind is growing in wisdom and virtue, and with that comes the question of what Religion will be in the future, since it has been for the finer and more sensitive spirits the motive power behind Morality. Governments that have ruled by Force and Fear have been able to live without moral sanctions, or to make their subjects believe that those sanctions consecrated them, but no free government has ever yet so lived and thriven, for it is by a reverence for the Powers Unseen and Eternal which impose those sanctions, that the powers of evil have been, however imperfectly, kept at bay and the fabric of society held together. The future of democracy is therefore a part of two larger branches of enquiry, the future of religion and the prospects of human progress.

The question, whether men will rise towards the higher standard which the prophets of democracy deemed possible, has been exercising every thoughtful mind since August 1914, and it will be answered less hopefully now than it would have been at any time in the hundred years preceding. That many millions of men should perish in a strife which brought disasters to the victors only less than those it brought to the vanquished is an event without parallel in the annals of the race. There has probably been since the fifth century no moment in history which has struck mankind with such terror and dismay as have the world-wide disasters which began in 1914, and have not yet passed away. The explanations of the facts are no more cheering than the facts themselves. Human passions have been little softened and refined by the veneer of civilization that covers them: human intelligence has not increased, and shows no sign of increasing, in proportion to the growing magnitude and complexity of human affairs. Knowledge has been accumulated, the methods and instruments of research have been improved, a wonderful mastery over the forces of Nature has been obtained, the world has become a more comfortable place to live in and offers a far greater variety of pleasures; but the mental powers of the individual man have remained stationary, no stronger, no wider in their range, than they were thousands of years ago, and the supremely great who are fit to grapple with the vast problems which the growth of population and the advances of science have created come no more frequently, and may fail to appear just when they are most needed.

This much, however, may be said regarding the question which directly concerns us here. It is not on democracy that the blame for these disasters ought to fall, nor have they darkened its prospect for the future, except in so far as they have disclosed faults in human nature, obstacles to human brotherhood, whose magnitude had not been realized. The seismic centre whence the successive earthquake shocks proceeded did not lie in any democratic country. The catastrophe was so tremendous, because due to the concurrent action of three explosive forces never before conjoined at the same moment—overweening military ambition, the passion of nationality and an outbreak of vengeful fanaticism from small but fiery sections of the industrial population. Such a conjunction of volcanic activities may not recur for ages.

Shaken out of that confident faith in progress which the achievements of scientific discovery had been fostering, mankind must resume its efforts towards improvement in a chastened mood, consoled by the reflection that it has taken only a few thousands of years to emerge from savagery, and less than half that time to rise above the shameless sensualities of the ancient world and the ruthless ferocity of the Dark Ages.

As respects progress in the science and art of free government, experience has established certain principles that were unknown to those who lived under despotisms, and has warned us of certain dangers unforeseen by those who first set up free governments; but when it comes to the application of these principles, and the means of escaping these dangers, the faults that belonged to human nature under previous forms of government have reappeared. Some gains there have been, but they have lain more in the way of destroying what was evil than in the creating of what is good: and the belief that the larger the number of those who share in governing the more will there be of wisdom, of self-control, of a fraternal and peace-loving spirit has been rudely shattered. Yet the rule of Many is safer than the rule of One,—as Cavour said that however faulty a legislative chamber may be an ante-chamber is worse—and the rule of the multitude is gentler than the rule of a class. However grave the indictment that may be brought against democracy, its friends can answer, " What better alternative do you offer ? "

Encouragement may be found in the reflection that such moral progress as history records has been made chiefly in the way of raising the sentiments and standards of the average man. Whereas in the realms of abstract thought and in those of science and of art it is to the great intellects that the world looks, popular government lives and prospers more by the self-restraint and good sense and good will of the bulk of the nation than by the creative power of great intellects; and whoever looks back three or six or nine centuries cannot doubt that in the civilized communities as a whole men's habits and moral standards have risen. Outbursts of crime and sin recur from time to time, but they come less frequently and are visited with a sterner condemnation. That the knightly virtues of courage and honour have suffered no decline is evident. The spirit of the citizen soldiers who in 1914 came willingly to give their lives for a cause in which the fortunes of mankind as well as of their own countries seemed to be at stake shone forth with a light brighter than in any former war. In this some consolation for many sorrows may be found.

No government demands so much from the citizen as Democracy, and none gives so much back. Any free people that has responded to the call of duty and come out of a terrible ordeal unshaken in courage, undimmed in vision, with its vital force still fresh and strong, need not fear to face the future.

The statesmen and philosophers of antiquity did not dream of a government in which all men of every grade should bear a part: democracy was for them a superstructure erected upon a substructure of slavery. Modern reformers, bolder and more sanguine, called the multitude to power with the hope and in the faith that the gift of freedom and responsibility would kindle the spirit self-government requires. For them, as for Christian theologians, Hope was one of the Cardinal Virtues.

Less has been achieved than they expected, but nothing has happened to destroy the belief that among the citizens of free countries the sense of duty and the love of peace will grow steadily stronger. The experiment has not failed, for the world is after all a better place than it was under other kinds of government, and the faith that it may be made better still survives. Without Faith nothing is accomplished, and Hope is the mainspring of Faith. Throughout the course of history every winter of despondency has been followed by a joyous springtime of hope.

Hope, often disappointed but always renewed, is the anchor by which the ship that carries democracy and its fortunes will have to ride out this latest storm as it has ridden out many storms before. There is an Eastern story of a king with an uncertain temper who desired his astrologer to discover from the stars when his death would come. The astrologer, having cast the horoscope, replied that he could not find the date, but had ascertained only this that the king's death would follow immediately on his own. So may it be said that Democracy will never perish till after Hope has expired.

INDEX

Abdul Hamid II., and the Khalifate, i. 82 *n.*
Able men brought to the front by the Parliamentary System, ii. 466
"Absent" voting, in Australia, ii. 183
Absolute Government, features of, i. 55
Abstract Ideas
    Attitude to, in the Dominions, i. 507, ii. 190, 245, 259, 323–4
    as influencing Evolution of Democracy, i. 24, 27, 31, 32, 36, 37, 39, 41
    Relative influence of, in England and France, i. 311, 312
Abstract Principles in Politics, lessons in, of History, i. 507
Achaean League
    Free Government in, i. 184
Acton, Lord, and The History of Liberty, i. 51
Adams, J. Q., ii. 94 *n.*
Adelaide, South Australia, ii. 167, 170, 250
Administrative Abuses
    Danger of, in Backward States, ii. 508–9
Administrative Extravagance, *see* Extravagance and Waste, *under* Democracies
Administrative Law, in France, operation of, i. 277–8
Administrative Skill, value of, Failure to appreciate, ii. 20, 66–7, 459, 524, 529, 540, *see also* Self-confidence
Advanced and Backward Races, increased Contact between, ii. 498
Advances to Settlers Act, New Zealand, working of, ii. 289, 296–7
Advertisement in Politics, ii. 556
Afghan Idea of Happiness, ii. 531
Africa, French Colonies in, i. 319
African Natives, Exclusion of, from Australia, ii. 215
Agathocles, Sicilian tyrant, ii. 542
Aggression, a Danger to Backward States, ii. 508
    Protection against, ii. 518
Agora, of Homeric Greece, i. 130, 337
Agricultural holdings, Australia, size of, ii. 169, 170, 180
Agriculturists
    French, i. 219, 220, 254
        Political Apathy of, i. 316
        Public Opinion among, i. 254, 295
    U.S.A., Characteristics of, ii. 119, *sqq.*
Agriculturists' Parties, i. 125, 254
Akbar, i. 25
Alaska, coal in, i. 456
Albania, Blood revenge in, i. 129 *n.*
    Idea in, of Happiness, ii. 531
Alcibiades, i. 206, ii. 559
Alcidamas, on Natural Equality, i. 61
Alcoholic Liquors, Prohibitory Legislation on, *see* Prohibition, *under* Countries

Alexander the Great, i. 108, 204
Alexander II., Tsar, and the war with Turkey, ii. 378
Algeria, Representation of
    Chamber of Deputies, i. 240
    Senate, i. 232, 233
Aliens, citizenship of, i. 144 & *n.*
All Russia Congress of Soviets, functions of, ii. 582 *sqq.*
Alsace and Lorraine, i. 221; no Prefects in, i. 276 *n.;* Representation of, in French Legislature, i. 240
Althorp, Lord, personality of, ii. 557 *n.,* 561
Ambition, Personal, and Party Spirit, i. 118
America, *see* Latin, North, South, Tropical, *and* U.S.A.
American Commonwealth, The, by the Author, ii. 1, 13 *n.* 1, 33 *n.,* 70 *n.* 1, 74 *n.,* 99 *n.,* 121 *n.*
American Constitutional Convention of 1787, ii. 416
American Declaration of Independence, i. 43, 44, 61, 138, 169, ii. 4
American and European Lands, having too few Small Landowners, i. 451
American Federation of Labour, ii. 578
American Judicature Society, the, ii. 92 *n.*
American People, the, Conditions among at Independence, ii. 4 *sqq.;* Pride of, in their newness, ii. 8
"American People," fallacy in the phrase, i. 145 *n.*
American Police Systems by Fosdick *cited,* ii. 453 *n.*
American Protective Association, i. 123
American Republic, beginning of national life of, i. 3
American Revolution, Influence of, on France, i. 212; unforeseen by Politicians, ii. 598
Anabaptists, Westphalian, i. 85
Anahuac, i. 225
Anarchism
    Causes of, i. 57 *n.*
    in Latin America, i. 85, 197, in Spain, i. 137, and in U.S.A., ii. 127 *n.* 1
    and Socialism, Common Aim of, ii. 571
Anarchist use of the Press, i. 94
Anchorites and Monastic Orders, causes producing, i. 58
Andorra, Valley of, Republic of, ii. 503 *n.*
Angles and Saxons in England, the Folk Mot of, i. 130, 337, ii. 8, 506
Anonymity in the Press, i. 102–3
Anselm, i. 83
Anti-Catholic Parties, U.S.A., i. 123
Anti-Clericalism, in Politics, i. 85, 137, 192, 199, 218 & *n.,* 236, 265, 290–1, 312, 315–6, ii. 6.

Anti-Clericalism—*continued*
　Parties to resist in France, Holland,
　　and Belgium, i. 88, 123,
　　ii. 347
Anti-Corn Law League, the, i. 120
Anti-Liquor Laws, U.S.A., ii. 141
Antipater at Athens, i. 182
Anti-Religious note in European Social-
　ism, ii. 571
Anti-Semitism in
　France, i. 217, 218, 291
　Switzerland, i. 403, 435
Anti-Slavery Party, U.S.A., Tolerance by,
　of Abuses, ii. 39
Appenzell, i. 328, 337
　Public Meeting in, of Freemen, i. 35
　Torture Chamber at, ii. 532 *n.*
Arabia, conditions in, ii. 514
Araucanian race, in Chile, i. 188 ; never
　conquered, i. 193
Arbitrary Power, security from, ii. 505
Arbitration, Compulsory, Courts of, and
　Working of, in
　Australia, ii. 195–6, 197, 223, 225 *sqq.*,
　　230, 232 *n.*, 302, 305 & *n.*,
　　305 *sqq.*, 323, 388
　New Zealand, ii. 226, 232, 299 *sqq.*
Arbitration Acts, New Zealand, ii. 299
　　sqq., 307 *n.* 1
Archons, i. 172
Areopagitica of Milton, i. 92
Argentina, Republic of, i. 187 *n.*
　American Influence on, i. 196, ii. 12 *n.*
　　1.
　Bicameral Legislature in, ii. 400
　a Democracy, i. 22
　Domination of the Capital in, i. 198,
　　ii. 577
　Economic advantages in, i. 194
　Intervention in, i. 196
　Landholders in, i. 198
　　Small, i. 451
　Manhood Suffrage and Proportional
　　Representation in, i. 198
　　n. 2
　Municipal Administration in, i. 197
　National Council of Administration in,
　　i. 198 *n.* 2
　New Constitution of 1919, provisions
　　of, i. 198 *n.* 2
　Party in, i. 196
　Political Civilization of, how effected,
　　i. 207
　Population, ethnic purity of, i. 193
　President, Legislature and Justiciary in,
　　i. 196
　　Powers of the President, i. 192, 197,
　　　ii. 469–70, 576
　Press influence in, i. 198, 437, ii. 118
　Progress in, ii. 512
　Public Life, Tone of, i. 197
　Railways in, i. 195
　Religious decay in, ii. 326
　Republican history of, i. 194–8
　a true Republic, i. 193
　under Rosas, i. 192
　Voting compulsory in, i. 196
　Wars of, i. 191 *n.*
Aristides, the Just, i. 180
Aristocracy, connotations of, i. 15
Aristocracy, Natural, of the Dominant
　Few, ii. 550
Aristophanes, on Democracy, i. 183
Aristotle, on Constitution and forms of
　　Government, i. 3, 9, 13,
　　165–6, 167 *n.* 1, 169, 170,
　　172 *n.* 1, 173, 181, 182 &
　　n., 183 & *n.*, 185; on
　　relativity of Justice, i. 62
　Model Democracy of, found in Switzer-
　　land, i. 366 *n.*

Armenia, New Republic of, ii. 575
Armies, Danger from, ii. 508, *see also
　　under Countries*
Arnold, Matthew, on Politics, ii. 338 & *n.*
Arrêtés, in France, i. 277
Arrondissements, *see under* France
Art, Democracy in relation to, ii. 519 *sqq.*
Asia
　French Colonies in, i. 319
　Roman Province of, delegates from, i.
　　167 *n.* 3
　Western, New Republics in, ii. 575,
　　602
Asiatic Immigrants, Problems connected
　　with, ii. 215–6, 311
Asiatics, Political Developments possible
　　among, ii. 499
Assemblies of Freemen, examples of, i.
　　35, 129–30, *see also*
　　Folk Mot, Landesgemeinde,
　　Thing, etc., *and* Legisla-
　　tures, *under Countries*
Assyrian monarchy, i. 25
Athens
　Assembly of, i. 121
　Civic Life of, basis of Plato's and other
　　views of Democracy, i. 13
　Defence at, i. 168, 172, 175 & *n.* 2,
　　181
　Democracy in, i. 13, 170 *sqq.*
　　Compared with that of U.S.A., as
　　　to suspicion of Power, ii. 20
　　End of, i. 170, 181, 182, ii. 601
　　Treatment by, of Allies, i. 56
　Domination of City of, Australian
　　parallels to, ii. 250
　Executive in, i. 171, 172, 181
　Great Leaders of, i. 179–80
　Indictments and Prosecutions at, i.
　　174–5, 178 & *n.*
　Judiciary at, i. 171, 176 & *n.*, 177 *sqq.*
　Juries at, ii. 480
　Legislature in, i. 171, 172 *sqq.*, *see
　　also* Assembly, *above*
　and Melos, ii. 369
　Orators of, i. 177 *n.* 2, 179–80, 183
　Period of Poetic glory in, ii. 522
　Popular Will in, how guided, ii. 546
　Public Life at, salient features of,
　　summarized, i. 183–6
　Republican Government in, i. 171 *sqq.*
　Safeguards of Legislation in, ii. 391–2
　Schools of, closing of, i. 182
　Short Terms of Office at, i. 172, 173,
　　175, 180
　and Syracuse, i. 36
　Tendencies influencing, i. 179
　Use at, of the Lot, i. 64 *n.*
　Voters at, average number polling, i. 176
　　Political Education of, i. 71–2
　Women's freedom in, ii. 525
Atkinson, Sir Harry, ii. 318
Auckland, New Zealand, ii. 266, 278 *n.* 1
Augsburg, ii. 537 *n.*, 538
Augustus, Emperor, i, 27, ii. 536, 600
　Famous men in reign of, ii. 522
Aurore, L', Australe, by Biard d'Aunet,
　　ii. 261 *n.*, 283 *n.*
Australia, Commonwealth of, ii. 166 *sqq.*
　Administration, Working of, ii. 255
　Agricultural holdings in, size of, ii.
　　169, 170, 180
　American Influence in, ii. 12 *n.* 1
　Arbitration, Compulsory in, Courts of,
　　ii. 195–6, 197, 223, 225
　　sqq., 230, 233 *n.*, 302, 305
　　& *n.*, 305 *sqq.*, 323, 388
　　Legislation on, in progress (1920),
　　　ii. 232 *n.* 1
　　Unsatisfactory Results of, ii. 230,
　　　242, 305–6

Australia—*continued*
  Asiatics and Africans excluded from, ii. 215, 311, *see also* Immigration, *and* White Australia Policy
  Attitude to Political misdoings in, ii. 252
  Birth-rate in, ii. 251
  Bounties in, Acts on, ii. 224–5
  Bribery and Corruption in, ii. 183, 255, 440
  Bush-rangers, ii. 171, 199
  Business, Fortunes made in, ii. 171
  Cabinet, *see under* Cabinet
  and Canada, comparisons and resemblances, i. 466, 479, 480, 487, 488, 492, 497, 499
  Capital and Labour in, relations between (*see also* Labour, *below*), ii. 231–2
  Changes in, Nature of, and Mode of effecting, ii. 256 *sqq.*
  City dominance in, i. 198, ii. 170, 250, 577–8
  Civic Apathy in, and its causes, i. 428, ii. 180 *sqq.,* 189, 244, 451
  Civil Servants and Trade Unions in, i. 277
  Civil Service in, ii. 174, 193 *sqq.,* 254, 260, 528
  Class Antagonism and Social Jealousy in, i. 309 *& n.,* ii. 171, 181, 190, 212–3, 249, 252 *& n.,* 253, 451, 457, 459, 562
  Class-government in (*see also* Labour, *below*), ii. 205–6, 218, 256–7, 263–4
  Climate of, ii. 168
    Droughts, ii. 167, 169, 220 *& n.,* 262
    Influence of, on Physical Type, ii. 168, 169
  Coal of, ii. 167, 170
  Coalition Government in (1909), ii. 206, 211
  Collectivism in, ii. 258
  Commonwealth, creation of, ii. 172
    Legal outlines of, ii. 173 *sqq.,* 177–8
  Compulsory Military Training in, Public Opinion on, ii. 175, 216, 252 *n.*
  Constituencies, usually single-membered, ii. 178, 183
  Constitution, Federal, of, i. 223, ii. 162
    Amendments to, ii. 175, 178, 179
    Proposed, by Labour Party, ii. 230, 239 *sqq.*
    Comparisons of, with those of other Lands and those of the Australian States, i. 459, ii. 178
    Interpretations of, ii. 174
    Machinery for altering, i. 459 *& n.*
    Separation of Powers in, ii. 22
  Constitutional System of, four distinctive points in, ii. 173
  Convicts formerly transported to, ii. 168 *& n.*
  Crime in, decrease of, ii. 254
  Death-rates in, ii. 167, 255
  Decentralization desirable in, ii. 435
  Democracy in, achievements of, ii. 173, 254 *sqq.*
    Characteristics of, ii. 243 *sqq.*
    Failures of, ii. 256
    Historical Evolution of, i. 33–4
    Lessons from, ii. 256 *sqq.*
    Special Characteristics of, and Future development under, ii. 256 *sqq.*
  Study of, i. 6–7

Australia—*continued*
  Direct Popular Legislation in, ii. 175, 418, 432 *n.* 2
  Economic Conditions in, effects of, ii. 168, 169, 180, 181, 245–6, 249, 256
  Economic Outlook of, ii. 260 *sqq.*
  Education in, ii. 199 *& n. sqq.,* 245–6, 255, 436
    General Level of, in Politicians, ii. 190, 213
  Eight-Hours Day in, ii. 204, 225
  Elections in
    Conduct and Cost of, ii. 183–4 *& nn.,* 255
    to Legislatures, ii. 176, 178, 186 *sqq.*
    of Local and other Officials, ii. 182, 198 *& n.*
    Triennial, ii. 176, 178, 191, 205
    Universal Suffrage for, ii. 178
  Electoral Districts in, ii. 183
  English Political Traditions in, i. 209
  English Sub-types in, ii. 168–9
  Ethnography of, ii. 166 *sqq.*
  Executive of, ii. 174
    Attitude of the People to, i. 487
    Complete dependence of, on House of Representatives, ii. 178
    Composition, ii. 175, 193
    Control of, by Parliament, ii. 175, 182
    No Veto possessed by, ii. 178
    General Character of, ii. 177 *sqq.*
    Democratic Features in, ii. 177–9
    Paternalism of, ii. 261, 263
    Powers of, ii. 173–4
    Extension of, Labour desire for, ii. 218, 230, 239 *sqq.*
    Seat of, present and future, ii. 175, 190, 437 *n.*
    and State Governments, Swiss parallels to, i. 342, 344, 356, 357, 361, 370
  Exports of, ii. 170, 217
  Federal Capital, ii. 175, 190, 437 *n.*
  Financial Policy in, ii. 222 *sqq.*
    Control of, by Assemblies, ii. 183–4, 188, 270
  Foreign affairs as affecting, ii. 172, 244, 372
  Forestry neglected in, ii. 255
  Frame of Government, ii. 166
  Free Trade and Protection in, Newspapers concerned with, ii. 248
  Gold of, ii. 167, 170
  Government Employees in
    Salaries of, and Pressure by, ii. 194, 195, 349
    "Slacking" by, ii. 235, 255, 588 *n.*
  High Court of, ii. 174, 177, 196, 197–8
  History of, ii. 166 *sqq.*
  House of Representatives, ii. 174 *& n.*
    Conduct of Business in, ii. 188 *& n.* 2
    Financial Powers of, ii. 188
    Members of
      Payment of, ii. 174 *& n.,* 178
      Quality of, ii. 187, 189 *& n.,* 190
    Vital Centre of Political Life, ii. 182, 188
    How impaired, ii. 188
  Immigration, into (early), ii. 168
    Australian attitude to, present-day, i. 456, ii. 170, 215–6, 224, 251, 311
  Income-Tax, progressive, in, ii. 220 *& n.*
  Industrial Legislation in, ii. 223, 224 *& n.,* 225 *sqq.*
  I.W.W. in, ii. 230
  Influences at work in, Economic and Social, ii. 179 *sqq.*

Australia—*continued*
Initiative, the, in, ii. 175, 218
Institutions of, Working of, Conditions affecting, ii. 180–1
Intemperance in, decrease of, ii. 255 & *n.*
Interstate Commissions of, ii. 177, 196
Irrigation Works in, ii. 236, 255
Isolation of, past and present, Results of, ii. 167, 244, 253
Judges in, Appointments, Salaries, Terms of Office, Removal of, Status of, etc., ii. 177, 197, 254
Judiciary in, Commonwealth and State, ii. 174, 177, 196 *sqq.*, 254, 386–7, 389, 528
Labour Class in, Migratory and Urban Character of, ii. 180, 181, 251
    Opinions and Interests of, ii. 246, 253
    Political Power of, as used by, ii. 451
Labour issues in, divisions due to, ii. 457
Labour Organizations in (*see also* I.W.W. *and* Trade Unions), Pressure exercised by, ii. 355–6
Labour Party in, evolution, advance, aims and methods of, i. 124, 488, ii. 276, 348, 571
    Caucus of, ii. 257, 316, 355, 451, 467
    Members of, in First Commonwealth Parliament, ii. 205
    Ministries from, ii. 173, 205, 206, 451, 467
        Maintenance of Law and Order under, ii. 99, 171, 199, 252, 362 & *n.*
        Pledges exacted by, ii. 208 & *n.*, 264
Land question in, Labour policy on, ii. 217, 218, 220–2
Law and Order in, Maintenance of, ii. 99, 171, 199, 252–3, 363 & *n.*
Lawyers, few, in Legislatures, ii. 189–90
Legislatures, *see also* House of Representatives, *above*, *and* Senate, *below*, *and under* States
Bicameral, ii. 174, 176, 182, 184
Differences between, how settled, ii. 409
Materialistic spirit of, i. 307, ii. 259
Members of
    Payment of, ii. 174 & *n.*, 176, 178, 454, increased, ii. 174 *n.*, 454
    Quality of, ii. 187, 189 & *n.*, 190, 191–2, 212–3, 247, 338
Parties in, ii. 203–4
    New character of, end of last century, ii. 204 *sqq.*
    Alleged Decline in, ii. 191
Respect not inspired by, ii. 256
Leisured Class absent from, ii. 189, 243–4
Liberal Party in, ii. 209, 316
Local Government in, ii. 198–9, 255–6, 576
Mandate of, for New Guinea, ii. 176, 244 *n.*
Manhood Suffrage in, ii. 172
Materialism in, i. 307, ii. 251, 259, 260
Mineral wealth of, ii. 167, 170

Australia—*continued*
Minimum Wage question in, ii. 227–8 & *n.* 1
Ministerial Instability in, ii. 191, 364–5, 452, 467 *n.* 1
Ministers, ii. 174, 175, 359
    Choice of, in, ii. 359–60
Money-Power in (slight), ii. 251–2, 260, 454, 485
Monopolist Combinations in, ii. 256
Municipal Government in, ii. 198, 440
Narrowness of outlook of, ii. 216, 252–3
National Character, ii. 167, 168–9, 171 *sqq.*, 190, 191–2, 212–3, 220, 243 *sqq.*, 249–51, 253, 261–2, 264, 362–3
National Debt, ii. 254–5
Natural Beauties of, ii. 250 & *n.*
Natural Wealth, ii. 167, 170
"New Protection" policy in, ii. 222 *sqq.*
Non-Political Authorities in, ii. 196–7
Officials
    Appointment and election of, ii. 174, 199
    Governor-General, ii. 174
Old-age pensions in, ii. 199
Parliament of, ii. 174 & *n.*, 258
Parliamentary Party Leaders in, authority exercised by, i. 255
Parliamentary system applied by, to Federation, i. 497
Parties in, ii. 202 *sqq.*
    Multiplication of, ii. 467, *see also* Labour, *above*
Party in, ii. 202 *sqq.*, 243–4
Party discipline in, ii. 191
Party feeling in, ii. 246
Party Government in, i. 115
Party Influence in, ii. 187
Party Organization in (*see also* Labour Party, Caucus of), ii. 453, 467, 556
Party organizations created in, to cope with Socialism, i. 450
Party questions in, ii. 202
Party Spirit in, and in U.S.A., ii. 470
Patriotism in, ii. 178, 218, 245, 259
Police of, ii. 219, 254
Political Committees in, i. 269, *n.*, how elected, i. 268
Political Connection of, with Great Britain, ii. 214–5 & *n.*
Political Loyalty in, ii. 251–2
Political Patronage in, ii. 195
Political Views of, past and present, ii. 171
Politicians in (*see also* Legislatures, Members of), i. 255, ii. 190, 191, 193, 194, 212–3
Politics in, Character of, i. 307, ii. 173, 187 *sqq.*, 243, 259
    Inattention to, *see* Civic Apathy, *above*
Popular Government in, Salient Features of, ii. 451
Population, original Stock, and Ethnic Homogeneity of, ii. 168–9, 243–4, 254, 325
    Distribution of, Conditions influencing, ii. 166, 167, 170, 180, 251, 315
    Occupations of, ii. 167, 169–70
    Physical characteristics of, ii. 168, 244, 246, 249
    Slow increase and Smallness of, ii. 168, 170, 216, 251, 253
Popular Sovereignty in, ii. 173, 178
Premiers of, Status of, ii. 193 & *n.*

Australia—*continued*
  Press Influence in, i. 103–4, 296, 437,
      ii. 118, 204, 246, 247–8,
      322
  Prices and Wages, relation between in,
      ii. 223–4, 228, 229, 261–2
  Professional Classes, Opinions and
      Interests of, ii. 247
  Prohibition question in, ii. 203
  Proportional Representation in, ii. 183,
      188 & n. 1
  Protection and Free Trade, Public
      Opinion on, ii. 217, 222 *sqq.*
  Protectionist Party, ii. 305
  Public Health in, ii. 255
  Public Life in, Tone of, i. 207, ii. 189
      sqq., 259–60, 338, 453
  Public Manners in, i. 429, ii. 190, 191
      & n., 199
  Public Opinion in, i. 488, ii. 180, 214
      sqq., 243 *sqq.*, 388, 456, 458
    Possible modication of, ii. 263–4
  Public Service Acts, ii. 195
  Public Services in, Promotion in, ii.
      195, 196
  Questions now before the People, ii. 223
  Railway Commissioners in, ii. 233
  Railways and their Administration in,
      ii. 233 *sqq.*, 251, 255
  Re-elections of Officials in, ii. 176, 183,
      185
  Referendum in, ii. 175, 182 n., 185 n.
  Religions in, ii. 168
  Reservation of Subject in, ii. 394
  Rich men holding off from Politics in,
      i. 428, ii. 451
  Roman Church's influence in, i. 88
  School Teachers in, ii. 201
  Second Chamber in, *see* Senate, *below*
  Self-Government in, ii. 172 *sqq.*
  Self-sufficing idea in, ii. 217
  Senate, Federal, of, ii. 174, 186 *sqq.*
    Elections to, ii. 178, 186 *sqq.*, 401
    Powers, ii. 401, 409
    Quality of, ii. 403
    Removal by withdrawals, ii. 413 n.
  Settlers in, Advantages enjoyed by,
      ii. 4
  Sheep-raising in, ii. 167, 169, 181, 216
  Short Views in, ii. 169, 251, *see also*
      Public Opinion
  Single Tax views in, ii. 221–2
  Small farmers in, political status of, ii.
      180
  Social Equality in, ii. 171, 181
  Spoils system in, i. 117
  Sport in, ii. 244, 245, 326
  Squatters in
    Conflict of, with Free Selectors, ii.
        202–3, 259
  Wealth of, ii. 171
  State Activities (Charities, Trading,
      etc.), i. 7, 11, ii. 126, 173,
      192, 199, 232 *sqq.*
  States of, *see also under Names*
    Assemblies of, ii. 176–7, 178, 191
        & n., 191–2
      Predominance of, ii. 184
    Constitutions of, ii. 172, 176, 177,
        178–9
      Alteration in, ii. 177, 178
      Compared with those of American
          States, ii. 179
      Democratic Features in, ii. 178
    Education in, ii. 199 *sqq.*
    Equal Representation of, ii. 174
    Federation of, ii. 172
    Finance in, Control of, by Assemblies,
        ii. 184
    Governments of, ii. 173–4, 176
      Powers of, ii. 173–4

Australia—*continued*
  States of—*continued*
    Questions dealt with before 1883,
        ii. 172
    Swiss parallel to, i. 330
    Governors of, powers of, ii. 176–7
    Judiciary in, ii. 177, 196
    Legislative Councils, ii. 176, 178,
        184–5
      Abolition desired by Labour, ii.
          185, 239
    Legislatures of, ii. 176, 178, 182,
        184
      Caucus in, ii. 355–6
      Elections to, ii. 176, 178, 401
    Personal Feelings as influencing
        Politics in, ii. 191
    Public Service Commissions in, ii.
        195
    Representatives of Annual Con-
        ference of, ii. 210
    Roads, Railways, and Tramways of,
        ii. 199
    Self-Government in, ii. 172
    "States' Rights" sentiment of, ii. 241
    Suffrages in, ii. 172, 178
    Unification project for, ii. 241
  Status of, as established by Peace
      Treaties and League of
      Nations, ii. 215 & n.
  "Stone-walling" in, ii. 188, 345
  Strikes and Strike Riots in, ii. 204,
      206, 218, 226, 256, 259,
      451, 452, 528
    Non-cessation through Compulsory
        Arbitration, ii. 237 *sqq.*
  Suffrages in, ii. 172, 174, 176, 177, 182
      & n., 183, 244
  Syndicalists in, ii. 230
  Tariffs in, ii. 172, 203, 217, 218, 222,
      223, 224, 259
  Taxation in, ii. 218, 220, 254, 259
  Territories administered by, ii. 176,
      244 n.
  Towns, Ports, and Cities of, relative
      sizes and importance of, ii.
      170
  Trade Disputes
    Compulsory Arbitration (*q. v. above*)
        in, ii. 225 *sqq.*
  Trade Union activities in, ii. 204 *sqq.*,
      207
    Privileges for, ii. 237 *sqq.*
  Traditions absent from, ii. 324
  Universities, ii. 201, 255
  Urbanization in, ii. 170, 180, 249, 250,
      251, 315
    Results of, ii. 451
  Voting Methods in, ii. 183
  Wages in
    Fixing of, and Boards for, ii. 223,
        225 & n., 226 *sqq.*, 258,
        259, 301–2
    Raising of, limit to, ii. 261
  War Efforts and Sacrifices of, ii. 252,
      259
  Wealth in, Distribution of, ii. 170–1
  White Australia Policy in, ii. 215, 224,
      243
  Women Voters in, influence of, etc., ii.
      172, 182 & n., 211 n.
Australia, *Problems and Prospects*, by Sir
    C. Wade, ii. 231 n. 2
Australian Liberal Union, the, ii. 209
Australian Workers Union, ii. 237 n.
Australie, La Nouvelle, by Voisson, ii.
    261 n., 283 n.
Austria, Empire of
  Fewness of actual Rulers in, ii. 544
  Foreign policy of, and its outcome, ii.
      372, 380

Austria, Empire of—*continued*
  Monarchical Oligarchy in, ii. 538
    Corruption in, ii. 540
  Monarchy of, ii. 535
    Constitution of, i. 21
  Racial Parties in, i. 124
  Republic of, ii. 575
  War with, as affecting German Democ-
    racy, i. 39
Authority
  Dethronement of, i. 46
  French attitude to, i. 306
  When Sacred, ii. 555 *n.*
Authorship, Leadership by means of, ii.
  554
Autocracies, Corruption in, ii. 453
  and Education of Peoples, ii. 517
  Evils of, remedied by Democracy, ii.
    562–3
  Rule in
    Direct, ii. 542
    Indirect, ii. 543
    Responsibility under, how secured,
      ii. 491
Autocracy, former, in China, ii. 500, 510–
  11
Average Citizen in Ideal Democracy, i.
  47–8
Average Man
  Athenian preference for, i. 181
  General conception of, i. 150
  Intelligence of, ii. 454
  as Ruler, i. 64, 207
  Sense of Civic Duty of, *see also* Civic
    Duty, ii. 454–5
  in U.S.A., ii. 8, 20 *et passim,* 119 *sqq.*
Azerbaijan, first Mussulman Republic, ii.
  575

Baboeuf, F. N., Communistic doctrines
  of, i. 218 *n.*
Backward Races and States
  Advances possible in, ii. 516–7
  Are they part of the People? i. 145
  and Democratic Government, and
    Equality, i. 68 & *n.,* ii. 498
    sqq.
  Dangers to be provided against, ii.
    508–9
  and the Logic of Events, ii. 518
  Expedients possible in, ii. 517–8
Bacon, Francis, ii. 522
Bagehot, W., *cited,* i. 228, ii. 335, 449 *n.,*
  472 *n.* 4
Ballance, Rt. Hon., —, Prime Minister,
  New Zealand, ii. 275, 283 *n.*
  Bold measures of, ii. 271, 299, 308
  Financial policy of, ii. 288
  Woman's Suffrage Bill of, ii. 308
Balmaceda, and the Chilian Civil War, i.
  193
Bankers and Heads of Businesses, Influ-
  ence of, in Oligarchies, ii.
  538 & *n.* 2
Bantu Races, i. 79 ; the Pitso of, i. 130
  & *n.* 1
Bar
  the, Influence of, ii. 87–8, 389
  Judges selected from, ii. 389
  Standard of, ii. 88, 155
Bar Association of New York, Reforms
  sought by, ii. 90, 163
Barbarian Kingdoms, 5th and 6th cen-
  turies, i. 27
Barren region, Canada, i. 455
Barrios, rule of, in Guatemala, i. 192
Basques
  Characteristics of, i. 286
  in Chile, i. 193
  Language of, area of, i. 209 *n.* 2

Basuto Race, the Pitso of, i. 130 & *n.* 1,
  371 *n.* 2, ii. 503
Beaconsfield, Earl of (B. Disraeli), i. 255,
  ii. 560, and the Eastern
  Question, ii. 378–9
  Extension of the Franchise by, ii. 567
  on Parties, i. 122
Beales, E., i. 30 *n.* 2
Bebel, A., *cited,* ii. 590
Bechuana Race, the Pitso of, i. 130 &
  n. 1
Beck, J. A., on Leadership, ii. 558 *n.* 1
Belfort, Territory of, Representation of,
  in Senate, i. 232
Belgium
  Class Bitterness in, ii. 457
  Clerical Party in, i. 88, 123, ii. 347
  Constitution of, i. 223
  a Democracy, i. 22
  Executive in, Popular Control of, ii.
    364
  Monarchy in, ii. 462
  Party Government in, i. 115
  Party Spirit in, ii. 470
  Senate in, Powers of, ii. 402, 406,
    407
  Suffrage in, i. 21
    Supplementary Vote, i. 63 *n.,* 152–3
Belgrano, in Argentina, i. 194
Benedek, Ingratitude to, of the Haps-
  burgs, ii. 559 & *n.* 2
Bentham, Jeremy, Political theories of,
  i. 46
Berlin, Cities counterbalancing, ii. 437
Bern, i. 328
  Junkers of, i. 427, 428
  Oligarchy of, i. 35, 329, 427
  Seat of Swiss Legislature, i. 347, 357
Berry, Sir G., ii. 191
Bezirk, the, in Switzerland, i. 334 *n.*
Bible, the, nature of, i. 87
Bicameral Governments, ii. 397 *n.,* 398
  sqq.
  Dominion, ii. 401, *see also* each
    Dominion
  European, ii. 339, *see also Countries
    named*
  Latin-American States, i. 194, 196, 200,
    and see under each Country
  U.S.A., *see that head*
"Big Business" (*see also* Money-Power),
  Influence of, in
  Monarchical Oligarchies, ii. 538 & *n.*
  U.S.A., ii. 24–5, 51, 64, 118, 485
  Public Opinion against, Canada, i. 482,
    499
Bilingual Difficulties of Canada, ii. 451
Bill of Rights, i. 224
Bills
  Inadequately Debated, U.S.A., ii. 58
  Private, *see* Private Bills
  Revision and Rejection of, by Second
    Chambers, i. 237, 246, ii.
    394–5, 408
Bismarck, Prince, compared with the
    great Democrats, ii. 541 ;
    Personality of, ii. 471 ; and
    Popular Government, i. 39 ;
    and the "Reptile Press," i.
    93, 103 ; Rule of, acquiesced
    in, ii. 600
"Black-legs," ii. 237
Blake, Edward, i. 478
Blanco, Guzman, President of Venezuela,
  i. 190
Block, the, in French politics, i. 254
Blood Feuds, i. 129 & *n.*
Boards, Municipal, U.S.A., ii. 16 ; small
  reason for, ii. 496
Bodley, J. E. C., book by, *cited,* i. 244 *n.*
Bolivar, i. 192

Bolivia, Republic of, i. 187 n.
  Area and Population, i. 206
  Political Status, i. 193, 207
Bolshevik Theory, The, by Postgate, cited, ii. 582
Bolshevism and Sovietism, ii. 582–3
Bonapartists, the, in France, i. 214, 215, 225, 291
Bordeaux, ii. 437
Borgia, Cæsar, ii. 369
Bosses, Political, in
  Canada, i. 475
  U.S.A., ii. 40, 65, 78, 82, 98, 101 sqq., 147, 157, 482–3
Boston, U.S.A., ii. 54
  Literary coteries of, ii. 54
  Police Strike at, 1919, ii. 362
Boulanger, General, the affair of, i. 216, 238, 291, 321, ii. 342, 602
Bounties, in Australia, Acts on, ii. 224
Bourbons, the, and their followers, i. 111
"Bourgeois" Democracies, denunciations of, ii. 580
Bourgeoisie, see under France
Boutmy, E., i. 6
Braganza dynasty, fall of, ii. 575
Brain-workers, elimination of, Labour views on, ii. 579 & n. 1
Brazil, Republic of, i. 7, 187 & n.
  Area of, i. 223
  Bicameral Legislature of, ii. 400
  Failure of Monarchy in, i. 200
  Government of
    Central, i. 201
    State, i. 201
  Language of, i. 187
  Needs of, i. 200
  Oligarchy in, i. 202, ii. 537–8
  Political capacity of Southern States of, i. 203, 207
  Political History of, i. 199 sqq.
  Population, Ethnic Elements in, i. 189 n. 2, 200
  Press influence in, i. 437
  Religion in, ii. 326
  Recent abolition in, of Slavery, i. 203
  a true Republic, i. 193
  Suffrage list in, i. 200
  Wars of, i. 191 n.
Breton Language, area of, i. 209 & n. 2
Bright, John, and the Crimean War, ii. 377; Economy expected by, from a Democracy, i. 314; Influence of, ii. 561; and Reform, i. 30
Brisbane, Queensland, ii. 170
British Cabinet, see Cabinet
British Constitution, see under Great Britain
British Counties and Cities, study of Political proclivities of, desirable, i. 289 n.
British Foreign Policy, see Great Britain, Foreign Policy of
British Isles
  Celts of, Kings of, i. 25
  Racial differences in, i. 210
British Parliament, see under Great Britain
British Privy Council, and a Council of State, i. 279
  Right of Appeal to, from Australia, ii. 196
British Provincial Newspapers, compared with French, i. 295
British Race, sub-types developed by, under new conditions, ii. 169
Browning, R., i. 324
Buck, E. A., on Civil Administration Code, U.S.A., ii. 137 n. 2

Buda-Pest
  Newspapers of, i. 293
  Parliamentary uproars at, i. 259
Buddhism, i. 82
  in Japan, attempted revival of, i. 88 n.
Budget
  French, i. 246
  Swiss, exempted from Referendum, i. 376
Buenos Aires
  Anarchists of, i. 197
  Dynamite outrages in, i. 197
  Growth and Dominance of, i. 195, 198, ii. 99 n. 1, 250
Bulgaria
  King of, despotism of, i. 22, ii. 358; fall of, i. 225 n.
  Legislature of, Unicameral, ii. 399
  Nominal Democracy of, i. 22
  Social Equality in, i. 427–8
Buonarotti, Michael Angelo, ii. 572
Burd, edition by, of The Prince, ii. 558 n. 2
Bureaucracy
  Causes and Evolution of, ii. 411, 576–7, 586–7
  of a Communist State, occupations and size of, ii. 589 sqq.
  in France, i. 274–6
  in Germany, i. 275
  Swiss aversion from, i. 363, 365, 384–5, 389, 431 n. 1, 444
Bureaux of
  French Chamber of Deputies, i. 245–6
  Swiss Legislature, i. 345
Burgundy, Transjurane, i. 346 n.
Burke, Edmund, i. 16, ii. 560, 598; on Democracy, i. 13; and the French Revolution, i. 47; on Members as not mere Delegates, ii. 350–1
Burnett, book by, on the Initiative, etc., in Oregon, ii. 142 n. 2
Burr, Aaron, ii. 559
Bush-ranging, Australia, ii. 171, 199
Business Corporations, U.S.A., forbidden to subscribe to Party Funds, ii. 51
Butler, Bishop, on the Nature of Things, ii. 549
Byron, Lord, i. 447
Byzantium, commerce of, i. 168

Cabinet of State Officers, U.S.A., ii. 137 & n. 1
Cabinets
  Composition of, ii. 462, 463
  Instability of (see also Ministerial Instability), causes of, ii. 348
  in Parliamentary, and Presidential Governments, ii. 462–3
  Resignations of, on censure of Minister, ii. 492 & n. 1
Cabinets and Cabinet system in various Lands
  Australian Commonwealth, ii. 174, 193, 194
  Australian States, ii. 176–7
  Canada, i. 459–60, 480, ii. 162
  France
    Formation of, i. 227
    Responsibility of, ii. 162
    Size of, i. 262
    Talent and reputation in, i. 262, 263
  Great Britain, ii. 461, 462, 464 sqq.
    French parallel to, i. 228
    Influence of, on House of Commons, i. 173
    Instability of, effects of, ii. 365 n.
    Nature of, i. 176
    Policy declared by, ii. 41

Cabinets—*continued*
  Great Britain—*continued*
    Powers of, ii. 449 *n.*
    Growth of, ii. 342-3, 576
    Source of, ii. 472 *n.* 4
    Responsibility of, ii. 162
  New Zealand, Maori Member of, ii. 267
  U.S.A., i. 494, ii. 137 *& n.* 1
    Ability in, ii. 94 *n.*
    Appointment to, ii. 18-19, 93, 94
      & n.
    Composition of, ii. 94
    Responsibility of, ii. 18-19
    Working of, ii. 93-4
Caciques, or local Bosses in Spain, ii.
  601 *& n.*
Cæsarism, still Attractive to the Masses,
  i. 322
Calan, Count de, *cited* on Politics in W.
  and N. W. France, i. 289 *n.*
Caledonia, Kings in, i. 25
Calhoun, J. C., i. 104 ; outstanding per-
  sonality of, i. 265
California, Boss rule in, ii. 82
Calvin, John, i. 332, 432
  Theocracy of, i. 84 *n.*
Camarina, and the oracle, i. 443
Canada, i. 455-6, **465**
  Aboriginals in, Treatment of, i. 486
  Abstract Ideas of little weight in, i.
    472-3, 495-6, 507
  Administrative Extravagance in, i. 499,
    501, ii. 452
  Administrative Offices in, Filling of, i.
    459 *sqq.*, 477, 493, and
    Multiplication of, i. 499
  Agricultural Discontent, recent, indica-
    tions of, i. 474 *& n.*, 475,
    see also Farmers' Party,
    below
  Asiatics excluded from, ii. 311
  and Australia, comparisons between, *see*
    under Australia
  "Big Business" disliked in, i. 482, 499
  Bilingual Difficulties of, ii. 451
  Birth-rate in, among French Canadians,
    i. 457, 467, 468
  "Bosses" in, i. 475
  Bribery and Corruption in, i. 241-2,
    366, 466, 477-8, 484-5, 489,
    497-9, 502, 534 *sqq.*, ii.
    183, 295 *n.*, 438, 441, 450,
    453, 478 *sqq.*, 541
  British Parliamentary System as worked
    in, i. 229, 455 *sqq.*, 492-3,
    497
  Cabinet of, *see under* Cabinets
  Candidates in, Choice of, for
    Legislatures, i. 475
  Local Government, i. 487
  Cities in, capable of forming Public
    Opinion, i. 490-1
  Large Populations, i. 456, 466
  Civic Sense in, i. 466, 468, 471 *sqq.*,
    479, 490 *sqq.*, 499-500
  Civil Administration in, improving, ii.
    528
  Civil Service in, i. 461-2, 490, 499 *sqq.*,
    ii. 254
  Civil Service Laws, Reform, i. 490
  Class-antagonism in, i. 466-7
  Climate of, i. 456
  Clubs, non-party, in, i. 473-4
  Coal of, i. 456
  Compromises in, i. 469-70, 472
  Compulsory Military Service in, ii. 361
  Constitution of, i. 223, 458 *sqq.*, 506-
    7
    Amendment of, ii. 175 *n.*
  Decorations deprecated in, i. 451
  Demagogism rare in, i. 501

Canada—*continued*
  Democracy in
    Historical evolution of, i. 34
    Study of, i. 7, 455 *sqq.*
  Direct Voting by the People not pro-
    vided for, i. 493
  Economic Conditions in, i. 456-7, 465
  Education in, i. 465-6, 470, 487, 501
    Local control of, ii. 436
  Elections and Electors in, i. 241, 463,
    474 *sqq.*, 487, 494-5
  Executive of, i. 460
    Appointments by, i. 461, 477
    Power of, over the Provinces, i. 459,
      483, 493
    Public Attitude to, i. 487
    Relations with the Legislatures, i.
      459 *sqq.*, 464, 494
  External affairs of, and relations with
    U.S.A., i. 469, ii. 372
  Farmers' Party and Movement in, i.
    125, ii. 340, 347-8, 483
  Finances of, i. 499, 500
    Control of, by Lower House, i. 459
  Foreign affairs of, *see* External Rela-
    tions, *above*
  Frame of Government of, i. 455 *sqq.*
  Government
    Federal, i. 458 *sqq.*, 494, ii. 435
      Dangers evaded by, i. 501, 505
      Democratic character of, compared
        with Australia and U.S.A.,
        i. 495, ii. 179
      Dissatisfaction with, causes of, i.
        502 *sqq.*
      Elections to, i. 475 *sqq.*
      Influence on, of Public Opinion, i.
        505
      Merits of, i. 469, 497, 500-2
      Powers of, i. 458-9, ii. 173, 174
      Problems before, i. 505
      Short life of, i. 507-8
      Working of, i. 477 *sqq.*
    Provincial, i. 462 *& nn.*, 463
  Grants and Subsidies in, i. 367, 481
    sqq., 499, 500, 504
  House of Commons, i. 460
    Financial Control exercised by, i. 460
    Life of, i. 460
    Members, *see under* Legislatures,
      below
    Party keenness in, i. 473
    Relation of, with the Executive, i.
      459 *sqq.*, 464
  Industrials in, i. 456, 466, 472
  Insurrections in, i. 464
  Judges, Appointments, Salaries and
    Status of, i. 461, 485-6,
    493, ii. 387, 389
  Judiciary, i. 459, 461, 485-6, 500, ii.
    528
  Labour Party in, i. 124, 474, ii. 378
  Labour troubles in, i. 465, 466
  Law and Order in, i. 486-7, 500, ii.
    199, 363
  Law Courts, i. 461
    Right of, to decide on Legality of
      Constitutional Provisions, i.
      485-6
  Legislatures, *see also* House of Com-
    mons, *above, and* Parliament
    and Senate, *below*
    Chief interests of, i. 482 *sqq.*
    Composition of, i. 248, 460
    Dissolution of, by Executive, i. 460,
      462, 494
    Dramatic Quality of, ii. 64
    Members of, Characteristics, Stand-
      ards and Status of, i. 478
      sqq., 499-500, ii. 337-8,
      343, 450-1

Canada—*continued*
  Legislatures—*continued*
    Members of—*continued*
      Payment of, i. 479, ii. 452
      Women, i. 460 *n.*
      Powers of, i. 460
      Procedure in, i. 481
    Provincial, *see* Provinces, Legislatures of
      Wisdom of, i. 500–1
  Local Government in, i. 487
  Local Improvements and Corruption in, ii. 440–1
  Local Subsidies in, i. 367
  Manufacturing in, i. 456
  Maritime Provinces, i. 456, 466
    French Canadians in, i. 458
  Materialism in, i. 476, 482, 488, 502, 504
  Ministerial Instability in, ii. 364–5
  Ministers
    Choice of, basis of, ii. 360
    Evolution of, i. 480
    Position of, i. 460
    Quality of, ii. 359
    Responsibility of, i. 494, ii. 451
    Scandals concerning, i. 489–90, ii. 479–80, 541
    Seats of, i. 460, 494
  Money Power in, i. 482–3, 485, 498, 499, ii. 454, 477, 484–6
  Mounted Police of, i. 486
  Municipal Government in, i. 487, 501, ii. 440
  National Character in, i. 478, 505, 506, 508, ii. 199, 363, *see also* Materialism, *above*
  Nationhood achieved by (1919–20), i. 469, 489
  Natural Wealth of, i. 455–6, 466, 492, 502
  Newspapers in, Provincialism of, i. 489
  Opportunism, alleged, of Statesmen in, i. 503 *sqq.*
  Parliament, i. 248, *see also* House of Commons *and* Legislatures, *above, and* Senate, *below*
  Parliamentary Party Leaders in, authority exercised by, i. 254–5
  Parties in, i. 471 *sqq.*, 474 *sqq.*
    Multiplication of, ii. 467
  Partisanship in, ii. 62
  Party in, i. 459, 460, 461, 464
    Effect on Provincial Politics, i. 499
    Mixed Elements in each Party, i. 470, 472, 488
    Working of, in the Legislatures, i. 472, 481, ii. 401–2
  Party and Non-Party Elections, i. 474–5, 487, 494–5
  Party Feeling, and Social relations in, i. 473
  Party Funds in, i. 477–8 *& n.*, 497–8
  Party Government in, i. 115
  Party Issues in, i. 471–2
  Party Organization in, i. 474–5, 501, ii. 453
  Party Spirit in, ii. 470
  Party Strength in, i. 466
  Party Strife in, centre of, i. 460–1
  Party Ties in, Loosening of, i. 474–5
  Patriotism in, i. 503
  Police Magistrates in, i. 485
  Political faults in, those of a New Country, i. 503 *sqq.*
  Political Institutions in, bases of, i. 455
  Political Patronage in, i. 363, 461–2, 489, 495
  Political Stability in, ii. 450

Canada—*continued*
  Political System of, compared with that of the U.S.A., i. 493 *sqq.*
  Politics in
    General Review of
      Criticism, i. 497 *sqq.*
      Praise, i. 487, 497
    insufficiently attractive to best Talent, i. 478–9, 499
    Principle needed in, i. 503–4
  Popular Government in, Salient features of, ii. 450–1
  Population of, i. 456, 457–8
    Cities of over 120,000, i. 456, 466
    French-speaking, Migration of, i. 468
    Growth of, i. 456, 457, 507–8
    Occupations of, i. 456
    Race Differences in, effects of, i. 158, 457, 463–4, 469–70, 472, 475–6, 488, 503, 506, 508
  Prairie Provinces, i. 455
    Grain-Growers' Associations in, i. 474 *n.*
    Immigrants to, i. 465
  Press of, Influence of, i. 488, 489
  Prime Minister of, compared with American President, i. 495
  Prohibition Question in, i. 470–1 *& n.*, 477, 491, 501
  Prospects before, i. 508
  Protection question in, views on, i. 466
  Provinces, *see also* Maritime, *and* Prairie Provinces, *above*
    Government of, i. 462 *& nn.*, 463
    Legislatures of
      Members of, i. 478
        Elections of, i. 475, 483
        Party in, i. 483
        Powers of, ii. 173–4
          over Finance, i. 483–4
      Powers over, of Federal Government, i. 459
      Procedure in, i. 483
      Standards of, i. 479–80, ii. 479, 541
  Public Affairs of, Interest taken in (*see also* Civic Sense, *above*), i. 465–6, 468, 469, 471 *sqq.*, 479, 490 *sqq.*, 500
  Public Life in, Tone of, i. 497 *sqq.*, ii. 338
  Public Opinion in, i. 287, 482, 488 *sqq.*, 491, 505, ii. 248, 389, 456
    Difficulty of forming, i. 505
    and Individual Liberty, Canada, i. 501
  Railways, Political Influence of, i. 465, 476, 482 *& n.*, 504, ii. 233
  Reforms in, i. 490
    Social, i. 491
  Relations of, to Great Britain and the other Dominions, i. 468, 470
  Religion in, influence of, i. 457, 458 *& n.*, 466, 467, 469–70, 475–6, 488, 503, 506, ii. 326 *n.*
  Religious Teaching in schools, Controversies on, i. 470
  Reserved Subjects, ii. 394
  Roman Catholicism in, i. 458 *& n.*, 467, 475–6
  Rural and Agricultural Conditions dominant in, ii. 450–1
  Senate of
    Composition, Powers, and Status, etc., of, i. 22, 460, 493, ii. 400 *n.*, 402, 409
    Nominations to, i. 462, 480, ii. 401
    Relations with, of the Executive, i. 460

Canada—*continued*
 Separation of Powers in, ii. 22
 Small Landholders in, i. 451, 457, 465,
  ii. 169–70, 221, 251
 Social and Economic Conditions in, i.
  455
 Spoils system in, i. 117, 461–2, 495
 Standard of Living in, i. 465, ii. 325
 Statesmen of, alleged Opportunism of,
  i. 503 *sqq.*
 Strikes and Strike Riots in, i. 466, 486,
  500, ii. 452
 Tariffs in, i. 465, 468, 471, 491
 Taxation in, i. 500
 and U.S.A.
  Relations between, i. 468–9, ii. 124
   & n. 2, 375
  Resemblances and Comparisons, i.
   457, 458–9, 462, 463, 466,
   474, 475, 479, 480, 482,
   483, 484, 486, 488, 489,
   492 *sqq.,* 498, 499 *sqq.,*
   505–6
 Universities of, i. 488
 Upper
  English sub-types in, ii. 169
 Veto practically absent in, i. 493
 Water power in, i. 456
 Wealth in, Distribution of, i. 457
 Western, ii. 325
  French Canadians in, i. 457, and the
   British Connection, i. 488,
   see also Race, *above*
 Prosperity of, i. 465, ii. 325
 Woman Suffrage in, i. 460 & *n.*
Canadian Bankers' Magazine, Article in,
  by Clark, referred to, i. 483
  n.
Canadian Boundary Question, peaceful
  Solution of, with U.S.A., ii.
  375
Canberra, seat of Australian Common-
  wealth Government, ii. 175,
  190, 437 *n.*
Candidates, Choice of
 Party Influences on, i. 113, 115
 Personality as Influencing, i. 113, 152,
  159, 171
 by Election or Nomination in
  Australia, ii. 183, 210
  Canada, i. 475, 487
  France, i. 249–50, 267
  Great Britain, ii. 338–9, 556
  Switzerland, i. 419 & *n.*, 427
  U.S.A., i. 474–5, ii. 28 *sqq.*, 36, 38
   sqq., 42, 49, 65, 129, 354
Canning, G., emergence of, ii. 556
Cantons, *see under* France, *and* Switzer-
  land
Capital, in Communistic views, ii. 570
Capital Cities, Domination of, i. 198, ii.
  170, 250, 437 & *n.*, 577
Capital Punishment in Switzerland, i.
  342, 436
Capitalism and
 Communism, ii. 570, 586 *sqq.*
 Revolution, ii. 598–9
Capitalists and Corporations
 Few in Canada, i. 456–7
 French and American, Influence of, on
  Politics, i. 457
Carbonari, the, i. 123 *n.*
Caribbean Republics, i. 187 *n.*, 191
 Not Democracies, i. 23
Carlyle, T., ii. 110, 568
Carthage
 Dominance of, ii. 250
 Government of, i. 166, 182
Case, The, for Labor (Hughes), *cited,* ii.
  208 *n.*
Caste Systems, i. 80, 83–4

Castile and Aragon, Causes arresting
  Democracy in, i. 38
Catherine II., ii. 536
Catholic Legitimists, *see* Legitimists
Catholic Party, Switzerland, i. 409
Catholicism, *see* Roman Catholicism
Catilina, i. 428
Caucus System
 Connotations of, i. 15
 "Going into," U.S.A., ii. 57
 in French Chamber of Deputies, ii.
  356
 Invention of, ii. 355
 Labour Party's, in Australia, ii. 316,
  356–7, 451, 467
 Party, U.S.A., Influence of, ii. 60
Caudel, M., on Civil Liberty, i. 314 *n.*
Cavour, Count, ii. 541, 608; Personality
  of, ii. 471
Celestine V., Pope, i. 136 *n.* 2
Celibacy of the Roman Catholic Priest-
  hood, i. 83
Celtiberians of Spain, Kings of, i. 25
Celtic Peoples, i. 130
 Contradictory Characteristics of, i. 221
  & *n.*
 Lack of Realism in, i. 312 *n.*, 447
Central America, *see* Latin America
Central Executive Committee of the All
  Russian Congress of Soviets,
  functions of, ii. 582 *sqq.*
Central Government, relation of, to Local,
  ii. 435 *sqq.*
Central Office of Political Parties, Great
  Britain's, ii. 556
Centralization
 in France, i. 237 *sqq.*, 244, 247, 258
  & *n.*, 264, 274, 280, 284,
  285, 320, ii. 447, 449
 Swiss dislike for, i. 335, 364, 412–13,
  435, 445
 U.S.A. Reform tending to check, ii. 137
Century, A, of Peace, by Prof. Dunning,
  ii. 124 & *n.* 2
Chaeronea, battle of, i. 170
Chairmen of Committees, U.S.A., powers
  and status of, ii. 56–7, 61
Chaka, the Zulu King, ii. 542
Chambers of Commerce, U.S.A., and Re-
  form, ii. 163
Chambord, Count de, and his adherents,
  i. 214–15 & *n.*
Character in Leaders, i. 139
 in Politicians, ii. 557 & *n.*
Charity, Private and Public, in New Zea-
  land, ii. 190
Charles the Bold of Burgundy, Swiss con-
  flict with, i. 36
Charles I., struggles of, with Parliament,
  i. 28, 29, 52
Charles V., ii. 523, 536
Charles X., i. 214, 319 *n.;* fall of, i. 29,
  214
Chartist agitation, i. 30 & *n.* 2, 32
Chatham, Earl of, Tone of Public Life
  raised by, ii. 487
Checks and Balances on Democratic Ma-
  jority Rule, ii. 390 *sqq.,* 398
  sqq.
Chicago
 Growth of, ii. 99
 Riots at, 1894, ii. 362
 Voting at, for Non-Party Ballot in Mu-
  nicipal Elections, ii. 139 *n.*
Chief Secretary for Ireland, and Irish
  Government, ii. 543 & *nn.*
Chieftain-rule, possibility of, in Latin
  America, i. 206
Chieftainship, in Europe, i. 25
Child Labour, Legislation on, by U.S.A.
  Congress, ii. 125

Chile, Republic of, i. 187 n.
  Administration in, i. 193–4
  Area and Population of, i. 188, 193, 206
  Army and Navy of, i. 194
  a Constitutional Republic, i. 193
  a Democracy (possibly), i. 22, 204
  Electoral Corruption in, i. 194
  Ministerial Responsibility in, ii. 463 n. 1
  Oligarchy in, i. 193, 201, 206, ii. 538
  Public Credit in, i. 194
  Universal Suffrage in, i. 193
  Wars of, i. 191
China
  Civilization in, ii. 509
  Composite population of, ii. 508
  Corruption in, past and present, i. 139, ii. 453, 477, 509, 516, 540
  Custom-abidingness of, ii. 511 & n. 2
  Danger to, of Aggression, ii. 508
  Democracy in, Size of Country in regard to, ii. 507, 510–11, 513, 516
  Education in, i. 79, ii. 502
  Family relations in, ii. 525
  Government of, Provisional, ii. 575 n.
  Money Power in (see also Corruption, above), ii. 508, 514
  National Characteristics in, ii. 509–10
  National Sentiment in, ii. 516
  Parliament of, Central, ii. 510–11
    Intellectual Quality of, ii. 514 n.
  Provincial Assemblies and Governors in, ii. 510–11 & n. 1
  Provisional Constitution of, ii. 575 n.
  as a Republic, ii. 500, 501–2
  Responsibility in, how to secure? ii. 507
  and Self-Government, i. 5, ii. 509–10, 516–17
  Superstition in, ii. 509
Chinese Empire, fall of, i. 5
Chinese in
  Australia, status of, i. 145
    Immigration of, into, why stopped, ii. 204
  New Zealand, ii. 311–12
Chinese War, 1857, British Public Opinion on, ii. 377
Christian Socialists, i. 86
Christian Theologians on Happiness, ii. 532
Christianity
  and Capitalism, i. 85
  and Civics, i. 91
  Ends and Means of, i. 86–7
  Essential qualities of, influence of, in Moral and Political Spheres, i. 89 sqq.
  Failures of, cause of, ii. 533
  of Latin American Indians, i. 189 & n. 2
  and Natural Equality, i. 28, 61, 62
  Never put into Practice, i. 87
  Roman attitude to, i. 81–2
  and the State, i. 82, 83 sqq.
Church, the, and the Training of Citizens, i. 75
Church and State
  Controversies between, and their outcome, i. 83–6
  Relations between, i. 81 sqq.
  in France, i. 217 sqq., 318
  Two deep-rooted tendencies in, i. 58
Church Disestablishment, in France, i. 217
Church Interests in
  Caribbean States, i. 191
  Latin American Republics, i. 191
  Mexico, i. 202

Churches, parties for, or against, i. 123 & n., see also Anti-Clericalism
Cicero, i. 428 ; on Bribing of Roman Juries, ii. 480 n.; on Democracy, i. 13 ; famous Orations of, i. 177 n. 2
"Cientificos," in Mexico, ii. 506 n.
Cité antique, La, by Fustel de Coulanges, i. 168 n.
Cities, see also Capital Cities, above, and Municipalities, under each Country
  Australian, sizes and importance of, ii. 170, 250
  Electors in, keenness a duty of, i. 132
  French Representation of, i. 232
  Great European, Intellectual influence of, ii. 250–1
  Mediaeval, Oligarchic rule in, ii. 537 & n. 1
  U.S.A.
    Boss rule in, ii. 101 sqq., 156
    Enormous populations of, ii. 577
Citizens
  First and nearest Duty of All, ii. 490
  Formation of, by Education and Training, i. 70 sqq., 74 sqq.
    Essentials to, i. 78
  Local Government as aiding, i. 132
  Political views of, modes of Perversion of, i. 417
  True, in Latin America, i. 188
Citizenship
  of Aliens, i. 144 & n.
  as Envisaged in an Ideal Democracy, i. 47–8
  Lessons on, of Christianity, i. 91
  Swiss, Admission to, i. 328–9, 331, 364 & n., 434 & n.
City, meaning of, ii. 109
City Assembly District, New York, ii. 33 n.
"City Charters," U.S.A., Character of, ii. 101
City Conventions, U.S.A., ii. 33
City Life, Greek, etc., tribal, early organization of, i. 25
City Management [Municipal] Government, U.S.A., ii. 16, 139–40 & n.
City Mobs, conduct of, no evidence against Democracy, ii. 559 n. 1
City Republics, Ancient, Australian parallels to, ii. 250–1
Civic Amenities, Neglect of, in New Zealand, ii. 278 n. 1
Civic Apathy and Abstention from Public Life, causes and consequences of, i. 24–5, 30, 31, 37, 39, 40, 41, 158, 185, 196, 240, 288, 295, 316–17, 323, 428, 444, 478, 479, ii. 28, 35, 36, 37, 39, 49, 52, 53, 64, 65, 100, 105, 107, 108, 109, 110, 112, 113, 119, 130, 135, 139, 157, 163, 180 sqq., 189, 244, 246 sqq., 318–19, 338, 411 sqq., 412 & n., 435, 442, 450, 454 sqq., 489–90, 546–7, 560, 599
Civic Duty
  Interest in, of the Average Man, scale of, ii. 547
  Sense of, in France, ii. 455
  under Popular Sovereignty, Expectation of, unfulfilled, ii. 112, 113, see also Civic Apathy, above

Civic Duty—*continued*
  Sense of—*continued*
    in Switzerland, strength of, i. 136–7,
        335, 340, 401 *n.*, 444, 446,
        454
    Traditional, i. 141–2
    in U.S.A., ii. 4, 15, 37, 454
Civic Education, i. 70 *sqq.*
  Possibilities of, at various stages, i.
      76–7
Civic Federations, U.S.A., and Reform, ii.
      163
Civic Religion, Rousseau on, i. 75
Civic Responsibility to the Whole People,
      ii. 489 *sqq.*
Civicism, and the Gospels, i. 86–7
Civil Administration, Efficiency of, in
        Democracies, ii. 527, 528–9,
        562
Civil Administrative Code, U.S.A., ii.
      137 *n.* 1
Civil Code in
  France, i. 256
  Switzerland, i. 336 *n.* 1, 341–2, 386
Civil Equality, i. 65
  Definition, i. 60
  in France, i. 316, ii. 158
  in Muslim countries, i. 66 *n.*, 82
  in Switzerland, i. 444
  in U.S.A., ii. 157
Civil Figures, rarely becoming Tradi-
        tional, i. 141
Civil Liberty, i. 52, 53, 55 ; in various
        lands, i. 314 *& n.*, 322, 501
Civil Officials, U.S.A., Impeachments of,
        tried by Senate, ii. 18
Civil Rights in Backward States, guaran-
        tees for, ii. 518
Civil Service, *see under Countries, see
        also* Government Employees
  Abuses, and possible remedy, ii. 343
  Bureaucratic tendencies of, ii. 437
  in Democracies, summary on, ii. 365–6
  Higher and Lower grades of, relative
        Purity of, ii. 479
  Quality of, in the Six Countries de-
        scribed, ii. 359, 360
  To whom Responsible, ii. 492
Civil Strife, as Destructive of Democra-
        cies, ii. 602
Civil War
  English, theories affecting, i. 32
  U.S.A., *see* War of Secession
Civilization
  Passion for Pleasure, alleged growth
        of, *pari passu* with, ii.
        603 *n.*
  Populations at different stages of, in
        one Country, ii. 508
Clan Organization, i. 25
Clark, M., K.C., article by, referred to,
        i. 483 *n.*
Class, Solidification into, of the Few, ii.
        549
Class Antagonism and Alienation
  Absent from Switzerland, i. 424
  Causes of, ii. 455–6
  Effects of, i. 159, ii. 474
  in Relation to
    Referenda, ii. 433
    Rule of the People, i. 149, 150
  in Various Countries
    Ancient Greece, i. 181
    Australia, i. 309 *& n.*, ii. 171, 181,
        190, 212–13, 249, 252 *& n.*,
        253, 451, 457, 459, 562
    Belgium, ii. 457
    Canada, i. 466–7
    England, i. 348, ii. 474
    France, i. 211, 212, 221, 287, 307–8,
        315, ii. 182

Class Antagonism and Alienation—*con-
        tinued*
  in Various Countries—*continued*
    Holland, ii. 457
    Italy, ii. 457
Class Benefits, sought by Labour Leaders,
        ii. 568–9
Class Cleavage emphasized by Labour and
        Socialist Parties, i. 124, 125
Class Distinctions, i. 60–1, ii. 114, 314–
        15, 331
Class Opinion
  in Australia, ii. 245 *sqq.*
  in Canada, i. 309–10
Class Rule in Australia (*see also* Labour),
        ii. 205, 218, 257, 263–4
  Defects of, ii. 539
Class Selfishness, Undiminished under
        Democracy, Illustrations of,
        ii. 562, 580–1
Class Solidarity of Labour, limitations of,
        ii. 311
Class Spirit, Developments of, ii. 578 *sqq.*
Class War, Doctrine of, ii. 164, 533, 574,
        578, 580, 581
  in Hungary, ii. 602
Classes, the, i. 20
  Enfranchised in Great Britain, apathy
        of, i. 30, 31
  Extinction of, Communistic desires for,
        ii. 570
  French, Disintegration within, i. 309
  Led astray by the Money Power, ii. 477
        sqq.
  Relations between, reversed, ii. 585–6
Clay, H., i. 265, 424
Cleisthenes, i. 170
Clemenceau, M., on the Brazilian Consti-
        tution, i. 200
Clericalism (*see also* Anti-Clericalism) in
        various Lands, i. 80–81 *sqq.*,
        88, 123, 191, 199, 217 *sqq.*,
        221, 287, 289–90, 292, 414–
        15, 419, 422, 423, 467, ii.
        347–8
Clerics, non-Roman, position of, in Can-
        ada, i. 466
Cleveland, Grover, President, U.S.A., i.
        104, ii. 67 ; and the Chi-
        cago riots, ii. 362 ; per-
        sonality of, ii. 472
Cliques, Political, in
  France, i. 307–8
  Scotland, i. 269
  Switzerland, i. 445–6
Closed Primaries, U.S.A., ii. 129–30, 131–2
Closure, the (*see also* Obstruction, etc.),
        ii. 57, 60 *& n.*, 188, 346
Clubs
  Canadian, Non-party, i. 473–4
  French, Influence of, on Public Opinion,
        i. 296
Coal in
  Australia, ii. 167, 170
  Canada, i. 456
  New Zealand, ii. 265–6, 295–6, 329
Coalition Governments in
  Australia (1909), ii. 206, 211–12
  Great Britain (1914–19), effect of lack
        of an opposition, i. 121
  New Zealand, during the War, ii. 276–
        7
Cobden, R., ii. 541 ; influence of, ii. 561 ;
        on the Crimean War, ii.
        377
Code Napoléon, the, i. 213, 220, 318
Coleridge, S. T., i. 447
Collective Life, and Christianity, i. 89
Collectivism
  Aims and Working of, i. 290, ii. 258,
        322–3, 585 *sqq.*

Collectivism—*continued*
Inadequate data for Study of, i. 12 & n.
and State Trading, ii. 233
College of Electors, U. S. A., ii. 69
Cologne, ii. 437
Colombia, Republic of, i. 187 n.
Political Level of, i. 193
Colonial Assemblies, North American, ii. 7
Colonial Group, in French Chamber of Deputies, i. 254
Colonies, French, *see* French Colonies
Colour Bar, not abolished by Democracy, ii. 562
Colour Majorities, i. 56
Coloured Citizens, U.S.A.
Status of, i. 144–5
Voting Rights of, ii. 23
Practical abolition of, ii. 17, 48, 50, 77 & n. 1, 113, 124, 499
Comitia, the, of Rome, i. 130, 337; Decline of, i. 179
Commerce, U. S. A., Federal Powers over, ii. 125
Commissars, Russian functions of, ii. 582
Commission of Selection for Senators suggested, ii. 414–15
Commissions of Legislatures
French, i. 237–8, 246 *sqq.*, 251, 255, 256
Swiss, i. 347
Commissions, Municipal, U.S.A., Election of Commissioners, ii. 441
Committee system of Municipal Government, ii. 440
Committees of Legislatures
French, i. 314
Swiss, Native criticism on, i. 446
U.S.A., i. 314
not reported, ii. 53
Working of, ii. 56
Committees, Party, U. S. A., ii. 34, 130, *see also* Primaries
Common enclosures, ii. 541
Common Interest and Common Duty, inculcated by Local Self-Government, i. 132, 133, 141
Commonwealth of Australia, creation of, ii. 172, *see also* Australia, *and each* State *under Name*
"Common Will," Source of, ii. 547–8 & n. 2, *see also* People, Will of
Communal Councils in
France, i. 282
Switzerland, functions of, i. 334
Communal Governments, Switzerland, Alleged Abuses, i. 368
Communal Rights in Land, i. 130
Commune, the, of Continental Europe, i. 131, 282
Commune, the, French, of 1871, i. 214, 219, 221
Communes, *see under* France, *and* Switzerland
Communism
Defined, ii. 585–6
and Democracy, ii. 585 *sqq.*
Ends and Means of, i. 87
in Goods, i. 66–7
and the Gospels, i. 86 *sqq.*
Inadequate data for Study of, i. 11, 12 & n.
Where most followed, ii. 571
Communist Party in Russia, power exercised by, ii. 583
Communist or Socialist Parties, i. 125
Communist State
Choice of, between Efficiency and Equality, ii. 593 & n.
Directing Officials, Duties of, ii. 591–2
Discipline and Obedience in, ii. 591–4

Communist State—*continued*
Functions to be Discharged by, ii. 589–91
Functions Discarded by, ii. 591
Moral virtues assumed by, ii. 588 & n., 591
Offences against, ii. 590 & n.
Private Property abolished in, ii. 570, 586–7 & nn.
Communist Views, on Capital and Private Property, ii. 570, 591 & n.
Communities, self-interest and, i. 46
Community, Civic Duty to, low place of, in Interests of Average Man, ii. 547, *see also* Civic Apathy
Community Spirit, past and present, i. 58–9
Companies, Incorporated, U.S.A., hatred of, powers of, ii. 127, 141
Comparative Free Government, by Prof. Ganaway, ii. 59 n. 1
Comparison of the Six Democratic Governments, ii. 446 *sqq.*
Compromise
in Canada, i. 469–70, 472
Greek aversion to, i. 184
Comptroller, the, in France, i. 211
Compulsion, no part of the Powers of Newspapers, i. 105
Compulsive Legislation, scanty, in Switzerland, i. 436
Compulsory Arbitration, *see under* Arbitration, *and under* Australia, New Zealand, *and* Norway
Compulsory Labour in Russia, Trotsky's defence of, ii. 574 n. 2
Compulsory Military Service, *see also under Countries*
Democracies imposing
Occasionally, ii. 361
Permanently, ii. 361
Compulsory Purchase of Land
Australia, ii. 221
New Zealand, ii. 285, 289
Conciliation Methods in Australia and New Zealand, ii. 177, 198, 226 *sqq.*, 299–300
Concord, U.S.A., and its Hog Reeve, ii. 490
Condemnation without Penalty at Athens, i. 176 n.
Condonation or Toleration of Offences, in Democracies, i. 139, 277–8, 314–5, 489–90, ii. 39–40, 89 & n., 90, 91–2, 100, 102–3, 109, 140, 154–5, 157, 252–3, 479, 525, 528–9, 541, 544–5
Conduct of Life, the Gospels on, i. 88–9
Confédération Générale du Travail, in France, ii. 578
Congregational Churches, lay share in managing, U.S.A., ii. 5
Congregational Theocracy of Calvin, i. 84
Congress, *see under* U.S.A.
"Congressional Caucus," French version of, i. 229
Congressional Committee U.S.A., ii. 32 n. 1
Leaders among, ii. 41
Congressional District Convention, U.S.A., ii. 33
Congressional Record, U.S.A., not read by the People, ii. 64
Conquistadores, the, i. 192, 202, ii. 581
Conscience and Fear to enforce Responsibility in Democracies, ii. 491
and Party Voting, i. 120 & n.

Conseil de Cabinet, France, i. 228
Conseil d'État, France, i. 213
Conseil Général
　France, i. 232, 235, 280, 282, ii. 401,
　　403
　Switzerland, i. 372
Conseil des Ministres, France, i. 228
Conseil du Roi, France, changed form of,
　i. 213
Conseils d'Arrondissement, France, i. 232,
　235, 281, ii. 401
Conservatism
　in France, i. 42, 210, 219, 220, 235,
　　237, 239, 256, 298, 315, ii.
　　364
　in New Zealand, ii. 315, 323
　in Switzerland, i. 389–90, 397, 422
Conservative Party
　Great Britain, ii. 347
　New Zealand, ii. 268–9
Considérant, —, doctrines of, i. 402 *n.*
Constantine of Greece, i. 22
Constantinople
　Mediaeval, Mobs of, ii. 558 *n.* 1
　Russian advance to, *circa* 1876, ii. 378
　Turkish capture of, i. 27, ii. 408
Constitution, connotations of, i. 16
Constitutional Government in the U.S.A.,
　by Woodrow Wilson, ii. 69
　n. 1, 73 *n.*
*Constitutional History and Law of New
　Zealand*, by Hight and Bam-
　ford, ii. 276 *n.* 1
Constitutional Laws, France, Scope of,
　i. 223–5, 232
Constitutions (*see also under each Coun-
　try*), ii. 10
　Unwritten or Flexible, ii. 10, 462
　Written or Rigid, ii. 10–11, 27, 384,
　　391, 396, 500
Construction, Socialist inexpertness in,
　ii. 572
Consuls, Roman, Checks on, ii. 392, 407 *n.*
Consumers and Wage-earners, Australia,
　relations between, ii. 223–4,
　228
Contentment, not induced by Democracy,
　ii. 533–4, 562
"Contingent" Voting in Australian States,
　ii. 183
Continuity in Policy, how secured in
　Switzerland and other lands,
　i. 356
Contrat Social of Rousseau, influence of,
　i. 36, 434, *cited*, i. 260 *n.*,
　ii. 548 *n.* 2
"Control of the Caucus," ii. 343
Conventions, U.S.A., ii. 33, 34, 131 & *n.*
　Delegates to, ii. 33, 129, 130
Conversation, Educational Value of, i. 72
Conveying Electors to Polls, ii. 482 & *n.*
Convicts, in early Australia, ii. 168 & *n.*
Convocation, Oxford University, Voting
　in, i. 151 *n.*
Cook Islands and New Zealand, ii. 313
Coolidge, Mr., article by, on Switzerland
　referred to, i. 329 *n.*
Corcyra, fierce Seditions at, i. 167 *n.* 2
Corporate Bodies, Force in, of Tradition,
　i. 135
Corrupt Practices Act of 1882 (Eng-
　land), i. 241
Corruption in various Forms in various
　Countries (*see also* Jobbery
　and Lobbying), i. 139, 152,
　177 *n.* 1, 180, 190, 194,
　216, 234, 242 & *n.* 3, 259,
　292–3, 300, 303–4, 314,
　325, 334, 349, 366, 405,
　417, 428, 444, 466, 479,
　481, 482, 484–5, 489, ii.

Corruption in various Forms in various
　Countries—*continued*
　50–2, 62, 80, 87, 88, 183–4,
　255, 438, 441, 450–1, 452–
　3, 477, 478 *sqq.*, 485 *sqq.*,
　493–4, 498, 516, 528–9,
　539, 541
　Administrative, Danger of, in Back-
　　ward States, ii. 508–9
　Direct, Bribery, etc., *see under
　　Countries*
　Indirect, Various Modes of (*see also*
　　Money Power), ii. 454, 480
　　sqq.
　in the New European States, ii. 509 *n.*
　Not Extinguished by Democracy, ii.
　　562
Corsica, Blood Revenge in, i. 129 *n.*
Cortes, Hernando, in Mexico, i. 192, 202
Cortes, the, Political groups in, ii. 343
Costa Rica, Republic of, i. 187 *n.*
Coulanges, Fustel de, book by, on Re-
　ligion and Politics, i. 167
　n. 2
Council, the, at Athens, i. 172 & *n.* 1,
　176
Council of Australian Liberal Union, ii.
　209
Council of State, in France, i. 278–9
Council of States
　Switzerland, i. 344
　　Elections to, and Powers of, i.
　　　344 *sqq.*
Councils
　Borough, New Zealand, ii. 277
　Cantonal, Switzerland, i. 337
　of Chiefs, and of Elders, in Ancient
　　Nations, ii. 398 & *n.*
　Communal, France, ii. 401
　of Conciliation, New Zealand, ii. 300
　　sqq.
Councils Elected, County, Rural, Muni-
　cipal, ii. 439–40
County Councils
　Great Britain, ii. 14
　New Zealand, ii. 277
Coup d'État, the, of Napoleon III., i. 224,
　231, 291
Cour de Cassation, France, i. 272
Court of Appeal
　France, i. 272, ii. 385
　Switzerland, i. 359
Court of Justice, functions as, of U.S.
　Senate, ii. 18
Courts of Arbitration and Conciliation,
　see Australia *and* New Zea-
　land
Courts of First Instance, Switzerland, i.
　359
Crime in Australia
　Decrease in, ii. 254
　Repression of, and Tolerance, ii. 525
Crimean War, British Public Opinion on,
　ii. 377
Criminal Justice U.S.A., Defects of, ii.
　88 *sqq.*, 155, 156, 453 & *n.*,
　528
Criminal Statistics, New Zealand, ii. 278
Cromwell, Oliver, *cited*, ii. 589
Crowd-mentality, and the Crowd-Will, i.
　147, ii. 545
Crown, the, English restriction on, i.
　310, 312
Cruelty, Administrative, Disappearance of,
　under Democracy, ii. 532
Cuba, Republic of, i. 187 *n.*
　and the U.S.A., i. 192, ii. 123–4, 376
Curti, Th., book by, on the Referendum,
　i. 317 *n.*, 387 *n.*, 402 *n.*
Curtius, self-devotion of, i. 136
Czech Party, in Austria, i. 124

Czecho-Slovakia, Republic of, ii. 575
  Constitution of
    Nature of, ii. 432 & n. 1
    Provisions in, as to Judicature, ii.
      385 n.
    Referendum provided by, ii. 432 n. 1
    Executive Head of State in, ii. 462
    Senate of, Direct Popular Election to,
      ii. 400–1

Dakota, North, Reforms in, ii. 126 n.,
  136
Dakota, South, Referendum in, ii. 424
Dalley, W. B., ii. 191
Dana, R. H., on Efficiency-gain, with competent Civil Service, U.S.A.,
  ii. 96 n.
Dante, cited on Money Power in Democ-
  racies, ii. 486 & n.; Peace
  the supreme good to, ii.
  531
Dauerreden (Obstruction), in Germany,
  ii. 345
d'Aunet, Biard, on the Future of Aus-
  tralia, ii. 261 n., 283 n.
Dead Virtues, ii. 604
Deák, F., i. 424
Deakin, A., ii. 191, 211
Death-duties, New Zealand, ii. 288
Debates
  in Congress, ii. 60
  not read by the People, ii. 64, 146–7
  Conduct of, in Greek Assemblies, i.
    175
  in Swiss Federal Legislature, i. 346–7
Debt, see National Debt
Decentralization, ii. 576
  Advantages of, ii. 343, 435–6
  Movement towards, in France, i. 285
    & n., ii. 435, 576
Decius, and the Samnites, i. 136
Declaration of Independence, U.S.A.,
  i. 43, 44, 61, 139, 169, ii.
  4
Declaration of the Rights of Man, by
  National Assembly of France,
  i. 43, 44
  Private Property included in, i. 49,
    218 n.
Declarations of War, Source of, in
  France and U.S.A., ii. 382
Decorations and Honours, absent from
  Switzerland, deprecated in
  Canada, i. 451
de Coulanges, F., book by, i. 167 n. 2
Decrees
  in France, i. 277
  Greek, i. 174, ii. 391
Defence, see also Armies and Navies under
  Countries
  Early Organization for, i. 129, 130
Defensor Pacis, by Marsilius of Padua,
  cited, ii. 599 & n.
de Girardin, E., i. 97 n.
Delane, J. T., i. 97 n.
Delegate theory of Representation, ii. 351
  sqq., Countries holding, and
  reverse, ii. 353 & n.
Delegates
  French, i. 232, 233, 235
  U.S.A., ii. 33, 35, 36, 129, 130
Demagogue, the
  Defined, ii. 554
  Where most frequent to-day, ii. 554
Demagogues
  Athenian, i. 180
  in Canada, i. 501
  in France and England, i. 321
  in Switzerland, i. 369, 444, 501
  in U.S.A. and elsewhere, ii. 470 & n. 2
Demes, the, i. 177

Democracies
  Best-administered, ii. 457–8, 464 n. 2,
    484–5
  the Chief Fault in, i. 132
  Dominated by, and Exempt from,
    Money Power, ii. 454
  Extravagance and Waste characteristic
    of, i. 483, 499 & n., ii. 200,
    290, 328, 331, 438–9, 452,
    458, 459, 464, 473
  Greek, origins of, i. 25
  Their attitude to the Law, ii. 84–93,
    362 sqq., see also Condona-
    tion and Law and Order,
    Maintenance of
  Leadership in, ii. 552 sqq., see also
    Few, the
  Majority Rule in, Checks and Bal-
    ances on, ii. 390 sqq., 398
    sqq.
  Not Valuing principles of Liberty for
    their own sakes, i. 56
  Oligarchies within, ii. 542 sqq.
  Present Tendencies in (see also Anarch-
    ism, Socialism, etc.), ii.
    575 sqq.
    Changes, ii. 576 sqq.
    New Forces, ii. 578 sqq.
  Rise of, within the British Empire,
    i. 4, 6
  Sentimentality of, ii. 90
  Tested by quality of Leaders, ii. 551,
    552, 561
Democracy, see also under Countries
  in the Ancient World, i. 165 sqq.
  Applicability of, to Backward Races,
    ii. 498 sqq.
    Advances and Expedients possible in
      place of, ii. 516 sqq.
    and the Logic of Events, ii. 518
    Pessimistic views of, ii. 514 sqq.
  Bases of, i. 143, ii. 489, 605
  Benefits of
    Negative, ii. 532
    Positive, ii. 531 sqq.
  in Canada more active than in U.S.A.,
    i. 495
  Change leading to origin and after-
    math of, i. 24, 27–8, 31,
    41, 42
  and the Communist State, ii. 585 sqq.
  Comparison of, with
    Monarchy, ii. 535–6
    Oligarchy, ii. 535, 537 sqq.
      Balance in favour of the former,
      ii. 540–1
  Conclusions on, ii. 561–3
  Connotation of, change in, i. 4
    Moral and Social, i. 23
  Contentment not induced by, ii. 533–4,
    562
  Definitions of, i. 20 sqq., 22–3, ii.
    555 n.
  Destructive rather than Constructive,
    gains from, ii. 606
  Disappointments in, i. 48–50
  Diseases, Defects, Failures and Suc-
    cesses of, i. 4–5, 38, 46, 62,
    ii. 28, 79 & n., 345 sqq.,
    456, 533 sqq., 562, 573–4,
    606
    Public Opinion the only Cure, ii.
      356–7
  Dulness of, ii. 520, 521
  and Education, i. 70 sqq., 78, 79
  and Efficiency, ii. 102, 459, 473, 524–5,
    528–9, 533, 539, 540, 593
  Evolution in, ii. 582
  Executive in, ii. 359 sqq.
  and Foreign Policy, i. 319, ii. 367
    sqq., 529

Democracy—*continued*
Fountain-heads of, i. 131
Future of,
Conjectures on, ii. 598 *sqq.*
Changing Tastes as affecting, ii. 604–5
Physiological Factors in, ii. 605
Predictions Vain, ii. 598–9
Reversion from, not Impossible, i. 42
Gifts of, to New Zealand, ii. 327–8
Growth of
Causes creating, i. 24 *sqq.*
Causes retarding or arresting, i. 38–40
Historical Evolution of, i. 12, 17, 24
Hopes for, Demands from, etc., ii. 455–6, 524, 573, 607 *sqq.*
Intolerance attributed to, ii. 519, 521, 522
Investigation into, i. 8
Methods of Enquiry, i. 9, 13 *sqq.*
Comparative Method, i. 17 *sqq.*
Later Phases of, ii. 564 *sqq.*
Latin American Republics as an argument against, i. 187–8, 192–3
Manners as influenced by, ii. 339, 452, 524–5
Material Changes affecting, ii. 564 *sqq.*
Materialism of, i. 303, 307, 481-2, 489, 504, ii. 173, 244, 251, 301, 326, 485, 521, 574, *see also* Labour, *under* Australia
Meaning of, ii. 550–1
as Means and End, ii. 602–3
Menace to, of doctrines of Class War and General Strike, ii. 581–2
Modern
Peace-loving, ii. 361–2
Tendencies in, ii. 575
Money Power (*q.v.*), chief Enemy of, ii. 486–7, 488
Morals as influenced by, ii. 525–6
New Aspirations, ii. 568 *sqq.*
Old Ideals of, Disappearing, ii. 574
Oldest, Simplest and Purest form of, i. 337
Party and Parties in, i. 111 *sqq.*
Permanence of, Arguments against summarized, ii. 601 *sqq.*
Press, the (*q.v.*), in, i. 72–3, 92 *sqq.*
Relation of, to
Equality and Liberty, i. 18
Letters, Art [and Science], ii. 519 *sqq.*
Relation to, of the Gospel teachings, i. 86–92
and Religion, i. 80 *sqq.*
Republic not the same as, i. 22
Responsibility in, Difficulty of Fixing, ii. 495, 496–7
Results of, ii. 527 *sqq.*
Safeguards of, ii. 487
Sole Advantage of, over other forms of Government, ii. 487
Spread of, ii. 575
Theoretical Foundations of, i. 43 *sqq.*
Things which discredit, ii. 103
True, Existence and Possibility of, discussed, ii. 546 *sqq.*
Value to, of Individual Liberty, i. 59
Virtues assumed by, ii. 605–6
Vital impulse of, i. 50
Weakness of, ii. 489–90
"Democratic," Connotations of term, i. 23
Democratic Advance, ii. 566–7

Democratic Government
Actualities of, reasons for Investigating, i. 4
Method of Investigation, i. 5 *sqq.*
Best training for, i. 79
Dangers threatening, i. 116 *sqq.*
"General Strike" and "Direct Action" counter to principles of, i. 322 *n.*
Types of, ii. 461 *sqq.*
Comparison as to Fulfilment of Will of the People, ii. 474–5
Points to consider regarding, ii. 464
Democratic Group, Switzerland, i. 409
Democratic Mistake, The, by Sedgwick, cited, ii. 491 & *n.* 1
Democratic Party, U.S.A.
Racial allegiance to, ii. 43
and Tammany, ii. 103 *sqq.*
Democratic States, Newly formed, *see* Europe, New Republics in
Democratic Theories in Modern Countries
First Proclamation of, i. 85
Spread of, to the New World, i. 85
the Two Pillars of, i. 70
Démocratie, La, en Nouvelle Zélande, by Siegfried, ii. 283 *n.*
Démocratie, La, et les partis politiques, by Ostrogorski, i. 123 *n.*, ii. 33 *n.*
Demos, use of term, i. 20; as Tyrant, Aristotle on, i. 183
Demosthenes, i. 170, 180, 182, 319
Denmark
Constitution of, i. 223
a Democracy, i. 23
Free Trade in, ii. 297
Party Government in, i. 115
Progressive Land Tax in, ii. 297
Second Chamber of, Power of, basis of, ii. 406
the War with, as affecting German Democracy, i. 39
Departmental Council, France, *see* Conseil Général
Departments, *see under* France
Deploige, —, i. 387 *n.* 1
Deputies, *see under* France
Dervish Fraternities, i. 80 *n.*
Despotism
and Dread of Education, i. 70–71
in the Eastern Empire, i. 27
French attitude to, i. 291, 321, 322, ii. 162, 358
of French Legislature, i. 230–1
Presidential, in Latin America, i. 190, 192
Principle of, ii. 491
Destruction, Socialistic skill in, ii. 571–2
Development, The, of the U.S.A., by Prof. M. Farrand, ii. 124 *n.* 2
Devotion to the Dynasty, the Japanese Ideal, i. 138 & *n.*
to the State, the Roman Ideal, i. 137
Diaz, Porfirio, President of Mexico, rule of, i. 203–4, 207, ii. 376, 512
Dicey, Professor, on the Conventions of a Constitution, i. 440 & *n.* 1
and Rait, Professors, book by, on the English and Scottish Union, ii. 396 *n.*
Dickens, Charles, and Western American manners, ii. 524
Dictators, Rise of, ii. 358
Dictatorship, Roman, U.S.A. parallel to, ii. 162
Diet, Swiss, i. 329

Dikasts and Dikasteries, Athens, i. 177, 178
Diplomacy
  Need of Expert Knowledge in, ii. 367, 368, 383
  Popular charges against, ii. 367 & n., 368 sqq., passim
  Secrecy in, ii. 367 & n., 368, 371 & n., 372, 383
  Abolition of, demand for, ii. 382–3
"Direct Action"
  Anti-Democratic, i. 322 n.
  Labour views on, in Australia, ii. 253
  Nature of, ii. 572–3
Direct Elections, of Officials, Representatives, and Senators, ii. 139, 161–2, 401, 403, 404
Direct Popular Control over Executives, ii. 363
Direct Popular Legislation, see Initiative and Referendum, see also under Countries
  Attractions of, ii. 577
  Chief Value of, Educative, ii. 433–4
  Demand for, Sources of, ii. 242, 262, 417–18
  General Reflections on, Pros and Cons, ii. 425 sqq.
  Modern Methods summarized and discussed, ii. 417 sqq.
  Objections to, ii. 145–6
    Replies to, ii. 146–7
  in Oregon, ii. 144 sqq.
  People's fitness for, as Tested by Referenda, ii. 422–3
  Results of, ii. 147 sqq.
  Where in Action, Methods of, and uses made of, ii. 417, 419 sqq.
  Working of
    Review of, and of its Methods, ii. 417 sqq.
Direct Presidential Primaries, U.S.A., ii. 70
Direct Primaries, U.S.A., ii. 77 n. 2, 130, 131 & n., 132–4
Directors, French Deputies as, i. 302
Discontent
  not allayed by Democracy, i. 4
  Provoked by Inequality, i. 37, 38, 45
  with Existing Government, Manifestations of, in France, i. 290–2
Discord, Internal, as Solvent of Traditions, i. 140
Disestablishment of the Church in France, i. 217
Disraeli, B., see Beaconsfield
Dissolution of Parliament on Censure of Minister, ii. 492 n. 1
Divine Right of Kings, i. 84, 144, 215
Divisions in House of Commons and House of Representatives, U.S.A., compared, ii. 470 n. 1
Divorce (see also under Countries), Greater Frequency of, in relation to Morals, ii. 525
Dockers' Strike, in England (1889), effect of, on Australian Trade Unions, ii. 204
Domestic Cares v. Civic Duty, Relative Interest taken in, ii. 547
Domestic Interest in Public Affairs, Value of, ii. 530
Dominican Order, i. 84
Dominions, the, see also under Names
  Bribery and Corruption in, ii. 478, 479, 480
  Executive vested in Cabinets in, i. 448
  Judiciaries of, High standard of, ii. 481

Dominions—continued
  Ministers Sitting in Parliament in, i. 261
  Parliamentary and Cabinet System in, ii. 461
  Party in, as compared with Party in U.S.A., ii. 45
  Political Connection of, with Great Britain, ii. 214–15 & n.
  Rise of, as Democracies, i. 4, 6–7, 26 & n.
    Historical Evolution, i. 42
    Social Equality in, i. 33, 61
    Status of, as recognized by the Peace Treaties and League of Nations, i. 489, ii. 215
Draco, i. 170
Dresden, ii. 437
Dreyfus Case, the, i. 217, 218, 291
Droz, Numa, book by, on Civisme, i. 76 n., 350
Druidical beliefs, i. 82 n.
Drummond, —, Life of Seddon by, referred to, ii. 300 n.
Dulness and Democracy, ii. 519–21
Dumping, Australian efforts to prevent, ii. 223 & nn.
Dunning, Prof., book by, on relations between Canada, Great Britain, and U.S.A., ii. 124 n. 2
Dutch Rule in Java, i. 205
Dutch Stocks in U.S.A., ii. 4
Duty and Power, former collocation of, i. 144
Dynasty
  Devotion to, the Japanese Ideal, i. 138 & n.
  Loyalty to, Parties rising from, i. 111

Eastern Empire, Acquiescence of, in Imperial rule, i. 27
Eastern Europe, Nationality in, Complications of, ii. 603–4
Eastern Question, Beaconsfield on, ii. 378–9
Eastern Question Association, the, i. 120
Ecclesiastical and Anti-Ecclesiastical Parties (see also Anti-Clericalism, Clericalism, and Roman Catholicism), i. 123
Economic Antagonism, i. 66
Economic Conditions, action of, on Politics, i. 195, 205, 207
Economic Distress not the cause of Labour Unrest, i. 197
Economic Dividing lines between Parties, tendency to, i. 125
Economic Equality (see also Private Property, Abolition, etc.), i. 38, 66–7, 316, ii. 564–5, 569 sqq.
Economic and Industrial Legislation, Improved Machinery for, desirable, ii. 474
Economic Issue, Interest in, dominance of, ii. 600, 601
Economy
  a Weak Point of Democracy, ii. 452, see also Extravagances, below
  secured by Swiss form of Government (q.v.), ii. 473
Ecuador, Republic of, i. 187
  Low Political Level of, i. 192, 204
Editors of Newspapers, Notable, i. 97 & n.
Educated Classes
  Duty of, ii. 459
  Objection of, to Public Life (see also Civic Apathy), ii. 455–6

Education, *see under Countries*
and Democracy, i. 70 *sqq.*, 78, 79
Elementary, Assignment of, to Local
    Authorities, ii. 435–7
Free, ii. 568
overestimated, as fitting for Democracy,
    i. 78
and Shrewdness, relative value of, in
    working a Democracy, ii.
    502
Standards set by, i. 135
Educational Inculcation of Civic Duty in
    Switzerland, i. 451
Educational Qualifications for Suffrage, i.
    63 *& n.*, 152, 194 *n.*
Educational Value of Local Government,
    see under Local Government
Edward III. and the Money Power, ii.
    538
Efficiency, Administrative
Concentration of Power Essential to,
    ii. 547
and Democracy, ii. 102, 459, 473,
    524–5, 528–9, 533, 539,
    540, 593
and Equality
    Choice between, in Communist
    States, ii. 593
    Form of Government most likely to
    Secure, ii. 464, 475
    under Monarchy, ii. 535
    under Oligarchies, ii. 102, 538–9, 540
    and Party Spirit, U.S.A., ii. 28
    Secured by Swiss form of Government,
    ii. 473
Egypt
Ancient
    Caste in, i. 81, 83–4
    Monarchy in, i. 25
Modern
    National Sentiment in, ii. 516
    Self-Government in, ii. 518
        Problems of, ii. 515
        Prospects of, ii. 513
Eight Hours' Day, in Australia, ii. 204,
    226
Election by Lot at Athens, by J. W.
    Headlam, i. 180 *n.*
Election Committees, ii. 30
Election Phenomena, different, according
    to locale, i. 13–14
Elections, *see also under each Country*
Aristotle's view on, i. 182 *n.*
Carrying of, a Party function, i. 113
as Expressions of Public Opinion, i.
    152, 156, 159 *sqq.*
Frequent, and their Effects, i. 397, 416,
    ii. 21, 31, 37, 49, 112, 135,
    161, 178, 191, 205, 364,
    411, 443–4, 450 *et alibi*
Indirect Corruption concerning, ii. 481
    & n. sqq.
Individual Responsibility for, ii. 496–7
Journalistic Influence on, i. 99
Money Power (*q.v.*) in, ii. 387, 454,
    457
Nature of, ii. 426
Party Funds for, i. 115
Elections of Judges (*see also* Judges),
    ii. 385–7
Electoral Anomalies and British Reform
    Acts, i. 29 *sqq.*
Electoral Colleges, France, i. 232 *& n.*,
    233, 235, ii. 403–4
Electoral Corruption, i. 139, 241–2, ii.
    478, 528
Direct, ii. 477–8
Indirect, ii. 480 *sqq.*
Electoral Districts, Australia, ii. 183
Electoral Franchise, U.S.A., wide Exten-
    sion of, ii. 19–20

Electoral Pressure on Candidates, ii. 349
Electoral Suffrage, Dependent on Local
    Conditions, ii. 506–7
as Natural Right, i. 49, ii. 506–7
Qualifications, Educational, etc., i. 63
    & n., 153, 194 *& n.*, ii. 277
U.S.A., ii. 47 *& n.*, 48–9
Electorate, Small Sections of, Results of,
    ii. 349
Electors, Guidance of, in Choice of Can-
    didates, i. 114–5
Electric Telegraph, as affecting Democ-
    racy, i. 92
Elizabeth, Queen, Ingratitude of, ii. 559
    n. 2
Elizabethan-Stuart age, glories of, ii. 522
Eloquence in Leaders, ii. 552–3
Power of, in Greek Republics, i. 179
Emerson, Ralph Waldo, Local office filled
    by, ii. 490
Emperor, the, and the Swiss, i. 328
Employees, Representation of, Australian
    view on, ii. 234–5 *& n.* 1
Employers
Australian Combinations, etc., of, ii.
    231
and Compulsory Arbitration, in
    Australia, ii. 230
New Zealand, ii. 306
and Employed in Australia, relations
    between, ii. 180–1
England, *see also* Great Britain
Abstract Ideas in, Slight Influence of,
    i. 311–2
Bases of Free Institution in, i. 142
Church Strifes, early, fought out in,
    i. 312
Class-antagonism in, past and present,
    i. 310
Common Law of, principles of, as af-
    fecting U.S.A., ii. 5
Conceptions in, of Liberty, i. 52 *sqq.*
Constitutionalism of, i. 138, 141
18th and 19th Centuries, Corruption
    in, i. 139, 241–2, ii. 452–3
Elizabethan Age in, ii. 522
Estates in, ii. 396, 398
Folk Mot in, i. 130, 337, ii. 8, 506
Freemasonry in, i. 123
Kings of
    Conflicts of, with the Popes, i. 83, 84
    Struggles of, with Parliament, i. 28
    sqq., 140
Law-abidingness in, and Devotion to
    Liberty and Law, i. 137–8,
    139, 310, 501, ii. 199
Leniency in, to Lawbreakers, ii. 363 *n.*
Local Self-Government in, i. 310–11
    Loss of its Popular Character, i. 131
    Small Units of, ii. 506
    Origin and History of, i. 130–1
Municipal Government in, Uniformity
    of, i. 171
National Characteristics in, i. 10, 137–
    8, 139, 310, 501, ii. 199
Oligarchic Rule in, i. 3, 4, 27 *sqq.*
Out-relief in, past problem of, ii.
    439
Parish and Parish Council in, i. 130,
    282
Party in, rise of, i. 113
    Social mixture in, i. 124, 311
Patronage in, i. 311
Place-hunting in, i. 370
Political Institutions of, as adapted by
    the Dominions, i. 7, *see
    specially* Canada
Political Level in, variations in, i.
    505–6
Popular Government in, progress of,
    history of, i. 28–32

England—*continued*
Primrose League in, i. 123 *n.*
Reliance in, on Precedents, i. 312
the Town in, i. 131 *& n.*
Tradition adhered to, in, i. 141
"English People," fallacy in the phrase,
   i. 145 *n.*
English and Scotch Poets, 18th and early
      19th Centuries, Stimuli of,
      ii. 522
English Political Institutions, Montesquieu
   on, i. 211
English-speaking Countries
   and Christianity, i. 85–6
   Democratic Principles assumed in, by
      the Roman Church, i. 88
   Elected Local Councils in, ii. 439–40
   Laws not largely Codified in, i. 318
   Party in, i. 113
   Popular Control over Executives lim-
      ited in, ii. 363–4
English tendencies influencing U.S.A., ii.
   4–5, 7–8
English Working-men Ignorant of their
   own power, ii. 567 *& n.*
Épuration of the Judicial Bench in
   France, i. 272, 273, 315, ii.
   385
Equality, *see also* Civil, Economic, Po-
      litical, *and* Social Equality
   in Civilized Communities, i. 60–7
   Connotations of, as to Individuality,
      etc., ii. 519–20
   and Democracy, i. 23, 45, 64 *& n.*,
      ii. 37
   Doctrine of, Abuse of, ii. 458
   and Efficiency, *see* Efficiency, *above*
   18th-Century ideas on, i. 37 *sqq.*, *see
      also* France
   Forms of, i. 38, 60 *sqq.*, 65 *sqq.*
   a Fundamental of American Democracy,
      ii. 8
   in Gospel Teachings, i. 88–9
   of Laws, Greek aim in Revolutions, i.
      25
   and Manners, i. 428–9, ii. 338, 524–5
   in North America, after its Independ-
      ence, ii. 4
   Not the Child of Nature, ii. 548
   Passion for Spread of, i. 68 *& n.*
      in France, i. 38, 68, 156, 254, 256,
      257, ii. 548
   Principle of, upset by Natural Facts,
      ii. 546–8
   in Savage and Backward Races, i. 68
      & n., ii. 498–9
   Sentiment of, created by Christianity,
      i. 90
   Strong, in Australia, ii. 171
   Swiss love for, i. 442, 445
Essays on Reform, i. 30 *n.* 1
Estates, the, in Mediaeval Assemblies, ii.
   398
Esthonia, Republic of, ii. 575
   Constitution of, provisions of, as to
      the Judicature, ii. 386 *n.* 2
   Delegate idea of Representation re-
      pudiated by, ii. 353
   Executive Head of State in, ii. 462
   Referendum in, ii. 399 *n.* 2
   Unicameral Legislature in, ii. 399 *&
      n.* 2
Étatisme, in Switzerland, i. 389, 412
   & n. 1
Euler, —, i. 434
Euripides, i. 71, 169 *n.*
Europe
   Bicameral Legislatures in, i. 228, ii.
      45
   Class-distinctions in, Disruptive force
      of, ii. 114

Europe—*continued*
Democracy in, Historical Evolution of,
   i. 25 *sqq.*, 34 *sqq.*
Early, Chieftainship in, i. 25
Labour Parties in, i. 124
New Republics in, since 1918, i. 4, 5,
   225 *n.*, ii. 575, 602
   Corruption in, ii. 508–9
   Efforts of, to establish Constitutional
      Governments, ii. 336
   Judiciaries of, ii. 385 *n.*, 386 *n.* 2,
      389
   Lessons from U.S.A., ii. 161 *sqq.*
   Parliamentary Government, adopted
      by, ii. 474–5
Predominance of, Menace to, of the
   Backward Races, ii. 498–9
South-Eastern, New Kingdoms of, *see*
   Bulgaria, Greece, Roumania
Stormy decade before (from 1920), i.
   454
European and American Ideas, percola-
   tion of, into Latin America,
   i. 210
European Cities, as Intellectual foci, ii.
   250–1
European Revolutionaries, Aim of, ii.
   568
European Wars 1792–1814, controversies
   raised by, ii. 5 *n.*
Europeans and Equality for Coloured
   Races, ii. 498–9
Excise Tariff Act of 1906, Australia, ii.
   223 *& n.*
Executive, or Party in Power, in Parlia-
      mentary Government, i.
      115–6
   in Democracies, ii. 358 *sqq.*
   Compared with that in an Oligarchy,
      ii. 541
   Quality of the Departments, ii. 358–9
   Summary on, ii. 365–6
   Defects of, in the Six Governments,
      ii. 452–3
   Sole power of, over Legislature in
      Parliamentary Government,
      ii. 464–5
   Tendency to look to, of Large Masses,
      ii. 576–7
Executive Council System of Government
      in Switzerland (*q.v.*), ii.
      461, 462–3, 473 *sqq.*
Executive Councils, *see under Countries*
Executive Equality, i. 63 *sqq.*
Executive Government, Instability of, ii.
   447, 448, 452, *see also* Min-
   isterial Instability
Executive Head of State in
   Parliamentary Governments, ii. 461–2
   Presidential Governments, ii. 462–3
   Swiss form of Government, ii. 461
Executive Strength, ii. 512
   French love for, i. 291
   in relation to the People, and to other
      Powers of the State, ii.
      363–4
Executives, *see also under each Country*
   Popular Control over, ii. 364
   Powers of, i. 56, ii. 464
   and Strikers, ii. 452
Executives and Legislatures, Balance be-
   tween, Disturbance of, ii.
   467
*Experiments in Government and the Es-
      sentials of the Constitution*,
      by Root, ii. 12 *n.* 2
Extravagance and Waste, Characteristic
      of Democracies, i. 483, 499
      & n. 2, ii. 200, 290, 328,
      331, 438–9, 452, 458, 464,
      473

Extremists
in French Politics, i. 268
Union of, in a Parliament, danger
from, i. 254

Faction, i. 111, 113 n.
Connotations of, i. 15
in Oligarchies, ii. 539, 540
Repression of, by the Law, i. 127
Factory Acts, New Zealand, ii. 297 n. 1
Facts and Forces creative of Popular
Government
Practical, i. 24
Theoretical, i. 24, 32, 36, 37
Newspaper manipulation of, i. 100–1,
109
Family Law, French, i. 318
Family Relations and Forms of Govern-
ment, ii. 525
Fanaticism, Danger from, ii. 507
Farmers' Party, and Movement, Canada,
i. 125, 474, ii. 340, 347
Farmers' Union Party, Australia, ii. 207
Farrand, Prof. M., book by, on Develop-
ment of U.S.A., ii. 124 n. 2
Fatalism of the Multitude, ii. 121 n.
Faure, Félix, on State Functionaries, i.
243 n.
Fear and Responsibility, ii. 491
Federal Army, Swiss, see under Switzer-
land
Federal Government, advantages of, ii.
435–6
Federal Handbook, of Australia, cited,
ii. 199 n., 222–3 & n. 1,
224 & n. 1, 228 n. 2, 240 n.
Federal States, in Spanish America, see
Brazil, and Mexico
Federation of Small States, Napoleon I.
on, i. 406–7
Ferdinand, Ex-Tsar, of Bulgaria, i. 22,
ii. 358, fall of, i. 225 n.
Ferri, E., adulation of, ii. 546
Ferry, Jules, position held by, i. 265 n.,
321
Feudal Rule, ii. 537
Judicial Functions under, i. 130
Feuillet, O., story by, cited on Centralization, i. 284 n.
Few, the, Dominance of, or Rule of (see
also Oligarchy), i. 20, 223,
ii. 499–500, 511, 541, 542
sqq., see also China and
Russia, Soviets, etc.
Filibustering, U.S.A., ii. 57, 60 n., 345
sqq.
Finance, see also under Countries, and see
Money Power as Differen-
tiating Function of Senates
and First Houses, ii. 402
Financial Associations of Origin of Rep-
resentation, ii. 349–50
Financial Control exercised
by Lower Houses, i. 349, 352, 460,
ii. 184, 188, 270, 402,
462
by U.S.A. Senate, ii. 60
Fines, at Athens, i. 179
Finland, Republic of, ii. 575
Executive Head of State in, ii. 462
Unicameral Legislature in, ii. 399
First Crusade, the, i. 147
First Decade of the Australian Common-
wealth, by Turner, ii. 225
n. 3
Fisheries, State, New Zealand, ii. 295
Fitness for Rule as coexistent with Po-
litical Equality, Theory of,
i. 28, 45, 63, ii. 20
Flag, National, of France, and the
Orleanists, i. 215 & n.

Flexible Constitutions, Countries having,
ii. 462
"Floor Leader," House of Representa-
tives, U.S.A., ii. 57
Florence, Mediaeval
Genius developed in, ii. 522
History of, ii. 537 n.
Money Power in, ii. 538
Republic of, Fate of, ii. 601
Use in, of the Lot, i. 64 n., 180 n.
Flowers, Australian, wealth of, ii. 250 n.
Folk Mot, the, English, i. 130, 337,
ii. 8, 506
Force, Physical, Menace of, to Democ-
racy, ii. 582
Ford, Prof. H. J., on the Canadian
Provincial and American
State Legislatures, i. 484
n.; book by, on American
Politics, cited, ii. 38 & n.
Foreign Affairs, see also under Countries
Conduct of, in Democracies, ii. 74
& n., 172, 359, 367 sqq.,
382, 383, 529
Interest in, resulting in Australian
Federation, ii. 172, see also
Papua
Mass Ignorance of, ii. 367, 369 sqq.,
382–3
Foreign Aggression, changed attitude to,
in U.S.A., ii. 123–4, 159
Foreign Policy, see also Foreign Affairs,
above
Committees and Commissions on,
ii. 382, 383
Control of, by Free Peoples, i. 40
in Democracies, ii. 367 sqq.
a Weak Point, i. 327, ii. 380, 528
Conclusions on, ii. 383
Ends and Means of, ii. 368 sqq.,
381 sqq.
Morality in, ii. 369
Popular Criticism of, and demands on,
ii. 367, 382
Possible Improvements in, ii. 382
Press Methods regarding, and Influence
on, i. 100, 103 n., 109, 158
n., 298, ii. 370
Foreign Relations
of Greek Republics, i. 206, ii. 74 n.
of Modern Democracies (see also under
Countries), ii. 601–2
under Monarchies, ii. 536
under Oligarchies, i. 184, ii. 74 n.,
371
of Roman Republic, ii. 74 n.
Foreign War, Destructive of Democracies,
ii. 601
Forest Cantons, the, i. 330, 331–2
Public Meeting in, of Freemen, i. 35
Forestry
in Canada, i. 456
State, New Zealand, ii. 297 & n. 2
Forms of Government, Influence of, on
Nations as Wholes, over-
estimated, i. 325–6
"Forty-seven Ronins, the," i. 138 n.
Fosdick, R. B., American Police Systems
by, cited, ii. 453 n.
Four Chambers of the Four Orders, old
Swedish, ii. 396
Fox, Charles James, ii. 560, 561, 569
Frames of Representative Government,
ii. 461 sqq.
Construction of, reasons for, ii. 490
Development of, ii. 505
France, Republic of
Abstract Ideas in, Force and Results
of, i. 37 sqq., 312
Acquiescence of, in Despotism of
Napoleon III., ii. 600

France—*continued*
Administration, Civil, in, i. 273 *sqq.*,
317, ii. 528
Anti-Clericalism in, i. 137, 218 & *n.*,
236, 265, 291–2, 312, 315–
6, ii. 6, 457
Anti-Semitism of, i. 217, 218, 291
Army of, i. 318
Service in, Compulsory, ii. 361
Arrondissements of, and their Admin-
istration, i. 276, 281,
285
Average Citizen in, in relation to Poli-
tics, i. 267
Bourgeoisie of
Class Antagonism of, i. 212, 221
Conservatism of, i. 220, 315, ii.
363–4
Influence of, on Politics, i. 298
Leaders of the Socialist Party from,
i. 218
Candidates in
Choice of, i. 113–4
Independence of, i. 250, 267
Cantons of, i. 280–1
Capitalists of, Influence of, *see* Money
Power, *below*
Centralization in, i. 212 *sqq.*, 244, 247,
258 & *n.*, 264, 274, 280,
284, ii. 447, 449
Chamber of Deputies of, i. 223, 232,
240 *sqq.*
Caucus System in, ii. 356
Characteristics of, i. 231, 244 *sqq.*
Check on, needed (*see also* Senate),
i. 321
Cleverness in, i. 323
Convoking of, i. 245
Debates and Scenes, in, i. 259
Decline of, i. 313, ii. 337
Dissolutions brought about by, ii.
492
Duration of, i. 240, 245
Election to, by Manhood Suffrage,
i. 240
Financial Functions of, i. 233, 236,
237, 246, ii. 402
Groups (*q.v.*) in, i. 227, 246, ii.
347–8
Intrigue in, i. 261, ii. 342
Members of
Classes and Views represented
among, i. 235, 248 & *n.*,
sqq.
Intellectual Standard of, i. 248–9
Number of, i. 232, 240
Officers of, i. 245
Powers of, i. 226, ii. 447, *see also*
Financial Functions, *above*
Procedure of, i. 245–6
Public Opinion in, i. 292
Relations with, of
President, i. 240
Senate and Executive, i. 233–4,
236 *sqq.*, 239, 240, 313,
314, ii. 492–3
Rules of, and their Working, i. 250
sqq.
Sections of, functions of, i. 245–6
Tone and Atmosphere of, i. 259
Work of, i. 256 *sqq.*
Church and State relations in, i. 217
sqq., 318
Cities of
Centres of Opinion, ii. 437
Representation of, i. 232
Civic Education, in, i. 76 *n.*
Civic Sense in, i. 317, ii. 455
Civil Liberty in, i. 314 & *n.*, 324
Civil Service of, i. 273 *sqq.*, 283–4,
303, 356, 366

France—*continued*
Civil Service of—*continued*
Permanent heads, Loyal Service given
by, i. 275
Salaries of, i. 275
and Trade Unions, i. 275
Class Antagonism in, i. 212, 221, 265,
287, 307–8, 316, ii. 181
Clerical Party in, i. 88, 123, ii. 347
Clericalism in, i. 85, 88, 123, 217
sqq., 221, 287, 289–90, 292,
467
Collectivist views in, i. 290
Colonies, Increase of, under Third Re-
public, i. 319
Representation of, i. 232, 233, 240
Commercial Classes of, Influence of,
on Politics, i. 298
Commissions of Chamber and Senate,
i. 235–8, 255, 256, Powers
of the Reporter in, i. 247,
ii. 56
Communes of, i. 239 & *n.*, 280, 281
sqq., ii. 440–1
Communism in, ii. 571
Conseil Général of, i. 235
Conservatism in, i. 219, 220, 236, 237,
239, 256, 298, 315, ii. 365
Constitution of, adopted in 1875, i. 43
sqq., 215, 216, 223 *sqq.*,
234–5
Amendment of, mode of, i. 223–4
& *nn.*
Discontent with, ii. 342
Earlier, i. 224, 278 *n.*
Constitutional Laws of, i. 223, 231–2,
passed without reference to
the Electorate, i. 224
Corruption in, i. 216, 234, 242 & *n.* 3,
259, 275, 302 *sqq.*, 303,
314, 317, ii. 438, 479
Council of State, i. 278–9
Councils, Local, in, *see also Conseil Gén-
éral, above*, i. 281–2, ii. 401,
404, 439–40
Customs Department of, Discipline in,
i. 276
Decentralization in, Movement towards,
i. 285 & *n.*, ii. 435, 577
Declaration by, on the Natural Rights
of Man, i. 43, 44, 218 *n.*
Delegates in, i. 232
Disproportion of, to Population, i.
232–3
Electing, chiefly Bourgeois, i. 235
Voting by, obligatory and remuner-
ated, i. 233
Democracy in, i. 6, 11, 22, 85
Achievements of, i. 309 *sqq.*, 317
sqq., ii. 532–3
Antecedents and Development of, i.
211 *sqq.*
Conservatism supporting, i. 42
Criticism and Comparisons, i. 309
sqq.
Defects alleged against, i. 313 *sqq.*
Historical Evolution of, i. 37–8
Swiftness of, i. 208
Influence of, on Political Thought,
i. 6
Lessons of, i. 320–1
Neither Monotonous nor Dull, ii.
521
Departments of, i. 220, 280 & *n.*
Normal Electoral Areas, i. 240
Regionalism of, i. 285 *n.*
Representation of, in Senate, i. 232
Self-Government in, i. 280 *sqq.*
Deputies in, i. 232
Age, Qualifications, and Disqualifica-
tions of, i. 245

France—*continued*
Deputies in—*continued*
Aims of, i. 249 *sqq.*
Character of, as distinguished from
    Senators, i. 235
Level of, Intellectual and Moral, i.
    301–2, 303, ii. 337
Names of those Voting in Divisions,
    records of, i. 247 & *n.*
Number of, i. 232, 240
Occupations of, in Chamber, etc., and
    Patronage exercised by, i.
    250, 255 *sqq.*, 269, 274–5,
    276, 311, 313–4, 321, ii.
    337, 410–11, 447
Payment of, i. 251
Personality, an asset to, i. 245
Press Relations of, i. 294
Sources of, and Preliminaries to Elec-
    tion of, i. 249 *sqq.*
Term of Office of, i. 235, 240
Despots and Dictators in (*see also*
    Boulanger *and* Napoleon
    III.), i. 283, 284, 291, 321–
    2, ii. 162, 358–9
Divorce in, i. 220, 325
Dreyfus Case in, i. 217, 218, 291
Economic Equality in, i. 38, 316
Education in, i. 217, 275, 303, 318,
    325
Secondary, i. 249
Secularism in, i. 76, 217, 243, 275,
    318, 325
Education Authorities in, ii. 436
Election in, of 1919, i. 288
Election Frauds in, i. 241, 242
Election Methods in, i. 216 *n., see also*
    Scrutin
Election Petitions in, i. 244 & *n.*
Elections in
Candidates' part in, i. 250
to *Conseil Général*, i. 281 & *n.*
not Costly, i. 267
Laws regulating, i. 240
Party influence on, ii. 441
Prefects' Influence on, i. 235, 243
    & *n.* 1
of President, i. 223
to Senate, i. 231 *sqq.*, 234–5, ii. 401,
    404
Two Types of, i. 268
Electoral Colleges in, i. 233, ii. 401
Electors, Registration of, i. 240
Eloquence in Parliament, ii. 553
Leaders brought forward by, ii.
    554
Epuration in, i. 272, 273, 315, ii.
    385
Equality in, and the Passion for it,
    i. 38, 68, 156, 254, 256,
    257, ii. 548
Results of, ii. 521
Executive of
Autocracy of, i. 278
Centralization of, i. 212 *sqq.*, 244,
    247, 258 & *n.*, 264, 274,
    280, 284, 285, 320, ii. 447,
    449
and Legislature in, Separation of, a
    principle, i. 230–1, *see also*
    Chamber and Senate, rela-
    tions between
Respect felt for, i. 138, 317
Stability desired for, ii. 342
Strength of, i. 319, ii. 363–4
Liked by the Nation, i. 278, 291,
    320
Vested in Cabinet in, i. 448
Executive Head of State (*see also*
    President), ii. 462
Finance of, i. 314, ii. 459

France—*continued*
Foreign Affairs in
Conduct of, i. 225, 319, ii. 382
Foreign Policy of, i. 319
as to Germany, ii. 372
Public Opinion on, i. 297–8
under Second Empire and after, i.
    319, ii. 372
Fraternity in, Present-day, i. 316
Freemasonry in, i. 123, 249, 270, 316,
    369
Government of, under
Ancien régime, i. 211–3
Consulate and First Empire, i. 213
Restorations, i. 213
Second Empire, i. 213
Third Republic, Frame of, i. 223 *sqq.*
Responsibility, Chain of, in, ii.
    492–3
"Groups" in, *see* Political Groups,
    below
Home of Learning, in Mediaeval days,
    i. 210
Huguenots expelled from, i. 211, 218 *n.*
    1
Income-Tax in, Strong objection to, i.
    237, 318
Industrialism in, i. 209
Industrials of
as Deputies, i. 303
Influence of, on Politics, i. 298
Public Opinion among, how formed,
    i. 296
Socialism among, i. 212, 214, 218,
    219, 220, 320
Intellectual Classes of, aloof from
    Politics, i. 287–8, 323
Public Opinion among, how formed,
    i. 296
Intendants in, i. 212
Interpellations in, i. 257–8, ii. 467
Journalism in, i. 292 *sqq.*, ii. 117
Judges in, i. 271 *sqq.*
Appointments of, Salaries, Tenure of
    Office, and Control over, i.
    271 *sqq.*, ii. 385
Épuration applied to, i. 272, 273,
    315, ii. 385, 479–80
Influences affecting, i. 304
of Lower Courts, Distrust of, ii. 479,
    528
Promotion of, i. 272, 304, ii. 388
Judiciary, Status, etc., of, i. 271 *sqq.*,
    304, 317, ii. 388
Senate's Functions as, i. 234, 239 *n.*
Justice in, Defects in Administration
    of, ii. 453
Labour Troubles in, i. 322 *n.*
Land and History, i. 208 *sqq.*
Laws and Decrees differentiated in, i.
    174 *n.*
Laws of Inheritance in, i. 274 *n.*, 318
Legislation
and Party in, ii. 45
since 1871, Value of, i. 318
Legislative Chambers of, ii. 42
Congestion in, ii. 346
Machinery in, *see* Chamber, *above,*
    and Senate, *below*
to whom Responsible, ii. 493
Legislature of, i. 223, 226
Corruption in, i. 300 *sqq.*, 314, ii.
    479
Decline of, i. 307, ii. 337, 339, 560
Dramatic quality of, ii. 63–4
Members of
Payment of, i. 251, ii. 174 *n.*, 454
Restrictions on, i. 302
Liberty as conceived of in, ii. 568
Lobbying in, ii. 483
Local Councils, Elected, ii. 439–40

France—*continued*
Local Divisions in, *see* Arrondissements, Cantons, Communes, Departments, etc.
Local Improvements in, ii. 437–8
Local Party Committees, function of, i. 114, 115, 235, 266, 268 *sqq.*
Local Party Organizations in, i. 261, 266 *sqq.*
Local Self-Government in, i. 131–2, 212, 280 *sqq.*, 311, 451–2
Late 18th Century, i. 212
Restricted action of, i. 274, 451–2, ii. 576, and the reasons, i. 220, 283, 315
Materialism in, i. 303, 307
Mediaeval, Estates in, ii. 398
Middle Classes, *see also* Bourgeoisie, *above*
Commercial, Professional and Plutocratic, Influence of, on Politics, i. 299
Ministerial Honour in, i. 300 *sqq.*
Ministerial Instability in, i. 236, ii. 342, 364, 447, 452, 468, 492–3
Ministers in
Cabinet of, i. 261 *sqq.*
Composition of, i. 226–7, 229, 238, ii. 359–60
of Defence in, Choice of, ii. 360
Wide Powers of, i. 277
Ministries in, Struggle against, i. 255 *sqq.*
Monarchy in
Oligarchical rule of, ii. 537
Defects of, ii. 539–40
Money Power in, i. 248, 294 & *n.*, 299, 301–2, 457, ii. 447, 454, 477 *sqq.*, 485
Municipalities in, i. 280, 281 *sqq.*
Debts of, i. 283
Napoleonic Rule in, ii. 536
National Assembly of, i. 224, 232
Compared with Swiss, i. 428, 429
Standard of (*see also* Legislature), i. 428
National Character
Contradictions in, i. 221 & *n.*
Types of, i. 210
National Defence in (*see also* Army *and* Navy), i. 318–9, ii. 361
National Life of, as shown in the Great War, i. 326
National Monopolies in, i. 276
National Unity in, i. 210
Natural Wealth of, i. 209
Distribution of, i. 209–10
Navy of, i. 318–9
Newspapers of, Characteristics of, i. 292 *sqq.*
Control of, by Statesmen, ii. 117
Offices in, Multiplication of, i. 260, 499 *n.* 2
Officials of
Bourgeois, origin of, 18th Century, i. 212
Delinquent, Special Tribunals for, i. 277–8, 315
Spying on, i. 306–7
Ordres du Jour in, i. 257
Organic Laws of, i. 232
Parliamentarianism disliked in, i. 239, 320
Parliamentary and Cabinet System of, ii. 461
Parties in, i. 235–6, 252 & *n.*, 253 & *n.*, 266, 311–2
Partisanship in, Vehemence of, i. 306, 316

France—*continued*
Party in, i. 451, ii. 45, 441
Party Discipline in, ii. 353
Party Funds in, i. 242 & *n.*, 249
Party Government in, i. 115, ii. 45
Party Influence on Local Elections, ii. 441
Party Organization in, ii. 453
no Use made of, by Ministers, ii. 467
Patriotism in, i. 222, ii. 457
Peasantry of, *see also* Peasants' Party
Influence of, on Politics, i. 298
Oppression of 18th Century and its results, i. 213
Place-hunting in, i. 250, 369
Police Methods in, i. 317
Political Cliques in, i. 308
Political Criticism in, i. 321, ii. 558
Political Development, 1789 to 1900, General Course of, i. 219–20
Political Equality in, i. 38, 316
Political Groups in, i. 235–6, 246–7, 251–2, 254, 255, 313, ii. 42, 45, 62, 347–8, 349, 354, 468
Political Ideals in, i. 138
Political Indifference in, i. 265, 287–8, 298, 304 *n.*
Political Life of, at outbreak of War, 1914, i. 220–1
Political Patronage in, i. 251, 258, 269, 274, 277, 284, 311, 313, 320, 363, ii. 337, 447
Politicians and Public Men of, Atmosphere surrounding, and Public Attitude to, i. 305–6
Politics in
Forces and Influences at work on, enumerated, i. 298–9
Variety in, i. 210
Vivacity of, i. 323
Popular Government in, Salient Features of, ii. 447 & *n.*, 448–9
Population of, Ethnic Elements in, i. 210
Prefects in, Functions of and Influence of, i. 213, 235, 243 & *n.* 1, 276, 277, 281, 282, 283, 315
President of, Election, Functions and Powers of, i. 223, 225 *sqq.*, 277, 278, 321, ii. 358, 472 & *n.* 3, 576
Press Influence in (*see also* Newspapers, *above*), i. 288, 292 *sqq.*, ii. 118
Money Power and, i. 294 & *n.*, 299
Prime Ministers of, i. 227–8, 230
Professional Politicians in, compared with American, i. 241
Proportional Representation as modified in, i. 240
Protectionist views in, i. 318
Public Life in
Brilliancy evoked in, ii. 455, 522
Causes deterring the Intellectuals from, i. 307–8
Tone of, i. 300, 304 *sqq.*, ii. 452
Traditions still influencing, i. 308, ii. 180
Public Opinion in, i. 151 *sqq.*, 236, 238, 278, 286 *sqq.*, 296–7, 302–321, ii. 113, 162, 457
Chief Currents of, i. 288–9
Divisions in, i. 158–9, 287, 290–1, on Foreign Affairs, i. 297
Formative Influences on, i. 292 *sqq.*, 296–7
Organs of Expression of, i. 292 *sqq.*
Types of, i. 288–9 *sqq.*

France—*continued*
Public Order in, Maintenance of, i. 317, 320, ii. 362
Racial and Linguistic Differences in, i. 209 & *n.* 2, 286–7
Railways in, ii. 231
Control exercised by, ii. 294
State Purchase of one, i. 237, 276
Regional Differences and Regionalism in, i. 264–5, 266–7, 285, 289 & *n.*, 307–8
Religious Antagonisms in (*see also* Anti-Clericalism, *above*), i. 217 *sqq.*, 221, 306–7, 310, ii. 114
Republican Party in, ii. 36
Responsibility, Administrative in, ii. 492
Roman Church's influence in, i. 88
Rousseau's influence in, i. 36
Second Chamber in, *see* Senate, *below*
Second Empire in (*see also* Napoleon III.), i. 242–3, 244, 314, 317
Secularism in, *see under* Education, *above*
Senate of, i. 223, Structure, Powers, Composition, E l e c t i o n, Status, Renewal of, i. 231 *sqq.*, 281 *n.*, ii. 185, 399, 402, 403, 406, 409
Abolition of, by whom and why demanded, i. 238
Atmosphere of, i. 238
Hopes raised by, unfulfilled, i. 239
Justiciary Function of, i. 234, 239 *n.*
Parties in, i. 234
Public Opinion in, i. 236, 292
Radicalism in, i. 236
Value of, as Check or Safeguard, i. 234, 239–40, 321, ii. 393, 447
Working of, i. 234 *sqq.*
Senators
Age, Average of, i. 238 & *n.*
For Election, i. 233
Character of, as Distinguished from Deputies, i. 235–6
Classes predominant among, i. 235–6
Numbers of, i. 232, 233
Status of, i. 238
Terms of Office, i. 233, 235
Separation of Powers in, i. 230–1, 247, 278 & *n.*, 313
Social Equality in, i. 38, 316
Social Importance in, of Officials, i. 361
Socialism and Socialists in, i. 214, 217, 218–9, 221, 235, 248, 250, 252 & *n.*, 253, 255, 268, 283, 290, 295, 299, ii. 353 & *n.*, 362
Anti-religious colour of, ii. 572
Insurrection due to, i. 219
Socialist Congresses in, ii. 340
Socialist Ministry of, in Strike, ii. 362
Spoils System in, i. 117
Strikes in, Riots, and *Sabotage*, i. 221, 317, ii. 362, 452
Sub-Prefects in, i. 276, 277
Suffrage in, i. 21, 213, 232, 233, 238, 269 *n.*, 281, 321–2, 325
Teachers in
Appointment of, and Influence of, i. 217, 243, 274
Higher Grade, i. 288, 307
Tendencies in Governing Politics, i. 253–4, 288, 291, 297
Tobacco Monopoly in, i. 276
Trade Unions in, and other Working Class Organizations, Legislation on, i. 318

France—*continued*
Trial by Jury in, less used than in England and U.S.A., i. 272 *n.* 2
Voters, Voting, and Voting Methods in (*see also* Elections, *above*), i. 232–3, 234–5, 241 *sqq.*, 247–8, 250 & *nn.*, 290–1, 297, 298–9, ii. 401
France, by Bodley, *cited*, i. 243 *n.*
France, la, contemporaine, by Hanotaux, i. 214 *n.* 1
Franchise, British, Extension of, i. 41–2, 70, ii. 567, *see also* Suffrage
Francia, rule of, in Paraguay, i. 192
Franciscan Order, i. 84
Franco-Prussian War of 1870, i. 213–4 & *n.* 1, 224, ii. 372
Effect of, on German Democracy, i. 39
Frankfurt, ii. 437
Parliament of, 1848–9, i. 312 *n.*
Franklin, Benjamin, Literary Influence of, ii. 554
Fraternity, anticipated under Democracy, but not secured, i. 38, 46–7, 62, 316, ii. 532, 574, 606
"Freak Legislation," U.S.A., ii. 143, 425
Frederick I., Emperor, and the Pope, i. 83
Frederick the Great, of Prussia, ii. 76, 369, 536
Last Personal ruler of Prussia, ii. 537; and Prussian Militaristic Spirit, i. 137–8
Prussian Oligarchy as followers of, ii. 539
Free Assemblies, the first, higher standard in, than in later ones, ii. 341
Free Constitutional Government
Forgetfulness of, Instances of, and Possible Recurrences of, ii. 599 *sqq.*
France the protagonist of, i. 6
Oligarchy within Democracy, ii. 550
Past and Present, i. 17
Present-day problems of, i. 5
Reversion from, to Monarchy, i. 12
Types of, in South Africa, before 1899, ii. 464 & *n.*
Free Institutions
English and Swiss, bases of, i. 142
Fusing power of, in Switzerland, i. 431
Free Passes, granting of, as Indirect Corruption, U.S.A., ii. 483
Freedom
Love of, faith in, exponents of, i. 59 & *n.*
of the Press, i. 58, 92–3
of Thought and Speech, under Democracy, ii. 532
Freemasonry, Continental, i. 123, 249, 270, 315–6, 369
English and American contrasted with, i. 123, 270
Freemen, Public Assemblies of (*see also under* Names), i. 35–6, 129–30, 169 & *n.*
Free Silver problem, U.S.A., ii. 44 *n.*, 115
Free Trade Party, Australia, ii. 205, 248
Predominance in Denmark, ii. 297
Freisinnige Partei, the decay of, ii. 600
French Assemblies of 1848 and 1871, Philosophic Thought exhibited in, i. 259
French Canadians
Birth-rate among, i. 458, 467, 468

French Canadians—*continued*
  and the British Connection, i. 488
  Distribution of, and Distinctness of, i. 457–8 & *n.*
French Convention, Governmental Method of, ii. 463 *n.* 3
French Crown, arbitrary and despotic powers of, i. 212 ; how replaced by Napoleon I., i. 213
French Directory, Governmental Method of, ii. 463 *n.* 3
French National Assembly of 1789 on Rights of Property, i. 218 *n.*
French Nobles, 18th Century, i. 212, 213
French Power in America, end of, ii. 5
French Republics
  Duration of, i. 208, 319 & *n.*
  Third
    Effect of, on Intellectual and Moral life, i. 323 *sqq.*
    Good and bad under, i. 309 *sqq.*
    How Consolidated, i. 215, 225
    Length of duration of, i. 320
    Menaced, i. 216, 217
    Parliamentary brilliance in, i. 248–9
French Revolutions
  First, i. 3, 29, 37, 46–7, 212, ii. 253
    American Influence on, ii. 3
    Anticipations from, i. 46–7, 49, 50
    Delegates, Mandates of, Provision for Terminating, ii. 149 *n.*
    Effects of, on Government, i. 212–3
    Influence of, in Germany, i. 39
    Rights of Property unquestioned in, i. 218 *n.*
    Spirit of, i. 46–7
      Late manifestations of, 1. 214
    Tradition of, Survival of, how modified, i. 221
    and Switzerland, i. 36, 329, 372–3, 393, 434
    Unforeseen by Politicians, ii. 598
  First, Second, and Third, Modern Socialism in relation to, ii. 570 *n.* 2
  Second, i. 37, 213
  Third, i. 37, 111, 213
  Fourth, i. 37
Freshfield, D. W., book by, *cited,* i. 372 *n.* 2
Frisia, Self-government in, i. 35
Fugger family of Augsburg, ii. 538

Gain, Illicit, and Politics, *see* Corruption
Galveston, U. S. A., Municipal Government in, ii. 16, 139–40 & *n.*
Gambetta, L., i. 265, 424 ; Anti-clericalism of, i. 217; on the Bicameral System, i. 239 ; Death of, i. 216 ; Fall of, i. 255 ; on Effect of Large Electoral Areas, i. 241 ; and the French Senate, i. 234 ; as Leader, i. 250, qualities of, i. 321 ; on the *nouvelles couches sociales,* i. 249
Gannaway, Prof., book by, on Comparative Free Government, ii. 59 *n.*
Garfield, President, ii. 67
Garibaldi, Giuseppe, i. 141, ii. 377
Gas Ring, the, Philadelphia, ii. 106
Gaucho Indians of Argentina, i. 195
Gaul
  Celts of, Human Sacrifices interdicted among, i. 82 *n.*
  Kings of, i. 25
  Unity of, as Country, i. 209

Gemeinde, where found, i. 282 ; American parallel to, ii. 14
General Councils of the Church, i. 83
General Elections, Great Britain, as affecting Party, ii. 45–6
General Labour Federation in France, i. 275
General Maxims, dangerousness of, i. 19
General Strike, the, ii. 164, 572, 581
"General Ticket" system, choice for Election of Presidents, U.S.A., ii. 18 & *n.*
Generals, Greek, re-election of, i. 172
Geneva, and Calvin, i. 84 ; Democratic Struggles in, i. 372 *n.* 2, 434 ; General Assembly of, i. 371-2 ; Popular Vote in, operation of, i. 400 *n.* ; Referendum and Initiative in, i. 392 *n.* ; Roman Catholics in, i. 332 ; and Rousseau, i. 36
Genius, and forms of Government, ii. 523
George, Henry, ii. 554–5
George III., i. 32, ii. 6, 485, 539
Georgia, New Republic of, ii. 575
German-Americans, ii. 114
German Bureaucracy, i. 40, 275
  Training and Ability in, ii. 361, 366
German Empire
  Civic Centres of Independent Opinion in, i. 296, ii. 437
  Constitution of, i. 21
  Fall of, i. 5
  Foreign Policy in relation to, ii. 372, 380
  Ministerial Appointments in, i. 356
  National unity under, i. 39, 40, 209
German Freemen, i. 25
German Government, Ministers of, Standard of, ii. 541
German Immigration into Switzerland, i. 331, into U. S. A., ii. 23
German Language in Alsace, i. 209 *n.* 2
German Morals of Sixty years ago, i. 325
German People and the desire for Political Liberty, i. 39–40
German Plutocrats, Intellectual Capacity of, ii. 538 & *n.* 2
German Poets and Scholars, the age of, ii. 522
German Socialists
  Aims of, i. 40
  Fidelity of, to Leaders, Michiels on, ii. 558 *n.* 2
  Leaders of Bourgeois Origin, ii. 546 *n.*
  Not specially Anti-Religious, ii. 571–2
  Views imported from Switzerland, i. 434
German-speaking Tyrolese in Italy, Status of, i. 145
German Stocks in U.S.A., ii. 5, 25 *n.*
German View of the State and Its Wisdom, i. 146
German Wage-Earners, efforts to Propitiate, ii. 569
Germans, Early, Councils and Meetings of, Tacitus on, i. 337 *n.,* 371, ii. 398 & *n.* 2
Germany
  Centralization in, i. 274
  Communism in, ii. 571
  Dauerreden in, ii. 345
  Divorce in, ii. 525
  Executive Head of State in, ii. 462
  Fewness of actual Rulers in, ii. 543–4, 545
  French Foreign Policy in relation to, ii. 372
  Gemeinde in, i. 282

Germany—*continued*
Home of *Imperium* in the Middle Ages,
i. 211 & *n.*
Kingship in, i. 25
Local Self-Government in, loss of
Popular character of, i.
131
Modern, History of Evolution and Ar-
rest of Popular Government
in, i. 39–40
Municipal Councils in, ii. 440
New Constitution of
Direct Voting by the People in, ii.
418, 577
Judicature in relation to, ii. 385 *n.* 1
Newspapers of, i. 293
Parties in, Multiplication of, ii. 347
Peasants' War in, i. 70
Presidential System of Government as
suited for, ii. 475
Pre-War, Monarchy in, ii. 535
Public Service of, not exempt from
peculation, i. 303
Relics of barbarism in till Napoleon's
day, ii. 532
Revolutions of 1848-9 in, i. 39, ii.
377
Roman Church's influence in, i. 88, ii.
347
Small Landholders in, i. 451
Social Importance in, of Officials, i.
361–2
Suffrage in, of Citizens, i. 75
Training in, of Citizens, i. 75
Upper, Old League of, i. 331, 453
Gersau, Independent Swiss hamlet, i. 334
Gibbon, E., ii. 598
Girondins, the, fate of, ii. 584
Gladstone, W. E., i. 104, 424; personal-
ity, etc., of, i. 255, 265, ii.
560 ; Emergence of, ii. 556 ;
Faith of, in Freedom, i. 59
n. ; on Character in a
Politician, i. 557 *n. ;* on
Parties, i. 122 ; on Reform,
i. 30
Glarus, Public Meeting in, of Freemen,
i. 35
"Go Slow" policy on State Collieries,
New Zealand, ii. 296 *n.,*
330
Godkin, E. L., i. 97 *n.*
Goethe, W. A., the age of, ii. 522 ;
Doctrines offending, ii. 568
& *n. ;* on Paris as Meeting-
place of Philosophers, i.
296 ; on Political Liberty
and Equality, ii. 568 & *n.*
"Going into Caucus," U.S.A., ii. 57
Gold in Australia, ii. 167, 170
Golden Age, the, i. 64, 148
Good Citizens' Clubs, U.S.A., and Re-
form, ii. 163
Good Government, Desire for, as cause for
Risings, i. 27 ; not Guaran-
teed by Popular Govern-
ment, i. 42 ; rather than
Self-Government, the real
desire of Peoples, i. 284, ii.
591, 600
Good Sense in Politics, i. 422 ; Nature of,
i. 389
Gospels, the, alleged Socialism in, i. 86
sqq.
Government
Chief Ends of, ii. 527
Declaration of, resting with the
Many, ii. 550
How far attained by Democratic
Government, ii. 527 *sqq.*
Frame of, *see under Countries*

Government—*continued*
Functions of, Extension of, ii. 576–7
New, i. 5
Government Employees, *see under* Civil
Service, Railways, etc.,
under Countries
Government of England, by L. Lowell,
cited, ii. 470 *n.* 1, 471 *n.*
Government of India Act of 1920, ii. 513
"Government Stroke," the, ii. 235, 236,
296 *n.* 1, 330, 588 *n.*
Government Subsidies (*see also* Bounties,
and Grants) to Local Au-
thorities, New Zealand, ii.
278
Governor-General
of Australian Commonwealth, powers
and status of, ii. 174, 193
of Canada, Functions of, i. 460
Governors
Chinese Provincial, ii. 510 & *n.*
of New Zealand, ii. 270
of States
Australia, ii. 176
U.S.A., ii. 13, 33, 67, 80–2, 162,
179, 342, 576
"Grain Growers of the West Association,"
in Canada, i. 474 *n.*
Grant, General, President, U.S.A., Military Fame of, ii. 555
Grants, Governmental
in Canada, i. 481 *sqq.,* 499, 500, 504
Discontinuance of, why advisable, ii.
491
Great Britain, *see also* England, Ireland,
and Scotland
and Australia, Reciprocal Ignorance of
one another, ii. 244–5
Bribery and Corruption in, i. 140, ii.
452–3, 477, 478, 485–6,
487, 528, 539–40
Cabinet of, *see* Cabinet
Canadian Connection with, i. 470
Civic Education in, i. 76 *n.*
Civil Liberty in, i. 322
Civil Service of, i. 311, 361, ii. 337, 365
Status, ii. 360
and Trade Unions in, i. 275
Compulsory Arbitration disliked in, ii.
231 & *n.* 1
Compulsory Military Service in, ii. 361
Constitution of, i. 223, ii. 10, 177, 342
Conventions, in, i. 440–1
Democratization of, i. 7, ii. 179
Flexibility of, ii. 462
Conveying Electors to Polls, ii. 481 *n.*
Decentralization desirable in, ii. 435
Proposals for, ii. 347 *n.*
Declarations in, of Policy, by whom
made, ii. 41
Democracy and Self-Government in, i.
11, 41–2
Causes of, Active, and Theoretical, i.
27–8, 31–2
Evolution of, i. 208, 309, ii. 458,
566–7
Gains under, ii. 532
Under Monarchy, i. 7, 22
Education in, ii. 436
Elections in, ii. 50, 379, 380, 478
Emigration from, to U.S.A., ii. 23
Epoch of Change in, i. 312–3
Evolution and Advance of, i. 208, ii.
567
in relation to Foreign Policy, ii. 376
Executive vested in the Cabinet in, i.
448
Foreign affairs in hands of, ii. 74 *n.*
Position and Powers of, during the
Great War (1914–18), ii.
155

Great Britain—*continued*
Foreign Policy of, ii. 74 *n.*
Influence on, of
Democracy, ii. 376 *sqq.*
Dominions, ii. 372
Government in, Popular, and Representative, ii. 350–1, 449 *n.*, 461, 462, 464 *sqq.*
House of Commons
Cabinet influence on, i. 173
Centre of Political Life, and Driving Force, i. 460, ii. 42, 342, 486
Members of, *see under* Legislature, *below*
Obstruction in, ii. 345–6
Origin of, ii. 396
Parties in, Multiplication of, ii. 347
Powers of, Origin and Growth, ii. 350, 397
Predominance of, i. 28 *sqq.*, ii. 179
Private Bills in, ii. 79, 337, 343, 492 *n.* 2
Scenes in, i. 259, ii. 338–9
House of Lords, i. 21
Origin of, ii. 396
Powers of, ii. 406
Limits of, ii. 397 *n.*
and Suffrage extension, i. 31
Intoxication in, ii. 255 *n.*
Judges in, Appointments, Salaries, Status and Traditions of, i. 271, 304, ii. 86 *n.* 2, 198, 386–7, 438
Judiciary of, Restriction on, i. 271
Labour Party in, i. 31, 311, ii. 348, 571
Law Courts, Confidence felt in, i. 138
Legislatures
Checks on, ii. 396–7 *& n.*
Compared with Swiss, i. 428
Decline of, i. 345, ii. 335, 337, 338, 339, 345, 346, 560
Dramatic Quality of, ii. 63–4
Independence of, i. 310
Members of
Influence exercised by, ii. 51
Names of those voting in Division, Record of, i. 247 *n.*
Payment of, i. 259, ii. 454
Relations of, with Constituents, ii. 351 *sqq.*, 410–11
Status of, Comparisons of, ii. 353
Liberty as conceived of in, ii. 568
Local Political Associations in, ii. 203–4
Local Self-Government in, i. 220, 452
Ministerial Instability, ii. 365
Ministerial Responsibility in, i. 231
Ministers
Impeachment of, ii. 392
Usually Members of Parliament, i. 261 *n.*
Ministries
Coalition, during the War (1914–1918), i. 121
Fall of, Causes of, i. 264
Formation of, i. 227, ii. 359–60
Monarchy in, i. 22, 227, ii. 461–2
Money Power in, Instances of, ii. 485–6
Municipal Government in, i. 192, ii. 444
Old-Age Pensions in, ii. 290
Oligarchy in, i. 3, ii. 537, 538, 539
Parish Councils in, i. 282, ii. 576
Parliament of, *see also* House of Commons, House of Lords, *and* Legislatures, *above*
Committees of Selection in, ii. 415 *n.*
Congestion in, i. 314

Great Britain—*continued*
Parliament of—*continued*
Eloquence in, ii. 553
Features of, i. 429
Party in, i. 113 *sqq.*
Party Leaders in, authority exercised by, i. 254
Political Groups in, i. 253 *& n.*, ii. 62
Popular figures in, i. 255
Powers of, in regard to the Dominions, i. 459–60, ii. 174, 175 *n.*
Voting in, i. 151 *n.*
Parties in, *see also under* Names
Forces consolidating, ii. 203, 204
Multiplication of, i. 266, ii. 347, 468
Partisanship in, ii. 62
Party in, as compared with Party in U.S.A., ii. 45
Party Conflicts in, ii. 45–6, 466
Party Discipline in, ii. 343, 353, 410
Party Feeling, not embittering Social relations in, i. 473
Party Organization in, ii. 30, 31, 203, 467, 470, 483
Party Spirit, Discipline and Organization in, compared with the same in U.S.A., ii. 470
Political Apathy in, to Democratic Changes, i. 30–1
Political Committees in, i. 269 *n.*
how Elected, i. 268
Political Connection with, of the Dominions, ii. 214–5 *& n.*
Postal Service, Electoral Pressure by, ii. 349
Power to issue Orders or Rules in, delegation of, i. 277
Press, the, in, Influence, etc., of, i. 104, 106–7, 296, 298, ii. 117–18
Prosecution in, of delinquent Officials, i. 277
Protectionist Intolerance in, ii. 44 *n.*
Public Life in, Tone of Past and Present (*see also* Bribery, *above*), ii. 179–80, 487
Public Opinion in, i. 287, 296–7, 488
Bulk of, generally justified by results, ii. 380
on Foreign Policy, Wars, etc., ii. 377 *sqq.*
Homogeneity of, i. 488
as affecting the Judiciary, i. 271
Unifying Effects of, i. 430
Wide bases of, ii. 250
Religious Strife in, i. 312
Representative Institutions of, as Model for Other Lands, ii. 336
Self-Government in, *see* Democracy, *above*
Spoils system in, i. 117
Suffrage in, Story of, i. 29
Extension of, i. 31, ii. 566–7
Universal, ii. 89
Taxation in, i. 3
Trade Unions, Triple Alliance of, ii. 578
Trades Union Congress in, effect of, on Decline of Legislatures, ii. 340
Trial by Jury in, i. 272 *n.*
and U.S.A., ii. 5 *n.* 2, 373
Upper Classes in, leadership of, ii. 314–15
Voters in, percentage voting, i. 250
Woman Suffrage in, i. 29, ii. 567
Working-Class Voters, majorities of, ii. 179

"Great Council of the Nation under the King in Parliament Assembled," ii. 394 n., 396
Great Lakes of Canada and U.S.A., agreements concerning, i. 469, ii. 375–6, 469 n. 1
Great Refusal, the, i. 136 & n. 2
Greatest Good of Greatest Number theory, i. 44–5
Greece
  Ancient, see also Greek Republics, below
    Agora of, i. 130
    Genius in, ii. 522
    Governments before Republics, i. 169
    Patriotism in, i. 184
    Prosecutions in, ii. 392
    Rule in, of the Average Man, i. 185
  Modern
    Constitution of (Rigid), ii. 391
    Democracy in, i. 22
    Executive Hereditary Head of State in (King), i. 225 n., ii. 462
    Dictatorship aimed at by, ii. 358
    Unicameral Legislature of, ii. 399
    and the War, i. 22
Greek Cities
  Kings of, i. 25–6
  Oligarchic and Democratic, opposition between, i. 36
Greek Colonies, Self-Government in, i. 166
Greek Commonwealth, The, by Zimmern, i. 175 n. 1
Greek Conception of Liberty, i. 51
Greek Constitutional History, Handbook of, by Greenidge, i. 180 n.
Greek Democracy, Faults of, i. 181 sqq.
Greek Oligarchies, Faults and Falls of, i. 26, 169, 180, 184–5
Greek Philosophers on Happiness, ii. 532
Greek Politics, Religious passion in, i. 82
Greek Republics (see also Athens), i. 165 sqq.
  Class (or wealth) parties in, i. 124
  Constitutions of, i. 170
    Characteristics, i. 171 sqq.
    Revision of, i. 224 n. 1
  Corruption in, i. 139, ii. 478
  Councils of, i. 172–3
  Decrees of, i. 174, ii. 391–2
  Defence of, i. 184
  Deposition of Officials in, ii. 149 n.
  Effect in, of Sophist teaching, i. 141
  Eloquence in, ii. 553
  Features lacking in, i. 181
  Foreign affairs in, ii. 74 n.
  Internal Strife in, i. 167 n. 2
  Judicial Machinery in, i. 176 sqq.
  Lot, as used by, i. 180 & n.
  Macedonian conquest, i. 170, 182, ii. 336
  News dissemination in, i. 168
  Organizations of the Citizens, i. 168
  Ostracism in, i. 171, 181
  Political Life of, contrasts with those of modern times, i. 167 sqq.
  Public Assemblies of, i. 169, 172–3, ii. 391, 398
  Powers of, i. 171 sqq.
  Regular Courts set up in, i. 130
  Short terms of office in, i. 173, 184
  Slavery in, i. 166
  Small size of, i. 166, 167 & n. 1, 171
  and Switzerland, similarities between, i. 442 n. 1
  Tyranny and Tyrants in, i. 180, 190

Greek Republics—continued
  Views of Democracy based on, i. 3, 7, 13
  Voting Methods in, i. 173, 176
Greek Views on Divers forms of Government, i. 185 n.
Greeks and Romans compared, i. 447
Greeley, Horace, i. 97 n.
Greenidge, A. H. J., book by, on Greek Constitutional History, i. 180 n.
Gregory VII., Conflict of, with the Emperor, i. 83 ; Personality of, ii. 76
Grévy, Jules, Presidency of, i. 215, 216, 230
Grey, Sir G., and New Zealand, ii. 273, 318, and the Franchise Extension, ii. 268
Grievances as causes for adoption of Democracy, i. 24, 26, 27–8, 29, 37–8, 39
  Opportunities for Voicing, in Backward States, ii. 518
Grisons, Canton of, i. 35, 334
Groups, Political (see also under Countries), Methods of, as to Candidates, ii. 354
Grutli, the Confederates of, i. 137
Guatemala, Republic of, i. 187 n., under Barrios, i. 192
Guelfs and Ghibellines, the, i. 111, 473
Guest, Dr. H., cited, on Communist control in Russia, ii. 583
Guild Socialism, Tenets of, ii. 587
Guthrie, W. D., cited, ii. 152 n.

Habit, how affecting the Individual, i. 134–5
  as Basis of Moral Action, i. 135
Habits, National, instances of, i. 139–40
Hadrian, ii. 536
Haiti, Republic of, i. 7
  Language in, i. 187 & n.
  Low Political Level of, i. 206
  Savagery in, i. 192 & n.
  U.S.A. and, i. 192 n., ii. 124
Hallam, H., ii. 335
Hamburg, ii. 437
Hamilton, Alexander, i. 3
Hamilton, Ont., Non-Party Club founded at, i. 473
Hampden, John, i. 141
Handworkers (see also Industrials), Changes affecting, ii. 565
Hanotaux, G., France contemporaine by, i. 214 n. 1
Happiness
  Democracy as making for, ii. 531 sqq.
  Ideals of, ii. 531–2, 591
Hapsburg, Counts of, and the Swiss, i. 34–5, 137, 328
Hapsburg Monarchy, The, by Steed, cited, ii. 559 & n. 2
Hapsburg Rule in Hungary, effects of, i. 39
Harrison, President, U.S.A., ii. 67 ; Military fame of, ii. 555
Harvard Law Review, referred to, ii. 228 n. 1, 230 n.
Hasbach, Dr., cited, 242 n. 3, ii. 538 n. 1
Hayes, President, U.S.A., ii. 67
Headlam, J. W., book by, on Athenian use of the Lot, i. 180 n.
"Hedging," Parliamentary, ii. 366 & n.
Heine, H., ii. 522
Heliaea, the, at Athens, i. 177
Helleno-Romans round Ægean Sea, i. 27
Helvetic Republic (see also Switzerland), the, i. 36, 329

Henry III., Emperor, personality of, ii. 76
Henry IV. and V., Emperors, and the Pope, i. 83
Henry IV. of France, ii. 536
Henry VIII., i. 84, ii. 599 n. 2
Heraclitus, cited, i. 14, 74
Herodotus, i. 20, 185 n.
Hichborn, F., book by, on the California Legislature of 1911, ii. 136 n.
Higgins, Mr. Justice, on the Australian Commonwealth Court of Arbitration, etc., ii. 228 n. 1
High Court, the, of the Australian Commonwealth, ii. 174, 177, 196–8
Hilty, Prof. K., i. 379 n. 1, 433 & n.
Hindrances to Good Citizenship, by the Author, i. 120 n.
Hines, W. D., address by, ii. 98 n.
Histoire politique de l'Europe contemporaine, by Seignobos, cited, i. 219 & n.
Historical Evolution of Democracy, i. 12, 17–18, 24 sqq.
History
　National Teaching of, i. 451
　as Reinforcement for Tradition, i. 141–2
　and Study of Democracy, ii. 19
　Teachings of, on Self-Government, ii. 503–4, 505 sqq.
Hobbes, Nathaniel, i. 16
Hoffähigkeit, i. 60
Holland, i. 39
　Class Bitterness in, ii. 457
　Clerical Party in, ii. 347
　Constitution of, i. 223
　a Democracy, i. 22
　Monarchy in, i. 227, ii. 461
　Party Government in, i. 115
　Place-hunting in, i. 370
　the Press in, i. 436
　Roman Church's influence in, i. 88
　Senate of, slender powers of, ii. 402
Holy Alliance, effect of, on Popular Government, i. 39
Holy Roman Emperors, conflicts of, with the Popes, i. 83
"Home Rule for Cities," U.S.A., ii. 139
Homer, Ideals of Happiness in poems of, ii. 531; on Monarchy in early Greece, i. 169
Homogeneity, Racial, in relation to Self-Government, ii. 502
Honduras, Republic of, i. 187 n.; and U.S.A., ii. 124 n. 1
Honesty, Civic, i. 78
Honour, rare, in Mediaeval Europe, i. 139
Hours of Labour (see Eight Hours Day), Reduction of, ii. 569
House of Commons, see under Canada and Great Britain
House of Lords, see under Great Britain
House of Magnates, see under Hungary
House of Representatives, see under Australia and New Zealand
Hudson Bay Company, Territories purchased from, Constitutions of, i. 462 n. 1
Hughes, Governor, of New York, ii. 81, 120–1
Hughes, Rt. Hon. W. M., book by, on Labour in Australia, ii. 208 n.
Hugo, Victor, i. 324, ii. 568
Huguenots, expulsion of, from France, i. 211, 218 n. 1

Human Nature, Conditions modifying, i. 17
　the "Constant" of the Social Sciences, i. 14–15
　"Constants" in, and the opposite, ii. 604
　How best Studied, i. 16
　Laws of, in relation to Communism, ii. 589
　Opposite Forces in, i. 58
　Tendencies of, persistence of, i. 185
Human Progress, views of, as affected by the Great War (1914–18), ii. 606 sqq.
Human Rights, doctrine of, less prominent now, than earlier, i. 38
Hundreds, English, ii. 506
Hungary
　Causes arresting Democracy in, i. 39
　Class War in (1919), ii. 603
　Estates in, ii. 398
　House of Magnates
　　Nominations to, ii. 400
　　Status of, ii. 406
　New Government not Settled in, ii. 575
　Religious Partizanship in, i. 435
　Revolution in, British Sympathy with, ii. 377
　Sovereigns of, i. 39, ii. 536
Hyde Park Railings, overturning of, i. 30 n. 2

Iceland
　Bicameral Legislature of, ii. 399
　Early Republic of, i. 36
　Free Government in, ii. 503
　the Thing of, i. 129 & n., 130, ii. 503
Icelandic Sagas, ideas in, on Happiness, ii. 531
Ideal Democracy, Conception of, continual influence of, i. 47–8, 50
Ideal Polity of Plato, i. 182
Idealism and Selfishness, the Struggle between, exemplified in the History of the U.S.A., ii. 164
Ideals
　Influence of, Historical instances of, i. 137–9
　Lack of, in Australasia, ii. 256, 324, 327, 331, 332
Ignorance of the Masses
　in relation to Foreign Affairs, ii. 367, 368, 370, 382–3
　Oligarchic use of, i. 70 n., ii. 540
　and the Suffrage, i. 63 & n. 1, 70 sqq.
Iliad, The, references to, i. 129 n., ii. 531
Illinois, Cabinet of State officials in, ii. 137 n. 2
Illiteracy as a disqualification for Civil rights, i. 71 sqq.
　When no Bar to Self-Government, ii. 503
Illumination, the Age of, i. 46
Immigrants, and Immigration, see under Countries
Impeachments at, and in
　Athens, i. 176
　Great Britain, ii. 392
　U.S.A., ii. 18, 20, 85
Imperial Defence, Strengthening of, ii. 214–15
Impressions of South Africa, by the Author, i. 371 n. 2
Income Tax, see under Countries
Independence
　Political and Individual, of the Swiss, i. 332, 340, 390, 420, 425–6, 431
　of Thought, Speech, etc., Intolerance of, i. 59

Independence—*continued*
Independence and Deference, the attitude of People to Leaders, ii. 561–2
Independents, the, Democratic views of, i. 28, spread of, to the New World, i. 28, 85
Independents, Party of, Australia, ii. 207
India
  British
    Fewness of Chief Administrators in, ii. 543
    Introduction into, of Democratic principles, ii. 499
    Literacy and Politics in, i. 73
    Religious sentiment invoked in aid of Politics in, i. 88 *n.*
    Self-Government for, i. 5, ii. 513
    Self-Government in
      Dangers to, ii. 508
      Prospects of, ii. 515, 518
    Vernacular Press of, restrictions on, i. 94
  Caste in, i. 80, 84
  Composite Population of, ii. 508
  Hill tribes of, and the Suffrage, ii. 507
  Land-allocation methods in parts of, i. 130
Indian Natives of Latin America, i. 188, 189 & *n.* 2, 191, 193, 194, 200, 201, 202, 203, 206
Indictment for Illegality, Athens, i. 174
Indifference as Destructive of Democracy, ii. 601–2
Individual Liberty and Individualism (*see also* Independence, *above*), i. 52, 53, 54–5
  Christian, i. 89
  and Democracy, i. 44–6
  French, i. 255
  Invasions of, i. 56 *sqq.*, ii. 569, 574 & *nn.*
  Not necessarily Secure under Democracy, i. 59, 322
  Relations of, with other Forms of Liberty, i. 55 *sqq.*
  in Switzerland (*see also* Independence, *above*), i. 331–2, 444, *and see* Switzerland
  in U.S.A., ii. 6, 7, 8
Individual Responsibility, ii. 489–90, 495
Individual Rights of Conscience, i. 58–9
Industrial Conflicts (*see also* Arbitration *and* Strikes), Prevention of, Methods of, in Australasia, ii. 226 *sqq.*, 299 *sqq.*, 304–5
Industrial Enterprises and State Aid (*see also* State Activities *under* Australia, *and* New Zealand), ii. 527, 529
Industrial Unions in Prussia, ii. 583
Industrial Workers of the World
  Australian counterpart of, ii. 237 *n.*
  and Compulsory Arbitration, ii. 230–1
Industrials and Industrialism (*see also* Labour and Trade Unions)
  in Canada, i. 456–7, 466, 472
  in France, i. 207, 213, 214, 218, 219, 220, 296, 298, 303, 320
Ine, King of the West Saxons, Laws of, i. 129 *n.*
Inequality
  Natural, i. 61–2
    Results of, ii. 548
  Social, in 18th Century, France, i. 212
Informers, *see* Sycophants
Ingratitude, Popular, and Monarchical, ii. 558 & *n.* 2, 559 & *nn.*

Inheritance, French Law of, i. 274 *n.*, 318
Initiative in Leaders, ii. 552–3
Initiative, the (*see also* Referendum), i. 49, 152, 159 *n.*, 449
  Party Influence on, i. 437
  Polling for, percentages of voters, ii. 144 & *n.*, 145, 421 & *n.* 2
  as Test of Fitness for Government, ii. 422–3
  Use made of, ii. 420
  Value of, Pros and Cons, ii. 427 *sqq.*
  in Various Countries (*see chiefly* Switzerland *and* U.S.A.), i. 373–5, 376–8, 401 *sqq.*, 484, 494, ii. 140 *sqq.*, 337, 395, 417, 419 *sqq.*, 449, 463 *n.* 2, 464, 473, 475–6
Injunctions, U.S.A., Mischief done by, ii. 87
Innocent III., Pope, personality of, ii. 76
Inquisition, the, i. 75
Insight, in Leaders, ii. 553
Institutions
  Best Type of, Search for, i. 10
  Working of, etc., need for Investigation of, i. 12
Insular Tropical Republics of the Western Hemisphere, i. 187 *n.*
"Insult to the Flag" argument, and the Chinese War of 1857, ii 377
Insurance, State
  N.Z., ii. 296
  Queensland, ii. 234 *n.*
Intellect, Oligarchy of, ii. 549–50
Intellectual Changes as affecting Democracy, ii. 565–6 & *n.*
Intellectual Classes, *see under* France
Intellectual Development, Acceleration of, ii. 518
"Intelligentsia," in Russia, ii. 506 *n.*
Intendants, in France, i. 212
International Relations (*see also* Foreign Affairs, Foreign Policy, etc., *and these under Countries*), under Democracy, ii. 562, 568
Interpellations in France, i. 257–8, ii. 467
Interstate Commission, Australia, ii. 177, 196
Interviewing, U.S.A., ii. 117
Ireland
  Blood Revenge in, i. 129 *n.*
  Education authorities in, ii. 436
  Government of, by the Few, ii. 543 & *nn.*
  Local Self-Government in, i. 131
  Political Recalcitrance in, Tradition of, rise of, i. 140 *n.* 1
  Racial Parties in, i. 124
  Roman Church's influence in, i. 88
  Royal Irish Constabulary in, ii. 439
Irish-Americans, ii. 114
Irish Home Rule Party, ii. 347
  and the British Opposition, ii. 366 *n.*
  Caucus invented by, ii. 355
Irish "People," fallacy in the phrase, i. 145 *n.*
Irish Union, the, ii. 539
Iron Bounties, Australia, ii. 224
Irresponsibility of Newspapers, i. 105, 109
Irresponsible Power, Danger of, in the Six Countries, ii. 459–60
Irrigation Works, in Australia, ii. 236, 255
Islam (*see also* Muslim, *and* Mussulman), i. 82–3
Ismail, Khedive, ii. 513
Israel, Monotheism of, i. 81

Italian Anarchists, hostility of, to the Roman Church, i. 85
Italian Cities, tribal organizations and Kings of, i. 25
  Mediaeval (*see also* Florence, *and* Venice), Tyrants of, i. 180, ii. 599
Italian Heroes of the Risorgimento, compared with the next generation, ii. 520
Italian Principalities, Corruption in, ii. 540
Italian Republics
  Overthrow of, by Tyranny, i. 180
  Regular Courts in, Functions of, i. 41
  Self-Government of, i. 83
  Use in, of the Lot, i. 180 n.
Italian subjects of the Swiss, stern rule over, i. 35
Italy
  Mediaeval
    Famous names of, ii. 522
    Home of the Priesthood, i. 211 & n.
    Party Spirit and the Tyrant in, i. 118
  Modern
    Anti-Clericalism in, i. 139, ii. 6, 571
    Carbonari of, i. 123 n.
    Chamber in, increased Subservience of, to Monarchy, ii. 343
    Class Bitterness in, ii. 457
    Communism in, ii. 571
    Constitution of, i. 223
    a Democracy, i. 22
    Eloquence in Parliament, ii. 553
    Executive in, Popular Control of, ii. 364
    Masonic Lodges in, Political Influence of, i. 123
    Monarchy in, i. 227, ii. 461
    Money Power in, ii. 343
    National Unity in, i. 209
    Party Discipline in, ii. 353
    Political Patronage in, ii. 337, 343
    Senate
      Nominations to, ii. 400
      Powers of, ii. 407, 408–9
        Relative to Lower House, ii. 401–2
    Small Landowners in, i. 451
    Socialism in, Anti-religious tone of, ii. 571
    Wars of Liberation of, British Sympathies in, ii. 377

Jackson, A., President, U.S.A., ii. 94 n., 128; General, Military fame of, ii. 555; and the Spoils System, ii. 29 n.
Jacobins, French, Corruption among, ii. 477
Jacobites, the, i. 111
James II., i. 111
Japan
  Awakening of, as precedent, ii. 517
  Buddhist revival attempted in, i. 88 n.
  Civic Education in, i. 75
  Devotion to the Dynasty, the Ideal in, i. 138 & n.
  Family relations in, ii. 525
  Ministerial appointments in, i. 356
  Monarchy in, limited, i. 24
Japanese in New Zealand, ii. 311
Java, i. 205
Jefferson, T., President, U.S.A., i. 424, ii. 25, 94 n. sqq.; Democracy a Religion to, ii. 533; Political Ideals of, ii. 568; Popular without oratory, ii.

555; on Small Landowners in U.S.A., i. 451 & n.; and the Spoils System, ii. 29 n.
Jesuit challenge to theory of Divine Right of Kings, i. 84
Jesuits, the, Swiss attitude to, i. 343, 369, 435
Jobbery and Log-rolling in Various Lands, i. 479–80, ii. 328, 337, 458
  Suggested Remedy for, ii. 343
John, King, and Magna Charta, i. 51
Johnson, Dr. S., ii. 598
Johnson, Senator, on the Choice of Minor Officers, U.S.A., ii. 136 n.
Jordan, Sir John, on Chinese Provincial Councils, ii. 510 n. 1
Joseph II., Ministers since, ii. 537
Journal of National [American] Institute of Social Sciences, cited, ii. 558 n. 1
Journalism, *see also* Newspapers, Press, *and this under each Country*
  as Factor in Leadership, ii. 554
  Truth in, i. 100
Journalists
  Ability of, how shown, i. 295
  Political, in France and England, i. 298
Juarez, Benito, President of Mexico, i. 189, 192, 203
Judges, *see also under each Country*
  Classes of, somewhat distrusted, i. 272, 273, ii. 385, 480
  Local, ii. 438, 453
  Qualities essential in, ii. 384, 385
    How secured, ii. 385 sqq.
  Selection, Appointment, Salaries and Tenure of office, summarized, ii. 384 sqq.
Judicial Functions among Early Nations, i. 129–30
Judicial Officials, Corruption of, ii. 480–1
Judiciary(ies), *see under each Country*
  in Democracies, ii. 384 sqq.
  Power over, of Executive, i. 56
Juges d'Instruction, i. 272 & n. 2
Juges de Paix, i. 271
Jugo-Slavia, Bicameral Legislature in, ii. 399
Jugurtha, on the power of Money, ii. 484
Julius Caesar, ii. 542
Juridical Rights of old French *Noblesse,* i. 212, 213, 280
Juries, *see under Countries*
Justice
  Administration of, by Democracies, ii. 527, 528
  and Doctrine of Natural Rights, i. 45–6
  and Equality, i. 62
  Faulty Administration of, ii. 453
  Inter-class, under Monarchy, ii. 536
  Relativity of, i. 63 & n.
Justinian, Athenian Schools closed by, i. 182

Kafirs, South African, Popular Assembly of, i. 371; Status of, i. 145
Kajar dynasty, in Persia, ii. 512
Kant, E., i. 108 n., ii. 522
Katkoff, Journalistic Services of, i. 103, ii. 554
Kenyon, Sir F., i. 172 n. 1
Kerosene Bounties, Australia, ii. 224–5
Kertch, i. 166
Khalifate, the, i. 82 & n.
King (or Kings)
  Able, Value of, and the Converse, ii. 536–7
  of Constitutional Countries, Powers of, i. 227
  Counsels of, Value of, i. 228 & n.

King (or Kings)—*continued*
Divine Right of, i. 84, 144, 215,
English
Judicial functions gradually re-
stricted to, i. 130
Position of, in the State, i. 228
Powers of, devolved on Cabinet, ii.
472 *n.* 1
Veto of, i. 461, ii. 174, 177, 394
King's Council, Executive Functions of,
France, i. 211
Kingship
in Asia, i. 25
in Europe, i. 25
in Greek Cities, i. 26
Kingston, C. C., ii. 191
Kleiner Rath, Swiss, i. 338
"Know Nothings," the, in America, i.
123, ii. 42
Knowledge
and Citizenship, i. 78
Not Teacher of Wisdom, i. 74
in relation to Political Capacity, i. 74
Koran, the, Nature of, i. 88
Kossuth, L., i. 141
Kumara, Seddon's Store at, ii. 273 & *n.*

Labour, *see under Countries*
Labour Conditions, attention to, ii. 529
Labour Confederations (*see also* Trade
Unions, etc.), Evolution,
Growth and Power of, ii.
577–8
Labour Congresses, tending to discount
Legislatures, ii. 340
Labour Department, New Zealand, Awards
of Compulsory Arbitration
Court enforced by, ii. 302
Labour Disputes, *see also* Strikes, *under
Countries*
Canadian Act on, i. 491
Causes of, i. 444, 465, 466
Compulsory Arbitration on, *see* Arbitra-
tion *and* Australia *and* New
Zealand
Direct Action in relation to, i. 322 *n.*
Labour Disputes Investigation Act, New
Zealand, provisions of, ii.
305
Labour Issues in Local Government, ii.
443
Labour Leaders and their Standard, ii.
212 & *n.*, 213, 245
Labour Leagues, in Australia, ii. 578
Labour Legislation, ii. 225 *sqq.*, 566–7,
568–9
Labour Party, *see also under Countries*
Australia
Caucus of, ii. 188, 193–4, 206, 208–9
& *n.* 1, 257–8, 262–3,
356–7, 450–1, 467
Chiefs of, Standard of, ii. 212 & *n.*,
213
Cohesion and Discipline of, i. 414
Conferences of Delegates for Election,
ii. 207
Discipline exerted by, ii. 207, 208
Interest of, in Education, ii. 200
Irish element in, ii. 206 *n.*
Organization of, Successes due to, ii.
209 *sqq.*
Organizations of, ii. 207 *sqq.*
Policies and Proposals, ii. 239, 240
sqq.
Power of, how built up, ii. 257
Proportional Representation repealed
by, ii. 183
Rule of, ii. 257
Schisms in, Signs of, ii. 261 & *n.*
Senatorial Elections carried by, ii.
187–8

Labour Party—*continued*
Australia—*continued*
Socialism of, ii. 236–7 & *n.*, 253,
258, 571
Success of, Causes of, ii. 210 *sqq.*
Coercion of Governments by, ii. 193,
195, 355–6, 572
Labour Parties, i. 32
Origins and aims of, i. 123–4, 125, 311,
ii. 347, 571
Labour Union Congresses, U.S.A., ii. 340
Labour Unions, Swiss, Socialist, i. 414,
415
Labour Unrest in Argentina, i. 197
Ladin Language, i. 330 & *n.*
Lagthing, Norway, slender powers of, ii.
402
Laissez-faire Doctrine
Canadian attitude to, i. 471
Discredited, not refuted, i. 57
Land
Allocation, etc., of, by Assemblies of
Freemen, i. 130
Local Control of, i. 130
Land Boom, in New Zealand, ii. 268, 283
Land Commission of 1905, in New
Zealand, evidence before, ii.
284
Land Legislation in New Zealand, ii.
283 *sqq.*
Land Questions in
Australia, ii. 216, 218, 220–2, 259
New Zealand, ii. 286 & *n.*, 328, 330
Land Sales, New Zealand, provisos con-
cerning, ii. 285
Land Tax
Australia, ii. 218, 220
New Zealand, ii. 288
Land Tenures, Australia (*see also* Land
Question, *above*), Party
Conflicts over, ii. 202–203
Landamman, Swiss, i. 337
Landesgemeinde, of the Swiss, i. 130,
337 & *nn.*, 371–2, 373, 374,
406
and the Referendum, i. 375, 393
Voting at, considered a Duty, i. 401 *n.*
Landowners
and Employers in Great Britain, and
their employees, ii. 180–81
and the Peasants in 18th Century
France, i. 212
Land-owning in Spanish America, i. 193,
196, 197–8, 203
Large Countries, Democracy in, Diffi-
culties of, ii. 502, 506, 507,
510
Initiative and Referendum Unsuitable
in, ii. 576
Lassalle, Ferdinand, i. 432, ii. 546
Latin America (Spanish and Portuguese),
Republics of, i. 7, 187 & *n.*
sqq., *see also under Names*
Latin-American Republics
Bicameral Legislatures in, i. 194, 196,
200
Clericalism in, i. 191, 199
Constitutions of, Provisions of, how
rendered ineffective, i. 189
sqq.
Corruption in, i. 139–40, 190
Defensive Forces of, i. 191, 193
Democratic Governments in, ii. 500
Early Settlers in, prospects of, ii. 4
Education in, i. 189, 190, 192, 200,
202, 203, 206
Elections in, i. 194, 196, 200, 203, ii.
478
Finance, Loans, Taxation, and Debt in,
i. 190
Future of, considered, i. 205–7

Latin-American Republics—*continued*
Heroes of the Independence of, i. 192
History of, i. 187 *sqq.*
Lessons of, i. 203 *sqq.*
Judges and Justiciaries of, i. 189, 190,
ii. 480
Legislatures in, i. 189, 190, *and see
under separate Republics*
Model of, ii. 336
Local Government in, i. 197, ii. 576
Not Democracies, i. 21–2, 23, 187,
192–3
Notable Men of, i. 192
Overseas Trade, of, in foreign hands,
i. 191
low Political level of, i. 204
Politically-interested Classes in, i. 188,
190
Popular Government arrested in, i. 39
Population of, Ethnic Elements in, i.
188, 189 & *n.* 2, 191, 193,
194, 200, 201, 202, 203,
206
President-dictators of, i. 190 *sqq.*, ii.
358, 469
Presidential Elections, ii. 472
Railways scarce in, i. 189 & *n.* 1
Real Republics among, i. 193 *sqq.*
Revolutions in, causes and effects of, i.
189, 190, 192
Socialism in, i. 197, 198, 199
True Citizens in, i. 188–9
Wars of, i. 191–2
Latin-European Immigrants into
Argentina, i. 195
Uruguay, i. 198
Latvia, Republic of, ii. 575
Laud, Archbishop, on Divine Right of
Kings, i. 87
Laurier, Sir Wilfrid, i. 255, 470, 473
Lausanne, Seat of the Swiss Federal
Tribunal, i. 357
Lavoisier, A. L., i. 65
Law, Scope of, in England, i. 310
Law and Order, Maintenance of, in the
Countries considered, i.
137–8, 139, 140, 310, 317–
8, 320–1, 458, 486–7,
500, 501–2, ii. 6, 7, 8, 83,
87–8 & *n.*, 89 & *n.*, 90,
91–3, 155, 156, 158, 171,
199, 252–3, 278, 328, 355,
362 & *nn.*, 363, 384, 439,
452, 453, 508, 527, 528,
545, 562
Law, the, British and French attitudes
to, contrasted, i. 310
Law, The, of the Constitution, by Dicey,
cited, i. 440 & *n.*
Law Courts, *see under Countries*
Laws
in Ancient Greece
Amendment of, and Prosecutions for
Infringements of, i. 174
of the City, ii. 391
Equality of, Watchword of Revolution, i. 26
and Decrees, distinction between, in
Greece, France, and Switzerland, i. 174 & *n.*
Lawyer-Presidents in Spanish-American
States, i. 195, 207
Lawyers in Parliaments, i. 248, ii. 189–
90
Lea, H. C., of Philadelphia, on Reform
and its Opponents, ii. 107
Leader of Opposition
in Canada, status of, i. 479
Recognized, Absence of, in French
Chamber of Deputies, i.
254–5

Leaders
Australian, Parliamentary, ii. 211–12
Choice of, ii. 551, 557–8
Educated, value of, i. 77
Functions and Duties of, ii. 560
Great, not specially produced by De-
mocracy, ii. 560
Influence of, on Tone of Public Life,
ii. 560–1
Ingratitude to, rare in History, ii. 558
& *n.* 2, 559 & *n.* 1
Lacking in
Australia, ii. 203, 259
France, i. 265
and Led, Relations between, ii. 561–2
Loyalty to, i. 111, 113 *n.*, ii. 558 & *n.*
2, 559 & *n.* 1
National, i. 126
Natural, ii. 506
Official, Ministers as, ii. 56
Personal Knowledge of, Few possess-
ing, ii. 557 & *n.*, 558
Popular, and Public Self-Confidence, i. 64
Power of, in regard to Importance of
Choosing, ii. 550–1
Qualities Essential in, i. 138–9, 161–2,
320–1, 323, ii. 366, 552,
553 *sqq.*
Different values given to, in Different
Lands, ii. 557–8
Sources of, ii. 505–6, 552, 554 *sqq.*
Leadership, *see also under* Switzerland
and U.S.A.
in Democracies, ii. 552 *sqq.*, *see also*
Few, the
Causes affecting, ii. 557 & *n.*, 558 & *n.*
1, 569
League of Nations
Admission to, of the Dominions, ii.
176, 215, 244 *n.*
Mandates given by, to and for
Australia, ii. 176, 244 *n.*
New Zealand, ii. 313
Persia considered, ii. 512 *n.* 1
Popular support essential to, ii. 383
and Prevention of Aggression, ii. 508
Swiss Entry into, submitted to Referen-
dum, i. 376, 438 & *n.*
League of Peasants, Switzerland, *see*
Peasants' Party
Leaseholder and Freeholder in New
Zealand, ii. 284–5, 287 *n.*
Lectures on the Constitution of Canada,
by Riddell, referred to, i.
483 *n.*
Lee, Robert E., Confederate General,
U.S.A., Southern Loyalty to,
ii. 559
Left or Radical Party, in Switzerland, i.
408 *sqq.*
Left Centre Party, in France, i. 215, 218,
229, 236, 410
Legal-mindedness of the Americans, ii.
21, 87–8
Legislation
Controversial, "Group" system as af-
fecting, ii. 348
Direct, by the People, Reforms designed
to secure, U.S.A., ii. 129,
140 *sqq.*, *see also* Initiative,
Recall, Referendum
Not duly Representative of Popular
Sentiment, i. 384 & *nn.*
Popular, in Switzerland, *see* Initiative
Popular Control over, *see* Referendum
Legislative Aims of Democracy, ii. 562
Legislative Caucus (*see also* Caucus, *and
under* Labour), ii. 354 *sqq.*
Legislative Chambers, Relations between,
and adjustment of differ-
ences, ii. 408 *sqq.*

Legislatures, *see also under Countries*
Anticipations from, ii. 336
Checks and Balances for, ii. 390 *sqq.*
Composition of, Changes in, in men, manners, and status (*see also* Decline, *below*), ii. 338 *sqq.*
Congestion of, ii. 346–7
Decline of, in the Countries considered, i. 180, 306, 307, 329, 478, 479, 499–500, ii. 52–3, 54, 64, 191 *n.*, 192, 317, 328, 335 *sqq.*, 346, 356, 359, 410–11, 412, 418, 555, 557, 560, 576
Defects and Diseases of, ii. 336 *sqq.*, 339 *sqq.*, 345 *sqq.;* the principal, ii. 410–11; Methods of discounting, ii. 412
Dominance in, of the Few (*q. v.*), ii. 545
Indispensability of, ii. 356
Influence of, on Public Opinion, ii. 248
Issues of Policy occupying, ii. 341
Members of (*see also under that head under Countries*), Corruption of, ii. 478–9
Powers Lost by, whither gone, ii. 342
Powers of, in
Parliamentary Governments, ii. 463 *& n.* 1, 464–5
Presidential Governments, ii. 463 *& n.* 2
Restrictions on nature and need of, ii. 390 *sqq.*, 393–4 *sqq.*, 396–7
Safeguards for, *see* Second Chamber
Talent in, Scarcity of (*see also* Decline, *above*), i. 307, ii. 555
Legitimists, in France, i. 214, 215, 225 *sqq.*, 288–9 *& n.*
Leipzig, ii. 437
Leo XIII., on the Civil Power in France, i. 217–8
Le Rossignol and D. Stewart, *cited* on State Socialism in New Zealand, ii. 283 *n.*, 286, 290 *nn.*, 292 *n.*, 295 *n.*
Lessing, G. E., ii. 522
Levelling Tendencies, alleged, of Democracy, i. 324–5; common under all forms of Government, i. 324
Liberal Party
Australia, ii. 205, 209, 210, 211–12, 218, 221, 316
Canada, Schism in, i. 474
Great Britain, i. 31, 409, ii. 347
New Zealand, ii. 268, 271, 315–6, 317, 348
Switzerland, i. 408 *sqq.*
Liberal-Labour Party, New Zealand, ii. 271, 283 *sqq.*, 289
"Liberal Union" in Australia, ii. 238
Liberalism, German, withering of, i. 40
Liberty, *see also* Civil, Industrial, Political, Press, etc.
Anticipations for, in Early U.S.A., ii. 3–4
Attainment of, ii. 568
Conceptions of, of Charles I. and of Parliament, i. 51–2
Connotations of, i. 15, 218 *n.* 2
Cooling of Enthusiasm for, i. 59
and Democracy, i. 23, 51, 185
Distinctions between uses of the word, and their bearing on one another, i. 51 *sqq.*
18th Century Theories on, i. 43–4
English conception of, i. 51 *sqq.*, 138
French conceptions of, i. 38, 316, ii. 568

Liberty—*continued*
Greek conception of, i. 51–2
Individual, secured by Democracy, ii. 562
Kinds of, relations between, i. 53 *sqq.* and Minorities, ii. 489
in New Phase of Democracy (*cf.* Russia), ii. 574 *& n.* 1
Spiritual, in the Gospels, i. 88–9
Swiss devotion to, i. 431, 454
Lieutenant-Governors of
Canada, i. 462 *& n.*, 463, 493
States, U.S.A., ii. 13 *n.* 2
Life of John Hay, by Thayer, ii. 374 *n.*
Life of Saussure, by Freshfield, i. 372 *n.* 2
Life of R. J. Seddon, by Drummond, ii. 283 *n.*
Lincoln, Abraham, President, U.S.A., i. 265, ii. 67, 120, 541, 561; and Chance, ii. 559–60; Declaration of, on Slavery, ii. 378; on Fooling the People, i. 150; as Orator, ii. 67
Liquor Legislation in New Zealand, ii. 276, 315, 317, *see also* Prohibition
Literacy and Politics in
Asiatic Democracies, i. 73
European Democracies, i. 71 *sqq.* as a Qualification for Civil Rights, i. 71 *sqq.*, 201
Literary Censorship of Communist State, ii. 590
Literature, Democracy in relation to, ii. 519 *sqq.*
Lithuania, Republic of, ii. 575
Living, Standard of, in the Dominions, i. 465, ii. 168, 169, 170–1, 245–6, 249, 256, 325 *n.* 2, 330–1
Loans, Foreign, i. 190, 207
Lobbying, and Corruption, ii. 479, 483
Local Administration or Local Self-Government, *see also* Municipalities *and see both under Countries*
Local Assemblies, Selection from, to higher Assemblies, *see* Soviets
Local Authorities, Patronage by, i. 320
Local Committees, i. 269, ii. 203 *et alibi*
Local Elections, Party Politics as influencing, i. 117, ii. 441–2 *sqq.*
Local Improvements, Corruption connected with, ii. 437–8
Local or Racial Parties, i. 124
Local Self-Government, *see also under Countries*
Aim of the Paris Communards, i. 219
Beginnings of, i. 129 *& n. sqq.*
Central in relation to, ii. 435 *sqq.*
Comparisons of, in different Lands, i. 211, 212, 310–1, 452
and Decentralization (*q.v.*), ii. 343, 576–7
Educative value of, i. 79, 132–3, 320, 335, ii. 14, 115–6, 160, 436, 442, 443, 448–9, 473, 555–6
Functions assigned to, i. 129 *sqq.*, ii. 435–6 *sqq.*
General Service rendered by, i. 132–3
Labour Issues affecting, ii. 443
Risks of, i. 284–5
Local Taxation, and Thrift, ii. 438
Localism in
Australian Politics, ii. 190, 245
U.S.A., ii. 7–8, 53, 54, 55
Locke, John, i. 16; Whig tendencies of, i. 28

Lock-outs, New Zealand, when Illegal, ii. 301

Log-rolling, U.S.A., ii. 62, 140, 143

London Borough Elections, difficulty of deciding on Candidate, i. 114 *n.*

London, Police of, Central Control over, ii. 439 *n.*

Long Parliament Government, ii. 463 *n.* 3

Lopez, rule of, in Paraguay, i. 191 *n.*

Lords of the Articles in pre-Union Scotland, ii. 396 *n.*

Louis XI., i. 192

Louis XIV., i. 37, ii. 536; Centralizing System of, followed by Napoleon I., i. 280; and the Civil Service, i. 274; and the Expulsion of the Huguenots, i. 211, 218 *n.* 1; reign of, as antecedent to French Democracy, i. 211; less costly than French Democracy, i. 314; glories of the Age of, ii. 522

Louis XV., Oppression under, ii. 532; Powers of the State under, ii. 542; Reign of, as leading up to Democracy, i. 212

Louis XVI., overthrow of, i. 37; and the Parlement of Paris, i. 311

Louis Napoleon, *see* Napoleon III.

Louis Philippe, an Elected Sovereign, i. 214; Foreign Policy of, i. 319; Length of Reign, i. 319 *n.;* overthrow of, i. 213, 219; Parliamentary brilliance in the days of, i. 248-9; Scandals in days of, i. 301; Suffrage during reign of, limited, i. 37-8

Low, S., Chapter by, in *American Self-Government*, ii. 99 *n.* 3

Lowden, Governor, on Civil Administrative Code, Illinois, ii. 137 *n.* 2

Lowe, Robert, ii. 191; on the Dull Level of Democracy, ii. 521; on Education for Voters, i. 70

Lowell, President A. L., book by, on Public Opinion and Popular Government, ii. 78 *n.;* on Voting-percentage in American Referenda, ii. 421 *n.* 2

Lowell, J. R., on the Ideal Man in a Democracy, ii. 524; on Tolerance in London, ii. 566 *n.;* on Voting, i. 151

Lowell, L., *Government of England*, by, *cited*, ii. 470 *n.* 1, 471 *n.*

Lower-Class Rule, present-day, ii. 585

Lower or First Houses, powers of, relative to Senates, ii. 401

Loyalty of Peoples to Leaders, ii. 558 & *n.* 2, 559 & *n.* 2

Swiss and Japanese, i. 137, 138 & *n.*

Lusitania, sinking of, ii. 375

Lusk, Major, book by, on New Zealand, ii. 283 *n.*

Luxembourg, Palais du, home of the Senate, i. 236

Luzern, i. 328

Lynching, U.S.A., ii. 90, 363, 452, 528

Lyons, ii. 437

Macaulay, Lord, ii. 335; on U.S.A. Government, ii. 178

M'Carthy, C., book by, on the Functions of a State University in Wisconsin, ii. 97 *n.* 1

Macdonald, Sir John, i. 255, 473, 478, 498

Macedonian overthrow of Athens, i. 170, 181, 182

Machiavelli, ii. 369; on Democracy, i. 13; on ingratitude of Princes and of Peoples, ii. 558 *n.* 2; Standards of, i. 139

Machine, the, U.S.A., *see* Party Organization *and* Party Machine

Mackenzie, —, i. 478

M'enzie, Rt. Hon. J., Land Legislation set on foot by, ii. 282 *sqq.*

McKinley, President, ii. 67; murder of, i. 94

MacMahon, Marshal, Presidency of, i. 214, 215, 230

Macy, Prof. J., on Direct Primary Elections, U.S.A., ii. 134 *n.*

Madagascar, French annexation of, i. 319

Madison, J., President U.S.A., ii. 94 *n.* 2, and the Spoils System, ii. 29 *n.*

Magna Charta, i. 137, 312, ii. 8; Liberty as secured by, i. 51-2

Magnum Concilium, the, ii. 396

Maine, Sir H., book by, on Popular Government, i. 187, 390 & *n.*, 397 & *n.* 2; on the Latin-American Republics, i. 187-8

Maine, State of, dispute over, ii. 375

Maires, French, Office and Functions of, i. 232 *n.*, 235, 249, 276, 277, 282 & *n.* 1, 283, 334

Majorities
Have they moral authority? i. 146
and Rigid Constitutions, ii. 11
Tyranny of, i. 487, ii. 121, 159, 355, 411, 521

Majority
Rule of
Checks and Balances for, ii. 390 *sqq.*
as Constituting Democracy, i. 20, 140-1
Criticisms on, i. 115-6
Drawbacks to, i. 53
the Logical Outcome of, and the Remedy, ii. 354-5
and Party Discipline, i. 115, 118 & *n.*, 120 & *n.*, 121
Will of, not the same as the Will of All, i. 297, ii. 548 *n.* 2

Majority Votes, when not representing a Complete Majority, ii. 355

Manchu dynasty, overthrow of, ii. 500 & *n.*, 501, 511, 514

Mandates, Election, i. 152
to Members of Parliament, ii. 351, 352

Manhood Suffrage
the Basis of Political Equality, i. 60
in Various Lands, i. 198 *n.* 2, 338, 441, ii. 13, 17, 47, 268, 269

Manlius Torquatus, example of, i. 136

Manners, Influence on, of Democracy, ii. 339, 452-3, 524

Manuel de Droit Civique, by Numa Droz, i. 76 *n.*

Many, the
Rights and Functions, Inexpugnable, of, ii. 550
Conception of, a revolt against oppression by the Few, ii. 548-9
Power Surrendered by, to the Few, ii. 547
Rule of, i. 20

Maori Race, New Zealand, ii. 265, 267 & n., 278 n. 2, 283, 311, 313
Mapoche Tribes of Chile, i. 188
Marcus Aurelius, ii. 536
Marcy, —, and the Spoils System, U.S.A., ii. 29 n.
Marseilles, i. 166, 168, ii. 437
Marsilius of Padua, ii. 599 & n.
Marvell, Andrew, on Public Opinion, ii. 122
Marx, Karl, bourgeois origin of, ii. 546 n.; French followers of, i. 290; wide Literary Influence of, ii. 554
Marxian Communists and the Russian Revolution, ii. 513
Mass Meetings, Communal, in German-speaking Swiss Communes, i. 333–4
Massachusetts
First Colonization of, ii. 4
and Initiative and Recall, ii. 147, 150
Masses, the, i. 20
Apathy of, to Political power, i. 24–5, 30–1, 32, 37, 39, 40, 41, see also Civic Apathy
Ignorance of, on Foreign Affairs, ii. 367, 369 sqq., 383
Matches, Monopoly in France, i. 276
Material Changes acting on Democracy, ii. 564 sqq.
Materialism of Democracy, i. 303–4, 307, 482, 488, 504, ii. 173, 244, 251, 301, 326–7, 521, 574, see also Labour, under Australia, and Industrials
Maximilian, Emperor, overthrow of, i. 192, 202
Mayors, see also Maires, above
American, Powers, Elections, etc., of, ii. 16, 33, 139, 140, 198 n. 3, 441, 496
Australian, Status of, ii, 198 & n. 2
Election or appointment of, ii. 440
New Zealand, Election of, ii. 276
Mazzini, Giuseppe, i. 141; on Authority, when sacred, ii. 555 n.; definition by, of Democracy, ii. 555 n.; Democracy a Religion to, ii. 533; and Educational worth of Self-Government, ii. 604; Faith of, in Freedom, i. 59 n.; Fraternally Religious Spirit expected by, ii. 606; Political Ideals of, ii. 568; Radicalism of, i. 16
Mediaeval City Oligarchies (see Italian Cities, see also Florence, and Venice), ii. 537 & n.
Mediocrity as result of Democracy, i. 324–5
Mediterranean Democracies, i. 165 sqq.
Meetings of the Early Germans, Tacitus on, i. 337 n. 1, 371, 391 & n. 2
Meetings, Political, in France, Britain, and America, i. 292
Melbourne, dominance of, ii. 250, 266; growth of, ii. 170; Present Seat of Australian Commonwealth Government, ii. 175
Member of Congress and of Parliament, relations of, with Constituencies, ii. 53, 55, 65
Member of Legislature, U.S.A.
as Delegate rather than Representative, ii. 54
Quality of, ii. 52
Members of Legislatures, Payment of, see Payment of Members

Members of Parliament
in New Zealand, drawback of the position, ii. 280 sqq., 320
Swiss, not Delegates, i. 348
Mental Activity as developed by Democracy, ii. 519, 520
Menteith, the Fause, i. 136 & n. 1
Merriam, Prof., on the Bosses and the Direct Primary Law, in U. S. A., ii. 134 n.
Mesopotamia, Conditions in, ii. 514
Mestizo population in Latin America, i. 189, 191, 193, 200, 202, ii. 500
Metternich, on Fraternity in France, i. 316
Mexico, Republic of, i. 187 n.
Administration, Election, etc., in, i. 202
Anti-clericalism in, i. 192, ii. 6
"Cientificos" in, ii. 506 n., 512
Civil Wars in, i. 201
Clerical and Anti-Clerical Party struggles in, i. 192
Constitution of, i. 202
Corruption in, i. 213, ii. 516
Ethnography and Ethnology of, i. 188, 201 sqq.
French Expedition, i. 192, 202, ii. 372
National Sentiment in, ii. 516
Party in, i. 111
Presidency in, of Diaz, and after, i. 203, 207, ii. 376, 512
Railway and Economic Development in, under Diaz, i. 202
Self-Government in, ii. 503
Danger to, ii. 508
Small Landowners in, i. 451
U.S.A. attitude to, ii. 124, 159, 373, 376
War against (1846), ii. 374
Micheli, H., book by, on Volksanfragen, i. 372 n. 1
Michiels, R., book by, on Political Parties, referred to, ii. 546 n., 547 n., 558 n. 2
Middle Ages, injustices of, why endured, i. 46
Migration in Canada, of French-speaking Population, i. 468
Miletus, craft of, i. 168
Militarism in Germany, i. 40; the Prussian Ideal, how founded, i. 137–8
Military Defence, France, i. 318
Military Organization
Athenian, i. 181
in Greek Republics, parallel to, i. 168
Military Presidents, of Latin-American States, i. 189, 193, 194, 196, 207
Military Service
Compulsory, in Australasia, ii. 175, 216, 252 n., 361
Universal, in Switzerland, i. 363
Mill, J. S., ii. 335; on Educative Value of Self-Government, ii. 604; and Majority Tyranny, i. 436
Milton, John, on unlicensed Printing, i. 92
Minimum Wage, in Australian States, ii. 225 & n. 2, 227–8 & n. 1
Ministerial Responsibility in Various Lands, i. 226–7; ii. 463 n. 1, 492 n. 2, 493–4
Ministers, see under each Country
under Autocracy, ii. 542–3
Continuity of, in Office, Switzerland, advantages of, i. 348, 351, 355–6, 440, 449

Ministers—*continued*
Dignity and power attaching to, in France, i. 262–3
Dismissal of, in France, Britain, and the Dominions, ii. 402
Forming a Cabinet, in
Parliamentary Governments, ii. 462
Presidential Governments, ii. 463
Popular Control of, *see also* Impeachment (Recall, *etc.*), i. 40
Presence of, in Legislatures, advantages of, ii. 465
Press relations of, i. 103–4, 293–4
Quality of, and Selection of, in Countries instanced, ii. 359 *sqq.*
Summed up, ii. 365
Ministrables, qualifications of, i. 262 & *n.* 1
Minorities
decisions by, in Socialist and Labour affairs, ii. 547 *n.*
and Individual Liberty, i. 57–8
and Proportional Representation in Switzerland, i. 413
Tyranny of, ii. 349
Mobs, why dangerous, ii. 495
Model Citizen, the, i. 47–8
Moderate men in Political Parties, i. 126, 127
Moderne Demokratie by Hasbach, *cited*, i. 242 *n.* 3, ii. 538 *n.* 1
Moderne Demokratie, by Zürcher, *cited*, i. 360 & *n.*
Modernism, Influence of, ii. 525
Mommsen, T., i. 324, ii. 522
Monaco, i. 166
Monarchical Ingratitude, ii. 559 & *n.* 2
Monarchical Oligarchies, i. 27 *sqq.*, ii. 538 *sqq.*, 543
Monarchical Rule
as Possibility in Spanish America, i. 205
Why probably adapted to China, ii. 511
Monarchist French Ministry of 1877, i. 242
Monarchist Party, France, i. 214 & *n.*, 215, 216, 225, 235, 252 & *n.* 1, 266, 289
Monarchy
in the Ancient World, i. 12
British, Democratic Character of, i. 7
Comparison with, of Democracy, ii. 535–7
Definitions of, i. 20, ii. 535
in Early Greece, i. 169
Failure of, in
Brazil, i. 200
Mexico, i. 190, 203, 205
Hereditary and Nominal, Advantages of, i. 200, ii. 465–6, 536–7
Instances of, i. 227, ii. 461
Merits of, ii. 536–7
Views on, in the Middle Ages, i. 36
Money Power in Politics, *see also under Countries*, i. 126, 450, 451, 468 *sqq.*
Chief Enemy of Democracy, ii. 486
Democracies Exempt from, ii. 454
Not extinguished by Democracy, ii. 146, 562
the Press as Instrument for, i. 98–9, 109
Relative Force of, in the Countries examined, ii. 454
Titles as Weapons of, ii. 484–5
Vitality of, Bases of, ii. 488
Monopolies, ii. 569
Monopoly in opinion, Tyranny of, dangers of, i. 107
Monotheism, Judaic, i. 81

Monroe, President, U.S.A., ii. 94 *n.* 2
Monroe Doctrine, a Political Tradition, i. 138
M. de Camors, by O. Feuillet, *cited*, i. 284 *n.*
Monte Video, Socialists of, i. 199
Montenegro, ii. 501 *n.*
Montesquieu, i. 6, 13; on English Political Institutions, i. 211; on the Principle of Despotism, ii. 491; on the Purchase of Judicial Posts, i. 271; on Republics and Monarchies, what each lives on, i. 314
Montreal
Municipal scandal in, i. 487
Population of, i. 456, 466
Moral Life of France, Effect on, of the Third Republic, i. 323, 325 *sqq.*
Moral Standards, effect on, of Party System, i. 117–8
Moral Virtues assumed by Communism, ii. 588 & *n.*, 591
Morality
and Divorce, ii. 525
and Religion in regard to the future of Democracy, ii. 606
Morocco, i. 319
Most, Johann, Conviction of, i. 94
Multitude, the, Fatalism of, ii. 121 *n.* 1
Munich, ii. 437
Municipal Bribery, U.S.A. (*q.v.*), ii. 480
Municipal Commissioners, Galveston Plan of employing, ii. 139
Municipal Councils, ii. 198, 440
Municipal Government, *see also* Municipalities, etc., *under Countries*
Committee System, ii. 440
Considerations on, ii. 439–41
in England, U.S.A., and ancient Greece, i. 171
Experts needed in, ii. 444
Watchfulness essential in, ii. 444
Municipal Government, by Dr. F. J. Goodnow, ii. 101 *n.*, 134 *n.*
Munitions of War, Manufacturers of, accusations against, ii. 484
Munychia, Macedonian Occupation, i. 181
Murder Trials, U.S.A., Defects in, ii. 88 *sqq.*
Music, unaffected by other intellectual movements, ii. 523 & *n.*
Muslim Sacred Law, i. 82
Mussulman Countries, Social Equality in, i. 66 *n.*

Nabobs, the, ii. 485–6
Naples, Kings of, ii. 536
Napoleon I., i. 37, 318, 319 *n.*, ii. 463 *n.* 3, 536, 598; Centralization of Power under, i. 213; Code of, *see* Code Napoleon; Council of State founded by, i. 278; Executive strengthened by, i. 280; Menace of, to England, i. 137; Opportunity and, i. 108; Reconstruction under, i. 213, 274; on Swiss Government, i. 372 & *n.* 3, 406–7; as Superman, ii. 542
Napoleon III. (Louis Napoleon), i. 319 *n.*; Alliance of, with the Roman Church, i. 85; and The American War of Secession, ii. 378; Bourgeois content under, i. 320; Corrup-

Napoleon III. (Louis Napoleon—*continued*
tion under, i. 303, ii. 540;
and the *coup d'État*, i. 213,
224, 231, 291; Fall of, i.
38; Foreign Policy of, i.
319, errors of, ii. 372; Journalistic hostility to, i. 294;
Ministers of, ii. 537; Morals
during Reign of, i. 325; Oligarchic rule of, ii. 540,
600; Plebiscites taken by,
i. 213, 291, ii. 472 *n.* 3;
Pressure on Voters under, i.
242; Scandals during Reign
of, i. 301; Support of, by
Universal Suffrage, i. 321–2
National Assemblies of African Races, i.
146, ii. 503
National Campaign Funds, U.S.A.,
Sources of, Legislation on,
ii. 482
National Character as affecting National
Institutions, i. 10; forma-
tion of, by Tradition, i.
136–7, 138–9
National Debt
Australia, ii. 254–5
New Zealand, ii. 289, 290 & *n.*, 292,
328
National Defence, in Democracies, Sum-
mary on, ii. 361–2, 365,
366
Departments Concerned with, in the
Six Countries described,
quality of, ii. 359, 361–2
National Democratic Convention, power
in, of Tammany Hall, ii.
104
National Ideals and Free Institutions, i.
141–2
National Leaders, i. 126
National Liberties, Temporary resigna-
tions of, dangers of, i. 140–
1
National Municipal Review, U.S.A., *cited*,
ii. 63 *n.*, 140 & *n.*, 137
n. 2
National Party, Australia, ii. 206, 209–
10
National (Party) Committee, U.S.A., ii.
32
National Patriotism in relation to Public
Opinion, i. 159
National Sentiment in Backward Coun-
tries, utilization of, ii. 516
National Unity
Sentiment of, co-operating with Ac-
tive Public Opinion, ii. 456–
7
Switzerland, i. 328, 330
"Nationalist" Antagonism in France to
Parliamentary System, i.
217
Nationalist Party, French, i. 253 *n.* 1,
292
Irish, i. 124
Nationalization, i. 108
American views on, ii. 126 & *n.*, 128
Australian Labour views on, ii. 218,
233, 234-5, 236
of French Railroad, argument against,
i. 276
Lessons on, from Public Management,
ii. 234
of Railways, Swiss Referendum on, i.
387
Nations
Effect on, of War, i. 140
Formation of, i. 130
Natural Equality, American Declaration
of Independence on, i. 61

Natural and Human Sciences, differences
between, i. 14–15 *sqq.*
Natural Inequity, i. 61–2, 65–6, ii.
548
Natural Justice and Political Equality, i.
62
Natural Leaders, ii. 506
Natural Rights
American and French Declarations on,
i. 43, 44, 218 *n.* 2
Doctrine of, i. 41, 48–9
Private Property among, in 1789,
present views on, i. 38
Negro element in Latin America, i. 188
n. 1, 200
Negro Republic of Haiti, i. 192
Negroes
Exclusion of, from Franchise, in Union
of South Africa, i. 22 *n.*, 34
in U.S.A., *see* Coloured Citizens
Nelson, Admiral, i. 141
Neo-Conservative Group in House of Com-
mons, 1880-85, i. 253 *n.* 2
Nepotism, alleged, of French Ministers, i.
263
Neutrality, Swiss, ii. 372–3
New Countries, Self-confidence (*q. v.*)
and Equalitarianism in, i.
65
New England
Democracy in, i. 28, 84–5
Dilution in, of English Stock, i. 140
Education in, ii. 5
Parish in, i. 130 & *n.* 2
Passion in, for Liberty, ii. 6–7
Political training in, i. 78
Religious sense in, ii. 6
Towns of, i. 147 & *n.* 2, ii. 55
Choice of Officials for, ii. 490
Evolution from, of the States, ii.
55
Self-Government in, ii. 490, 506
Town Meetings of, i. 337, 452 *n.*, ii.
440, 506
Newfoundland, Religion in, ii. 326
New Guinea, and Australian Federation,
ii. 172, 244
Australian Mandate for, ii. 176
"New Protection," the, in Australia, ii.
222 *sqq.*
New Republics and Instability of Minis-
tries, ii. 364
New South Wales
Coal-miners' Strike of 1910, effect on
Politics of, ii. 206
Constitution of, ii. 172
Courts of Conciliation and Arbitration
in, ii. 226–7
Export trade of, ii. 170
Free Trade views in, ii. 203
Legislature of, ii. 176
Labour Member in, ii. 204
Minimum Wage in, ii. 225 *n.* 2
Population of (1901), ii. 186
Religion as Political factor in, ii. 206 *n.*
Roman Catholic Schools in, ii. 200
Site for Federal Capital provided by,
ii. 175
State Mining in, ii. 234
Voting Methods in, ii. 182–3
Women Voters in, Numbers Voting, ii.
211 & *n.*
News-dissemination, past and present, i.
168–9
Newspaper Editors, notable, i. 97 & *n.*
Newspapers, *see also* Journalism *and*
Press, *and the latter under
Countries*
Commercialization of, i. 95, 98
in Democracies, Use and Misuse of, i.
92 *sqq.*

Newspapers—*continued*
Desiderata in, i. 96–7
Dual functions of, i. 95–6 *sqq.*
External Influences on, i. 98–9, 109
and Foreign Policy, i. 100–2, 103
Influence of, i. 101–2 *sqq.*, 105–6, 109
Partisanship in, i. 72–3, 96–7, 99 *sqq.*, 107
as Political Educators, i. 72–3, 74
Prestige of, i. 102–3
Public Confidence in, i. 72–3, 96–7
Traditions of, how maintained, i. 106
New York Assembly, Status of, i. 480
New York City
Boss domination in (*see also* Tammany), ii. 81–2, 102 *sqq.*, 112
Expansion of, ii. 99
Reforms in, how carried out, ii. 121
New Zealand, ii. 265 *sqq.*
Advances to Settlers Act, operation of, ii. 296–7
to Workers, ii. 297
Agricultural dominance in, ii. 451
Arbitration, Compulsory, in Courts of, ii. 225–6, 232, 299 *sqq.*, 305–6, 329
Dictum on, of the Chief Justice, ii. 307 *n.* 1
Asiatics Excluded from, ii. 311
Birth-rate and Death-rate in, ii. 325 *n.* 2
Borough Councils in, ii. 278
and the British connection, ii. 323, 324–5, 326
Chinese in, ii. 311
City Amenities neglected in, ii. 278 *n.* 2
Civic Apathy in, i. 157, ii. 319–21, 454
Civil List Act of 1908, provisions of, as to Maori representation, ii. 267 *n.*
Civil Service of, ii. 277, 279 *sqq.*, 345
Participation of, in Politics, ii. 281–2
Class Antagonism and Class Distinctions in, ii. 314–5, 459, 562
Climate of, ii. 265
Coal in, ii. 358
State Mining of, ii. 295, 329
Coalition Ministry in, during the War, ii. 277, 315
Collectivism not an aim in, ii. 322, 323, 324
Compulsory Military Service in, ii. 361
Compulsory Purchase of Land in, ii. 285, 289
Conciliation Commissioners, ii. 299–300
Conservatism in, ii. 276, 315, 323
Constitution of, i. 223, ii. 462, before 1890, ii. 269–70
Corruption practically absent from, ii. 318–9, 320–1, 453
Crime in, ii. 278
Death-Duties, ii. 288
Democracy in, ii. 265 *sqq.*
Evils of, escaped in, ii. 331
Gifts of, ii. 327–8
Historical Evolution of, i. 33–4
Steps leading to, ii. 267 *sqq.*
Study of, i. 6
Results of, summarized, ii. 322 *sqq.*
Divorce in, ii. 326 *& n.* 2
Early History of, ii. 267
Education in, ii. 277 *sqq.*, 325, 328, 331
under Local Authorities, ii. 436
Religious Teaching in Schools, contest over, ii. 278–9, 317

New Zealand—*continued*
Elections, ii. 269, 316
Cost of, ii. 318
Electoral qualifications for Mayoral Elections, ii. 277
Ethnography of, ii. 265–6
Executive Council, Maori members of, ii. 267 *n.*
Experimental (semi-Socialistic) Legislation in, ii. 282–3 *sqq.*
Facts absent from, which colour Political Questions in Europe, ii. 313–5
Financial Administration in, ii. 267–8, 275–6, 285–7 *sqq.*, 328, 331
Foreign affairs of the Empire influenced by, ii. 372
Frozen Mutton, Export of, ii. 270
Gold, etc., in, in, ii. 265, 267
Government of, ii. 315
Merits and Defects of, ii. 328, 331
Salient Features of, ii. 450, 451
Working of, ii. 313 *sqq.*
House of Representatives
Composition of, ii. 267, 269, 317–8, 349
Elections for, ii. 316
Maori Representation in, ii. 267, 269
Membership, etc., of, ii. 267 *& n.*, 269, 270
Powers of, ii. 267, 269, practically unlimited, ii. 270, 315
Supremacy of, ii. 331
Women Candidates of, ii. 308 *n.* 2
Immigration into, ii. 267
Checks to, ii. 309, 324, 328
Seddon's policy on, ii. 308–10
Income-Tax, ii. 288
Jobbery in, ii. 288
Judges and Judicature of, ii. 328, 386–7, 528
Labour Legislation, ii. 297 *n.* 2
Labour Organization in, ii. 322
Labour Party in, ii. 276
Activities of, ii. 276, 278, 316
Aims of, ii. 311, 571
Land in, State Ownership of, ii. 284 *sqq.*
Land Boom in, ii. 268, 270, 283
Land Commission of 1905 in, Evidence before, ii. 284
Land Legislation in, ii. 283 *sqq.*
Law-abidingness of the Native-born in, ii. 278
Leaders in, chief qualifications of, ii. 553–4
Legislative Council of, ii. 267
Functions and Membership of, ii. 270
Lack of attraction of, ii. 319–20
Recent modification of, ii. 320 *& n.* 1
Status of, since 1890, ii. 272
Legislatures
Checks on, ii. 393
Criticism of, ii. 317 *sqq.*
Decline in, ii. 317, 328, 338
Members of, Payment of, ii. 317, 452
Standards of, i. 480, ii. 338
Liquor Legislation in, ii. 276, 315, 317
Living, Standard of, in, ii. 325 *& n.* 2, 326, 330–1
Local Government in, ii. 277, 278, 328
Local Improvements in, and Corruption, ii. 294, 438
Lock-outs, when Illegal in, ii. 301
Mandate of, for Western Samoa, ii. 313
Manhood Suffrage in, ii. 268
Maori aborigines of, ii. 265, 266, 267 *n.*, 278, 283, 311, 313
Maori Land Reserves in, ii. 267, 283
Maori Wars, ii. 267

New Zealand—*continued*
Ministerial Instability in, ii. 365
Ministries in, ii. 270, 359
Municipal Government in, ii. 278 *n.* 2, 279, 440
National Characteristics, ii. 313, 322, 324 *sqq.*
National Debt of, ii. 289, 290 & *n.* 4, 328
Nationalization in, of Industries, ii. 126
Natural Beauties of, ii. 297, 327
Natural Wealth of, ii. 265–6, 330–1
Old-Age Pensions in, ii. 290 & *n.* 1
Parliament of, *see* House of Representatives, Legislative Council, and Legislatures, *above*
Composition of, ii. 269
Functions of, and Subjects dealt with, ii. 267 *sqq.*
Maori Representation in, ii. 267 & *n.*
Parties in, ii. 268–9, 276–7, 315 *sqq.*
in Municipal Elections, ii. 278
State of, on Elections of 1919, ii. 277 & *n.* 1
Party Spirit in, ii. 316
Pastoral industries of, ii. 265–6
Patriotism in, ii. 332
Pauperism and the Poor Law in, ii. 290
Police in, ii. 278
Political Patronage in, ii. 275–6, 280
Politics of
Idealism lacking in, ii. 324, 328, 331, 332
Writers on, ii. 283 *n.*
Population of
Distribution, Rural and Urban, ii. 315, 325 & *n.* 1
Homogeneity of, ii. 313, 325, 331
Police and Crime in relation to, ii. 278
Sections of, ii. 322
Slow increase in, ii. 325 *n.* 2, 328
"Pork Barrel" methods in, ii. 295 *n.* 1
Post and Telegraph Services, appointments to, ii. 280
Preferential treatment of British Imports in, ii. 287
Press influence in, ii. 322
Private Wealth in, ii. 325
Propertied Classes in, influence of, ii. 314–5, 323
Proportional Representation in, in Municipal Elections, ii. 278
Protection in, ii. 287, 297–8, 304
Provincial Councils in, ii. 267, 268
Public Funds in, Seddon's Manipulation of, ii. 275–6
Public Life
Lack of Attraction in, ii. 318–9
Tone of, ii. 320–1, 337–8
Public Opinion in, ii. 276, 456, 457, 459
on Arbitration, ii. 305–6
Articles of Faith of, ii. 323 *sqq.*
on Immigration, ii. 309 *sqq.*
on Land, ii. 286
Summarized, ii. 327
Public Service in, Number of Employees, ii. 279
Public Works Department, scope of, ii. 289, 290, 292
"Push," the, in, ii. 314
Railway Board in, ii. 292–3
Railways in, ii. 268, 291 *sqq.*
Appointments to, ii. 280
Cost of, for Construction, Pensions, etc., ii. 282, 291–2, 293, 294
Employees of, Problems connected with, ii. 293, 294
Minister for, ii. 293

New Zealand—*continued*
Religion in, ii. 326
Revenue, Sources of, ii. 268, 287 *sqq.*
"Right to Work," claim in, ii. 297 *n.* 2, 316
Second Ballot Act of, repealed, ii. 318 *n.*
Self-Government bestowed on, ii. 172
Senate of, Relative Powers of, ii. 402
Settlers in
Advances to, ii. 289, 296–7, 329
Early, ii. 4, 267, 324–5
Sheep-farming, and Mutton-exporting Trades of, ii. 266, 270
Short views taken in, ii. 269, 291, 323, 331
Small Farmer in, ii. 283, 286
Conservatism of, ii. 276, 315
Small-holding problem in, ii. 270
Social Conditions in, Improvement in, ii. 303
Democratic Party in, ii. 297 *n.* 2, 317
Social Equality in, i. 33, ii. 323
Socialists of, ii. 316–7
"Spoils" System absent from, ii. 280
Sport, love of, in, ii. 326
State Activities, Industries, etc., in, i. 6–7, 11, ii. 272, 274–5, 277, 282 *sqq.*, 290, 291 *sqq.*, 304–5, 576–7
Extension of, wide, ii. 173; Desire for further, ii. 569 *sqq.*
Results of, Summarized, ii. 328–9 *sqq.*
State Aid, Reliance on, Schemes encouraging, ii. 297
State Employees, Number of, ii. 279
State Land, tenants of, ii. 284
State Ownership of Land in, ii. 284 *sqq.*
State Socialism in, ii. 324, 451–2
"Stone-walling" in, ii. 318
Strike riots in, ii. 452
Strikes in, ii. 269, 271, 282, 299, 301, 303–4, 305, 307, 308, 323, 329, 451
of State employees, ii. 295 & *n.* 2
When Illegal, ii. 301, 305
Subsidies to Local Authorities in, ii. 278
Succession Duties, ii. 288
Syndicalists in, ii. 316, 323
Tariffs in, ii. 268, 287, 297–8, 304
Taxation in, ii. 268, 288–9, 311
Trade Unions in, ii. 269, 271
and Compulsory Arbitration, ii. 299 *sqq.*
Large numbers outside of, ii. 304, 322
Power, etc., of, ii. 322
Preference to, ii. 301
Traditions lacking in, ii. 326
Universal Suffrage in, ii. 328
University of, ii. 279 *n.*
Wages in, Fixing of, ii. 302 *sqq.*
Tariffs as affecting, ii. 297–8
War Loan, magnitude of, ii. 289, 332
in the Great War (1914–18), ii. 332
Wealth of
National, ii. 255–6, 330
Private, ii. 325
Woman Suffrage in, ii. 308 & *nn.*
Workers, Advances to, ii. 296–7
Working Class Legislation, ii. 275
New Zealand, by Sir R. Stout, ii. 277 *n.* 3, 278 *n.* 1, 283 *n.*
New Zealand in Evolution, by Scholefield, ii. 283 *n.*
New Zealand Federation of Labour, and the Waihi Gold Mine Strike, ii. 305 *n.*

New Zealand Hansard, ii. 292 *n.*
New Zealand Official Year-Books, ii. 283 *n.*
Nicaragua, Republic of, i. 187 *n.*
  and the U.S.A., ii. 124 *n.* 1
  under Zelaya, i. 192
Nicholas I., Czar, ii. 377
Nicias, i. 180
Night Riders, U.S.A., outrages by, ii. 91
Nomothetai, the, i. 174
Nonconformity, British, i. 312
Non-legal bodies interfering with Legislatures (*see also* Labour Caucuses, Party Organizations, Tammany, etc.), ii. 281 & *n.*, 282, 467, 576, 578
Non-Party Ballot for Municipal Elections, Chicago, ii. 139 *n.*
Non-Party Legislation, U.S.A., ii. 42
Non-Political Authorities in Australia and U.S.A., ii. 196–7
Normans, the, characteristics of, i. 286–7
Norsemen, the Thing of, i. 130, 337, ii. 506
North America, *see also* Canada *and* U.S.A.
  Beginnings in, of Democracy, ii. 3 *sqq.*
  Gifts to, of Nature and of a Splendid Past, ii. 4 *sqq.*
  Rousseau's influence in, i. 36
North American Colonies, English Oligarchy and, ii. 539
North Atlantic Fishing Rights, Arbitration on, ii. 375
Northern Territory, Australia, ii. 176
Norton, C. E., *cited* on Tolerance in London, ii. 566 *n.*
Norway
  Compulsory Arbitration in, ii. 226, 307 *n.* 2
  Constitution of, i. 223
  a Democracy, i. 22
  Emigration from, to U.S.A., ii. 23
  and Iceland, i. 36
  Lagthing of, slender powers of, ii. 402
  Monarchy, democratic, of, i. 22, 227, ii. 461, 535
  Money Power slight in, i. 444, ii. 254 *n.* 1, 454
  Party Government in, i. 115
  Place-hunting in, i. 370
  the Press in, i. 436
  Professional Politicians, few in, i. 425
  Self-governing Groups in, ii. 503
  Self-Government in, i. 35
  Social Equality in, i. 60, 66, 427
  Stor Thing in, ii. 402 *n.*
  Suffrage in, i. 21
  Thing of, i. 130, 337, ii. 506
Nos Libertés politiques, by Caudel, *cited*, i. 314 *n.*
Nouvelle Australie, La, by Voisson, ii. 261 *n.*
Nova Scotia, Bicameral Government in, i. 462, ii. 400 *n.*
Novo Nikolaievsk, rapid growth of, ii. 99 *n.* 1
Nursing the Constituency, ii. 482 ; not practised in Switzerland, i. 418

Obstruction, Parliamentary, ii. 188–9, 345–6, 356, 467
O'Connell, Daniel, i. 424
Offences, Familiar, public attitude to, i. 139
Official Candidatures in France, i. 242, 245
Official or Clerical Influence on French Elections, i. 241, 242, 243

Official Dereliction, how dealt with, in France and elsewhere, i. 277–8, 314–5
Official and Legislative Corruption, where found, ii. 508–9 & *n.*, *see also* Corruption *and* Jobbery
Officials
  Choice of, by Appointment, Election, and Nomination, *see also* under each Country
  in Small and Large Communities, Responsibility for, ii. 490
Old Age Pensions in
  Australia, ii. 199
  Great Britain, ii. 290
  New Zealand, ii. 290 & *n.* 1
"Old League, the, of Upper Germany," i. 331, 453
Old Liberals Party of Switzerland, i. 409
Oligarchic Working of Party, U.S.A., ii. 46
Oligarchy and Oligarchies, i. 22
  Aristotle on, i. 185
  Connotations of, i. 15
  Corruption under, ii. 539–40
  Definition of, i. 20
  Democracy compared with, ii. 535, 537 *sqq.*
  Evils of, remedied by Democracy, ii. 562, 563
  Fall of, how caused, i. 26, ii. 540, 549
  Forms of, ii. 549–50
    as Possible for Spanish America, i. 205–6
  of the Future, speculation on, ii. 538
  Ignorance of people an advantage to, i. 70, ii. 541
  of Intellect, ii. 549–50
  Merits and Demerits of, ii. 538–9
  in Monarchy, i. 3, 27 *sqq.*, ii. 542–3
  Party under, i. 111
  Possible rise of, by a Law of Nature, ii. 603–5
  Probable, after attempt at Democracy in a Backward State, ii. 516
  Purity in, ii. 540–1
  Strength of, ii. 489
  "Understandings" in, i. 440–1 *n.* 1
  in Various Countries
    in Brazil, i. 200–1
    Carthage, i. 166
    Chile, i. 193, 201, 204, ii. 537
    Greece, i. 25, 26, 169–70, 181, 184–5
    Southern States, U.S.A., i. 32–3
    Switzerland, i. 35, 329, 427
    Venice (*and see* Italian Cities), i. 70 *n.*, ii. 538, 540
Omar, dictum of, as adapted to Second Chambers, ii. 399 & *n.* 1
One Big Union, Australia, Aims of, Opposition to, ii. 237 *n.*
Ontario
  Churchgoing in, ii. 326
  French Canadians in, i. 457
Open Primaries, U.S.A., ii. 129–30, 131–2
Operation of the Initiative, Referendum, and Recall in Oregon, by Burnett, ii. 142 *n.* 2
Opinion, *see also* Public Opinion
  Monopoly in, Tyranny of, i. 107
  Value of, in relation to Value of Votes, i. 152
Opportunity, Art of Seizing, Instances of, i. 108 & *n.*
Opposition, the
  Australian, Consolidation of, ii. 206
  British, duties of, i. 116
  Canadian, i. 460

Opposition—*continued*
in Democracies, Methods of, ii. 345
　　sqq., 365
in Parliamentary Government, i. 115
Party Discipline in, i. 120–2
Swiss, i. 350, 424
Value of, i. 121–2
Opposition Minority Parties, coalescence
　　of, effect of, i. 414
Optimate Rule in Rome, by whom de-
　　stroyed, ii. 540
Optimism of the Americans and Swiss,
　　i. 445
Orange Free State
Military Organization in, i. 168
Money Power slight in, ii. 254 & *n.*
One of the two best-administered De-
　　mocracies, ii. 458, 464 *n.,*
　　484
Orange Party in Ontario, i. 472
Orators, Athenian, i. 177 & *n.* 2, 179–
　　80, 182
Oratory as means of Political Education,
　　i. 72
Order, *see* Law and Order
Ordres du Jour, in France, i. 257
Oregon
British-American Dispute over, ii. 375
Direct Popular Legislation in, and the
　　outcome, ii. 144 *sqq.*
Organic Laws, France, Amendment of,
　　Method of, i. 232
Organization essential to Rule, ii. 546
Orleanists, the, in France, i. 214, 215,
　　216, 225
Orthodoxy, Political and Theological, i.
　　75
Ostracism, Greek, i. 171, 181
Ostrogorski, M., book by, on Democracy
　　and Party Politics, i. 123
　　n., ii. 33 *n.*
Oxenstierna, *cited,* ii. 542

Paine, T., i. 38 ; Literary Influence of, ii.
　　554
Palais Bourbon, Home of the Chamber of
　　Deputies, i. 236, 306 *n.*
Palestrina, period of, ii. 523 *n.*
Pampas, the, of Argentina, i. 194
Panama, Republic of, i. 187 *n.*
Panama Canal
Repeal of Act concerning, ii. 376
Scandals in France, Political effects of,
　　i. 217, 301
Papal Infallibility and the Swiss Ultra-
　　montanes, i. 408
Papua or New Guinea, Australian admin-
　　istration of, ii. 176, 244 *n.*
Paraguay, Republic of, i. 187 *n.*
Church interests in, i. 191
under Francia, i. 192
Political Level of, i. 192
Population of, Indians in, i. 191 *n.*
War of, losses of population in, i. 191 *n.*
Parents and Old People, Respect for, as
　　Lessened by Democracy, ii.
　　525
Paris
Administrative weight of, i. 220
Centre of Political Thought, i. 19, 296
Class-war outbreaks in, i. 265
Communards of
Insurrection of, 1871, i. 215, 219
Commune of
Delegates from, i. 232
Insurrection of, 1871, i, 215, 219
Regulation of, i. 282
as "Mother of Revolutions," i. 37–8,
　　213, 221, 282, 290
Unable to make one to-day (1920),
　　i. 320

Paris—*continued*
Municipality of, Scandals of, i. 317
Parlement of, and Louis XVI., i. 311
Schools of, mediaeval fame of, i. 211
Paris, Count of, and his Supporters, i.
　　215, 216
Parish, The, in England and New Eng-
　　land, i. 130, 282, ii. 14, 15
Parish Church under Local Control, i. 130
Parish Councils, English, and Dominion,
　　i. 282, ii. 440
Parkes, Sir H., and New South Wales, i.
　　255, ii. 191
Parlement of Paris, and Louis XVI., i.
　　311
Parlements, Provincial, French, i. 280
Parliament and King, Struggle between,
　　in England, i. 28, 52
Parliamentarism, in France, i. 313
Faults of, i. 239
Tendency adverse to, in, i. 291, ii. 342
Parliamentary and Cabinet System of
　　Government in Great Brit-
　　ain, ii. 461, 462–3, 464 *sqq.*
Parliamentary Committee, Great Britain,
　　Powers of Chairmen, ii. 56
Parliamentary Countries
Eloquence in, ii. 553
Leaders in, Emergence of, ii. 555 *sqq.*
Parliamentary Government
in Australia, ii. 176, 451
Legislatures under, Powers of, ii. 462,
　　464–5
Merits and Demerits of, ii. 465 *sqq.*
Parliamentary and Presidential Systems,
　　Common root of, ii. 472
Parliamentary Proceedings, Reporting of,
　　in France, i. 295
Parliamentary System, Adoption of, by
　　New European States, ii.
　　475
Parnell, C. S., i. 424, and Party Disci-
　　pline, ii. 356
Parties, *see* Political Parties, *below, see
　　also under Names*
Partisanship, *see also under Countries*
in Newspapers, i. 96–7 *sqq.*
in Public Speaking, i. 97, 99
Party, i. 111 *sqq.*
Countries in which Overworked, i. 450–
　　1, ii. 46
in Countries with Representative Gov-
　　ernments, functions of, i.
　　113–4, 115
Dissolution into Groups (*q.v.*) of, ef-
　　fect of, i. 121–2
Evils due to, i. 116–9, Mitigated by,
　　i. 119–20
Executive Head Outside in Parliament-
　　ary Governments, ii. 466
How best Serving a Country, i. 128
Inevitability of, i. 119, 122 & *n.*
Irresponsibility of, ii. 110–11, 388
National, Extension of, to Local Elec-
　　tions, i. 117
in Parliament, i. 113 *sqq.*
and the People, Leaders' Duties in re-
　　gard to, ii. 560–1
in Power, Scope of, in Different Coun-
　　tries, i. 115
Preparatory work of, i. 119–20
Publicity and Expenses of, i. 126
Strength of, nature of, ii. 354 ; ad-
　　vantages of, i. 466
Party Chief or Leader
Attitude to, in Switzerland and else-
　　where, i. 409–10
and Foreign Policy, ii. 371
Opinions reacting on, i. 122
Power of, in Democracies, ii. 544–5
Talent rare in, Talleyrand on, ii. 555

Party Control of Party Spirit, i. 127–8

Party Conventions, U.S.A., ii. 129–30

Party Discipline, i. 115, 118 & n., 120
& n., 121, 155
British, ii. 343
Effect of, on Legislatures, ii. 338, 339
Non-existent in French "Groups," i.
254
Objection to, of the Better Educated,
ii. 456
Relative Strictness of, in Great Britain,
France, and U.S.A., ii. 470

Party Funds, i. 114, 126, ii. 484–5
Absence of, in Switzerland, i. 415

Party Loyalty
Canada, i. 473, 493
U.S.A., ii. 40, 135

Party Machine, the U.S.A., i. 494, ii.
94–5, 133, 337, 388
Building up of, ii. 203
Methods of, ii. 495
and Party Organization, ii. 38 sqq.
Powers of, how limited, ii. 72
Public Disgust at, ii. 127–8

Party Managers, functions of
England, i. 114
U.S.A. (see also Boss), ii. 40, 49

Party Obligation, work on, by the author,
i. 120 n.

Party Organization, see also under Countries
Dominance in, of the Few, ii. 545–6
& n., 547
and Independence of Members, ii. 54,
350 sqq.
Influence of, in Local Politics, ii. 441
sqq.
Merits and Defects of, ii. 453
Power of, and Checks on, i. 127–8, ii.
458–9
and Professional Politicians, ii. 458
Responsibility as enforced by, ii. 496
Use made of, in the Countries dealt
with, ii. 467

Party Pledges, ii. 41 & n., 261–2, 455–6

Party Spirit
False estimates of, how arrived at, i.
127
Influence on, of Referendum, ii.
394–5
in Parliamentary and Presidential Governments, ii. 466, 470
and Passive Resistance, i. 118 n.
Powers of, Checks on, i. 127–8
Public Opinion confused by, i. 178–9,
ii. 382–3
Strength of (see also Party Strength of,
above), in Democracies, ii.
453
as Substitute for Thinking, i. 490

Party Strife, Educational aspect of, i.
119

Party System, see also Parties, Party Or-
ganization, etc., etc.
Criticisms on, i. 115 sqq.
Organization of, i. 113 sqq.

Party Ties, Referendum as loosening, ii.
432 n. 2

Party Voting, i. 116–7, 118 & n., 120
& n.
Influence on, of the Referendum, ii. 422

Party Workers, U.S.A., Three Classes of,
ii. 38

"Passive Resistance" and Party Spirit,
i. 118 n.

Pastoralists, Australia, wealth of, ii. 171

Pastors, Swiss, Elections of, for Short
Terms, i. 335

Paternalism, ii. 125, 261, 263, 330

Pathan race, Blood Revenge among, i.
129 n.

Patriotism of Democracies, ii. 178, 218,
245, 259, 562 (see also
under Countries)

Patronage, Political (see also under Coun-
tries), i. 115, 117, 270, 274,
ii. 436
Defects due to, ii. 458
Development of, ii. 577
Possible Remedy for, ii. 343

Payment of Members of Legislatures, i.
175, 250–1, 259, 344, 347,
479, ii. 13, 18, 21, 65, 174
& n., 176, 178, 190, 269,
317, 339, 452, 454

Peace
Conditions favouring in early days of
U.S.A., ii. 5–6
as Ideal of Happiness, ii. 531–2
Not secured by Democracy, ii. 562–3

Peace Treaties 1919, and 1920, as affecting the Status of the Do-
minions, i. 469, ii. 215

Peace of Westphalia and Swiss independence, i. 36

Peasantry, French
Conservatism of, i. 210, 219, 220, 298,
315
Oppression of, 18th Century, i. 212,
results in Class Antagonism,
i. 213

Peasants' Party, in Switzerland, i. 125,
409, ii. 340, 348

Peasants' War in Germany, i. 70

Pedro II., Emperor of Brazil, i. 199

Peel, Sir R., i. 104, 122, 255, 265, ii.
560–1

Pennsylvania
Assembly of, Status of, i. 298
"Boss" power in, ii. 78, 82
Germans in, ii. 5, 25 n.

Penrose, Senator, on Municipal Efficiency
in relation to Politics,
U.S.A., ii. 106 n.

Pensions, see Old Age, and under Countries

People, The, i. 143 sqq.
Direct Election by, to Legislatures, ii.
404
Direct Legislation by, see Direct Popu-
lar Legislation
Faith in, i. 144
Causes for, i. 148 sqq.
Criticisms on, i. 146–7
Origins of, i. 148–9
Majesty of, i. 144
Party system as working among, i.
113 sqq.
Power of
Governments in which acting
Directly, ii. 463–4
by Delegation, ii. 473
Increase in, ii. 566–8
Restrictions on, modern attitude to,
i. 49
as Source of Power, Doctrine of, ii.
599 & n.
Sovereignty of
Basis of Democracy, i. 143, 152, ii.
40, 462
in Australia (q.v.), ii. 173, 176, 182,
263
Embodied in Rigid Constitutions, ii.
11
Fatalistic faith in, results of, ii. 397
in Greek Republics (q.v.), i. 173–4,
185
Methods of exercising, i. 151 & n.,
Criticisms on, and replies to
them, i. 151–3
Not extending to Local affairs in
France, and why, i. 283–4

People—*continued*
  Sovereignty of—*continued*
    Party Organizations' respect for, ii.
      34
    in Switzerland, i. 341 *sqq. passim,
      see also* Initiative *and* Ref-
      erendum
    Working of, in U.S.A. (*q.v.*), ii. 19
      sqq., 51, 92–3, 112, 127–8
  Will of, ii. 548
    Expression of
      in Backward States, ii. 518
      in Communist States, ii. 594 *sqq.*
      by Voting (*q.v.*), i. 145, 159–60,
        161–2, ii. 51–2
      as brought out by Swiss System
        (*q.v.*), ii. 476
    Fallacies concerning, ii. 548 *n.* 2
    Which form of Government best
      gives effect to, ii. 464
    Wisdom ascribed to, i. 143–4, 145–6,
      149, ii. 411; American be-
      lief in, ii. 8, 20, 30, 31, 37,
      60, 96, 100–1, 120, 125,
      141–2, 158, 159, 163–4
People's Non-Partisan League, Dakota, ii.
  136–7
Pericles, i. 172, 180, 181, 182, 183 *n.*,
  184, ii. 456 *n.*
Périer, Casimir, President, on the pow-
  ers of the French President,
  i. 230
Persecution, i. 53 *n.*, 81, 85
Persia
  Corruption in, ii. 516
  Democratic outlook in, ii. 511
  Education in, ii. 502–3
  Monarchy in, i. 25
  National Sentiment in, ii. 516
  Parliamentary Government in, ii. 500,
    failure of, ii. 511
  Religious persecution in, of the Sassa-
    nid Kings, i. 81
Personal Importance, Sense of, Evolution
  of, i. 69 & *n.*, 79
Personality, i. 136, 138–9, 140–1, 158
  of Presidents, Importance of, ii. 471–2
Peru, Republic of, i. 187 *n.*,
  Area and Population of, i. 189 & *n.* 1,
    193, 205
  Church interests in, i. 191
  Political Level of, i. 193
  Wars of, i. 191
Peruzzi, the, loans by, to Edward III., ii.
  538
Peter the Great, Choice by, of Ministers,
  ii. 536
Philadelphia, Misgovernment in, and Re-
  form, ii. 106 & *n.*
Philanthropic Impulse, felt by, in U.S.A.,
  Outcomes of, ii. 126 *sqq.*
Philip of Macedon, i. 170, 182; on the
  Power of Gold, ii. 477,
  480–1
Philip II., ii. 107
Philippine Isles
  Cession of, to U.S.A., ii. 123, 374
  Education in, i. 79
  Literacy and Politics in, i. 73
  Self-Government in, and the Logic of
    Events, ii. 518
  Self-Government for, i. 49, ii. 499
  Prospects of, ii. 515–7
Phocion, i. 172, 180, 182, 183
Phoenician Cities, Tribal Organization
  and Kings of, i. 25
Phoenician Rule in Carthage, i. 166
Picketing, Peaceful, and other, ii. 483 *n.*
Picts, Kings of, i. 25
Pilgrimages, in France, i. 217
Piraeus, port of, i. 175

Pitso, the, of the Bantus and Basutos, i.
  130 & *n.* 1, 371–2 & *n.* 1,
  ii. 503
Pitt, W., i. 265, 424, ii. 471, 560, 561
Pius IX., on the Orleans Flag, i. 215 *n.*
Place-hunting
  Not an active motive in Canada, i.
    472–3, 475
  alleged, in Switzerland, i. 369, 445
Platform-speaking, Increase of, Effects of,
  on Legislatures, ii. 340
Plato, i. 16, 181; on Defects of Greek
  Republics, i. 182, ii. 521;
  on Democracy, i. 13, 185 &
  n. 1; on Formation of Po-
  litical Habits, i. 75; on
  Forms of Government, i.
  165
Pleasure, Passion for, alleged growth of,
  with growth of Civilization,
  ii. 603 *n.*
Plebiscites, French, i. 213–14, 291, ii.
  472 *n.* 3
Plural Voting, absent from Australian
  Commonwealth, ii. 178
Pluto and Plutus, Dante's reference to, ii.
  486 *n.*
Pocket boroughs, ii. 467
  Abolition of, ii. 486
Poic merit of, ii. 556
Poincaré, Raymond, on the burdens of
  French deputies, i. 258 *n.* 2
Poland
  Causes arresting Democracy in, i. 39
  Executive Head of State in, ii. 462
  New State of, ii. 575
  Rulers of, ii. 536
Poles in German Empire, Status of, i. 145
Police forces, *see also under Countries*
  Central or Local Control of, ii. 439
Policy, Traditions of, i. 138–9
Polish Party in
  Austria, i. 124
  Germany, ii. 347
Polish Revolution (1848–50), British
  sympathy with, ii. 377
Political Action
  Advantages of, over Strikes, ii.
    568–9
  by Labour and Socialist Parties, ii.
    568–9, 572
Political Agents, rare, in Switzerland, i.
  425
Political Assassination, Press Advocacy
  of, i. 94
Political Associations, *see* Parties *and*
  Party Organizations
Political Changes, causes of, ii. 564 *sqq.*
Political Chief, Mexico, Functions of, i.
  202
Political Community, meaning discussed,
  i. 20–1
Political Education
  Factors of, *see* Local Self-Government,
    Newspapers, Orators, Press,
    Reading, Schools, Universi-
    ties, etc.
  Greek, i. 71–2
  Modern, i. 72–3
Political Equality, defined, i. 60
  Faith in, in U.S.A., Defects and Suc-
    cesses due to, summarized,
    ii. 157 *sqq.*
  Gain from, ii. 568–9
  Greek passion for, i. 169, 172
  and Natural Inequality, i. 65–7
  No Means of testing Fitness for, i. 63
Political Force, Attempt to estimate, ii.
  544
Political Institutions, Influence of, on
  Individuals, ii. 529 *sqq.*

Political Jobbery, see Jobbery, see also Lobbying and Political Patronage
Political Labour Leagues, in Australia, ii. 207, 210
Political Leaders, see Leaders
Political Leadership, Evolved from Social, ii. 504–5
Political Liberty, i. 52, 54
  Relations of, with other forms of Liberty, i. 55 sqq., 149
  Value to, of Individual Liberty, i. 59
Political Morality, U.S.A., ii. 100, 108
Political Organizations, see Party Machine and Party Organization, above
Political Orthodoxy, i. 75
Political Parties (see also under Names, and see Parties under Countries), i. 111 sqq.
  Book on, by Michiels, cited, ii. 546 n., 547 n. 1, 558 n. 2
  Continuity of, how retained, i. 112–3
  Future of, i. 122 & n.
  Labour (q.v.), or Class, i. 123–4, 125
  Legalization of, in the Russian Duma, i. 127
  Loyalty to, i. 111, 113 & n.
  Multiplication of (see also Groups), i. 125, ii. 347 sqq., 468
  New
    Local or Racial, i. 124
    Religious or Ecclesiastical, and the reverse, i. 123
    Strength of the former, i. 126
    Socialist or Communist (q.v.), i. 125
  Old
    Disruption of, i. 122, 125
    Scope and Type of, i. 111 sqq.
  Organization essential to, i. 126
  Origins of, i. 111–2
  Reasons for existence of, i. 112
  Representative Governments all worked by, ii. 462
  Types of Men distinguishable in, i. 126
  Value of, i. 122 & n.
  Vigour of, Four Forces conducing to, i. 112–3 & n.
Political Patronage, see Patronage, above and under Countries
Political Propaganda, cost of, i. 126
Political Science, i. 10
  Chief Contributions to, by the U.S.A., ii. 27
Political Sectionalism, effect on, of Popular Voting, ii. 427
Political Terms, Difference in, from Scientific, i. 15
Political Virtue, Traditions of, soon forgotten, i. 141
Politicians
  Character in, i. 139, ii. 557 & n.
  Considerations controlling, i. 105
  Education of, General Level of, in Australia, ii. 190, 212–3
  Failure of, Chief Cause of, ii. 366
  Highest and rarest quality among, i. 162
  Opportunities of, for Influence, as compared with that of the Press, i. 104
Politics
  Action on, of Economics, i. 196, 204, 205–7
  Few who take interest in, whence, Rule by the Few, ii. 549
  Indifference to, Examples of, and possible recrudescence of, ii. 599 sqq., see also Civic Apathy

Politics—continued
  Interest in, will it last?, ii. 599 sqq.
  Money the sinews of, i. 127
  Practical, Training of, in knowledge of Human Nature, i. 16–7
  Professionalism in, i. 259, 260, ii. 77 n. 2, 453–4, 458
  Religion as Influencing, i. 80 sqq., 112, 141, ii. 507
    and the Formation of Groups, ii. 347–8
  Rooted in Psychology, i. 15
  Secret Societies and, i. 321
  Terms in, associations of, i. 4, 15
  Why not a Science, i. 14
Polity of the Athenians, by Aristotle, i. 172 n. 1
Polytechnikum, at Zürich, i. 368
Polytheism, i. 81
Poorer Classes, Exploitation of, a Danger in Backward States, ii. 508
Popes, the, conflict of, with Secular Rulers, i. 83
Popular Assembly, Government by (see also each form of Assembly), ii. 461
Popular Choice of Leaders, ii. 550–1
Popular Constitutional Initiative, see Initiative
Popular Control of Foreign Affairs, demand for, ii. 367, 383
Popular Demonstrations in France, i. 292
Popular Election by the Whole Nation, or by an Assembly, discussed, ii. 472 & n. 2
Popular Government, see People, the, Direct Legislation by, Sovereignty of, Will of, etc. under People above, also Initiative and Referendum
  Defects observable in, ii. 446, 452–4
  Executive as the weak point in, discussed, ii. 358 sqq.
  Facts and Forces
    Creative of, i. 24 sqq.
    Retardative, or Arresting, i. 38–41
    in General, observations on, i. 8 sqq.
    Mental and Moral Coefficients affecting, ii. 446, 454 sqq.
  Origins of, i. 129–31
  Progress of, in the Modern World, i. 27 sqq.
  Realities of, how best studied, i. 16
  Salient Features of those considered, ii. 446, 447 sqq.
Popular Government, by Maine, cited, i. 187–8, 390 & n.
Popular Government, its Essence, its Permanence, and its Perils, by Ex-President W. H. Taft, cited, ii. 88 n., 89 n., 152 n.
Popular House, Countries in which Ministers are controlled by, ii. 401
Popular Opinion and Popular Government, by A. L. Lowell, ii. 78 n.
Popular Powers, Negative character of, ii. 550–1
Popular Representation, Equal and Disproportioned, instance of, i. 232
Popular Self-Government
  Early, i. 129–30
  Functions retained by, i. 130
Popular Sovereignty, see People, Sovereignty of, above
Population-quality, change in, as affecting Traditions, i. 140

Populations
  Best fitted to exercise Self-Government,
    Characteristics of, ii. 503
  Large and at Different Levels, Public
    Opinion weak in, ii. 507-8,
    514-5
Populists, U.S.A., ii. 42
"Pork Barrel, the," i. 499 n. 1, ii. 63
    & n., 295 n. 1
Portugal
  a Democracy, i. 22, ii. 575
  Executive Head of State in, ii. 462
  Second Chamber in, Indirect Election
    to, ii. 401
  Socialism in, Anti-religious colour of,
    ii. 571
  Suffrage in, i. 21
  Ties with, of Brazil, advantages of, i.
    200
Portuguese America, see Latin America
Postgate, R. W., book by, on Bolshevism,
    cited, ii. 582 sqq.
Poverty, a Safeguard of Democracy, ii.
    448-9, 457-8, 484-5
Power
  Concentration of, Essential to Effi-
    ciency, ii. 546-7
  Derived from the People, doctrine of,
    in abeyance, ii. 599 & n.
  Long Possession of, and Staleness, ii.
    276
  Passing to the Few, ii. 264, 546-7,
    549-51
  Width of, in Communist States, ii.
    594-5
  Worship of, i. 144
Practical Forces, Creative of Popular
    Government, i. 24 sqq.
Precedent, English reliance on, i. 311-
    12
Prefects, French, i. 213, 235, 242-3 & n.,
    276, 277, 281, 315
Prefectural Council, France, i. 276
Preferential Majority Voting for Senators,
    Australia, results of, ii. 188
    n. 1
Preferential Primaries, U.S.A., ii. 70 n. 3
"Preferential" Voting, in Australian
    States, ii. 183
Presbyterianism, origin and nature, i,
    84
President, or Presidents, see also under
    Countries
President of the Council, France, choice
    by, of Cabinet Ministers, i.
    261-2
President of French Chamber of Deputies,
    Functions of, i. 245
Presidential Election, in various Coun-
    tries, ii. 472 & n. 3
Presidential Primaries, U.S.A., ii. 545
Presidential System
  Cabinets in, ii. 462-3
  Demerits of, ii. 468-9, 494-5
  Distinctive quality of, ii. 475
  Legislatures in, ii. 463
  Merits of, ii. 470
  Responsibility in U.S.A., Chain of, ii.
    493 sqq.
  States favouring, ii. 475
  in U.S.A., and other States, ii. 461,
    464 & n. 1
Presidents
  Dictatorship of, i. 203, see also under
    Latin-American Republics
  of French "Groups," small authority
    of, i. 254
  Party influence and, ii. 466
  Status and functions of, ii. 468, 469,
    471, 472
  Checks on, ii. 468, 471

Press, the, see also Journalism, News-
    papers and Press, under
    Countries
  Agent of Political Purity, ii. 480-81,
    487
  Attitude of, to
    Spanish-American affairs in 1898,
      and to
    Transvaal affair, 1899, i. 100 & n.
  in a Democracy, i. 72-3, 92 sqq., 103-
    4, 105, 108-9
  Freedom of, i. 58, 92-3
  Influence of, on
    Democracy, Summary, i. 108-10
    Foreign Policy, i. 100, 109, 297, ii.
      370-71
    Politicians, favourable or otherwise,
      ii. 556-7
    Politics, in regard to Decline in
      Legislature, ii. 338-9, 340
    Voters, i. 119
  Invaluable Services of, i. 109-10
  Irresponsibility of, i. 105, 109, 110
  Monopoly, danger of, i. 107-8
  Public confidence in, i. 103, 109
  Public opinion as ascertained from, i.
    156
  Relative Authority of, i. 106
  Subornation and Control of, by Money
    Power, etc., i. 93-4, ii. 454,
    457-8, 483-4, 486
Priesthood, Roman Catholic, not a Caste,
    or Oligarchy, i. 83-4
Primaries, U.S.A.
  Closed, ii. 130, 131-2
  Direct, ii. 130-1 & n.
  Open, ii. 131
  Unofficial, ii. 131
Primary Assemblies, Safeguards on, ii.
    391
Prime Ministers, Personality and Status
    of, as compared with those
    of Presidents, ii. 471-2
Primrose League, the, i. 123 n.
Prince, The, by Machiavelli, Burd's edi-
    tion, cited, ii. 558 n. 2
Prince Imperial, the, and his Supporters,
    i. 214-5, effect on them of
    his death, i. 216, 291
Private Bills in
  France, i. 301
  Great Britain, ii. 79, 337, 343, 492
    n. 2
  U.S.A., i, 301, ii. 58 & n., 79 & n.,
    80
Private Opinion, divergent from Public
    Opinion, i. 155
Private Property
  Dominion action as to, see Land, etc.,
    under each Dominion
  and Economic Equality, i. 38, 66-7, ii.
    579
  Gospel teaching on, i. 86
  Insecurity of, U.S.A., ii. 155
  Views on, of
    Communists, ii. 570, 579, 587 & nn.,
      591
    Democrats, i. 38, 48, 66-7
    First French Revolutionists, i. 218
      n. 2
    French Peasantry, i. 219
Problems of To-day, by Storey, ii. 294 n.
Proceedings of Massachusetts Constitu-
    tional Convention, on Initia-
    tive, etc., ii. 147 n.
Procureur-Général, French, i. 272
Professional Classes
  Australian, Opinions and Interests of,
    ii. 247-8
  French, Influence of, on Politics, i. 288,
    298

Professional Politicians, i. 259, 260, ii. 77 *n*. 2, 453-4, 458
  Non-Existent in
    British Dominions, ii. 452
    Switzerland, i. 496, ii. 454
  Not necessarily made by Payment, i. 259
  Rise of, Causes leading to, ii. 454, 458
Progress and Poverty, by Henry George, long-lasting Influence of, ii. 554-5
Progressives, U.S.A., ii. 42
Prohibition, *see under Countries*
Proletarian Dictatorship, ii. 574, 579
Proletariate, the, the Communistic Ideal, ii. 570
  Early equivalent of People, i. 148
  Revolution theory, ii. 579 & *n*. 2
Propaganda, Dangers of, i. 155, ii. 459-60, 483-4
Property, *see Private Property, above*
Property Qualifications for Voters, i. 29, 32, 33, 63 & *n*. 1, 64 ; Aristotle on, i. 183 *n*. 1; in Australia, ii. 176 ; in Belgium, i. 63 & *n*. 1, 153
Proportional Representation in Various Countries, i. 153 *n.*, 198 *n.* 2, 340, 409 *n.*, 413-14, 444, ii. 50-1, 183, 188 & *n*. 1, 278
Prosecutions, in
  Greek Republics, i. 174, 178 & *n.*, ii. 392
  U.S.A., ii. 439
Prosperity, Stabilizing effect of, i. 195
Protection, Views on, in Various Lands, i. 471, ii. 203, 204, 205, 217, 222 *sqq.*, 287-8 & *n.*, 297-8
Protestant Ideas on
  Divine Right of Kings, i. 84
  Equality, i. 90-1
Proudhon, P. J., French followers of, i. 290; on the Human desire to be governed, ii. 548 *n*. 2 ; on Private Property, ii. 587
Provincial Newspapers, French and British, Characteristics of, i. 295
Prussia
  Acquiescence of, in Bismarck's rule, ii. 600
  Class Distinctions in, i. 60-1
  Militarism, the Ideal of, i. 137-8
  Liberals, of, Conflict of, with Bismarck, i. 39
  Monarchical Oligarchy in, ii. 538 & *n*. 2
  Efficiency secured by, ii. 539, 541
  Monarchy of, Theoretical and Practical, ii. 538 & *n*. 1
  Refusal in, of Electoral reforms, i. 40
Prytany, the, i. 173, 174
Psalms, the, Ideals in, of Happiness, ii. 531
Psychology
  of Habit, i. 135
  in relation to Politics, i. 15
Public Bills, U.S.A., ii. 58
Public Conduct, Ideals of, how inculcated and reinforced, i. 135 *sqq.*
Public Duty, the first, ii. 490, *see also* Civic Sense, *under Countries*
Public Elementary Education in England, Establishment and Extension of, i. 70, 71
Public Elementary Schools, Civic Education in, i. 76
Public Franchises, U.S.A., ii. 80

Public Health, ii. 529
Public Honesty, Want of, ii. 452-3
Public Institutions, Central or Local Administration of, ii. 438-9
Public Lands, Problem of, throughout the ages, ii. 222, 286
Public Life
  Abstention from, etc., *see* Civic Apathy
  Best Men not recruited for, in Democracies, ii. 180, 189, 204, 243, 331, 344, 455-6, 560, 562
  Improvement of, in Democracies, ii. 366, *see also under Countries*
  Tone of, Formative Agencies, i. 305, ii. 487
  Traditions of, still active in England and France, ii. 180
  Vulgarization of, Causes of, ii. 456
Public Manners, ii. 338-9, 436
Public Meetings as Guides to Public Opinion, i. 155
Public Offices, and the Spoils System (*q.v.*), i. 117
Public Opinion (*see also under Countries*), i. 151 *sqq.*
  Action of, on
    Class Antagonisms, i. 158
    Class Selfishness, ii. 580-1
    the Few, ii. 544
    International Politics, i. 158 *n., see also* Press influence on Foreign Policy
    Party (*q.v.*), i. 118 & *n.*, 119
  Chief Defect of, i. 162
  Civic Centres of, ii. 437
  Comparative force of, ii. 456
  Continuous Operation of, i. 154-5, 160, 161-2
  Definition of, i. 153
  Examples of, i. 154
  Growth of, i. 156
  Homogeneity as creating, ii. 502
  How best Ascertained, i. 156-7
  Makers of, i. 287, 288
    Exceptions to, in France, i, 287, 288
  Ministerial perception of, i. 155, 161
  Numbers essential to formation of, ii. 506 *n.*
  Oscillations of, ii. 364-5
  and Publicity, Chief Arms of a Democracy, ii. 487
  Sole effective restraint over Money Power, ii. 483-4
  Strength of, ii. 416
    How to Gauge, i. 156
    in Small Communities, i. 504
  Talk as Formative of, i. 72, 296
  Value of, ii. 456
  Vigilance of, in Small Communities, ii. 448-9
  Wise, Formation of Conditions requisite for, i. 152, 162
Public Opinion and Popular Government, by Lowell, ii. 421 *n.*
Public and Private Ownership of Transportation, pros and cons of, ii. 234
Public Service Commissioners and Assistants, functions of, New Zealand, ii. 281
Public Service Commissions, in Australian States, ii. 195
Public Services, *see under Countries, see also* State Activities, *under Countries*
Public Speaking, influence of, relative to that of Newspapers, i. 96, 99, 104-5

Public Spirit, i. 78
  as Guarantee of Political Purity, ii. 486
Public Utilities, ownership of, Constituting a Democracy, i. 23 n.
Public Works, Construction of, Local or Central, ii. 438
Publicity, see also Press
  Essential to Responsibility, ii. 507
  and Party, i. 127
  Passion for, in U.S.A., ii. 119
  and Public Opinion, Chief Arms of a Democracy, ii. 487
Puerto Rico, cession of, to U.S.A., ii. 374
Puritans
  Democratic ideas of, i. 28
  English, influence of, on the New England mind, i. 33
  Grievances of, i. 29
  Individualism of, as operating in U.S.A., ii. 7–8
Purse, the, Oligarchies of, ii. 549
"Push, The," in New Zealand, ii. 314

Quebec Province
  French Inhabitants of, Characteristics of, i. 457, 458, 466–8
  Legislature of, i. 462
    Second Chamber of, ii. 400 n.
  and Prohibition, i. 471 & n.
Queensland
  Legislature of, ii. 176–7
  Railways in, ii. 233
  Referendum in, applications of, ii. 185 & n., 262 n.
  Religion only Political factor in, ii. 206 n.
  Self-Government set up in, ii. 172
  State Insurance Office in, ii. 234 n.
  Sugar Subvention in, ii. 224
  Voting Methods in, ii. 183
Questions in Parliament, ii. 465, 487, 492
Questions for a Reformed Parliament, i. 30 n. 1

Race, Influence of, on
  Formation of "Groups," ii. 347
  Manners, ii. 524
Race Difference
  in Canada, effects of, i. 159, 457, 464, 469–70, 472, 488, 502, 506, 508
  as affecting Public Opinion, i. 159
Race Factor, the, ii. 523
Race Fusion, Problem of, i. 209 & n. 2, ii. 605
Racial Admixture in U.S.A., Early Days, ii. 5
Racial Divisions, and Party, i. 111, 124
Racially-distinct subjects, are they The People?, i. 145
Radical Democrat, typical, Political Creed of (1830–70), ii. 145
Radical Group, in House of Commons, 1870–80, i. 253 n. 2
Radical Party, Switzerland, i. 414–5
Radicalism, Shades in, i. 125
Radicals, French, i. 236, 290
Railways, see under each Country
Raison d'État, in France, i. 310
Ranke, L. von, i. 324, ii. 522
Reading, i. 78
  as Substitute for Thinking, i. 72, 157
Realism, Nations showing, i. 447
Reason, the Age of, i. 46
"Recall," the American, ii. 141, 149 sqq., 449, 493, 496
  Swiss parallel to, i. 338
"Red Feds," New Zealand, ii. 316

Redistribution of Seats
  Australia, ii. 183
  Great Britain, i. 30, 31
Reed, T. B., and the U.S.A. Speakership, ii. 57
Re-Elections, Countries favouring, see Australia, Switzerland, and U.S.A.
Reeves, Rt. Hon. Pember, book by, on State Experiments in Australasia, ii. 283 n., 299
Referendum (see also Initiative), i. 49, ii. 399 & n. 2, 493 (see specially Chap. XXIX. Vol. I. and Chap. LXV. Vol. II.)
  in Australia, ii. 175, 182 n., 185, 218
  Canada and, i. 484
  Demand for, Support essential to, ii. 429 & n.
  in Esthonia, ii. 399 & n. 2
  in Large Populations, Difficulties of, ii. 432, 576
  Nature of, i. 152, 160, 373, 437
  in New Zealand, ii. 315
  Non-existent in France, i. 238
  Possibilities of, in
    Legislation, ii. 355
    Municipal Matters, ii. 426
  in Switzerland, i. 338–9, 348, 355, 363, 371 sqq., 403, 410, 412 sqq., ii. 142, 410, 417 sqq., 440, 449, 463 n. 2, 464, 473, 475, 493, 576 (see also Ch. XXIX. Vol. I. and Ch. LXV. Vol. II.)
  Cantonal, i. 373–4 sqq.
  Circumstances conducing to its Success, i. 449–50
  Cost, i. 379
  Creation of, i. 373
  Deductions from, i. 384
  Demand for, ii. 429 & n.
  Working of, i. 374 sqq., 421, 442
    Application to entry into League of Nations, i. 436–8 & n.
    Effect on Party, ii. 421–2
    Matters submissible to, ii. 419, 420
    Matters withheld from, i. 374, 375 & n. 2, 376, 399, 405 n. 1
    Obligatory, i. 392 n., 400, ii. 530
      at Zurich, i. 391
    Optional, i. 375, 381, 392, 400
    Voting for, i. 380 sqq., 422
      Polling of Voters, i. 379 & n. 1, 380, 391, 396, 398, 416–7, 422, ii. 421 & n. 2, 434
    Tendencies revealed by, i. 387 sqq.
    Two deductions from, i. 383–4
  as Tests of Popular fitness for Government, ii. 422–3
  in U.S.A., i. 387 n. 1, 388, 393, ii. 140 sqq., 337, 342, 417, 419, 422, 449–50, 463 n. 2
    Exempted subjects, ii. 142
    Results, ii. 142, 143 & n. 1, 144 sqq.
  Use made of (see also under Countries above), ii. 419, 420
  Restrictions on, Suggested, ii. 430 & n. 2
  Value of, ii. 425 sqq.
Referendum, Le, by Curti, i. 373 n.
Reform in Canada, why apparently flagging, i. 490
Reform, The, of Legal Procedure, by M. Storey, ii. 453 n. 1
Reform Acts, British, i. 29 sqq., ii. 486, 532, 540, 557 n.
  No Keen Popular Demand for, i. 30, 31
Reform Party, New Zealand, ii. 277, 285

Reformers
Philosophers as, i. 16
Revolt of, dual Nature of, i. 84
Reforms
English method of making, i. 311–12, 323
U.S.A., see under U.S.A.
Regency, the, Morals during, i. 325
Regierungs Rath, Swiss, i. 338
Regionalism, French, i. 264, 267, 285
Regionalist Party, Catalonia, i. 124
Regulus, self-devotion of, i. 136
Reichstag, the, Parties in, Multiplication of, ii. 347 & n.; and Popular Control, i. 39
Reid, Sir G. H., ii. 191, 211, on Rudeness in N.S. Wales Legislature, ii. 191 n.
Religion, see also under Countries
and the formation of Groups, ii. 347
underlying Impulse of, i. 144
Influence of, in Politics, i. 80 sqq., 111, 140–1, ii. 507
Religious Beliefs, Roman attitude to, i. 81
Religious Intolerance in Spain, i. 137
Religious Liberty, i. 52, 54
and the English Puritans, i. 58
Relations with other forms of Liberty, i. 55 sqq.
Religious Orders, i. 80–1
Swiss Laws on, i. 343, 435
Religious Struggles in England and France, contrasted, i. 311–12
Vitalizing Influence of, ii. 599
Religious Teaching in Schools
Australia, ii. 200, 202
Canada, i. 470
New Zealand, ii. 278–9, 317
Renan, E., i. 324
Reporter, the, in French Chamber of deputies, i. 246
Representation, Parliamentary
Origin of, ii. 350 & n.
Various views of, ii. 350 sqq.
Representative Assemblies
Domination of, by Party, Australia, ii. 173
and Responsibility, ii. 495
Safeguards on, ii. 391
Representative Character of Second Chamber, authority derived from, ii. 406
Representative Governments
Anticipations from, ground for, ii. 341
Leading Examples of, ii. 335, 336
Points to consider in regard to, ii. 464 sqq.
Types of, ii. 461 sqq.
Features of
Common, ii. 461–2
Distinctive, ii. 462–4
Unknown in Greek Republics, i. 167 & n. 3
Representative Institutions, why Essential, ii. 344
Representatives, Parliamentary (see also Members, under Legislatures under Countries), Status and Duties of, ii. 351 sqq.
Parliamentary
Choice of, ii. 506
Payment of, see under Countries
Unpaid, in Chile, i. 194
"Reptile Press," German, i. 93, 103
Republic, not identical with Democracy, i. 22
Republican Party
France, i. 85, 253, 266, 268, 290, 295, 340

Republican Party—continued
U.S.A., i. 124, ii. 42 n. 1, 43, and Tammany, ii. 105 & n.
Republics
Ancient, see also Athens, and Greek Republics, i. 165 sqq.
Bellicosity of, ii. 361
Eloquence in, ii. 553–4
Ferocity of Dispute in, ii. 252–3
Modern Governments, Modelled on, i. 3
New European, see under Europe
Spanish American, i. 187 & n., sqq., and see Latin America
Reservation of Subjects from Legislatures, i. 386–7, 389
Responsibility
Chain of, ii. 490 sqq.
in Democracies (see also under Countries), Basis of, ii. 489 sqq.
Enforcement of, ii. 495 sqq., 507
Individual, ii. 489–90, 495
under Parliamentary Government, ii. 463 & n. 1, 466
Principle of, Nature of, ii. 590–1
and Publicity, ii. 507
and State Business Activities, ii. 577
under which System best secured?, ii. 470–2
Revenge, Spirit of, in Modern Democracies, ii. 580
Revenue, Raising of, controlled by Lower Houses, ii. 462
Reverence, decay of, and possible reappearance of, i. 68–9
Revolutionary Movements, present-day (1920–21), i. 5, ii. 448
Revolutions (see also French, and Spanish-American Republics)
Aims of, ii. 504
Continental, Anti-religious Character of, how evoked, i. 85
Democracy the best guarantee against, in U.S.A., ii. 164; but not rendering impossible, ii. 562–3
Economics as extinguishing, i. 195–6
European, ii. 567
British Sympathies with, ii. 377
Habits of Thought and Action engendered by, i. 322 & n., 323
of North America, and the Revolutionary War, i. 32, 33, 85, ii. 4, 8, 11
of the Proletariate, ii. 579 & n. 2
Revue politique de l'École Libre des Sciences Politiques, articles in, i. 289 n.
Rewards in relation to Efficiency, ii. 442 n., 485, 491
Rich, the,
in Australia, Opinions and Interests of, ii. 180, 181, 189, 190, 212, 246
and Poor Parties of, Ancient and evolving, i. 124, 125
and Taxation, i. 178 n.
Richelieu, Cardinal, and the French Civil Service, i. 274
Riddell, Mr. Justice, book by, on the Canadian Constitution, i. 462 n., 483 n.
Right to Work, Claim of, ii. 569, in New Zealand, ii. 316
Rights of Individuals, problem of, i. 54
Rights of Man (see also Natural Rights), Doctrine of, American and French Declarations on, i. 33, 218 n. 2, unheard of, in the Ancient World, i. 26

Rigid Constitutions, ii. 10–11, 21, 391, 462
  Position of Judiciaries under, ii. 384–5
  Restrictions involved in, ii. 396
Rings, in Politics
  Canada, i. 475
  Switzerland (rare), i. 444
  U.S.A., ii. 78, 98, 102–3 *sqq.*, 130, 138
Rise and Growth of American Politics, by Prof. H. J. Ford, ii. 38 *n.*
Risorgimento, the Italian, heroes of, ii. 520
Rittinghausen, —, doctrines of, i. 402 *n.*
Robespierre, significance of his Sobriquet, ii. 477
Roman Catholic Church in
  Australia, ii. 199, 200, 206, 244
  Belgium, i. 88
  Canada (*q.v.*), i. 88, 458 & *n.*, 467, 475
  Latin America, i. 191, 199
  U.S.A., ii. 114
Roman Catholic Emancipation, ii. 539
Roman Catholicism and Buddhism, resemblances of, i. 82
Roman Law
  followed by French Canadians, i. 458
  Influence of, in France, i. 310
  Never adopted in Britain, i. 313
Roman Parallel to Boss rule in U.S.A., ii. 102
Roman Writers, period of the most illustrious, ii. 522 & *n.*
Romans
  Characteristics of, i. 10, 447
Rome
  Ancient, Imperial, and Republican, i. 182
  Caesarism in, i. 322, ii. 336
  Class Distinctions in, i. 60
  Comitia of, i. 130, 337
  Conduct of Foreign affairs in, ii. 74 *n.*
  Constitution of, i. 166
  Corruption in, i. 139, 177 *n.* 1, ii. 477, 480 & *n.*, 484
  Decay of Tradition in, Causes of, i. 140
  Democracy never thoroughgoing in, i. 26
  Devotion to the State in, instances of, i. 136
  Eloquence in, ii. 553
  Empire of, ii. 600
    Provincial disturbances in, by Military Adventurers, i. 264
  Faithfulness in, to Tradition, i. 140
  Legislature of, Balances to, ii. 391, 392
  Oligarchy of, ii. 538
    Why broken down, i. 26–7
  Republic of
    Demoralised by Money Power, ii. 484–5
    Fall of, results to Self-Government, i. 26–7
    Land Problems of, ii. 222
    Law of, resemblances to, of English Common Law, i. 502
    Voting Methods of, i. 145–6
  Republic of—*continued*
    Women's Freedom under, ii. 251
    Working of, i. 440–1
    Senate of, Counterbalances to, ii. 392
    and Foreign relations, ii. 371, 538–9
    Power of, basis of, ii. 407 & *nn.*
  Slavery in, i. 167
  and the Theory of Popular Sovereignty, ii. 417
Romano-Germanic Emperor, republics under sway of, i. 35, 36

Romansch Language, i. 330 & *n.*
Roosevelt, President T., on "Malefactors of Great Wealth," ii. 110 ; Personality of, i. 104, ii. 472
Root, Senator E., book by, on Government and Constitution of America, ii. 12 *n.* 2, 152 *n.*
Rosas, President, rule of, in Argentina, i. 192, 194, 195
Roscher, W., i. 13
Rossignol and Stewart, book by, *cited,* on New Zealand Affairs, ii. 280 & *n., et passim, in notes*
Rotorua Geyser Region, New Zealand, Nationalization of, ii. 295
Round Table, The, cited, ii. 237 *n.*
Rousseau, Jean Jacques, i. 6, 38 ; and Christianity, i. 90 ; on Direct Popular Government, i. 372 ; and the Doctrine of Popular Sovereignty, ii. 417 ; on Censorship of Literature, ii. 590 ; on "Common Will," ii. 547–8 & *n.;* Communal Spirit expected by, ii. 606 ; Influence of, i. 36, 46, 85, 434, ii. 554–5 ; on Non-existence of a true Democracy, ii. 548 *n.* 2 ; on Popular Government, i. 372, 393 *n.;* on Public Services and private advantage therefrom, i. 260 *n.*
Royal Irish Constabulary, ii. 439
Royalists, French, *see also* Monarchist
  loss of Ground by, i. 216
Ruchonnet, —, i. 350
Rulers, real (*see also* Few), Fewness of, ii. 542
Rumania, Democratic backwardness in, ii. 567
Rural Local Authorities, i. 132, *see also* Parish, Town, etc.
Rural Police, absence of, in U.S.A., ii. 91, 156
Rurales, the, in Mexico, i. 202
Russia
  Present Day (1921)
    Administrative Cruelty persisting in, under New Rule, ii. 532
    Anarchism in, ii. 571
    Bolshevism in, ii. 582–3
    Communists in, ii. 587 *n.*, View of, on the Average Man, i. 65
    Compulsory Labour in, Trotsky's defence of, ii. 574 *n.* 2
    Corruption in (and under Tsarist rule), i. 139, 325, ii. 453, 477, 480, 508–9, 540
    "Democracy" in, i. 11, 73
    Size of country in regard to, ii. 507, 514
    Unfitness for, example of, ii. 513
    Education in, i. 73, 79, ii. 502–3
    Government Censorship in, ii. 590
    Industrial Unions in, ii. 583
    "Intelligentsia" in, ii. 506 *n.*
    the Mir in, i. 130
    National Sentiment in, ii. 516
    Orthodox Church in (1920), i. 88
    and Persia, ii. 511–2
    Plutocratic influence slight in, ii. 538 *n.* 2
    Press and Ministerial relations in, i. 103
    Productive Capacity of, i. 209 *n.* 1
    Proletarian Dictatorship in, ii. 579 & *nn.*
    Revolution in, and after, ii. 501–2

Russia—*continued*
  Present Day—*continued*
    Self-Government for, i. 5
    Pessimistic view on, ii. 515–6
    Socialism in, Anti-religious tone of,
      ii. 571
    Soviets and Soviet Rule in, ii. 474,
      500–1, 580 & n., 582–4
  Tsarist
    Bureaucracy in, ii. 372, 538, *and see*
      Corruption, *above*
    Civil Service of, ii. 360–1
    Corruption in, *see above*
    Finance under, i. 314
    Foreign policy of, and the outcome,
      ii. 372, 380–1
    Monarchy (*Autocratic*) in, ii. 377,
      535, 536
      Fall of, i. 5, ii. 380–1, 500, 501
  Russo-Turkish War of 1876, British Pub-
    lic Opinion on, ii. 378–9

Safety against External Attack, as se-
    cured by Democracy, ii. 527,
    528
St. Augustine, i. 87, 108 n.
St. Gothard Railway, Political Importance
    of, to Switzerland, i. 412
    n. 2
St. Paul, i. 61, 108 n.
St. Thomas Aquinas, i. 108 n., 393 n.
St. Thomas of Canterbury, i. 83
Saladin, i. 25
Salamis, Battle of, ii. 499
Salaries of Officials, (*see also* Payment of
    Members of Legislatures),
    various ranks in various
    Lands, *and see under Official
    Classes*, i. 275, 361, ii. 14,
    16, 156, 200
Salvador, Republic of, i. 187 n.
    Political Level of, i. 192
Samoa, Western, New Zealand's Mandate
    for, ii. 313
San Domingo, Republic of, i. 187 n.
    U.S. influence in, i. 192
San Francisco
    Boss and Ring rule in, ii. 105
    Civic Amenities neglected in, ii. 278
      n. 1
San Marino, ii. 503 n.
San Martin, i. 192, 193
Sand, George, on Diffusion of Talent in
    France, i. 323
"Scabs," ii. 237
Schérer, E., on Democracy as producing
    Mediocrity, i. 323
Schiller, J. C. F., von, i. 447, ii. 522, 568
Schlesinger, M., *cited*, ii. 567 & n.
Scholefield, G., book by, on New Zealand,
    ii. 283 n.
School Committees, U.S.A., ii. 15
School-Teachers, *see* Teachers, *under
    Countries*
Schwytz, Democracy of, i. 35
Science
    Democracy in relation to, ii. 519 *sqq.*
    Physical, Swift Advance in, ii. 564
Scotland
    Government institutions in, pre-Union,
      ii. 396 n.
    Kings of, i. 25
    Political *fainéants* in, i. 157
Scoto-Irish Stock in U.S.A., ii. 4
Scottish Provincial Newspapers, Com-
    pared with French, i. 295
Scottish Traits in New Zealanders, ii.
    325–6
"Scratching" at U.S.A. Elections, ii. 49
"Scrutateurs," Swiss, i. 345
Scrutin d'arrondissement, i. 182 n., 241

Scrutin de liste, i. 182 n., 216 n., 241
Secession, War of, in U.S.A., *see* War of
    Secession
Second Ballot Act, New Zealand, repeal
    of, ii. 318 n.
Second Chambers, *see also* Senates, *under
    Countries, and below*
    British Example followed in, ii. 398–9
    as Checks on Popular Government, i.
      21, ii. 393–4, 398 *sqq.*, 416
    Creation of
      Conditions preventing, ii. 416
      Methods of, ii. 399 *sqq.*, 413–4
    Desiderata in, ii. 412 *sqq.*
    Direct Election to, Drawbacks of, ii.
      402–3
    Directly formed, ii. 406
    in Federal States, ii. 400
    Functions and Powers of, i. 237, 336,
      ii. 395, 405 *sqq.*, 408–9
      Classification of, ii. 400–2
      Three Theories of, ii. 408–9
    Indirectly formed, ii. 407
    Nomination to, ii. 400–1
      Drawbacks of, ii. 402–3
    Present-Day reasons for maintaining,
      ii. 410 *sqq.*
    Utility of, ii. 412 *sqq.*
Secondary Schools, Civic Education in, i.
    76–7
Secret Commissions, ii. 479
Secret Diplomacy, ii. 367 & n., 368, 371
    & n.
    Abolition of, Popular demand, ii. 382
    Need for, ii. 383
Secret Societies (*see also* Freemasonry,
    under Democracy), i. 322
Sects, i. 80 n.
Secularism in Education, *see under* Aus-
    tralia, France, New Zealand
Sedan, i. 213
Seddon, Rt. Hon. J., Prime Minister,
    New Zealand, and his Poli-
    tics, ii. 272, 273 *sqq.*, 282–3
    & n., 287, 289, 290, 292,
    294–5 & n., 296, 299, 304–
    5, 308 & n. 1, 324
Sedgwick, A., *The Democratic Mistake* by,
    cited, ii. 492 & n. 1
Seignobos, M., book by, on Political
    History in Contemporary
    Europe, *cited*, i. 219 & n.
Selectmen, U.S.A., ii. 14
Self-Confidence
    in Democracies, i. 63, 64, ii. 521, 524,
      528
    as Qualifying for Leadership, ii. 554
Self-Governing Institutions
    and Backward populations, i. 5
    Plants of Slow growth and Struggle,
      ii. 501–2, 515, 516–7
Self-Government
    Basis of, ii. 505
    Early Instances of, ii. 506
    Educative Value of, i. 446, ii. 529–30,
      see also Local Self-Govern-
      ment
    Effective only when desired by the
      Masses, ii. 501–2, 513
    Evolution and Growth of, ii. 502 *sqq.*
    Meaning of, in practice, i. 53
    Possible weariness of, ii. 603
    Value in, of Tradition and Training,
      ii. 162–3
Self-Interest, Danger of, ii. 458–9
Self-Reliance, evolution of, ii. 518
Selfishness of Modern Democracy, ii.
    310
Selim I., and the Khalifate, i. 82 n. 2
Semi-Nomadic Races, Government among,
    ii. 514

Sempach, Battle of, i. 137
Senates, *see also* Second Chambers, *and under Countries*
  as Checks on Lower Houses, ii. 395-7
  Powers of, relative to First Houses, ii. 401-2
  Ideal, Selection of, Methods suggested, ii. 413 *sqq.*
Seniority
  in Civil Service Promotion
    Australia, ii. 194
    New Zealand, ii. 281
    Deference paid to, in U.S.A., reason for, ii. 60
Sentimentality towards Criminals, U.S.A., and elsewhere, ii. 89 & *n.*, 90, *see also* Condonation
Senussi, the, i. 80 *n.*
Separation of Powers, Doctrine of, followed in
  France, i. 230-1, 242, 277-8 & *n.*
  Rome, ii. 391, 393
  Switzerland, ii. 22
  U.S.A., i. 138, 494, ii. 12, 19, 20-1, 43, 121, 162, 391, 392-3, 396-7, 468-9, 474-5
Serbia, Social Equality in, i. 427-8
Servius Tullius and the term Proletariate, ii. 579 *n.* 2
Settlers, *see also under Countries*
  Individualism of, ii. 7
Seward, W. H., i. 104
Shakespeare, W., Age of, ii. 521
Sheep-farming, *see under* Australia, *and* New Zealand
Sheep-shearers, Australia, ii. 181
Sheldon, —, on Bible support for Divine Right of Kings, i. 87
Shelley, P. B., ii. 568
Shire Councils, Australia, ii. 199
Short Ballot movement, U.S.A., ii. 136
Short Terms of Office, *see under* Athens, Switzerland, *and* U.S.A.
Short views, in Australasia, ii. 251, 269, 291, 323, 331, 371
Siberia
  Cities of, growth of, ii. 99 *n.* 1
  Composite Population of, ii. 508
Siegfried, A., book by, on Democracy in New Zealand, *cited*, ii. 275 *n.*, 283 *n.*, 300 *n.*, 320 & *n.*
Siéyès, Abbe, on Second Chambers, ii. 399
Signs of the Times, The, Address by Ex-President Taft, ii. 127 *n.* 2
Simplon-Loetschberg Railway, privately owned, i. 342
Sin, changed views on, ii. 525
Single Chamber rule in England, i. 32
Single Tax, supporters of, on Taxation of Land, ii. 222
Single-Tax Law, U.S.A., ii. 141
Sinn Fein Party, i. 124
Size of Countries in relation to Forms of Government (*see also* Switzerland, Orange Free State, etc.), ii. 356, 473 *sqq.*, 501, 502, 504, 505-6, 508, 510-1, 514, 576
Slave-holding Party, U.S.A., and the Mexican War, ii. 374
Slave States of American Union and Brazil, parallel between, i. 201
Slavery
  Britain ends, ii. 532
  in Europe, i. 26
  in Greek Republics, i. 166
  and Natural Equality, i. 61-2
  and Natural Inequality, i. 62
  and the Rights of Man, i. 169
  in Spanish America, i. 188 *n.*, 201
  in U.S.A., ii. 5, 6, 23, 197

Slavs, Polish and Serbian, i. 447
Slip Ticket, the, in U.S.A., ii. 49
Small Landholders
  Canada, i. 451, 457, 465, ii. 170, 251
  Lack of, in Australia, ii. 251
  New Zealand, Land for, ii. 284 *sqq.*
Small Landowner, Problem of, Swiss solution of, i. 451
Small States, Value of, to Democracy, ii. 444-5
Smith, Goldwin, i. 102, 122 *n.*
Snap Elections and Public Opinion, i. 159
Social Changes, acting on Democracy, ii. 564 *sqq.*
Social Conditions
  in America after the War of Independence, ii. 5
  in New Zealand, Improvements in, ii. 303
  and Political Institutions, ii. 506
Social Democratic Party
  in Germany, i. 40
  New Zealand, ii. 317, and the "Right to Work," ii. 297 *n.* 2
Social Environment, Unifying force of, in U.S.A., ii. 113-4
Social Equality
  Bases of, i. 65-6
  in the British Dominions, i. 33, ii. 181
  Defined, i. 60-1
  European Countries in which greatest, i. 427-8
  in Islam, i. 82
  in Switzerland, i. 337, 433 *sqq.*, 444
Social Inequalities, i. 66, 212, 213
Social Influences commanded by Money Power (*q.v.*), ii. 485
Social Reconstruction, ii. 570 *sqq.*
Social Responsibility, Lost Sense of, effect on Legislatures, ii. 339
Social Structure as Factor in Self-Government, ii. 502
Social Welfare in New Zealand, by Lusk, ii. 283 *n.*
Socialism and Socialists, *see also under Countries, and* State Socialism, *below*
  and Anarchism, Common Aims of, ii. 571
  Anti-religious Colour of, ii. 571-2
  and Christianity, i. 86 *sqq.*
  Economic bases of, i. 125
  of Labour Leaders, ii. 236-7 & *n.*, 571
  Modern, in relation to the three French Revolutions, ii. 570 *n.* 2
Socialist Methods, ii. 572
Socialist Ministry, French, firmness of, in dangerous Strike, ii. 362
Socialist Parties, i. 125, 266, 414
  Evolution and bases of, ii. 348
  Methods of Action possible to, ii. 571-3
  Sects among, ii. 572
Solon, i. 182
Sonderbund, the, i. 329 *n.* 2, 342 *n.*
Sonderbund War, in Switzerland, i. 329 & *n.* 2, 350
Sophocles, on Life, ii. 534 & *n.*
South Africa, Public Opinion in, Race difference as affecting, i. 158
South African Republics, Parsimony of, i. 435
South African War, the, ii. 363 *n.* 1
  British Public Opinion on, divisions in, i. 118 *n.*, ii. 353, 379
  Chief Cause of, i. 144 *n.*
South America, *see also* Latin America
  Republics of, i. 187 *n.*
South Australia
  Civil Service Examinations in, ii. 194

South Australia—*continued*
Legislature of, ii. 176
Manhood Suffrage in, ii. 172
Ministerial Changes in, ii. 190–1
Party Struggles in, ii. 207
Self-Government set up in, ii. 172
South Carolina, i. 21
South-Eastern Europe
Self-Government in, ii. 501 *n.*
Status of the People in, i. 21
South German Princes, Swiss conflicts with, i. 36
South Slavonic Methods of Land-Allocation, i. 129
Southern States, U.S.A.
Negro Problem in, ii. 124
Political Attitude of, Present-day, ii. 6
Souveraineté Populaire, La, by Micheli, referred to, i. 372 *n.* 1
Soviets, *see* Russian Soviets
Spain
Anarchists of, i. 85, 137, ii. 600–1
Anti-Clericalism in, i. 85, 137, ii. 6, 571
Celtiberians of, Kings of, i. 25
Communism in, ii. 571
Corruption in, ii. 540
Democratic backwardness in, ii. 567
Elections in, ii. 600–1
Empire of, lost, i. 188, 189, 192
Executive of, Popular Control of, ii. 363–4
Intolerance in, ii. 522, 523
Local Party in, i. 124
Monarchy in, ii. 461, 536
National Unity in, i. 209
in North America *circa* 1792–1814, ii. 5
Political Groups in, ii. 343
Race differences in, i. 430
Religious Intolerance in, i. 137, ii. 522
Republic in, ii. 600–1
Senate of
Nominations to, ii. 400
Power of, Bases of, ii. 407
Small Landowners in, i. 451
Socialism in, ii. 600–1
Anti-religious colour of, ii. 571
Theological Orthodoxy in, i. 75
U.S.A. and, ii. 123, 373, 374
Universal Suffrage in, ii. 343, 600–1
Spanish America, *see* Latin America
Spanish-American War, the, ii. 123, 374
Sparta, i. 75
Speaker, the, of
Australian House of Representatives, ii. 188 & *n.* 2
House of Representatives, U.S.A., i. 173, ii. 41, 57
Special Convention, Swiss Disapproval of, i. 382 *n.*
Specialists, need of, i. 64–5
Spencer, Earl, ii. 557 *n.*
Spiritual Freedom, Idea of, inculcated by Christianity, i. 89, 90–1
Spoils System (chiefly in U.S.A.), Working of, i. 117, 361, 461, 495, ii. 29 *n.*, 38, 60–1, 78, 94, 135, 136, 366, 436, 528
Sport in Australasia, ii. 244, 245, 326
Squatters, *see under* Australia
"Squeeze," the, in China, ii. 509
Standards of Conduct, i. 135, 136
Standing Committees, Canada, i. 484
Standing Orders, Great Britain, ii. 79
Star Chamber, the, i. 52
State, the,
as Business Concern, ii. 587 & *n.*
Devotion to, the Roman Ideal, i. 136
as Employer, Position of, in face of Strikes, ii. 578
Political Coercion of, by Labour, ii. 568–9

State Action (*see also* State Activities *under* New Zealand), Effect of, on Individual, i. 56 *sqq.*, ii. 285, 330
State Assembly District Convention, U.S.A., ii. 33
State (or National) Committees, U.S.A., ii. 131 *n.*
Platforms of, ii. 40–1
State Conventions, U.S.A., Delegates from, for Presidential Elections, ii. 33 & *n.*, 70
Platforms of, ii. 40–1
State Employees
Control and Dismissal of, ii. 491
Individual Responsibility of, ii. 490–1
Influence exercised by, ii. 577
Slacking by (Government Stroke), i. 183 & *n.*, ii. 235, 293–4, 295–6 & *n.*
Stimuli operating on, ii. 591
State Experiments in Australia and New Zealand, by Pember Reeves ii. 283 *n.*
State Purchase of Railway in France, i. 237, 276
State Senatorial District Convention, U.S.A., ii. 33
State Socialism (*see also under* Countries), i. 38–9
Dislike for, of French Senate, i. 237
Inadequate data for Study of, ii. 11, 12 & *n.*
State Socialism in New Zealand, by Rossignol and Stewart, *cited,* ii. 280 & *n., et passim in notes*
State Trading (*see also* State Activities, *under* Australia *and* New Zealand), ii. 529, 569; book *cited* on, ii. 593 *n.*
States
Australian, and U.S.A., *see under those Countries*
Independence of, Preservation of, and Foreign Policy, ii. 369
Various Aims of, ii. 595–6
States-General, in France, i. 310
Statesmen in New Countries, Standards by which to be judged, ii. 189–90
Statutes, Constitutionality of, Right of Canadian Courts to pronounce on, i. 486
Steed, W., *Hapsburg Monarchy* by, *cited,* ii. 559 & *n.* 2
Steering Committee, U.S.A., ii. 57
"Stonewalling," and the Closure, in Australia, ii. 188
Stor Thing, Norway, ii. 402 *n.*
Storey, M., books by, ii. 294 *n.*, 453 *n.*
Story of the California Legislature of 1911, by F. Hichborn, ii. 136 *n.*
Stout, Sir R., on Municipal Government in New Zealand, ii. 277 & *nn.*, 278 & *n.* 1, 283
Strength, importance of, in Rulers, ii. 550
"Strike," special meaning of, in U.S.A., ii. 79–80
Strike, General, Anti-Democratic, i. 322 *n.*
Strikes
Australian, Political repercussion of, ii. 204–5
Extended range of, ii. 569
as Tools of Labour or Socialist Parties, ii. 572–3
Sympathetic, ii. 572 & *n.*
with Violence, ii. 362 & *n.*, 363 & *n.*

1

Strikes and Strike Riots in
Australia, ii. 204, 206, 218, 226, 230
sqq., 256, 259, 451, 528
Stuarts, the, and their followers, i. 111
Studies in History and Jurisprudence, by
the Author, referred to, i.
129 *n.,* 224 *n.* 1, ii. 464 *n.*
Subscriptions by M.P.'s, as Indirect
Corruption, ii. 482
Subventions, *see also* Bounties *and* Grants
Discontinuance, why suggested, ii. 343
Swiss, i. 363, 367
Succession Duties, New Zealand, ii. 289
Suffrage
Character of, as determining what is a
Political Community, i.
20–1
Educational and Property Qualifications
for, i. 29, 30, 32, 33, 63 &
n. 1, 70–1 *sqq.*
Electoral Fitness for, ii. 499–500, 507
Equal and Universal, apparently un-
avoidable, i. 153
Extensions, Great Britain, i. 30 *sqq.,* 42
and Labour Legislation, ii. 569
Ignorance and, i. 63 & *n.,* 70 *sqq.*
Suffrages, *see under each Form, and under
each Country*
Suffragettes, excesses of condoned, ii.
363 *n.*
Sugar Bounties and Export Duty, Aus-
tralia, ii. 224
Supplementary Votes in Belgium, i. 63 *n.*
Surtax, Graduated, in U.S.A., ii. 288–9
Sweden
Constitution of, i. 223
a Democracy, i. 22
Emigration from, to U.S.A., ii. 23
Estates in, ii. 398
Party Government in, i. 115
Monarchy in, ii. 461
Second Chamber in
Indirect Election to, ii. 401
Origin of, ii. 396
the Ynglings of, i. 25
"Swing of the Pendulum," in Politics,
ii. 364
Swiss Confederation, *see also* Switzerland,
below
Recognition of, i. 36, 329
Swiss Delegates in Paris, 1801, Speech to,
by Napoleon I., i. 372,
406–7
Swiss Guards, at the Tuileries, 1792, i.
137
Swiss Guides, Intelligence of, i. 432
Swiss League of Mutual Defence, i. 328–9
Switzerland
Administration in, i. 333 *sqq.,* ii.
493 *n.,* 528
Administrative Cases in, how dealt
with, i. 358 & *n.*
Administrative Council in, i. 338, ii.
463
Administrative Talent in, how secured
for the Nation, i. 355–6
Aliens in (*see also* Immigration, be-
low), i. 144 *n.*
Naturalization of, i. 333
Army of, and System of Defence, i.
342, 352, 363 & *n. sqq.,*
443, 451
Cost of, i. 364, 366
Élite of, i. 363, 364
Organization of, i. 363 & *n. sqq.,*
451, ii. 396
Abuses, alleged, connected with, i.
368, 445
Central Control of, i. 352
Reserves, i. 363, 364
Strength of, i. 364

Switzerland—*continued*
Assemblies in, *see Gemeinde, and*
Landesgemeinde, *below*
Budget excepted from Referendum, i.
376
Bureaucracy disliked in, i. 363, 365,
384–5, 389, 431 *n.* 1, 445
Candidates in, Choice of, i. 114, 419
& *n.,* 420 & *n.,* 427
Cantonalist Feeling in, i. 337, 435
Cantons of, i. 329, 330, 333, 335 *sqq.*
Assemblies of, i. 333 *sqq.*
Constitutions of, i. 335–6, 338, 375
n. 1
Councils of, i. 35–6, 339, ii. 406,
439–40
Payment of Members, i. 339
Elections in, i. 339 *sqq.,* 362, 398,
414, 422–3
Equal Political Rights of, i. 329–30
Governments of, i. 335 *sqq.*
Alleged abuses in, i. 368–70
Lessons from, ii. 506
Rights and Powers of, i. 330 *sqq.*
Working of, suggested Changes in,
i. 441–3
Initiative as applicable to, i. 373–4,
375, 376–8, *sqq.*
Judiciaries of, i. 338, 359 *sqq.*
Local Self-Government in, i. 334
Names of, i. 335 & *n.*
Political Life in, i. 411–13
Populations of, i. 335 & *n.*
Public Service a Duty in, i. 340
Referendum in, i. 373–4
Representation of, in Federal Legisla-
ture, i. 335, 344
Spirit of Intrigue in, ii. 448
Subventions by, to Employees, i. 363
Subventions to, from Federal Funds,
i. 343, 367
Capital Punishment in, i. 342, 436
Centralization disliked in, i. 335, 365,
435, 445
Cities of, alliance of, with the Three
Cantons, i. 328
Citizenship of, Admission to, i. 329,
331–2 & *n.* 1, 333, 364 &
n., 434 & *n.*
Civic Education in, i. 76 & *n.*
Civic Sense in, Strength of, i. 137,
287, 335, 340, 401 *n.,* 422,
443–4, 446, 451, 454, ii.
246, 455
Civil Code of, i. 336 *n.,* 342, 386
Civil Service of, i. 352, 361 *sqq.*
Relations of, to Political Life, i.
361–2
Status of, i. 365 & *n.,* 366
Class-hatred absent from, i. 423–4
Clerical party of, Influence, etc., of, i.
414, 419, 422, 423
Communes of, Local Self-Government
in, i. 333 *sqq.*
Councils of, i. 334, ii. 439–40
Compulsory Military Service in, i. 363,
ii. 361
Compulsory Voting in, i. 380, 417, ii.
530
Conservatism in, i. 389–90, 397, 432,
ii. 475
Constitutions of, at different times *see
also* Federal Constitution,
below, and Cantonal, *above,*
i. 36, 329–30, 372, 4$6–7, 408
Constitutionalism in, i. 142
Controversial Issues in, i. 412–13
Corruption rare in, ii. 374, 453
Council of States in, i. 344, ii. 400
Composition and Powers of, i. 344
sqq.

Switzerland—*continued*
  Councils in, *see under* Cantons, *and*
      Communes, *above, see also*
      Federal Council, *below*
  Decentralization in, i. 329, ii. 448
  Demagogism rare in, i. 501
  Democracy in, Antiquity, Character,
      Evolution, Success, and
      Faults of, i. 3, 7, 34–7, 77–
      8, 133, 446, ii. 12 *n.* 1,
      448–9, 458
    Examples from, i. 447 *sqq.*
    Future of, i. 453–4
    Merits and Demerits considered, i.
      443 *sqq.*
    Unique features of, i. 7
  Direct Legislation in, by The People,
      i. 338, 341, 344, 347–8,
      355, 363, 365–6, 371 *sqq.*,
      438, ii. 175, 464
    Arguments on, and Origin of, re-
      capitulated, i. 393 & *n.*
      sqq.
    Methods of (*see also* Landesgemeinde,
      below)
    A. Referendum, i. 373, 374 *sqq.*,
      422
    B. Initiative, 373, 374, 376 *sqq.*,
      401 *sqq.*, ii. 421 & *n.*
  Divorce in, i. 385–6, ii. 525
  Early conflicts in, i. 36
  Education in, i. 335, 342, 444, 451,
      ii. 373
  Elections in, all kinds, i. 334 & *n.* 2,
      338 *sqq.*, 344, 347, 361,
      398, 414–5, 416, 418, 422–
      3
    Conduct of, i. 418
    Cost of, i. 418
    Frequency of, i. 416
    Party Influence on, i. 414 *sqq.*
  Equality in, love for, i. 442, 445
  Étatisme in, i. 389, 412 & *n.* 1
  Ethnography and Ethnology of, i. 327–
      8, 331–2
  Executive of, i. 343, 351 *sqq.*, 436,
      439
    Compared with American and British,
      i. 448
    Party Influence on, i. 422
    Executive Council, *see* Federal Council,
      below
  Federal Constitution of, i. 170, 223,
      327, 330, 336, 338, 341–
      3
    Amendments of, opposed by and pro-
      posed by Initiative and Ref-
      erendum, i. 348, 373, 374,
      383 & *n.*, 384 *sqq.*, ii.
      421
    Authorities comprised by, i. 343 *sqq.*
    Changes proposed in, i. 443
    Federal Tribunal in relation to, i.
      357–8
    Prescription of, on Cantonal Con-
      stitution, i. 375 *n.*
    Revision-procedure, i. 341–2
    Rights under, of Cantons, i. 326–7
    Separation of Powers in, ii. 22
  Federal (Executive) Council of, i. 226,
      344 & *n.* 2, 351 *sqq.*, ii.
      455, 461, 473, 474
    Advantages secured by, i. 355–6, 440,
      448, ii. 473
    Allegations adverse to, i. 367
      sqq.
    Composition and Function of, i. 351–
      2, 448–9 & *n.*
    Finance controlled by, i. 349, 352
    Foreign Policy of, i. 364–5, ii.
      373

Switzerland—*continued*
  Federal (Executive) Council of—*con-
      tinued*
    Membership of, i. 347–8, 351–2, 440;
      in 1920, i. 449 *n.*
    Overloading of, i. 367
    Usages of, i. 440–1
  Federal Government, i. 341 *sqq.*
    Frame of, and Working of, i. 343
      sqq., ii. 435–6, 448, 461,
      463, 473 *sqq.*
    Applicability of, to other Coun-
      tries, ii. 454–6, 473–4
    as expressing Popular Will, ii.
      464, 473, 474–5
    Powers of, Concurrent with those
      of Cantons, i. 336, 342
  Federal Legislature of, i. 336 & *n.* 1,
      344 *sqq.*, ii. 463–4
    Cantonal Representation in, i. 336,
      344
    Constitutional Limitations on, i.
      347–8
    Debates in, i. 346, 379
    Evolution of, ii. 473
    Intellectual Level of, i. 351
    Members of, Elections of, i. 344,
      347
      Character of, i. 426–7
      Not considered as Delegates, ii.
        353
      Numbers in each House, i. 344
      Payment, i. 344
      Qualities shown by, i. 345 *sqq.*
      German-, and French-Speaking,
        i. 345–6
    Methods of dealing with Bills, etc.,
      i. 348–9, 352
    Party Action in, i. 421
    Power of, over the Federal Tribunal,
      i. 358
    Proceedings in, i. 346 *sqq.*, 429
  Federal Tribunal of, i. 343 & *n.* 1, 356,
      357 & *nn.*, 358–9
  Finance Bills, dealt with by Federal
      Council, i. 349, 352
  Financial Parsimony of, i. 388, 392,
      415, 435, ii. 528
  Foreign Affairs and Policy of (*see also*
      Neutrality *below*), i. 342,
      351–2, 353 & *n.*, 412, ii.
      74, 372–3, 473
  Freemasonry in, i. 369
  Freemen of, Assemblies of, *see Ge-
      meinde*, Landesgemeinde,
      Councils in Cantons *and*
      Communes, *and* Federal
      Council
    Salient Features of, ii. 448, 461
  Forest Cantons, Popular Assembly Gov-
      ernment in, i. 35, 335–6,
      337–8, ii. 461
  French Revolutionary Influence on, i.
      35–6, 328, 372–3, 393, 434
  Government, Popular, in, *see also* Coun-
      cils, *under* Cantons *and*
      Commune, *see also* Federal
      Government*; above*
    Federal, i. 327, 329–30, 341 *sqq.*
    Local, i. 333 *sqq.*
    and Administration in General, i.
      366 *sqq.*
  History of, Outline of, i. 34 *sqq.*, 328
      sqq.
  Immigration into, i. 332, 409, 434,
      444
  Initiative in (*see also that head, and
      under* Direct Legislation,
      above), ii. 420 *sqq.*
  Institutions in, *see* Federal Council,
      Initiative, *and* Referendum

Switzerland—*continued*
  Institutions in—*continued*
    Question of fitness of, for other
      Lands, i. 447–9, ii. 473–4
  Italian subjects of, i. 35, 56
  Jesuits in, i. 343, 435
  Judges in, Cantonal and Federal, of,
    i. 338, 356, 357, 359, 362,
    ii. 385 *sqq.*
  Judiciary, Cantonal, *see under* Cantons, *above*
    Federal, Status of, etc., i. 343 & n.
      1, 356 *sqq.*, 486 n., ii. 528
  Justices of the Peace in, i. 359
  Labour Party in, ii. 348
  Labour Troubles in (1919), i. 444
  Landesgemeinde of, i. 130 & n., 170 n.,
    337 & nn., 371–2, 373, 374,
    375, 393, 401, 406
  Languages used in, i. 330, 335–6
  Law and Order in, Maintenance of, i.
    401, ii. 363, 528
  Laws in
    Disallowed only by Referendum, i.
      338, 374, 376 n.
    Distinguished from Decrees in, i.
      174 n.
    on Religious Orders, i. 343
    and Resolutions, Referendum as applicable to, i. 375 *sqq.*
  Leaders, Political, in, i. 424, 432, ii.
    315, 469, 555–6
  and League of Nations, i. 376, 437–8
    & n.
  Legislatures, *see* Cantons, Councils, and
    Governments of, *and* Federal Legislature, *above*
  Local Abuses, alleged, in, i. 368–70
  Local Self-Government in, past and
    present, i. 327–9, 331, 333
    sqq.
    Democracy in relation to, i. 133
    Educative Effects of (*see also* Civic
      Sense, *above*), i. 335, 432,
      446, ii. 448, 555–6
  Manhood Suffrage in, i. 338, 441
  Ministers and Ministries in, Position,
    Re-Election, and Stability
    of, i. 348, 351, 352, 399,
    401, 410, 440, 451, ii. 359–
    60
  Money Power practically inoperative
    in, i. 444, ii. 254 n., 260,
    448–9
  Municipalities of, Government of, i.
    332–3, 443
  National Assembly of, i. 344, 345, 428–
    9, ii. 473
  National Characteristics, i. 331–2, 335,
    340, 345–6, 388, 389, 390,
    392, 393, 420, 424–5, 430
    sqq., 434 *sqq.*, 447, 467, ii.
    558, 561
  National Council of
    Elections to, Sessions of, Members
      paid, etc., i. 344 *sqq.*
    Groups in, i. 409 n.
    Powers of, i. 345 *sqq.*
    Radical Strength in, i. 409 & n.
  National Unity in, i. 327–8, 330,
    446
  Neutrality of, i. 353 & n. 2, 363, ii.
    372–3
  Noble Families of, and Politics, i. 427,
    ii. 315
  Officialism disliked in, *see* Bureaucracy,
    above
  Officials in, Appointments and Choice
    of, i. 361
  Oligarchy and Democracy in, Alliance
    between, i. 34

Switzerland—*continued*
  Parties in, i. 347, 348, 350, 408 *sqq.*,
    413
  Party in, i. 340–1
    Influence of, Manifestations and
      Methods of, i. 341, 394–5,
      414 *sqq.*, 418 *sqq.*, 421–2,
      423
    Long predominance of one, and the
      results, i. 350, 424–5, 440,
      442 *et alibi*
    Opposition in, i. 350, 424–5, 442
    Organization in, i. 414–5, 446
  Pastors and School Teachers, Elections
    of, for Short Terms, i. 334
    & n., 335
  Patriotism in, i. 137, 328, 331, 332,
    424, 446, 454
  Patronage in, i. 362–3, 367–8
  Peasants' Party in, i. 125, 409,
    ii. 348
    Congress of, ii. 340
  Penal Code, in Preparation (1919), i.
    336 n.
  Pensions not approved of in, i. 363,
    367
  Police of, under Cantonal Rule, i. 338
  Political Equality in, i. 327 & *passim*
  Political Institutions in, i. 333 *sqq.*,
    439 *sqq.*
    Concluding Reflections on, i. 440
    sqq.
  Politicians of, Status of, i. 340, 347,
    348
  Politics in
    Cheapness of, i. 415
    Purity of, i. 410, ii. 275
    Religion as influencing, i. 328–9,
      342–3, 369, 381, 385, 400,
      409–10, 413, 430, 435,
      444
  Polling in, for Elections, Referenda,
    etc., i. 250, 380, 381, 382–
    3, 422, 449–50
  Popular Government in, Salient Features of, ii. 448
  Population of, i. 449
    Ethnic Elements of, i. 327–8, 330,
      331–2, 345–6, 430
    Occupations of, i. 331
  Presidents of, Position, Powers, and
    Pay of, i. 226–7, 351–2
    and Vice-Presidents, i. 344 *sqq.*
  Press Influence in, i. 380, 436–7, ii.
    557
  Professional Politicians absent from, i.
    425 *sqq.*
  Proportional Representation in, i. 340,
    409 n., 413–4; views on, in
    1919, i. 444
  Public Life in
    Purity of, i. 366, 446, ii. 276
    Tone of, i. 366, 428 *sqq.* 443–4
    Wisdom the Note of, ii. 455
  Public Manners in, i. 445
  Public Meeting of Freemen in certain
    Cantons in, i. 35–6, *see also*
    Landesgemeinde
  Public Opinion in, i. 287, 296, 430 *sqq.*,
    444–5, ii. 242, 372–3,
    452
  Public Service in, i. 338–9, 340, 354,
    361, 362, 363, 415, 417–8,
    424, 425, 426, 446
  Public Works in, i. 443
  Railways of, National property, i. 342,
    349, 361, 362, 386, 412 &
    n. 2
  Re-election of Officials in, i. 339, 347,
    352, 356, 362, 419, 426,
    440, 448, 450

Switzerland—*continued*
Referendum in, *see under* Direct Legislation, *above*, *see also* Chap. XXIX. Vol. I. *and* Chap. LXV. Vol. II.
Religions in, i. 328–9 & *n.* 2, 332 & *n.* 2
Constitutional provisions concerning, i. 342–3
Religious Influence in Politics, *see under* Politics, *above*
Reserved Subjects in, ii. 394
Resolutions, Urgent and other, in, i. 375 & *n.* 2
Roman Church's Influence in, i. 342–3
Salient Characteristics of, i. 331
Self-Government in, i. 34, 327 *sqq.*, *passim*, ii. 503 *n.*
Senate of, Council of State, i. 344, ii. 400
Separation of Powers, i. 338, ii. 21–2
Short Terms of Office in, i. 334–5, 338, 356, 359, 361, 416, 440
Social Equality in, i. 61, 66, 337, 428, 433 *sqq.*, 444
Socialism and Socialist Party in, i. 364, 409 & *n.*, 410, 412, 414, 415, 423, 434, 449 *n.*, 450
Sovereignty of the People in, i. 185, *see also* Direct Legislation, *above*
State Socialism disliked in, i. 435
Subventions in and to Cantons, i. 343, 367
Tariffs in, i. 349–50, 365, 413
Territories comprised in, ii. 473 & *n.*, 503 *n.*
Trial by Jury in, i. 342, 360
Universal Military Service in, i. 363, 451, ii. 361
Voters in, Independence of, i. 34
War of Secession, 1847, i. 408
War of 1914-18 as affecting, i. 353–4, 444–5
Wealth in, Distribution and Taxation of, i. 445 & *n.*, 447
Sycophants, the, at Athens, i. 178
Sydney, N.S.W.
Dominance of, ii. 250, 266
Export trade of, Growth of, ii. 170
"Sympathetic" Strikes, ii. 572
Syndicalism in U.S.A., ii. 127 *n.* 1
Syndicalists
Australia, ii. 230
New Zealand, ii. 316, 323
Syracuse, i. 36, 166, 169 *n.*
Voters of, i. 71

Tableaux politiques de la France de l'Ouest, by Siegfried, i. 242 *n.* 2
Tacitus, on the Meetings of the early Teutonic Peoples, i. 337 *n.* 1, 371, ii. 398 & *n.* 2
Taft, Ex-President W. H., book by, on Popular Government, ii. 88 *n.*, 89 *n.*, 152 *n.* 1
on Defective Criminal Justice, U.S.A., ii. 88 & *n.*, 89 *n.*, 453 *n.*; on the Money Power in U.S.A., ii. 127 *n.* 2
Tahiti, Chief's rule in, ii. 503
Taine, H. A., i. 6, 13, 284, 324
Talk as forming Public Opinion, i. 71–2, 156, 296
Talleyrand, on Scarcity of Talent among Party Chiefs, ii. 555
Tammany Hall, Influence of, ii. 103–4 *sqq.*, 110

Tammany Ring, the, U.S.A., ii. 104–5
Tariffs, *see under* Countries
Tasmania
Civil Service in, ii. 194
Democracy in, Historical Evolution of, i. 33–4
Legislature of, ii. 176–7
Population of (1901), ii. 186
Proportional Representation in, ii. 183
Public Opinion in, ii. 245
Railways in, ii. 233
Self-Government set up in, ii. 172
Taxation, *see under* Countries
Taylor, General Z., President, U.S.A., Military Fame of, ii. 555
Teachers, Australian, salaries and status of, ii. 200, 201
Teachers' Union, Swiss, i. 334 *n.* 2
Teaching Orders, Dissolution of, in France, i. 217
Tennyson, Lord, no successors of, i. 324
Thayer, W. R., on the Senate and Foreign Policy, U.S.A., ii. 373–4 & *n.*
Thebes, i. 170
Themistocles, i. 180, 184
Theoretical Foundations of Democracy, i. 43 *sqq.*
Thesmothetai, the, i. 174
Thiers, Adolphe, i. 214, 215, 226
Thing, the, of Norse Races, i. 129, 130, 337, ii. 506
Thinking, definition of, i. 72
Thoughts on the Union between England and Scotland, by Dicey and Rait, ii. 396 *n.* 1
Thucydides, *cited*, i. 167 *n.* 2, 183, 185 *n.*, ii. 456 *n.*
Tibet, Buddhism in, i. 82
"Tidal Wave," in Politics, U.S.A., ii. 364
Tilden, S. J., on Boss Tweed and Tammany, ii. 104
Times, The, cited, ii. 583
Timocracy in Early Greece, i. 170
Tithings, ii. 506
Titles as weapons of Money Power, ii. 484
Tobacco monopoly in France, i. 276
Tocqueville, A. de, i. 3, 6, 13, 320, ii. 30
on American Democracy, i. 284, ii. 3; on Love of Equality and of Liberty, i. 68; on the Status of the French President, i. 230; on the U.S.A. Senate, ii. 59; on the Tyranny of the Majority, i. 436, ii. 121–2, 159, 521
Tolerance of Abuses, *see* Condonation, etc.
Tolstoi, Count Leo, Influence of his Writings, ii. 554
Toronto, population of, i. 456, 466
Torture chambers, ii. 532 & *n.*
Tory Party, the, ii. 347; origin of, i. 113; Social Mixture in, i. 124, 313; views of, on Franchise Extension, i. 31, ii. 576
Town Meetings of New England, i. 377, 337, 452 *n.*, ii. 440, 506
Towns and Communes, Directly Elected Officials of, ii. 439–40
Towns and Townships (*see also* Cities), *see under* Australia, *and* U.S.A.
Toynbee, P., *cited* on Dante, ii. 486 *n.*
Tozer, H. F., Commentary of, on Dante, *cited,* ii. 486 *n.*

"Trade, a," in U.S.A., Senate, ii. 61
Trade and Labour Councils, Congress of, New Zealand, ii. 316
Trade Unions and Unionism, *see also under Countries, and see Labour*
Evolution from, of Labour Parties, i. 123–4
Powers of, ii. 546 *& n.*, 565, 569
Right of Peaceful Picketing of, risks from, ii. 363
Triple Alliance of (G.B.), ii. 578
Tradition(s) and Authority
as Base of Power of Second Chambers, ii. 405–6
Causes destroying, i. 140
Definition of, i. 137
Influence of, on the making of Citizens, i. 75, 77
in relation to Democracy, i. 134 *sqq.*
as Forming Tone, in Public Life, i. 305
Traditions
Good and Bad, i. 135 *sqq.*, 139–40
Influence of, Historical Instances of, i. 137–8
Lacking in Australasia, ii. 324
Operation of, in English Politics, i. 312
Rise and decay of, i. 140
Train Robberies, U.S.A., ii. 91
Trajan, ii. 536
Trans-Australian Railway, ii. 233 *n.*
Transport (*see also* Railways, *under Countries*)
Control of, Private and Public, ii. 233–4
Transvaal, the
Form of Government in (*pre* 1899), ii. 464 *n.* 1
Military Organization in (same date), i. 168
Suffrage in, i. 21, 144 *n.*, 145
Treaties and Commissions
between Canada and U.S.A., i, 468–9
Submission of, to the Senate, U.S.A., ii. 18, 61, 381–2
Submission of, to Swiss Referendum, i. 375–6, ii. 373–4 *& n.* 1
Treaties of Westphalia, i. 329
"Treating" at French Elections, i. 242
Treaty of Berlin, ii. 378
Treaty of Versailles, 1919, i. 376
Trebizond, i. 166
Trent affair, Queen Victoria's counsel on, i. 228–9 *& n.*
Trial by Jury
in France, i. 272 *n.*
in Switzerland, i. 342, 360
Trials, Criminal, U.S.A., ii. 88 *sqq.*
Tribal organization, i. 25–6
Tribunes, Roman, ii. 392–3
Triple Alliance [of Unions], Great Britain, ii. 578
Tripotage, in France, i. 302
Tropical South American Republics, i. 187 *n.*
Trotsky, L., on Compulsory Labour in Russia, ii. 574 *n.* 2
Trusts, Amalgamations and Monopolies, ii. 569
State Trading *versus*, ii. 232 *sqq.*
Tsardom, Russian, downfall of, i. 5, ii. 500, 501
Tunis, i. 319
Tupac Amaru, Insurrection of, i. 192
Turkey
Corruption in, ii. 453
Government in, ii. 377, 500
Monarchy in, before 1905, ii. 535
Turkish atrocities and the Russo-Turkish War, ii. 378

Turkish Domination in Hungary, effects of, i. 39
Turner, H. G., book by, referred to, ii. 225 *n.* 1
Tweed, W. M. (Boss Tweed), and the Tammany Ring, ii. 105
Tyranny and Republics, i. 180
Tyranny of Demos
Aristotle on, i. 183
Evils of, ii. 517
Tyranny of the Majority, i. 436, ii. 121, 159, 355, 411, 521
Tyrants, Greek, i. 180, 189

Ulster Protestants in Virginia, etc., ii. 6
Undesirable Immigrants Bill, of 1891, New Zealand, ii. 309
Unemployment
Government liability as to, Australian view on, ii. 236
New Zealand demands concerning, ii. 297 *n.* 3
State action concerning, effects of, ii. 297
Unicameral Legislatures, *see* House of Representatives, *see also* Unitary Governments, *below*
"Unification of Australian States," project for, ii. 241
Union of South Africa
and the British Election of 1905, ii. 379
Constitution of, i. 223
a Democracy, i. 22 *n.* 1
Government of, Powers of, ii. 173
Parliamentary System in, i. 497
Senate of, Powers of, relative, ii. 402
Unitary Governments, ii. 203, 241
Second Chambers in, ii. 400
United Federation of Labour, New Zealand, ii. 316
United States of America, i. 187, ii. 1, 3 *sqq.*
Administrative Boards in, for control of Parties, i. 127–8
Anti-Catholic parties in, i. 123
Army and Navy, the, ii. 361
the President the Chief of, ii. 74
Average Man, the, in, ii. 119 *sqq.*
Bar, the, in, ii. 65
Censorship exercised by, ii. 88
Judges chosen from, ii. 389
Standard of, ii. 88, 155, 386, 389
Bar Association in, and Reform, ii. 90, 163
"Big Business" in, Influence of, ii. 127, 141, 465, 485, *see also* Money Power, *below*
Bills inadequately debated in, ii. 58
Boss Influence in, ii. 40, 65, 78, 80, 81–2, 101 *sqq.*, 157, 482–3
Cabinet in, i. 449, 494, ii. 41, 93, 359
Disconnection of, from Congress, i. 449, ii. 19
French parallel to, i. 228
and Canada
Relations between, i. 468–9, ii. 124 *& n.* 2, 375
Resemblances and Comparisons, i. 457, 458–9, 462, 463, 466, 474, 475, 479, 480, 482, 483, 484, 486, 488, 489, 492 *sqq.*, 498, 499 *sqq.*, 505–6
Candidates in, Choice of, Methods of, i. 113–14, ii. 17–8, 28–9 *sqq.*, 36, 39 *sqq.*, 42, 49–50, 65, 129, 354
Capital in, accumulation of, ii. 23–4, 171

United States of America—*continued*
Capitalists of, *see* "Big Business,"
 above, and Money Power,
 below
Central Executive lacking in, 1776–89,
 i. 329
Child Labour Acts of, ii. 125
Cities of (*see also* Immigrants *and*
 Municipal, *below*), Rapid
 Growth of, Results of, ii. 99
 & *n.* 1, 100 *sqq.*, 441 *sqq.*
Civic Sense in, i. 157, ii. 5, 15–16, 36,
 37, 52 *sqq.*, 113, 116, 263,
 450, 454–5
Civil Equality in, ii. 12 *sqq.*, 19–20,
 158
Civil Liberty in, i. 322, ii. 12 *sqq.*, 19–
 20
Civil Order in (*see also* Law and Or-
 der, *and* Lawlessness, *and*
 Lynching), ii. 83 *sqq.*
Civil Self-Government of (*see also* Lo-
 cal Self-Government, *be-*
 low), practice of, ii. 5
Civil Service, Federal
 Permanent, Organization and Work-
  ing of, ii. 93, 94 *sqq.*, 360
 Reforms affecting, ii. 95
 Salaries in, ii. 95
 Summary on, ii. 365–6
Civil War of, *see* War of Secession
Class Antagonisms of, ii. 114–15 & *n.*
 1
Closure in, Rules for, in Congress, ii.
 57, 60 & *n.* 2
Coal in, i. 456
Coloured Population of
 Distribution of, ii. 5 & *n.*
 Practical Exclusion of, from Fran-
  chise, ii. 17, 48–9, 50, 77
  & *n.* 1, 114, 124, 499
Committees in, ii. 34, *see also under*
 Names
Committees of Congress, *see under*
 Congress, *below*
Congress, *see also* House of Representa-
 tives, Legislatures, *and* Sen-
 ate
 Cabinet not connected with, i. 449,
  ii. 19
 Candidates for, Nomination and Elec-
  tion of, ii. 17–18, 33–4
 Closure in, Rules for, ii. 58, 60 & *n.*
 Committees of, ii. 56
  "Steering," i. 173
 Compared with French and Australian
  Legislatures, ii. 41, 178–9
 Composition of, i. 248, ii. 17–18
 Debates in, ii. 60
  Not read by the People, ii. 64,
   146–7
 Decline of, and Causes, i. 307, ii.
  52–3, 54, 64, 342
 Defects in, i. 345, ii. 52–3, 54, 64,
  154, 157–8
 Eloquence in, ii. 553–4
 Legislation by, invading States'
  Privileges, ii. 125
 Members of
  Payment of, ii. 18, 65–6
  Quality of, ii. 52 *sqq.*
 Ministers excluded from, i. 261, 262
 No "Groups" in, i. 59, 252–3
 "Peculiar and Essential Qualities of,"
  ii. 12
 Political Corruption rare in, i. 479–
  80
 Popular Attitude to, ii. 52–3, 62–3
 Powers of, ii. 12, 21, 74, 173
 Limitations in, ii. 20–1 & *n.*, 493–4

United States of America—*continued*
Congress—*continued*
 President's relations with, ii. 64, 75,
  364
 and the Recall, ii. 149–50
 Rise in, of Party, i. 113
 Scenes in, i. 259
 Usages in, Origin of, i. 441 *n.*
 Woman Member of, ii. 47–8
Congressmen, Patronage of, ii. 95–6
Constitution, Federal, of, i. 3, 6, ii.
 10–11
 Abstract Conceptions in, i. 507 & *n.* 2
 Amendments of, ii. 17, 48, 59 & *n.*,
  124–5, 176, 186 *n.*, 337
 Comparison of, with those of Aus-
  tralia and Canada, i. 459,
  461, 4, ii. 179
 Effect on, of the Referendum, ii.
  143
 Machinery for Altering and Inter-
  preting, i. 459 & *n.*, ii. 27,
  83–4, 393–4, 409–10
 as Model for those of
  Spanish-American Republics, i.
  189, 204
  Switzerland, i. 341–2
 Nature of, i. 170, 223, ii. 10, 16–17
  83–4
Constitutional Government in, book on,
 by Woodrow Wilson, ii. 69
 n., 73 *n.*
Conventions (*see also* National, *and*
 Party, *below*), ii. 33–4, 129
 sqq.
Corruption in, i. 241–2 & *n.* 1, 479,
 ii. 50–1, 62, 79–80, 88,
 452–3, 480, 541
Counties in,
 Elections of Officials of, ii. 15
 Importance of, in the South, ii. 55
 Local Government of, ii. 14
  Defects of, ii. 98 & *n.*
Criminal Law in, Lax Enforcement of,
 ii. 88 & *n.*, 89 *n.*, 155–6,
 453 & *n.*, 528
Delegates in, ii. 33–4, 35, 36, 129,
 130
Demagogues in, ii. 470 & *n.* 2
Democracy in, i. 11, 23 & *n.*
 Bases of, i. 3
 Beginning, ii. 3 *sqq.*
 Early, ii. 567, 571
 Characteristics instilled by, ii. 121–2
 Compared with that in Canada, i. 495
 Defects, ii. 27, 154–5
 Causes of
  Non-Political, ii. 157 *sqq.*
  Political, ii. 155 *sqq.*
 Fundamental Principles of, ii. 8–9
 General Review of, ii. 154 *sqq.*
 Historical Evolution of, i. 32–3
 Slow Evolution of, i. 208
 Successes of, ii. 158 *sqq.*
 Ideas contributing to, ii. 158 *sqq.*
 Supervenient Changes as modifying,
  ii. 22 *sqq.*
Development of, book on, by Farrand,
 ii. 124 *n.* 2
Difficulties of, in application of Demo-
 cratic Principles, ii. 499–
 500
Diplomatic relations of, ii. 375–6
Direct Election in, applications of, i.
 493, ii. 59–60, 139–40, 161–
 2, 342, 401, 402–3, 449–50
Direct Popular Legislation in (*see also*
 Initiative *and* Referendum,
 below), ii. 129, 140 *sqq.*,
 147–8, 409–10

United States of America—*continued*
Direct Primaries in, ii. 77 *n.* 2, 131 &
   n., 132–4
Divorce in, ii. 526
Dominance in, of the Few, ii. 545
Education in, under Local Authorities,
   ii. 436–7
Election Expenses in, Legislation on,
   ii. 482
Elections in, in General, Methods, Cost,
   etc. of, i. 226, ii. 7–8, 13,
   14, 15–16, 17, 18, 28 & *n.*,
   30, 31, 32, 49 *sqq.*, 59–60,
   68 & *n.* *sqq.*, 85–6, 100,
   101 *n.*, 102, 129–30, 133 &
   nn., 135 & *n.*, 139–40, 161–
   2, 342, 348, 401, 402–3,
   404–5, 441 *sqq.*, 449–50,
   472 & *nn.*
   Frequency of, Reasons for, and
      Results of, ii. 21, 31, 37,
      49–50, 112, 449–50
   Three Sets of, ii. 49, *see also* Presi-
      dential, *below*
Elective Administrative Offices in, i.
   274, 493
Electoral Suffrage in, ii. 47 & *n.*,
   48–9
Electoral System (*see also* Elections,
   above), Capital Fault of, ii.
   135
Electors, powers of, i. 495
English in, changes in, ii. 168–9
Executive in
   Choice of, i. 115
   in relation to Judicature, i. 459 &
      n., ii. 84, 394
   Powers of, when greatest, ii. 76
   vested in the President, i. 448
   Responsibility of, i. 231
   Veto of, ii. 179, 393, 394, 468 *n.*
      2, 470
Executive Officials, Selection of (by
   Appointment or Election),
   ii. 18, 49, 66, 77
Federal Constitution, *see* Constitution,
   above
Federal Courts of, ii. 386
   Foreign Praise of, ii. 450
Federal Government, *see* Government,
   below
Federal Legislatures, *see* Legislatures,
   Federal
Federal Officials, *see under* Officials
Federal Senate, *see* Senate, *below*
Federal System, Others modelled on, ii.
   335–6
Finance in, Senate's Powers over, ii.
   60
Fitness for Office little heeded in, i.
   64 *n.*, ii. 20, 37, 156, 158
   et alibi
Foreign Policy of, ii. 123–4, 159, 373–
   4, 376
   Presidential Powers concerning, ii.
      74, 373–4, 376
Foreign Relations Committee of Senate,
   ii. 373, 381
Freak Bills rejected in, by Referenda,
   ii. 138, 425
Freemasonry in, i. 123
Government
   Federal or National
      Frame of, ii. 10 *sqq.*, 16, 19, 29–
         30, 44, 47, 162, 436
         as affected by Recall of Deci-
            sions, etc., ii. 152 & *n.*,
            153
         Belief in which constructed, ii.
            29–30
         Firmness of, ii. 162

United States of America—*continued*
Government—*continued*
   Federal or National—*continued*
      Frame of—*continued*
         Powers of, Growth and Limita-
            tion of, ii. 21, 124–5
         Stimulus given by, to Popular
            interest in Public Questions,
            ii. 113
      Law and Order under, ii. 356–7
      Macaulay's dictum on, ii. 178
      Salient Features in, ii. 449–50
      Subjects reserved to, ii. 385
      Tone of, ii. 452
      Working of, ii. 47 *sqq.*
   State, *see under* States, *below*
   Growth of, in 19th Century, i. 4
Heroes of Lofty Character in, i. 139
House of Representatives, Federal, ii.
   17, 56–7, 401
   the Few in, ii. 545
   Powers of, in relation to those of
      the Senate, ii. 401
Houses of Representatives of States,
   see under States, *below*
Idealism and Selfishness in, Struggle
   between, ii. 164
Immigrants into, i. 451, ii. 23, 40,
   48–49, 109–10, 160, 164,
   441, 450, 571
   Exclusion of undesirable, ii. 311
   Rights of Eastern Asiatic, Insecurity
      of, ii. 91
Impeachments in, ii. 13, 18, 20, 85,
   86, 151 & *n.* 1
Income-tax in, ii. 125
Influence of, in Cuba and Haiti, i. 192
   & *n.*
Initiative and Referendum in, *see under*
   States, *below*
Interstate Commerce Commission, Aus-
   tralian Copy of, ii. 196
Interviewing in, ii. 117
Journalism in, ii. 117
Judges in, *see also under* States, *below*
   Federal
      Appointment, Election of, Salaries,
         Status, Terms of Office, etc.,
         i. 493, ii. 19, 49, 83 *sqq.*,
         101, 138, 158, 385–6, 449
      Impeachment of, ii. 85, 151 & *n.*
         1
      Promotion of, i. 304
      Qualities needed in, ii. 84–5
      Recall as applied to, ii. 19, 141,
         152 *n.*, 153
      Re-election of, ii. 86
   Local (*see also* States, Judges of,
      below), ii. 14, 15
Judiciary
   Federal and State, ii. 19, 83 *sqq.*
   Defects in, ii. 87 *sqq.*
      Tolerance of, ii. 92–3
   in relation to Executive, i. 459 & *n.*,
      ii. 83–4, 394
   Reform movement as affecting, ii.
      90, 92 *n.*, 137 *n.*, 138 *n.*
   Restrictions of, i. 271
Juries in, ii. 88, 89
   "Fixing" of, ii. 89, 480
Justice in, Defects in, ii. 87–8 & *n.*,
   89 *n.*, 92–3, 155, 156, 157–
   8, 453 & *n.*, 528
Labour Disputes in, ii. 127 *n.* 1
Labour Organizations, Nationalism ad-
   vocated by, ii. 126
Labour Party, ii. 41 *n.*, and Socialism,
   ii. 115 *n.*
Labour Troubles threatening in (1920),
   ii. 164
Labour Union Congresses in, ii. 340

United States of America—*continued*
Law and Order in, Maintenance of, and
Defects in, ii. 6, 7, 83 *sqq.*,
90, 91, 156, 157, 362–3,
452, 528, see also Lynch-
ing, *below*
Law Courts of, ii. 27, 84–5, 150
Supreme Court, ii. 19, 85
Lawyers (*see also* Bar, *above*) Influence
of, on Public Opinion, ii.
116
Leaders, in relation with Average Men,
in, ii. 561
Leadership in, ii. 41–2, 60–1, 111,
136
Lack of Official, ii. 57
Training for (*see also* Local Self-
Government, *below*), ii. 450,
555–6
Legislatures, see also Congress, House
of Representatives, Senate,
etc.
Federal, ii. 17, 52 *sqq.*
Attitude to, of the People, ii. 52,
62 *sqq.*, 418
Decline in, ii. 335–6, 343
Possible Remedies, ii. 343
Dissolution of, i. 494
"Filibustering" in, ii. 57, 60 *n.*
2, 345 *sqq.*
Legislation by
Methods of, and Value of Re-
sults, ii. 52, 56, 58
Non-Party, ii. 42, 158–9
Materialism in, i. 307
Members of, ii. 52 *sqq.*
Payment of, ii. 174 *n.*, 339–40
Popularly elected, ii. 36
Quality of, ii. 52 *sqq.*, 63, 64
Municipal, ii. 16, see also Municipal,
below
State (*see also under* States), ii. 12–13
Liberty in
Social and Political, ii. 158 *sqq.*
"Lobbying" in, ii. 483, 488
Local Authorities in, i. 220
Education under, ii. 436
Local Committees, ii. 203–4
Local Improvements in, and Corrup-
tion, ii. 437–8
Local Self-Government in (*see also*
Municipal, *below*), i. 133,
220, 452, ii. 7–8, 14 *sqq.*,
97, 98 & *n.*, 199
Educative Results of, ii. 450, 555–6
Fundamental Principles carried out
in, ii. 20
Non-Party Elections for, ii. 15, 28 *n.*
Party Influence on Elections in, ii.
15, 441 *sqq.*
Three Types of, ii. 14 *sqq.*
Localism in, ii. 7, 15, 30 *sqq.*, 54, 55
"Log-rolling" in, ii. 62, 140, 143
Lynching in, ii. 90, 363, 452, 528
Majority Tyranny in, ii. 159, 521
Manhood Suffrage in, ii. 13, 17, 47,
77, 401
Materialism in, *circa* 1820–60, ii. 521
in Legislatures, to-day, i. 307
Mayors of, functions of, Elections of,
etc. (*see also* Municipal
Self-Government), ii. 16
Veto of, ii. 16
Mexican Affairs, and Restraint shown
over, ii. 159, 373, 376
Mexico, War with, in 1846, ii. 374
Ministerial Instability in, ii. 364, 452
Ministers in
Excluded from Congress, i. 261, 262
Responsibility of, ii. 493–4
Scandals (past), concerning, ii. 480

United States of America—*continued*
Money Power in (*see also* "Big
Business," *above*), i. 456–7,
ii. 24, 127 & *n.* 2, 141, 155,
156, 157, 171, 442, 450,
454, 478, 485
Municipal Government in (*see also*
Chicago, Galveston, New
York, Philadelphia, etc.), i.
132–3, 171, ii. 14–16, 97,
98 *sqq.*
Book on, by Goodnow, referred to,
ii. 101 *n.*, 134 *n.*
Commissions System of, ii. 441
Defects in, Causes and Conse-
quences, i. 133, 317, ii. 99
sqq., 107 *sqq.*, 110–11, 119,
127–8, 138–9, 155, 156,
157, 441–2, see also Immi-
grants
Two forms of, ii. 15–16
Municipal Officers in, ii. 15–16, 33,
100, 101 *n.*
Municipalities of, see also Chief Cities
under Names
Morality, Political, of, ii. 108
Reforms in, ii. 129, 138 *sqq.*
Ring and Boss rule in, ii. 98
Vigilance Committees of, ii. 444
National Characteristics, ii. 3–4, 6 *sqq.*,
21–2, 37, 38, 119 *sqq.*, 160,
361, 376, 423
National Committees of (*see also* Com-
mittees, *above*), ii. 32, 41–2
National Convention of (*see also* Party
Convention, Functions, etc.,
of), ii. 33, 34, 41, 42, 46,
69 & *n.* 1, 70 *nn. sqq.*, 81,
131 & *n.*
National Defence in, ii. 74, 361
Nationalization views in, ii. 126, 127
Natural Resources of, ii. 23
Negroes of, see Coloured Citizens, *above*
Nominating Conventions in, ii. 33 *sqq.*
Nominations in, ii. 32 *sqq.*, 74
of Presidents unsuccessfully tried, ii.
472 *n.* 1
Non-Party Associations of Business
Men in, i. 473–4
Officials in
Federal
Attitude to, of People, ii. 5, 7–8
Choice and Appointment of,
Methods of, and Reforms
aimed at, i. 64 *n.*, ii. 19,
20, 129, 135 *sqq.*, 490
Direct Election of, Lessons from,
ii. 161–2
Removal of, see Recall, see also
Impeachment
State, see under States, *below*
Parish and Town in, i. 131 & *n.*
Parties in, see also under Names
Balance of, and absence of Groups, ii.
42, 62, 348
Criticisms on, i. 116–7
New, ii. 348 *n.* 1
Old, Historic, i. 124, 266, ii. 348
Partisanship in, ii. 28–29, 61, 62, 63,
118
Party in, ii. 27 *sqq.*, 46
Growth of, ii. 24, 25–6
Influence of, on
Foreign Affairs, ii. 373–4
Senatorial Elections, ii. 28, 404
State Elections of Judges, ii. 86
Inspirers of, i. 265–6
Legal Recognition of, ii. 131 *sqq.*
Public Opinion not ruled by, ii. 114–5
Rise of, i. 113
Party Committees in, ii. 32 & *n.* 1

United States of America—*continued*
Party Conferences in (*see also* National, *above*), ii. 340
Party Convention in (*see also* National, *above*), Functions of, ii. 11, 68–9 & *n.*, 80, 102–3, 339
Party Discipline in, ii. 353, 470
Effect of loss of, ii. 121
Party Feeling and Social Relations in, i. 473–4
Party Funds in, restrictions on, ii. 52, 482
Party Gatherings in, Status of, ii. 40–1
Party Machine in (*see also* Tammany)
Public attitude to, ii. 39, 40, 127–8, 129, 133
Responsibility within, ii. 495
Party Organization in, i. 477, ii. 26, 27, 31–2, 42, 49, 65, 96, 99 *sqq.*, 340, 453, 482–3
and Choice of State Officials, ii. 494–5
Defects in, ii. 134–5, 155 *sqq.*
Extra-legal Power of, ii. 42–3, 162, 449
Four Roots of, ii. 135
Influencing Elections, ii. 15, 27 *sqq.*, 32, 441 *sqq.*, 494–5
and the Judicature (*q.v.*), ii. 386
Main Features of, ii. 77 *sqq.*
Members of Legislatures as Nominees of, ii. 54
as affecting Municipalities, ii. 99–100
Ossification of, 123
and the Party Machine, ii. 39 *sqq.*
Postulates of, ii. 129–30
Reforms aimed at, ii. 129 *sqq.*
as Selecting Leaders, ii. 555–6
Strength of, i. 501, ii. 449, 470
Unifying Action of, ii. 39–40, 44, 99, 110
Party, Primary, ii. 31, 32–3 & *n.*
Functions of, ii. 33, 132 & *n.*
Objections to, ii. 133
Party Control of, ii. 102–3
Reform of, Efforts for, ii. 37, 129 *sqq.*
Senatorial, ii. 60 *n.* 1
Working of, ii. 34 *sqq.*
Party Platforms, ii. 40–1 & *n.*
Party Policy
by whom declared, ii. 41
in whom resting, ii. 45–6
Party System in, ii. 27 *sqq.*, 44, 45
Paternalist tendencies in, ii. 125 *sqq.*
Patriotism in, ii. 113
Patronage in (*see also* "Pork Barrel" *and* Spoils System), i. 320, ii. 29 & *n.*, 61, 80, 93, 94–5, 113, 365, 366
Pensions Scandals in, i. 500–1, ii. 58, 528–9
Personal Rights in, Insecurity of, ii. 91, 155–6
Police in, ii. 91, 439
Political Characteristics, ii. 21–2
Political Committees in, i. 268, 269
Political Equality in, ii. 8–9, 158
Political Institutions of, *see* Constitution, etc., etc.
Geographical and Economic Changes as affecting, ii. 22 *sqq.*
Political Reforms in, ii. 129 *sqq.*
Political System of, compared with that of Canada, i. 493 *sqq.*
Political Traditions of, i. 138–9
Polling in, ii. 50–1
for Initiative, ii. 144 & *n.*, 145
Poorer Class in, improvement in conditions of, ii. 24 *n.*
Popular Government in, Salient Features of, ii. 449–50

United States of America—*continued*
Popular Sovereignty in (*see also* Direct Legislation, Direct Voting, *and* Initiative and Referendum), i. 4, ii. 12
Devotion to the Idea of, i. 495
Historical Evolution of, i. 41–2
Principle of, Working of, ii. 158
Rule of, in Party Organization, ii. 34, 36, 68
as Secured in State Constitutions, ii. 12 *sqq.*, 19–20
Population
Ethnic Elements in, i. 451, ii. 5, 17, 23 & *n.*, 25 & *n.*, 48, 49, 99 & *nn.*, 113–14, 331, *see also* Coloured Population *and* Immigrants
Expansion of, ii. 22
Immigrant
Difficulties due to, ii. 127 *n.* 1, 156
Ideas introduced by, ii. 115–16, 127 & *n.* 1, 164
Party Unification of, ii. 40, 43, 99, 110
and Tammany Hall, ii. 104
Small Landowners (*q.v.*), a stable element in, i. 451
"Pork Barrel," The, in, ii. 63 & *n.*, 295 *n.* 1
Presidency of, ii. 66
Qualifications for, ii. 66 *sqq.*, 555
President of
Election of, *see* Presidential Elections, *below*
Executive Vested in, i. 448
Functions, Powers, and Status of, *see also* Veto of, *below*, i. 226–7, 231, 449, 494, 495, ii. 18, 19, 41, 43, 66 *sqq.*, 74 & *n.*, 162, 342, 360, 373–4, 376, 462–3, 468 & *n.* 2, 471–2, 493–4
Fears concerning, ii. 75
Restrictions on, Checks on, ii. 17–18, 73, 162, 364, 468–9 & *n.* 2
Model on which created, ii. 472 *n.* 4
Nomination of, tried unsuccessfully, ii. 472 *n.* 1
Patronage of, ii. 29, 94
Re-Eligibility of, ii. 469 & *n.* 2
Relations with Congress of, ii. 64, 75, 364
Responsibility of, to the People, i. 231, ii. 471, 493–4
Veto of, ii. 18, 74, 179, 393, 394–5, 396, 468 *n.* 2, 470
Presidential Elections, Candidates, Nominations, Polling, etc., i. 227, ii. 18–19, 27–8, 32, 33, 34, 51, 64, 66, 67 *sqq.*, 131, 135 & *n.*, 472 & *nn.*
Presidential System of Government in, ii. 66 *et passim*, 461, 462–3, 468, 470, 474–5
"Presidential Timber," ii. 70 & *n.* 1
Press, the, in, Influence, Methods, and Status of, i. 103, 106–7, 489, ii. 113, 116, 117 *sqq.*, 119, 557
Private Bill Legislation, ii. 79 & *n.*, 80
Professional Politicians in, i. 260, 447
Prohibition in, i. 471, ii. 42, 99 *n.* 3, 125 & *n.*, 159
Proportional Representation in, ii. 50–1
Protectionists in, Tolerance of Abuses by, ii. 39–40, 106
Public Affairs of, General Interest in, ii. 113, *see also* Civic Sense, *above*

United States of America—*continued*
Public Life in
Dearth of Talent in, ii. 36, 155, 157,
see also Legislatures, Decline in, *above*
Tone of, i. 307, ii. 156–7, 164–5,
487, 515–6, 560
Public Opinion in, i. 287 & *n.* 1,
296, 297, ii. 81, 112 *sqq.*,
162–3, 249, 456–7
Assumptions in, i. 158–9
Better instructed than in Europe, ii.
115–16
Changes in, ii. 122 *sqq.*
as Check on President, ii. 75
on Enforcement of Law and Order,
ii. 362–3
and Foreign Affairs of, ii. 373, 374–6
General Rightness of, ii. 380
Independent of Party, ii. 115
Influence of, on Presidential Election,
ii. 69–70, 72, 73
Influence on, of
Business men, ii. 115, 116 *n.*
Newspapers and the Press, ii.
117 *sqq.*
Universities, ii. 115–16 & *n.*
Power of, as to Reforms, ii. 96,
140
Tendencies to be Noted in, ii. 123,
124 *sqq.*
the True Ruler in, ii. 122
Two classes of, ii. 115 & *n.* 2, 116
& *n.*
Unifying Effect of, i. 430
on the Wars of the last Hundred
Years, ii. 374–5
Race Difficulties in, *see* Coloured Population, *and* Immigrants,
above
Races unassimilated by, ii. 113–14
Railways in
Political Control of, ii. 294
Presidents of, ii. 102
Private Ownership of, ii. 234
State Management of, during the
War, Cost of, ii. 294 *n.*
"Recall" in, application of, i. 494,
ii. 20, 141 *sqq.*, 148–9 *sqq.*,
424, 449–50, 493, 496
Reforming Spirit, Reform Movement,
and Reforms in
Aims, Objects, and Agencies of, ii.
80, 95 *sqq.*, 164
Beginnings of, ii. 122–3
affecting Civil Service, results of, ii.
95 *sqq.*
Difficulties of, ii. 153–4
Leaders in, ii. 116–17
Most dangerous Enemy of, ii. 107
in Municipal Government, ii. 129,
138 *sqq.*
Public Opinion and, ii. 96, 140–1
Recent Movements, ii. 129 *sqq.*
Temporary (*see also* Tammany), ii.
105, 106
Three Moving forces of, ii. 127–8
Religious Differences in, ii. 6, 114
Religious Sense in, Strength of, ii. 6
Responsibility in, of
Executive, i. 231
Party Machine, ii. 495
President, i. 231, ii. 471, 493–4
Subdivision of, ii. 493–4, *see also*
Separation of Powers, *below*
Roman Catholics in, ii. 114
Second Chamber, *see* Senate, *below*
Secretary of State for Foreign Affairs,
ii. 373
Selectmen, Elections of, ii. 14
Senate, Federal, ii. 17–18, 399–400

United States of America—*continued*
Senate—*continued*
Composition, Choice, Election, etc.
of, i. 281 *n.*, ii. 17–18, 58
sqq., 125, 186 & *n.*, 286,
342, 401, 403
Party Influence on, ii. 28, 403, 404
Function and Powers of, ii. 19, 58
sqq., 401
as Check on President, i. 234, ii.
18, 162, 468 *n.* 2
as to Foreign Affairs, ii. 18, 61,
74, 373–4, 381
to Declare War, ii. 381
Judicial, ii. 18, 20
to Reject Bills, ii. 409
Relative to those of House of
Representatives, i. 493, ii.
60, 409
Indispensability of, ii. 61
Leadership in, ii. 60–1
Members of, ii. 59
Payment of, ii. 18
Quality, Status, and Opportunities
of, ii. 52, 59–60, 61, 62
Origin of, ii. 59
Renewal by retirements, ii. 59, 413 *n.*
Superiority of, to what due, ii. 59–60
Senates, State, *see under* States, *below*
Senatorial Primaries in, ii. 60 *n.* 1
Seniority in, Deference to, ii. 60
Separation of Powers in, i. 138, 494,
507 *n.* 2, ii. 12, 19, 21,
22, 43, 121, 162, 391, 393–
4, 396–7, 449–50, 468–9,
474–5, 493–4
Short Ballot movement in, ii. 136
Short Terms of Office in, ii. 9, 13, 14,
16, 19, 20, 29, 31, 49,
77 *n.* 2, 85, 92, 94, 95,
101, 102, 112, 138, 156, 158
Slavery in, and its Consequences, *see*
Coloured Population, *above*
Small Landowners in, i. 451–2 & *n.*,
ii. 170, 221, 251
Social Equality in, i. 61
Socialism, Socialists, etc. in, ii. 108,
115, 126–7 *n.* 1, 571 & *n.*,
see also Immigrants
Spoils System in, i. 117, 461, 475, ii.
29 & *n.*, 38, 94, 366, 436,
see also "Pork Barrel" *above*
States of
Administrative Officials of, *see*
Officials, *below*
Budgets of, Reforms concerning, ii.
137 & *n.* 1
Cabinet of State Officers, ii. 137 &
n. 1, 138
Civic Education in, i. 76 *n.*
Civil Service in, i. 493, ii. 97
Comparison of, with
Canadian Provinces, i. 493 *sqq.*
Swiss Cantons, i. 334 *passim*
Compulsory Voting in, ii. 530
Constitutions of, ii. 11–12 *sqq.*, 173
Working of, ii. 47 *sqq.*, 77 *sqq.*
Corruption in, ii. 448–9, 452–3, 479,
480
Councils not always existent in, ii.
440
Defects in, ii. 154 *sqq.*, 363, 452, 453
Direct Popular Election in, i. 493,
ii. 463 *n.* 2
Direct Popular Legislation in, *see*
Initiative and Referendum,
below
Elections in, i. 493–4, ii. 12–13, 49,
77, 80–1, 463 *n.* 2, 494–5
Evolution of, ii. 7–8, 55
Finance of, ii. 78

United States of America—*continued*
States of—*continued*
Government of
Frame of, i. 493 *sqq.*, ii. 463 &
n. 2
Working of, ii. 47 *sqq.*, 77 *sqq.*
Governors of, Election, Nomination,
Functions, Powers, and
Status of, i. 338, 493, ii. 13,
34, 66, 80–2, 93, 162, 342,
increase in Powers of, ii.
496, 576
Veto of, ii. 80, 179, 396
Houses of Representatives in, ii. 13,
79, 401
Impeachments of Officials Tried in,
by Senates, ii. 13, 20
Initiative and Referendum in, i.
387 *n.* 1, 394, 484, 493–4,
ii. 141, 143, 337, 342, 394,
395, 417 *sqq.*, 449, 463 *n.*
2, 576
Cost of, ii. 142
Polling for, ii. 144 & *n.*, 145, 421
& *n.* 2
Use Made of, ii. 419 *sqq.*
Judges of, Selection, Appointment,
Salaries, and Status of, ii.
13–14, 85–6, 156, 388, 389,
438, 449, 453, 480, 541
Judiciaries of
Defects and their Causes in,
Summarized, ii. 154–5, 156,
158, 453, 528
Quality of, ii. 85–6 *sqq.*
Legislatures of, ii. 13
Conduct of, ii. 78
Faults of, ii. 140–1, 154 *sqq.*, 336,
479
Remedies for, ii. 140 *sqq.*
Limitations on, ii. 21 *n.*, 336–7
Members of,
Quality of, ii. 77 & *n.* 2, 78
Women, ii. 47–8
Popular Distrust of, ii. 141
Power of, whither gone, ii. 342
Private Bill Legislation in, ii. 79
& *n.*, 80
Manhood Suffrage in, ii. 13, 17, 47,
77, 401
Officials of
Election, Appointment, Salaries,
and Functions of, ii. 13, 14,
80–1, 97, 136 *n.*, 463 *n.* 2,
490, 494–5
Reforms in Method of choosing,
ii. 135 *sqq.*
Irresponsibility of, ii. 494–5
"Recall" as used in, *see that head,
above*
Representation, equal, ii. 17–18,
174
Rights reserved to, Narrowing of, ii.
125 & *n.*
Senates of, Elections to, Powers of,
and Status of, ii. 13, 77,
186, 401
Quality of, ii. 77, 402–3
Respect for, ii. 406
Social Reform Legislation in, ii. 79
Southern, Negro Problem in (*see also
Coloured Population, above*),
ii. 499
Suffrages, varying in, ii. 17
Varying Sizes of, i. 335
Vote-counting in, ii. 472 *n.* 2
Western, attitude of, to Railways, i.
482
Manners in, *circa* 1840, ii. 524
"States' Rights" Sentiment in, ii.
241

United States of America—*continued*
Suffrages in, *see* Manhood, Universal,
and Woman
Swiss Examples worth note by, i. 448,
449, 450
Tariffs in, and Party Politics, ii. 28,
39–40, 106
Taxation in, ii. 100, 288–9
Territorial Expansion and Economic
Changes in, ii. 22–5
Results of, on Political Institutions,
ii. 25–6
Tolerance in, of Abuses, ii. 36–7, 40,
103, 108–9, 140, 154, 157,
363–4, 452, 453 *et alibi*
Town, Towns, Townships, *see also*
Cities *and* Municipalities
Elections in, ii. 15–6, 28 *n.*
European parallel to, i. 282
Local Government of, ii. 14, 15, 16
Localism of, ii. 7
States evolved from, ii. 7, 55
Town Meeting in (*see also under* New
England), ii. 7, 14, 15
Trial by Jury in, i. 272 *n.* 2, ii. 88,
89, 480
Trusts in, ii. 569
Universal Suffrage in, ii. 13, 17, 174,
178, 182, 244
Universities of, Status and Influence of,
i. 488, ii. 96, 97, 115–16 &
n., 201
Urbanization of, ii. 577
Vetos, *see* Executive, Mayor, Presi-
dential, State Governor, etc.
Voters and Voting Methods in, i. 145,
251, ii. 47, 48–9
War, Declarations of, ii. 74
and the War of 1914–18, ii. 113–14,
121 & *n.*, 124, 375
War of Secession, or Civil War (*see also
that head*), ii. 121 & *n.*,
122–3, 125, 197
Ward Committees in, ii. 32, 110
Ward Primaries, Delegates from, ii. 33
Wars of, since 1846, ii. 361–2, 374–
5
Woman Suffrage in, ii. 17, 42, 47 &
n., 48
Universal Suffrage, *see also under Coun-
tries*
as Panacea, Failure of, ii. 506–7,
533
Universities, *see also under Countries*
Civic Education in, i. 77
University Clubs, U.S.A., and Reform, ii.
163–4
Unterwalden, Democracy of, i. 35
Upper Class, absence of, in Australia, ii.
180
Upper Germany, Old League of, i. 331,
453
Urbanization, effects of, ii. 577
Uri, Democracy of, i. 35
Uruguay, Republic of, i. 187 *n.*
Church interests in, i. 191
a Democracy, i. 22
Government, Legislature, Faction, etc.
in, i. 112, 199, ii. 469
Insurrection of 1910 in, i. 199
Parties in, Origin of, i. 112
Political Civilization of, i. 207
Population of, Ethnic purity of, i. 188,
198
President's power in, i. 199, ii. 469–70
Progress in, ii. 512
Railways in, i. 198
a True Republic, i. 193
Democracy evolving in, i. 198
Wars of, i. 191 *n.*
Civil, i. 199

Vallées et Suzeraintés, see Andorra
Valour, Traditions of, i. 135, 138
  Permanence of, i. 141
Van Buren, M., ii. 94 *n.* 2
Vancouver, population of, i. 466
Venezuela, Republic of, i. 187 *n.*
  Boundary troubles of, 1895, ii. 375
  Low Political Level of, i. 192, 204
Venice, Mediaeval, ii. 537 *n.*
  Foreign Affairs in, ii. 74 *n.*, 371
  Oligarchic rule in, i. 70 *n.*, ii. 538–9, 540–1
Vestry, English, American Evolution from, ii. 14
Veto
  of Executives, i. 461, ii. 13, 16, 18, 20, 74, 80, 174, 177, 178, 364, 392–3, 394–5, 396, 468 *n.* 2, 470
  Popular, in Switzerland (*see also* Referendum), i. 373
  of Roman Tribunes, ii. 392
Victoria, Australia
  Civil Service in, ii. 194
  Export and Trade Centre of, ii. 170
  Gold in, ii. 167, 170, 181
  Legislature of, ii. 176
  Ministerial Changes in, ii. 190–1
  Party Struggles in, ii. 202
  Protectionist views in, ii. 170, 203
  Railwaymen's Pressure in, on Legislators, ii. 195 & *n.*
  Self-Government established in, ii. 172
  Voting in, ii. 182–3
Victoria, Queen, i. 229 & *n.*
Vigilance Committees of American Cities, ii. 444
Village rule, in China, ii. 510
Village Schoolmaster, the, in France, and Elections, i. 243
Vinet, A. R., i. 434
Virgil, *cited*, i. 148
Virginia
  First Colonization of, i. 32, ii. 4
  Passion in, for Liberty, ii. 6
Vogel, Sir Julius, and Communications in New Zealand, ii. 267; Financial policy of, ii. 267–8, 283, 291
Voisson, —, on the Future of Australia, ii. 261 & *n.* 1, 283 *n.*
Volksanfragen, Swiss, i. 372 & *n.* 1
Voltaire, and Christianity, i. 89, 90
Vorarlberg, and Swiss Confederation, i. 364 & *n.*
Vote-catching, Methods of, ii. 458, 467, 540, *see also* Nursing the Constituency *and* Corruption, Indirect
Voters, *see also* Electorate, Electors, Polling, *and under Countries*
  Education for, two views on, i. 70
  Education of, by Party Strife, i. 119
  Influence on, of the Press, how countered, i. 119, *see also* Press Influence, *under Countries*
  Intimidation of, i. 152
Votes
  Equality of value of, i. 161
  Supplementary, in Belgium, i. 71 *n.*
Voting
  Compulsory, in Argentina, i. 196
  as the Expression of the Will of the People, i. 146, 151–3, 160, 161
  Legal Authority going with, i. 146
  Methods, *see* Suffrages, *and that head under Countries*
  at Non-Parliamentary Elections, i. 159 *n.*

Voting—*continued*
  with a Party, i. 116–17, 118 & *n.*, 120 & *n.*, 155
  Popular, Effect of, on Constitutional Government, i. 398–9
Vox Clamantis, cited on State Management of Industries, ii. 593 *n.*

Wade, Sir C., book by, on Compulsory Arbitration, ii. 231 *n.* 2 ; on State Undertakings, ii. 235 *n.* 2
Wage-earning Class, Australia, ii. 451, *see also* Industrial, Labour, *under* Australia, Working Class, etc.
Wages
  Higher, aimed at, Methods employed, ii. 568–9
  Trotsky's view on, ii. 574 *n.* 2
Wages Boards, *see under* Australia
Wagnière, M. G., on Democracy in Geneva, i. 372 *n.* 2
Waihi Gold Mines, New Zealand, Strike at, ii. 305 & *n.*
Waldeck-Rousseau, M., i. 255, 264, 265 *n.*, 321
Walpole, Sir R., ii. 477, 539
War
  Christian teaching on, disregarded, i. 87
  Destructive of Small States, ii. 445, and Democracies, ii. 604, 605
  as an Ideal of Happiness, ii. 530 *sqq.*
  National Changes effected by, i. 140–1
War, the Great (1914–18)
  Compulsory Military Service imposed during, by U.S.A., Great Britain, and some Dominions, ii. 175, 361
  Executive dominant during, in Great Britain, ii. 179
  Issues of, determined by the Few, ii. 544
  Lessons of, ii. 215, 606, 607, 608
  Swiss Precautions during, ii. 372–3
War Loan, New Zealand, magnitude of, ii. 289, 332
War Service, as qualification for Leadership, ii. 555
War of Independence (U.S.A.), ii. 7
War of Liberation, German hopes from, i. 39
War of Secession (Civil War), U.S.A., ii. 6, 17, 23, 30, 42, 121 & *n.* 2, 122, 125, 159, 197
  British Public Opinion on, Cleavage in, ii. 377–8
  Napoleon III., and, ii. 378
  Pension Scandals after, i. 500–1, ii. 58, 528–9
Ward Elections, ii. 441
Wars
  Newspaper action regarding, i. 100
  of Latin-American Republics, i. 191 & *n.*
Washington, George, ii. 561 ; Cabinets of, ii. 94 *n.* 2 ; Election of, as President, ii. 69 ; Personality of, ii. 472 ; Tradition formed by, i. 139
Waste and Extravagance in Democratic Finance, i. 483, 499 & *n.* 2, ii. 328, 331, 438, 452, 457, 458
Wat Tyler's rising, i. 70, 309
Water Power, in Canada, i. 455–6
Wealth
  Distribution and Sources of, Changes in, ii. 564–5

Wealth—*continued*
  Great, Two Consequences of, ii. 541 *n.*
  Power of, *see* Money Power
  Redistribution of, why useless, ii.
    570 *& n.* 1
Webster, Daniel, Personality of, i. 265
Wellington Club, New Zealand, ii. 318
Welti, as Popular Leader, i. 350 ; on
    Popular Voting, i. 396
Western Australia
  Courts of Conciliation and Arbitration
    in, ii. 226–7
  Labour majorities in, ii. 206
  Legislature of, ii. 176
  Public Opinion in, ii. 245
  Population-distribution in, ii. 167
  Self-Government set up in, ii. 172
  State Trading in, ii. 234
  Voting Methods in, ii. 183
  Women's vote in, ii. 182 *n.*
Westphalia
  Anabaptists of, i. 85
  Treaties of, as affecting Switzerland, i.
    329
Whigs, or Whig Party, the, i. 28, ii. 347
  Doctrine of, on Constitutional Changes,
    i. 323
  Origin of, i. 113
  Social mixture in, i. 124, 311
  Watchword of, original sense of, i. 52
"White Australia" Policy, ii. 215, 224,
    243
White Caps, U.S.A., Outrages by, ii. 91
Will of the People, *see* Popular, etc.
William the Conqueror, i. 83
William I. and II., German Emperors and
    Divine Right of Kings, i. 84
Wilson, Woodrow, President of the
    U.S.A., ii. 67
  book by, on Constitutional Govern-
    ment in the U.S.A., ii. 69
    n., 73 *n.*
  on Equal Representation of States in
    the Senate, ii. 59 *n.*
Wilson Scandal in France, Political
    Effects of, i. 216, 230
Winkelried, Arnold von, at Sempach, i.
    137
Winnipeg, Population of, i. 466 ; Strike
    at, in 1919, i. 466, 486, 500
Wisconsin Idea, The, by C. M'Carthy, ii.
    97 *n.* 1

Wisdom, Collective, ascribed to the Peo-
    ple, i. 144, 150 ; Criticisms
    on, i. 145–6, *see also* Self-
    Confidence
  Not Sought by the People in their
    Leaders, ii. 555
Witan, the, ii. 350
Woman Suffrage, *see also under Countries,*
    i. 49, 163, ii. 308
  and the Relative place of Civic Interest,
    ii. 547
  Under Consideration in some Swiss
    Cantons, i. 338 *n.*
Women, Status of, in Athens and Rome,
    ii. 525
Wordsworth, W., i. 324, ii. 568 ; on the
    Revolutionary period, i. 47 ;
    on Swiss Liberty, i. 454
Working Class alone represented in
    Russian Soviets, ii. 582–3

Xenophon, i. 183

Ynglings, the, i. 25
Yuan Shi Kai, failure of, cause of, ii.
    500 *n.*

Zealots, in Political Parties, i. 126
Zelaya, rule of, in Nicaragua, i. 192
Zemstvos, Russian, ii. 513
Zimmern, A. E., book by, on the Greek
    Commonwealth, i. 175 *n.* I
Zinoviev, Mr., *cited,* on the Russian
    Soviets, ii. 582–3
Zug, Public Meeting of Freemen in, i.
    35
Zürcher, Dr. E., book by, *cited,* i. 360
    & n.
Zürich
  Elections in, i. 420
  Initiative in, i. 403–4, 405 *n.,* 412–13
  Liberalism of, i. 35
  Municipality of
    Enterprise of, i. 334
    Party difficulties in, i. 449
  Non-citizens dwelling round, i. 332 *n.* I
  Oligarchy of, i. 35
  Referendum in, i. 391 *& n.,* 392, 406,
    412
  and the Swiss League, i. 328–9
  Voting in, percentage of, i. 391 *& n.,*
    417